INNOVATION CORRUPTED

Malcolm S. Salter

Innovation Corrupted

The Origins and Legacy of Enron's Collapse

HARVARD UNIVERSITY PRESS

Cambridge, Massachusetts, and London, England   2008

Publication of this book has been supported through the generous
provisions of the Maurice and Lula Bradley Smith Memorial Fund.

Library of Congress Cataloging-in-Publication Data
Salter, Malcolm S.
    Innovation corrupted : the origins and legacy of Enron's collapse / Malcolm S. Salter.
        p.   cm.
    Includes bibliographical references and index.
    ISBN-13: 978-0-674-02825-8 (alk. paper)   1. Enron Corp.—Corrupt practices.   2. Enron
Corp.—Management.   3. Business ethics—United States.   I. Title.
    HD9502.U54.E579225   2008
    333.790973—dc22   2008004259

Contents

Acknowledgments

For their assistance and support, I want to acknowledge the helpful readings and comments of many friends and colleagues, including Chris Argyris, Dwight B. Crane, Brian Hall, Tamar Frankel, Robert Glauber, Jerry R. Green, Paul M. Healy, Joseph Hinsey IV, Jay W. Lorsch, Gregory S. Miller, Jeremy P. Nahum, Lynn S. Paine, Krishna G. Palepu, Thomas R. Piper, Robert Pozen, William A. Sahlman, Bruce R. Scott, W. Mason Smith, and Guhan Subramanian. Mason Smith, who read each and every chapter multiple times, raising important questions and offering many insightful comments on human behavior in organizations, deserves special thanks for being such an intellectually generous and persistent friend. Several of these readers have questioned my framing of specific issues or some of my interpretations and conclusions. All have offered constructive counsel and enriched my line of approach. The Enron case history supports a diversity of interpretations, and I have benefited greatly from these views. However, the views expressed here are mine and mine alone.

Tables D.1 and 2.1 previously appeared as exhibits 4 and 6 in Harvard Business School Case No. 9-904-036, "Innovation Corrupted: The Rise and Fall of Enron," and are reproduced by permission.

Figure 1.1 was prepared by Mars and Co. and appears by permission.

In preparing this study, I have also been ably assisted by several research associates. Lynne C. Levesque provided invaluable assistance at the front end of my research, conducting extensive library, media, and archival research and summarizing materials that have found their way into various chapters of this book. She was a critical coauthor of the Harvard Business School case study on Enron's collapse, which became the primary building block of this book. Maria Ciampa also contributed to the initial Enron case study, focusing on the stock-based compensation of Jeffrey Skilling and

Kenneth Lay during the final two years of Enron's existence, when serious internal cash-flow problems and profit pressures developed. Perry Fagan was invaluable in helping me map the Sithe transaction, described in Chapter 1, and in charting the course of Enron's ethical drift, the subject of Chapter 4.

Jason Mahon deserves special acknowledgement. For almost two years he served as my most important research and discussion partner. He is also coauthor of several chapters dealing with Enron's board (Chapter 5), the role of financial intermediaries (Chapter 6), and Enron's public watchdogs (Chapter 7). Jason is a remarkable young researcher, and a major contributor to this book.

I would also like to salute two of my editors. Michael Aronson, Senior Editor for Social Sciences at Harvard University Press, sought me out in the early stages of my research and provided support and guidance to me through several years of writing, reformulation, and rewriting. In addition, Sandra Hackman did a superb job working with me in rewriting and condensing a very long "final draft" of the book. With her remarkable mastery of both detail and story line, we were able to reduce the word count by a third!

Without the patience, good humor, and support of my wife, BJ, this book could never have happened. Over the past five years BJ has spent countless evenings, weekends, and vacations listening to my evolving ideas and lingering questions about the Enron case. With an incisive comment or two, she was always able to help clarify my thinking and writing. She also cheerfully tolerated my many prolonged absences from family life required to research and write this book. I can't imagine that any researcher, writer, and teacher has ever been so cheerfully and intelligently assisted in the living of both family and professional life.

Finally, I am most grateful for the financial support provided to me by the Division of Research and Faculty Development at the Harvard Business School. Despite this generous funding, this book should not be taken as an official report of that school or of Harvard University. Rather, it should be considered the intermediate product of a single faculty member pondering the meaning of the Enron story for twenty-first-century American capitalism and the management of contemporary enterprise. We still have much to learn about and learn from Enron's remarkable history. It is my hope that this book places a brick on the road to greater understanding of the essential ingredients of effective and ethical administrative leadership.

INNOVATION CORRUPTED

Introduction

Until its collapse in the fourth quarter of 2001, Enron Corp. was the world's dominant energy trader, accounting for about one-quarter of all energy trading in the United States. By pioneering the development of large-scale energy trading, Enron was able to transform itself from an "old economy" gas pipeline operator to a "new economy" financial intermediary and market maker. In the process, Enron's revenues grew from $13.5 billion in 1991 to a reported $101 billion ten years later. During the last five years of the millennium, Enron delivered more than a 500 percent total return to shareholders. It was also a prominent member of published lists of America's most admired and innovative companies.

At the beginning of 2001, Enron's market capitalization was $63 billion. One year later its stock was worth only pennies to its unfortunate shareholders, and the company then held the dubious distinction of being the largest bankruptcy in American economic history. A corporate icon of the 1990s had collapsed, not only swiftly but ignominiously, leaving a trail of frantic efforts to hide losses on a host of questionable transactions with off-balance-sheet partnerships, allegedly fraudulent accounting, and insider trading; and evidence of serious conflicts of interest on the part of Enron's most senior financial executives.

Although much already has been written about Enron's rise and fall, four important questions pertaining to corporate governance and control remain unanswered:

1. What kinds of management behavior and processes led Enron down the path from truly innovative to deceptive management?

2. How could Enron's board of directors have failed to detect the business, ethical, and legal risks embedded in the company's aggressive financial strategies and accounting practices?
3. Why did Enron's external watchdogs—security analysts, credit-rating agencies, and regulatory agencies—fail to bark?
4. What actions can prevent Enron-type breakdowns in the future?

This book attempts to answer each of these questions. In contrast to previous books by investigative reporters and former employees, which present timeline narratives of Enron's collapse, my goal is to explain *why* Enron collapsed, and the *lessons* of this calamity for the governance and control of public companies—those owned by outside shareholders.

This is a daunting and fascinating task, as Enron presents one of the most complicated challenges to forensic accounting that I have seen in four decades as a business school professor and industry consultant. In addition, the precise truth about Enron remains elusive. There is much that we still do not know, for example, about the true economic performance of Enron's various business units and structured-finance transactions. There are some facts about the Enron case that we may never know, such as the personal knowledge and intent of Enron CEOs Jeffrey K. Skilling and Kenneth L. Lay and other Enron executives in making and ratifying key business decisions. As a result, men and women of experience and wisdom differ on what part of Enron's strategy was successful and what was not, and what was legal and what was not. Finally, as all practicing historians know, establishing the true facts of such a complex case is not only a legal challenge but also a political one: we all bring different values to bear in interpreting stories like Enron's, and agreeing on the truth requires considerable debate.

Despite these challenges, the broad contours of the Enron story are clear enough to invite reflection on the origins and legacy of this momentous case history. At its core, this story is about thoughtless and incompetent leadership, the ethical drift that inevitably followed, and a breakdown in oversight and control by the company's board of directors and external watchdogs. It is also a story about how the lives of thousands of highly skilled and professional employees can be shattered by the missteps and inattention of a small number of officials at the top of an organization. In telling this story, I focus on the administrative practices and behaviors of those responsible for Enron's collapse rather than on the legal merits of subsequent criminal convictions and ongoing appeals.

Enron's collapse involved the corruption of a remarkable strategy of innovation. That corruption was the result of a gradual erosion of integrity and candor that took place in response to a combination of factors: poorly designed financial incentives that encouraged excessive risk taking without accountability for results; a corporate culture wherein senior managers encouraged limits-testing and, in certain instances, both tolerated and promoted deception; and pressures to disguise unexpected write-downs of overvalued commodity contracts and risky merchant investments, cash-flow shortfalls, and escalating debt.

The tipping point in Enron's drift into deceptive financial accounting and reporting came in 1997. In that year, Enron's profits took a nosedive for the first time in its history, and the company's chief financial officer, Andrew Fastow, created the first of many off-balance-sheet partnerships and related financial transactions designed to bolster Enron's reported profits and cash flow and maintain the company's investment-grade credit rating. More violations of generally accepted accounting principles (GAAP) and rules of the Securities and Exchange Commission (SEC) followed. Enron executives also made careless mistakes—some supported by outside advisors and investment bankers who, in essence, colluded in designing and executing transactions that disguised the company's true financial condition. Most of these questionable transactions went undetected and undeterred by Enron's board of directors and regulatory agencies.

What makes the telling so interesting is that Enron's senior management straddled many gradations of ethical behavior, with a good deal of this behavior lying in the murky borderlands where rules are ambiguous, the spirit of the law can be widely interpreted, and outside auditors can find reasons for approving transactions that have deceptive characteristics.[1] With Skilling and Lay urging aggressive exploitation of existing rules while lobbying for fewer rules and less oversight by regulatory agencies, Enron lived in an ever-expanding grey area between right and wrong, with many opportunities for executives to make costly mistakes both for themselves and the corporation.

During the trial of Skilling and Lay in the spring of 2006, the jury faced the difficult challenge of working through the legal ambiguities that figured prominently in the government's case (plus many others that escaped inclusion). Despite these ambiguities—which included, for example, the use and disclosure of off-balance-sheet partnerships, corporate reorganizations that concealed business failures, and so-called prepay transactions to bolster reported earnings—government lawyers were able to convince the jury that the details of Enron's compliance with legal rules were secondary to a general pattern of deceptive behavior that was either masterminded or approved by Skilling and Lay.

In reaching this conclusion, the jury sent two strong messages to CEOs. The first was that they can be convicted of conspiracy to defraud investors not only for making misleading statements to investors and the SEC, but also for financial policies and practices that might not be incontestable breaches of the law. In essence, the jury's verdict reflected the legal principle that in matters of alleged fraud, intent to deceive trumps compliance with arcane legal rules.[2] This verdict is consistent with the long-established ethical principle that the moral status of an act should be judged not only by its consequences, but also by the intentions of the actor.[3] The second message was that CEOs should not expect to escape responsibility for the devious or deceptive acts of others (such as CFO Fastow), even though they may not have been present when the offending acts were committed. In other words, the captain goes down with the ship.[4]

Skilling and Lay were found guilty on May 25, 2006, in federal court on multiple counts of fraud, conspiracy to commit fraud, and, in Skilling's case, two counts of insider trading. The fraud charges involved lying to investors, the SEC, credit-rating agencies, and employees about the true financial position of the company, and using off-balance-sheet entities to fraudulently manage reported earnings.

Yet behind the headlines lie many important details that can help explain how the Enron story ended the way it did. Indeed, the Enron story is a source of great learning about the damage that can be created by the kind of thoughtless and, in some ways, inexperienced leadership that poisoned Enron. That makes Enron a far more interesting and informative case than other contemporaneous corporate scandals, such as WorldCom, HealthSouth, Tyco, Adelphia, or Cendant, as it involves delinquency and carelessness beyond the straightforward accounting shenanigans and looting of those cases.

For these reasons, the Enron story is not only an important indicator of where twenty-first-century capitalism can go astray, but also, at base, a story about *us*. After decades of studying the practice of management, I am convinced that very few of us who live in the world of competitive product markets and unforgiving capital markets have not encountered the management behavior and business policies that became so toxic at Enron.

For example, all of us involved in the business world (and other competitive endeavors, as well) are subject to the overconfidence and hubris that led Enron into many high-risk gambles, especially after a roaring success like the one Enron experienced in its early years. We are all similarly vulnerable to denial and defensiveness when our personal reputations are at stake—tendencies that blinded Skilling and Lay to organizational problems and contributed to intolerance of internal dissent regarding the company's controversial financial strategies. As self-interested individuals, we are also all susceptible to incentives that improve our economic well-being and tempt personal opportunism, and many such incentives operated at Enron.

Enron is also about us because many in the business community, including those closest to Enron, simply failed to question the performance of its business model, despite indicators of trouble. Enron was a company that never earned its cost of capital, even when computed on the basis of its inflated earnings reports. According to this metric, it destroyed economic value year after year. Nor did Enron's cash flow ever keep up with its reported earnings. Although this is not unusual for successful startups experiencing hypergrowth, Enron was not a true startup. The company ran an established natural gas pipeline business, and acquired many going concerns in the power generation and water businesses in the United States and abroad. The simple fact is that Enron's profit margins were narrow and declining, and its modest earnings were way out of proportion to the rapidly growing scope and scale of its investments.

Such indicators of distress are not difficult to detect, even within the obscure management commentary and footnotes in Enron's annual reports. With notable exceptions, however (such as the short sellers of Enron's stock), most of us uncritically bought the Enron story as company officials presented it to us. As employees, directors, and advisors, or as intermediaries, business reporters, and business school professors, our failure to question Enron's performance makes us, in a very real sense, participants in the delinquent society that surrounded Enron.

Enron is also a story about us because this company chose to live in an ethical and legal zone that many of us could easily cross into, either because of a desire to gain maximum advantage by exploiting the ambiguities of legal rules and social custom, or through simple ignorance and thoughtlessness. Owen D. Young—the visionary capitalist and founding chair of RCA and NBC, and later chair of General Electric—defined this zone over eighty years ago as the "shadowed space" or "penumbra" between the clear light of rightdoing and the clear light of wrongdoing, where the law is unclear and the spirit of the law is open to interpretation.[5] It was in this penumbra that Skilling, Lay, and many of their colleagues lost their way.

Because of these complexities, it is too easy to think that the criminal convictions of former Enron CEOs Skilling and Lay for fraud will, by themselves, deter similar calamities. That's because much of the behavior that brought Enron down was not illegal. Enron's collapse is as much about incompetence as it is about fraud, and courts have only a limited role to play in protecting shareholders and employees against breakdowns in corporate governance and control.

It is also too simple to conclude that the appropriate remedy for Enron's mistakes and ultimate collapse lies with more regulation of corporate affairs. In the wake of Enron, Congress enacted the Sarbanes-Oxley Act of 2002 to strengthen monitoring and control of public companies by boards of directors. Whatever its eventual impact on board behavior, we need not—and cannot—rely on legislatures to prevent the kinds of problems that destroyed Enron. Solutions to those problems lie not in drafting new laws but rather in the far more complex task of creating, in company after company, organizational processes and structures that promote effective management and ethical behavior. This book attempts to show why that is so.

For readers who have not followed the Enron story as closely as I have, the following plot summary will set the scene for a more in-depth analysis of the origins of Enron's collapse, and of measures that can protect against Enron-type breakdowns in the future. To experienced Enron watchers, this summary will be familiar.

Enron was created in 1985 through the merger of two existing gas pipeline companies. The CEO and "founder" of the new company was Kenneth Lay, who had served as a naval officer in the Pentagon, and who had earned a PhD in economics at the University of Houston before joining the Federal Power Commission in Washington. Lay later switched to the private sector, and worked his way up through the energy industry to become CEO of Houston Natural Gas, one of Enron's predecessor companies. He was widely known as a free-market advocate and an outspoken lobbyist for deregulation.[6]

Jeffrey Skilling succeeded Lay as CEO in 2001. He had begun working with Enron in 1986 as a consultant with McKinsey & Co., and joined Enron in 1990 when Lay made him president of Enron's new trading operations. A graduate of Southern Methodist University and Harvard Business School,

Skilling quickly won Lay's confidence with financial acumen and innovative ideas on trading natural gas. Skilling was known within McKinsey as a talented and charismatic consultant with a brash, in-your-face persona. According to Tom Peters, the bestselling management writer who had worked with him at McKinsey, Skilling "could out-argue God."[7]

Before 1997, Enron was an innovative and profitable player in the newly deregulated natural gas industry. Skilling's big idea was to create fluid and transparent markets for commodities like natural gas that were burdened with highly inefficient delivery systems. In time, the company supported this basic concept with EnronOnLine, a Web-based trading platform that instantly became the world's largest e-commerce system in 1999. Skilling also created a Gas Bank, to provide a "reserve requirement" to back up supply commitments. Enron had a major advantage over competitors as a middleman between producers and consumers because it operated one of the nation's largest natural gas pipeline networks. These innovations enabled Enron to develop and run a futures market for natural gas and create derivative supply contracts that could help customers manage the risks of demand volatility and price swings more effectively than ever before. In this way, Skilling and his colleagues solved a major contracting problem between the producers and users of natural gas, and the rewards were great.

This initial success prompted Enron to extrapolate its business model to other markets. In 1994, Enron officials started trading wholesale electricity, after Congress deregulated the industry and Enron analysts estimated the electricity market to be ten times larger than the natural gas market. Diversification into water utilities and broadband soon followed, as did expansion to other countries that promised to deregulate and privatize energy production and distribution.

Unfortunately, applying the company's middlemen skills to other commodities and developing power projects in diverse markets proved a significant challenge. Still, supreme overconfidence and perverse financial incentives led to a gladiator culture in which executives proposed—and risk managers and the board of directors approved—a growing number of risky gambles with high expected returns. Meanwhile, building on intense lobbying to encourage further domestic deregulation and limit federal oversight of the energy industry, Skilling encouraged Enron executives to exploit recent SEC rule changes, as well as current tax rules, to the hilt.

Many of Enron's investment gambles failed to satisfy its voracious appetite for cash to support its commodity-trading operations, and in 1997

profits declined. This prompted the company to sell overvalued, underperforming assets to off-balance-sheet partnerships controlled by CFO Fastow—
a conflict of interest approved by the board. The idea was to use these mind-
numbingly complex entities to manage reported earnings, minimize
reported debt, and maintain the company's all-important credit rating and
overvalued stock price. Enron also used the off-balance-sheet entities to
hedge its more successful investments—to avoid having to report any declines in their value. The problem was that many of these hedges were not
real, because Enron was essentially hedging with itself.

The idea of a hedge normally is to contract with an outside party that is
prepared—for a price—to take on an investment risk. The outside parties
with which Enron hedged—the so-called Raptor partnerships—were funded
almost entirely with Enron's own stock, an unusual arrangement approved
by the board. This meant that if the value of Enron's investments and its stock
fell at the same time, these off-balance-sheet partnerships would be unable to
meet their obligations. That is precisely what happened in 2000 and 2001,
when two of these hedges were unable to cover Enron's shortfalls.

To help disguise the company's deteriorating financial position, many
outside advisors and bankers either colluded in or acquiesced to these questionable transactions. Enron's sophisticated risk analysis and control system
also experienced serious breakdowns. These breakdowns, along with management's increasing aversion to truth telling, isolated the board from many
evolving realities. In addition, Enron's supernormal growth and skyrocketing stock price made it difficult for most directors to challenge management's strategy and tactics. Still, board members understood that Enron was
trying to move underperforming assets and potential investment losses off
its balance sheet, and red flags should have alerted them to the fact that the
company was short of cash as well as profits. Yet Enron's board failed to detect and prevent violations of accounting principles and rules.

On January 1, 2001, the board appointed Skilling CEO of Enron. After
Enron's stock declined that spring and summer, an increasingly distraught
and volatile Skilling abruptly quit as CEO, claiming personal reasons. Board
chair Lay resumed his role as CEO. As Enron's stock price fell during 2001,
both Skilling and Lay claimed that everything at Enron was fine—even that
its stock was woefully undervalued. That, of course, was not the case.

In the third week of October, Arthur Andersen, Enron's highly compromised outside auditor, "discovered" several large accounting irregularities
related to the off-balance-sheet partnerships. This forced Lay to announce a

$544 million charge against earnings, and a $1.2 billion write-down in shareholders' equity, largely related to the impending closure of the Raptors. Enron collapsed into bankruptcy within weeks, as its trading partners quickly lost faith—proving, once again, that even a hint of negligence or misconduct can be devastating to a company. As Skilling correctly observed, there was a "run on the bank," but not before he and Lay reaped $173 million and $78 million, respectively, from sales of stock and exercised options during 2000 and 2001 (they had cashed out more gains earlier).

In the end, the Justice Department took more than three years to master the financial complexities and legal ambiguities of the Enron case, and to indict Skilling, Lay, and former chief accounting officer Rick Causey. Federal prosecutors claimed that Enron used the Raptors and other off-balance-sheet entities to inflate its reported earnings from the third quarter of 2000 through the third quarter of 2001 by more than $1 billion. The government also claimed that the Raptors did not hold the required amount of independent equity, thereby invalidating their purpose. An examiner appointed by the bankruptcy court claimed even larger-scale violations of GAAP and SEC regulations.

In a plea bargain with government prosecutors, former CFO Fastow admitted that he and others knew that the Raptors were not independent from Enron, and that they therefore should have been included in the company's financial statements. Fastow admitted that this scheme overstated Enron's earnings, and to enriching himself at the expense of Enron's shareholders.

Enron's accounting violations were matched by poor investment decisions. Had Enron's balance sheet from December 31, 2001, been prepared according to GAAP, the company would have had to report about $5 billion in write-downs of impaired investments and uneconomic hedges. Before declaring bankruptcy, the company lost another $5 billion in new power generation, water, and broadband businesses. Yet shareholders never charged board members with a legal breach of their fiduciary duties in failing to oversee these investments and ensuring that Enron complied with accounting rules.

As of November 2006, five banks had paid dearly for their collusion— agreeing to pay shareholders and the SEC nearly $7.5 billion to settle suits claiming that they aided and abetted Enron's deceit—but without admitting guilt. Andrew Fastow had identified two more banks as colluding institutions. A worse fate awaited Arthur Andersen, which was forced to close its doors after a federal jury convicted the auditor of obstruction of justice in the Enron case.

Just weeks before the criminal trial was to begin, in January 2006, Causey, who had been mounting a united defense with Skilling and Lay, defected and negotiated a plea bargain. On July 5, 2006, ten days after his conviction in Houston federal court, Lay died in Aspen, Colorado, from a massive heart attack. That left Skilling standing alone, to be sentenced to twenty-four years in prison. For cooperating with the prosecution, Andrew Fastow saw his plea-bargained ten-year sentence reduced to six years. Skilling, who received four times Fastow's sentence for trying to defend himself, promised a vigorous appeal. Causey was sentenced weeks later to a five-and-a-half-year prison term for his role in Enron's fraud.

Throughout the trial, Skilling and Lay strenuously denied knowledge of any conspiracy to defraud shareholders, despite the fact that fifteen of thirty-four other Enron executives indicted for conspiring to defraud share-holders had already entered guilty pleas. Skilling and Lay argued that these fifteen plea bargainers were all honest men who, like Causey, had been bullied into false confessions by the "witch hunt" tactics of the Justice Department. Lay maintained to his dying day that he was innocent of all charges brought against him. Skilling held fast to a similar position. On September 14, 2007, Skilling submitted a 60,000-word appellant brief demanding that his conviction be reversed and that his case either be dismissed or retried outside Houston under "lawful procedures and a properly instructed jury." On March 3, 2008, Skilling filed a Supplemental Brief arguing that recently unsealed notes of Fastow's interviews with the Enron Task Force showed that government prosecutors had willfully suppressed evidence that would have enabled Skilling to challenge Fastow's incriminating testimony in court and defend himself against the government's conspiracy charges.

How Enron, Skilling, and Lay got into such a mess is the subject of this book. So, too, is how to avoid such pervasive breakdowns in corporate governance and ethics and their enormous social and economic costs.

Part I of the book addresses the origins of Enron's collapse. This investigation shows how the forces that pushed the company along the pathway from innovative to deceptive management originated in specific business policies, as well as the dysfunctional behavior of Enron's leaders, advisors, bankers, and internal and external watchdogs.

Chapter 1 traces how Enron's early innovations mutated into what can only be described as reckless, high-risk gambling. Chapter 2 shows how this transformation stemmed from financial incentives that spurred this gambling with shareholders' money, keyed excessive executive pay to the wrong performance goals, and deepened a deadly addiction to pumping up the company's stock price through a variety of obfuscating maneuvers.

Chapter 3 shows how these perverse incentives, along with other bungled business policies and practices, contributed to a corporate culture that tolerated and sometimes encouraged deception. The ultimate deceits, of course, were the violations (and near violations) of GAAP and SEC rules on financial accounting and reporting. Chapter 4 traces the pathway of Enron's ethical drift, identifying 1997 as the tipping point when the company first used structured financial transactions to disguise its true financial condition.

Chapter 5 analyzes the failure of Enron's board of directors to detect and deter this ethical drift by monitoring corporate affairs and fulfilling its responsibilities on behalf of shareholders. Chapter 6 reveals how members of the investment banking community colluded with Enron executives in disguising the company's true financial condition. Chapter 7 explains how outside financial analysts, credit-rating bodies, and regulatory agencies missed, for the most part, the dark side of the Enron story.

Part II of the book addresses three central implications of the Enron story, as revealed in Part I. The first relates to the lack of oversight by Enron's board of directors. Chapter 8 argues that a potentially powerful remedy for the governance breakdown that afflicted Enron as a *public company* can be found outside the legislative and legal arena, in the neighboring world of *private companies*. This remedy is best observed in formerly public companies that—aided by professional buyout firms—have been taken private and armed with active directors who pursue common-sense governance practices that have stood the test of time. In arguing for the private-equity model of corporate governance, I do not suggest that boards of public companies can or should copy it directly. Public and private companies clearly differ markedly in their ownership structures, and in the rules governing director independence. I do suggest, however, that directors of public companies can adapt key aspects of the private-equity governance model, to ensure that they fulfill their oversight responsibilities.

Chapter 9 addresses a second set of implications of the Enron story related to executive compensation. Warren Buffett has called executive compensation "the acid test of corporate governance." The Enron case provides a dramatic example of executive compensation veering off the track. Chapter 9 makes specific recommendations for designing executive pay in public companies, including the effective use of stock-based compensation and comparative performance measures, and the need to balance turbocharged incentives with turbocharged controls.

Chapter 10 addresses a third implication of the Enron story for contemporary business: how to preserve ethical discipline when the legal rules of the game are ambiguous, and executives stand to reap enormous rewards by exaggerating or camouflaging a company's true economic performance. Both conditions existed at Enron, and it was not the only firm to inhabit that shadowed space. Chapter 11 offers multiple examples of the company's life in the penumbra between clear rightdoing and clear wrongdoing, where Skilling, Lay, and many of their colleagues lost their way. The chapter then outlines organizational processes that are critical to reinforcing ethical discipline, and that were noticeably lacking at Enron despite its nicely printed code of ethics.

The research for this book is based largely on an extensive library of public information amounting to millions of pages, supplemented by interviews with former Enron executives. Internal Enron documents from various sources have also fallen into my hands in the course of my research, and these extend and deepen the other information.

The public information falls into several categories, including:

- Documents subpoenaed by various congressional committees in the aftermath of Enron's bankruptcy. These documents include minutes from meetings of the board of directors and its finance and audit committees, copies of presentations to the board or its subcommittees by Enron executives, presentations to investors in Enron's off-balance-sheet partnerships, and other internal documents on the status of Enron's business and merchant investment portfolio.
- Testimonies of former Enron executives and directors subpoenaed by various congressional committees, given under oath and risk of perjury, and related to the company's business model, financial transactions, and management.
- Testimonies from individuals associated with the SEC, Enron's various bankers, and credit-rating agencies.
- Reports of various House and Senate committees based on these documents, personal testimonies, and the work of their research staffs.
- The response of Enron's directors to the report of the Permanent Subcommittee on Investigations of the Senate Governmental Affairs Committee.

- The Powers report, produced by the Special Investigative Committee of the Board of Directors of Enron Corp. in the months immediately following Enron's bankruptcy.
- The four-volume report of Neal Batson, the examiner appointed by the New York State Bankruptcy Court. This report covers a wide range of subjects, ranging from technical analysis of accounting practices to the behavior of Enron's board of directors.
- Court documents and decisions from both domestic and foreign jurisdictions.
- State and federal statutes, and related law review articles.
- Books by investigative reporters and former Enron employees, technical articles from trade journals, and thousands of articles from the business and financial press (including the *New York Times, Wall Street Journal, Financial Times, Houston Chronicle, Fortune, the Economist,* and many more periodicals in the United States and abroad). Many skilled and experienced reporters have doggedly pursued the Enron story, leaving a record worthy of careful inspection.
- Extensive videotaped interviews of Kenneth Lay and Jeffrey Skilling at the University of Virginia's Darden School of Business Administration and at Harvard Business School.
- Transcripts of the Skilling/Lay criminal trial, held in Houston during the spring of 2006.
- Skilling's appeal of his May 25, 2006, conviction.
- The Department of Justice's rebuttal to Skilling's appeal.
- Skilling's December 21, 2007, reply to the DOJ's rebuttal brief.

Over the past two years, I have interviewed some two dozen former executives, in encounters lasting from one hour to several days. I began by meeting with former students employed at Enron, and then by following their suggestions for interviews with more senior and knowledgeable executives (some agreed to meet and some did not). As my research questions became clearer, I sought more targeted interviews related to Enron's accounting and board practices. This approach then mutated into a policy of speaking with anyone with information relevant to my emerging themes.

In pursuing this strategy, certain rules of the game emerged. The first—admittedly controversial and contrary to my natural instincts—was to refrain from pursuing interviews with indicted executives during the pretrial period. While their testimony might have added important nuance to my story, I did not want to be open to influence by those whose legal stakes were so high. In addition, I wanted to be respectful of a grand jury investigating many of these individuals. Finally, because key Enron executives were contesting each other's testimonies, I thought it best not to place myself in the midst of controversies that were best left to the courts. At the time of my research, federal prosecutors had charged thirty-four executives with various acts of fraud and conspiracy. This resulted in fifteen guilty pleas, five jury convictions, two acquittals, and eight others awaiting trial.

A second, related rule was to refrain from contacting another 114 executives whom the government alleged were part of a broad conspiracy to defraud Enron's shareholders. My rationale was the same as that for avoiding the already indicted executives.

These two rules have limited my ability to pursue a dozen or so executives who appeared to be central players in Enron's business strategies and its post-1997 drift from innovation to reckless gambling to deceptive management. Without their direct testimony, which may become available in the future under different legal circumstances, I have had to piece together the origins of Enron's collapse from the publicly available information and interviews with executives who were both unindicted and willing to meet.

I have solicited comments on chapter drafts from a small group of faculty colleagues, former Enron executives, and experienced corporate executives and directors who have come to know my work and who possess distinctive, technical competence in matters related to the Enron story. While this process in no way ensured complete accuracy or authenticity, it has afforded me a second opinion from those who were involved in either managing Enron or assessing from the outside what was going wrong.

As a final comment on sources and methods, I need to stress that I have relied on information that was available to me at the date of printing. Additional information may appear now that a grand jury is no longer hanging over the heads of former Enron executives. Jeffrey Skilling, for example, has already contested, in the course of his appeal, the facts and interpretations on the basis of which he was convicted. Enron's directors also vigorously dispute reports on their role in Enron's collapse.[8] None of these arguments can, however, alter the fundamental fact that something was terribly wrong at Enron and that the persons in charge did not prevent it.

The Origins of Enron's Collapse

Part I analyzes the failings of the myriad actors who bear some responsibility for the Enron debacle, and the roots of their failures. The evidence presented in the next four chapters suggests that before fraud at Enron there was fatal thoughtlessness and incompetence among its executives. Understanding the scope of Enron's managerial incompetence is key to understanding the company's ethical drift, and the subsequent indictments, plea bargains, and convictions of mid-level and top-level executives. Indeed, the evidence presented here suggests that Enron's collapse resulted less from a criminal conspiracy carefully planned by Enron's leaders (as found by the jury in the criminal trial of Jeffrey Skilling and Kenneth Lay) and more from a pattern of deceptive behavior that unfolded in incremental steps over time, as a result of pride and hubris, a host of unprofitable new ventures and bad investment decisions, poorly designed and administered incentives, a culture of deceit, and breakdowns in performance measurement and control systems at a time when Enron had trouble meeting its aggressive earnings targets.

The ensuing three chapters address the stunning lack of attentive oversight of these matters by Enron's board of directors, the collusion of its bankers in disguising the company's true financial condition, and the failure of public and private watchdogs to protect the interests of Enron's employees and shareholders and the public at large.

Passive behavior as both decision makers and overseers was a hallmark of Enron's board. When unsure of the risks of aggressive investments and questionable accounting policies, and when vaguely worded or highly technical reports created confusion, board members were content to rely on other directors' perceptions rather than to seek clarification. The directors also manifested submissiveness and lack of deliberation in monitoring off-balance-sheet partnerships, and in their apparent fear of stepping on the toes of operating executives. One board member who did dare to question management's representations was viewed as being "too negative" and essentially asked to resign.

Long-standing personal relationships and emotional bonds with Ken Lay precluded deliberate assessment of Enron's executive leadership, and effectively defined a compliant and noninterventionist role for the board.[1] Indeed, once the media conferred rock-star status on Enron's senior executives, the board effectively became their entourage. The result was that the directors allowed fixable problems to fester into uncontrolled cancers that wounded vital corporate organs. In so doing, Enron's directors broke their bond of accountability to the company's owners, and their bond of stewardship on behalf of its employees.[2]

This failure does not imply that Enron's board was populated by bad people. To the contrary, what is notable about this case is that the directors who caused such great harm by failing to take precautions against predictable and preventable misconduct were—outside the context of Enron's board—principled and responsible leaders in the worlds of business, education, medical research, and public service.[3] Neither does this failure suggest that the behavior of the directors was unique to Enron. Indeed, one of the most intriguing facets of the Enron story is that its directors suffered from many of the same maladies that plagued the boards of other large, publicly owned corporations during the late 1990s. What *is* unique about Enron, however, is the vast scope of its unsuccessful gambles and unmonitored financial maneuverings, and the enormity of destruction in value that resulted.

Responsibility for the Enron story is not limited to those who worked within the walls of the company's Houston headquarters every day, or to those who populated the boardroom several times a year. Actors outside the corporate hierarchy also enabled Enron's inept management and financial deception, interacting with Enron to varying degrees and in different contexts. Some actively provided assistance, while the passivity of others allowed problems to balloon unchecked. Some spent a great deal of time working hand in hand with Enron executives, while others had only intermittent and superficial contact with the company. What each had in common was the understanding that, at some level, they had a responsibility to protect shareholders, the marketplace, and other stakeholders from the misdeeds of corporations. As we will see, not all these watchdogs are created equal, not all watch the same areas, and not all were watching.

Perhaps the most culpable were the private professionals that provided Enron with outside expertise. These lawyers, accountants, and bankers collaborated with Enron to help it achieve its financial goals. The bankers provided infusions of cash through complex financial structures of questionable legality, the accountants approved aggressive accounting choices, and the lawyers signed off on all of it. Each of these parties is primarily profit driven and owes limited duties to the public. Their goal is to maximize their own bottom line while helping clients achieve their particular goals. Though they are deeply knowledgeable about regulations in their particular spheres, they often use that knowledge to maneuver clients around regulatory landmines and constraints.

Governmental entities such as the Securities and Exchange Commission, and quasi-governmental entities such as the credit-rating agencies, serve the public interest more directly than bankers and accountants, and must shoulder some responsibility for failing to warn the public about the dangers that Enron's business tactics posed to investors. However, although these public watchdogs performed their duties torpidly, they are less culpable than the private watchdogs because they were not active participants in misdeeds: theirs were errors of complacency.

Overwhelmed regulatory systems were vulnerable to manipulation and evasion—particularly at Enron's creative hands. Different agencies failed to piece together chunks of data that posed no concern when viewed independently to see the broader picture, and therefore missed or ignored indications of wrongdoing. Attention from these guardians of the marketplace is no guarantee that they will alert the public to problems ahead of time. However, the scale of irregularities within the Enron story makes it difficult to understand why the watchdogs charged with protecting the public interest were quiet for so long.

CHAPTER 1

From Innovation to Reckless Gambling

In the face of Enron's dramatic collapse and public disgrace, it is easy to forget that the company was a highly innovative enterprise for much of the 1990s. This chapter focuses on the innovations that transformed this old-line operator of natural gas pipelines into a new-economy trading company. Enron's successful entry into trading natural gas provided a platform for the company's later expansion into other commodity markets, and its emergence as a leading-edge commodity trader.

This strategy generated explosive growth. However, it also failed in two important respects. First, the successful strategy Enron developed for the natural gas business ran into some serious problems when applied to electric power and never really worked in the broadband and water markets. Second, the company never came close to earning a return on capital employed in its business (ROCE) equal to the cost of that capital (WACC or weighted average cost of capital) during the 1990s (see Figure 1.1). Indeed, Enron as a whole does not appear to have earned its own cost of capital on a sustained basis.[1] Thus, most of the company's various innovations—all backed by substantial capital investments—failed to create real economic value for its shareholders.

Before analyzing the roots of these failures, this chapter explains the natural gas strategy itself, largely put together by Jeffrey Skilling during the early 1990s. This strategy enabled the company to establish a dominant competitive position as an intermediary or middleman between producers and consumers in newly deregulated energy markets. In its early application, this strategy had all the markings of a winner. However, the inexperience of Enron's most senior leaders in setting up and operating new businesses, coupled with the hubris or supreme overconfidence that followed early successes in natural gas, led the company across the frontier of thoughtful innovation into a world of increasingly risky gambles.

Early Innovation: Skilling's Natural Gas Strategy

Back in 1989, Jeff Skilling's big idea was to create a fluid market for natural gas in the wake of industry deregulation and an unshackled trading environment, from which Enron would emerge as the dominant middleman. Before deregulation, more than 75 percent of gas sales to wholesalers and large end users had occurred through the spot market, with significant volatility in prices.[2] *Gas producers,* however, operated under federal price controls and pipeline companies under long-term contracts that obliged them to buy specified amounts of gas from producers at stated prices. This arrangement discouraged the production of natural gas and constrained demand.

To facilitate both the freeing of prices at the producer level (which began when Congress passed the Natural Gas Policy Act of 1978) and the movement of natural gas around the country more efficiently, in 1985 the Federal Energy Regulatory Commission (FERC) started giving incentives to long-

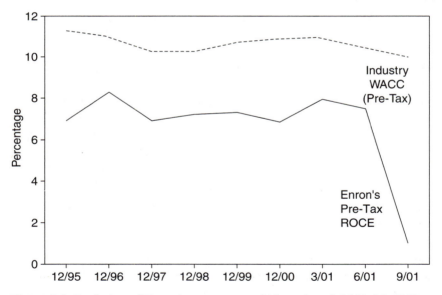

Figure 1.1 Evolution of Enron's return on capital employed, 1995–3Q 2001. Excludes one-time charges, gains on sales of assets. Includes interest income, equity in earnings of affiliates, and assets/liabilities from risk management on a net basis. Sources: 10Ks, 10Qs, Mars & Co. analysis.

distance pipelines to provide third-party transportation services to shippers who had made their own gas supply arrangements at a federally approved price.[3] Seven years later, in April 1992, FERC completed the process of deregulating natural gas sales with Order 636 mandating open access to the natural gas pipeline system. With prices now deregulated at the wellhead and access to distribution assured at a standard price, more natural gas could be sold in more markets under more competitive conditions.[4] Although this left many pipeline companies, including Enron, with overpriced, long-term supply contracts to contend with, deregulation created enormous opportunities for those who recognized them.

Skilling—then still an energy consultant at McKinsey & Co.—saw that deregulation would lead to an increased supply of gas, and that new utilities would want to burn that gas to make electricity. All that was needed was an intermediary to aggregate supplies from gas producers and then guarantee reliable delivery to utilities and other large-scale consumers. Skilling knew that Enron was well placed to play such a logistical role by tying together supply and demand, and by figuring out the most cost-effective way to transport gas to its destinations.[5] Indeed, Enron was already in the logistics business, as the following example shows:

> In 1999, Peoples Gas Light & Coke Co. of Chicago, a local distribution company, signed a five-year gas procurement deal with Enron. Enron took over Peoples' scheduling of gas pipelines and storage assets that Enron then could use to meet commitments for a broad array of other customers. In the meantime, it procured gas daily as Peoples needed it, provided working capital, handled accounts receivable and payable, managed storage, and financed the gas in storage.[6]

Skilling's key insight was that Enron could capture the intermediation role by using brains rather than by owning physical assets. To his way of thinking, Enron's traditional strategy of ensuring reliable delivery of natural gas with plants and pipelines was an old-fashioned, "asset-heavy" way of doing business. This insight developed into Enron's "asset-light" strategy for natural gas.

Three elements of Skilling's asset-light strategy were critical to its success: a guaranteed source of supply, efficient distribution, and market-making capabilities. Enron had aspects of all three elements covered. The critical distribution element—gas storage facilities and pipelines—was already in place: as a result of the merger that created it, Enron possessed the largest natural gas pipeline network in the country. The first and third elements constituted Enron's greatest innovations.

To line up sure sources of supply (and supply insurance), Skilling's boldest idea was to propose, in 1989, a Gas Bank that Enron would use to buy and sell gas for future delivery. He knew that Enron—like a commercial bank and its reserve requirement—did not need 100 percent inventory to back up supply contracts. The Gas Bank was, in essence, Enron's reserve requirement, composed of pooled gas supplies from various sources—some purchased under standard long-term contracts, some secured through Enron's innovative Volumetric Production Payments (VPP) program.

Under VPP, Enron paid cash to producers for specified future amounts of oil and gas. This cash advance was secured not by the producing company but by its production fields. This arrangement had two benefits: first, Enron would be repaid in gas rather than cash, enabling it to lock up long-term supplies; second, securing its loans with oil and gas protected Enron from the risk that the producer would go bankrupt.[7]

The Gas Bank, supported by VPP, was a promising idea. The up-front cash payments enabled thinly capitalized producers to drill more wells and guarantee more supplies to the Gas Bank under both standard and VPP contracts. With more guaranteed supplies of natural gas on the market, gas-fired power plants became more attractive to lenders. As more debt-financed gas plants were built, gas consumption would rise, which would mean more business for Enron's pipeline business. A complete virtuous circle was in place.

That brings us to market making, the third leg of Skilling's evolving energy strategy. Enron's innovation in market making was the creation of standard contracts with buyers based on long-term contracts with suppliers. Before this innovation, with which other marketers were also experimenting, gas suppliers and customers could take up to nine months to negotiate long-term contracts, and legal fees on both sides were enormous. Standardized contracts enabled Enron to sign, seal, and deliver supply agreements in as little as two weeks, and at lower cost. The faster Enron could close deals, the more liquid it would be, because it would not have to hold as much inventory for possible delivery after deals were signed. And the more liquid Enron could be, the lower its debt and interest costs, and the higher its profit margins.

Enron also promoted the firm contract. Before its entry into gas trading, delivery contracts were often interruptible: when gas prices surged, suppliers could default, either because they could no longer make money on the contract, or because they had found a buyer willing to pay more. To build trust with customers, Enron offered contracts that guaranteed gas deliveries unless interrupted by "acts of God," such as hurricanes. Fulfilling such contracts was not always easy, but Enron knew it was the only way to develop a functioning gas market.

Buying and selling gas were only part of Enron's market making. Another important strategy was breaking up long-term supply contracts into smaller segments and selling off pieces to suit specific customers' needs. By designing such "derivative products" (similar to stripped treasury bills, whereby principal and interest are sold separately), Enron—along with a few other natural gas marketers—could help customers manage volatility in demand, prices, and liquidity. For example, Enron could enter into a long-term contract with an oil or gas producer, and sell part of that guaranteed supply to a customer that needed a two-to-three-year contract, and another part to a customer interested in a ten-year deal.

(In finance, a derivative is basically a contract that promises payment from one investor to another, contingent on a future event such as a price increase or change in interest rates. The value of a derivative is determined by fluctuations in the underlying asset. The most common underlying assets include stocks, bonds, commodities, currencies, interest rates, and market indexes. Futures contracts, forward contracts, options, and swaps are the most common types of derivatives. Because derivatives are just contracts between two parties, just about anything can be used as an underlying asset. There are even derivatives based on weather data, such as the amount of rain or the number of sunny days in a particular region. Derivatives are generally used to hedge risk, but also can be used for speculative purposes. Determining what risks exist in an investment and then handling those risks in a way best suited to your investment objectives is typically referred to as "risk management"—an activity in which Enron invested very heavily.)[8]

Skilling took the core idea of the Gas Bank to CEO Kenneth L. Lay, and recommended that Lay hire him to run the new venture. They quickly agreed to launch the proposal on Skilling's terms, and on August 1, 1990, Skilling joined Enron as chair and CEO of the new Enron Finance Corp. into which the Gas Bank was integrated. (Enron Finance was later renamed Enron Capital & Trade Resources, in which Skilling received a 5 percent phantom-equity stake.)[9]

One of Skilling's next steps at Enron was to petition the Securities and Exchange Commission (SEC) for permission to adopt mark-to-market accounting—until then authorized only for financial institutions.[10] Under mark-to-market accounting, Enron would book the entire revenue and profit stream from a contract the year it was signed (discounted for the risk of default and potential interruptions in payments). That approach contrasted markedly with traditional accrual accounting, in which revenues and profits were recorded each year during the contract.[11] After active lobbying by Enron, and by Arthur Andersen on Enron's behalf, the SEC granted permission to use mark-to-market accounting for natural gas trading from 1992 forward.

Enron became the first nonfinancial public company to adopt the technique, and Skilling quickly hired a team of sophisticated analysts who could figure out how to value long-term contracts.[12] In fact, Enron used mark-to-market accounting to record most trades, including three-to-twenty-year contracts, which eventually accounted for 30 percent of the company's trading volume.[13]

Success was almost immediate: gas sales surged, as buyers no longer faced the risk that gas prices would fluctuate. By 1992 Enron was the largest marketer of natural gas in North America, able to sell ten-year, fixed-price contracts with average prices as high as $3.50 per 1,000 cubic feet, even though current prices were as low as $1.30. Thanks to the large margins on this fast-growing book of business, Enron's reported earnings from gas sales and trading jumped from $29 million in 1990, before interest and taxes (or 3.7 percent of total earnings), to $122 million in 1992 (12.4 percent of total earnings).[14] At its peak, Enron's gas-trading business reportedly had three hundred main clients.[15]

The Gas Bank and mark-to-market accounting put Jeff Skilling on the map. Those practices also established Enron as the first major innovator in the natural gas business in years. And once the company became the leading natural gas trader, it was a natural step to expand its capabilities into trading *energy*—which, in the first instance, included electricity.

With secure sources of supply, efficient distribution, and leading-edge trading and contracting all coming together, Skilling realized that it was important to get big quickly. Bigger players would be stronger competitors because they could select the best, lowest-cost solutions for customers from a diversified portfolio of suppliers. Skilling also understood that because margins on commodity-related transactions are typically narrow (and would shrink further as new entrants imitated Enron), the way to make money was to build volume—and the faster the better, to prove the merit of the business model to Ken Lay and Enron's board.[16] Finally, Skilling believed that Enron could eliminate its risk if its trading portfolio were properly hedged (by purchasing, for example, assets whose prices tended to move in the opposite direction of those in the portfolio). The intended result was an investor's dream: low risk, high return.

Skilling's asset-light strategy did not replace, but rather built on, Enron's traditional asset-heavy gas transport and power generation businesses. Using its distribution system and operational efficiencies, the company built market share while steadily increasing profits. Over time, even as its hard-asset side of the business declined as a percentage of total sales, it continued to account for a major proportion of corporate profits.[17] Indeed, these operations generated solid returns and cash flows even after Enron's bankruptcy.[18] Meanwhile, Skilling's idea of using industrial assets as a wedge for developing trading and finance businesses quickly gained traction with Lay and Enron's traditional pipeline executives, and guided the company's rapid entry into deregulating energy markets around the world.

The Debut of EnronOnline

Fast forward to November 1999, when the company introduced Enron-Online, its new Web site. A logical extension of the company's gas-trading business, EnronOnline became the largest e-commerce entity and trading platform in the world within a few weeks of its launch.

Developed by Louise Kitchen, a confident and impatient thirty-year-old Brit who had been Enron's head natural gas trader in Europe, and a thirty-person team based in London and Houston, EnronOnline transformed Enron's trading business by enabling it to close deals in seconds. During the first five months of 2000, hundreds of traders used this Web site to execute 110,000 transactions involving more than eight hundred different products with a total value exceeding $45 billion.[19] EnronOnline quickly became the toast of cyber-space, cannibalizing 60 percent of the company's traditional phone/fax/e-mail energy transactions and totaling more than the revenues of eBay, Amazon, Dell, and Cisco combined.[20] By 2001 Enron's gas marketing unit was the nation's largest, selling 25 percent of all U.S. wholesale natural gas.[21]

When Skilling first heard of Kitchen's efforts, he let it be known that he was not interested in an automated trading system that applied the technology of E*Trade and Charles Schwab to commodities. Enron had made good money as a market maker by influencing price and volume from one side of a trade—as a buyer or seller. Skilling doubted that creating a neutral marketplace where Enron would execute trades for other companies without acting as a principal was a profitable idea. But when he understood that anyone who bought gas from EnronOnline would be buying it from Enron, and that any gas sold on EnronOnline would be sold by Enron, he bought the idea.[22]

It is easy to underestimate what was required to make this idea work. The technology had to be bulletproof, so that with one click the computer network would flawlessly process a trade that might be entered in London, recorded in Houston, and confirmed back in London, where the books would be kept in this example. Enron also had to ensure that its contracts for each commodity met the needs of both trading parties. EnronOnline had to conform to different laws in the United States, Great Britain, and the other European countries in which it operated. And its architects needed to differentiate EnronOnline from a regulated exchange, so that added complications wouldn't kill the project.

EnronOnline began with natural gas and electricity—for which large, liquid markets already existed—and gradually ramped up to other products. As their repertoire of trading skills expanded, Enron officials applied their knowledge and middleman skills to other traditional commodities. After starting with U.S. gas, the Web site added Canadian gas, U.S. electricity, Nordic electricity, coal, pulp and paper, and plastics. Over time, Enron expanded into an increasing array of less traditional products as weather hedges (to insure, for example, ski lodges against a lack of snowfall).

EnronOnline displayed bid and ask prices for each contract, so customers would not think Enron was manipulating the market or ripping them off. Traders liked the transparency, and EnronOnline had more than 450 active customers within two months of its launch. During 2000, its first full year of operation, the Web site executed 548,000 transactions with a value of $336 billion, and had become the company's most important business.[23] EnronOnline also quickly became the place to go for accurate, up-to-the-minute prices for dozens of products. Few commodity traders failed to keep one of their screens permanently tuned to Enron's Web site.

Both EnronOnline and the Gas Bank turned out to be powerful drivers of Enron's growth. The Gas Bank launched Enron into orbit as a leading energy trader, while EnronOnline facilitated Enron's development into a broad-line commodities trader. According to Enron, profits from its energy-trading operations in the fiscal year before its collapse were $2.3 billion. Such returns would have made Enron Wholesale Services (the crown jewel of Skilling's asset-light strategy, of which EnronOnline was only a part) one of the most profitable U.S. companies as a stand-alone entity. In both endeavors, Enron was able to stake out an early competitive advantage, not just as the first mover but also through innovative ideas supported by new contracting and trading technologies.

This spectacular launch and growth notwithstanding, there are several troubling questions about the wholesale services business. First, it is not entirely clear how profitable Enron's trading operations actually were. Although Wholesale Services generated $2.3 billion in income in 2000 (before interest and taxes), aggressive use of mark-to-market accounting inflated trading profits.

Mark-to-market accounting—which records the entire value of long-term contracts today—requires making many assumptions about the future prices of commodities.[24] Such assumptions can be credible in liquid markets, where traders use a "forward price curve." However, such assumptions are difficult to justify in illiquid markets, where a forward price curve is at best a very rough estimate.[25] (Such assumptions are also difficult to hedge.) To offset those concerns, Enron's chief risk officer was responsible for validating traders' forward price curves and for seeking outside verification whenever possible.[26] However, this control system experienced costly breakdowns and misjudgments under bureaucratic pressures described in Chapter 2. To complicate this picture, Enron started transferring bad transactions to off-balance-sheet partnerships, to avoid reporting write-downs on its income statement.

Moreover, although the commodity-trading and derivatives business grew dramatically throughout the Skilling era, the spreads on individual trades were narrowing, thanks to Enron's policy of making prices transparent, and the entry of competitors into Web-based energy trading. Smaller trading spreads meant that Enron needed higher and higher trading volumes to sustain profit levels. And, as trading volumes rose, the company was forced to raise more and more debt to keep the business going. Because it stood in the middle of each trade, Enron had to carry an increasing amount of various commodities on its books as volumes increased. Sometimes this inventory failed to move for days and even weeks until it could get the prices it wanted. By the end of 2000, the company's long-term debt exceeded $8 billion, and that figure skyrocketed to just under $10 billion in the first quarter of 2001. Enron's interest expense alone was $835 million in 2000. Prorating part of this amount to Wholesale Services would reduce its reported—and overstated—profits significantly.

It is also unclear whether Enron actually created a large, new market for natural gas and later electricity—or merely the appearance of such a market. During 2001, for example, a vastly greater volume of natural gas was traded on paper than moved physically. Heavy emphasis on trading futures and derivatives can produce that result, but that is exactly the point: the market for risk-management instruments appears to have vastly exceeded demand for the underlying commodity. Although this is characteristic of all commodity markets, the size of the multiple in this case is remarkable: one market participant told me that the ratio of gas trades to deliveries was 43–1! The same dynamic appears to have been at work in power trading. In 2002, the year after Enron's collapse and the inflated trading during the California energy crisis, the volume of power trades fell by 70 percent—suggesting that the market had found a much lower equilibrium.[27]

So, when we acknowledge Skilling's brilliance as the principal architect of Enron's gas strategy, and the company's success as an innovative energy and commodity trader, we should avoid exaggerated financial claims. The company's true track record emerged only after a full restatement of its financial reports was submitted to the bankruptcy court. Some insiders seriously doubt that Enron's trading operations were ever profitable in its later years.

Enron clearly became less profitable as it grew. The company's ROCE peaked at slightly over 7 percent in 1992. After Enron radically increased its investment in electricity-producing assets (see below), its ROCE fell to 4–5 percent through 1996.[28] This return then rose to 6.35 percent in 1999 but collapsed again to less than 5 percent in 2000. Thus Enron was consistently failing to earn a ROCE commensurate with the cost of that capital, even as its revenues were rising by more than 40 percent per year and aggressive mark-to-market accounting was inflating its reported profits.[29]

From Innovation to Hubris

As noted above, Enron's success in natural gas encouraged its managers to try to replicate its business model in other industries, such as electricity, coal, steel, paper and pulp, plastics, water, and broadband. According to Skilling, these markets shared some characteristics. They tended to be fragmented and undergoing significant change, such as deregulation. Distribution channels were highly complex, capital intensive, and dedicated to a single commodity. Sales cycles were lengthy. Supply and service contracts tended to include loosely defined performance guarantees. Prices were not transparent—most deals were struck in the strictest confidence without public disclosure. And even buyers who needed some flexibility in managing their supplies and price risks were typically saddled with long-term, fixed-price contracts. The result was a high degree of market inefficiency—and the potential for substantial profit margins.

Because these markets appeared to share important characteristics, Skilling argued that Enron could apply the same logistics system, risk-monitoring system, and back-office and accounting systems to expand its trading business: "If you have the same general [market] characteristics, all you have to do is change the units. Enron has a huge investment in capabilities that can be deployed instantly into new markets at no cost."[30]

Skilling had plenty of reasons to be confident. Wasn't he the person most responsible for transforming Enron from an old-line pipeline company into a new-economy growth machine? Didn't his innovations spur Enron's revenues to rise to more than $30 billion by 1998, and its market capitalization to triple during the mid-1990s? For Skilling, the message was straightforward: no matter how complicated a trading environment, Enron employees could use their considerable knowledge base to figure out how to enter it successfully. Or, as Skilling told a November 2000 management conference, "Enron had found the one successful business model that could be applied to any market."[31]

Skilling's side of the house consisted of executives who had grown up in a transaction-oriented culture, in which every day and every hour brought winners and losers at the trading desk. His inner circle of executives and analysts, along with the young MBAs they hired, were celebrated as winners both inside and outside the company because of their innovative trading deals and proprietary trading technology. They had witnessed the successful development of EnronOnline, the most sophisticated trading platform the world had ever seen, and they had seen how this platform achieved almost instant success in the marketplace. Many had already made a great deal of money through large bonuses and stock options. This was heady stuff for Skilling's young team.

If nothing else, Enron put its money where its mouth was, entering just about every deregulated industry and trading space around the world. Yet, despite claims of a generally applicable business model, Enron's rush to commoditize other markets turned out to be difficult and risky. As its reach severely exceeded its grasp, its ventures into electric power generation, broadband, and water turned into costly failures.

These failures appear to have been fueled by extreme overconfidence and related narcissism. How deep this hubris ran within Enron is difficult to say.[32] But a look at Enron's failures suggests that arrogance and appetite for risk clouded the company's collective judgment about where and how to invest its capital. Many of Enron's investments in deregulating markets were fraught with peril, and many of the assumptions used by Enron executives to justify their deals assumed that nothing would ever go wrong—that political delays in building plants would never occur, that cost overruns were unlikely, that government partners would never seek to renegotiate contracts, that technologies would never fail to work as planned, and that markets would never fail to develop as imagined.

Electricity

Enron saw investing in gas-fired power plants as a natural extension of its gas-supply business, and a precursor to expanding into the electricity-trading business. Indeed, long before the company started trading electricity and electricity derivatives, it controlled and operated power plants in Virginia and Massachusetts as well as the Houston area. By 1990 Enron was building power generating capacity at Teesside, in the United Kingdom, along with facilities to process natural gas.

Deregulation of the electric power industry broke apart an integrated supply chain, and enabled companies such as Enron to choose which parts to operate. In lobbying for electricity deregulation, Enron advocated splitting utilities into three separate businesses: power generation, long-distance transmission, and distribution wires to local homes and businesses.[33] The company thought that if private power plants were owned separately from power distribution lines, and if those lines could provide transport services to any number of competing power markets, more competition would exist and prices to end users would fall. Businesses logically would be most interested in energy savings, with residential customers next. Enron intended to go after these segments in that order, backed up by an expert trading and financial services (risk management) operation.

The company had launched its electricity-trading operation in 1994, after obtaining an SEC exception from the Public Utility Holding Company Act of 1935 because it was primarily trading electricity rather than producing it. Electricity trading looked attractive to Enron for several reasons. First, the company was acquainted with power plants. Second, it knew a lot about trading commodities whose prices fluctuated around the country owing to weather and supply problems (called "basis risk"). Third, the wholesale electricity market was extremely volatile, and given volatility and pricing disparities across markets, Enron sensed profitable opportunities as an intermediary.[34] Fourth, Enron correctly thought that the natural gas and electricity industries would converge as a result of electricity deregulation, an inevitable decline of the price of electricity at the consumer's meter, increased substitutability of electricity for gas by consumers, and the greater possibilities of electric power generating plants selecting gas as their fuel of choice. (Gas and electricity traders were soon sitting side by side at Enron and at other commodity-trading companies as well.)[35]

Enron continued to invest in power plants during the mid-1990s as a supply base for its trading operations. By the end of the decade, Enron had built with local partners twenty-six new power plants—ten in the United States and sixteen overseas—and the company was the number one marketer of electricity in the United States.[36] Unfortunately, two of these power plant investments—the Dabhol power project in India and the acquisition of Portland General, an electric utility in Oregon—ended up losing significant amounts of money.

Overseas Expansion

Following its successes in the deregulated natural gas industry in the United States and its early experience in transferring its wholesale gas marketing expertise to the developing electric power market, Enron trained its sights on the deregulating natural gas and electricity markets abroad. The goal, according to Enron International CEO Joseph Sutton, was to pursue future growth where it was greatest—outside the United States and Europe.[37] While Enron had a variety of power projects stretching across the globe, the two largest were Teesside in the United Kingdom, successfully started in 1993, and Dabhol in India, a two-phase project scheduled to start up at the end of 1996. Dabhol ended up being a very troubled and costly venture. Several other international power projects met similar fates.

When India decided to open its electricity market to foreigners, after years of shortages and losses from poorly managed power systems, Enron and its coinvestors, GE and Bechtel, saw a major opportunity. In 1993—after eighteen months of negotiation and more than thirty trips to India by the then Enron International chief Rebecca Mark—Enron signed a contract to build the Dabhol power plant and to sell all its electricity at a guaranteed price to the Maharashtra State Electricity Board (MSEB) for twenty years. The project would include the world's largest gas-fired power plant, located two hundred miles south of Bombay.

Maharashtra was India's third-largest state, and the Dabhol project was to be the cornerstone of Enron's activities throughout the country. Because Dabhol would be a major customer for liquefied natural gas (LNG), the project included construction of a modern port facility that could unload large tankers, and a plant for regasifying imported LNG. Enron anticipated that this facility would become the hub of a wholesale and retail natural gas network throughout India.[38] Enron also intended to link the largest power plant on the subcontinent with an LNG operation in the Middle East. Dabhol represented a grandiose vision.

The World Bank refused to finance the two-phased project, arguing that it was too large and would cost the MSEB too much, because Enron had negotiated a high price for the electricity. The consortium nevertheless managed to line up $643 million in debt financing for the 740-megawatt first phase, and also planned a 1,444-megawatt second phase. Enron owned 80 percent of the project, while GE and Bechtel each contributed 10 percent.

Immediately after the contract was signed, critics contested it on the grounds that

1. the state had awarded the contract to Enron in a closed, uncompetitive process,
2. the MSEB had to purchase the gas even if it didn't need the supply,
3. the guaranteed price of the gas was too high,
4. local and state governments had ignored standard environmental approvals, and
5. the national government had to pay Enron if the MSEB defaulted.

In short, the public thought the deal too sweet for Enron. After a political party opposing the Dabhol power plant won a critical state election, construction was suspended while various suits and countersuits worked their way through local courts. In the interim, interest payments and project delays were costing Dabhol Power Co. $250,000 a day.

A new plan devised in 1995 set a much lower price for electricity and a maximum 30 percent ownership stake for the MSEB.[39] However, the board never honored its commitment to take its required Dabhol output. The MSEB also fell $240 million behind in payments for the electricity it did draw, because the power had become more expensive owing to higher oil and naphtha costs, demand was lower than expected, and locally owned power plants produced electricity more cheaply. Enron shut down the operation in June 2001, just before completing the second phase. By then the consortium had invested $2.9 billion in Dabhol, and Enron faced as much as $900 million in equity write-offs.[40] Enron was also on the hook for an unspecified amount of project-related debt.

Instead of realizing its dream of opening the Indian subcontinent to a vast energy market and then dominating it, Enron faced the reality of a huge, idle power facility on its balance sheet and major write-offs. The returns that had looked great on paper when the Dabhol contract was negotiated simply did not appear. Striking profitable deals might have been Enron International's long suit, but Dabhol revealed the difficulties inherent in making the terms of large-scale investments stick. Dabhol also typified Enron's remarkably bad run of troubled international power projects: the power plant in China that never operated commercially; the gas power plant in Cuiabá, Brazil, that ran hundreds of millions of dollars over budget; the power plant in the Dominican Republic that was idled for a time; the Polish power plant venture that the government ordered but had trouble paying for; and the planned power plants in Indonesia and Croatia that never materialized.[41]

Enron's power plant in Cuiabá deserves special comment because it exemplified the company's attitude toward risky gambling. By 1998 Enron was considering extending its business model to South America. One of its first moves was to invest close to $700 million in building the Cuiabá plant. When the Brazilian government announced its intention to sell state-controlled energy assets in June, Enron jumped on the opportunity. After being briefed on a proposal to acquire Elektro Electricidade e Serviços S. A., Brazil's sixth-largest electricity distributor, Skilling decided to bring the potential acquisition to Enron's board. Skilling saw a company that could serve as both critical access to Brazil's electricity grid and a building block for a new South American energy-trading operation.

In the end, Enron paid nearly twice the minimum price set by the Brazilian government—$1.3 billion for 90 percent of the voting shares and about 40 percent of the economic interest. Even far more important than this rich price was the method of financing. The plan was to finance the entire purchase price with dollar-denominated debt borrowed from banks—parts of which Enron would then sell to third parties. This scheme added currency risk to the pricey deal's business risk. If the real, Brazil's currency, collapsed, the value of the debt would remain the same, but the value of Elektro's cash flow in dollars would fall—making it more difficult for Elektro to cover its principal and interest payments.[42] In fact, an 8 percent devaluation of the real against the dollar occurred on January 13, 1999. Prices on the São Paulo stock exchange fell within minutes, and when the decline ended, Enron had lost more than half its investment.[43]

Domestic Expansion

Enron's troubled push into power generation and distribution to support the trading and sale of electricity was not limited to overseas markets. In the United States, Enron moved quickly to exploit opportunities created by the Energy Policy Act of 1992, which ushered in a new era of competition in generating electric power.[44] The act created a new class of independent ("exempt") power producers that were free to sell energy to any utility, although not directly to consumers. The act also required utilities to open up their transmission systems to any seller of electricity.

These provisions might have appeared to reshape the electric power industry along the lines of the deregulated natural gas business, but there were important differences. Because electricity cannot easily be stored, it is more difficult to trade than natural gas.[45] It is also more difficult to transport over long distances.[46] In addition, electricity prices are far more volatile than natural gas prices, and contracts for future deliveries were usually not viewed as firm (short-term contracts were considered firm, and were traded widely like contracts for natural gas, pork bellies, and soybeans).

Electricity traders also found it much more difficult than natural gas traders to sign big customers to profitable long-term contracts. Nor was there any real way to make serious amounts of money by trading electricity without owning power plants—mainly because in many states it was against the law to trade power without owning it.[47] Finally, in marked contrast to the natural gas business, the electricity business was deregulated not on the federal level but by individual states, where political action was decidedly local, and entrenched utilities jealously guarded their turf. For all these reasons, electricity trading presented a more complicated landscape than gas trading.

Enron nevertheless jumped in, and by 1994 had begun trading electricity. Deal originators led by Ken Rice began trying to line up long-term power deals with utilities, but discovered that many prospective customers were still unwilling to provide access to their transmission lines. To get into the electric power club, Skilling decided to add a major public utility to its portfolio of power generation plants. In 1995 Enron began boasting—even before securing a large power generating base—that it was going to grab 20 percent of the wholesale electrical power market.[48] In pursuit of this goal, the company announced a huge new venture in July 1996: it had reached an agreement to purchase Portland General Electric, an Oregon-based utility, for $2.1 billion and the assumption of $1.1 billion in debt. The purchase price represented an extraordinary 48 percent premium for shareholders. The idea was to combine Enron's gas trading, risk management, and logistics expertise with Portland General's expertise in power generation, transmission, and distribution.[49]

The company also looked to the acquisition to backstop its trading and finance activities. Although Enron had enormous gas reserves to support its many gas trading deals, it owned only a few independent power plants and wind farms scattered around the country. Situated near California—the first state to deregulate its electric power industry—the utility would presumably put Enron in a favorable geographic position to attack this market. What's more, the acquisition preserved the option of leading the way in future restructuring of the industry, if it so chose, by selling off the power generation business and keeping the trading and distribution businesses for itself.

Unfortunately, by just about any strategic or financial measure, this gamble was a failure. When Enron tried to sell off Portland General's power plants, the Oregon Public Utility Commission flatly rejected the idea, on the grounds that separating the retail market from secure sources of supply was too risky, and that selling the company's hydroelectric plants to a third party would threaten Oregon's advantage as a low-cost power producer.[50] To make matters worse, neither the Oregon nor California markets turned out to be as lucrative as originally thought.

So, in the summer of 2001, five years after making a major commitment to domestic power generation, Enron put the entire company up for sale. Northwest Natural Gas agreed to acquire Portland General for $1.9 billion and the assumption of $1.1 billion of its debt, leaving Enron with a capital loss of more than $200 million.[51] This loss was soon to expand. After Enron declared bankruptcy in December 2001, the purchase agreement was dissolved by mutual consent. A year and a half later, a bankrupt Enron announced a final write-down of Portland General totaling $1.8 billion.[52]

Although Portland General was usually profitable during the years when Enron owned it, the utility's loss in market value ended up costing Enron 50 percent of its equity investment. Worse, any strategic benefits were negligible. If Enron had acquired Portland General to learn the electricity business, it was an expensive lesson at a time when the company was increasingly short of cash. As a former managing director put it, "We didn't need to buy a company to get a few electricity traders. That's like if you want a glass of beer, you buy a brewery."[53]

Like Dabhol, the Portland General affair cost Enron shareholders hundreds of millions of dollars. How could the very executives who prided themselves on astute political analysis and effective lobbying have had such a tin ear? How could executives who touted their ability to create and exploit new markets have had such a severely impaired vision of profitable growth opportunities in power generation? Of the many possible explanations, the one that stands out in both cases is that senior executives overestimated their own insights and undervalued the risk of failure, and proved incapable of working through the surprises and bad luck that accompanied expansion into power generation.

Enron's Big Bet on Retail

Although not its most expensive miscalculation, Enron's foray into the retail distribution of energy is perhaps one of the most revealing instances of overconfidence getting the best of its senior leadership. In March 1997, two months after becoming president and COO, Skilling took a big swing at developing a new business by establishing Enron Energy Services (EES) as a separate unit, to capture the retail side of the domestic energy market. Its mission was to provide electricity, gas, and energy management directly to homes and businesses. Skilling put Lou Pai, one of his most trusted deputies from Enron's trading world, in charge.

Both Skilling and Lay had a lot at stake in this new enterprise, having received sizable grants of phantom equity, and hoping to take EES public to cash in. They believed that states would soon open up their power markets, and they intended to turn Enron into a consumer brand. They were badly mistaken. By 2001, only a quarter of the U.S. power market had opened up, and prospects for further openings had virtually evaporated.[54]

When states were slow to deregulate energy markets and allow new entrants to compete by tapping out-of-state supplies, Enron was forced to shift its branding hopes from homes to businesses. But it was never clear how Enron was going to make money from a business-to-business version of EES. Providing electricity at a discount through long-term contracts just didn't add up, when the retail part of the business was often a money loser, and states were refusing to deregulate their markets. The only way Enron could sell at discounted prices was to buy electricity from a local utility and resell it at a loss—hardly a road to riches.

Despite this setback, Enron persisted in writing supply contracts that combined sales of electricity and gas with energy-management services. Among many high-profile institutions that signed on to these "total energy outsource contracts" lasting four to ten years were the University of California, Lockheed Martin, Ocean Spray, Owens Corning, Chase Bank, IBM, and the Catholic Archdiocese of Chicago.

According to one account, EES kept score of progress in this business through "total contract value." This metric represented the cost of the energy and infrastructure a customer had outsourced to EES over the life of a contract. If Enron agreed to supply $500 million worth of electricity to a large corporation over ten years, for example, that $500 million became the value of the contract, even if Enron was likely to lose money on it.[55] And lose money Enron did! EES reported pretax losses of $119 million in 1998 and $68 million in 1999.

By paying the 170 EES deal originators on the estimated profitability of their contracts, Enron encouraged them to close long-term deals quickly, and many unprofitable deals were struck under this incentive regime. What's more, because its customers were scattered across the country, Enron had little opportunity for economies of scale in delivering energy. Worse, the company's billing procedures totally broke down, with customers' checks often unopened and uncashed, sending accounts receivable through the roof. Finally, when California electricity prices skyrocketed in the summer of 2000, EES incurred staggering losses because Lou Pai had bet that prices would drop.[56] (In contrast, traders at Enron Wholesale's far larger and more experienced trading desk had bet that prices would rise in California and cleared hundreds of millions of dollars for the company.)[57] By mid-2000 Pai had virtually disappeared from EES, failing to show up for work as his personal life took control of his calendar.

According to one investigative reporter, internal investigators estimated that Enron was facing more than $500 million in book losses.[58] To disguise those losses from speculative trading and grossly overvalued contracts that were immediately marked-to-market, Skilling and Pai's successor, Dave Delainey, decided to merge EES's trading function with Enron Wholesale Services, the company's principal commodity-trading operation.

In retrospect, both the strategic and economic logic of EES look highly questionable. Neither fundamental economics nor managerial capabilities could support Skilling's hopes of extending his energy-based business model down the value chain from sales to utilities, to sales to consumers. Skilling's big bet on retail energy did not come close to being viable.

Enron's senior executives—many of whom were as short on experience in operations as they were long on deal-making expertise—revealed a truly misplaced self-confidence. By persistently overestimating their ability to expand Enron's original business model to the production, distribution, and trading of electricity, they ended up losing a bundle of money for shareholders and diverting top-level attention from more productive activities. Nor were the company's problems in extending its basic business model limited to electricity and the energy sector. In applying the business model to broadband and water, Enron fared far worse.

Broadband

Skilling told analysts during Enron's annual meeting on January 19 and 20, 2000, that the U.S. market for bandwidth "intermediation" would grow to $68 billion by 2004, and that Enron would quickly control 20 percent of this market, plus part of the international market as well. He also predicted that this business would generate more than $1 billion in operating earnings by 2004, plus another $3.5 billion from the emerging content services side of the business. He calculated that the two segments of the broadband business were worth $29 billion—or an extra $37.00 a share. Not surprisingly, two hundred outside securities analysts rushed to call their trading desks, and Enron's stock price immediately rose 26 percent, to a high of $67.25.[59]

Ken Lay reiterated this message at PaineWebber's annual energy conference one month later. Enron, he insisted, intended "to become the world's biggest buyer and seller of bandwidth, just as we have become the world's biggest buyer and seller of electricity and natural gas."[60] As further explained in Enron's 2000 annual report, its goals were to

1. deploy the most open and efficient global broadband network,
2. be the world's largest marketer of bandwidth and network services, and
3. be the world's largest provider of premium content delivery services (including movies and sports events).

Enron would achieve all this by becoming the first provider of global broadband connectivity through the Enron Intelligent Network—a "network of networks" that would provide switching capacity between independent networks, for low-cost scalability. The resulting broadband operating system would give Enron the ability to provide bandwidth in real time, control access and network quality for Internet service providers, and monitor and control the flow and quality of applications as they streamed over the network. Of course, Enron also planned to develop a large-scale bandwidth intermediation business that included dark (unactivated) fiber, circuits, Internet protocol services (transporting data packets according to IP standards), and storage capacity. Finally, the company planned a joint venture with a U.S. video retailer to deliver movies and other on-demand content over the Enron Intelligent Network.

Despite Lay's bravado, a fiber network that cost more than $1 billion to assemble reported only losses. During the first nine months of 2001 alone, Enron Broadband Services lost over half a billion dollars, and Enron wrote off some $1 billion in broadband-related assets after declaring bankruptcy in December 2001.[61] Yet as late as July 2001, Paul Racicot, vice president of global bandwidth risk management for Broadband Services, was boldly proclaiming that Enron was still going to rule the world of broadband. Mimicking Skilling, Racicot boasted: "Anything we want to intermediate, we can."[62]

Enron, it is worth noting, was not the first energy company to plunge into the broadband business. A decade before Enron's entry, Tulsa-based Williams Companies recognized that it could use its pipeline routes to string fiber-optic cable. By 1995 it had built up such a successful network that it sold its fiber-optics business to WorldCom for $2.5 billion in cash.

Enron entered the broadband business in 1999, after acquiring Portland General, when it discovered that a small group was building a fiber-optic ring around that city. Enron executives jumped on the idea of expanding this urban network into a long-haul business. In its SEC filings, Enron stated that it believed that skills developed in merchant energy services could yield operating efficiencies for Enron and other participants in the developing bandwidth market.[63]

As with electricity, the natural gas and broadband businesses had some similarities. Both had been controlled by monopolies in markets now being deregulated. Pipelines and fiber networks also shared two requirements: complex switching systems to deliver products throughout the country, and skilled marketers who could sell capacity to promising customers. However, Enron executives apparently overlooked or minimized major operational differences.[64]

Unlike electricity and natural gas, broadband was experiencing overcapacity: the amount of installed fiber cable in the United States quadrupled between 1996 and the end of 2000.[65] Swarms of companies were laying cable, including Level 3, Extant, Qwest, Broadwing, Global Crossing, and Williams—all direct competitors of Enron. None of this seemed to discourage Lay, who told *Fortune* in January 2000 that Enron would exploit broadband the way it had exploited electricity—implying that the company would become the nation's largest supplier of broadband in only four years.[66]

Whereas natural gas flowing through pipelines is a fungible commodity, with prices posted on exchanges around the country, photons traveling through fiber are packaged into highly differentiated images and priced outside public view. Price and reliability were the most important factors in trading energy, but security and service, together with reliability, were the key success factors in broadband. Because it did not own curb-to-curb fiber, Enron could ensure neither security nor reliability. Further complicating matters, the telecom business only had a handful of accepted hubs—in contrast to natural gas and electricity networks, which could rely on well-established pooling points around the country. Most fiber networks also had different termination points, which made interconnectivity an enormous problem for wholesale traders. Enron addressed this by building pooling points into its network, but its claims to have solved the problem were not borne out.[67]

Finally, it was never clear why the telephone companies that owned most of the fiber would want to trade with Enron, if that meant revealing how they were pricing their supply of broadband. Such transparency could only aggravate the telecoms' falling prices and profit margins. With the telecoms holding back, Enron had fewer potential parties for broadband trades, making the market far less fluid than that for energy.

McKinsey & Co. reportedly warned Skilling to avoid climbing on the broadband bandwagon. McKinsey noted that not only did the service requirements of fiber-optic cable (which Enron wasn't particularly good at or even interested in) differ from those of gas pipelines, but that the cost of streaming a movie into a private home was so high that no market existed for the service in the first place. Skilling and his team nevertheless pressed on, telling McKinsey: "You just don't get it."[68]

In the end, Enron's promotional claims for its broadband infrastructure and capabilities masked a low level of demand. Not only were telecoms reluctant traders, but falling broadband prices provided few incentives to trade broadband to lock in long-term prices. The fundamental purposes served by Enron's trading model were thus essentially irrelevant in this market, nor was there enough business to support the mammoth investments Enron was making. To make matters worse, the test market for delivering video content to homes turned into a financial fiasco for both Enron and its partners in that joint venture.[69]

Once again, Enron's efforts to extend its intermediation strategy beyond natural gas ended up losing hundreds of millions of dollars for shareholders. These losses reflected not only bad timing and collapsing demand, but also a brash attempt to become the world leader in a market in which Enron had limited experience, and that required massive investments just to get into the trading game.

Although whatever similarities that existed between energy and broadband were largely superficial, these apparent similarities—coupled with the hype surrounding the Internet—served as a convenient distraction for unsuspecting investors and managers. This distraction appears to have worked well. Few investment analysts criticized Enron's broadband strategy, and there is no public record that anyone within the company raised cautionary flags.

Water

Enron entered the water business on October 2, 1998, with the $2.4 billion cash acquisition of Wessex Water, a small but profitable utility headquartered in Bath, England. After searching for more than a year, the Water Development Group in Enron International targeted Wessex as the centerpiece of a global water treatment and distribution business. This business—under the eventual leadership of Rebecca Mark—turned out to be another example of Enron's belief that it could successfully enter an emerging market with a blockbuster acquisition before testing the market and its own operational skills. This venture also reflected the same cockiness that brought down other failed Enron subsidiaries. According to J. Paul Oxer, former vice president of international development at Azurix: "The incentive was to make deals happen, not make deals work. . . . We kept flitting from thing to thing to find the next big deal instead of focusing on operating the company."[70]

Enron apparently saw water as the commodity of the next century, and thus a natural extension of its gas and electricity trading businesses. The global water business was a $300 billion industry supposedly about to be deregulated and run by private companies. Mark argued that there was a global shortage of usable water; that demand would grow along with national economies; that opportunities were everywhere, including in Britain, Germany, Brazil, and the United States; and that there were synergies with energy. After acquiring a water utility, Enron could use its risk management and trading skills to buy water in surplus regions and sell it in deficit regions.

The Wessex acquisition offered Enron a chance to replay its basic business strategy: learn a new market by buying a well-respected utility, squeeze inefficiencies out of facilities previously owned by government, and develop and dominate sales and trading of the underlying commodity. In other words, Enron would do for water what it had done for energy—except facing far less competition. This claim overlooked the fact that two French companies, Lyonnaise des Eaux and Vivendi, had been in business for nearly a century, and already serviced 160 million people around the world.[71]

What's more, Enron's water strategy was clearly neither a natural nor an easy extension of its gas and electricity strategy. Unlike those resources, water is a highly variable commodity (in taste, salinity, and turbidity), and water treatment is difficult to standardize and therefore expensive. Many people also view access to water as a birthright, and are simply not willing to pay a lot (or at all) for it. Local communities tend to jealously guard their jurisdiction over water supplies, some for religious or historical reasons. Thus it was never clear that such a sensitive commodity could trade freely, unfettered by laws and tradition.

Also unlike gas and electricity, few countries have nationwide water pipeline systems, and governments did not order the water company owners to open existing pipeline systems to third parties. Implementing a growth strategy would therefore require massive investments in water lines, with returns years away—not exactly what Enron needed in its world of quarter-to-quarter growth in earnings.

But invest Enron did. Within a year of acquiring Wessex Water, the company committed another $647 million to six acquisitions in Canada, Mexico, Argentina, Brazil, and Germany, designed to create a global footprint. All told, Enron bet $3.3 billion on this strategy, with Mark forecasting a 20 percent return, versus an industry average of 10 percent.[72]

To help finance this commitment, Enron put all its water businesses operating under the Azurix name into a holding company called Atlantic Water Trust, in which it held a 50 percent voting interest. A special-purpose entity called Marlin Water Trust purchased the remaining 50 percent interest. Marlin sold $1.15 billion in notes and certificates to five institutional investors to raise its 50 percent share. Structuring the ownership of Azurix in this way enabled Enron to keep debt off its balance sheet, even though it controlled the business.

On June 9, 1999, less than a year after its creation, Azurix was taken public at $19 per share, raising $695 million and giving the company a valuation of nearly $2 billion. Atlantic Water Trust owned roughly two-thirds of the company, with Enron retaining a 33 percent interest.[73] Enron took its share of the capital to retire its debt, leaving Azurix with just over $464 million with which to retire its debt and to spend on acquisitions.

Things began to go downhill quickly after the initial public offering (IPO). Because part of the IPO receipts went to retiring debt, Azurix was cash-starved from the outset. Profits declined at Azurix throughout 1999 and early 2000, and Atlantic Water Trust reported a $328 million loss on its two-thirds share in Azurix on December 31, 2000. Most of this loss was attributable to a write-down of "impaired assets" in Argentina. During the spring and summer of 2000, Azurix's stock price plummeted when privatization of water supplies failed to materialize in Florida, Texas, and California, and unexpected changes, such as capped water prices, curbed profit opportunities in other parts of the world.

By August 25, the day that Rebecca Mark resigned (or was squeezed out) as CEO of Azurix, the stock closed at $4.94. Azurix was forced to take itself private at just over $8 a share, leaving it with nearly 100 percent debt. Two years later, in June 2002, a bankrupt Enron sold Wessex Water, the jewel in Azurix's crown, for $794 million.[74] Because Enron had paid $2.4 billion for Wessex in 1998, this transaction represented a $1.6 billion loss. But Wessex was only Azurix's most significant money loser: the company eventually recognized many more capital losses related to water assets in Argentina and Germany.

Enron's water strategy represents yet another failure in its efforts to extend its business model. According to Chris Wasden, former Azurix managing director, this business simply did not have the capacity to earn the returns that Mark had claimed it could. Because Enron was not interested in deals that earned less than 15 percent, Mark pressed her employees to come up with ways to meet that target.[75]

Enron had also paid dearly for water assets, beginning with the Wessex acquisition. The purchase price of Wessex was 36 percent over the publicly traded value—based partly on other acquisitions in the industry, and partly on synergies and savings built into Mark's valuation model. But according to one M&A executive who worked on the Wessex acquisition, the company was so efficient that little incremental value could be squeezed out of the company.[76]

Similarly, Mark apparently overpaid for a major acquisition in Argentina in order to secure a position in Latin America. Various sources reported that her bid was two to three times higher than that of the second-place contender. Due diligence also failed to uncover an unusually low collection rate on customer bills (40–50 percent in Argentina, versus 90 percent in the United Kingdom) and a fragile business infrastructure.[77] Although Mark strongly contests the threefold overpayment, claiming that the competing bids were for different pieces of the Argentinean utility's market, she does admit to a much smaller overpayment to deter Enron's two largest (French) competitors. Whatever the precise figure, the acquisition premium, coupled with bad luck, led to a write-down of the Argentinean asset from its $438 million purchase price to zero—putting Mark's career in serious jeopardy.

Another factor contributing to the failure of this "natural extension" of Enron's business model was that U.K. regulators ordered Wessex to cut its rates by 12 percent—a major blow to a business that was supposed to throw off tons of cash. And even though Azurix's trading aspirations were low, it also experienced great difficulty applying the Enron trading model to the water business. The deal flow was thinner than expected, and its Web-based trading platform, Water2Water.com, never gained traction.

Then there was the issue of Azurix's corporate overhead. Mark reportedly spent freely building, redesigning, and decorating Azurix's offices in the United Kingdom and North America. She decided, for example, to build an elegant new stairway between two floors of Azurix's headquarters, at a cost of $1 million. Some wags referred to this as Rebecca's "stairway to heaven." This was soon outdone by $5.2 million spent on Azurix's new London offices.[78]

Most important, perhaps, Mark clearly hit a patch of bad luck with Azurix. Its Argentinean assets soon became impaired, owing to internal sabotage at a Buenos Aires utility, where employees destroyed all customer billing records, and algae contamination in a reservoir not controlled by the company forced it to stop billing for odiferous but otherwise unharmful water.

Finally, as noted, Azurix was consistently strapped for cash. According to Mark, Azurix's principal problem was that it did not have enough capital to stay in the game. She claims that after the IPO and several refinancings that enabled Enron to recoup some of its investment, the company dried up as a source of capital. Mark nevertheless apparently felt obligated to rush into acquisitions to validate Wessex's expertise and Azurix's strategy. The overpayments associated with these transactions—besides the minimal trading revenues in the United States, and high infrastructure investment requirements in the rest of the world—doomed Enron's water strategy. Wall Street lost faith in it rather quickly, as did Azurix's board (which included Skilling, Lay, and Enron director Herbert Winokur), but not before much damage had been done.

Totaling and Explaining the Losses

Enron's forays into electricity, broadband, and water—each of which resulted in hundreds of millions of dollars of operating and capital losses—totaled nearly $6 billion (see Table 1.1). This total does not include substantial operating and capital losses related to New Power Co., Enron Energy Services, international assets other than Dabhol, a large portfolio of merchant assets, and a restatement of operating results because of accounting errors over five years. Those accounting errors had led Enron to inflate its reported net income by $591 million beginning in 1997. Of that amount,

Table 1.1. Summary of operating and capital losses in selected electric power, broadband, and water ventures (in billions of dollars)

Source	Losses
Dabhol	$0.9
Portland General	1.8
Wessex	1.6
Broadband (operating losses)	0.5
Broadband (write-offs)	1.0
TOTAL	$5.8

$287 million was related to Azurix, and $180 million to restructuring Broadband Services.[79] This brings publicly reported operating and capital losses in electric power, broadband, and water to well over $6 billion.

In the end, other business failures dwarfed even those losses. In a report to the U.S. Bankruptcy Court, Stephen F. Cooper, Enron's interim CEO and chief restructuring officer, acknowledged that restating Enron's balance sheet from November 2001 in accordance with generally accepted accounting principles (GAAP) would require about $14 billion in write-offs related to all accounting errors and massive cuts in overhead. A restatement would also require another $8 billion to $10 billion write-down of risk management assets. Even if only a small percentage of those write-downs pertained to the four ventures above, Enron's efforts to adapt the business model developed for the natural gas market to other deregulating markets now look disastrous.[80]

How could such massive losses happen? No doubt both bad luck and bad timing came into play. However, a combination of hubris and subsequent misjudgments of risks and returns—amplified, perhaps, by the contagious emotions of the Internet boom—help explain many of the problems Enron created in just about every aspect of its corporate affairs.

This is not to say that Enron did not have plenty of true experts and skilled players, especially in the company's traditional natural gas and pipeline operations and newer risk management disciplines. But those players were not the ones at corporate headquarters, from Ken Lay on down, who made repeated claims that Enron could intermediate any market, that

Enron would grab 20 percent of the electric power market, that Enron would become the world's biggest buyer and seller of bandwidth, and that Enron would achieve twice the industry's average return on investments in water treatment and distribution.

Enron's leaders were not, of course, unique in their vulnerability to hubris. Many successful people and organizations face this peril. Hubris, in the business setting, typically involves a kind of supreme overconfidence that blocks systematic analysis of opportunities and risks.

Hubris in business differs from optimism in subtle but important ways. According to *Webster's* dictionary, optimism is "an inclination to put the most favorable construction upon actions and events or to anticipate the best possible outcome." Optimism is a common characteristic of entrepreneurs, day traders, venture capitalists, and even military officers.[81] Because optimists typically remain robust in the face of adversity, optimism can have survival-enhancing effects in business. According to one study, "Founders who can behave 'as if' the activity were a reality—producing and directing great theater as it were—may convince others of the tangible reality of the new activity."[82] Optimism can also influence customers, employees, and financial backers to support a new endeavor.

Hubris, on the other hand, has survival-destroying effects. Hubris can lead to spectacular, irreversible error. In Enron's case, hubris was most evident in senior executives' serious misreading of similarities between the natural gas business and the power generation, broadband, and water businesses with respect to price behavior, contracting, distribution, capital requirements, consumer attitudes, and local politics; overestimation of the opportunities and underestimation of the risks of each business; and the exaggerated view of their own ability to compete successfully in multiple product markets with a single business model. Skilling's claim at a management retreat that "Enron has found the one successful business model that can be applied to any market" is perhaps the most revealing evidence of leadership's hubristic, and ultimately destructive, mindset.[83] Also revealing was Skilling's claim that EnronOnline was a platform for all kinds of markets, and that "Enron could be the market maker for the world!"[84] The supreme confidence reflected in this aspirational claim ended up delivering large-scale value destruction for Enron shareholders.

Enron's hubris and commitment to highly generalized notions of strategy were there for all to see as far back as 1999, when management offered ethereal definitions of the company's business model. Skilling and CFO Andrew

Fastow often explained that Enron's business was "risk intermediation." Enron's description of its business model in its 1999 annual report was even more vague—virtually devoid of any substantive content:

> Enron is moving so fast that sometimes others have trouble defining us. But we know who we are. We are clearly a knowledge-based company, and the skills and resources we use to transform the energy business are proving to be equally valuable in other businesses. Yes, we will remain the world's leading energy company, but we will also use our skills and talent to gain leadership in fields where the right opportunities beckon. . . . We are participating in a New Economy, and the rules have changed dramatically. What you own is not as important as what you know. Hardwired businesses, such as energy and communications, have turned into knowledge-based industries that place a premium on creativity.[85]

Thus Enron's senior executives established few, if any, boundaries for investment ideas, save the general notion that the greatest opportunities lay in deregulating and otherwise inefficient commodity markets. Such ephemeral boundaries perpetuated the myth of Enron's ability to do whatever it wanted in the "risk intermediation" business. In the absence of more specific guidelines tailored to corporate capabilities, the company not surprisingly experienced large investment losses outside its original gas business.

Hubris and muddled thinking about corporate strategy were all the more lethal because many of Enron's leaders lacked the administrative experience and follow-through that running new businesses require. I remember Henry Kissinger once telling a class I attended as an undergraduate that "in foreign policy, execution dominates conception." So, too, the four ventures detailed here suggest that Enron's senior executives were more successful at conceiving and negotiating deals than at running the businesses. Put more succinctly, Enron had become a deal shop.

Rebecca Mark's team at Enron International, for example, scoured the world for attractive power projects. After identifying a suitable project, she and her team developed it for a fee, financed the project for another fee, offered to operate the project for a fee, and collected a fee for managing the ever-present joint venture between Mark's Enron Development subsidiary and its equity partners. The company collected many of these fees before a project produced or transported any gas or electricity. Although this deal making required various skills, operating the new projects successfully was not in the mix. While we do not know the combined performance of

Enron's portfolio of sixteen overseas power projects, we have already noted the failures of significant projects that were revealed in the business and financial press. As Chapter 2 will show, it is no exaggeration to say that Enron's incentives rewarded employees for closing deals at least as highly as running successful businesses.

Enron's attention to operations was also compromised by the resignation of COO Richard Kinder in 1996, after a falling out with Lay. In the wake of Kinder's departure, no one at the top had any real experience operating a business: not Ken Lay, who primarily focused on regulatory and public affairs; not Jeff Skilling, a highly successful consultant but not yet tested as an executive in complicated, capital-consuming businesses; not Andrew Fastow, who had virtually no training as a corporate CFO. Fastow's background included a stint in asset securitization and structured finance at Continental Illinois Bank. His primary activity at Enron was structured finance; that is, devising transactions that raised both equity capital and debt on favorable terms for its off-balance-sheet partnerships. Notably absent was deep experience (or interest) in treasury functions or managing a disciplined resource allocation process.

Ironically, *CFO* magazine bestowed on Fastow its Excellence Award for Capital Structure Management, for designing the innovative structured finance transactions that eventually led to his downfall. More to the point, deal architecture is probably the least important aspect of a chief financial officer's job. An effective CFO at Enron would establish performance metrics and milestones for routinely monitoring the company's strategic and merchant investments. With the exception of the deal approval process, which was subverted when top management anointed a particular venture (see Chapter 2), there is little public evidence that Fastow ever led or participated in a systematic review of existing businesses. Indeed, the company seemed to lack any conceptual framework for determining the success or failure of new businesses once they were launched. Lack of systematic oversight at the top allowed Enron's enthusiasms and overconfidence to reign unchecked.[86]

The implications of this pattern of behavior are important. They suggest that whatever misdeeds or fraudulent activities Enron executives engaged in, the root of the company's troubles and eventual collapse was not premeditated crime, but rather hubris and a certain recklessness or fearlessness and the lack of operating experience. Certainly, investments in new gas pipelines, gas trading, and even electricity trading—areas in which Enron had operating experience—should be considered intelligent gambles, which are well accepted as normal activities of business. However, investments pursued without relevant operating experience; without deep, specific knowledge on the part of project overseers at corporate headquarters; and without effective risk controls—such as the aforementioned electric power projects and the excursions into the water and broadband businesses— crossed the line into the zone of reckless gambles. (Arthur Andersen apparently judged Enron's use of mark-to-market accounting to be a controlled risk. This turned out to be a major misjudgment, mainly because initial valuations of contracts were systematically inflated.)[87]

As Chapters 3 and 4 show, gambling or speculative behavior in business often takes on unethical characteristics when decision makers fall short of established goals.[88] Given Enron's single-minded emphasis on growing reported earnings per share, the gambling behavior of the fifteen senior corporate executives subsequently indicted by federal prosecutors (and perhaps more on the government's unindicted coconspirator list) took the form of betting on financial management and reporting strategies designed to obfuscate the company's true economic condition.

Reckless Gambling in Financial Management

Perhaps the most significant example of Enron's reckless gambling is the way top management chose to hedge merchant investments in power plants, the Internet, and other technology companies often far from the company's expertise. These hedges—designed to offset fluctuations in the value of these investments, and thus in reported net income—played a central role in the company's eventual collapse. Although controversial among Enron's risk management experts, the hedges nevertheless won approval from Skilling, Lay, and Enron's board of directors.

Uneconomic Hedges

Enron's hedging activities had a productive and proper beginning. As a gas production and distribution company, Enron had always tried to hedge against declines in gas demand and prices. It did so by offsetting a commitment to buy natural gas today (say, one hundred million cubic feet for $25,000) with a contract to sell a similar amount in the future at the same price (or, ideally, a higher one). This type of hedge—based on a futures contract to buy or sell something at a specific price on a specific date—has been in use since the 1800s, when farmers started looking for ways to guarantee the prices they would receive at harvest time six to nine months later.

It was an easy step for Enron to move from hedging as a producer and distributor of natural gas to hedging as part of an expanding derivatives business and investments in new operating companies. Once Enron decided to intermediate the natural gas and electricity markets, Enron traders began jumping in and out of energy contracts just to profit from the ups and downs in contract prices. Long before EnronOnline catapulted the company into the role of principal market maker in newly deregulated commodity markets, hedging was a well-understood, broadly practiced skill at Enron. Indeed, it was part of the company's DNA, as it was at just about every other energy company.

However, over time Enron's financial managers shifted their attention from pure commodity hedges to hedging a wide variety of merchant investments with off-balance-sheet partnerships, or special purpose entities (SPEs). Some of these were so improperly structured that when they failed in October 2001, Enron was forced to write off $1.2 billion. That unexpected write-off marked Enron's turn onto the road to eventual collapse.

The Rhythms hedge—one of Enron's earliest hedging transactions using SPEs—is a case in point. In March 1998, when Enron invested $10 million in Rhythms NetCommunications, a provider of high-speed Internet access, it was still a private company. With a cost basis for Rhythms of $1.85 per share, Enron began to realize massive profits when the company went public at $21.00 a share in April 1999. The stock reached $69.00 by the end of the first day of frenetic trading. Enron's investment in Rhythms was worth $300 million by the end of May.

Because Rhythms was not expected to become profitable in the near future, and because Enron was prohibited from selling its Rhythms shares before the end of 1999 owing to a lockup agreement, Skilling wanted to hedge Enron's investment against a drop in share price. However, few Rhythms shares were changing hands, so the market was too illiquid to support normal options trading. To solve this problem, Fastow proposed creating an off-balance-sheet partnership called LJM (after the first initials of his wife and two children) to serve as a hedging counter-party for Enron. This limited partnership would be capitalized with appreciated Enron stock. LJM (and its subsidiary, Swap Sub) wrote Enron an option to sell 5.4 million shares of Rhythms stock at a set price of $56 per share.

In theory, if the value of Enron's investment in Rhythms declined and Enron exercised this "put" option, LJM would have to buy Enron's entire position in Rhythms at $56 a share. The rub was that LJM's ability to make good on the Rhythms put rested largely on the value of Enron stock. If the value of Enron shares fell along with the value of the Rhythms investment, LJM would be unable to fulfill the put. And that is exactly what happened: this accounting hedge failed as an actual economic hedge, and contributed to the company's massive write-off in October 2001.[89]

Specialists within Enron's Risk Assessment and Control (RAC) group quickly realized that hedging investments with one's own stock does not typically qualify as a true economic hedge.[90] Vincent Kaminski—head of a research group within RAC, who Skilling asked to price the put option—went to his boss, Rick Buy, with concerns about the deal. In his blunt way, Kaminski reportedly told the RAC head that the Rhythms option idea was "so stupid that only Andrew Fastow could have come up with it."[91] Buy told Kaminski that Fastow had not only conceived the LJM hedging deal but also proposed to run the partnership. This was a clear conflict of interest, as LJM would be engaging in transactions with Enron. At Buy's request, Kaminski agreed to review the entire transaction.

After he and a colleague reviewed the deal over a weekend, Kaminski strongly recommended to Buy that Enron not proceed with the Rhythms hedge. Beyond Fastow's obvious conflict of interest, Kaminski concluded that LJM was unstable, in that Enron would be completely exposed to a large loss on its Rhythms investment if the value of its own stock and that of Rhythms stock declined together. Once again he called the deal "stupid," although he did not think it would be illegal.

Buy assured Kaminski that his objections would be passed on to top management before Enron's board reviewed the deal. We do not know whether Kaminski's message was passed on, but we do know that Fastow presented the idea to the board's finance committee on June 28. Fastow pointed out that he would serve as LJM's general partner, but that he would not benefit from any gains in Enron stock. The full board approved the deal after waiving the company's ethics code, which prohibited corporate officers from taking a financial interest in transactions involving Enron. After hearing complaints about how Kaminski's research group operated "like cops," Skilling then transferred Kaminski and his team out of RAC, so Kaminski could not review deals involving LJM or other partnerships.[92] This effectively silenced the strongest internal critics of Enron's flawed financial management.

The Rhythms hedge served as a prototype for even larger hedges that Fastow created with four new SPEs known as the Raptors (raptors were small prehistoric dinosaurs with hind legs and large claws adapted for grasping and tearing at prey). These partnerships were designed to hedge Enron's rapidly expanding portfolio of merchant investments and stock holdings by entering into derivatives, including swaps, puts, and collars.[93] In so doing, these SPEs would keep fluctuations in the value of these investments off Enron's balance sheet, which had to be adjusted each quarter under mark-to-market accounting.

Three of the four Raptors were again capitalized with Enron stock. A fourth, Raptor III, was capitalized with the stock of a company called New Power, another investment Enron was attempting to hedge. Enron set up New Power to house its residential and small commercial businesses, and planned to turn it into an Internet-based marketing company.[94] Like many of the merchant investments Enron moved off its balance sheet, New Power was expected to be unprofitable until it could amortize its enormous startup costs over a customer base. With typical enthusiasm for its own ideas, Enron envisioned revenues of $10 billion for New Power by 2005, which would put the company in a class by itself as a successful dot-com startup.

New Power went public in October 2000 at $21.00 a share, with Enron retaining a 44 percent stake. Before the IPO, Enron took steps to hedge its investment in New Power as it had with Rhythms. But Raptor III, the hedging counterparty, was capitalized with New Power stock transferred to it by Enron. (Enron received a promissory note from Raptor III in return.) Because Raptor III valued its New Power shares at $10.75 (owing to certain restrictions on its shares), the SPE was able to declare an immediate $246 million gain on paper after the IPO. This gain enabled Raptor III to engage in at least $246 million worth of hedging.

Other aspects of this transaction enabled Enron to initially lock in gains of $370 million on its New Power stock. However, like the Rhythms hedge, if New Power stock declined, Raptor III would be unable to pay Enron for declines in *its* New Power stock. As with Rhythms, no one at Enron with decision-making authority thought that the securities would fall in value. However, New Power's stock price declined from the day it was issued. By March 2001 the price was $6.20, rendering the Raptor III credit impaired. Although Enron delivered more of its shares to Raptor III to shore up its capital, the New Power hedge ultimately failed, and Enron's $370 million gain was eventually wiped out.

In both the Rhythms and New Power cases, Enron created a vicious cycle in which it depended on SPEs to prop up both its earnings and stock price, while the SPEs' financial health depended entirely on the value of either Enron stock or that of the hedged investment. In other words, Enron was hedging risk with itself. Executives thus had strong incentives to keep Enron's stock trading at high (and even inflated) levels, because if Enron's stock price fell below a predetermined trigger price, it had to either contribute more stock to the SPE or close it and the underlying hedges.

All told, Enron used the Raptor SPEs to offset a $1 billion decline in the value of several investments during 2000 and the first three quarters of 2001.[95] However, as the stock of Enron and New Power declined during the spring and summer of 2001, the hedging obligations of the Raptor SPEs exceeded the value of the assets available to satisfy those obligations. On September 28, 2001, Enron calculated that the Raptors' combined assets were about $2.5 billion, and their combined liabilities about $3.2 billion. Enron therefore decided to close all four Raptor partnerships—which required adding a $710 million charge to third-quarter earnings ($544 million after taxes). Another $1 billion write-down reflected the fact that Andersen had found that the Raptors did not comply with GAAP, while a further $200 million stemmed from the closing of the Raptors. (See Appendix A for more on the Raptors and the controversy surrounding them.)

Threats to Enron's Creditworthiness

From its inception, Enron had been preoccupied with its creditworthiness—a hangover from the heavy use of debt to finance the original merger between Houston Natural Gas and InterNorth, other acquisitions financed by junk bonds, and a $350 million buyout of a potentially hostile bidder in 1987. Enron's fast-growing trading business only fed the company's voracious appetite for debt.

This appetite reflected several business requirements. First, running and expanding a trading business is virtually impossible without an investment-grade credit rating. Without large amounts of readily available debt, Enron would have had to post enormous amounts of collateral in order to secure, for example, ten-year energy swaps between itself and another party. Enron's credit rating served as a proxy for its future ability to fulfill such swaps. Were Enron ever to receive a below-investment-grade credit rating, not only would its supply of capital decline, but the rising cost would eat up profit margins on the swaps. Indeed, without a large supply of relatively low-cost capital, Enron's business model simply would not work.[96]

If Enron were to lose its investment-grade credit rating, it might have to repay—as opposed to simply recollateralize—billions of dollars of debt.[97] In the end, that is what happened. When Jeff Skilling later testified before Congress that Enron's collapse was the result of a classic "run on the bank," he had it just about right.

In retrospect, it seems almost inexplicable that a credit-sensitive company such as Enron would design such credit-threatening hedges with SPEs. The company's directors also showed a surprising lack of curiosity about the strategy the Raptors would use to sell Enron shares, if needed to pay the Raptors' obligations. It is as if the directors and managers forgot that in the real world, the credit quality of one's trading partners matters a great deal, and they failed to see that the hedges were fundamentally flawed.

As a financial intermediary, Enron had significant positions in both primary contracts and derivative contracts, which were marked to market and fluctuated in value daily.[98] To survive, Enron needed to write and trade such contracts with virtually no risk that it would default. If its default risk were to rise, its role would cease to have value. By pledging its common stock as collateral for the debt-funded, off-balance-sheet partnerships that purchased many of its most risky assets, Enron was positioning itself for total collapse. A falling stock price would immediately erode the credit guarantees that the pledged stock was intended to shore up.

With Enron's overhyped stock, a default in one of the partnerships was a disaster waiting to happen. (In January 2000, management claimed that its stock—then at an all-time high of $86—was really worth $126, or more than one hundred times its trailing twelve-month earnings per share.) A credit failure in Enron's off-balance-sheet partnerships—coupled with major write-downs in net income and shareholders' equity—was bound to spook every banker with lines of credit extended to Enron. In the end, it did.

Enron's creditworthiness was further threatened by its increasingly risky hedging strategies as its derivatives business expanded. Over time, Enron moved from requiring a matched book or pair of hedged investments on a transaction-by-transaction basis to what is called a synthetic matched book. In such a book, investment risks are hedged across a full portfolio of investments. Synthetic matched books are more likely than transaction-by-transaction matched books to break down. In Enron's case, they did break down, and those breakdowns turned out to be significant.[99]

As Enron's derivatives business grew and the connections between various hedges became more complex, the risk of inadequately modeling those connections rose. Faulty modeling could yield a mismatch rather than a matched book. This apparently occurred, as Enron wrote off $8 billion to $10 billion in risk management assets after its bankruptcy.

Excessive Risk Taking in New Business Development

Reckless financial management was not limited to the structuring of Enron's hedges—it infected operating businesses as well. The story of National Energy Production Co. (NEPCO) and its $5 billion in contingent liabilities provides a case in point.

Enron purchased NEPCO in 1997 for $1 million, and organized the acquisition as a subsidiary of Enron Engineering & Construction Co. (EE&CC). The idea of acquiring this full-service engineering and construction company belonged to Larry Izzo, an executive in the long-standing EE&CC. Izzo proposed using NEPCO to build gas-fired power plants in the U.S. heartland and on the West Coast, as supply insurance for periods of peak demand. Rather than simply contract with other companies to build the plants that it would operate, Enron figured that it might as well capture any profits to be made from plant construction.

What started life within Enron as an in-house construction company soon became a general builder of power plants for other companies. By 2000 NEPCO was number four in annual construction revenues, after Bechtel, Black & Veatch, and Foster Wheeler, although its revenues were only half those of the industry leader. Between 1997 and 2001, NEPCO's aggregate revenues increased from about $200 million to over $2 billion.

Building large power plants on a turnkey basis—that is, for other owners— entailed a great deal of risk; and the larger the project, the greater the risk of missing deadlines and other performance milestones. In the years after NEPCO's purchase, the average size of turnkey projects rose rapidly from $60 million to more than $400 million, yet profit margins and cash flow were constricting, mainly because of disorganization accompanying NEPCO's rapid growth. In a word, NEPCO's growth outran its management's competence.

The guarantees it extended to customers on project completion time and plant performance constituted NEPCO's principal sources of competitive advantage. After Enron's bankruptcy, it was discovered that these guarantees had quickly escalated to about $5 billion in potential liabilities. Yet NEPCO's top management was unaware of this sum until declining margins set off alarm bells as Enron was searching for assets to sell to meet its own cash-flow problem.

As a wholly owned subsidiary, NEPCO's guarantees were a liability for Enron. In other words, Enron ended up being the guarantor of NEPCO's performance on every construction contract. As NEPCO came to rely on "selling guarantees," backed by its parent's creditworthiness to gain advantage over competitors, Enron's liabilities skyrocketed. Because NEPCO never disclosed these guarantees in footnotes to its intercompany financial statements (presumably because it thought the guarantees were costless!), the level of its contingent liabilities took Enron totally by surprise. Indeed, a full schedule of these guarantees was not completed until six months after Enron's bankruptcy, when NEPCO itself filed for bankruptcy. It is shocking that no one within NEPCO or Enron really knew the extent of the outstanding guarantees until two years after the start of the rush to build non-Enron plants. By then, the sponsor of the acquisition and one of the architects of NEPCO's strategy (Larry Izzo) had been paid off and was long gone.

The recklessness surrounding the acquisition and development of NEPCO is noteworthy because it shows the pervasiveness of Enron's commercial naiveté, deal orientation, and lack of financial discipline. These shortcomings affected virtually every part of the company, including operating divisions and subsidiaries two steps removed. Enron's problem with reckless gambling was endemic, and its deal culture was not limited to trading.

The Roots of Reckless Financial Management

How do we explain such reckless financial management? Was the same hubris that led to the unprofitable extensions of Enron's natural gas business model responsible for the disastrous hedges? Did executives truly believe that there were no limits to the use of structured-finance deals to meet Enron's ever-expanding risk management needs? How could senior executives and the board have assumed that Enron's business concepts and financial returns were sufficiently risk free to pledge the company's own securities as guarantors for its businesses? What kind of organizational culture and governance practices spawned and sustained this overweening self-confidence and lack of prudence?

Enron's foolhardy extrapolation of an initially successful business model, and its seemingly reckless gambles with its balance sheet and credit rating, could have several sources. One might well have been a mode of reasoning that inhibited learning and failed to detect and correct error. Under what my Harvard colleague Chris Argyris terms "defensive reasoning," tacit premises are tested, if at all, against the self-referential logic used to create them. The result of such reasoning is what Argyris calls "escalating misunderstanding": a compulsion to repeat errors that are then covered up through lack of transparency and denial.[100]

Another potential source of Enron's predilection for reckless gambling is a defective decision-making strategy known as "the gambler's fallacy." Identified in a famous study by Twersky and Hahnemann, the gambler's fallacy entraps a decision maker who believes that chance is a self-correcting process: that is, that a deviation in one direction will follow a deviation in the other. This defective thinking gives rise to illusions about the probability of future events—such as the assumption that because it rained more than normal last month, it will rain less than average next month, and thus be a great time to take a vacation.[101] Other defective decision-making strategies identified by Twersky and Hahnemann include projections of success based on insensitivity to sample size (for example, thinking that because intermediation worked in natural gas, it must work the same way in electricity), and disregard of possible unfavorable outcomes (facing up to "model error," in the case of broadband).

Finally, we cannot discount the possibility that Enron executives and managers simply believed that luck was on their side. Enron's early corporate history included plenty of big hits—some planned, some just plain lucky—in that the company avoided disaster at the last moment. The Sithe transaction is an example of the latter case, where luck—along with a lack of full disclosure and fast thinking by Enron executives—turned a deteriorating gamble into a winning play (see Appendix B).

These are intriguing thoughts, not inconsistent with the behavioral analysis in Chapter 4. But we cannot investigate such explanations of Enron's recklessness without first considering the extraordinarily perverse incentives at work within the company during the late 1990s. It is to that subject that we now turn.

CHAPTER 2

The Impact of Perverse Incentives

Enron's drift from innovative to deceptive management stemmed from many causes. One of the most important was the performance management system created by Jeffrey Skilling and Kenneth Lay.

Performance management systems typically include a method for measuring individual or group performance, and a set of financial and nonfinancial rewards tied, in some way, to designated performance measures. The actual relationship between measures and rewards in each system determines its incentive effects.

At Enron, Skilling created a system of strong incentives—including very large payoffs—based on his deeply held belief that business success depends on cultivating an innovative environment that spurs creativity and risk taking. Unfortunately, in its implementation, Enron's system of financial incentives also led to a gladiator culture in which increasingly risky gambles found support, personal opportunism ran rampant, and risk management processes broke down at the most inopportune times.

In this chapter, I show how financial incentives at Enron had enormously perverse effects on individual and group behavior, and contributed directly to the company's evolving culture of deceit. I start by describing how Enron's incentive system fit into the company's overall approach to corporate management. I then show the impact of this system on the behavior of deal originators and traders in the commodities business, project developers in the power generation business, and risk managers who were responsible for vetting all new business deals and transactions. I end by discussing how the richness and depth of Enron's executive bonuses and stock option program—coupled with the company's overvalued stock price—adversely affected its corporate culture. In particular, short-term time horizons mutated into an organization-wide obsession with current stock price and an addiction to growth at all costs.

Enron's Core Management Approach

Enron relied heavily on two management processes: a performance management system rooted in a vision of how best to attract, develop, and retain exceptional people, and a risk management system rooted in advanced financial technologies. The company had no formal corporate strategic-planning process, but rather a single, superordinate goal: "to create markets in commodities where there are inefficiencies," according to Skilling.[1]

Enron's employees—all its employees—were its strategic planners, Skilling and Lay maintained. Insisted Lay: "You must have the very best talent and then let them develop a good strategy."[2] Skilling added that with an open, internal market for talent, highly mobile employees would find new business opportunities. "You can understand your strategy by looking at personnel reports," he explained. "By the time strategic planners find out about something, it's too late." By observing where people are moving, Skilling maintained, senior managers could put the needed financial resources behind them.[3]

Skilling was averse to any rigidity that might constrain Enron's dynamism or impede swift decision making, believing that "a vertical communication system doesn't work in a dynamic organization." He therefore gave managers of business units "plenty of responsibility with only the broadest of parameters,"[4] encouraging them "to develop their own strategies" and "set their own rules."[5] Business units had the freedom to structure their own deals and new ventures until corporate was expected to come up with cash to finance them.[6]

Essential to this management approach was a high level of trust between Skilling and Lay, and between them and their subordinates. As we shall see, though, this mutual trust and respect turned out, in critical instances, to be more imagined than real.

Recruitment and Performance Evaluation

At the time of its collapse in 2001, Enron was widely known to have a deep reservoir of talent. Its traders included not only a full complement of MBAs but also dozens of PhDs, nuclear scientists, and meteorologists who could help predict energy demand and the weather, construct weather derivatives (hedges against weather-related changes in the demand for natural gas and electricity), and time trades to take advantage of the greatest profit opportunities.[7] Lay was a long-time proponent of hiring "the best and the brightest." He often repeated: "There is no substitute for talent. . . . If you have the best talent and a reasonably good strategy, everything else works out."[8]

Enron began to pay special attention to building its intellectual asset base in the early 1990s. The company created an Analysts and Associates Program modeled after similar programs in the investment banking industry. Begun with 3 undergraduates and 2 MBAs in 1990, the program had grown to 250 undergraduates and 250 MBAs by 2001. The vast majority of participants in this program were hired to work in Enron's fast-growing trading-related businesses, rather than in the old-line oil and gas and pipeline businesses or Enron's overseas power plant projects.

Experienced operations and line managers typically recruited program candidates, screening them for intelligence, a strong work ethic, problem-solving ability, and a sense of urgency. Once on board, new analysts and associates rotated through different groups every six to twelve months until they found a more permanent position. Because most of these recruits were headed toward Enron's new trading-related businesses, all had to spend a short rotation learning how to structure complicated commercial transactions.[9] Skilling considered this program "the source of Enron's competitive advantage."[10]

The program was also designed, according to a former Enron executive, to put recruits on a pedestal "so they would develop a sense of superiority." A two-week orientation not only lured recruits with $20,000 signing bonuses and prospects of annual bonuses of up to 100 percent of salary, but also strove to impress on the newest elite Enron's image as "a cosmopolitan, global company with unlimited possibilities."[11] Recruits were barraged with Enron's lists of accomplishments: *Fortune*'s "most innovative company" for six years running; number 29 on its list of fastest-growing companies; number 22 on the list of best companies to work for; number 18 on the list of most admired companies. Recruits were told that Enron's stock price was woefully undervalued—easily worth $120 a share (the price never broke through the $90 level)—and that they were lucky to have been chosen to join such a remarkable company.

A key component of Enron's approach to managing this talent was its performance evaluation process, modeled after the one Skilling had learned at McKinsey & Co., the renowned management consulting firm where he had been a partner. This semiannual feedback system rested on "360-degree" reviews: evaluations from peers, customers, supervisors, and supervised employees. Employees could also submit self-assessments. This system was intended to eliminate bias, identify top performers for future promotion and average or poor performers for remedial action, allocate pay equitably, and lay the groundwork for future recruiting needs.[12]

Rolled out for the energy trading businesses and corporate departments in 1997, the performance evaluation system applied to about 8,000 of Enron's 24,000 employees by 2001, leaving the traditional pipeline, oil and gas exploration, and overseas operations to their own processes. However, although it did not cover all employees, the performance review committee (PRC) process exerted a significant impact on organizational behavior, as it encompassed Enron's fastest-growing and most innovative divisions.

Under this system, PRCs comprised of about twenty higher-level employees met twice a year for as long as three weeks at a time to rank employees according to several criteria:

- innovation/entrepreneurship
- communication/setting direction
- teamwork/interpersonal skills
- leadership/vision/values
- business/organization skills
- analytical/technical skills

Supervisors developed preliminary rankings for their employees based on reviewers' feedback. PRCs overseeing groups of individuals with similar job titles then met to evaluate their performance, based on the value each person added to the organization. There was a target distribution of how many employees should fall within each category. Thus each business unit had to submit its top 10 percent and bottom 10 percent of employees.[13]

Ranking decisions during PRC meetings had to be unanimous. Rising stars in the top two (of six) categories typically received nearly double the bonuses of employees in the middle categories, although the PRC process was not formally linked to bonus awards. Top performers were often encouraged to look for and take on bigger challenges in the company wherever they existed. Employees who fell into the bottom 20 percent were in danger of being let go (although as Enron expanded rapidly and turnover grew, low performers were in less danger of termination).[14]

"You have to constantly show that you are adding value to the organization," explained Skilling. "That value can come in the form of new business ideas that make money, or from doing the old business well and maintaining the organization while others go on to build a new business. And you get the benefit of the doubt for trying something new."[15]

Skilling and Lay relied heavily on this performance management system to set and communicate strategic direction, and to promote specific skills and capabilities. "Through the PRC we can make clear this is what we value and this is what we compensate for," Skilling explained. "If you're off on a tangent, that's reviewed [and] you get feedback."[16] "In most organizations," he added,

> you have a vertical chain of communication. Your struggle is how to send messages to everyone when those messages sometimes have to come through managers who might not "get it." This is a major problem in fast-moving organizations. To fix this, you have a horizontal performance evaluation system with a committee of twenty people who "get it," who understand performance that is consistent with organizational values. With this approach you can cut out the noise; you have better communication, move faster, and get the right jobs done.[17]

Skilling saw this process as both a communication vehicle and a safeguard against office politics. "It kept a disabling boss from communicating the wrong messages," he explained. "An employee's career is not in the hands of his or her boss; it's in the hands of the committee."[18]

Despite these espoused advantages, however, Enron's approach to both recruitment and performance evaluation exerted several perverse effects. First, the self-congratulation and hype surrounding recruitment fertilized whatever arrogance new recruits brought to the job.

Second, although some Enron employees thrived in the PRC environment and felt that it was a good way to cull deadwood, others both inside and outside the company felt that it was a ruthless rank-and-yank system. According to one senior executive, during the PRC process "people were routinely treated as objects or commodities, loyalties were regularly sacrificed, and moral contracts were rarely honored."[19]

The PRC process was also seen as extremely political—precisely what Skilling had hoped to avoid. Because decisions had to be unanimous, strong advocates could hold up the proceedings fighting for their employees, while weaker advocates would see their employees emerge with lower ratings. For example, Andrew Fastow reportedly refused to cite evidence and provide backup for his judgments, as stipulated by the PRC format. "When his guys were criticized," recalled a former senior executive, "Andy just dug his heels in." If Skilling didn't rein Fastow in, the group would often just cave and give Fastow's people the top ranking to wrap up the meeting and go home.

The extreme mobility of Enron employees intensified the political wrangling. "Managers have to deliver good bonuses to their best guys to keep them," explained an Enron associate who had worked closely with Skilling. "Everyone's horse-trading. I need this guy; I'll vote for your guy if you vote for mine.' "[20] The PRC process also became, in some instances, a management tool for rewarding loyalists and punishing dissenters:[21]

> Managers would gather in conference rooms at downtown Houston hotels such as the Hilton or Doubletree. A human resources representative would flash pictures of employees on a screen and managers would then dissect each one. The HR departments would collect the results and compare them against a "preferred distribution" curve that Enron had concocted.
>
> That was when the blood sport began. Inevitably, the managers' curve was more generous than Enron's ideal. A number of employees given strong reviews would have to be downgraded to conform to the company's suggested bell curve.
>
> The managers would argue over employees as they sought to reshuffle the rankings. Typically, a manager would begin by praising the employee and listing all their accomplishments and then move on to a few weaknesses.
>
> "The minute you said 'but,' the floodgates would open and [the other managers] would attack," a former Enron manager recalls. "If you weren't on the team, the managers could absolutely crucify you." . . .
>
> The process often pitted managers against each other as they lobbied for their employees. Supervisors who did not win good rankings for their charges would soon discover that people would transfer out of their departments. They then stood to suffer in their own subsequent evaluations.[22]

In the absence of appeals, the result was extremely low morale among employees who fell below the top two categories, or who perceived their assessments as unfair.[23] An outside firm that conducted focus group interviews during the summer and fall of 2001 reported that "employees at the associate manager, director, and VP level . . . see a morale crisis among their colleagues," and identified the PRC as a key contributor. This report found that "at its heart, the PRC is seen as a *punitive* process, not an incentive policy. It is *not* viewed as a reward system. It is *not* viewed as a meritocracy. It *is* viewed as a punishment."[24]

Third, annual turnover in jobs held by employees ranked "superior" or "excellent" ran as high as 20 percent. Because these employees were encouraged to move to positions where they felt they could add more value and generate as much revenue as possible—often without their supervisors' permission—high performers often changed jobs two or three times in two years.[25] In seven quick years employees could jump from associate to trader to manager to director and, ultimately, to head of a new business unit.

Skilling maintained that this movement "strengthen[ed] Enron, with better matches of employees' talent with the job." He emphasized that "in a hierarchical organization, if the job description doesn't fit, you're stuck," adding: "I'd prefer to let people go where they are interested, where they are supported."[26] Enron therefore instituted a policy whereby titles were not tied to specific positions but moved with employees.[27] Skilling lauded this policy for encouraging people "to move to new, small start-ups and keep their old titles."[28]

Yet how could Enron build up enough experience and knowledge to create successful enterprises when high performers were circulating around the company in free-agency mode, looking for new challenges, and 10–15 percent of employees were leaving Enron in the wake of poor evaluations? How could supervisors evaluate the true performance and potential of someone who remained in a job for less than a year? In most cases, they could only do so with great uncertainty.

Take the case of Louise Kitchen, who at age 31 had led the development of EnronOnline in 1999, and was named CEO of Enron N. A. in August 2001—her seventh promotion in five years. Even given the entrepreneurial environment of Enron's online trading business, it is difficult to imagine what track record could have qualified her for such a key general management position just as Enron was entering a period of maximum organizational stress and loss of investor confidence.

Fourth, Enron's high rate of job rotation was matched by a high rate of organizational change. Employees complained that five to six reorganizations in an eighteen-month period had led to chaos, and that they had difficulty seeing how they fit into the company's future because the game plan seemed to be constantly changing. According to one VP, "As a company, we're still suffering from small-business syndrome. We're a major corporation still acting like a dot.com start-up."[29]

In the course of this continuous reorganizing, ever younger and less-experienced people became heads of business units. Many either didn't fully understand their new jobs or didn't know to whom they reported. A former executive recounts how more seasoned Enron employees responded to the hype surrounding the company's inclusion among *Fortune*'s 100 Best Companies to Work for in America with an alternative characterization: the Bizarre Social Experiment.[30]

By the summer of 2000, this social experiment had created a "crisis" and an "emergency" within the company, according to the employee attitude study. From associate to vice president, employees complained of instability. In their own words: "The left hand doesn't know what the right hand is doing." And "there is a sense of chaos in our everyday work. It's a symptom of the lack of an overriding strategy at the top, and it's starting to define practically everything."[31]

Fifth, with many young recruits striving to get on the fast track, make large sums of money, and move on to a new venture, Enron exposed itself to a mortal managerial sin: discouraging accountability. Many highly touted entrepreneurs never stayed put long enough to see and manage the results of their new ventures, as the PRC process rewarded employees for completing a deal or transaction rather than making it work.[32] According to one commentator, "Employees gravitated toward projects that could show results within the six-month review cycle, an attitude described as, 'if it's not going to happen by then, don't talk to me about it.'"[33]

Finally, the PRC process depreciated the very collaborative qualities that it supposedly valued. Once the marathon performance review sessions began, what really counted was money. Observed an executive from Enron Capital and Trade involved in reviews of traders and deal originators, "If they were making money and being total jerks to people, we'd always forgive them for that. They might be a 5 in teamwork, but if they were a 1 in earnings, they were a 1. If you weren't doing deals, we had trouble valuing your contribution to the company."[34]

Nowhere was the lack of teamwork more problematic than in the relationships between deal originators and traders in Enron Capital and Trade. Because the PRC process rated originators and traders with the same title together, and the financial stakes were so high (a ranking of 2 or 3 could cost a vice president a six-figure sum), the process often fostered fights about the relative worth, brains, and dedication of originators and traders. These battles amplified cultural differences between origination teams and traders and reinforced a certain ruthlessness and selfishness. Originators, who worked months building customer relationships and negotiating deals, tended to view traders as "bloodless mercenaries." Traders, for their part, tended to view originators as dinosaurs destined for extinction and themselves as agents of market efficiency.[35]

The Pay-for-Performance System for Originators and Traders

Adding the company's financial incentives to this mix reveals the true dimensions and toxic results of Enron's evolving performance management system. Skilling strongly believed that monetary rewards were the greatest motivator, and he designed a compensation system that played to that motivation. One managing director recalls Skilling telling him: "I've thought about this a lot, and all that matters is money. You buy loyalty with money. This touchy-feely stuff isn't as important as cash. That's what drives performance."[36]

Skilling's view is actually not so distant from that of many organizational economists.[37] However, like most credible behavioral propositions, dysfunctional outcomes can occur when such notions are carried to extremes or otherwise poorly applied. And perverse outcomes clearly resulted from the method Skilling chose to compensate Enron's 400–1,000 deal originators.

As in-house entrepreneurs who created and sold long-term commodity contracts and structured finance deals, originators were the princes of Enron. Their promotion ladder was not unlike that of investment bankers. Analysts stepped onto the first rung right out of college; associates were typically hired out of MBA or other graduate programs. Subsequent rungs elevated analysts to manager, director, and vice president. At the top of the ladder were managing directors—analogous to partners in old-line private banks. The salary for an average, early-career originator at the managing director level was in the $150,000–$200,000 range, with bonuses as high as $1 million in a good year, yielding a five-to-one ratio of bonus to salary. For senior originators (and traders—see below), the ratio was closer to ten-to-one (see Table 2.1). With bonuses running from five to ten times salary, one thing is clear: originators were working primarily for bonuses and other incentives, not for salaries.

Although Enron's use of incentive compensation is not unusual, the size of the bonus multiples for both average and top-level originators is. But there's more. Annual bonuses for originators at all levels were based on the

Table 2.1. Compensation of top-level originators and traders, 2001

Individual	Function	Salary (1)	Bonus (2)	Long-Term Incentive (3)	Deferred Income (4)	Deferral Payments (3)	Loan Advances (6)	Other (7)	Expenses (8)	Director Fees (9)	Total Payments
Belden, Timothy N.	Trader	$213,999	$5,249,999	—	$(2,334,434)	$2,144,013	—	$210,698	$ 17,355	—	$5,501,630
Detmering, Timothy J.	Originator	210,500	425,000	$ 415,657	(775,241)	875,307	—	1,105	52,255	—	1,204,583
Dietrich, Janet R.	Trader	250,100	600,000	556,416	—	—	—	473	3,475	—	1,410,464
Dimichele, Richard G.	Originator	262,788	1,000,000	694,862	—	—	—	374,689[a]	35,812	—	2,368,151
Donahue, Jeffrey M. JR.	Originator	278,601	800,000	—	(300,000)	—	—	891	96,268	—	875,760
Fallon, James B.	Originator	304,588	2,500,000	374,347	—	—	—	401,481	95,924	—	3,676,340
Garland, C. Kevin	Originator	231,946	850,000	375,304	—	—	—	60,814	48,405	—	1,566,469
Humphrey, Gene E.	Originator	130,724	—	—	—	2,964,506	—	—	4,994	—	3,100,224
Kitchen, Louise	Trader	271,442	3,100,000	—	—	—	—	93,925[a]	5,774	—	3,471,141
Lavorato, John J.	Trader	339,288	8,000,000	2,035,380	—	—	—	1,552	49,537	—	10,425,757
Leff, Daniel P.	Originator	273,746	1,000,000	1,387,399	—	—	—	3,083	—	—	2,664,228
McConnell, Michael S.	Originator	365,038	1,100,000	554,422	—	—	—	540	81,364	—	2,101,364
Muller, Mark S.	Originator	251,654	1,100,000	1,725,545	(719,000)	842,924	—	947	—	—	3,202,070
Shankman, Jeffrey A.	Trader	304,110	2,000,000	554,422	—	—	—	1,191	178,979	—	3,038,702
Sherriff, John R.	Trader	428,780	1,500,000	554,422	—	—	—	1,852,186[b]	—	—	4,335,388

(1) Reflects items such as base salary, executive cash allowances, and benefits payments.

(2) Reflects annual cash incentives paid based on company performance as well as other retention payments.

(3) Reflects long-term incentive cash payments from various long-term incentive programs designed to tie executive compensation to long-term success as measured against key performance drivers and business objectives over a multiyear period, generally 3–5 years.

(4) Reflects voluntary executive deferrals or salary, annual cash incentives, and long-term cash incentives as well as cash fees deferred by nonemployee directors under a deferred compensation arrangement and deferrals under a stock option or phantom stock unit in lieu of cash arrangement.

(5) Reflects distribution from a deferred compensation arrangement due to termination of employment or to in-service withdrawals as per plan provisions.

(6) Reflects total amount of loan advances, excluding repayments, provided by the debtor in return for a promise of repayment. In some instances the terms of the promissory notes accommodates repayment of the option with company stock.

(7) Reflects items such as payments for severance, consulting services, relocation costs, tax advances, and allowances for employees on international assignment (i.e., employment agreements as well as imputed income amounts for such things as use of corporate aircraft).

(8) Reflects reimbursements of business expenses as well as fees paid for consulting services.

(9) Reflects cash payments and/or value of stock grants made in lieu of cash payments to nonemployee directors.

a. Payments include international assignment related amounts.

b. Payments to Sherriff include international assignment—related payments imputed for calendar years 2000 and 2001 within the 12-month period.

Source: Adapted by the author, with the assistance of a former Enron executive, from Payment to Insiders, Schedule of Financial Affairs, Enron Corp., submitted to New York Bankruptcy Court, May 17, 2002, Case No. 01–16034.

present value of deals completed during the year. That is, Enron estimated future cash flows from multiyear deals and used those totals as the principal basis for determining current bonuses. This arrangement was facilitated by mark-to-market accounting, which enabled Enron to post the present value of long-term contracts on its books immediately, rather than spreading revenues over the life of the contracts. This practice encouraged some originators to shade the valuation of deals by selecting forward energy price curves and discount rates to show the present value of profits and cash in the most favorable light. According to one former member of Enron's celebrated Risk Assessment and Control Group, originators

> usually aren't trying to come up with the real value of the deal; they are trying to meet their individual bonus targets. . . . If the people in the business units wanted to survive the PRC process and meet their bonus targets, they often needed to inflate the deal value. . . . With inflated deal value they could deliver bigger earnings. More specifically, they could deliver bigger earnings to senior management, who in turn would deliver them to Wall Street and investors.[38]

Traders, who were rewarded in large part but not solely on the profitability of their trading books, had an important role in the deal-valuation process—especially where originators' deals involved long-term commodity contracts. For shorter term contracts (up to eighteen months in duration), where forward price curves were readily available from the New York Mercantile Exchange, traders played a limited role in making price assumptions and valuing originators' deals. But for contracts with time horizons stretching far beyond that of the NYMEX futures market (such as the Sithe transaction described in Appendix B), deal originators and their risk managers had to rely on pricing models based largely on the educated guesses of traders who were responsible for managing the inventory and associated risks of Enron's future commitments to buy and sell gas (and other commodities). In these situations, where all assumptions about supply, demand, price, regional differences, and transportation costs were open to both debate and gaming, traders ended up playing a large role in determining the profitability of originators' deals.[39] In addition, with significant future profits up for grabs, opportunities for traders to shift spoils among themselves and deal originators were legion.[40]

Under this system, many of Enron's top traders were taking home bonuses in the $2 million to $3 million range in good years. In 2001 John D.

Table 2.2. Annual gains/losses and bonus payments for 20 natural gas traders, 2001

Employee Receiving Payment	Natural Gas Gain/Loss 2001 (in millions)	Payment Amount
Arnold, John D.	$843.1	$8,000,000
Bass, Eric P.	5.5	400,000
Brawner, Sandra F.	(96.3)	525,000
Clark, Chad T.	9.7	150,000
Cowan, Michael R.	8.3	200,000
Cuilla, Martin L.	15.3	325,000
Dorland, Christopher	1.5	150,000
Ermis, Frank J.	101.6	850,000
Grigsby, Michael D.	(296.1)	200,000
Lambie, Chris D.	(77.2)	50,000
Lewis, Andrew H.	53.5	650,000
Martin, Thomas A.	54.95	1,100,000
May, Lawrence J.	30.0	850,000
McKay, Bradley T.	(1.5)	300,000
McKay, Jonathan	(3.6)	175,000
Neal, Scott M.	(4.43)	225,000
Schwieger, James E.	189.5	650,000
Shively, Hunter	29.3	1,750,000
Storey, Geoffrey C.	772.0	650,000
Tholt, Jane M.	23.4	200,000

Source: Enron Corp., Schedule of Financial Affairs, submitted to Bankruptcy Court, May 17, 2002, Case No. 01–16034, and FERC Data Extracts, D04–56-GAS, P&L by trader, at www.ferc.aspensys.com.

Arnold, a West Coast gas trader who realized approximately $840 million in "trading profits" for Enron, was paid an $8 million bonus. Although a complete picture of the full range of bonuses paid to traders across Enron's various trading desks is not publicly available, Table 2.2 presents the range of bonuses for twenty natural gas traders who received *retention* bonuses after Enron's bankruptcy was reported to the bankruptcy court. According to Enron officials involved in wrapping up the bankruptcy, these retention bonuses were approximately equal to the bonuses these traders would have normally earned through the first three quarters of 2001. The table therefore understates "normal" full-year payments.

Table 2.2 reveals that the relationship between annual trading gains and bonuses was crude: a simple, formula-based bonus system was clearly not in force. For example, Andrew Lewis, James Schwieger, and Geoffrey Storey each received $650,000 despite very different trading gains. And the extraordinary bonuses Thomas Martin and Hunter Shively received seem way out of line with their performance. (Their positions as heads of the Texas and central trading desks, respectively, might provide a partial explanation. Heads were responsible for the gains and losses of traders executing transactions in a particular commodity group and geographic area.) Scott Neal, head of the east trading desk, was less fortunate.

In his testimony before the Commodity Futures Trading Commission on August 19, 2002, pursuant to an Investigative Subpoena, the highly compensated John Arnold offered one possible explanation of the low correlation between trading gain and bonuses. Subjective judgments about the quality of profits achieved and the extent to which a trader helped out in deals traded by others at the same desk were apparently made by the leaders of Enron's trading operations when allocating bonuses to traders. The quality of profits principle was explained (somewhat disjointedly) by Arnold as follows: "If my trading profits were that I got lucky or that I had one position that I got lucky on at the end of the year, that's less valuable than if I made steady money every day. Because part of what you are paying someone for is their future success as well. Compensation is a tool to retain talent. So if someone makes money every day, you are more confident that they're going to make money in the future versus somebody with very volatile profits."[41]

In the end, Enron's well-paid professionally mobile traders were important partners for originators. It was often traders who decided which assumptions to plug into originators' deal valuation models. The further into the future originators had to project cash flows and profits, the more their calculations rested on traders' judgment calls. With prospects of immediately boosting their mark-to-market profits, traders and originators had a shared incentive to be optimistic with their forecasts of future energy prices and cash flows. And since both parties participated handsomely in the estimated profitability of their deals but not in any future losses, the incentives to take risks were correspondingly high. Enron's system for compensating originators exerted another perverse effect: because the system ranked their accomplishments semiannually and provided rewards on a twelve-month cycle, originators had little incentive to nurture promising deals that took a long time to sign. In fact, the last thing aggressive originators wanted was a transaction that lingered in limbo. Quipped an MBA who had gone through the associate analyst program: "If you hold onto a deal too long, it looks like you've got nothing better to do."[42] As originators turned into deal machines, they paid less and less attention to customer relationships, and Enron developed a reputation for ruthlessness and selfishness with utilities, its principal customers.

Weaknesses in Enron's Risk Management System

By the mid-1990s Enron prided itself on being the most innovative company in the energy industry. By the end of the decade Enron saw its innovations reaching across several industrial sectors, supported by an organization whose idea-generating and risk-taking capabilities were widely touted.

This strategy entailed many risks, including unproven demand for new product offerings, uncertain future price movements, unpredictable interest rates, counterparty credit risks where hedges were involved, and overpayment resulting from competitive bidding for existing businesses. Accounting practices involving off-balance-sheet partnerships—set up to help manage the reported cash flows and debt associated with Enron's new businesses—were also high risk.

Given the company's permissive management philosophy, it is not surprising that Skilling worked hard to put a centralized risk management system in place. However, although this system was widely celebrated, it turned out to be one of Enron's greatest weaknesses. Specifically, Enron's risk management system failed to protect the company from transactions promoted by deal originators and traders working under perverse financial incentives.

The impetus for developing a sophisticated risk management system gained strength in 1997, after the company took a $675 million write-off on a contract for North Sea natural gas. Following this embarrassment, Skilling assembled a collection of financial and risk assessment analysts, business managers, and lawyers into an independent group known as Risk Assessment and Control (RAC). RAC was headed by chief risk officer Rick Buy, who reported directly to Skilling.

The RAC group was responsible for analyzing the financial and nonfinancial risks of all significant Enron businesses, projects, and contracts, including proposed commodity deals and capital-intensive investments.[43] According to Skilling: "You get fired if you do something that doesn't go through RAC."[44] Once up and running, a staff of 150 analyzed and monitored transactions involving some 8,000 counterparties and $20 billion in revenues. RAC's annual budget was more than $30 million.

The RAC process for evaluating risks and potential rewards gave rise to a deal approval sheet—known as DASH—for all large capital transactions. A DASH was essentially a recommendation that a transaction go to Enron's senior managers (and sometimes the board) with a list of five or six key risks.[45] Lay and Skilling typically weighed in on proposed new businesses and large transactions that came their way, but only after the deals had been through the RAC process.[46]

To help manage the risks of each deal, as well as the company's overall risk position, RAC developed a comprehensive information system known as RisktRAC. This system broke trades and contracts into 1,217 separate trading portfolios—or books—for different commodities, depending on the interest rate, time horizon, location, and price risk. Traders who specialized in particular products managed the risk exposure for each book.[47] A research group built pricing models and other tools to help traders decide whether to trade, hedge, or hold particular investments or product groups.

RisktRAC also repriced the books each night and produced reports showing the firm's positions in the morning. According to David Port, former head of market risk at Enron, this enabled RAC to display each "commodity group's market and credit risk in real time to traders, senior management, and risk managers."[48]

On paper, this risk management system undoubtedly looked rock solid. In practice, however, it turned out to be remarkably weak. Even while creating an illusion of organizational competence, Enron's well-publicized process proved virtually impotent in stopping the company's reckless gambling.

The Powers report—produced for the board of directors after Enron's bankruptcy—criticized both RAC and its procedures for approving projects. For example, the board required that no transaction with an off-balance entity could proceed without surviving the deal approval process. The Powers report faults RAC head Rick Buy and his group not only for failing to follow prescribed procedures, but also for designing a deeply flawed process that promised little control. For example, RAC did not require originators to document efforts to find bona fide, unrelated hedging partners for Enron assets. The RAC process also posed questions with boilerplate conclusions ("Was this transaction done strictly on an arms-length basis?"), and set unreasonably low standards of compliance ("Was Enron advised by a third party that this transaction was not fair, from a financial perspective, to Enron?").[49]

What's more, many senior managers did not take the risk management system seriously. A former Enron managing director told *Fortune* reporters McLean and Elkind that "RAC was a hurdle, a speed bump, but not an obstacle. If a deal had overwhelming commercial support it got done. I treated them like dogs and they couldn't do anything about me. The process was there, sure, but the support wasn't. If RAC had complained about me and I got paid $100,000 less bonus, I would have changed. Never happened. I told my guys to fuck 'em." A former RAC vice president concurred: "We didn't approve shit." Offered another veteran originator: "RAC existed to keep analysts happy, to keep the story alive."[50]

Some internal observers attribute RAC's weaknesses to that of its leader, Rick Buy, known to be a soft-spoken fellow who was uncomfortable with confrontation. When his analysts raised issues with a deal, Buy would reportedly take them up the chain of command. But in confrontations with senior traders and originators, he always backed down. "Buy was a decent guy but not smart enough or strong enough to be in that position," remarked a former Enron senior executive. "Rick's the right guy to evaluate the risk. He's not the right guy to stand down the guys who want their deals done. They'd ram it down his throat."[51]

According to interviews by McLean and Elkind, Buy didn't want to be seen as someone who said no to a deal—even insisting that saying no was not part of his job description. He eventually told his staff that RAC's charge was simply to describe a transaction, analyze its risks and possible returns, and tell senior management: "You guys make up your minds."[52]

Buy's voice was also muted at the board level, despite the fact that the directors believed that "numerous groups monitor[ed] compliance with procedures and controls and regularly . . . update[ed] Mr. Buy."[53] The minutes of board and committee meetings reveal that Buy rarely reported on transactions between Enron and off-balance-sheet partnerships like LJM, despite the fact that the board had given Buy explicit responsibility for reviewing all such transactions.

In one notable instance Buy actually kept the board in the dark about investment risks and accounting shenanigans. This case involved Enron's investment in Mariner Energy, an oil and gas company that performed deepwater exploration. Enron bought Mariner in 1996 for $185 million. Enron North America executives later revalued this highly speculative investment upward—to conveniently convert these increases into mark-to-market income. By the second quarter of 2001, the Mariner asset was assigned a carrying value of $376 million, based on a model not supported by RAC. In fact, RAC valued Mariner in the range of $47 million to $196 million.

By the third quarter RAC's average valuation of Mariner and that shown as the book value differed by nearly $230 million. (Enron eventually had to take a $257 million write-off on Mariner.) Despite this enormous undocumented revaluation and departure from established risk management accounting, Buy did not bring the matter to the attention of the board. According to knowledgeable Enron executives, neither did he disclose to the board many other such violations of internal controls.[54]

The combination of Enron's deal-making culture and Buy's weakness proved disastrous for Enron. Few deals that originators brought to RAC were flatly rejected; debate usually focused on how to make the deals work. And RAC lost its reputation for independent oversight. After completing their analysis of a deal, RAC executives typically circulated their draft comments, and deal makers actually had the right to edit them. Indeed, RAC often drafted deal approval sheets with originators at the table suggesting language. To save their reputation, risk managers often resorted to reporting a range of potential outcomes.

RAC also had limited control over what originators and business unit managers reported to senior managers, who often asked them to squeeze more profits out of their deals by "tweaking the numbers." The fact that many transactions involved unusual commodities and periods of time greased this process. At the end of 2000 or early 2001, RAC reportedly made a presentation to senior management expressing concern about the systematic overvaluation of deals. Although the meeting generated a commitment to help business units prepare their deal proposals, no one mentioned the problem to the board's audit committee.[55]

To further complicate RAC's efforts, the volume of contracts was so high that risk managers could often do little more than check an originator's arithmetic—let alone question underlying assumptions about forward prices and risk. This problem was especially acute a few days before the close of a quarter, when entire deals often arrived, leaving risk managers little time to scrutinize transactions involving hundreds of millions of dollars, and putting enormous pressure on them to sign off because the company needed to hit its numbers. (These end-of-quarter deals became known as "Friday night specials.")

Did Skilling realize how ineffective his risk analysis and control operation was? It is difficult to imagine that he did not understand at some level.

According to McLean and Elkind, Skilling told associates that Buy wasn't strong enough to stand up to the deal makers; when he left Enron, Skilling even told Lay to replace Buy with someone tougher and more aggressive. So why didn't Skilling replace Buy? He apparently believed he could compensate for Buy's weakness by aggressively challenging deals himself. That was one of Skilling's most self-defeating delusions.

Skilling sometimes personally approved transactions of which he was openly skeptical, especially if they were backed by one of his trusted deputies. "I don't like this deal. I hate this deal!" Skilling would announce in a meeting. Then he would look over at the senior deal maker backing the transaction and tell him he was getting a pass. "If you really want to do it, this is your silver bullet. But I'm going to hold you responsible."[56] What's more, according to Jordan Mintz, general counsel of Enron's finance unit the year before the company collapsed, Skilling consistently failed to sign off on LJM deal approval sheets, as required by the board.[57] Thus Skilling's compliance with his own risk management procedures was apparently highly selective.[58]

Besides Buy's management style and Skilling's unpredictable behavior, the 360-degree PRC process also apparently motivated some of Enron's risk assessment managers to let deals go unchallenged, to avoid being criticized as uncooperative and unentrepreneurial. In other words, many RAC professionals labored under fear of reprisal for fulfilling the group's mission. Risk controllers who gave originators a hard time could get knocked down from the first or second to the third or fourth performance level—enough to make a six-figure difference in their annual bonuses. Consider the reported behavior of Angela Schwarz, the aggressive head of commercial markets within Enron Energy Services (EES):

> There were risk controllers within EES whose job was to approve the terms and the pricing that went into the contracts. Despite reservations, they often yielded to Ms. Schwarz. Many believed it was senseless to challenge her because senior management had tilted toward sales in their effort to find earnings of any quality. Further, Ms. Schwarz and her boss, Jeremy Blachman, were feared for the power they wielded in the PRC. "People didn't want to knock down deals that Jeremy or Angela did because everyone knew they could be ruthless during PRC," says one EES internal risk officer.[59]

Apparently similar practices prevailed in Enron's other energy trading businesses and its Broadband Services division.[60]

Thus did Enron's widely touted risk management function become a corrupted enterprise. Yet there is no evidence that this serious organizational failing was either acknowledged by top management or identified in Arthur Andersen's annual report to the board on Enron's internal controls.

In fact, Arthur Andersen's external oversight of Enron's deal valuations was becoming increasingly ineffective. It is not clear that Andersen had the expertise to assess trades at the extreme edge of what originators and traders could get away with. Neither is it clear that Andersen could have convinced Enron to book and mark its deals to market more conservatively. As one originator put it, Andersen "didn't know the difference between pushing the limits and playing it safe."[61]

The combination of Enron's PRC process, short-term performance metrics, and lack of market knowledge by internal and external risk controllers created an environment in which originators, traders, and risk managers had reasons to collude, explicitly and implicitly, to inflate current profits. That was especially true for risk managers because of the sensitivity of challenging the roughly eighty traders who accounted for 90 percent of Enron's reported profits in 2000. Why kill the goose that lays the golden eggs? In this environment, it is hardly surprising that many originators became less concerned with finding profitable projects and controlling risk than with booking as many high-value deals as possible.[62]

The costs of doing so soon became obvious, as underestimates of the cost of capital and overstatements of future cash flows led to write-downs of unprofitable contracts and projects. Less obvious, perhaps, was the addiction to growth that this environment nurtured. With reported profits spiking upward until a severe downturn in 1997, and then recovering in 1998, Enron had to continue the rapid increase in its reported revenues and profits to keep Wall Street's confidence and Enron's stock price up. In this vicious cycle, pressure for growth led to aggressive deals with overstated returns, which in turn required more such deals to cover shortfalls related to write-downs of previously booked deals.

Providing a precise accounting of overstated profits stemming from such trading behavior and lax risk controls is difficult, given the sheer volume of transactions. However, according to Stephen Cooper, Enron's post-bankruptcy CEO, redoing the company's balance sheet from December 31, 2001, according to generally accepted accounting procedures (GAAP) would require "a significant write-down of assets . . . which current management estimates would be approximately $14 billion." Cooper attributed about $5 billion to $6 billion of that amount to "valuations of several assets, the historical value of which current management believes may have been overstated due to possible accounting errors or irregularities." My own analysis shows that at least $4 billion of the $5 billion to $6 billion stems from mark-to-market overvaluation of assets.[63]

The Negative Effects of Executive Bonuses

Enron's executive bonus system was a fairly standard pay-for-performance scheme. As a financial services operation, Enron was certainly not unique in its approach. Where it might have been unique, however, was in the size of the feast. Furthermore—as with bonuses for originators, traders, and risk managers—bonuses for senior executives brought markedly perverse pressures to bear.

Enron executives were extremely well paid. Total compensation of the top two hundred employees—including salary, bonus, stock options, and restricted stock—rose dramatically from $193 million in 1998 (after the first decline in profitability and liquidity scare) to more than $1.4 billion in 2000. Cash bonuses to executives totaled $750 million in 2000, including $430 million in normal bonuses plus $329 million under a Performance Unit Plan (PUP) (see below). Although Wall Street firms typically pay out large percentages of profits to outstanding producers, Enron's total profits that year were only $979 million.

In 2001—Enron's bankruptcy year—bonuses for individual executives reached as high as $5 million and $8 million, in two separate instances, before gains from stock options. At least forty-eight executives received bonuses of $1 million or more.[64] As was the case with deal originators and traders, bonuses for senior executives in good years also averaged five times base salary.

According to Enron's proxy statements, factors influencing annual executive bonuses included "funds flow, return on equity, debt reduction, [and] earnings per share improvements."[65] Since the company's off-balance-sheet transactions and questionable accounting methods affected each of these performance metrics, top executive bonuses were closely tied to the company's use of these transactions.

The compensation committee of the board of directors set the bonuses for Enron's most senior executives. Below this top echelon, annual bonuses for executives in businesses other than Enron International, transportation, and oil and gas operations were tied indirectly to the PRC process. Whatever the source of bonus recommendations, Enron executives often pocketed significant wealth even before their significant gains from stock options. Enron's (sketchy) proxy statements show, for example, that Mark Frevert, CEO of Enron Europe, received $5.3 million in cash bonuses, plus $5.5 million in "other" cash compensation from 1995 through 2000. When Frevert left the company in 2001, he received additional cash payments totaling $17.4 million, including $7.4 million in deferred compensation, consulting fees, severance, and imputed income (personal use of corporate jets).[66] Rebecca Mark, who launched many of Enron's energy projects outside the United States, received cash bonuses of almost $3.5 million in 1998—nearly 5.3 times her $660,000 salary.[67]

Skilling and Lay, of course, held the top spot on the cash compensation scale. From 1995 through 2000 they received $17.6 million and $12.1 million, respectively. Gains from stock options and grants netted each hundreds of millions of dollars more.

Executive bonuses were paid from an annual fund tied to Enron's after-tax profits (except at Enron International, where executive bonuses were largely linked to the completion of power projects). Before 2000, bonuses were funded as a percentage of each business unit's net profit, but this created problems for business units with little or no profits but significant market (shareholder) value. To help solve that problem and ensure that Enron executives would accept assignments in all parts of the company, the single corporate funding pool was established.[68] By the end of 2000, the board's compensation committee had set the corporate-wide bonus pool at 27 percent of after-tax profits—up from 11 percent in 1996. The pool allocated to the most senior (so-called Section 16) officers was 5 percent of recurring after-tax profits.[69]

Once the board approved funding for annual bonuses, the Office of the Chairman determined the allocation for each operating group. Payouts were based on the performance of each business unit (or corporate performance, for corporate executives), and, with the exception of Skilling and Lay, each individual's performance as determined through the PRC process.[70]

On the surface, such a pay-for-performance system appears to align executive and shareholder interests. However, this compensation system included enormous incentives for executives to maximize short-term results, to expand the use of off-balance-sheet entities as a way of managing Enron's income statement and balance sheet, and to ignore many of the values and administrative foundations required for a successful business organization. The details of executives' contracts show how the company reinforced these and other highly questionable incentive effects.

BONUSES FOR LARGE-SCALE PROJECT DEVELOPERS. Except for those paid to Skilling and Lay, most large bonuses paid to executives outside Enron's trading operations went to lead developers of large-scale power and, eventually, broadband projects, which required years to become operational. Enron Development Corp.—renamed Enron International in 1996—developed many of these projects.

In its early years, Enron was forced to rely on developers outside the company to create power projects, given a limited supply of internal talent. These outsiders—such as John Wing, who cut his teeth in GE's power business and later worked for Ken Lay at Houston Natural Gas—operated under profit and equity participation contracts based on the actual success of the ventures.[71]

That compensation pattern changed after Enron began to rely on in-house talent to develop large-scale power projects (most of which happened to be overseas). Under the new arrangement—introduced by COO Richard Kinder and known as the Project Participation Plan—project development executives received tens of millions of dollars in bonuses *at the closing of deals,* whether or not they turned out to be profitable. The plan's details are important.

Payments to project development teams were triggered by (1) financial closure of the project, (2) completion of construction, (3) commencement of commercial operations, and (4) the sale or transfer of the project. Initially, the awards for any of the milestone events were paid in three installments: 70 percent by April 15 after the plan year in which the right to receive the payment arose; 20 percent (plus interest) by March 31 of the following year; and 10 percent (plus interest) by March 31 of the next year. By the mid-1990s, these percentages were changed to two 50 percent payments. The payment at financial closure was generally 8 percent of a project's estimated net value, as was the payment for commercial operation, minus any bonus at financial closure. Thus the plan normally paid out 8 percent of a project's net value. (Annual awards were reduced by projects' direct costs, and by write-offs during the year.)[72]

The idea behind this new approach was to avoid giving project developers a permanent equity-like claim on future cash flows, as Wing had received. However, several perverse features of this plan stand out. First, because developers received a considerable bonus at a project's financial closing, before it became fully operational as a business entity, the incentive to close deals—rather than running them profitably—was high.

Second, Enron's incentives favored very large deals (like Dabhol) over small deals, because bonus payouts were based on projects' estimated future cash flows. Third, the fact that corporate directors or senior executives in Houston had unilateral authority to set project valuations for bonus payouts meant that senior project developers had strong incentives to forecast above-average returns and fully accommodated risks in their initial proposals to the corporate office for funding.

Fourth, 30 percent of bonus payouts for completing construction and commencing project operations could be revoked or canceled if a project was deemed unprofitable. This implies that project developers had some managerial control over the profitability of their projects once they became fully operational business entities. However, project developers did not see themselves in that role, nor did they have the authority to play it effectively.

Thus the Project Participation Plan was a pay-for-performance scheme for signing large power plant deals and meeting construction deadlines, rather than for operating profitable businesses for Enron, and the rewards were significant. Although there was a $20 million cap on payouts to executives for any single project, awards for top developers ran as high as $5 million to $7 million per project.[73]

Former executives of Enron Development Corp. (EDC) rebuff the claim that team members overstated the net present value of projects. These executives argue that outside parties typically vetted project proposals, along with specialists in tax, accounting, and finance at Houston headquarters and on the board. These outside parties included the Export-Import Bank and the International Finance Corp., which provided equity insurance for overseas power and pipeline projects; banks, which financed 80–90 percent of these projects through loans; and equity partners, which invested 10–20 percent of project funds, as GE and Bechtel did in the Dabhol project. The exposure of these parties would have spurred them to push for conservative estimates of revenues and cash flows. One executive remarked: "We had very rigorous third-party oversight. In fact, we were lucky to have any deals at all!"[74]

EDC executives also claimed that the commodity trading operation was the principal source of perverse incentives at Enron, since corporate headquarters did not rely on third-party reviewers to vet commodity deals. Moreover, in marked contrast to international power projects, the elapsed time for originating and developing gas deals was only days—too short a time to fully evaluate their risks and returns.

What's more, these executives claimed, if EDC's role was to develop projects, then why not pay accordingly? Project-specific development fees helped retain good people, and were consistent with EDC's mission. "We were being paid to be a project development shop," a former EDC executive explained, "and we knew it," adding: "We were also viewed with suspicion. For this reason, many of our plants and newly completed projects were taken away from us by the folks in Houston, which only reinforced our role and self-perception as a pure development or deal shop." Another executive pointed out: "We needed money at the closing because deals took two to four years to develop, and there were lean years in between bonuses when teams were living on relatively low salaries."[75]

However, given the sizable payoffs associated with project closings, and the lack of rewards and penalties for actually running new projects, the bias toward originating large new ventures was inevitable. EDC and Enron International executives also received extra compensation for acquiring existing businesses—reinforcing their strong incentives to close deals. Coupled with the natural desire to beat out other buyers, these incentives may have spurred Enron to overpay for major acquisitions. Such deals included Enron's pricey purchase of an Argentinean water utility, and the 36 percent premium over publicly traded value it paid for Wessex Water, which eliminated any possibility that Azurix would profit from post-acquisition efficiencies.[76]

BONUSES FOR BROADBAND EXECUTIVES. The power plant development business wasn't the only part of Enron's nontrading activities where executives received bonuses based on projects' net present value. Executives at Broadband Services (EBS) received bonuses totaling at least $10 million after claiming $111 million in expected returns from a new video-on-demand venture in late 2000 and early 2001.[77] Six months later the company wrote off the claimed $111 million profit as a complete loss. The unit was phased out, and the chief financial officer and head accounting manager were later indicted for accounting fraud.[78]

Here again, paying bonuses when executives' projects were signed delivered a slanted message. Except for a risk management assessment at the project proposal stage, few people at EBS seemed to care deeply and think rigorously about how a deal was structured, how much it cost, or the likelihood that expected returns would materialize. The overwhelming interest was in closing deals quickly—and, better yet, keeping them off the balance sheet.

SKILLING'S BONUS ARRANGEMENT. Skilling's bonus plan provided plenty of incentive for him to become the leading proponent of mark-to-market accounting, which eventually played a key role in Enron's billions of dollars of overstated value. According to the company's 1990 proxy statement, Skilling's original contract stipulated that he would receive cash bonuses based on increases in the value of Enron Financial Corp.—the company he was hired to create. He would receive $10 million if the net worth of the new company grew to $200 million, and $17 million if it grew to $400 million. Because of aggressive valuing of future revenues and profits, mark-to-market accounting enabled Skilling to report the maximum growth for his new unit.

Although Enron's proxy statements shed little light on bonuses actually paid out to Skilling, he appears to have received $2.5 million in cash under this plan in 1995, and nearly $6 million in restricted stock in 1996. Proxies from earlier years do not provide information on his bonuses, but he probably received rising payments as Enron Financial Corp. grew. He also apparently received comparable cash awards as a result of internal reorganizations.[79]

Apart from his belief in mark-to-market accounting, Skilling had strong personal incentives to push both the board's audit committee and Arthur Andersen to approve this practice. His next step was to petition the Securities and Exchange Commission (SEC) for permission to adopt the practice—until then authorized only for financial institutions. Skilling argued that mark-to-market accounting was more appropriate than traditional accrual accounting for matched purchases and sales—not only because of the embedded hedge, but also because traditional accounting allowed companies with unmatched portfolios to create the financial outcome they wanted merely by selling winning positions while holding onto losers.[80] After active lobbying by Enron and Arthur Andersen on Enron's behalf, the SEC granted Enron permission to use mark-to-market for natural gas trading from 1992 forward.[81]

Whatever the strength of Skilling's argument, mark-to-market accounting enabled Enron to report fast-growing profits even when much of the cash from commodity contracts would not flow in for years. While such accounting was new to the gas-trading business, banks had long booked profits on oil, currency, and interest-rate swaps before realizing them. But what made the Enron situation so problematic were the incentives built into Skilling's bonus contract and those of his senior colleagues. These incentives encouraged a sharp focus on revenue growth and size rather than predictable operating cash flow, as a driver of company value, and the corporate-wide practice of booking overstated deals that eventually needed to be written-down. And because Skilling's contract included no clawback provisions, which gave the company the right to take back paid bonuses if the transaction triggering the original bonus turned unprofitable, he suffered no penalties or accountability for these write-downs.

In the end, Enron lost its ability to generate enough profits and cash flows to run its businesses. It tried to hide the ballooning debt required to run its trading operations, but eventually collapsed when bankers and investors lost confidence in the company's management. In retrospect, we can see that the seeds of this financial collapse were sown years earlier in the bonus contracts written for Skilling and his colleagues.

Stock Options and Stock Price Mania

The obsession with short-term performance and exploiting mark-to-market accounting spawned by Enron's bonus system was magnified by its stock option practices. In fact, the company's bonus plan and stock option schemes were closely linked, because Enron encouraged employees to take their bonuses as stock and stock options. The result was that much of the pay of top executives—like that in many other companies during the 1990s (and today)—took the form of stock options and grants. For example, in 2000 equity-based awards accounted for 66 percent of Lay's total compensation, and about 75 percent of Skilling's.[82] This was consistent with the company's goal of placing 75 percent of the total compensation of the most senior executives "at risk"—that is, based strictly on profit targets, stock price performance, and total shareholder return (capital appreciation plus dividends). The latter criteria directly determined the grants of stock-based performance units to these executives.

To this end, more than one hundred senior executives who worked for Enron between 1998 and 2000 held phantom equity in addition to stock options. Phantom equity was designed to track the value of business units that have no stock of their own. These executives could convert this phantom equity into Enron common stock or cash at certain times.[83] For example, when Skilling became chair and CEO of Enron Capital Trade and Resources (the company's wholesale gas and electricity trading operation) on January 1, 1996, he was granted phantom options, which he could sell back to Enron in four equal amounts over a four-year period.[84]

Enron's SEC filings reveal that some payouts under the phantom stock plan were huge. For example, Skilling received a phantom option stake in Enron Energy Services (which sold gas and electricity directly to small industrial, commercial, and residential customers) that totaled 5 percent of the unit's net worth. Skilling converted this stake into $100 million of Enron common stock in 1998, after he helped persuade the California Employees' Retirement System and Ontario Teachers Pension Plan to invest $130 million in the unit.[85]

Although this form of payment focused attention on increasing the net worth of the division, it also reinforced the company's deep preoccupation with its stock price. Furthermore, inasmuch as these phantom shares didn't cost Enron managers a nickel, they had a strong incentive to aggressively invest other people's money.

Under a longer-term PUP, senior executives also received multimillion-dollar bonuses for hitting target stock prices—further reinforcing this obsession.[86] Each year, executives were granted bonus units whose value depended on Enron's total shareholder return over four years—compared with that of a peer group of eleven companies. For example, the value of units granted in 1997 rested on Enron's total shareholder return between 1997 and 2000.[87] If Enron's return ranked first compared with the peer group, each unit was worth the maximum of $2. If Enron's return ranked third, the units were worth $1. If Enron ranked lower than sixth, the units were worth nothing. The units also had no value if Enron's total stockholder return trailed the ninety-day return of U.S. Treasury bills over the same period.

Because of mergers and divestitures, four of the eleven firms in the peer group in 1997 had changed by 1999.[88] These changes prompted the board's compensation committee to alter executives' long-term incentives—placing even more emphasis on share price. For example, whereas compensation under the original plan was capped, the new plan consisted of restricted stock and stock options whose value was limited only by the price of Enron stock.[89] The restricted stock was also subject to accelerated vesting. For example, if Enron met its annual profit targets in 1999 through 2001, one-third of the restricted stock grant would become vested as soon as the following January 31.[90]

Kinder's and Lay's 1994 option packages—which included $1.2 million in options for Lay and another $1 million for Kinder—would vest more quickly if Enron's earnings grew at least 15 percent each year. For example, rather than vesting in 2000 after five years, as prescribed by the 1994 Stock Option Plan, one-third of these options would vest each year that the company met the growth target.[91]

The company often resorted to selling productive assets to meet the 15 percent target. For example, between 1994 and 1996 Enron sold down its 50 percent stake in Teesside to 28 percent, folding the gains into its earnings.[92] Because the Teesside power plant was one of the company's most successful power projects, this move compromised long-term gains for other shareholders in favor of short-term gains for senior executives.[93]

Lay's 1996 employment agreement included a powerful incentive to increase the company's stock price as well as its earnings. On the surface, this incentive does not look especially radical. Under the agreement, Lay could exercise 80 percent of the stock options on or after November 1, 2003—making for a seven-year holding period. However, he could exercise one-third of the options if Enron's total shareholder return for any given year equaled or exceeded 120 percent of the average return of the S&P 500. These conditions vastly shortened Lay's vesting period and greatly accelerated his payout. Even if Enron did not meet this standard, Lay could receive the same payout if Enron's *cumulative* total shareholder return equaled or exceeded the cumulative adjusted average S&P return. The obvious message was that supernormal short-run gains in stock price would lead to quick, supernormal returns for the CEO.[94]

Enron's overall executive compensation program—particularly its stock option program—had features that advocates of compensation reform often applaud. Payouts of cash and equity-based awards were closely linked to shareholder value and earnings targets, an index or peer group, and—in the case of Lay's 1996 agreement—special benefits if Enron's total return exceeded the S&P's by 20 percent on either a yearly or cumulative basis. In other words, relative performance (and, for Lay, premium performance) was an importance metric. This aspect of Enron's policy was quite progressive: most companies do not design their equity-based pay for performance to include these features. When option grants are not based on a peer group, executives can receive windfall gains because of an overall rise in the stock market.[95] Similarly progressive was Enron's policy of expecting executives to hold Enron stock with a value at least equal to their annual salary—ensuring that they had some annual compensation and personal wealth at risk.[96]

However, whatever the positive features of Enron's executive compensation plan, its emphasis on stock price and accelerated vesting created a severe short-term bias and serious moral hazard. Because stock options pay off only on the upside but—unlike stock—do not penalize recipients on the downside, a rich stock option program with accelerated vesting tempts executives to take the money and run, shifting too much of the company's cash flow from shareholders to managers.[97] Such an approach also provides incentives for executives to manipulate reported earnings to meet performance thresholds.[98] The result was that managers became obsessed with Enron's stock price.

This obsession spread far beyond the top executives' suite. In 1998 Lay announced that if the company hit certain earnings targets over several years, employees would receive twice their annual salaries in Enron shares. The predictable result was that nothing became more important at Enron than hitting quarterly performance targets. Because the company's earnings were inherently volatile owing to its deal-making and trading operations, these targets became more and more challenging and led to many distortions in both strategy and financial reporting.

The Project 50 Stock Option Program, introduced in January 2000, turbocharged these perverse incentives. This program gave employees a one-time grant of fifty stock options when Enron's stock price reached $50, after the 1999 two-for-one stock split. Intended as a thank-you from Lay for contributions to Enron's success as a global energy and communications company, he said that "it would not surprise me if our stock continued to $50 milestones after two-for-one splits on an even more frequent basis. In fact, anything is possible, if we are focused, if we work together, as a team, as One Enron."[99] Perhaps the best evidence of the obsession with Enron's

Table 2.3.   Stock sales of Enron executives, October 19, 1998, through November 19, 2001

Name	Position at Enron	Gross Proceeds
Lou Pai	CEO, Enron Energy Services	$270,276,065
Ken Lay	Chairman, Enron Corp.	$184,494,426
Rebecca Mark	CEO, Azurix	$82,536,737
Ken Rice	CEO, Enron Broadband Services	$76,825,145
Jeffrey Skilling	CEO, Enron Corp.	$70,687,199
Mark Frevert	CEO, Enron Europe	$54,831,220
Stan Horton	CEO, Enron Transportation	$47,371,361
Joe Hirko	CEO, Enron Communications	$35,168,721
J. Clifford Baxter	Vice-Chairman	$34,734,854
Andy Fastow	Chief Financial Officer	$33,675,004
Rick Causey	Chief Accounting Officer	$13,386,896
James Derrick	General Counsel	$12,563,928
Rick Buy	Chief Risk Officer	$10,656,595
Mark Koenig	Executive Vice President	$9,110,466
Cindy Olson	Executive Vice President	$6,505,870
Steve Kean	Executive Vice President, Chief of Staff	$5,166,414
Jeff McMahon	Treasurer	$2,739,226
Michael McConnell	Executive Vice President	$2,506,311
Kevin Hannon	President, Enron Broadband Services	Unknown
Greg Whalley	COO, Enron Corp.	Unknown
	TOTAL	$953,236,438

Source: Adapted from Robert Bryce, *Pipe Dreams,* New York: Public Affairs, 2002, p. ix. Bryce's data came from *Mark Newby et al. v. Enron Corp. et al.;* SEC filings; congressional testimony; and Enron press releases. Costs incurred in exercising the options and selling stock meant that executives' net proceeds were lower.

stock price was Lay's decision to place a large electronic quote board displaying the price in real time (along with commodity exchange prices for oil and gas) at the entrance to corporate headquarters.[100]

Table 2.3 reveals how equity-based pay affected the wealth of Enron's most senior executives over a three-year period. Proceeds from stock sales dwarfed cash received as salary and bonus. For example, Lay's gross proceeds from stock sales were ten times his salary and bonus; Rice's were fourteen times salary and bonus; Skilling's, five times; Stan Horton's, ten times; and Mark Frevert's, five times. Given these enormous gains, it was almost inevitable that several key executives would leave as their interests diverged from those of shareholders, employees, and the company. For example, Ken Rice resigned from Enron in 2000, and Lou Pai and Jeff Skilling departed in June and August 2001, respectively.

My analysis in Table 2.4 shows that during the twenty-one-month period leading up to Enron's collapse, Lay pocketed more than $175 million from net sales of Enron stock while receiving an additional $34 million in stock, and option grants with a value in excess of $21 million. Skilling pocketed in excess of $78 million from net sales of Enron stock while receiving an additional $13 million in stock grants and $24 million in option awards.[101]

Over half these gains occurred during the nine months leading to Enron's bankruptcy, when both Lay and Skilling were strongly promoting Enron's stock. This was also when Lay and Skilling were vigorously defending Enron's great prospects even as the company was trying to manage its way out of a rapidly deteriorating financial condition. In early 2001, for example, Skilling argued before analysts and investors in San Francisco and Houston that Enron stock was worth at least $126 a share—nearly 50 percent higher than its current value—because of its broadband, energy services, and other new business ventures.

Shortly after this event, on CNN's *Moneyline* on February 5, reporter Willow Bay asked Skilling where he thought the stock should be trading. The stock was then priced in the low $80s, with a price-to-forward-earnings multiple of 67.1—an extremely rich valuation by both market and energy-sector standards. (The S&P energy sector had a 16.2 multiple on the same date.) Skilling responded:

> I think there are a number of parts of our business that are being under-estimated by the Street. Our wholesale [energy business] has had a 50 percent growth rate for the last decade. We think that it should be valued more in our stock price. Our retail [energy] business, which is brand new, is growing 100% a year, and we think that should be valued higher. And then [the] broadband business has got enormous potential for the future.[102]

On March 26, after Enron's stock had skidded from about $80 per share to $55, Skilling complained to the *Wall Street Journal* that the slide was crazy,

Table 2.4. Stock grants and cash from net sales and swaps of Enron stock by Lay and Skilling, 2000–2001

	2000	2001	2000–2001 Total
Lay	• Cash generated from open market sales of stock awards and exercised options, plus sales back to Enron, totaled $86,440,316.	• Cash generated from open market sales of stock awards and exercised options, plus sales back to Enron, totaled $86,722,842.	• Cash generated from open market sales of stock awards and exercised options, plus sales back to Enron, totaled $173,163,158.
	• Stock grants at then current market value of $7,500,024	• Stock grants at then current market value of $26,575,306	• Stock grants at then current market value of $34,075,330
	• Option grants at a Black Scholes value of $12,645,893	• Option grants at a Black Scholes value of $8,967,499	• Option grants at a Black Scholes value of $21,613,392
Skilling	• Cash generated from open market sales of stock awards and exercised options totaled $60,726,478.	• Cash generated from open market sales of stock awards and exercised options totaled $17,510,530.	• Cash generated from open market sales of stock awards and exercised options totaled $78,237,008.
	• Stock grants at then current market value of $3,500.036	• Stock grants at then current market value of $9,500,060	• Stock grants at then current market value of $13,000,096
	• Option grants at then current Black Scholes value of $17,116,854	• Option grants at then current Black Scholes value of $7,133,952	• Option grants at then current Black Scholes value of $24,250,806

Source: Author's analysis from SEC Forms 4 and 5 and information in the Global Access database (www.primark.com). The Black-Scholes model is a mathematical model of the market for an equity or share of stock, in which equity's price changes in a more or less random fashion.

and that the company's "core businesses" were all in "great shape." By 4:00 PM Enron stock had risen by 8 percent, to $59.40, in response to Skilling's pep talk.[103] When Enron reported second-quarter earnings slightly above estimates on July 12, Skilling confidently told the Associated Press: "The strong growth you've seen from Enron in the past will continue."

Skilling was either out of touch with Enron's operations or preoccupied with its short-term market value. Available evidence suggests the latter. Three and a half months earlier, on April 1, Enron's finance committee had told the full board that 64 percent of merchant assets were "underperforming," 54 percent were operating "below expectations," and 10 percent were "troubled"—the lowest category. (By August 13, just days before Skilling resigned, the finance committee reported that 67 percent of merchant assets were "underperforming," of which 45 percent were "troubled.")[104] To deliver this report on April 1, the committee must have begun related studies months earlier. It is highly unlikely that Skilling, as CEO, was unaware of either the studies or the report.[105]

Skilling's public comments after his resignation reveal what everyone who followed Enron already suspected: that he took the company's stock price drop personally: "I put a lot of pressure on myself [for the decline]. I don't think I would have felt the pressure to leave [if the stock price had remained up]."[106]

After Skilling's departure, Lay picked up where Skilling had left off. In an August 24 interview with *Business Week* after a 14 percent drop in Enron's stock, to $36, Lay was asked whether any "accounting or other issues that have yet to come to light" might be affecting Enron's stock. Lay responded:

> There are absolutely no problems that had anything to do with Jeff's departure. There are no accounting issues, no trading issues, no reserve issues, no previously unknown problem issues. The company is probably in the strongest and best shape that it has ever been in.[107]

Again, on September 26, Lay called the stock "an incredible bargain" and told employees, "The third quarter is looking great."[108] He added that he had bought Enron stock within the last two months. (He had acquired it by exercising 215,240 options.) Only three weeks later, Enron was forced to report a third-quarter loss and a $1.2 billion write-off related to trades and investments by partnerships set up by Fastow.

Figure 2.1 provides a clue as to why Lay, Skilling, and the entire executive team were fixated on Enron's stock price. Until 1997, the average exercise price of stock options held by Skilling and Lay was modestly in the money (meaning that the market price was greater than the exercise price of the option), as one might expect for a growth company. After 1998, however, as Enron's stock price began a dramatic ascent, the stock options held by Skilling and Lay—and presumably every other senior executive and director—were way in the money, representing extraordinary paper wealth. Thus these executives had ample incentive to talk up the stock—used to build new homes, invest in venture capital deals, and pledge donations to local charities. This incentive was clearly much stronger than the incentive to let the stock settle to a price more closely reflecting the historic valuation of energy companies, utilities, and trading houses.

The costs to executives of failing to meet Wall Street's expectations for quarterly earnings were enormous in terms of both bonus awards and capital wealth. As Enron's investments in power plants, water, broadband, and other ventures turned bad; as profits from trading fell because of growing competition; as the company required a rising stock price to finance rapidly expanding trading; as its credit rating and the cost of borrowed money became a key driver of profitability and survivability—as all these pressures converged in the late 1990s—the same incentives that had encouraged deal originators and traders to pursue long-term commodity contracts and test the outer limits of legal and conventional business practice began to work on Enron's top executives. Enron crossed these outer limits as the

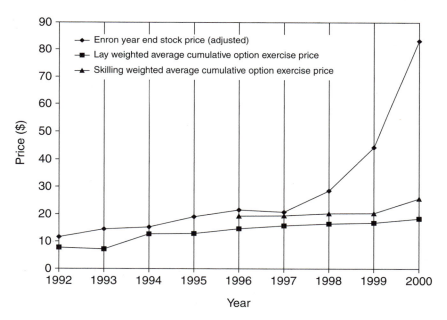

Figure 2.1 Enron stock price versus cumulative weighted option prices for Skilling and Lay, 1992–2000.

organization developed two deadly addictions: a broadly based addiction to growth at all costs and an addiction shared, perhaps, by a much smaller group of executives to disguise Enron's true financial position. These twin addictions festered in a developing culture of deceit, which is the subject of Chapter 3.

The Evolving Culture of Deceit

Enron was touched by the overheated economic conditions that prevailed during the late 1990s. These conditions included

- a high-tech fever that fueled images of a new economy based on new ways of thinking and radical innovations in products and services;
- a booming stock market that doubled between 1995 and 2000, nourishing dreams of unparalleled opportunities for becoming rich;
- a propensity for taking on huge risks financed by venture capitalists willing to spend unprecedented amounts of cash on the next new thing;
- an enthusiasm for capitalism and free markets (deregulation), despite the election of a supposedly liberal Democrat as U.S. president; and
- the idealization of CEOs and their companies, and entrepreneurs and their startups, by a business press in need of a steady flow of entertaining news.

For many business newcomers, the message was that you were either in the new game and on the track to becoming rich, or you were on the sidelines and not worth taking seriously.

However, although the irrational exuberance of these years was real, what is most important about the Enron story is not what was going on outside the organization, but what was going on inside it. Deregulation of the energy business created many new opportunities that Jeffrey Skilling and Kenneth Lay thought they could exploit, but it is in *how* they exploited these opportunities and acted as institutional leaders that the truth about Enron's breakdown lies.

I have already traced the company's slide from remarkable innovations in the natural gas market to the hubris that led to costly misadventures in new

95

markets and reckless gambling with its balance sheet and credit rating. Buried in this story of hubris and recklessness is a supreme irony: for all its idiosyncrasies and remarkable business failures, the Enron organization behaved exactly as one would predict, given the nature of its key management processes.

The next two chapters elaborate this story line and document Enron's drift into deceptive management. We have seen that perverse incentives go a long way toward explaining many of the company's blunders in strategic and financial management. What I have yet to explain is how and why Enron became so involved in elaborate attempts to cover up its true financial position when its turbocharged growth strategy and heavy capital investments failed to generate the expected returns and cash flows. These misrepresentations included violations of generally accepted accounting principles (GAAP) and rules of the Securities and Exchange Commission (SEC) on recognition of revenue and profit, disclosure of debt and other contingent liabilities, and the use of special purpose entities and other transactions to mask the company's true financial position.[1] According to federal prosecutors, many of these violations constituted fraud.[2]

In this chapter I set the scene by first describing the organizational setting in which Enron's deceptive financial management and reporting arose, focusing mostly on the chaos affecting decision making during the late 1990s. This commentary provides insight into what enabled and motivated senior financial executives to pursue both subtle and not-so-subtle cover-ups of the company's failings. I also show how the defensive behavior of CEO Ken Lay encouraged accounting and reporting deceptions to become part of Enron's standard repertoire. In this, Enron was no different from most other organizations. For it is how leaders respond to unexpected problems, manage internal conflicts, and face crises that reveals the essence of their leadership style and establishes the organization's mores.

I present three case histories that show how top management began to circumvent and then violate accounting rules, and then I analyze the key accounting techniques Enron used to inflate reported earnings and disguise accumulated debt. I use this information to assess the claims by the court-appointed bankruptcy examiner regarding the scale of Enron's fraud. An assessment of the examiner's extensive report is important because the true extent of Enron's fraud remains unclear. Not only is the scale of accounting deception claimed by the examiner open to criticism because the company's creditors paid his professional fees, but no truly objective party has tried to quantify the scale of Enron's fraud. A more independent analysis might show, for example, that the examiner's quantification of the scope of Enron's fraud is considerably overstated. Despite this complication, plus the fact that considerable ambiguity remains over whether or not the financial strategies and accounting practices used by Enron were, in fact, illegal, the examiner's report *does* provide a wealth of information pertaining to Enron's questionable accounting practices. It also sheds considerable light on Enron's emergent culture of deceit.

Administrative Chaos

The recurring phrase Enron executives used to describe the company's decision making was perpetual chaos. Skilling was highly averse to any policies that might constrain or impede swift decisions. Believing that a vertical command and control system was ineffective in a dynamic organization, he gave managers of business units a great deal of responsibility and imposed few constraints, encouraging them to develop their own strategies and set their own rules. Indeed, business units were free to structure their own deals and new ventures up to the point when they needed to secure corporate financing.

The source of many new initiatives, this approach to business development also generated confusing investment guidelines and priorities for those responsible for day-to-day operations. If employees examined the company's annual reports to shareholders, they would have read first about the Gas Bank, then the gas-trading platform, then the entry into electric power, overseas power projects, the water business, and broadband—producing a perpetual flow of new ventures that was supposed to make Enron, as the sign on corporate headquarters boasted, the World's Leading Company (formerly the World's Leading Energy Company).

That this ever-changing, boundary-less operating environment afforded many opportunities for misunderstandings and conflicts to develop around business strategy should come as no surprise. After the launch of Enron Broadband Services (EBS) in 2000, for example, conflicting visions of its objectives developed between the Houston corporate office and the seat of this expensive new venture in Portland, Oregon. Although the goal of the executives running EBS was to develop the ultimate broadband network, the goal of corporate executives was far more circumscribed: to create an organization that could trade bandwidth. Executives held at least three conflicting visions of the purpose of the division's Broadband Operating System (BOS). Some executives viewed BOS as the sum of all the functions on the Enron network, while others thought it was a software interface that enabled outside programmers to use those functions. Still others thought BOS was simply the name of an industry Internet protocol.[3] In the world of startups and new ventures, companies typically resolve such basic differences before pursuing massive capital spending, not after spending the funds.

Enron's chaotic operating environment included uneven application of financial controls. In Chapter 1, we saw that top executives of the NEPCO plant-building subsidiary discovered $5 billion worth of construction guarantees only when accounting and finance specialists at headquarters were preparing the unit for sale to raise much-needed cash. Corporate officers never signed or filed many deal-approval sheets for large off-balance-sheet transactions, as required by Enron's Risk and Control group.[4] Even more shocking, Enron's capital budgeting process resulted in enormous unplanned overruns, such as the $4 billion overrun on a $1 billion budget that caught the board's finance committee by surprise at the close of 1999.[5] More evidence of Enron's deep-rooted sloppiness and administrative chaos emerged during the final weeks before the company's collapse. When Jeff McMahon, Enron's newly appointed chief operating officer, was trying to stave off a credit meltdown in October 2001, he could not find a complete schedule of current maturities on outstanding debts.

To make matters worse, Enron's new treasurer, Raymond Bowen, discovered when he took office at that same moment that Enron was not systematically tracking its cash on a daily basis.[6] When Bowen asked why, one executive from the treasurer's office reported that no one had ever asked him to focus on it. Similarly, no one in Enron's Global Finance operation appeared to have a clear sense of the number or terms of total-return swaps—transactions in which purchasers of assets could essentially force Enron to take them back—on the books, exposing the company to unknown liabilities. Nor did anyone create a list of all the triggers that would require Enron to issue stock to off-balance-sheet entities, assume debt, or otherwise take on new obligations if the company's stock price or credit rating were to sink.[7] In short, despite highly sophisticated value-at-risk computations on Enron's trading positions, the company had no system for tracking all its assets, liabilities, and exposures.

Nor, apparently, did the chaos stop there. One former member of Enron's Finance Group recounted this apocryphal story: A friendly banker often called around Thanksgiving to wish members of the treasurer's office a happy holiday, and to remind them that a $200 million payment was due the next day. "Oh, yes, of course," would be the casual reply, after which total panic would ensue as everyone ran around trying to raise the cash.

The effects of chaotic decision making and perpetual firefighting were felt by Enron's rank and file. In an October 21, 2001, memo summarizing the findings of an employee survey, Frank Luntz of the Luntz Research Companies reported to Ken Lay and other senior executives that "your employees at the associate, manager, director, and VP level made it very clear to us that they see a morale crisis among their colleagues at Enron." Although this unease undoubtedly reflected the rapid fall in Enron's stock price during 2001, Luntz began his report by emphasizing the degree to which instability and chaos were perceived to characterize the organization. He wrote, "One theme stood out clearly above everything else: chaos, instability, and uncertainty. In their own words: *This can sometimes be a good thing, but most of the time it's dysfunctional and disorganized. The left hand doesn't seem to know what the right hand is doing.*" Luntz added that "it was very clear that this sense of instability is not a new phenomenon. Rather, for better and now for worse, it has become part of the Enron culture."[8]

A Deficit of Management Competence at the Top

The chaos at Enron during the late 1990s partly reflected the fact that the composition and role of the management "team" overseeing day-to-day operations changed continually. Coincident with these changes were important—and in the end costly—changes in Lay's leadership role.

During the company's early years, the rate of turnover among top executives was not unusual. John Seidl was appointed COO in 1985 and he left in 1990; his successor, Richard Kinder, remained until 1996. However, in the wake of Kinder's departure, the pace of top management resignations accelerated rapidly, forcing Enron to continually reinvent itself at the top. Fewer than half of the thirty-four senior executives listed in Enron's 1999 annual report had remained when the company filed for bankruptcy two years later.[9] When he resigned in August 2001, Skilling was the sixth senior executive to depart that year, leaving only two seasoned managers with significant operational experience reporting to Lay.[10] Establishing and maintaining knowledgeable monitoring by top management just as Enron was facing severe competitive and financial hurdles was clearly a challenge.

By the time management turnover reached its zenith, Lay's role as CEO had changed in a way that had dire consequences for corporate governance and control. As far back as 1990, when he made Kinder president and COO, Lay had indicated that he wanted to "devote more time to long-term and strategic planning and development of new business opportunities." Kinder's role was to oversee day-to-day operations, with Lay continuing as chair and CEO.[11] Described as "a detail man with a head for numbers and a somewhat controversial reputation predicated in part on his demanding performance standards," Kinder was regarded as Lay's virtual equal, the kind of disciplined operating executive needed to balance Lay's external interests.[12] This division of labor at the top appeared to work for Enron.

When Skilling was named COO in 1997, and CEO in February 2001, Lay was content to continue the arrangement struck with Kinder. His new deputy would have full responsibility for domestic operational activities and, later, international operations as well, with the understanding that Skilling would keep Lay apprised of major issues.[13] With day-to-day operations entrusted to Skilling, Lay could continue to focus on local and national economic policy and politics and high-profile philanthropic activities. However, this division of labor severely diminished Lay's ability to monitor the work of his executive team during the most critical time in the company's history. An interview conducted during the board's investigation after the company's collapse revealed Lay to have been so uninvolved that he learned about major transactions by key employees from the newspaper. Lay repeatedly stated that he did not know or could not recall numerous facts about Enron's operations.[14]

From the outside, Skilling's looked to be the right team in the right place at the right time. To help him run the financial side, Skilling brought in Andrew Fastow, who became Enron's chief financial officer in 1998 at age 38, from Continental Bank. Fastow quickly earned a reputation as a brash, intimidating executive who liked to say that capitalism was about survival of the fittest. Skilling's team also included chief risk officer Richard Buy, who had come from Banker's Trust, and chief accounting officer Richard Causey, who had earlier been in charge of Andersen's audit of Enron. Skilling's management team quickly and consistently earned recognition from both industry peers and awards from the business press.[15] For example, in 1999 *Fortune* ranked Enron first nationwide in the quality of its management. Notwithstanding significant turnover at the top, Lay must have been proud of the team to which he had delegated the company's day-to-day management.

Internal assessments of Enron's management were less benign. There was considerable anxiety among senior members of Enron's financial staff over the management of the off-balance-sheet partnerships. In one well-documented incident, Enron treasurer Jeffrey McMahon complained to Skilling in a meeting on March 16, 2001—long after many of Enron's off-balance sheet partnerships had been created—that he was having great difficulty dealing with Fastow.[16] Fastow was McMahon's boss as well as the general partner of the LJM partnerships that helped finance the Raptor off-balance-sheet entities (described in Chapter 1).

"The LJM situation has gotten to a point that is untenable for me and my group," McMahon protested, after having been involved in several difficult negotiations with Fastow as the general partner representing LJM. "I'm pressured to do deals that I don't believe are in the best interests of the shareholders. . . . To continue, I must know that I have the support from you and there won't be any ramifications."[17] McMahon asked Skilling to either remedy the situation or move him elsewhere in the company. McMahon had already approached Fastow on several occasions about conflicts of interest in transactions involving the LJM partnerships, proposing options for reducing or eliminating these conflicts, but Fastow had ignored his concerns and remedies.

To McMahon's dismay, Skilling failed to support his request for intervention, taking his concern to be principally a matter of financial compensation. Thus Skilling passed on an important opportunity to seriously examine the conflicts of interest that eventually helped to sink the corporation. Skilling offered many excuses: that Fastow's more substantial economic stake in Enron than in the LJM entities would presumably lead him to place Enron's interest ahead of those of the partnerships; that Enron's risk-management processes would uncover important conflicts of interest; that the LJM partnerships had been approved not only by Enron's board but by its outside auditors at Arthur Andersen and the attorneys at Vinson & Elkins. However, excuses aside, Skilling simply failed to exercise the disciplined oversight of matters that could permanently compromise the company's integrity that one might expect of an experienced CEO.[18]

Defensiveness and Pain Avoidance

Like Skilling's, Ken Lay's approach to dealing with crises that threatened Enron's institutional integrity exacerbated its culture of chaos and instability.

Lay's approach is perhaps best described as pain avoidance—a form of defensive behavior that fostered Enron's culture of deceit. This culture lived underground, shielded from public view by the gloss of internal and external claims about Enron's innovative management model.

Prominent psychiatrist Scott Peck observed, "What makes life difficult is that the process of confronting and solving problems is a painful one."[19] Being forced to recognize personal error, admit failure, and experience loss of control often engenders narcissistic anguish. Being forced to change one's view of the world and even of oneself, especially as one relies on winning strategies developed to cope with the world as one has come to see it, can engender extreme psychological discomfort. Fear of psychological pain drives many of us, consciously or unconsciously, to avoid problems in our professional and personal lives. We minimize rather than face them head-on or we procrastinate, hoping they will somehow disappear.

According to decision theorists Irving Janis and Leon Mann, such psychological stress profoundly affects normal patterns of information processing. When decision alternatives pose threats of serious risk, they observe, "Loss of hope about finding a better solution than the least objectionable one will lead to defensive avoidance." Janis and Mann define defensive avoidance as selective inattention or forgetting, distortion of the meaning of warning messages, construction of rationalizations that minimize negative consequences, and avoidance of vigilant search. Defensive avoidance often leads to procrastination, "buck passing," and "bolstering," or magnifying the attractiveness of a chosen course of action and diminishing that of alternatives.[20] All three behaviors are in evidence in the Enron story.

The concept of defensive avoidance is consistent with Jensen and Meckling's notion of pain avoidance.[21] According to these organizational theorists, when we are in a defensive, pain-avoiding regime, we are frightened, fear losing our self-esteem, make decisions that generally leave us worse off, and learn too slowly. We are unable to confront problems early because we are unwilling to put aside something pleasant or less painful for something more painful. Brain scientists tell us that this behavior is grounded in biological foundations such as the flight-or-fight mechanism, which has contributed to human survival for millions of years.[22]

When behaving defensively, we typically deny that we are acting to avoid pain, and refuse to acknowledge responsibility for our errors or mistakes. We tell ourselves that things are going just fine, and perpetuate this state of mind by failing to encourage any testing of our convictions.[23] Because we often do not realize when we are in a state of pain avoidance, we don't recognize our actions to be self-defeating, and make no attempt to alter our not-rational, unproductive behavior. This, we will see, was the case with Ken Lay, who appears to have had a well-developed capacity for self-delusion about harsh truths he did not want to face. One Enron executive is reported to have observed that Ken Lay "invents his own reality."[24]

People who tend to behave defensively cling to beliefs in the face of overwhelmingly contrary evidence. Defensive behavior is thus not rational and unproductive.[25] An instructive example is negative feedback. Most people who say they are open to identifying and discussing their errors and weaknesses actually resist such feedback—either by denying responsibility or attacking the messenger. Defensive behavior of this sort should not be considered random: people who routinely decline negative feedback also tend to systematically overrate themselves within peer rankings.[26] In the case of Enron, we will see how Ken Lay and some of his key executives systematically refused to confront investment mistakes and their own incompetence, and constructed cover-ups to make things appear better than they were.

When we are in a rational, productive regime, we become creative enough to find ways around new constraints. We are willing to make calculated trade-offs to maximize our self-interest. We make mistakes but learn from them, reducing their number in the future. When behaving productively, we generally think things through in a calm, reasoned way that fosters learning.

Most people learn how to strike a balance between these competing behavioral regimes. But when defensive avoidance dominates personal or organizational behavior, huge mistakes inevitably follow, leading to massive value destruction. As we shall see, the history of Enron, like the histories of GM, Kodak, and AT&T during the 1990s, reveals the difficulties of leaders of major corporations in using information and absorbing knowledge. In each of these cases, recasting management's view of reality was apparently too painful to implement in a timely fashion.

Indeed, some of us will go to extraordinary lengths to avoid facing problems, "proceeding far afield from all that is good and sensible in order to find an easy way out, building the most elaborate fantasies in which to live, sometimes to the total exclusion of reality."[27] This defensive, pain-avoiding behavior—proceeding far afield from all that is good and sensible—corrupted the ethical mores of the Enron organization.

Four instances of classic defensive behavior led Lay and the Enron organization to subtle and not-so-subtle cover-ups of problems. Each of these incidents constitutes a defining moment in the evolution of Enron's culture of deceit. Together they illuminate the relationship between pain avoidance and ethical drift at Enron.

Joseph Badaracco has eloquently termed a defining moment as one that "reveals something important about a person's basic values and about his or her abiding commitments in life." In such a moment, people tend to reveal their priorities among the many competing values at work in their personal and business worlds. Defining moments can also reflect and define "the values of the communities in which they have lived." More than finely crafted statements of corporate purpose and values, the decisions that managers make when values and interests compete send "strong messages to their organizations about how things really work and about how to get ahead." In Badaracco's words, "Defining moments can matter as much to the life of an organization as they do to the life and career of a manager," as these messages define the true purposes of the organization and how it will pursue them.[28] The defining moments for Ken Lay and Enron stretched from the organization's inception to the weeks preceding its collapse.

Defining Moments of Enron's Culture of Deceit

The Valhalla Oil-Trading Fraud (1987)

In retrospect, perhaps the most important defining moment for Ken Lay was his handling of the oil-trading scam discovered at a distant New York trading operation.[29] This incident occurred shortly after Enron acquired the forty-person business, located in Valhalla, New York, as part of the 1985 merger of Houston Natural Gas with InterNorth that created Enron.

In the early days after the acquisition, Lay assumed that the distant Valhalla was professionally run and accounted for, and left lead trader Louis Borget largely unsupervised. But unbeknownst to Houston, Borget, treasurer Thomas Mastroeni, and several others had begun to manipulate the books to reap substantial bonuses.

Here's how the scam worked: Borget set up offshore shell companies that created sham transactions and phony profits for Valhalla. Borget, Mastroeni, and a few others split bonuses of $3.1 million on reported profits in 1985, Valhalla's first year of ownership by Enron, and $9.4 million in 1986. To hide the deed, Borget kept two sets of books. However, the scam began to unravel in January 1987, after a New York bank called an internal Enron auditor to inquire about cash transfers of $2.7 million from Enron's accounts to Borget's. A few weeks later, Ken Lay asked Borget and Mastroeni to meet with him to discuss the suspicious dealings.

Under questioning, Borget and Mastroeni claimed that everything was legal, and that they were simply trying to reserve profits to meet future targets after fulfilling their 1986 targets.[30] Their response is remarkable because that kind of profit manipulation is both unethical and illegal. It is all the more remarkable that Borget's boss in Houston characterized these managers' actions as "sincere efforts on their part to accomplish the objectives of transfer of profitability from 1986 to 1987."

Rather than fire Borget and Mastroeni on the spot, Lay sent them back to the trading desk with a team of internal auditors to conduct further investigations. They were soon joined by a team of auditors from Arthur Andersen, which reported its findings to the audit committee of Enron's board in April 1987. The team's report stated that Borget and Mastroeni had "demonstrated the ability" to do deals "explicitly for the purpose of transferring company funds and deferring company profits." The report further concluded that although the team did not find any "additional unrecorded commitments, we cannot give you assurance that none exist."[31]

The minutes of the audit committee's meeting indicate that after a full discussion, "management recommended that the person involved be kept on the payroll." In other words, Lay apparently decided not to terminate Borget, perhaps because he badly needed the earnings Borget could generate. Enron was carrying a great deal of debt from its takeover of Inter-North, which Enron had financed with high-yield (junk) bonds. Under the terms of this bank loan, Enron had to earn at least 1.2 times the interest on its debt each quarter.[32] Enron also wanted to prevent a drop in reported earnings and cash flow, and was trying to raise more loans, which disclosure of massive trading losses would have jeopardized. The motives for a cover-up were clearly in place.

The Valhalla scandal did not end with Lay's decision to retain Borget and his team. Although Houston later took direct control of Valhalla's cash, other problems soon developed. Under growing pressure to produce profits, Borget began placing large trading bets, and consistently ended up on the wrong side of the market. He tried to save his trading book by "doubling down," thereby lowering the cost, but the volatile oil market continued to work against him.[33] By the time Houston got wind of what was going on, Valhalla's trading position could have wiped out almost all of Enron's 1987 earnings. Lay had to send one of Enron's star traders to Valhalla to close down the bad trading portfolio, and in doing so the trader discovered six dozen sham trades that exposed Enron to deliveries it could not fulfill. Even though the star was able to work off many of the unit's unfunded liabilities, Enron was still forced to announce a Valhalla-related $85 million charge against earnings.

When Lay later called an all-company meeting to discuss the Valhalla matter, he told the crowd that he had been blindsided by events, which is probably true. However, what was not discussed was why Borget had not been fired on the spot, or at least after the audit committee received the Andersen team's report. That omission only compounded the adverse effects of Lay's decision not to fire Borget and his coconspirators. Lay's clear message to employees was that rising earnings were more important than sound ethics. Lay's failure to deal decisively with this rogue trading behavior became part of Enron's cultural lore.

This incident presented Lay with two defining moments: when Borget's scam was discovered, and when the all-company meeting was called to explain events. In both instances the embarrassment of facing and revealing reality—and the huge trading losses that would have occurred just as Enron was trying to establish credibility in the capital and product markets—were apparently too great for Lay. By refusing responsibility and instead adopting the role of victim of deceit, Lay perpetuated the conditions that had fostered the scam in the first place. His defensive, pain-avoiding behavior set a tone that had enormous adverse consequences for his organization and its stockholders a decade later, when traders and originators were routinely overstating the value of deals to inflate their own bonuses.

As a footnote to this story, Borget later pled guilty to a number of criminal charges, and was sentenced to a year in prison and ordered to pay some $6 million in restitution. Mastroeni was sentenced to two years' probation.

Conflict Management at Enron Global Power and Pipelines (1995)

Enron Global Power and Pipelines was in the business of buying and operating power plants and pipelines in developing countries.[34] The company was created and spun off from Enron in 1994, with Enron retaining 52 percent ownership, and the rest of the shares publicly traded.

Enron Global Power's CEO, James Alexander, a former Drexel Burnham investment banker, had helped finance the merger between Houston Natural

Gas and InterNorth, and then engineered a takeover defense for Enron immediately after the merger was consummated. After joining the new Enron, Alexander rose through the ranks with support from Rebecca Mark, who had promoted the company's overseas "asset-heavy" acquisition program.

As CEO of Global Power, Alexander naturally believed that he should defend shareholders' interests when they conflicted with those of Enron—which became increasingly common during the mid- to late 1990s. Enron often asked Global Power to purchase poorly performing power plants. The price Enron set was typically the full cost of development rather than market value, which was sometimes much less. Alexander's complaints to COO Richard Kinder reportedly drew criticism of Alexander as a disloyal executive.

In 1995 Alexander reportedly went to Lay to complain in person about the conflict of interest he was being forced to live with, as well as rumors that executives were inflating the price of power projects to increase their compensation. Lay listened coolly and ended the meeting abruptly, saying he would take the matter up with Kinder. Shortly thereafter, key members of Alexander's staff were placed under Skilling, who was running Enron's trading operations. This triggered the resignation of Alexander's controller, who refused to sign any financial documents that had not been prepared by staff under his supervision. After losing his control staff, Alexander himself resigned. He had probably been trying to pay as little as possible for assets "offered" by Enron for as much as possible. This tension, and Alexander's bargaining power, might have led his bosses to decide to get rid of him, buy back Enron Global Power, and sell interests in its power assets to third parties.

This story again reveals Lay's (and Kinder's) failure to address serious conflicts of interest—in this case between Global Power's shareholders, who were being asked to take ownership of sub-par properties, and Enron, which was trying to raise cash and boost earnings by selling questionable investments in overseas power plants at prices above market value. Alexander was asking Lay to mediate between the conflicting interests of two sets of owners, and to confront the complicity of Enron managers who forced Alexander to violate his own fiduciary responsibilities. Lay apparently never did so. Had Global Power shareholders known what Alexander knew about overpaying for acquisitions, Alexander would have been subject to legal action.

Though we have no knowledge of what Lay actually reported to Kinder or any other Enron executive about his meeting with Alexander, the outcomes suggest two forms of classic pain-avoiding behavior. First, Lay apparently took no steps to personally intervene, choosing instead to pass the problem on to his chief operating officer. In recusing himself from a serious matter of corporate governance and ethics, Lay avoided

1. admitting that his company had been involved in improper, self-serving financial transactions,
2. working out rules to prevent such a conflict of interest from arising again, and
3. suffering the public embarrassment of restating Enron's earnings to make restitution to Global Power's public shareholders.

Second, Kinder appears to have avoided the substantive issue entirely by re-assigning personnel to forestall future complaints by Alexander. By failing to address Alexander's conflict of interest, Lay and Kinder effectively ended up siding with those responsible for the untenable situation. And Lay once again chose to avoid direct confrontation with the facts during a defining moment.[35] As with the Valhalla fiasco, his actions clearly revealed his ambiguous moral priorities and established questionable standards for the corporation.

Earnings Management at Enron Capital & Trade (1995–1996)

By the summer of 1996, Enron Capital & Trade's (ECT) considerable success in trading gas had encouraged competitors to enter the business. The natural gas market was also becoming more efficient. Yet even though this should have meant smaller profit margins and lower bonuses, Enron's traders continued to live in a world of great wealth, high levels of testosterone (few were older than thirty), and routinely foul language. The trading floors, according to Sherron Watkins, who had recently been assigned to ECT's finance group, "had the feel of a locker room crossed with the court of the Sun King."[36] Presumably, Jeff Skilling was the Sun King. Having successfully lobbied Skilling to raise limits on speculative trading set by Enron's board, and to take over managing trading records from deal originators, traders viewed themselves as "better—smarter, tougher, meaner—than the rest of the company."[37] In good times, top traders made more money than either Skilling or Lay.

However, by the end of 1995, even its intense narcissism and arrogance could not protect ECT's trading operation from rumors circulating on Wall

Street that it was losing money. Although Lay strongly rebutted these rumors, ECT had already made repeated efforts to manage its earnings—that is, to shift profits from month to month and year to year.

The first indication of overt earnings management on the trading side occurred late that year, according to Watkins, when a young associate who oversaw interest-rate books on the trading desk rushed into her office in a panic.[38] The associate's job was to ensure that trading gains and losses balanced every day, by hedging the risks of interest-rate fluctuations that directly affected the value of traded commodity contracts. But that day his trading book was mysteriously $70 million short—the funds had simply disappeared from the account. Watkins immediately called ECT accounting and was told that nothing was amiss: Enron was simply "correcting and fine-tuning" curves showing the future price of natural gas, to shift some of the funds made in 1995 into 1996 earnings. The money would be returned to the associate's account after the New Year.

Suddenly the locker room style and bad manners of the trading floor seemed beside the point to Watkins. The real point was that overvaluing and misrepresenting trading results had become routine strategy for managing earnings. No one on the trading side of the business doubted where the ethical center of Enron lay: making the profit Enron had forecasted superseded any responsibility to report its true financial position.

Just six months later Enron faced another awkward situation that required fancy reengineering of reported earnings. The company's quarterly profit goal was $100 million, but trading mistakes (including unsuccessful bets on the price of gas) had put ECT $90 million in the hole, bringing the total shortfall in earnings to $190 million. Enron had never before missed its earnings targets. In the wake of many panicky meetings, ECT transaction accountants came up with the idea of covering trading losses by revaluing some equity investments in power plants, natural gas projects, and energy stocks that had been buried in the JEDI (Joint Energy Development Investments) partnership.

Under the cover-up, Enron would simply apply mark-to-market accounting, which it routinely used for long-term oil and gas contracts, to its merchant investments. All the company needed to do was redefine JEDI from a core corporate asset to assets held for resale in an existing market. Doing so would allow the company to include unrealized gains in the value of those assets in its income statement: assets bought in 1995 for $100 million were suddenly worth 50 percent more.[39] Crisis averted!

This aggressive and unethical approach to earnings management in December 1995 and the summer of 1996 is especially noteworthy because Enron was grooming its future leaders at ECT, and the ensuing diaspora from that unit revealed and spread many of the company's true values. For example, when he succeeded Kinder as COO in 1997, Skilling appointed Lou Pai, his deputy at ECT, to head Enron Energy Services, the company's new retail operation. Ken Rice, another Skilling protégé, became chief of ECT's North American operations, and eventually head of Enron Broadband Services. Rice was among the first senior executives indicted for manipulating Broadband Services' reported 1999 earnings. These executives had claimed that the division had products ready to ship and video ready to stream over the Internet, and that it could meter and bill customers, even though it had no such products or capabilities.

In retrospect, the transgressions of 1995–1996 qualify as a defining moment in the evolution of Enron's corporate culture. ECT managers explicitly chose to cover up their volatile earnings and trading mistakes rather than face the pain and embarrassment of full disclosure. In the long run, both they and the entire company paid dearly for their flawed judgments and behavior.

Responses to Internal Dissent over Accounting and Disclosure (2001)

On August 14, 2001, just after Skilling had resigned as CEO, vice president for corporate development Sherron Watkins expressed concern in an unsigned letter to Lay that the company was about to "implode in a wave of accounting scandals," and that "the business world will consider the past successes [of Enron] nothing but an elaborate accounting hoax."[40]

In what came to be known as her whistleblower letter, Watkins elaborated on (1) aggressive valuation, booking, and disclosure of profits from derivative transactions involving off-balance sheet-partnerships, and (2) the adverse effects of capitalizing these partnerships with Enron stock or stock rights, whose falling value was triggering the need for equity infusions. Watkins also revealed that Enron treasurer Jeff McMahon was so agitated over conflicts of interests embedded in the LJM partnerships that he complained to Skilling and "laid out five steps he thought should be taken if he was to remain as treasurer." Three days later, according to Watkins,

"Skilling offered him the CEO spot at Enron Industrial Markets and never addressed the five steps with him."

Shortly after writing her anonymous letter, Watkins revealed her identity, and on August 22 she met with Lay, a follow-up memo in hand. In this memo, Watkins pointed out that Fastow and his partners in the LJM partnerships had already recouped their investments by making a substantial profit on the Raptor deals, and that they no longer had any "skin in the game." This meant that Enron bore all the risk, which was high and rising.[41]

Lay forwarded a copy of the unsigned letter to Enron's general counsel, who decided that the company should retain an outside law firm to conduct an investigation. Notwithstanding Watkins' warning that it had a vested interest in the outcome, Vinson & Elkins, which Enron had paid $35 million in fees during 2001, was retained based on its detailed knowledge of the company and LJM matters. V&E's task would be to determine whether the facts raised by the letter warranted further independent or accounting review.[42]

Over two weeks, V&E interviewed eight Enron officers (six at the executive vice president level or above), two Andersen partners, and several in-house Enron lawyers, and examined selected documents. V&E then interviewed Watkins, distributed copies of Watkins' letter to Andersen for comments, and held follow-up interviews with CFO Fastow and Richard Causey, Enron's chief accounting officer. In its report to Enron, V&E concluded that the company's accounting was "creative" and "aggressive" but not "inappropriate from a technical standpoint." V&E also concluded that the facts did not warrant "further widespread investigation by independent counsel or auditors," although the "bad cosmetics" of transactions with the Raptor partnerships and poor performance of many assets placed in these partnerships created "serious risk of adverse publicity and litigation."[43]

In reviewing V&E's examination of the Watkins incident, the special investigative committee of Enron's Board of Directors later concluded:

> With the exception of Watkins, V&E spoke only with very senior people at Enron and Andersen. Those people, with few exceptions, had substantial professional and personal stakes in the matters under review. The scope and process of the investigation appear to have been structured with less skepticism than was needed to see through these particularly complex transactions.[44]

Watkins wasn't the only Enron official warning top management of improprieties in the company's off-balance-sheet partnerships. As early as

1999, Vince Kaminski, who headed the research group that analyzed Enron's risk-management and trading operations, was rejecting transactions as bad deals for Enron. In the fall of 2001, Kaminski was maintaining within Enron that some of "the partnership arrangements had gone from being merely 'stupid' for Enron and its shareholders to being fraudulent."[45] Kaminski's concerns apparently came to a head at an employees' meeting on October 22, 2001, when he proclaimed to Lay and other top managers that the partnership arrangements under discussion were "terminally stupid" and "improper." He apparently pushed this view so persistently that another senior executive admonished, "Enough, Vince."[46]

Jordan Mintz, a senior attorney also concerned about Enron's off-balance-sheet partnerships, apparently chose not to voice his concerns as boldly as Watkins or Kaminski or to alert the board, even after Skilling declined to sign documents required for approving the deals, and failed to respond to memos and phone calls asking for an explanation. "I tried to work within the system," he testified before a House Energy and Commerce subcommittee.[47] However, Mintz did hire outside lawyers at Fried Frank to "take a fresh look" at the deals. The contents of and internal audience for Fried Frank's report are not known, but Mintz is believed to have turned over copies to the FBI and the Securities and Exchange Commission.[48]

It is not unusual for CEOs to leave accounting details to their chief financial and accounting officers, but the concerns raised by Watkins, Kaminski, and Mintz involved more than details. All three raised fundamental questions about the credibility of Enron's accounting and reporting practices, and the loss of investor confidence that would inevitably follow disclosure of Enron's real financial position. Yet despite the seriousness of the dissenters' accusations and predictions, Lay took the easy road in responding to the Watkins letter, avoided personal involvement, and asked his general counsel to take care of matters, who turned to his trusted advisors, V&E and Arthur Andersen. This was a major mistake on both the general counsel's and Lay's part. Lay ceded to others his responsibility as CEO to protect Enron's institutional integrity, while the general counsel created an unnecessary conflict of interest and a barrier to objective review. In the end, both failed by "proceeding far afield from all that is good and sensible in order to find an easy way out"—that is, by creating a culture of deceit. A less defensive and deceitful but more painful path would have been to call for an independent review of the accusations, and to publicly acknowledge any irregularities. Lay paid for temporarily avoiding embarrassment, and the chagrin of Enron employees, with the collapse in fifteen days of what had taken fifteen years to build.

The Crucial Deceit: Alleged Violations of Accounting Principles and Rules

Consistent with Lay's pattern of sidestepping difficult problems, and the ubiquitous fear of a credit downgrade, accounting maneuvers were a persistent attempt to disguise the realities of a company that had accumulated unprofitable long-term contracts, uneconomic hedges, and failing merchant investments. Many of Enron's alleged accounting violations involved transactions with special purpose entities (SPEs), whose raison d'être was to mislead investors and the financial community by hiding losses from speculation in technology stocks, disguising huge debts incurred to finance unprofitable new businesses, and inflating the value of other troubled businesses such as broadband. Any one of the above can contribute to a company's collapse. Yet nothing is more likely to seal a company's fate than the use of accounting tricks to hide bad decisions.[49]

Enron employed many such ruses to misrepresent its true financial state. Perhaps its most transparent attempt occurred on October 16, 2001, when it announced third-quarter earnings of $393 million, or $0.43 per share. Buried deeper in the release was the news that Enron had actually *lost* $618 million, or $0.84 per share. Enron converted this net loss into recurring net income by excluding $1 billion of expenses and losses as "non-recurring." Once spotted by experienced analysts, this accounting maneuver essentially doomed the company, as they knew intuitively what Bala Dharan of Rice University had shown the accounting world: that that kind of earnings reporting is often a company's desperate attempt to hide underlying problems from investors.[50]

More alarming and misleading than Enron's earnings reports were its history of cutting accounting corners, and its extensive use of accounting and reporting techniques to disguise its true financial position (see Table 3.1).[51] Some of this equivocation was driven by leaders' unwillingness to face serious problems, and their fear that unprofitable new business strategies and failing speculative investments in broadband and other technology would, if discovered, impair the company's credit rating. Others—such as the infamous Chewco transaction—were hidden from Lay, Skilling, and even chief accounting officer Causey, or only casually reviewed by these parties.[52]

Table 3.1.   Motives underlying Enron's alleged accounting violations

Motive #1: Managing Enron's Credit Rating

- Failing to disclose the nature and extent of off-balance-sheet partnerships operated by the CFO
- Excluding the debt of nonqualifying SPEs from the balance sheet and corporate financial reports
- Failing to disclose the full extent of contingent liabilities (i.e., debt that would come due if Enron's stock price and/or credit rating dropped below a specified level) and their potential effects on Enron's liquidity and capital availability
- Misrepresenting debt as "minority interest" rather than debt on the balance sheet
- Executing transactions that were loans disguised as commodity trades and treating them as trading liabilities rather than debt and the cash received as "cash flow from operations" rather than "cash flow from financing"

Motive #2: Managing Enron's Need for Cash and Earnings Volatility Related to Mark-to-Market Accounting

- Treating transactions as asset sales without actually transferring the risks of ownership
- Engaging in transactions that purportedly hedged Enron's risk in certain investments but, not being true economic hedges, were designed to keep losses from those investments off the books

Three early transactions with SPEs reveal the kinds of mistakes and deceptive accounting that marked Enron's path to larger-scale misrepresentation of Enron's true financial position.[53]

Project Braveheart

In July 2000, Enron created a joint venture with Blockbuster, the video rental chain, to supply content and traffic to Enron's new fiber-optic network.[54] Enron chair Kenneth Lay called the arrangement "the killer app for the entertainment industry," while Blockbuster chair John Antioco termed it the "ultimate bricks-clicks-and-flicks strategy."

The vehicle for financing this twenty-year joint venture was an SPE, code-named Project Braveheart (the legal name was EBS Content Systems). Public corporations often use SPEs to develop new businesses, or to sequester debt and other risks off the books. However, Project Braveheart could qualify as an off-balance-sheet SPE only by meeting two conditions of the Financial Accounting Standards Board. First, an independent owner must supply at least 3 percent of the SPE's assets (and that 3 percent must remain at risk throughout the life of the entity). Second, this independent owner must exercise control of the entity. Because it did not want to add the Braveheart partnership to its balance sheet, Enron needed to meet this 3 percent rule.

Enron assigned the Braveheart partnership a value of $125 million, based on projected revenues and earnings. Given this initial valuation, the partnership needed $3.74 million in outside equity to meet the 3 percent independent ownership rule. NCube—a company controlled by Oracle's Larry Ellison—provided more than half that amount by supplying critical computer hardware worth $2 million. The remaining $1.74 million was to come from a second partnership known as SE Thunderbird LLC, in which Enron had a 71 percent stake. To meet the 3 percent outside-money rule, Enron moved $7.1 million from Thunderbird to Braveheart. This transaction seemed to fulfill the 3 percent rule. However, because Enron controlled the supposedly independent owner, it did not.[55]

Nor did the irregularities surrounding Project Braveheart end with its financing. At its peak, the venture provided only about one thousand test customers with movies in four U.S. cities—revealing a clear lack of commercial viability. Enron withdrew from the partnership within eight months of its launch, claiming that Blockbuster could not convince major studios to supply their hottest films. Enron's exit left its Braveheart partners with substantial losses—but not before Enron claimed $111 million in gains during the fourth quarter of 2000 and the first quarter of 2001, based on estimates of future revenues. These reported gains limited the overall losses incurred by Enron's young broadband division. However, when Enron reported a write-off of $544 million against third-quarter earnings on October 16, 2001, it included Braveheart losses in the total, essentially reversing the $111 million in claimed profits. Kenneth Rice, former CEO of Enron Broadband Services, and Kevin Hannon, the unit's former COO, pled guilty to charges of securities fraud, and agreed to testify against several EBS associates sued by the U.S. government for fraudulent reporting and issuing false statements related to the Braveheart transaction.

Chewco Investments

The Chewco transaction marks the tipping point in Enron's drift toward fraudulent management.[56] Chewco Investments—created as an off-balance-sheet partnership—enabled Enron to boost its reported earnings by $28 million (of $105 million total) in 1997, by $133 million (of $703 million) in 1998, by $153 million (of $893 million) in 1999, and by $91 million (of $979 million) in 2000. This partnership also helped cut Enron's reported debt by $711 million in 1997, $561 million in 1998, $685 million in 1999, and $628 million in 2000. Chewco was shut down in the third quarter of 2001, after it was discovered to have violated accounting rules.

In the mid-1990s, Enron created Joint Energy Development Investments (or JEDI), with the California Employees Pension Fund (CalPERS). Both parties invested $250 million in power plants, natural gas projects, and energy stocks, earning more than 20 percent per year. (CalPERS contributed cash; Enron, twelve million shares of its stock.)

In 1997 CalPERS expressed interest in investing $500 million in JEDI II, a new Enron partnership, but wanted to cash in its first JEDI investment, then worth $383 million. To raise that amount, Enron created Chewco Investments (named after the Star Wars character Chewbacca), an SPE partnership of Enron and undisclosed outsiders. Chewco's investors did not have the required $383 million, so JEDI II lent Chewco $132 million, and Enron guaranteed a $240 million loan to Chewco from Barclays Bank.

To qualify as an off-balance-sheet SPE, outside investors had to contribute 3 percent of Chewco's capital (the remaining $11.4 million of the $383 million). When no willing third parties could be found, CFO Fastow invited Michael Kopper, Enron's head of structured finance, to become the required "outside" investor, working through several intermediary partnerships. This was the first time that Enron's finance group used an SPE run by an Enron employee to keep a significant investment partnership off Enron's financial statements—this time without prior approval by Enron's board. Kopper invested $125,000 and arranged to borrow the remaining $11.4 million from Barclays Bank, through two partnerships (Big River Funding LLC and Little River Funding LLC). The Barclays loans were treated as "funding agreements," enabling Chewco and Enron to characterize them as equity—not uncommon in SPE financing.

Concerned about the security of its loans, Barclays required Chewco to fund reserve accounts with $6.6 million in cash collateral. Although this satisfied Barclays, the collateral reduced the amount of outside equity at risk by $6.6 million, thereby disqualifying Chewco from meeting the 3 percent rule.[57]

It is not entirely clear whether this failure resulted from poor judgment, negligence, or the fact that Enron employees put their own economic interests ahead of their obligations to Enron. However, when Andersen auditors discovered this disqualifying event in the fall of 2001, Enron was forced to repurchase Chewco's stake in JEDI and move all Chewco's assets and liabilities back onto its books. This resulted in a $400 million write-down of previously reported profits for 1997 through 2000. Meanwhile Kopper reaped a $10 million return on his $125,000 investment—not including $1.5 million in management fees he received during the life of the partnership.[58]

Enron Energy Services

Former trading head Lou Pai was named head of Enron Energy Services (EES) after three prior chief executives (including Andy Fastow) failed to jump-start this new venture, set up in 1997 to manage the power needs of large corporations. Instead of plain old retail energy sales, EES aimed to finance, construct, operate, and maintain entire energy infrastructures for clients such as Lockheed Martin Missiles, the San Francisco Giants' Pacific Bell Park, the Archdiocese of Chicago, and Ocean Spray. Through a strategic alliance, EES also provided a full range of energy and facility maintenance services to CB Richard Ellis Commercial Real Estate and its industrial clients.[59]

It is not clear how this venture was to make money, as EES planned to sign management deals that guaranteed customers ever-lower energy costs over ten years. In fact, according to former finance executive Sherron Watkins, EES paid cash back to ensure that its clients achieved an immediate 10 percent savings in energy costs.[60] Although EES expected to make up the difference over the life of the contract, it predictably reported operating losses in 1997 and 1998, and no one knew when the venture would begin to operate in the black.

Enron executives pushed Andersen to permit EES to mark to market the electricity it expected to sell under its long-term contracts. The idea was to classify these energy-management contracts as FAS 125 deals, which would enable the company to use fair-value accounting and book unearned profits. However, FAS 125, issued by the Financial Accounting Standards Board in 1996, applied only to financial assets. More than 30,000 words long, this standard was subject to interpretation—something Enron had become quite good at. Jeff McMahon, who had come to Enron from Andersen, figured out how to wrap financial contracts around the cash flows expected from power plants (the first being Teesside in the United Kingdom), enabling Enron to effectively book all expected future profit streams in one year.

Though not a flagrant violation of GAAP, Enron's use of FAS 125s nevertheless masked EES's true economic performance. And Enron does appear to have violated GAAP in accounting for other EES transactions—thereby overstating the mother company's 1997 net income by some 63 percent. Here, in simplified form, is what happened.

In 1997, the JEDI II partnership and the Ontario Teachers Pension Fund invested in EES by buying shares. According to GAAP, companies in the "developmental stage" cannot claim a gain on the sale of such shares.[61] And it seems clear that EES had not moved beyond the developmental stage, having run up considerable startup losses in 1997. Thus, Enron's subsequent recognition of a gain on sales of equity to JEDI II and Ontario Teachers appears to be a violation of GAAP.

JEDI II and Ontario Teachers paid Enron their commitments in three installments. Andersen concluded that although Enron had transferred all the EES shares in 1997, it could not claim the entire gain that year, because it had not yet collected all the money. Andersen believed the SEC to be clear that a gain on the sale of an asset must reflect actual cash collected. In recognizing the entire gain in 1997, Enron simply did not comply with GAAP. Had it done so, the company would have reported gains of $20 million in 1997 through 1999—rather than the entire gain of $61 million in 1997, thus overstating its income for that year by 63 percent.[62]

The Spread of Deceptive Accounting Techniques

The Braveheart, Chewco, and EES transactions merely suggest Enron's casual approach to compliance with GAAP. The examiner appointed by the bankruptcy court, and the indictments of CFO Fastow by the U.S. Department of Justice, catalogued many more serious violations.[63]

After studying thirty-seven "structured" transactions, the examiner concluded that Enron routinely relied on six accounting techniques to manage its need for cash, credit rating, and volatile earnings generated by mark-to-market accounting.[64] The company's most important goal, in the examiner's judgment, was to manage its credit rating. Many of these transactions entailed stunningly complex interpretations of existing rules, while others required judgments on critical accounting issues not explicitly addressed by GAAP. Together these six techniques exemplify what Peck sees as the extraordinary lengths to which some people go to avoid facing problems, "proceeding far afield from all that is good and sensible in order to find an easy [easier] way out."

The examiner's job was to establish Enron's true financial performance, thereby laying the foundation for adjudicating creditors' claims. The court also directed the examiner to consider potential legal actions available to Enron shareholders.[65] Neal Batson's conclusions are not statements of fact or binding on any party, including the bankruptcy court and a jury: they are *possible* interpretations of the facts he assembled, made with the likelihood that claims would be successful in court.[66]

FAS 140 Transactions

According to the court-appointed examiner, transactions structured under FAS 140 rules enabled Enron to remove illiquid assets from its balance sheet without relinquishing control over them. In other words, Enron continued to treat assets it had "sold" as part of its holdings.[67]

These transactions entailed selling assets to SPEs. In most cases, the SPE borrowed 97 percent of the purchase price, and issued equity for the remaining 3 percent. Enron typically obligated itself to repay the loan through a total-return swap: it agreed to make payments to the SPE equal to its scheduled debt payments. Meanwhile Enron remained entitled to all gains produced by the transferred assets, except those due to the holders of the 3 percent equity.[68] Enron marked the total-return swap to market—enabling it to report increases and decreases in the value of the investment on its balance sheet and its income statement.

The court-appointed examiner argued that Enron's use of such transactions resembled loans to itself more than sales of assets. Enron's lawyers opined that the transferred asset had been "legally isolated" from the transferor, in the event of bankruptcy. However, the examiner concluded that these legal opinions "were limited in scope and analyzed only certain steps and specific entities rather than the transaction in its entirety." In fact, according to the examiner, "legal isolation was not achieved and, consequently, Enron's accounting treatment was improper."[69]

The examiner also concluded that if Enron's FAS 140 transactions were considered loans, it would have to return assets valued at some $500 million to its creditors after bankruptcy. Enron's balance sheet would also have to include the amounts the SPEs borrowed in these transactions—$1.1 billion of which remained outstanding at the time of bankruptcy. Finally, Enron would have to reclassify $1.2 billion in cash flow from those transactions as cash flow from financing operations.[70]

Tax Transactions

According to the examiner, Enron's second deceptive accounting technique had no business purpose other than to increase reported earnings. Enron often acquired assets that it did not need, and that were not part of its business operations—such as interests in mortgage loans and aircraft leases—to take advantage of GAAP rules on accounting for income taxes. The examiner put the total impact of such transactions on Enron's income at nearly $900 million through September 2001.

The examiner's report cites many examples, but two of the more straightforward types of transactions impart a sense of Enron's purposes and practices. The first type involved selling pools of real estate to investors, to claim future tax benefits as current pre-tax income. From 1997 through September 2001, Enron generated $144 million of income in this manner.[71] The examiner concluded that recording future tax deductions as current income was misleading, and not in compliance with GAAP.

The second type of tax transaction involved transferring assets—usually to SPEs—to "step up" the tax basis of large assets, such as Enron's headquarters buildings in Houston. Such a transaction usually creates a tax shield through larger depreciation. However, because the transfers were structured so that any benefit to Enron in federal income tax would not occur for many years, Enron did not deduct higher depreciation. Instead, the company reported the present value of those future tax benefits—amounting to $460 million from 1997 to September 2001—as an increase in after-tax net income.[72] Here again, the examiner concluded, this accounting did not comply with GAAP.

What is most striking about these (simplified) examples is how closely they parallel Enron's practices in valuing commodity trades: booking the present value of estimated benefits from contracts that extend years into the future. Enron apparently used a standard set of plays to manage its reported earnings and shareholders' equity. The playbook appears to have been kept by Enron's corporate tax department, which over time became an important profit center, with its own revenue and profit targets.[73] Robert J. Hermann, former Enron vice president for taxes, has testified that transactions originating in Enron's tax department became "kind of like cocaine," on which Enron's top management got hooked.[74]

Enron's tax department had two other important characteristics. First, although Enron structured its earliest tax transactions aggressively, they initially complied with GAAP, and were used at that time by hundreds of public companies. However, only two of eleven transactions reviewed by the examiner fit this characterization. The remaining nine, beginning in 1997, did not comply with GAAP. In other words, Enron moved from a world of aggressive but proper accounting practices to a world of highly questionable practices. What drove this conversion from compliant to deceptive behavior within Enron's tax department? Chapter 4 addresses that question.

The second important characteristic is that Enron's tax department became fertile ground for outside promoters of transactions that exploited highly nuanced tax laws. Indeed, third parties—including Andersen, Bankers Trust/Deutsche Bank, and Chase Securities—initially promoted all the tax transactions after 1997. So lucrative were Enron's tax initiatives that Bankers Trust was apparently willing to serve as both professional advisor and investor in improper tax strategies, reaping other benefits while also receiving $40 million in fee income.[75] Outside promoters also often hired Andersen's New York office to consider the accounting treatment of a hypothetical transaction—after which Enron engaged Andersen to approve the accounting treatment for the actual transaction.[76]

Enron's tax transactions—along with its FAS 140 transactions—reveal a record of systematic and continuous testing of accounting and disclosure by both Enron and its advisors. In other words, we are looking not at a series of isolated lapses, but at consistent policy and practice from 1997 onward. As we will see, this record was only the tip of the iceberg.

Hedging Transactions

As Chapter 1 showed, Enron attempted to hedge drops in the value of some investments by entering into contracts with SPEs owned indirectly by Enron and LJM II. These hedges were examples of flawed accounting as well as flawed corporate finance.

The LJM II partnership, created and managed by CFO Fastow, acquired energy and communications assets primarily owned by Enron. Third parties unrelated to Enron capitalized LJM II. Besides investing in these assets, LJM II also invested in structured-finance vehicles such as the Raptors. Fastow's LJM II partnership eventually set up four Raptor SPEs as hedging vehicles for Enron—capitalized by 55 million shares of Enron stock worth about $1 billion. Herein lies a significant accounting problem.

According to the examiner, LJM II should have been considered a related party to Enron under GAAP, and Enron should have added the SPEs participating in the hedging contracts to its balance sheet, thereby eliminating the benefits from this technique. The examiner concluded that Enron's accounting for the Raptors' hedging transactions wrongly raised reported net income by $346 million—or 35 percent—in 2000.[77]

Share Trust Transactions

Enron first used this accounting technique in the Marlin transaction, which it created to refinance some $900 million of debt incurred to buy water businesses operated through Azurix Corp. (see Chapter 1). The Marlin Trust was a Delaware business trust funded primarily by debt and a small amount of third-party equity that enabled Enron to move acquisition-related debt and the Azurix assets from Enron's balance sheet. The trust was set up as a co-owner with Enron of a holding company for Azurix. Marlin used the proceeds of the debt and equity it raised to repay a portion of the debt that Enron used to acquire Azurix assets. Enron indirectly guaranteed Marlin's debt. The examiner claimed this treatment of off-balance-sheet debt may have been permissible under a narrow interpretation of GAAP rules, but that Enron failed to properly disclose its contingent liability to provide funds to repay Marlin's debt until the third quarter of 2001.[78]

Enron adapted this technique in Whitewing, a structure created to purchase $1.6 billion of assets. Once again, in its implementation of the share trust Enron was seen by the examiner as having violated GAAP.[79] Enron retained significant control over Whitewing's investments, even though outside investors could appoint 50 percent of the board and approve purchases and sales. Thus the structure should have been part of Enron's balance sheet.[80] Enron had again created the appearance of independence while retaining control over transferred assets.

According to the examiner, improper use of the share trust technique increased Enron's 2000 funds flow by $418 million, and kept $4.2 billion of assets and $4.8 billion of debt and other liabilities off its balance sheet of December 31, 2000.[81]

Minority-Interest Transactions

This technique—implemented through a holding company structure similar to that used with shared trusts—enabled Enron to borrow money while showing the loan as a "minority interest" on its balance sheet. This placement was significant, because credit-rating agencies treated minority interests as a hybrid form of equity rather than debt. The examiner concluded that this technique enabled Enron to misrepresent $1.7 billion of debt on its balance sheet of December 31, 2000. This preserved favorable debt-equity ratios used by agencies to evaluate the company's creditworthiness.

Prepay Transactions

Although a significant portion of Enron's profits came from commodity trading, cash flows from these trades—especially longer-term contracts—lagged profits reported under mark-to-market accounting. To remedy this timing gap, Enron used prepay transactions to raise cash for current use. From 1992 through 2001, the company used prepays to obtain at least $8.6 billion in financing.[82] Both the bank examiner and a Senate subcommittee argued that Enron used these prepays to disguise the magnitude of its debt and inflate its reported net cash flow. Indeed, of the $5 billion outstanding from prepays on June 30, 2001, only $148 million appeared as debt on Enron's balance sheet. And prepay transactions, according to the examiner, accounted for *all* of Enron's net cash flow from operations in 1999, and 32 percent of that cash flow in 2000.[83]

JPMorgan Chase and Citigroup worked with Enron to develop transactions that allowed the banks to advance funds equal to those that specific energy trades might realize in the future. The banks typically routed these prepayments through an intermediary, or "conduit entity." Through a complex series of swap contracts, Enron effectively agreed to repay the funds over time, with interest.

In their simplest form, the prepays boil down to a circle of three transactions that transferred price risk of the underlying commodity, so that no party incurred extra risk. In the absence of price and credit risk, the examiner concluded that the prepays to Enron basically amounted to debt.[84]

Assessments of the accounting for these prepay transactions conflict. The examiner concluded that Enron's accounting treatment did not comply with GAAP, because the company recorded the prepays as risk-management liabilities rather than debt. He further concluded that Enron should have reported the transactions as cash from financing activities rather than from operations.[85] However, a British High Court judge held the opposite. In a suit arising from transactions between Mahonia Ltd. (an energy trading company created, operated, and controlled by J. P. Morgan) and Enron, Justice Jeremy Cooke ruled that Enron's choice of accounting was a plausible interpretation of GAAP.[86]

Both Batson and Cooke agreed that no GAAP rule is directly relevant.[87] The conflicting views hinge on whether the three transactions involved in each prepay should be considered one transaction. If yes, then Enron improperly accounted for the cash flow. If seen as three separate trades, then Enron's accounting was permissible.

The examiner took the view that the three transactions should be considered together because "all three were entered into at the same time, all involved the same quantities or notional amounts, and none would have been entered into but for the other two." The net effect was to provide Enron with a loan from a bank, which received repayment plus interest. He contended that the substance of the transactions did not match their form, and thus that no extension of GAAP rules could justify Enron's choice of accounting.[88]

Justice Cooke found that the three legs of the Mahonia transaction could be considered independent, and thus that the substance-over-form analysis was inappropriate. "There is no suggestion that the contracts were in any sense of the word a sham, so these rights and obligations were enforceable in accordance with the terms of the transactions with results which are very different from an ordinary loan. . . . It follows from my finding that Enron's accounting for the prepays . . . did not constitute a breach of US Securities law."[89]

The examiner's conclusions leave open the possibility that the transactions were fraudulent—as do prior decisions in U.S. jurisdictions. Indeed, U.S. case law has established that compliance with GAAP is not an absolute defense against claims of fraud.[90] Regardless of what verdict a U.S. court might reach, the prepay transactions are prime examples of Enron's penchant for pushing the accounting envelope to the point of bursting.

The Financial Impact of Enron's Addiction to Deceptive Accounting

To quantify the impact of Enron's improper accounting techniques, the examiner recomputed the company's reported results so that they complied with GAAP. He also reversed the impacts of the hedges and tax-driven transactions on net income and cash flow in 2000.

This analysis revealed that the six accounting techniques contributed *96 percent* of Enron's reported net income, and *105 percent* of its reported funds flow from operations, that year. The examiner also concluded that these transactions enabled Enron to understate its debt by more than half: it would have been $22 billion rather than $10 billion on December 31, 2000.[91] These astounding conclusions reveal the extraordinary extent to which Enron allegedly went to manufacture income and disguise debt through deceptive accounting and reporting.

It is important to note that structured-finance transactions using SPEs are not inherently illegal or improper. Indeed, they are often an efficient means for companies to raise funds while reaping accounting and tax benefits. What *is* improper, however, is using such transactions to report results that a company does not achieve. That is the basis of the examiner's allegations of fraud.[92]

Many employees were apparently well aware of Enron's dissimulations—some even joked about their pervasiveness. According to vice president Sherron Watkins, the giant green leaf overlay on the lush tropical scene on the cover of Enron's 1997 annual report quickly became known internally as "the fig leaf" obscuring the company's financial status and performance.[93]

Fig leaf or not, the bank examiner's assessment of Enron's fraud is probably overstated. To test his claims, let's assume for the moment that most Enron financial executives thought that pushing accounting rules in the search for new and more effective structured-finance products was standard practice in leading companies. Let's also assume that these executives were not trying to misrepresent Enron's true financial position—a difficult but useful assumption. Let's even hold aside the question of whether top management knew how close to violating GAAP and SEC rules Enron's financial

Table 3.2. Analysis of court appointed examiner's findings regarding Enron's accounting violations during fiscal 2000 (in Millions of dollars)

Selected financial information	Income	Funds Flow from Operations	Debt	Equity
As Reported in Financial Statements	$979	$3,010	$10,229	$11,470
Examiner's Adjustments by Accounting Technique				
FAS-140 Asset Sale Transactions (A)	(352)	(1,158)	1,353	(352)
Tax Transactions (A)	(269)	(61)		(547)
Noneconomic Hedges (B)	(346)		(150)	(518)
Share-Trust Transactions				
Marlin (C)	55	81	2,559	(113)
Whitewing (D)	(25)	(499)	2,312	(1,473)
Minority Interest Transactions				
Rawhide (fees), (B)			740	
Zephyrus, (C)			500	
Choctaw (fees), (C)			500	
Total, Minority Interest Transactions			1,740	
Prepay Transactions (E)		(1,527)	4,016	
Examiner's Total Adjustments to Reported Results	(937)	(3,164)	11,831	(3,003)
Examiner's Estimate of Actual Results	$42	(154)	$22,060	$8,467

Author's Revisions to Examiner's Adjustments[a]

Examiner's Estimate of Actual Results	$42	(154)	$22,060	$8,467
Reversal of Examiner's Accounting for FAS-140 and Tax Transactions (A)	$621	$1,219	$(1,353)	$899
Adjustments based on treating Marlin as a qualifying SPE	$(55)	$(81)	$(2,559)	$113
Reversal of Examiner's interpretation of GAAP regarding Whitewing (D)	$25	$499	$(2,312)	$1,473
Author's Estimate of Actual Results[b]	$633	$1,483	$15,835	$10,952

Note: Letters in parentheses following accounting techniques listed in upper panel refer to reasons for possible downward adjustment listed in lower panel.

a. I have added back and/or subtracted dollars based on the examiner's own identification of transactions and accounting practices where reasonable people could differ with respect to GAAP and SEC compliance.

b. Neither the examiner's analysis of the effects of these six accounting techniques on Enron's fiscal 2000 financial statements nor my revisions of this analysis are intended to be a restatement in accordance with GAAP. It is not possible to fully understand Enron's use of structured finance transactions involving SPEs without consideration of the specific purposes of those transactions—which was, in a general sense, to manage Enron's reported financial condition.

executives were on a daily basis from 1997 onward—also a difficult assumption to substantiate. How much can we reduce the size of the alleged fraud by assuming the absence of malevolent intent? The answer is that the examiner's findings can easily be seen as excessive.

A close reading of all 15,000 pages of his report by a reviewer sympathetic to Enron would reveal that many of the alleged accounting violations involve legitimate points of dispute. Table 3.2 compares the examiner's findings with my reclassification of the transactions based on a friendlier reading. I give the benefit of the doubt to Enron that the accounting for the FAS 140 and tax transactions was both ambiguous and correct. My reclassification concurs with the examiner that the noneconomic hedges and prepay transactions were inappropriately accounted for. Under this view, accounting violations would account for 33 percent—rather than 96 percent—of Enron's reported income for 2000.

Similar reversals of the examiner's adjustments to Enron's reported funds flow would leave $1.5 billion rather than $3 billion. And Enron would have understated its reported debt by only 50 percent rather than 105 percent that year.

If we go even further and assume that the U.K. court's judgment of the prepay transactions was correct, then allegations of fraudulent accounting and reporting by Enron would appear to be completely without basis. The company could be criticized only for inept and incomplete disclosure of its finances, not manipulation.

However, Andrew Fastow's plea agreement with federal prosecutors shows how incorrect that argument is. Fastow unequivocally admitted guilt in conspiring with others at Enron to improve the appearance of its financial statements. He did so by generating improper earnings and funds flow, inflating market prices for assets, and improperly protecting Enron's balance sheet from poorly performing and volatile assets. Fastow also admitted that his principal purpose (beyond self-enrichment) was to mislead investors and others about Enron's true financial position, thereby inflating its stock price and fraudulently maintaining its credit rating.[94]

Fastow's plea bargain is limited to entities under his direct control; I can only speculate about the scope of conspiracy and malicious intent beyond them. Available evidence suggests that the true fraud at Enron was far more than the unrealistically friendly assumptions point to, but also much less than what the examiner claimed.[95]

Despite these caveats, the scope of Enron's accounting violations suggests a deep interest on the part of management in disguising the company's true financial position. Had Enron reported unvarnished numbers, its stock price would have certainly fallen and its credit rating would surely have been jeopardized—resulting in a much higher cost of capital and diminished access to debt, for which Enron had a voracious appetite. While not necessarily life threatening, these outcomes would have created enormous capital losses for shareholders and Enron employees alike and diminished Enron's financial prospects considerably.

When reviewing Enron's compliance (or noncompliance) of GAAP, we also need to remember that Enron was accused of failing to comply with SEC rules as well. These alleged securities violations included failure to disclose (1) the nature and extent of the company's dependence on off-balance-sheet arrangements for its liquidity and capital resources, (2) Enron's obligations under these arrangements, and (3) their impact on the company's liquidity and capital availability. Companies normally disclose such items in footnotes to their financial statements, or in the SEC-mandated management discussion and analysis section of those statements.[96]

How can we explain the scope and persistence of Enron's addiction to deceptive accounting practices? Part of the answer relates to the pattern of defensive behavior established by Ken Lay from Enron's very inception. Part is also attributable to the perverse incentives that both motivated and amplified a latent tendency within the Enron organization to cheat. A third explanation is Enron's desire to prevent a downgrade to its credit rating at all costs, which intensified perverse incentives to take abnormal risks.

The accounting rules surrounding SPE transactions are so technical, and the structures so complex, that every transaction may have presented a "miss-by-an-inch, miss-by-a-mile" situation for the corporation and its advisors. Still, under those conditions, and given that these transactions were critical to maintaining Enron's credit rating, reported profits, and stock price, top management and the board should have carefully vetted their risks and rewards. Such vetting does not appear to have occurred.

The actual path of Enron's drift into fraudulent accounting and reporting is the subject of much speculation. My own reading of the record suggests a pathway from prudent to perhaps imprudent but by all means ethical management, through a period of serious bumbling by Enron's top leaders, to a buildup of enormous pressure to cover up cash-flow shortfalls that resulted from top management's poor investments, execution capabilities, and oversight. I see progress along this pathway being driven by large doses of managerial carelessness and intolerance for internal dissent, coupled with the need to place increasingly risky bets with a growing number of SPEs to satisfy all the conditions needed to maintain the company's investment-grade credit rating.

Enron at its inception was neither a conspiracy nor an axis of evil, but rather drifted into managerial and ethical lapses as its leaders avoided coping with difficult business realities by trying to cover up unprofitable commodity contracts, rising cash-flow shortfalls related to underperforming investments in power plants and water utilities around the world, highly volatile and risky merchant investments in broadband and other technologies, and escalating debt and other financial liabilities. The tipping point in the company's attitude toward playing by the rules occurred in 1997. Numerous events that year provided the incentive and rationale to shift from a more-or-less standard practice of limits testing in accounting and financial reporting to outright financial manipulation and violation of GAAP and SEC rules. Chapter 4 elaborates this argument.

Ethical Drift

The examiner appointed by the bankruptcy court found that the circle of responsibility for Enron's financial misrepresentations encompassed the company's chairman, chief operating officer, chief financial officer, chief risk officer, chief accounting officer, Arthur Andersen, in-house attorneys, outside attorneys, outside financial institutions, and, on some matters, the outside directors. All told, by the time the Skilling/Lay criminal trial began in January 2006, 34 Enron executives had been named in a mix of civil and criminal cases brought by such diverse claimants as former Enron employees, Enron shareholders, the U.S. Department of Justice, the Securities and Exchange Commission, the U.S. Department of Labor, and the Commodities Trading Commission. Fifteen of these executives pleaded guilty, five were convicted in jury trials, and two were acquitted.[1] The government alleged that the conspiracy to defraud shareholders included another 114 Enron executives, although their names were not made public.

One of the plea bargainers was Andrew Fastow, who was indicted on ninety-eight counts of securities fraud, money laundering, and tax charges. He admitted on January 14, 2004, that he had looted Enron, and promised to help federal prosecutors go after other Enron executives. Under the terms of his plea bargain, he agreed to serve ten years in prison and forfeit just under $30 million in cash and property.

A second senior executive, David Delainey, who ran Enron's trading business and later its failed retail energy unit, also entered into a plea bargain with government prosecutors after being indicted for deceptive reporting of Enron's financial performance and insider trading. Finally, a third senior officer, Rick Causey, Enron's former chief accounting officer, entered into a plea bargain with federal prosecutors in December 2005, only a few weeks before the start of his conspiracy trial, which had been bundled together with that of

Skilling and Lay. Causey pleaded guilty to securities fraud, and the plea deal called for a sentence of seven years, which could be reduced to five years if he cooperated fully with the government. Causey also agreed to forfeit $1.25 million. And, of course, both Skilling and Lay were convicted of participating in widespread schemes to mislead government regulators and investors about the company's earnings (although they vigorously contested those charges).[2]

Although many Enron officials, along with outside advisors and bankers, helped develop or approve the transactions that obfuscated the company's financial condition, a relatively small group among the thousands at Houston headquarters—working under the supervision of Fastow and Skilling— drifted across the ethical line separating truth telling from misrepresentation and deceit.

In the fall of 1997, a severe cash crunch and slowing growth drove these senior executives to begin searching for strategies that would preserve the appearance and reality of Enron as a new type of company representing the next stage in U.S. capitalism, in which newly deregulated markets, new ways of thinking, new technologies, and new forms of finance would help America work faster and cheaper and make the folks rich who "got it."

As Enron's newly appointed chief operating officer, Skilling's specific challenge in 1997 was to figure out how to keep the company's profit machine running, boost its stock price, and maintain its credit rating amid the worsening cash crunch. The latter stemmed largely from the organization's apparent inability to curb operating expenses, to balance outlays for capital investments with cash flow, and, to a lesser extent, by the unfortunate timing of a request from the California Employees Pension Fund (CalPERS) to cash out of an energy investment partnership. Also looming were ominous signs that the extension of Skilling's successful natural gas strategy to electric power trading and power plant development in North America and overseas would not generate the expected profits and cash flow.

By the fourth quarter of 1997, Enron's situation was so dire that it had begun to execute—through off-balance-sheet partnerships—transactions aimed at "managing" or manipulating its reported operating earnings and cash flows, in violation of generally accepted accounting principles (GAAP). Also beginning in 1997, the company failed to make appropriate public disclosure of these partnerships under applicable standards. These earnings manipulations and reporting failures mark the beginning of Enron's many misrepresentations of its true financial position.[3]

In searching for ways out of the cash crunch, Skilling and his closest associates were subject to preexisting conditions favorable to financial obfuscation and manipulation. Beyond the company's history of denial and cover-up, these conditions included a conflict between Enron's goals of achieving the high price-earnings ratio typical of high-growth companies, and maintaining an investment-grade credit rating typical of stable companies with predictable and recurring earnings. Underlying conditions also included accounting and financial conventions that Skilling and his colleagues could exploit to report steady growth in earnings for an inherently volatile deal-making and trading business; and a board of directors, chaired by Ken Lay, that was not predisposed to closely monitor the activities of Skilling and his team.

Conflicting Objectives

Enron's 2000 annual report boldly lays out Enron's conflicting business objectives.[4] On page 2, management proclaims its commitment to high earnings growth: "Enron is laser-focused on earnings per share, and we expect to continue strong earnings performance." Yet twenty-five pages later management tells shareholders that maintaining Enron's credit rating is a central objective: "Enron's continued investment grade status is critical to the success of its wholesale business as well as its ability to maintain adequate liquidity." Unfortunately, these two goals conflicted, because assuming rising levels of debt to fuel growth increases the risk of default, which puts a company's credit rating at risk.

Because of preference and feasibility, Enron was not free to tap sources of capital other than debt. It was extremely reluctant to finance its enormous capital expenditures by issuing stock, for fear that such dilution would harm the stock price. The company was also unable to finance its capital needs with earnings, because these were largely mark-to-market earnings, which generated little actual cash flow.

Nor could Enron raise capital by selling merchant investments in power plants and new ventures around the world (such as Dabhol), because a high proportion of these were either underperforming or highly illiquid. Thus debt became Enron's only viable source of capital for investments in its targeted growth areas: wholesale services (commodity trading), retail energy services, transportation services, and broadband.

The dilemma was that large amounts of debt on Enron's balance sheet would seriously impair the investment-grade credit rating that was critical to the company's wholesale business. Without such a rating, Enron would have to start posting collateral. To avoid this, it relied increasingly on transactions with special purpose entities (SPEs) to raise debt, because it did not have to disclose these transactions on the company's balance sheet.

To complete this vicious circle, the more debt Enron raised, the more important it became to show steady earnings to support its credit rating. This tension—built into everyday life at Enron—was a strong incentive for Skilling and his financial staff to use transactions with SPEs to manage reported earnings, and to disguise the company's true debt and other financial obligations.

Accounting Practices

As noted previously, mark-to-market accounting enabled Enron to assign aggressive market values to all contracts extending into the future. Mark-to-market accounting is straightforward when analysts can easily calculate the market value of contracts, but becomes much more complicated when applied to over-the-counter trades and sophisticated long-term contracts, which many of Enron's trades were.

Whatever the merits on either side of the considerable debate over whether Enron's use of mark-to-market accounting was lawful, or whether such aggressive accounting can be defended, originators and traders certainly had strong short-term incentives to overvalue the firm's long-term contracts, and thus overstate current earnings. From a corporate governance perspective, the valuation process looks a lot like the mouse guarding the cheese. Indeed, according to Stephen Cooper, Enron's chief restructuring officer during bankruptcy, the company overvalued its risk-management assets by as much as $8 billion to $10 billion![5]

Enron's application of mark-to-market accounting had several toxic effects that disposed the organization to deception and fraud. First, from 1991 onward, the company's rapid growth—its market value rose from $2.65 billion in 1990 to $8.26 billion in 1994—was hugely dependent on aggressive valuations generated by mark-to-market accounting. Once such accounting set highly optimistic values for long-term contracts and hard-asset investments, the only way to increase reported earnings was to value new contracts and projects even more optimistically. Enron's use of mark-to-market accounting also tended to accelerate earnings in mature energy markets that were growing at only 2–3 percent per year—a powerful incentive to deliver future growth through creative accounting and reporting maneuvers. Over time, these practices gave rise to a perverse culture of accounting fiction.

By 1997 Enron's deal originators and traders, and Skilling himself, had six years' experience using mark-to-market accounting on the trading side of the house to feed Enron's escalating need for growth. What's more, the sharp focus on short-term earnings growth as a driver of stock price was entirely consistent with Skilling's and other executives' personal payoff, given that much of their compensation came in the form of stock.

Perhaps most pernicious was the payment of bonuses to deal originators and developers of new businesses based on aggressive valuations of large-scale power projects, some of which were marked to market. After these originators and developers had collected inflated front-end bonuses, there was "no juice left" (in the words of one executive) to squeeze out of projects to pay performance-based bonuses to executives for actually running the businesses. Talent therefore gravitated away from operations toward the vastly more lucrative job of bringing in high-value contracts and projects, leaving Enron exposed to growing and unattended risks on the operating side of the house.

Board Oversight

The use of mark-to-market and fair-value accounting to keep profits and executive bonuses flowing was facilitated by lax oversight from the board of directors—especially of the true purposes and impacts of Enron's SPEs. As Chapter 5 will reveal, a significant body of evidence suggests that the board was out of touch with the realities of Enron's diverse and complex operations despite its distinguished membership. Skilling and his colleagues could hardly have been unaware that most directors operated in a hands-off manner, and that he and his team were relatively unfettered in perfecting their policy of living at the edge of creative finance and accounting. By 1997, Enron had crossed the line between limits testing and out-and-out deception.

1997: The Tipping Point

Enron journeyed into the realm of fraud by way of predisposition, but not entirely by premeditation.[6] It succumbed incrementally during the late 1990s, when it was not much different from a host of dot-coms and tele-coms that were gambling for large gains based on staking a leading position in emerging technologies and markets.

Almost as soon as he walked in the door of Houston Natural Gas in 1984, Ken Lay began to commit large amounts of capital in the belief that dere-gulation was imminent, and that when the price of natural gas reflected its true value, the companies with the most extensive pipelines would be calling the shots. This same investment logic was operating a decade later. Like Amazon.com investing large amounts of capital in electronics and lo-gistics infrastructure to spur a run to profitability, and telecoms betting huge sums to establish the first seamless network of broadband fiber, Enron de-cided to bet big to fill out its gas pipeline network, develop a presence in electric power, and create new technologies to support its skyrocketing commodity-trading business.

However imprudent and grandiose these investments might appear now, there was nothing unethical or fraudulent about them over Enron's first dozen years. Hubris, muddled thinking, and systematic investment errors may have led the company to lose billions of dollars on new business ven-tures, but nothing in its history suggests that Skilling, Fastow, or any other Enron executive intended to deceive shareholders before 1997. Until that year, the worst that Enron could have been accused of was misguided in-vesting, poor execution, and aggressively testing the limits of acceptable practice.

Enron's story is thus not one of avowed swindlers, of an Ivar Kreuger (the Swedish Match King of the 1930s), a Billie Sol Estes (who illegally cornered the salad oil market in the 1950s), a Robert Vesco (the mutual fund swindler who ran off to Costa Rica with investors' money in the 1960s), or the Banco Ambrosio (which developed a large money-laundering business in the 1980s). Enron's drift toward fraudulent management—prompted by the de-teriorating performance of its many business ventures and merchant invest-ments, and by an unexpected cash crunch—was subtler and more common, and therefore more instructive.

Figure 4.1 traces Enron's path from gambling more or less prudently to gambling ever more imprudently for large gains, until too many bungled investments in power and merchant-banking deals—along with recurring cash-flow shortages and mounting pressure for steady increases in reported profits—drove it briefly from the top-left into the top-right quadrant. Now gambling to survive, Enron management looked to its cadre of MBAs and lawyers to exploit ambiguities in GAAP and SEC rules to present the company's financial position in the most favorable light.[7] The skills of living at the edge of compliance with such rules, perfected during this time, served Enron all too well when a dramatic decline in reported profits—along with turbocharged incentives embedded in executive contracts and a pressing need to maintain the company's credit rating—created enormous pressure to resume reports of steadily rising profitability.

Four signal events define the point at which Enron crossed the line from gambling for large gains to gambling for survival, and toward this end systematically and persistently violated GAAP and SEC rules:

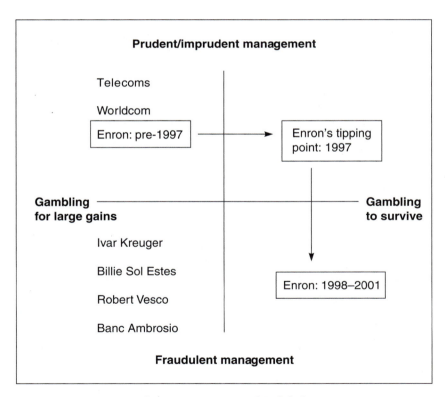

Figure 4.1 Enron's ethical drift.

1. Skilling's replacement of COO Rich Kinder;
2. a cash-flow crunch that demanded dramatic action;
3. the Chewco transaction, approved by the board on November 5, 1997, which served as a prologue and precedent; and
4. Enron's explosive use of SPEs and deceptive accounting techniques to raise large amounts of undisclosed debt and manage its reporting earnings.

Of these, the Chewco transaction stands out as the critical point of departure for Enron's descent into the realm of fraudulent management.

Skilling's Ascent to COO

When COO Richard Kinder resigned in late 1996, he was succeeded by Skilling, who had, of course, developed and run the gas-trading side of the house. Perhaps coincidental with his appointment as COO, Skilling and other employees became beneficiaries of the 1997 Performance Unit Plan, which promised huge payoffs if the company's stock price rose. The plan understandably focused all attention on Enron's stock price. This objective was reportedly reinforced by the practice of enabling key executives to value their stock options daily on their personal computers.

By all accounts, Kinder and Skilling embodied cultural opposites. Described as a tightwad who understood the value of cash as well as profits, Kinder was said to be able to hear "the sound of a nickel rolling along the sidewalk two blocks away." Kinder reportedly ensured that the cash Enron spent on new projects roughly equaled the amount it earned from operations. In 1996, the last of Kinder's seven years as president, he added little to Enron's long-term debt. That year the company earned more than $1 billion in cash from operations, while its outstanding debt totaled $3.3 billion.

Skilling's approach to financial management was a study in contrasts. During 1997, his first year as president and COO, Enron's capital expenditures nearly doubled, to $1.4 billion, while debt jumped to $6.25 billion (see Figure 4.2). Meanwhile interest expense rose 44 percent, from $290 million to $420 million. Although the company's debt as a percent of total capitalization remained constant, hovering around the 0.5 mark, after 1997 mark-to-market and accounting abuses inflated Enron's reported earnings and equity accounts (the value of earnings retained in the business). Given this record, it is fair to say that Enron's leverage increased significantly after Skilling seized the reins.

Under Skilling, expenses also exploded. One Enron executive estimated that the company's annual cost of overhead ballooned to $1.8 billion world-wide in the late 1990s.[8] Of this expense, $750 million went to consultants and professional services. Hundreds of deal originators and executives flew around the world in first-class seats and stayed in deluxe hotels. Entertain-ment costs for visits to strip bars in Houston, ski trips to Aspen, and team-building motocross outings were charged at will. Enron Capital & Trade (ECT) spent $2 million for flowers in a single year. "If you met your earnings target, you'd get your bonus," observed a former gas-marketing executive at ECT, "even if you spent twice your budget for expenses."[9] Reflected one internal auditor: "The excess was obscene. We were just pissing away money."[10]

Excess thus became a way of life under Skilling: flights in corporate jets, limousines on constant call, personal concierge services. He fretted that fru-gality discouraged original thinking. "I don't think we should be doing stupid things," he remarked, "but I don't think a penny pinching environ-ment is one that fosters creative ideas. We are not the Wal-Mart of the nat-ural gas business. We are the Mercedes-Benz of the natural gas business."[11]

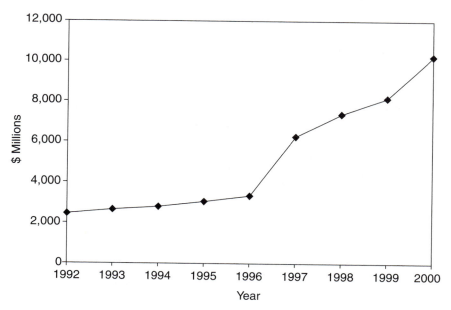

Figure 4.2 Enron's post-1997 run-up in reported outstanding debt.
Sources: Enron annual reports, various years.

Enron's largest spending category was investments in asset-heavy projects in the United States and abroad. In 1997 Enron completed the $3 billion acquisition of Portland General Electric and bought back shares of Enron Global Power and Pipelines. The company also acquired a 33 percent stake in Queen Sands Resources, an independent energy company, and bought Zond Corp., a leading wind energy company. In all, Enron spent more than $3.8 billion in cash and stock acquiring new assets in 1997.

Capital expenditures in existing businesses—including investments in power plants in Guam, India, Turkey, Puerto Rico, Italy, Britain, Poland, and Brazil, and expansion of commodity and derivatives trading in coal, water, pulp and paper, and weather—also rose from $878 million in 1996 to more than $1.4 billion in 1997. In 1998 Enron entered the global water business by acquiring Wessex Water, in a cash deal that topped $2 billion.

An important cultural shift accompanied the dramatic change in spending habits under Skilling. According to one observer: "The elevation of Skilling was a crucial moment for Enron. It represented the triumph of his trader's mentality."[12] This shift reflected a virtual takeover of Enron's top management—in business units other than pipelines and transportation—by executives who lived in the traders' world. Skilling's protégés Ken Rice and Mark Frevert took control of wholesale trading businesses in North America and abroad. Although they had significant trading experience, these were not seasoned operating executives. Lou Pai, another successful trader, had limited experience in the retail energy business, yet Skilling installed him at the helm of the beleaguered Enron Energy Services (EES).

Skilling's new headquarters was also populated with executives who had absorbed a trader's view of the world, having been hired into the trading side of the business. The two most important such executives were Rick Causey, chief accounting officer, who had spent five years at Skilling's ECT; and Rick Buy, chief risk officer, also an intimate of Skilling's from ECT. Skilling centralized risk analysis—previously spread throughout the organization—under Buy. Andy Fastow, another finance executive from the transaction side, also owed his job and career to Skilling, who made him a senior vice president in the finance group in 1997, and then promoted him to CFO in March 1998. Fastow had previously failed at his only operating assignment at Enron Gas Services.

A former corporate officer watching developments from overseas observed that Skilling's new leadership team not only consisted almost entirely of executives groomed on the trading side of the house, but was notably "short on operating executives and long on youth and inexperience."[13] With Skillingites filling eleven of the twenty-six top management slots at Enron by the end of 1997, the shift away from Kinder's precise, penurious, hands-on operating style was palpable.[14]

Enron's Cash Crunch

During 1997, the year after Skilling became COO, cash flow from operations turned negative, and Enron seemed to become less profitable as it grew. In the first quarter of 1997, Enron's negative cash flow totaled $142 million. By the second quarter it had soared to $523 million, and by the end of the third quarter it had reached $588 million. To complicate matters, Enron took a second-quarter restructuring charge of $675 million stemming from an impaired North Sea gas deal.[15]

Net income also fell from $584 million in 1996 to $105 million in 1997, while earnings per share dropped from $1.15 to just $0.16. By the end of 1997, Enron's stock price had stalled at around $19.00—or $2.00 lower than before Kinder's departure. In fact, Enron had been underperforming its peers in the natural gas sector since 1993.

When Causey voiced concern over the company's cash situation, Skilling reportedly told him: "Cash doesn't matter. All that matters is earnings."[16] By Halloween 1997, however, Skilling realized that he had to do something radical to bolster the company's cash position.

Matters came to a head when Skilling also had to find a way to fund a major transaction on the merchant investment side of the business. In the mid-1990s, Enron had created Joint Energy Development Investments, or JEDI, a partnership with CalPERS. JEDI's investments of $250 million in power plants, natural gas projects, and energy stocks were earning more than 20 percent per year.

In 1997, CalPERS wanted to invest $500 million in a new Enron partnership, JEDI II, but first wanted to cash in its half interest in JEDI I, worth $383 million. How could Enron raise the funds to cash out CalPERS while keeping any new debt and the highly leveraged JEDI partnership off the balance sheet? Skilling turned to his senior vice president for finance, Andy Fastow, for a financial solution.

The Chewco Partnership

Fastow's solution was to create Chewco Investments, which evolved into a devilishly complex deal. As described in Chapter 3, this special purpose entity (SPE) was designed to raise enough debt to pay off CalPERS' JEDI I investment. Under Fastow's plan, JEDI II would lend Chewco $132 million, and Enron would guarantee a $240 million loan to Chewco by Barclays Bank, to help pay off CalPERS. Together with $11.4 million representing the 3 percent of risk equity required to qualify as an off-balance-sheet entity, the $372 million of debt would capitalize Chewco at the $383 million required to pay off CalPERS. In addition, sequestering this debt in a separate partnership ensured that it would not appear on Enron's balance sheet.

Barclays, however, was concerned about the security of its loan, so it required—in a secret side agreement—$6.6 million in cash collateral from Enron. When this arrangement was discovered several years later, it disqualified Chewco from meeting the 3 percent rule, as the funds from outside investors had to be "at risk." This discovery, along with other irregularities in the management of Chewco, forced the entire transaction to be unwound and financial statements to be restated.[17]

Chewco also enabled Enron to place significant amounts of additional debt off-balance-sheet and, to boot, helped Enron artificially inflate its reported earnings. In March 1998 Enron recognized a lump sum of $25.7 million in income by taking the present value of some of the management fees it would receive from JEDI through June 2003, not unlike the up-front profits recorded in a mark-to-market transaction.[18] Enron also was able to book throughout the life of the partnership significant income from the appreciation of Enron stock held by JEDI, which would not have been allowed by accounting rules had JEDI had been consolidated into Enron.[19]

The Chewco transaction set an important precedent. Were I to assign a precise date to Enron's tipping point, it would be November 5, 1997, when the Enron board approved the Chewco partnership. On that date—after outside counsel Vinson & Elkins rushed to draw up paperwork for the deal within 48 hours—Skilling and Fastow reportedly presented the transaction to the board's executive committee during a conference call. By all indications, the board's consideration of Chewco was brief.

According to the meeting's minutes, Herbert Winokur, a member of the executive committee and chair of the finance committee, was traveling and had to excuse himself from the call, as his flight was boarding. Although he asserted that he was "familiar with the topics to be covered at the meeting," Winokur indicated that he had not yet received the "supplemental material sent late in the morning on the date of the meeting."[20] He said he supported Skilling's and Fastow's recommendations, but would meet with them the next morning to discuss the transaction.

During the conference call with Enron's diminished executive committee, after providing background on the JEDI partnerships, Skilling called on Fastow to discuss the recommended Chewco transaction. Fastow reviewed the project's economics, financing arrangements, and corporate structure, and disclosed that Enron would provide a corporate guarantee for a $383 million bridge loan that JEDI I would use to cash out CalPERS, and another guarantee for the $240 million loan from Barclays Bank to Chewco. He recommended that the executive committee approve these guarantees. In addition to Fastow and Skilling, Lay and other Enron officers attended this meeting, although Lay arrived after the Chewco discussion had already begun.[21]

From the minutes, it is not clear how much the committee discussed the Chewco transaction before approving it. The transcript simply reads: "A discussion ensued." However, it is unlikely that the committee could have discussed a transaction of this complexity in great detail over the phone, especially given the absence of the finance committee chair.

With the Chewco transaction approved by the board, Enron's reported cash flow received a much-needed boost. By mid-February 1998, Enron's stock price was on a steady upward rise, prompting an analyst to call it a "growth stock." By April, five months after the Chewco deal was approved, Enron's stock had risen 21 percent. Thus the Chewco transaction killed two birds with one stone: Skilling retained CalPERS as a core investor in energy development projects, and the deal helped maintain the appearance of Enron's financial strength.

The Powers committee, appointed by the board to investigate Enron's bankruptcy, gathered information suggesting that the unlawful structure of the Chewco deal resulted from deliberate choices. Many employees professed no recollection of the $6.6 million in cash collateral requested by Barclays Bank and put up by Enron, which eventually disqualified Chewco as a valid SPE. However, this group included the Enron officer who signed the December 30 letter of agreement and authorization for the $6.6 million wire transfer, and other employees reported that the transaction had been openly discussed. SPEs had also been around for quite some time, and would have been familiar to financial engineers such as Fastow.[22]

The Chewco transaction marks the beginning of aggressive use of SPEs to keep as much debt as possible off the corporate balance sheet, and to manage reported cash flow and earnings. It also marks the time when Enron's financial strategies edged over the line from limits testing to clear noncompliance with established and widely understood accounting rules.

The Chewco transaction also marks a turning point in conflicts of interest at the highest levels of Enron management. Fastow initially planned to participate in the transaction by serving as an outside equity investor and general partner. Indeed, he had tried to participate in off-balance-sheet partnerships created to buy Enron assets as early as 1995. To Fastow, investing his own money in Enron deals was no different from investment bankers' contributing personal funds to deals they put together. If it was okay on Wall Street, it should be okay in Houston.

However, Enron's law firm, Vinson & Elkins, had nixed that idea, on the grounds that Enron was not an investment bank. Two years later, in 1997, V&E advised Fastow that Enron would have to disclose his direct involvement in Chewco on public financial statements. To skirt that problem, Fastow proposed that Michael Kopper assume the role of outside equity investor, because he was not an executive officer of Enron, and thus the company would not have to disclose his involvement. (Several other junior executives also ended up investing in Chewco.)[23]

The government claimed that Kopper violated his duty to provide honest services to Enron and its shareholders when he funneled a portion of the $1.5 million in fees he received as managing partner of Chewco to Fastow's wife, plus a portion of the $400,000 "nuisance/arrangement fee" Enron paid Chewco for consenting to an amended agreement. These kickbacks totaled $54,000 and $67,000, respectively.[24]

Chewco's violation of the 3 percent outside-ownership rule, its key role in managing Enron's 1997 earnings, and the inherent undisclosed conflicts of interest involving participating investments by Enron executives were not its only noteworthy aspects. The transaction was also a deadly symptom of the terminal disease that gripped Enron in 1997: top management's failure to pursue many important details surrounding Chewco's unusual ownership structure and to fully inform the board of a major transaction's extraordinary features. Even though board minutes reveal that Chewco was discussed at the board's executive committee with Skilling and Lay present, salient facts of the transaction were apparently omitted. With this omission, the pervasive sloppiness and resulting deceit surrounding Chewco was complete, and the pattern established for limited and misleading reporting to Enron's board of many other transactions of doubtful merit and legality.

The Chewco imbroglio, and the shifts in strategy, personnel, and management behavior that accompanied Skilling's hands-off style as COO, are dramatic examples of the attitudes and behaviors that eventually brought Enron to its knees. Chewco also marks the point in Enron's ethical drift when its most senior executives, both wittingly and unwittingly, crossed the line from aggressive but largely compliant financial management to persistent manipulation of the company's financial performance and reporting. Chewco was also the direct antecedent of the LJM and Raptor partnerships, which played a key role in Enron's eventual collapse.

Direct Descendents

As with Chewco, Fastow designed the LJM1 and LJM2 partnerships as private equity funds with deception and conflicts of interest as two of their most salient characteristics. The mission of these off-balance-sheet partnerships was to invest in deals that Enron wanted to remove from its books. Again, like Chewco, Fastow would control the funds, finding ways as managing director for himself, friends, and colleagues to participate as coinvestors.

Other features of these funds appealed to Fastow and his superiors. As standing funds, the partnerships would eliminate the need for Enron to round up new investors every time it wanted to sell assets. The funds would also allow Enron to close deals swiftly—managing reported earnings and disguising bank debt more flexibly than ever before. And by structuring the partnerships as standing entities, Enron could minimize banking fees and other transaction costs. These features inclined Enron to make the LJM partnerships its principal tools for managing earnings. The partnerships also provided rich opportunities for Fastow to pursue undisclosed personal gain at the expense of the company he served as CFO.

Overall, like Chewco, LJM1 was rife with blatant conflicts of interest, self-dealing by Fastow and his associates, and misrepresentation to Enron's board.[25] Thus the Chewco partnership was but a stepping-stone on the path to the vastly more destructive LJM partnerships.

LJM1 was created less than two years after Chewco as a hedging vehicle for Enron's Rhythms NetCommunications investment, a small broadband startup that had just gone public and risen substantially in market value. No other parties were available to hedge Enron's stake in Rhythms, and thus reduce the company's exposure to a decline in Rhythms' market value and write-downs on its balance sheet.

Fastow set up LJM1 with $1 million of his own money and $15 million from two outside investors. To create the Rhythms hedge, LJM1 created a subsidiary, LJM Swap Sub, which would sell Enron a put option on the entire Rhythms investment. The put gave Enron the right to force Swap Sub to buy Rhythms stock at $56 a share in June 2004—thereby enabling Enron to limit its reported losses if the Rhythms stock fell below that price. To compensate Fastow and his partners for assuming that risk, Enron transferred 3.4 million shares of its own stock, valued at $276 million, to LJM1, which transferred about half that amount to Swap Sub. Enron thus used the value of its own stock to buy the hedge—called a "dirty hedge" in Chapter 1.

Enron's board approved this structure and a $500,000 management fee for Fastow without any dissenting votes. Fastow's insistence to the board that he would receive "no current or future (appreciated) value" from the Enron stock held by LJM1—although he would serve as its general partner—turned out to be a colossal misrepresentation.

The government's indictment of Fastow claims that as the Enron shares held by Swap Sub temporarily soared from $56 to $70, he and his outside partners schemed to siphon off funds beyond those needed to cover the Rhythms put. According to the indictment, Fastow's initial $1 million investment, made in the spring of 1999, yielded him an $18 million distribution in July 2000. Although the partnership made only two more deals with Enron, Fastow's secret take totaled $25 million. His deputy, Michael Kopper, received $12 million, while other Enron accounting and finance executives received lesser amounts.

LJM1 was quickly followed by the much larger LJM2, an all-purpose private equity fund designed to help Enron manage risk in its investment portfolio, and its flow of funds, reported earnings, and financial flexibility. As with Chewco and LJM1, Fastow continued to mix personal business dealings with Enron's interests.

Fastow and two other Enron executives were the general partners of LJM2, with Fastow serving as the managing partner.[26] However, this time the board asked Enron's chief accounting officer and chief risk officer to approve all transactions between Enron and LJM2, and asked the board's audit committee to review all LJM2 transactions annually. Given this oversight, and the right of investors to oust Fastow and limit his fees to those typical of private equity funds, the board approved the new off-balance-sheet partnership on October 12, 1999. The board also granted Fastow permission to serve as both general partner of LJM2 and CFO of Enron, despite conflicts of interest stemming from negotiated transactions between the partnership and the corporation, on the grounds that this arrangement would not adversely affect the interests of the corporation.[27]

Over the next eighteen months, LJM2 executed more than twenty transactions with Enron valued at hundreds of millions of dollars. Enron could not find any other party to agree to many of these deals, and used LJM2 extensively, like its predecessor partnerships, to manage its earnings. The partnership also played a key role in helping Enron disguise its true economic performance by moving troubled assets off its balance sheet. LJM2 enabled Enron to book the profits and cash flow it needed to maintain its credit rating and stock price and make the targets that Wall Street expected.

Another of LJM2's uses was to provide the required 3 percent outside capital for the Raptors, the four SPEs Enron used to hedge its rapidly expanding portfolio of merchant investments and stock holdings. LJM2's major investors, which included Chase Capital, GE Capital, JP Morgan Capital, Merrill Lynch, Dresdner Bank, and Morgan Stanley, collectively committed $30 million to each Raptor partnership, in return for a promised annualized return of at least 30 percent.

Fastow let Enron's lead banks know that failure to commit capital to LJM2 would adversely affect future banking relationships. Under this threat, most fell into line, and ended up in the highly privileged position of knowing more about LJM2's structure than Enron's own board. What these outside investors learned—and Enron's own directors did not know—was that LJM2 would be managed "on a day-to-day basis by a team of three investment professionals who all currently have senior level finance positions with Enron."[28] Here, again, the pattern of deception established in the Chewco transaction continued.

Fastow also revealed aspects of the partnership that the board could never have imagined to Merrill Lynch's private-equity team, which was lining up investors for LJM2. These were that: (1) Fastow would be spending far more than the three hours per week on LJM2 affairs announced earlier; (2) LJM2 was to be Fastow's ticket out of Enron into the private-equity world;

and (3) although Fastow was obligated to represent Enron in its negotiations with LJM2, he would "always be on the LJM side of the transaction." Amazingly, these revelations were recorded on videotape.[29]

Reported internal rates of return on the four Raptors were 193 percent, 278 percent, 2,500 percent, and 125 percent, respectively. These returns reflected substantial and rapid transfers of cash from the Raptors to LJM2. However, later events call these reported returns into question. Enron repurchased five of seven merchant investments sold by the partnerships after the close of the 2000 accounting period—revealing the Raptors' true colors as vehicles by which Enron could transfer volatility in market value but not economic risk.

By early 2001, Fastow's strategy of capitalizing the Raptor partnerships with Enron's own stock—and agreeing to deliver more stock if the value of the Raptor investments fell—was revealed as incorrect not only from an accounting perspective. (A business normally cannot recognize gains in the value of its own stock on its income statement.) The strategy also represented flawed financial management. As the price of Enron's overhyped stock fell along with the value of its merchant investments, the Raptors' ability to meet their obligations to Enron diminished, even after Enron forked over more stock to shore up the Raptors' creditworthiness. By late summer 2001, continuing declines in the stock of both Enron and its merchant investments produced a credit deficiency for the Raptors of hundreds of millions of dollars. Fastow's strategy of trying to use gains in Enron's stock to avoid recognizing losses on its merchant investments was failing catastrophically.

At the same time, Andersen and Enron accountants discovered a substantial accounting error. Although Andersen had previously approved Enron's posting of the Raptors' IOUs as notes receivable, and thus gains in shareholder equity, Andersen concluded in September 2001 that some of the notes should have been shown as reductions in shareholders' equity. This presumably reflected the fact that Enron's contingent contracts to deliver stock to the Raptors were in fact liabilities. Andersen decided that some $1 billion of more than $2 billion in Enron stock committed to all four Raptor partnerships had been incorrectly accounted for. Correcting this error contributed to the $1.2 billion reduction in shareholder equity announced at the end of the third quarter.

As the value of the assets held by LJM2 and the Raptors fell during the summer of 2001, their ability to repay Enron diminished. On September 28,

2001, Enron calculated that the Raptors had assets of about $2.5 billion, and liabilities of some $3.2 billion. The company decided to wind down all four Raptor partnerships and post a pretax charge to third-quarter earnings of $710 million ($544 million after taxes), on top of the aforementioned $1.2 billion write-off.

Despite the eventual collapse of the Raptors and liquidation of LJM2, Fastow profited handsomely. He later admitted to receiving $22 million in income from LJM2. To complete the circle of self-dealing and deceit, the board had no inkling of his true compensation until the *Wall Street Journal* reported in October 2001 that Fastow was reaping "potentially huge financial rewards" from participating in LJM2. During a conference call hastily arranged with two of Enron's outside directors, Fastow finally admitted to the $22 million, making his acknowledged earnings from both LJM partnerships more than $45 million. Other estimates have put his take at more than $60 million.

This slice of Enron's financial history reveals that the pattern of self-dealing and deception that characterized the company during the late 1990s started with Chewco and reached its zenith with the LJM partnerships. Along the way, Enron committed many more alleged violations of GAAP and SEC rules (as Chapter 3 noted), and engineered many more cover-ups of poor performance. Much of this questionable behavior occurred through some 2,400 off-balance sheet-entities spawned after 1997.

The Exploding Reliance on SPEs

Whetted by the Chewco and LJM transactions—with their conflicts of interest and accounting irregularities—Enron's appetite for SPEs became voracious. According to insiders, Enron created about one hundred primary SPEs after 1997, and each typically spawned twenty to thirty spin-offs. Thus the number of off-balance-sheet entities in Enron's accounting system at the time of bankruptcy had reached roughly 2,400.

Enron's accounting violations escalated apace with its use of SPEs. Indeed, the company matched its growing reliance on SPEs after 1997 with expanding reliance on the six key accounting techniques identified by the bankruptcy examiner (and noted in Chapter 3). The examiner set 1997 as the beginning of Enron's major GAAP violations.

With Skilling's appointment as COO in 1997, Enron embarked on a strategy of developing and acquiring new businesses, many internationally based.[30] To further this aggressive expansion while protecting its balance sheet, and thus its credit rating, Enron came to rely on SPEs as its primary vehicle for raising debt capital and bolstering liquidity.[31]

The best indicator of the company's heavy reliance on SPEs as a source of covert debt is a presentation to bankers on November 19, 2001, just one month before Enron filed for bankruptcy. At that meeting, Enron revealed that its off-balance-sheet debt totaled $25 billion, with $14 billion of that amount incurred through transactions with SPEs.[32]

Enron officials were savvy enough to present their growing reliance on SPEs in a favorable light. In a February 17, 1998, presentation to Moody's, the company stated that it was focusing on "streamlining the corporate financial structure, simplifying and better articulating core business fundamentals and facilitating investors' ability to financially model Enron."[33]

The bankruptcy examiner did not concur with Enron's representations to Moody's. "Ultimately, Enron engaged in a series of SPE transactions that did anything but 'streamline' its corporate financial structure. Rather, its financial structure became increasingly complex and more difficult to understand."[34] The examiner could have added that Enron's financial obligations to these entities, if its stock price fell, made it more vulnerable to market downturns and turbulence.

The SPEs also helped the corporate office in Houston generate, more or less at will, gains in revenues and profits—both critical to maintaining Enron's stock price and credit rating—by buying merchant investments and trading contracts (at inflated prices). These transactions also enabled Enron to move failing merchant investments in power plants and equity participations in other public companies off the balance sheet.

According to the bankruptcy examiner, Enron's proceeds from transactions with key SPEs from 1996 to 2001 topped $16 billion (see Table 4.1). (As Chapter 3 noted, the examiner's worst-case bias may have inflated the figures.) These transactions enhanced both liquidity and earnings.

Chewco Investments and the LJM partnerships were thus only the beginning of Enron's extensive use of SPEs to enhance reported earnings and avoid disclosing corporate debt (and contingent liabilities). This deceit was enormous: Enron's $25 billion in off-balance-sheet debt at the time of bankruptcy was twice that disclosed in its financial statements. Also undisclosed were the terms of this debt: that it would become due if Enron's stock price or credit rating dropped below specified levels. These conditions had the potential to greatly damage Enron's liquidity and capital availability, as the company's meltdown revealed.[35]

Table 4.1.   Proceeds to Enron from key SPE transactions, 1996–2001 ($ million)

Year	Prepay	FAS 140	Share Trust	Minority Interest	Related Party	Tax	Total
1996–1998	800	n/a	1,150	1,250	383	411	3,994
1999	1,300	n/a	1,500	1,000	287	248	4,335
2000	1,790	1,274	1,150	500	350	158	5,222
2001	1,130	525	915	n/a	n/a	n/a	2,570
Total	5,020	1,798	4,715	2,750	1,020	817	16,120

Note: These data do not capture all of the SPE transactions created by Enron during this time period. Tax data include only current period proceeds and not expected benefits beyond the period indicated.

Source: Appendix D to U.S. Bankruptcy Court, Southern District of New York, *In re Enron Corp.,* Chapter 11, Case No. 01–16034 (AJG), "Final Interim Report of Neal Batson, Court-Appointed Examiner" (November 4, 2003), pp. 74–102.

Gambling to Survive

In sum, the expanding use of SPEs after 1997, the growing number of improperly accounted for transactions with them, and the failure to disclose their true purposes and the extent of their hidden liabilities reflected the propensity of Enron's senior executives to risk serious violations of GAAP and SEC rules when the company's survivability was at stake.

Although the roots of this deceptive behavior ran deep in its cultural history, Enron's attitude toward risk taking with accounting rules shifted dramatically when Skilling assumed the top operating job and promptly had to solve pressing cash-flow and earnings problems. Any tendencies to compromise the spirit of these rules were reinforced when many of the investments initiated or approved by Skilling and his team turned out to be blunders. As Enron's financial situation deteriorated, senior executives had powerful incentives to pursue risky accounting gambles designed to cover up and touch up the financial picture, to protect the company's credit rating.[36]

Once Skilling took over, a traders' mentality came to dominate the senior executive ranks. Investments surged to support the company's aggressive growth goals and the flow of large, front-end-loaded bonuses to senior executives. Debt levels also surged, because financing investments by issuing stock would have diluted Enron's reported earnings per share. Increasingly risky bets and unprofitable commodity trades were used to sustain a profit stream previously beefed up with overvalued contracts marked to market.

Within a few years, many of Enron's hard-asset investments in power, water, and broadband at home and abroad were failing to generate expected returns, while margins in Enron's vast commodities-trading business were declining. The company soon needed to hedge seemingly profitable merchant investments through SPEs it controlled, because it could not find independent counterparties. At the same time, impaired assets needed to be managed and liabilities disguised. Following this trail, Enron's accounting drifted across the unmarked frontier between aggressive but accepted practice and murkier territory, where the company routinely concealed gains and losses in its core businesses and made major misrepresentations of its true financial position. The goal: to resurrect the promise and potential of the new Enron.

Traveling the path from gambling for large gains to gambling for survival required only a slight shift in purpose and attitude, but in the end the search for a way to endure as a new-economy company consumed Enron's resources, revealed the inherent weaknesses of its business model, and led inexperienced, perversely compensated, and increasingly frantic executives to find ever more creative fixes for their financial statements. This path toward manipulating and obfuscating financial results from 1997 onward—this ethical drift—was probably inevitable, despite the sophisticated risk-management group assembled by Skilling.[37]

Enron's culture of hubris, high-risk gambles, denial, and extreme defensiveness was already well established by the time Skilling and his team of former commodity traders replaced Kinder. All that was needed to reveal the dark side of Enron's modus operandi were a few setbacks. Indeed, recent research on goal setting shows that Enron executives followed a pattern of behavior similar to one convincingly elucidated by laboratory experiments. These experiments show that decision makers are more likely to engage in unethical behavior when they fall short of a goal, rather than when they have met it or are merely trying to do their best.[38]

The behavior of Enron's senior executives reveals these probabilities in practice. In the face of an unexpected collapse in operating profit in 1997, and the adverse impact on the company's stock price and credit rating, senior managers were more likely to engage in financial misrepresentations than if they had met their goals, or if those goals had not been so prominent in the Enron psyche and day-to-day affairs. This cheating, which multiplied

after 1997—this *gambling for survival*—was either not spotted or intentionally ignored by the company's internal risk-management and audit staffs,
whose critical oversight was weakened by a contentious and highly political
performance review process. These choices also persisted amid deeply
flawed board oversight, the subject to which we now turn.

CHAPTER 5

The Directors' Failure

The responsibility of our board—a responsibility which I expect them to fulfill—is to ensure legal and ethical conduct by the company and by everyone in the company. That requirement does not exist by happenstance. It is the most important thing we expect from board members.

—Kenneth Lay, chair of the Board, Enron Corporation

Read today, this passage seems ironic.[1] How better to describe Enron's deeply flawed corporate governance than to say that the board of directors failed "to ensure legal and ethical conduct by the company and by everyone in the company"?[2]

Despite this failure, none of the nineteen outside directors who served on Enron's board during the years leading up to the company's bankruptcy were charged by shareholders with a legal breach of fiduciary duty.[3] The lack of litigation does not, however, let Enron's directors off the hook for poor oversight of corporate affairs, nor does it eliminate the controversy surrounding Enron's board. No less than four formal investigations—by a special committee of Enron's board of directors, two Senate committees, and an examiner appointed by the New York Bankruptcy Court—cited significant failures by Enron's board.[4]

Enron's outside directors strongly contested all such allegations. For example, the directors argued that the Senate subcommittee investigating their role in Enron's collapse had manipulated the facts, and that any shortcomings in the board's performance stemmed from betrayals by Enron's executive team, which intentionally withheld information. The directors further argued that they relied on advice from Arthur Andersen, Enron's auditor, and Vinson & Elkins, its legal advisors (see Appendix C).[5]

In the absence of a formal legal process aimed at establishing whether or not Enron's directors breached their fiduciary duty, questions surrounding the behavior of Enron's directors cannot be fully resolved. However, we do have sufficient evidence on the public record and sufficiently clear standards of director performance—drawn from both legal and management principles of effective corporate governance—to take a second look at how they fulfilled their oversight responsibilities. What this examination reveals is that Enron's directors failed to act in accordance with many of the principles or ideals of effective corporate governance.[6]

This conclusion should not be interpreted to mean that there was a legal breach of directors' fiduciary duties. Making such a legal determination is not the intent of my analysis, and, in any case, a careful reading of the record reveals that there are many uncertainties surrounding the behavior and blameworthiness of Enron's directors. But what my examination does reveal is that Enron's directors acted in ways that fell short of many ideals of effective corporate governance, thereby contributing to the serious social injury caused by Enron's collapse. This social injury included the destruction of over $60 billion in shareholder value, the complete loss of employees' retirement savings, widespread layoffs, and a diminution of public trust in business institutions.

At first glance, the directors' lack of effective oversight seems inexplicable. How could they have failed to detect and deter Enron's reckless gambling, perverse incentives, devious financial maneuvers, and ethical drift? This question is particularly compelling because nothing in the profile of Enron's board suggests that its members were ill-equipped to fulfill their responsibilities as directors of a public corporation. Six of the company's thirteen nonexecutive directors had served sixteen to eighteen years at the time of the company's bankruptcy. The chairs of the board's vitally important Finance and Audit committees were pursuing distinguished careers in the nation's leading financial and academic communities. One director represented Enron's largest institutional shareholder; another was a former British secretary of state for energy and a leader in the houses of Lords and Commons; and two others were former CEOs of major companies acquired by Enron. What's more, potential conflicts of interest—whether related to consulting contracts, Enron's philanthropic activities, or seats on regulatory bodies before board membership—were, in the grand scheme of things, minor (see Appendix D).

Indeed, if studies and guidelines by academics and by professional organizations are any indication, the Enron board appeared to be a model of corporate governance. Many board structures recommended by experts were in place, save for the then-rare separation of CEO and board chair roles, and designation of a lead director. The board averaged eighteen members from 1997 to 2001, a slightly higher number than recommended—justifiable given the complexity of Enron's businesses.[7] The board also created the recommended committees (including audit, finance, compensation, nomination, and corporate governance), as well as an executive committee, and staffed them with outside directors.[8] The board and committees met regularly, reviewed and approved or rejected proposals, saw that Enron adopted a code of ethics, and monitored audits, disclosures, and executive performance.

Unfortunately, the board did not perform any of these responsibilities very well. The board failed to detect and deter violations and questionable applications of accounting principals and rules. It failed to question the wisdom of hedging merchant investments with the company's own stock rather than with bona fide counterparties. It failed to monitor board-approved conflicts of interest inherent in CFO Andrew Fastow's role in off-balance-sheet partnerships. It failed to see and react to many red flags—such as rushed attempts by executives to move assets with low returns off the corporate balance sheet, to reduce reported debt, and to sell billions of dollars of assets to raise cash—all revealing deteriorating economic and ethical performance. This chapter explains how these failures occurred.

In so doing, I first identify the legal and managerial principles that help define what makes for effective director oversight and corporate governance. I then argue the case for the directors' failure of effective governance by describing their role in two important transactions—Rhythms NetCommunications and Raptors—designed to hedge losses in Enron's merchant banking investments.[9] My analysis shows that outmoded board processes, directors' compensation, a lack of mastery of key aspects of Enron's evolving business model, and behavioral predispositions prevented Enron's directors from seizing ample opportunities to detect and deter ethical drift and subsequent fraud. This conclusion conflicts markedly with the directors' rebuttal to the Senate report, and with the findings of the board's own special investigative committee in the months immediately following Enron's bankruptcy.

This analysis of the directors' conduct serves as a springboard to suggestions in the final three chapters regarding how to prevent Enron-type breakdowns. These suggestions specifically show how to improve board oversight in ways that go beyond the rules promulgated by the Sarbanes-Oxley legislation, how to productively manage financial incentives for executives, and how to preserve ethical discipline in the modern corporation.

Criteria for Assessing Director Performance

Sorting out the board's role in Enron's collapse requires a set of criteria for evaluating director performance. I draw these criteria from principles underlying legal and managerial ideals of effective corporate governance. Some of these have their roots in legal precedent, but my goal in applying these criteria to Enron's directors is to argue neither legal compliance nor dereliction of duty. Rather, I seek to develop a more general picture of how well Enron's directors served the interests of Enron's shareholders.

Performance Criteria Reflecting Legal Principles

Most advanced industrial societies have set legal standards for fiduciaries, including the boards of public corporations, that provide a modicum of protection to beneficiaries, such as shareholders. (A fiduciary is "one who owes to another the duties of good faith, trust, confidence, and candor.")[10] In the United States, standards of director performance come from multiple sources: hard-hitting standards of liability pursuant to corporate law, federal law/regulation that can result in criminal sanctions (jail or fines) as well as civil sanctions (fines and other penalties), tort law and other common law concepts that can result in individual liability for deficient conduct (damages), and aspirational standards reflected in the Model Business Corporation Act. Directorial standards of performance built on the traditions of Anglo-Saxon law are typically expressed in terms of fiduciary duties.

U.S. legal standards of fiduciary duty appear low when compared to the aspirational standards and best practices promoted by various professional organizations. These low standards—along with other protections—reflect the interest of the courts in encouraging esteemed professionals and others with years of business experience to serve in oversight roles, and to eliminate judicial interference in business decisions, benefiting not just specific companies but the economy as a whole.

Of the fiduciary duties recognized by Oregon law (Enron was incorporated in that state), seven have potential relevance to Enron's board.[11] These seven duties cluster into two groups: conduct duties and task duties.[12]

Conduct Duties

1. *Duty of care:* Directors must act as a prudent and competent person would in the same line of business under similar circumstances.[13]
2. *Duty of good faith:* Directors must act with an actual intent to promote corporate welfare.[14]
3. *Duty of loyalty:* Directors must put the corporation's interests ahead of their own—that is, avoid conflicts of interest.[15]

Task Duties

1. *Duty to make informed business decisions:* This is a two-part obligation. First, directors must comply with the duties of care, good faith, and loyalty in adequately considering all reasonably available information before making a decision on behalf of the corporation.[16] Second, the substance of each decision must reflect a rational business purpose—that is, not be "so beyond the bounds of reasonable judgment that it seems essentially inexplicable on any [other] ground."[17]
2. *Duty of candor (also known as the duty of disclosure):* Directors must be honest, candid, and complete in their public and direct communications with stockholders.[18]
3. *Duty to monitor:* This duty comprises one-half of the directors' oversight function. The board's continuing obligation is to remain attentive to and informed about the corporation's activities.[19]
4. *Duty to inquire:* This is the other half of directors' oversight function. The board is obligated to actively seek explanations for troubling facts or circumstances that would arouse suspicion in a similarly situated reasonable person.[20]

The duty to make informed business decisions deserves special comment.[21] When directors' conduct is challenged with respect to business decision making, the so-called "business judgment rule" often comes into play. This rule protects directors from being liable for well-intentioned decisions that simply didn't work out due to miscalculations or other mistakes. Put slightly differently, the rule ensures that the *substance of a decision* reached through proper process is all but completely protected from judicial review. Plaintiffs seeking damages from directors must therefore prove that directors' *decision-making process* was grossly negligent or that they acted in bad faith.

While the principal themes of the business judgment rule are, one way or another, embedded in states' business corporation acts, they do not literally constitute a "duty" that directors might "breach." Rather, they are what one scholar has called "conduct highways." For example, when directors' conduct is challenged, the plaintiff will not assert that the business judgment rule was breached, but the defendant directors can invoke the business judgment rule in their defense. This defense only comes into play, however, where a specific, substantive decision is at issue.[22]

Under this doctrine, courts focus mainly on the process leading to a challenged decision. A court may set aside a procedurally sound decision only if it was made without good faith. A lack of good faith may be inferred if a decision is so beyond the bounds of reasonable judgment that it cannot be explained. But such conclusions by courts are rare.[23]

Directors are therefore required to adequately consider all reasonably accessible information before making decisions on behalf of the corporation's owners.[24] The depth of consideration and quantity of information needed to discharge this duty depend on the circumstances; there is no prescribed technique for becoming informed. "Both the method and measure—'how to' and 'how much'—are matters of reasonable judgment for the director to exercise."[25]

The four task duties—decision making, disclosure, monitoring, and inquiry—provide a useful framework for organizing an assessment of how well Enron's directors served as agents for shareholders. Table 5.1 summarizes how the legal considerations of care and good faith, the two most relevant conduct duties in the Enron case, can be applied to an assessment of directors' task fulfillment.[26] In the next section I identify five additional considerations drawn from managerial rather than legal principles.

Table 5.1. Performance criteria reflecting legal principles

Directors' Task Duties

Directors' Conduct Duties	Decision Making	Disclosure	Monitoring	Inquiry
Duty of Care	The duty of care is breached when directors act, or fail to act, without adequately considering all reasonably available information.[a]	The duty of care is breached when the board intentionally misleads shareholders by misstating or omitting material information.[b]	State courts have been reticent to establish a duty of care standard to avoid discouraging board service by qualified persons, relying instead on a duty of good faith standard to encourage effective monitoring.[c]	The duty of care is breached if the board fails to recognize "red flags" that would "put a prudent man on his guard" against harm to the corporation.[d]
Duty of Good Faith	The good faith duty is breached when a decision goes so beyond the bounds of reasonable judgment that it can only be explained by the actor's lack of intent to promote corporate welfare.[e] Conflicts of interest are typically present.	The duty of good faith is breached when directors knowingly mislead shareholders through misstatements or material omissions.[f]	A breach of good faith is characterized by either sustained inattention to the corporation's business or a complete abdication of monitoring responsibilities.[g]	The duty of good faith is breached when directors consciously disregard a known risk.[h]

a. See *Aronson*, 473 A.2d at 812. See also *Brehm v. Eisner*, 746 A.2d 244, 264 (Del. 2000) ("Due care in the decision-making context is process due care only").

b. *Zirn v. VLI*, 681 A.2d 1050, 1062 (Del. 1996). See also *Arnold v. Society for Savings Bancorp., Inc.*, 650 A.2d 1270, 1287–88 (Del. 1994).

c. See *Caremark*, 698 A.2d at 971 ("Such a test of liability—lack of good faith as evidenced by sustained or systematic failure of a director to exercise reasonable oversight—is quite high. But a demanding test of liability in the oversight context is probably beneficial to corporate shareholders as a class, as it is in the board decision context, since it makes board service by qualified people more likely, while continuing to act as a stimulus to *good faith performance of duty* by such directors").

d. See *Devlin*, 130 P. at 45.

e. See *West Point—Pepperell*, 542 A.2d at 780.

f. *Malone*, 722 A.2d at 10.

g. See *Caremark*, 698 A.2d at 971 ("In my opinion only a sustained or systemic failure of the board to exercise oversight—such as an utter failure of the board to attempt to assure that a reasonable information and reporting system exists—will establish the lack of good faith that is a necessary condition of liability").

h. *Graham*, 188 A.2d at 130 ("It appears that directors are entitled to rely on the honesty and integrity of their subordinates until something occurs to put them on suspicion that something is wrong"). See also *McCall v. Scott* ("*McCall II*"), 250 F.3d 997, 1001 (6th Cir. 2001).

Performance Criteria Reflecting Managerial Principles

Complementing performance criteria drawn from the legal arena, many professional bodies that serve public corporations—including the Conference Board, the Business Roundtable, the New York Stock Exchange, and the Organisation for Economic Co-operation and Development—have attempted to codify the meaning of good board performance with a decidedly managerial twist. These performance criteria address the role of directors in reviewing and guiding corporate strategy; formulating major plans of action, risk policies, and annual budgets; setting performance objectives; monitoring financial results; and overseeing major capital expenditures, acquisitions, and divestitures.[27]

The exercise of these responsibilities is a form of decision control. This term refers to the process by which senior executives or a board of directors approves plans and capital investments proposed by operating managers, and monitors the results.[28] Effective decision control requires that directors attend to three key activities when evaluating and approving proposals that have percolated up through an organization:

- Assessing the relevant opportunities and risks
- Establishing or validating current and future resource requirements
- Establishing performance targets and milestones

These activities have their roots in basic capital budgeting and resource allocation processes. Indeed, it is difficult to imagine any meaningful approval process that does not include such fundamental determinations.

Once corporate directors have approved a plan or specific course of action, virtually every code obligates them to monitor progress. This task imposes two additional responsibilities.

- Periodically reviewing approved projects with respect to preestablished targets and milestones, and measuring overall corporate progress against performance indicators
- Analyzing deviations from what is expected

As with the approval process, it is difficult to imagine a monitoring system—at any level in an organization—that would not measure progress toward targets and provide feedback, to enable managers to adjust resource commitments and processes to produce outcomes that more closely approach expectations.[29] Forward-looking metrics such as targets and milestones help directors fulfill their obligation to monitor projects, and to focus on those that do not conform to expectations.

These five principles of effective decision control provide practical criteria for measuring a board's performance beyond those suggested by the law. The inclusion of these principles or governance ideals in our analytical framework will help reveal a board's willingness to master the disciplines and seek out the information needed to support—and impose on the corporation—its members' reasoned decisions. As recently suggested by Chancellor William B. Chandler of the Delaware Chancery Court in the Walt Disney Co. case, "the aspirational ideals of good corporate governance practices for boards of directors that go beyond the minimal legal requirements of corporation law are highly desirable" even though they do not define standards of legal liability.[30]

Directors' Behavior Related to Decision Making

The public record of board decision making related to off-balance-sheet partnerships and structured-finance transactions shows that Enron's directors fell short of important ideals of effective corporate governance. Two examples illustrate this problematic behavior: the Rhythms hedge, and the four hedging arrangements collectively known as the Raptors—all of which played a significant role in the company's eventual meltdown. (Appendix A describes the Raptor structures in detail.)

The Rhythms and Raptor transactions involved off-balance-sheet partnerships, or special purpose entities (SPEs), that were capitalized with Enron's own stock. The company used these entities as hedging counterparties to offset risky and poorly performing merchant portfolio investments that—because of Enron's inflated use of mark-to-market accounting— posed serious hazards to income and Enron's credit rating.[31]

The board approved the Rhythms hedge in late June 1999, after Enron's $10 million investment in Rhythms NetCommunications had grown to $300 million, representing 7.6 percent of Rhythms' outstanding stock and 50 percent of its public ownership.[32] As noted in Chapter 1, Enron wanted to hedge this investment against a drop in the price of the Rhythms shares. However, given the size of the stake and the relative illiquidity of the stock, no unrelated counterparties for such a hedge were readily available.[33]

To solve this problem, Fastow came up with the idea of creating an off-balance-sheet partnership—LJM1—to serve as a hedge counterparty. A few months later—believing that the Rhythms hedge had been successfully designed and implemented—the board approved the first of the Raptors partnerships, to hedge losses in Enron's rapidly expanding portfolio of merchant investments and stockholdings. In addition, with the approval of the executive committee of the board (which included Lay and Skilling) and the affirmation of the full board, Fastow became the managing partner of the LJM1 partnership that held the Rhythms hedge, and subsequently the LJM2 partnership that provided the 3 percent of at-risk equity in the Raptors that Enron needed in order to deconsolidate the entity under accounting rules.[34] Fastow thereby became, in essence and in fact, Enron's hedging partner while serving as the company's CFO.

To avoid a highly probable default by LJM1 on the Rhythms hedge, the company was forced to unwind (or cancel) the hedge in the first quarter of 2000. By early 2001, it became apparent that the Raptors were similarly impaired, because they had been used to hedge troubled merchant investments, and because the strategy of using Enron's own stock to capitalize off-balance-sheet partnerships was badly flawed. As the price of Enron's hyped stock fell along with the value of its merchant investments, so, too, did the Raptors' ability to pay off their obligations, even after Enron forked over more stock to shore up their creditworthiness. In late summer 2001, the continuing decline in the value of both Enron's stock and its merchant investments created a credit deficiency in the Raptors partnerships totaling hundreds of millions of dollars. Enron was facing a death spiral, even though it previously claimed to have earned $1.1 billion in transactions with the Raptors during 2000–2001—or 73 percent of the company's reported pretax earnings.[35]

At the same time, Andersen and Enron accountants discovered a serious accounting error. Andersen had earlier approved Enron's posting of IOUs under the Raptor hedges as "notes receivable," and thus additions to shareholder equity. However, in September 2001 Andersen and Enron concluded that some of the notes receivable should have been shown as reductions in shareholders' equity—since the Raptor hedges included a contingent contract to deliver Enron stock to the Raptor entities under certain conditions and should thus be considered liabilities. Correcting this error contributed to the $1.2 billion reduction in shareholders' equity announced at the end of the third quarter. When Enron's finance staff calculated the Raptors' combined assets at about $2.5 billion, and combined liabilities at about $3.2 billion, the company decided to wind down all four Raptor partnerships. This meant that Enron posted a pretax charge to third-quarter earnings of $710 million ($544 million after taxes)—along with the $1.2 billion write-off. These charges and equity write-offs, along with write-downs of overvalued assets in the water business and restructuring charges at broadband, thrust Enron onto the road to bankruptcy.

The directors' approval of the Rhythms hedge and other transactions with the Raptor partnerships shows how the board's decision-making process produced devastating consequences. The hedging activities with Fastow's partnerships preserved the pristine façade of Enron's balance sheet, but since the partnerships were not truly unrelated or independent entities and the hedging transactions were thus not true economic hedges, all was not as it seemed. Fortunately for the directors, the business judgment rule and director exculpation provisions protected them from any legal liability.[36] However, even though the directors' decisions appear legally defensible, an important principle closely akin to the legal duty of care appears to have been dishonored—at least as it relates to reasoned deliberation of the robustness of the hedges secured by the value of Enron's own stock and the true business purpose of the LJM and Raptor partnerships (hedging versus moving underperforming investments off Enron's balance sheet).

Viewed as a decision control rather than a legal matter, the board's decisions to approve the Rhythms and Raptors transactions are even more vulnerable to criticism. When evaluating such proposals, directors are expected to weigh their opportunities and risks, establish or validate current and future resource requirements, and create performance milestones for approved projects. Enron's directors appear to have failed to take these steps. The directors counter that company executives withheld critical information from the board. However, although that often appears to have been the case, the board's flawed information-gathering system also disabled its decision-making process.[37]

The first flaw was the board's apparently common practice of squeezing packed meeting agendas into relatively short time frames. For example, the one-hour board meeting on June 28, 1999, covered the Rhythms hedge, a related code-of-conduct waiver for Fastow (see below), a two-for-one stock split, Enron's ongoing reorganization, and a proposal to build the first independent power plant in the Gaza Strip.[38] The board clearly approved the Rhythms hedge under less-than-perfect circumstances. Drawing on statements from the directors, the bankruptcy examiner described the situation thus:

The special meeting at which the Board authorized the Rhythms transaction was held by telephone and lasted only one hour. During that time, seven topics were considered. . . .

The Board made decisions, and approved resolutions, with respect to all agenda items except [one]. . . . There is no record of how much time was spent on each topic.

To prepare directors for the 10:00 A.M. Monday Board meeting, the corporate secretary faxed each Outside Director forty-eight pages of materials on Friday afternoon between approximately 4:00 P.M. and 9:00 P.M. central time. These materials included twelve pages about the Rhythms transaction and twenty-one pages about [another agenda item]. In addition, four of the Outside Directors who were on the Compensation Committee also received an additional twenty pages in preparation for a special meeting of that committee, which was held from 9:00 A.M. to 10:00 A.M. immediately preceding the special Board meeting. The proposed transaction was not reviewed by the Finance Committee before it was introduced to the entire Board.[39]

Recalled director Lord Wakeham: "I was there by telephone, over a transatlantic telephone line, which is not the best of arrangements."[40] "I was in transit and I was at a pay phone on the side of the road in Northern Virginia and the light was fading," recollected director Gramm. "It was physically more difficult hearing, and my papers weren't exactly standing still in front of me. It was not an enclosed payphone."[41]

Raptor I was presented to the finance committee on May 1, 2000 (see Appendix E). Also covered in that ninety-minute meeting were an LJM2 update, an analysis of Enron's credit rating, a plan to monetize $1 billion in investments, a request for approval of $1 billion in new debt, a review of the transaction approval process, and a review of discrepancies in projected valuations between Enron Energy Services and Risk Assessment and Control (RAC). The committee voted to recommend Raptor I to the full board.[42]

The following day, during an almost four-hour meeting, the board approved a five-part resolution proposed by director Winokur on behalf of the finance committee, including Raptor I.[43] The directors also discussed fourteen other issues, including updates from three other committees and reports on five business units, two international lawsuits, and a tax dispute in Argentina.[44]

In a thirty-five-minute special telephone meeting on June 22, 2000, the executive committee considered and approved "(i) the purchase of a power plant in Texas and related long-term power contracts; (ii) the election of two new officers; (iii) the utilization of power barges in Nigeria and construction of related facilities; (iv) Raptor II; and (v) the issuance of up to $1 billion of additional debt securities."[45] Raptor II was never presented to the full board for approval, but no directors appear to have objected to implementing the structure.[46]

Given these intense agendas, the Rhythms and Raptor transactions could receive only cursory consideration, and the directors appear to have engaged in little discussion of the risks they entailed and the resources they required before approving them.[47] Nor did the board establish performance standards for any of the hedging operations. Although not egregious enough to violate legal standards, these procedural shortcomings did impede the board's consideration of all aspects of the proposals, and thus fell far short of the ideals of effective board oversight and conrol.[48]

As another example, internal documents show that the board was told that Enron was contractually bound to neither sell nor hedge Rhythms stock between April 6, 1999 (the date of Rhythms' IPO), and November 9, 1999.[49] However, the transactions composing the hedge were executed during June 1999—well within this lockup period.[50] Yet the directors' sworn statements to the bankruptcy examiner, and the meeting minutes for June 28, 1999, do not indicate that this issue received any discussion.[51]

The most troubling aspect of the relationship between Enron and the LJM partnerships was the board's approval of unusual conflicts of interest involving Fastow's service (viewed by some as exceptions to the company's code of ethics) on three different occasions. These approvals allowed Fastow to continue serving as Enron's CFO while acting as the general partner and leader of the LJM partnerships.[52] Because Fastow knew what assets Enron wanted to sell, how badly and how soon Enron wanted to sell them, and whether they had alternative buyers, he could exert pressure on Enron personnel negotiating with LJM. Indeed, the Powers committee reported, "We have been told of instances in which [Fastow] used that pressure to try to obtain better terms for LJM, and where people reporting to him instructed business units that LJM would be the buyer of the asset they wished to sell." The committee also reported "at least 13 transactions between Fastow and LJM2 in which individuals negotiating on behalf of Enron reported directly or indirectly to Fastow."[53]

Enron's Code of Ethics prohibited company executives from assuming positions that involved such conflicts of interest without the approval of the chair of the board and the CEO.[54] Ratification by the board itself was not required, but Arthur Andersen, Enron's outside auditor, refused to approve the Rhythms transaction without the directors' approval of Fastow's role.[55]

Permitting a company executive to bargain from the other side of the table is not inherently improper, as long as the transaction is fully disclosed and receives approval from disinterested directors. However, when the board fails to weigh the risks, consider other courses of action, and create means for monitoring the impact of the conflict of interest, it subjects the company and its shareholders to serious hazard.[56] Herein lies the board's greatest collective failure.

The process by which the board reached its decision to ratify the Rhythms and Raptor hedges fell far short of the diligence suggested by managerial ideals of effective governance.[57] Enron's directors appear to have been content to go through the motions rather than be true advocates for the corporation and its shareholders. In this instance, the directors' failure of effective governance took the form of decisions based on cursory reviews of information. These decisions caused serious financial problems that ultimately suffocated the corporation.

Although the Rhythms and Raptor transactions diminished earnings volatility on Enron's balance sheet, the directors' approval violated the ideals of good faith because the transactions were not true economic hedges.[58] They were cosmetic: they enabled Enron to preserve gains previously recorded under mark-to-market accounting, in an attempt to disguise from credit agencies and investors the company's true financial condition.[59] In fact, Ben Glisan, the former Enron treasurer who pleaded guilty to charges stemming from the Raptor transactions, admitted that the transactions violated generally accepted accounting principles (GAAP) in having "no true business purpose."[60]

If the function of the transactions was to protect the company from investment losses, as the directors seem to have believed, approving deals that exposed Enron to even greater losses is an unusual form of protection. The directors who understood this should have questioned the rationale for these proposals; those who did not should have asked for explanation. Had they engaged in appropriate discussion, the directors might have come to a more complete understanding of Enron's predicament. Without such discussion, the board believed that the Rhythms transaction had been successfully implemented, and repeated the same mistakes in approving the Raptor transactions.[61]

The board has offered no justification for the transactions, beyond stating that they "made sense for Enron and were in the best interests of the Company's shareholders."[62] The defenses articulated in the directors' response to the Senate report on their role in Enron's collapse are equally weak. Although the directors testified that they had relied on a fairness opinion drafted by PriceWaterhouseCooper in approving the Rhythms transaction, this opinion was written after the board had approved the transaction. Indeed, none of the outside directors had seen the opinion before testifying before the bankruptcy examiner more than three years later.[63] When it approved the Rhythms transaction, the board was relying only on Fastow's assertion that the PriceWaterhouseCooper opinion would be favorable.

Directors have also pointed out that they were entitled to rely on the opinion of Enron's accountant, Arthur Andersen, on accounting matters.[64] That is true. However, there is no evidence that the board received an opinion from Andersen on the Rhythms transaction.[65] And although Arthur Andersen expressed comfort with the Raptor I structure, Andersen's input is relevant only on the accounting aspect of the transaction.[66] The directors failed to decide whether the Raptors transactions made business sense in light of all considerations.

The Rhythms and Raptor transactions are emblematic of shortcomings in the board's decision making. The level of diligence necessary to understand what they were approving was absent. There is no evidence that the directors considered whether those transactions represented a good use of corporate resources.[67] And the board's failure to set explicit performance standards left it without a means of weighing the transactions' ongoing risks and viability, as well as their appropriateness as models for other deals.[68] Thus it is very difficult to claim that Enron's directors complied with the ideals of effective oversight in making informed business decisions.

Nor did the directors take any of the three steps required by standards of effective decision control when they approved the Rhythms and Raptor transactions. Ultimately, the declining market value of Rhythms Communications and Enron stock dragged the hedging counterparties—and Enron itself—down with them.

Directors' Lapse Related to Disclosure

Shareholders make investment decisions based partly on information supplied by the corporation, and most are not in a position to verify that information. For this reason, principles governing disclosure, also known as candor, require that directors be honest, accurate, and complete in public and direct communications with stockholders.[69] Financial statements and other documents filed with the Securities and Exchange Commission (SEC) are among the most important of such communications. In this context, disclosure means describing a material event or state of affairs in language that is clear enough to enable the reader to understand its importance and effect.[70]

Simply making the reader aware of an event or its status is not always sufficient from a purely legal perspective. Nor do disclosures that are adequate under GAAP and SEC rules necessarily fulfill all legal requirements. The relevant standard is not "whether [the accounting firm's] report satisfies esoteric norms, comprehensible only to the initiate, but whether the report fairly presents the true financial position of [the company], as of [the date of the challenged document], to the untutored eye of an ordinary investor."[71]

Unfortunately for shareholders, Enron's vague proxy statements, and the footnotes to its Form 10-K financial statements filed with the SEC on related-party transactions from 1999 to 2001, fell short of corporate governance ideals. Company and directors finalized both types of disclosures through a cycle of revisions.[72] The proxy statements—which the board had the opportunity to examine—originated from the office of Enron associate general counsel Rex Rogers. The footnotes to the draft financial statements were produced by Enron's financial reporting group. The board's audit committee reviewed and discussed these drafts with Enron management (see Appendix F).[73] All directors were required to sign off on Enron's forms 10-K and 10-Q during the three-year period.[74]

The Powers report concluded that Enron's disclosures of related-party transactions were "fundamentally inadequate."[75] The disclosures omitted details that investors would likely have considered material.[76] Enron's second-quarter 2000 10-Q, for example, identified CFO Andrew Fastow only as a senior officer of Enron who was the managing member of the general partners of the limited partnership with which Enron was transacting.

The 10-Q also suggested that the listed transactions were comparable to those struck with other unrelated third parties, but the document offered no supporting facts.[77] The Financial Accounting Standards Board (FASB) has provided some guidance on this matter in Standard 57, which expressly prohibits making such claims without a proper basis in fact.[78] The language in Enron's SEC filings is a particularly serious problem for disclosures related to the Rhythms transaction, because board members knew that the company was having trouble finding an unrelated third-party hedging partner.[79] If Enron's directors knew that the form cited unrelated third parties, and that the hedge could not be entered into under similar terms with other hedging counterparties because of their lack of interest, then they came very close to violating the principle of candor by misleading shareholders about the nature of a material transaction.

Enron's directors clearly approved publicly filed documents that contained incomplete representations of several related-party transactions. What is not clear is whether the directors suspected that their disclosures were misleading. Because the documents were prepared without a rigorous review process, and the board's outside advisors thought the documents disclosed enough information, the board might have believed that its SEC filings adequately described relevant events and arrangements for educated readers. As it turned out, they did not. Once again, board members' miscomprehension of at least their aspirational obligations and refusal to seek clarification prevented them from recognizing and correcting a fundamental flaw.

Directors' Lapse Related to Monitoring and Inquiry

Under Oregon law, corporate directors are responsible for overseeing the general affairs of the corporation.[80] This oversight obligation includes two task duties identified earlier in this chapter: the duty to monitor, and the duty to inquire. The former refers to the board's obligation to remain attentive to and informed about the corporation's activities. The latter requires that directors investigate information that implies that the corporation has problems. These duties are invariably linked—with the duty to inquire typically triggered by information discovered through the duty to monitor.

The Enron board appears to have taken the minimum action required to discharge these duties—but only barely, leaving the ideals of good-faith oversight compromised. They created information-gathering systems—poorly functioning though they were—and appear to have paid attention to the information brought to them. No evidence proves that the directors were aware of problems within the organization. Had they been aware, that knowledge would have triggered an obligation to inquire.

From a decision-control standpoint, the board's performance looks demonstrably worse. One reason that Enron required debt-reducing and earnings-enhancing transactions was that it had largely disregarded its capital budgeting and monitoring processes until RAC tallied up the impaired investments in 2000. The board apparently did not treat the budgetary information it regularly received as performance targets, and seldom created performance standards or milestones for the investment projects and financial transactions it approved. This made it virtually impossible for directors to systematically monitor the company's capital investments and, later, to pick up the scent of brewing troubles.

Monitoring

Directors are generally considered to have failed to execute their monitoring responsibilities only if they have abdicated their responsibilities or exhibited sustained inattention to corporate concerns.[81] Such abdication or inattention indicates a lack of good faith, and exposes directors to the claim of legal breach.[82] "Directors may not shut their eyes to corporate misconduct and then claim that because they did not see the misconduct, they did not have a duty to look."[83] However, directors are not expected to search for inadequacies or noncompliance with corporate systems.[84] The issue is whether the board takes reasonable steps to keep itself informed—not whether it pursues measures to remedy a problem.

According to this definition, Enron's directors appear to have satisfied minimum standards of their obligation to monitor corporate affairs. However, the board's oversight appears to have been far less adequate from a decision-control perspective, as there is no evidence that directors established diagnostic measures for evaluating the progress of the initiatives they approved. Here is where the ideals of effective governance were most seriously abrogated.

The board and its committees met five times annually, scheduled other meetings as required, and followed a detailed audit and compliance calendar. Enron's outside directors estimated that they spent one hundred to four hundred hours annually preparing for and attending board and committee meetings.[85] Enron typically sent the outside directors volumes of information in preparation for meetings.[86] Such information might stack more than a foot high for directors serving on more than one committee.[87] The directors indicated that they "read the materials and were generally impressed by the level of preparedness of their colleagues."[88]

Meetings were well attended. "From 1997 through the fall of 2001, there were 24 regularly scheduled board meetings, with perfect attendance at 10 of these meetings, one director absent from nine of the meetings, and two directors absent from five of the meetings."[89] Full board meetings averaged between four and five hours; committee meetings, around ninety minutes.[90]

Unfortunately, as noted, board and committee meetings tended to have crowded agendas, and typically included presentations by both Enron executives and outside experts. Board members themselves seemed to feel the need to spend more time together. In anonymous 2001 self-evaluations, directors wrote:

> This is a great board (in my opinion). And, if anything, more meeting time would be nice. It is a working board and lots going on in the company!
>
> We may need to meet beyond noon more often, to allow for in-depth briefings, and to leave sufficient time for special reports to present risks, hurdles, alternative scenarios, and requests for specific advice.
>
> I think I would support a move to six meetings a year (but not too strongly).[91]

Thus the directors' own observations support the conclusion that they fell short of an important standard of effective board governance—that directors will serve as informed and attentive watchdogs of corporate interests.

Senior managers and directors alike had incomplete information about the risks of each new transaction and business venture because Enron's RAC system failed to work as designed. This governance gap widened once the Fastow-controlled LJM partnerships were created and approved. The board initially imposed few controls on Fastow's participation in the LJM funds and Enron's transactions with those off-balance-sheet entities. The board also approved the Rhythms hedge and Fastow's participation in the LJM1 partnership without introducing any diagnostic controls.[92]

Transactions with the LJM2 partnership were similarly subject to few controls. On October 12, 1999, the board approved Fastow's participation in LJM2 on the condition that (1) Rick Causey, Enron's chief accounting officer, and Rick Buy, the company's chief risk officer, review all of Enron's transactions with LJM2; and (2) the audit committee review each of those transactions annually.[93] These controls had been proposed not by a director but by Fastow himself, in his presentation to the finance committee the previous day.[94] One director indicated that he had considered Fastow's fiduciary duties to Enron to constitute a third control.[95]

Later board presentations identified other controls that could protect Enron's interests in deals with Fastow's partnership groups. In presenting LJM3 to the finance committee on October 6, 2000, for example, Fastow listed six "mechanisms that had been put in place to mitigate any potential conflicts" between his roles in Enron and LJM3:

1. Fastow's fiduciary responsibilities to [Enron]
2. The ability of the office of the chairman to ask Fastow to resign from the LJM funds at any time
3. The required approval of Buy, Causey, and Skilling for all transactions between the company and the LJM funds
4. An annual audit and compliance committee review of [Enron's] transactions with the LJM funds
5. A review of Fastow's economic interest in [Enron] and the LJM funds to be presented to Mr. Skilling
6. The absence of any obligation for Enron to transact with the LJM funds[96]

The finance committee voted to recommend that the board ratify the third LJM partnership and Code of Ethics waiver for Fastow—if these six controls were supplemented by two others suggested by Norman P. Blake Jr., a veteran of eight other boards; and Herbert S. Winokur Jr., who had served on the boards of Enron and its predecessor Houston Natural Gas since 1984.[97] Blake recommended that the finance committee conduct quarterly reviews of transactions between Enron and the LJM partnerships. Winokur recommended that the compensation committee review Fastow's compensation by Enron and the LJM partnerships.[98] Although LJM3 was never formed, the meeting minutes indicate that these eight controls were intended to apply to transactions between Enron and all LJM partnerships, not just LJM3.[99]

Four months later, in February 2001, Causey told the audit committee that Enron was relying on the following new controls to protect itself in transactions with the LJM funds:

1. LJM senior professionals do not ever negotiate on behalf of [Enron].
2. [Enron] professionals negotiating with LJM report to senior Enron officials separate from Fastow.
3. Numerous groups monitor compliance with procedures and controls and regularly update Fastow and Buy.

4. [Enron] regularly consults with internal and outside counsel regarding disclosure obligations.[100]

On the same day, Fastow made similar representations to the finance
committee, and stated that the LJM2 control system was effective.[101] It is
unclear why these four new controls were necessary. Nor is it clear why
neither Causey nor Fastow mentioned the six control mechanisms discussed at the finance committee meeting on October 6, 2000, and whether
the directors questioned that omission.

In any event, the controls intended to regulate transactions between
Enron and the LJM partnerships were implemented in a shoddy fashion.
For example, Causey—who was supposed to review LJM2 transactions
on behalf of Enron—approved a decision by other executives, including
Fastow, to keep information about certain transactions from the board.[102]
Moreover, the audit committee's annual reviews of Enron's transactions
with the LJM partnerships appear to have been largely ceremonial, with the
committee content to accept brief reports from Causey and Arthur Andersen. No pubic records show that the finance committee ever undertook
the quarterly reviews suggested by Blake in October 2000.[103]

Other controls mentioned at the October 2000 meeting were not properly
executed. According to discussion at the finance committee meeting on October 6, Skilling was to approve all transactions between Enron and the
LJM funds. Before the House subcommittee on February 7, 2002, and later
at his fraud trial, Skilling testified that he believed that Enron did not require his approval to transact with the LJM funds.[104] Nevertheless, Skilling
did not oppose Fastow's representation at the finance committee meeting
that he was to be involved in the LJM approval process.[105] Enron's legal department seems to have had a more precise view: it created LJM approval
sheets that included a signature line for Skilling, to supplement the normal
sheets required for all Enron transactions.[106] A memo from Jordan Mintz in
the legal department of Enron Global Finance (dated May 22, 2001) reveals
that he, too, expected Skilling's sign-off.[107] However, Skilling signed only
three of eighteen publicly available LJM approval sheets.[108]

Although both the compensation committee and Skilling were charged
with monitoring Fastow's LJM-related compensation, neither took steps to
learn how much he actually received until media reports surfaced in the fall
of 2001.[109] In his June 28, 1999, presentation to the board, Fastow indicated
that he would receive $500,000, plus 2 percent of the limited partners'

invested capital.[110] The committee took few steps to verify this information (see below). Instead, it submitted general inquiries to Enron staff about outside compensation reported by all Section 16 officers.[111]

Viewing the behavior of Enron's directors as an exercise in decision control suggests several conclusions. The board failed to seriously review transactions between the corporation and the LJM partnerships, which were loaded with risks of self-dealing and potential conflicts of interest. One notable omission was the board's apparent failure to notice and question the fact that Skilling had not signed the vast majority of the LJM approval sheets, as requested by Enron's legal department. The board created few performance standards or milestones to assess the progress of approved hedges, merchant investments, and operating policies. The board's unwillingness to comply with its own mandates to compel management to fulfill its obligations—and to push to better understand the risks of doing business with one of the company's own top executives—reflect a weakness of will and compromised approach to corporate governance.

The board did create some metrics to evaluate Fastow's compensation from the LJM partnerships, but Fastow himself supplied the data. More important, the compensation committee—which had been delegated responsibility—failed to determine whether Fastow's compensation was within the parameters he had laid out.

Inquiry

When a board becomes aware of information that "would awaken suspicion and put a prudent man on his guard," directors have a responsibility to investigate.[112] Such information is generally referred to as a "red flag."[113] Once aware of a red flag, directors have an obligation to actively seek explanations for troubling facts or circumstances.[114]

As with any subjective analysis, proving directors' awareness of red flags is largely an exercise in implication. The ability to recognize a red flag might depend on a particular director's experience in the business segment of concern.[115] The duration and magnitude of a red flag might also help establish whether directors were aware of it.[116]

Despite these inevitable ambiguities, it appears that Enron's board satisfied the minimum standards of performance set forth by legal principles pertaining to the duty to inquire. However, viewed from the standpoint of decision control, the directors' performance looks remarkably different.[117]

Their claims notwithstanding, the record shows that the outside directors knew or should have known that the company's balance sheet was often close to veering out of control and endangering Enron's credit rating, and that executives were taking drastic measures to maintain the veneer of financial fortitude. The directors should have inquired into the depth of these problems much earlier than they did.

Although outside directors neither requested nor received regular reports comparing nondiscretionary capital expenditures to budgeted amounts, they did receive information showing significant budget overruns, according to the bankruptcy examiner. Meeting minutes and other materials show that the board was aware that Enron's capital investments were over budget by $5.052 billion in 1998, $3.921 billion in 1999, and $2.309 billion in 2000.[118] The finance committee also received periodic reviews of year-to-date capital investments compared with budget.[119]

The bankruptcy examiner concluded that "the Finance Committee appears to have done little review of Enron's debt maturity schedules, and the Outside Directors appear to have little knowledge of the true size of Enron's total obligations."[120] That no one at Enron—including executives and directors—seems to have paid much attention to the company's capital budgeting and monitoring processes largely accounts for the need to pursue transactions with related parties in the first place.[121] Moreover, having established no metrics beyond overall funds-flow targets, the board was not positioned to effectively probe many of the risks posed by financial transactions.

Directors also failed to pursue red flags related to the timing of cash flows and the purpose of transactions with off-balance-sheet entities. Statements by directors imply that the board was aware of the purpose of these transactions. Consider the sworn statement by Robert A. Belfer, a member of the finance committee, to the bankruptcy examiner:

> It was a little disturbing to have these [transactions] come so close at the end of the year, but there was some discussion of that, as I recall, and the idea was to not put ourselves in a position like that again if we could avoid it.[122]

In testimony before the Senate Governmental Affairs Subcommittee of Investigations, Robert Jaedicke, chair of the audit committee, recalled that the timing of the Rhythms hedge was important, "because [Enron executives] did not want to be in the position of having a fair value investment, a stock on their books, a mark-to-market, without a hedge. . . . the hedge should have been put on by the end of June."[123]

There are also indications that the board was aware that Enron executives were using transactions with SPEs to conceal the company's true financial condition, in possible violation of securities laws.[124] The board understood that the disclosure of these transactions was precarious because it depended on fluctuating accounting rules and interpretations.[125] The board also knew that the SPE transactions "apparently were designed to accomplish favorable financial statement results, not to achieve bona fide economic objectives or transfer risk," and expressed concern about the use of the transactions to meet the expectations of rating agencies.[126] Yet there is no evidence that Enron's directors attempted to blow the whistle on obfuscating transactions or ask for a review of the company's financial strategy. If they had, they would have been obligated to investigate further, to avoid legal charges that they consciously disregarded known risks.

The large discrepancies between budgeted spending and actual spending should also have spurred the board to call for changes in the investment process. In failing to inquire into these variances in the capital budget, Enron's board fell far short of the ideals of effective internal governance and control.

Explaining the Directors' Lapses

The directors' failure to detect and deter problems embedded in the Rhythm and Raptor transactions and Enron's overall ethical drift was rooted in organizational anomalies, administrative practices, and behavioral tendencies that made the board both a victim of and major contributor to the company's governance breakdown.

Organizational and behavioral factors (noted in Chapter 3) included a deficit of experienced operating officers stemming from poor selection and high turnover; frequent organizational changes; an incestuous relationship between the company and its outside auditor; and the inability of Skilling and Lay to tolerate or learn from dissent. Along with the culture of deceit that developed from Lay's repeated inability to nip misrepresentation and conflicts of interest in the bud, these factors helped create a wall of denial and silence between Enron's top management and the board, and cut it off from the evolving realities of Enron's operations. This wall was buttressed by outside auditors and lawyers, who obscured the fact that the company was taking significant accounting risks.

This picture of Enron's directors as victims of a hoodwinking by top management and outside advisors is, however, woefully incomplete. Far from being passive victims, board members furthered the company's governance breakdown. They perpetuated outmoded board processes. They ratified and were subject to an inflated stock-based compensation plan that made it increasingly difficult for them to challenge management as the price of Enron stock soared from 1997 to 2000. Many failed to master the details of the company's complex financial maneuvers designed to promote growth in reported earnings in the face of declining operating margins. And the directors failed to demand explanations for the risks implicit in the use of SPEs, to attend to readily available information that should have aroused suspicions in experienced business leaders, to think critically about deal structures, and to monitor conflicts of interest that they themselves had approved. Enron's directors also tended to treat senior executives with great deference—a tendency rooted in longstanding personal relationships and emotional bonds with Ken Lay.

As the board became compliant, it allowed fixable problems to fester into uncontrolled cancers that wounded vital corporate organs.[127] Enron's nonexecutive directors thus broke their bond of accountability to the company's owners, and their bond of stewardship on behalf of its employees.[128]

Outmoded Board Processes

As Enron's business model evolved, the board failed to revise its antiquated decision control and oversight processes. Procedures that might have served the corporation and its shareholders well when Enron was a predominantly domestic pipeline operation turned out to be inadequate as the company internationalized and took on many of the characteristics of a high-risk, transaction-oriented financial services firm.

Enron was not unique in its inability to adapt to changes in its business model.[129] A study conducted by Colin B. Carter and Jay W. Lorsch just as the wave of accounting scandals washed over the business world found that even corporate boards that followed best practices often spent inadequate time determining their optimal design. Thus many corporate boards remained rooted in increasingly outdated structures and processes.[130] In Enron's case, it was the combination of outmoded board processes with other characteristics of its governance regime that proved to be so destructive.

There is not (and cannot be) a single best approach to board-level decision control and oversight. However, it is reasonable to expect board processes to reflect the nature of the decisions that occur within a particular business. For example, the more complex and continuous the flow of investment decisions that put a public corporation's business model and reputation at risk, the more time its board will need to spend reviewing and ratifying the array of proposals from management and monitoring outcomes.

That is precisely where the formal processes of Enron's board failed to support its directors' responsibilities. Many of management's proposals involving the funding of new businesses (such as electric power, broadband, and water utilities), the creation of SPEs (such as LJM1 and LJM2), and the transfer of assets and related debt among corporate and off-balance-sheet entities (such as the Raptors) involved strategic, financial, accounting, and legal aspects that needed to be vetted not only by specialists inside and outside the company but also by the board itself. As these proposals became more innovative, more frequent, and more likely to put the company's future at risk, the mismatch between the time required to vet and monitor them and the time available to do so certainly expanded. In the end, Enron's finance committee simply could not do its job effectively in the five ninety-minute meetings per year preceding a full board meeting, or the informal telephone conferences between meetings. The same holds for Enron's audit committee, which faced an ever more complex array of accounting and reporting decisions. (See Appendices E and F for a summary of the agenda and meeting times of finance and audit committees for which minutes are publicly available.)

Enron's adherence to the five-meetings-a-year format followed by most boards of U.S. public corporations gave rise to a serious governance gap. In preserving its traditional meeting format after 1997, the board denied itself the chance of fully understanding the complex web of financial and legal assumptions embedded in numerous proposals presented for approval—aside from uncovering irregularities in these transactions.[131] As the purpose, structure, and expected outcomes of investment decisions and related investment vehicles became more complex, the short and crowded bimonthly meetings of the finance and audit committees made it increasingly difficult for directors to seriously vet, ratify, and monitor Enron's expanding schedule of capital commitments.

Compensation of Nonemployee Directors

Just as the board's internal processes made it difficult for Enron's nonemployee directors to detect and deter the company's ethical drift, so the directors' compensation arrangements may have discouraged a swift shutdown and disclosure of ill-conceived financial and accounting strategies designed to disguise failed bets in the electricity distribution, water, broadband, and telecommunications businesses. Indeed, a look at how Enron directors were compensated suggests that their incentives to go along with efforts by senior executives and outside advisors to disguise the company's true financial condition were as strong as their incentives to uncover, fix, and disclose the company's deteriorating business fundamentals.

A large component of many directors' compensation was stock-based. This approach is typically celebrated as a way of aligning directors' interests with those of shareholders, whose agents they were.[132] However, depending on holding provisions specifying how long stock grants and exercised options must be held, stock-based compensation can also promote a focus on short-term earnings—and even encourage inflation of reported earnings to drive up beneficiaries' stock price and wealth position. Even worse, when a company is highly overvalued and its stock options represent enormous capital gains, directors have a strong incentive to support management's use of "access to cheap debt and equity capital to engage in excessive internal spending and risky negative net present value investments that the market thinks will generate value." This, in turn, can encourage misrepresentations and fraudulent practices to sustain the appearance of rising growth and profitability.[133]

Evidence suggests that this dynamic might have been at work in Enron's case. Nonemployee directors received both annual fees and equity grants. From 1999 to 2001, they were awarded annual fees of $50,000. Committee chairs received another $10,000, and individual directors an additional $1,250 for each meeting they attended.[134] Beginning in 1997, directors had to divert 50 percent of their annual fees to a deferred phantom stock option account. Phantom stock was treated as if the director had purchased shares of Enron common stock. Participants could specify during the first quarter of the year after a "termination event" (retirement, death, disability, or termination) how deferred accounts were to be paid. Directors could take their remaining fees in cash or defer them under various plans.[135] Most chose one deferred compensation plan or another over cash.[136]

Between the "50 percent deferred" phantom stock option rule governing their annual compensation, voluntary diversion of their remaining annual service fees into additional deferred stock plans, and supplemental annual grants of stock options and phantom stock, Enron's directors were deeply invested in the company's stock. By mid-August 2000, Enron's seven longest-serving and most respected nonemployee directors had between $2.6 million and $3.2 million of equity value in deferred accounts.[137] One year later—before Lay announced the company's surprising third-quarter write-offs—these equity values had dropped, on average, to just over $900,000. (The averages understate the stock ownership of director Robert Belfer, who sold Belco Petroleum to Enron in 1985 and retained a large stake of Enron stock. Belfer was Enron's largest shareholder and the majority owner of Enron's outstanding convertible preferred stock.)

Although small compared with the value of the stock-based compensation of Enron's most senior executives, these financial stakes were nevertheless considerable. The operative question is whether this sizable stake influenced directors' decision-making and oversight roles.

At its peak market value of $70 billion, Enron's equity was overvalued by as much as $40 billion, and management was increasingly unable to generate enough sales and profit growth to support that valuation.[138] Even without a formal analysis showing that Enron's market price was out of line with its fundamental value, the directors would have had trouble missing a $40 billion overvaluation of a company that was failing to earn its cost of capital. At that point their choices were straightforward. They could try to talk the stock price down by informing Wall Street that it was out of line with Enron's underlying economics and short-term prospects, or they could do anything and everything to maintain the inflated stock price.

Few boards have ever shown the courage to reset the market value of a company's equity by forcing disclosure of information that would ratchet down Wall Street's expectations.[139] In this case, telling the truth about the company's economic condition would have led to a precipitous decline in stock price and the wealth positions of all involved. Thus the directors had plenty of incentives to support "earnings management"—which at Enron surpassed the normal smoothing of earnings that had become more or less standard for many senior executives and audit committees of public companies. Once Enron started sprucing up its earnings by reporting financial gains as operating income, hiding debt in its off-balance-sheet partnerships, and hyping the performance of struggling new ventures such as broadband, the board had few financial incentives to reverse field.

Lack of Mastery and Deference to Management

Whatever the impact of directors' overvalued equity holdings, and the organizational factors affecting the board's knowledge and modus operandi, at some point directors' behavior becomes a matter of individual choice.[140] For reasons noted below, many of Enron's directors chose to delegate understanding of the company's practices to members they perceived as more experienced.

This lack of deep understanding of Enron's business and financial strategies was compounded by a reticence to clarify and carefully consider the company's investment risks, the true purposes of the off-balance-sheet partnerships created after 1997, and related accounting rules of the game. The inevitable result was a shift in the balance of power from nonexecutive directors to the company's most senior executive officers. This shift severely diminished the effectiveness of board monitoring and yielded many poor investment decisions.

The trappings of model corporate governance largely masked the directors' lack of mastery and their reticence to confront management. One of the most important lessons of the Enron story is that whatever a board's organizational context, composition, and internal processes, the directors' intentions and commitment matter most. Unless directors' diligent endeavors nourish effective corporate governance principles, the board will not have the strength to discharge its responsibilities.

To say that Enron's directors were ill intentioned or took no efforts to promote the company's well-being would be incorrect. However, owing to their deference to top management, board members made significant decisions on numerous occasions without seeking clarification of information they did not understand. Confusion appears to have been an acceptable state of mind.

For example, some directors recalled not understanding the Rhythms hedge when it was proposed during the board meeting on June 28, 1999.[141] Many directors would presumably have benefited from more time to study the proposal's details. Though other directors disputed Jaedicke's contention that immediate approval was necessary so the company would not have unhedged stock or mark-to-market assets on its books, the minutes (perhaps predictably) do not indicate that a director formally requested more time or expressed confusion.[142] In any case, had the directors forced management to explain the Rhythms proposal more fully, a broader and deeper understanding of the transaction would have been achieved and the transaction and its fallout might have been avoided.

Confusion was also rampant regarding the Raptors. Lay understood that they were noneconomic hedges, meaning that they were not hedges at all.[143] Director Winokur, in contrast, indicated that he understood the connection between Enron's stock price and the credit capacity of the hedge vehicle.[144] However, director Blake stated that he thought "that economic risk was transferred in the transaction . . . because otherwise, I don't believe that Arthur Andersen would have approved it."[145] Although the presentation materials on Raptors I and II made clear that the hedging capacity of the counterparty was dictated by the value of Enron stock, the directors apparently never reconciled their disparate comprehension of the materials.[146] In fact, in their statements to the bankruptcy examiner and interviews with the board's special investigative committee, the directors did not recall debating the economics of the transactions.[147] Thus the board approved transactions that lacked economic reality without a grasp of their true structure.

Directors' statements to the bankruptcy examiner also reveal unresolved confusion regarding the ongoing relationship between Enron and the LJM1 partnership. Meeting minutes note that "LJM may negotiate with the Company regarding the purchase of additional assets in the Merchant Portfolio," and the board presentation itself referred to the possibility that LJM1 could "negotiate with Enron for purchase of additional merchant assets."[148] Several directors recalled these details.[149] But others, including Lay, John Mendelsohn, and Winokur, believed that the Rhythms hedge would be the only transaction between the two entities.[150] That the directors took away such vastly different conceptions of the Enron/LJM1 relationship suggests that they did not collectively understand what they were approving or rejecting—a circumstance likely aggravated by the company's information-gathering problems.

Similarly, as discussed above, the directors did very little to clarify and monitor the compensation Fastow received from the LJM1 partnerships.[151] Fastow had promised in his presentation to the board that he would not benefit from the Enron stock transferred to LJM1.[152] At minimum, information about Fastow's LJM1 compensation would have verified his compliance with this promise.[153] It would have also kept the directors in touch with the expanded business dealings between Enron and its controversial, CFO-managed off-balance-sheet partnerships.

Director LeMaistre, chair of the compensation committee, which was responsible for reviewing the compensation Fastow received from his involvement in the LJM partnerships, indicated that he did not pursue the matter further because he thought Skilling, Lay, and the audit committee were doing so.[154] It is unclear how LeMaistre developed the belief that the audit committee was involved. Lay—who recalled being shocked to learn that Fastow had made $30 million from the LJM2 partnerships—said he refrained from making direct inquiries into Fastow's compensation because he thought Fastow had been hesitant to participate in the LJM funds.[155] Skilling recalled receiving "conceptual information" on two occasions, but felt that establishing a definitive number would have been too difficult because LJM was making long-term investments.[156]

Given confusion about Fastow's role in the LJM partnerships, Enron's directors should have, at minimum, ensured that Enron was protected against the use of inside information in negotiating transactions with LJM. However, the board established no controls until the creation of LJM2 in connection with Raptor I. The directors apparently assumed that the company's accounting department would act if the payments Enron received from the LJM1 transactions were too low.[157] All the controls put in place by the outside directors (and cited in their response to the Senate report on the board's role in Enron's collapse) occurred well after initial approval of the Rhythms hedge, indicating a remarkably lax approach to board oversight.[158]

The board was not much better when it came to understanding its role in the public disclosure process. Enron's outside directors misconstrued their duty as simply to make the public aware of the company's state of affairs. Lacking a rigorous process for reviewing and revising the company's SEC filings, the board must have believed that the information was sufficient for educated readers. It was not. Once again, the board's miscomprehension of its obligations and failure to seek clarification prevented it from recognizing and correcting a fundamental flaw.[159]

Had the directors challenged management to explain and clarify information, even cursorily, major flaws would likely have been revealed. Instead, the directors failed to take the initiative, and opportunities passed.

Why would a board fail to ask probing questions? The public record suggests possible answers to this critical question. Perhaps the desire to avoid group conflict and the risks of being deemed "too negative" pushed Enron's

directors into a habit of mind that prevented informed reflection and deliberation. According to Irving Janis—widely respected for his research on the
behavior of presidential advisors—such feelings are central to a psychological process he coined as "groupthink."[160]

Groupthink, an important concept that has reached cliché status, inhibits
people from questioning the purposes and morality of their behavior. Such
inhibitions occur in cohesive groups in which members share a feeling of
belonging, decision-making procedures are inadequate, and a high level of
decisional stress causes members to rely on each other to ease anxiety and
feelings of inadequacy. These conditions were all in play on Enron's board.

Organizations subject to groupthink tend to believe in their inherent
morality and correctness and defer to their leaders' vision—much the way
that directors came to view Ken Lay and Jeff Skilling as evangelists and he-
roes in their quest to enhance social welfare by changing energy markets
through deregulation. Under these conditions, groups also tend to develop
overconfidence and an illusion of invulnerability. When time is short and
decision issues are complex, the group's built-in optimism can help simplify
or minimize the required judgments—witness the Enron board's approval
of many risky projects. Feelings of group solidarity can also lead to collective
rationalization and the absence of rigorous inquiry and self-criticism, as
seen in the audit committee's failure to monitor Enron's related-party transactions, and the compensation committee's failure to monitor Fastow's pay.

Finally, groupthink can restrain frank discussion and lead to denuncia-
tion of criticism, and the rejection or expulsion of group members who
"don't get it." Corporate boards are no different from other groups in these
norms.[161] At Enron, Jerome Meyer, one-time CEO and chair of Tektronics,
offered not to stand for reelection in 2001 when told by Lay that Skilling
thought Meyer's questioning too critical of management.[162] The fact that
criticizing management could get one escorted out of the group was probably not lost on the other outside directors.

Directors' personal attachment to Lay might also have contributed to the
board's inability to function as an oversight body.[163] More than a third of
Enron's board had served as directors of Houston Natural Gas (HNG) when
Lay was CEO (before the merger between HNG and InterNorth which created Enron). These directors were all susceptible to seeing Lay as a policy
whiz kid who had served as assistant energy secretary in Washington, and
as a bright young executive who rose to senior positions at Florida Natural
Gas and the Transco pipeline company before being called in to save a

troubled HNG. Once Lay succeeded in wresting control of the HNG/Inter-North merger and was made chair and CEO of the new company, these directors came to view Lay as an effective leader and authoritative voice—although he had only limited knowledge of who was actually building businesses at the new Enron.

The tendency of Enron's directors to avoid criticizing Lay was, of course, not unique.[164] According to Lorsch, "Directors are expected above all to treat the CEO with respect, which means not embarrassing him or her in a board meeting." Given this tacit prohibition, the usual manner for expressing displeasure with a CEO is to ask penetrating questions—just the method that Enron executives suppressed.[165] In failing to contest this censorship, the board deprived itself of valuable information that could have informed its strategic decisions, and permitted the corporate ship to drift closer to the rocky financial shoals that ultimately sank it.

What's more, according to Lorsch, "Even though most directors are highly talented and experienced, they're rarely familiar enough with a particular business to assess [management] proposals properly."[166] When complicated data supplied by management compound this lack of familiarity, directors tend to acquiesce to peers who seem to better understand the issue.[167]

According to the court-appointed examiner, "Several of the Outside Directors testified that they might not have understood an area of the company's operations or a particular matter, but they were not concerned because they expected someone else on the Board did."[168] For example, audit committee member Ronnie C. Chan indicated that he did not ask for clarification of an auditing issue because he considered Robert Jaedicke, John Duncan, and Wendy Gramm relative experts in accounting.[169] This reliance on peers seems somewhat misplaced: Jaedicke did have an extensive accounting background, but neither Duncan nor Gramm had notable accounting experience.[170]

All these influences appear to have been present in the Enron boardroom. Management proposals—particularly those related to the structured-finance SPE deals—often entailed specialized issues that exceeded directors' knowledge. And management frequently presented information to directors in a lengthy and confusing format that impeded directors' ability to extract relevant information and ask insightful questions.[171] Remarkably, several directors told the examiner that none of their colleagues had the knowledge or experience to independently evaluate the sophisticated accounting maneuvers.[172] Whether directors think a perceived expert seems comfortable with an issue or keep quiet for fear of appearing inept, the result is the same.[173] The simple questions—which are sometimes the most revealing—go unasked.

CEO control of the information a board receives often exacerbates its reluctance to recognize predicaments.[174] Lay was heavily involved in shaping the board's preparatory packets and meeting presentations.[175] Given Lay's reticence to face difficult problems, the way he framed this information tended to reflect an optimistic—indeed, inflated—view of Enron's position. It is not surprising, therefore, that his directors were ill-informed about the deteriorating performance of Enron's large portfolio of merchant investments until well into 2001—months after RAC had documented the problem.[176]

However, although directors lacked timely knowledge of the company's deteriorating investment performance, the risks of the SPEs, and even the full extent of its indebtedness, they were well aware that Enron's complex accounting measures were akin to nitroglycerin—volatile and unstable, with the potential for disastrous results should something jar them. Management's reactions to opposing views likely tempered any individual director's enthusiasm for promoting a change in financial strategy.

Enron's problems did not emerge overnight, though it might have seemed that way to directors who became aware of their magnitude only after published reports surfaced in the fall of 2001. The board's failure was to remain blind to problems that developed gradually. Absent some clear event to ignite board activity, corporate directors typically find it difficult to recognize that a problem exists, accept that changes must be made, and unify to counter the power wielded by the CEO.[177]

Lorsch has observed that director unity is the most significant source of a board's power, because it enables members to collectively challenge senior management.[178] Indeed, as Janis pointed out in his study of presidential advisory groups, knowing that others share the same point of view reassures group members that their analysis is accurate and eases the pain of difficult choices.[179] This also means that the costs to the group when any member breaks consensus can be high.[180] The work of both Janis and Lorsch helps explain the directors' failure to take more steps to feel out and debate each other, and to see the company's brewing financial and conflict-of-interest problems before they reached the boiling point.

The lack of director accountability at Enron and other U.S. companies has exerted a profound effect on corporate governance reforms, including

Sarbanes-Oxley. Yet the limited legislative debate leading up to its passage reveals that Congress failed to understand many of the critical factors that contributed to Enron's collapse—particularly the directors' lack of mastery of many aspects of the company's administrative and financial affairs. Adopted in July 2002, less than a year after the Enron scandal broke during a period of media frenzy and a free-falling stock market, there was virtually no testimony from business leaders with deep understanding of the origins of Enron's collapse and other contemporaneous scandals. As a result, we cannot expect these new rules to protect us from future Enrons. For example, Sarbanes-Oxley places a great deal of emphasis on the expanded use of independent, nonexecutive directors, but one of the problems with this requirement is that many truly independent directors may not have the kind of specific business knowledge required to monitor corporate operations in a disciplined fashion. In Enron's case, one of the causes of its governance breakdown was the lack of mastery of the company's financial strategies at the board level, which was acknowledged by Enron directors in their 2001 self-assessment.[181] Thus, where mandated director independence crowds out director knowledge and experience (with all conflicts of interests disclosed), the risks of a breakdown in board monitoring and control may well increase.

True reform will require fundamental changes in corporate governance practices that rebalance the power between board chairs and nonexecutive directors—changes Congress and the courts cannot mandate. Chapter 8 will show how such fundamental reforms have been stress-tested for years in the private equity community.

CHAPTER 6

The Collusion of
Financial Intermediaries

Many of the outside professionals Enron employed in the conduct of its business affairs either colluded with or acquiesced to efforts by Enron executives to misrepresent the company's true financial condition.[1] Enron's auditor, the now-defunct Arthur Andersen, for example, was widely criticized for approving the accounting treatment of many questionable transactions, and for failing to be more vocal about concerns raised by its own employees regarding the risks and conflicts of interest inherent in several of Enron's unique financial structures.[2]

Enron's legal advisors sparked similar criticism. Perhaps because it handled the superficial investigation prompted by Sherron Watkins's infamous "smoking gun" memo, Vinson & Elkins, Enron's primary outside counsel, bore the brunt of public condemnation of the legal community's role in helping Enron.[3] A more significant indictment concerns the law firm's repeated dissemination of favorable opinions regarding Enron's structured-finance transactions.[4]

However, although Enron's accountants and attorneys earned the criticism directed at them, their actions occurred away from the epicenter of these deals. Closer to the core of Enron's deceit were the financial intermediaries who actively participated in designing and implementing transactions aimed at misrepresenting the company's true financial position. This chapter examines their role.

The chapter's investigation reveals a breakdown in the internal checks and balances of Enron's bankers. Enron's banking business was so large that some banks, at least, appear to have sought to boost their share of the company's debt and equity financings by coming up with creative ideas to strengthen its balance sheet, improve its cash flow, and take advantage of the tax code. Creative bankers also seem to have considered Enron a hot property because it was doing exciting and innovative deals that they might apply elsewhere. For these and no doubt other reasons, the extensive public record reveals aggressiveness among Enron's bankers, and a shift in power from employees responsible for maintaining credit and financing integrity to those responsible for sustaining customer relations.

How Bankers Aided and Abetted Enron's Fraud

When a company improperly reports cash flows generated by or used in financings as cash generated from typical business operations [then] investors, analysts and credit rating agencies will be misled as to the financial health of a company and its ability to meet future commitments on cash.—*Lynn Turner, former chief accountant of the SEC*[5]

Enron engaged numerous financial advisors, underwriters, and commercial bankers. Its long list of "regulars"—as well as those aspiring to that group— enabled it to play one banker off another, punish banks if their analysts published less-than-flattering stock reports, and entice bankers to coinvest in off-balance-sheet partnerships.

Financial intermediaries qualifying as Enron regulars during the 1990s included Donaldson, Lufkin & Jenrette; JPMorgan Chase; Barclays; BT/Deutsche; Canadian Imperial Bank of Commerce; Royal Bank of Scotland; and Toronto Dominion. Credit Suisse First Boston, JPMorgan Chase, Goldman Sachs, Citigroup, Merrill Lynch, Bear Stearns Cos., and Commerzbank also worked to varying degrees with Enron on letters of credit and derivative-trading transactions.[6]

Many of these banks competed aggressively for a piece of Enron's huge banking business. In the five years leading up to its bankruptcy, Enron took on loans totaling almost $36 billion, while also issuing $21 billion in publicly owned debt and just over $3 billion in equity.[7] Given the fees and income from this massive flow of transactions, the rewards for regulars were clearly significant. At least six banks recorded revenues of $60 million or more from Enron-related activities during this five-year period. Citigroup generated more than three times that amount, posting nearly $190 million in revenue from its relationship with Enron.[8]

Many of the transactions between Enron and its coterie of bankers complied with generally accepted accounting principles (GAAP) and rules of the Securities and Exchange Commission (SEC). However, other transactions were clearly designed to disguise or otherwise misrepresent reported profits, cash flow, and debt. To shed light on this darker side, I describe several transactions in which two of Enron's most important bankers, Citigroup and Merrill Lynch, participated. These complex transactions were put together in December 1999, just as Enron was preparing its final accounting for the year. As we will see, each was designed to look proper, but also to produce the desired effect on Enron's publicly reported balance sheet and income statement.

In the case of Merrill Lynch, both the bank and Enron resorted to allegedly secret verbal understandings to protect the accounting treatment of a particular financial transaction as a *bone fide* asset sale and source of reportable profits. As for Citigroup, the bank designed a structure that enabled Enron to record loan-like financing as equity-like financing—and thus avoid reporting this debt on its balance sheet. However, as in the Merrill Lynch case, Citigroup required Enron to provide guarantees that it would repay the disguised loans.

After describing these transactions, I analyze what they tell us about the nature of the collusion between Enron and some of its most important financial advisors and intermediaries. This analysis reveals that banks colluded with Enron in three ways. First, they knew that Enron wanted to produce financial reports that would mislead those who read them, including credit-rating agencies, and helped Enron to structure transactions to accomplish that. Second, the banks ignored risks associated with these transactions identified by their own internal control systems. Third, banks helped Enron maintain a positive market image by pressuring their own analysts to recommend the company to clients as a solid investment.

Though these banks did not suffer the mortal fate of Arthur Andersen, the aftermath of Enron's implosion found them beset by expensive legal settlements and sullied reputations. For example, Citigroup agreed to pay Enron shareholders $2 billion to settle its portion of a class-action lawsuit, and anted up another $101 million in a settlement with the SEC.[9] JP-Morgan Chase and Canadian Imperial Bank of Commerce agreed to pay Enron shareholders fines topping $2 billion. At the time of this writing, Merrill Lynch had not yet resolved its shareholders' suit, but had agreed to pay the SEC $80 million to settle its claims.[10] (On March 19, 2007, a three-judge panel of the Fifth Circuit Court of Appeals ruled that the conduct of Merrill Lynch, while "hardly praiseworthy," was not liable for any fraud committed because it did not make any false statements about the fraud.[11]

In June Supreme Court justices put off a hearing of an appeal brought by Enron shareholders in their class action suit.)

By early August 2005, five of Enron's banking partners had agreed to pay shareholders, the SEC, and Enron itself a total of nearly $8.7 billion in cash, fines, disgorgement of gains, interest, and dropped claims against Enron (see Tables 6.1, 6.2, and 6.3). None of these bankers admitted any guilt in assisting Enron's fraud.[12]

Citigroup and the Nahanni Transaction

With more than $1 trillion in assets and nearly 300,000 employees, Citigroup is a financial titan.[13] The bank provides financial assistance to other companies through its Global Corporate Banking unit.[14] Buried within this unit and operating through Salomon Smith Barney, a Citigroup subsidiary, is the Global Energy & Power Group, which managed the company's relationship with Enron.[15]

Citigroup was clearly an important financial partner to Enron, participating in at least thirteen transactions with special-purpose entities (SPEs). In 1999, Enron cited Citigroup as its "primary banking relationship" that year.[16] Central to this relationship was the so-called Nahanni transaction, completed in December 1999.

Table 6.1.   Banks' settlements with Enron investors

Defendant	Settlement Figure
Canadian Imperial Bank of Commerce	$2.4 billion
J. P. Morgan Chase & Co.	$2.2 billion
Citigroup	$2 billion
Lehman Brothers	$222.5 million
Bank of America	$69 million
Settlement Total:	$6.892 billion

Note: As of August 19, 2005. Investors have recouped just over $7 billion through the class-action suit, including settlements with other parties such as Arthur Andersen and Enron's outside directors. See August 2, 2005, press release from the University of California Board of Regents, "UC Secures $2.4 Billion Settlement with CIBC in Enron Fraud Case," available at www.universityofcalifornia.edu/news/2005/aug02.html.

Table 6.2. Banks' settlements with the SEC

Bank	Settlement
Canadian Imperial Bank of Commerce	$80 million in total ($37.5 million in disgorgement, a $37.5 million civil penalty, and $5 million in prejudgment interest)
J. P. Morgan Chase & Co.	$135 million in disgorgement, penalties, and interest
Citigroup	$101 million in disgorgement, penalties, and interest
Merrill Lynch	$80 million dollars in disgorgement, penalties, and interest
Settlement Total	$396.0 million

Note: As of August 19, 2005. SEC suits claimed that banks aided and abetted Enron in disguising its true financial, thereby defrauding investors. As of August 2005, settlements with banks not listed in Table 6.1 were still outstanding.

Citigroup understood that many Enron transactions were intended to obscure the company's financial condition.[17] Citigroup further understood that helping Enron structure these transactions in certain ways could lead those who read its financial reports to draw incorrect conclusions.[18] Citigroup's reference to Nahanni as "year-end window dressing" describes precisely the role it was designed to play.[19]

In late 1999, Enron needed additional capital, but wanted neither to damage its credit rating by taking on more loans nor to dilute earnings per share by issuing new stock. Thus the company looked to structured-finance transactions to borrow money without having to increase its reported debt.[20] This was the original impetus for three "minority-interest transactions" designed by Citigroup and implemented in consecutive Decembers.[21] (Such structured finance transactions enabled Enron to show loans as "minority interests" or holdings on its balance sheet.) Enron did not record as debt any portion of the roughly $1.75 billion it obtained from Citigroup through these transactions. For its role, Citigroup collected $25 million in structure fees and $4.7 million in underwriting fees.[22]

The Nahanni transaction essentially converted loans into ownership interests. Citigroup loaned money to Nahanni, an SPE established for Enron (see Figure 6.1).[23] This loan was limited to 97 percent of the SPE's assets, so

Table 6.3. Banks' settlements with Enron

Bank	Cash payment from bank to Enron	Value of dropped claims[a] by bank against Enron	Fee paid by bank to Enron for rights to transfer its claims to a third party	Value of creditor claims transferrable to a third party	Net value to Enron[b] (cash plus subordinated claims minus transferred claims)
J.P Morgan Chase & Co.	$350 million	$660 million	$0	$0	$1,010 million
Toronto Dominion Bank	$70 million	$56 million	$60 million	$320 million	($134 million)
Canadian Imperial Bank of Commerce	$250 million	$40 million	$24 million	$80 million	$234 million
Royal Bank of Canada	$25 million	$0	$24 million	$114 million	($65 million)
Royal Bank of Scotland	$42 million	$309 million[c]	$0	$0	$351 million
TOTAL:	**$737 million**	**$1,065 million**	**$108 million**	**$514 million**	**$1,396 million**

Note: Enron made these claims against banks that submitted claims as creditors in Enron's Chapter 11 proceedings. The clash between Enron's estate and the banks has been dubbed the "megaclaims litigation." Enron allege that the banks aided and abetted breaches of fiduciary duties, aided and abetted fraud, and engaged in civil conspiracy. Conservatively assuming that Enron will wholly satisfy the transferred claims, the net value of the settlements is just under $1.4 billion.

a. A dropped claim is technically a claim that has been subordinated to other creditors' claims. In the bankruptcy context, subordination is when otherwise superior claims are moved behind inferior claims. Subordinated claims are paid only after the superior claims have been satisfied. Bankruptcy courts subordinate claims to remedy misconduct by creditors that has harmed the debtor or other creditors. Since subordinated claims are the least likely to be paid, they are considered as dropped claims in calculating the net benefit Enron receives from these settlements.

b. Net value equals a cash payment, plus value of banks' dropped claims against Enron, plus fees paid to Enron for rights to transfer its claims to a third party, minus the value of claims that could legitimately be transferred according to banks' acquired rights.

c. RBS agreed to pay subordinate claims totaling $329 million, in return for a $20 million payment from Enron.

Enron would not have to add Nahanni to its balance sheet.[24] Outside investors (probably arranged by Citigroup) contributed the remaining 3 percent of Nahanni's assets as equity.

Nahanni was the minority shareholder in an Enron subsidiary called Marengo, in which Enron was the majority shareholder. Nahanni contributed all its assets to the Marengo subsidiary, which loaned the capital to Enron. To complete the transaction, Enron consolidated Marengo in its

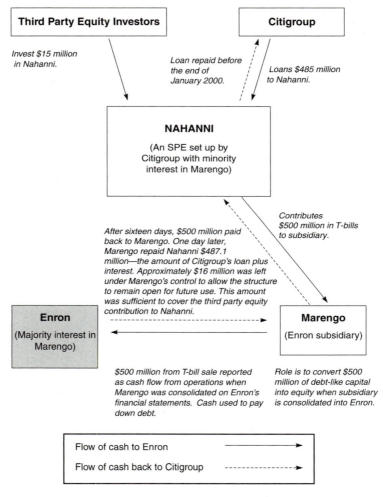

Figure 6.1 Flow of cash to and from Enron in Nahanni transaction.

financial statements, thereby converting a reportable loan into an unreported intercompany loan.[25]

Nondebt treatment was the only benefit Enron had derived from the two other minority-interest transactions Citigroup created.[26] However, Citigroup tinkered with the structure of Nahanni to provide another advantage. During September 1999, Citigroup learned that Enron needed to prop up its cash flow from operations by the end of the year.[27] Citigroup knew that credit-rating agencies compare cash flow to earnings expected from marked-to-market assets—to determine whether those earnings are likely to actually materialize.[28] Citigroup also understood that to create the needed cash flow from operations, the Nahanni structure would have to include a sales transaction (see Figure 6.1).[29]

The Nahanni structure therefore included a feature not present in earlier minority-interest transactions. In late 1999, Citigroup loaned $485 million to Nahanni, the minority shareholder in Marengo, and located outside investors to supply the 3 percent equity, or $15 million, needed to allow Nahanni to remain off Enron's balance sheet. However, Citigroup instructed Nahanni to invest the $500 million in Treasury bills, rather than contribute the cash directly to Marengo.[30]

Citigroup also instructed Enron to define T-bills as permissible assets in its merchant investment portfolio. When Marengo sold the T-bills, it was now selling a merchant asset.[31] As with the sale of any other such asset, Enron could record the revenue as cash flow from operations. Thus, when Enron added Marengo to its financial statements, the T-bill sale boosted reported cash flow from operations in 1999 by $500 million—or nearly 70 percent.[32] This was the "year-end window dressing" to which Citigroup had referred.

As it was creating the deal, Enron sought an additional benefit. It wanted to use the $500 million to pay down outstanding debt.[33] Citigroup agreed only after Enron offered a $500 million letter of credit guaranteeing that it would repay the equity and debt Citigroup had invested in Nahanni.[34] Internal Citigroup correspondence suggests that the bank knew before agreeing to the deal that Enron might want to use the capital to reduce existing debt.[35] And indeed, the transaction improved Enron's debt-to-equity ratio by 16 percent.[36]

The problem with this seemingly attractive deal was, of course, that the $500 million Enron received was inappropriately accounted for—by design. Three facts reveal that the $500 million was a temporary financing transaction, rather than cash flow from the sale of an asset. First, Citigroup documents show that the bank knew Enron wanted an infusion of cash to make its financial statements more photogenic for a year-end snapshot.[37]

Second, Marengo repaid 97 percent of Nahanni's contribution less than one month after the initial T-bill transfer.[38] And third, when Enron unwound the transaction (by reversing the cash flows between Citigroup and Enron), it did not reverse the original accounting treatment categorizing the proceeds as cash flow from operations. Instead, Enron took a $500 million reduction in cash flow from financing. The SEC found this misrepresentation unlawful.[39]

In using the $500 million to reduce existing debt, Enron created a second accounting problem. To avoid having to consolidate Nahanni on its balance sheet, it needed the 3 percent equity contribution from third-party investors to remain "at risk." The letter of credit Enron obtained to pacify Citigroup destroyed that quality, as it guaranteed that Enron would repay Nahanni's entire investment in Marengo, including the equity contribution in Nahanni itself. Though the letter was not directly intended to protect third-party investors, it effectively did so. Without any at-risk equity, Enron should have consolidated Nahanni on its balance sheet.[40]

Merrill Lynch's Electricity Transactions

Like Citigroup, Merrill Lynch is a banking behemoth. Through its subsidiaries and affiliates, the holding company provides investment, financing, advisory, insurance, and related products and services worldwide. By 1999 its two business segments—the Wealth Management Group and the Corporate and Institutional Client Group—employed 63,800 people and managed assets totaling more than $1.4 trillion.[41]

In mid-December 1999, Merrill Lynch engaged in two simultaneous transactions with Enron. One involved the purported sale of three barge-mounted power plants moored off the coast of Nigeria; the other, a swap of electricity contracts. A primary purpose of both was to help Enron meet its financial goals for the year.[42] Enron booked some $60 million in earnings from these transactions.[43] Merrill Lynch collected $9.3 million in fees for its role in the two deals, though this was roughly half the figure to which the parties agreed when the deals were struck.[44] The amount is nevertheless nearly one-quarter of the revenues Merrill received from Enron in 1999.[45]

Merrill Lynch also viewed engaging in these transactions as a way to deepen its relationship with Enron.[46] Merrill's manager of the Enron relationship stressed in an internal memo that the Nigerian barge transaction was a way to "differentiate [Merrill] from the pack and add significant value."[47] Merrill was also vying to become Enron's financial advisor for private equity in its telecommunications subsidiary.[48] Being there for Enron during a time of need seemed to be a savvy step.

This strategy worked. Before the two sets of transactions, Enron had ranked Merrill Lynch as a tier-3 bank.[49] By the end of 1999, Merrill Lynch ranked ahead of all other financial institutions as Enron's top fee earner. Merrill's Enron-linked revenues reached $40 million that year—up from $3.1 million and $2.2 million, respectively, for 1998 and 1997.[50]

For participating in the two sets of transactions with Enron, Merrill Lynch and several executives were charged by the SEC with aiding and abetting accounting fraud.[51] The bank settled its portion of the case immediately, agreeing to pay $80 million in penalties, interest, and allegedly ill-gotten gains. Merrill Lynch also agreed to a permanent antifraud injunction prohibiting future violations of federal securities laws.[52] In November 2004, four Merrill executives were convicted of fraud and received jail sentences. (In early 2006, three of the four were released on bond pending their appeal, and on August 1 an appeals court vacated their convictions on grounds of faulty legal procedure.)

THE NIGERIAN BARGE TRANSACTION

In late 1999, Enron treasurer and executive vice president Jeffery McMahon contacted Robert Furst, a relationship manager at Merrill, to solicit the bank's participation in a transaction involving power-generating barges off the coast of Nigeria.[53] Enron had been negotiating to sell the barges to the Tokyo-based Marubeni Corp., but could not complete the sale by the end of the year, which meant that Enron would not be able to claim the transaction in its quarterly earnings.[54] Enron wanted Merrill Lynch to purchase an interest in the barges before the end of the quarter as a "bridge to permanent equity."[55]

In a preliminary discussion, McMahon shared three details with Furst. The transaction would enable Enron to book $12 million in earnings; Merrill Lynch would "hold" the asset for a maximum of six months; and the investment would yield a 22.5 percent rate of return for Merrill.[56] The deal was consummated on December 29, 1999, despite some reluctance on the part of James Brown, head of Merrill's Strategic Asset Lease and Finance

Group, and its Debt Market Commitments Committee.[57] Under the agreement, Merrill agreed to purchase—through a collection of off-balance-sheet partnerships—a 90 percent interest in future cash flows generated by Enron's three floating power plants.[58] To do so, Merrill needed to put up only $7 million of the barges' purchase price of $28 million, with Enron essentially covering the remainder.[59]

Six months later, on June 29, the LJM2 E-Barge partnership (related to the LJM2 partnership run by Enron CFO Andy Fastow) purchased Merrill's $7 million equity interest in the three Nigerian barges for $7.525 million.[60] The $525,000 premium equaled 15 percent annual interest on the original $7 million investment for the six-month period.[61] The $250,000 Merrill received in advisory fees for this transaction brought its total return to 22.14 percent.[62]

Federal prosecutors later charged four former Merrill Lynch bankers and two former Enron executives with conspiring to commit fraud.[63] At the heart of the matter were complicated accounting issues related to the transfer of risk. Put most simply, prosecutors argued that because Enron guaranteed to take Merrill Lynch out of the deal in six months and also guaranteed its return, Merrill never incurred any risk. Thus Enron could not classify the transaction as a sale and book it as revenue. (Under SEC guidelines, a company cannot recognize a transaction as a sale if the risks of ownership do not pass from seller to buyer.)[64]

The Merrill Lynch executives maintained that Enron had made no unusual guarantees to Merrill, and had agreed only to make best efforts to find a third-party purchaser for Merrill's portion of the deal.[65] However, considerable evidence suggested that Enron had indeed made the promise.[66]

On November 3, 2004, the four former Merrill Lynch executives and one Enron executive were convicted in a U.S. district court of fraud and conspiracy charges in connection with the Nigerian barge transaction.[67] A few months later the convicted defendants were sentenced to an average of thirty-nine months in prison and fined a total of $3.3 million.[68] Merrill Lynch had also previously agreed to pay stiff financial penalties to the government. (The conviction of three executives was reversed in August 2006 by the U.S. Court of Appeals for the 5th Circuit on obscure procedural grounds—namely, that the jury shouldn't have been instructed that the defendants denied Enron of the intangible "honest services" they owed the company. However, in his written opinion Judge Grady Jolly included an important disclaimer: "This opinion should not be read to suggest no dishonest, fraudulent, wrongful or criminal act has appeared." In April 2007 U.S. District Court Judge Ewing Werlein ordered a retrial of the case.)[69]

THE ELECTRICITY TRADES

Around the time that Enron executive vice president Jeffery McMahon contacted Robert Furst, Cliff Baxter, president of Enron North America, was in touch with Dan Gordon, a managing director in Merrill's Derivatives Trading Unit, about a proposal involving electricity trades.[70] When all was said and done, Enron booked gains of about $50 million from these trades.[71] According to Merrill attorney James B. Weidner, Baxter told Merrill employees that besides boosting earnings, the trades would enable Enron to keep certain power plants off its balance sheet.[72]

According to a memo prepared by Gordon for Merrill's Special Transaction Review Committee (STRC), the deal consisted of two call-option contracts.[73] Merrill would purchase a physically settled option (meaning that electricity rather than its cash value would be physically delivered) from Enron, and Enron would buy a financially settled option from Merrill.[74] Gordon noted that "the proposed transaction is back-to-back and therefore is delta-neutral."[75] Jeff Kronthal, head of Merrill Lynch's Global Derivatives Group, told the bankruptcy examiner that this meant the options were equally "in the money" (profitable) and "out of the money" (unprofitable).[76]

As in the Nigerian barge transaction, Merrill Lynch played no role in creating the structure of the electricity trades. However, Enron agreed to pay Merrill fees totaling $17 million for participating in the trades. The fees would not be paid up front, but rather as premiums on the two option agreements.[77] The contracts were structured so that neither was exercisable until September 2000.[78] Merrill Lynch apparently was aware that these options would likely not be exercised, but rather would be unwound—or nullified—after they had served their accounting purpose.[79]

Though stories vary on the exact timing—some say February, some May—in early 2000, as expected, Enron sought to unwind the deal, but with a twist. Enron did not want to pay the $17 million fee.[80] Merrill Lynch asserted that the fee was warranted because the deal was laced with significant trading and operational risks.[81] But Gordon's memo to the STRC had not mentioned any risks, and an internal Merrill e-mail indicated that the fee amount was determined by the size of the trade and "the benefits enjoyed by Enron as a result of the transaction."[82] A later e-mail described those benefits as helping Enron "make earnings for the quarter and year (which had great value in their stock price, not to mention personal compensation)."[83] Enron and Merrill Lynch eventually settled on $8.5 million, half of the amount originally agreed on.[84]

The legal question surrounding this transaction centers on the accounting principle of revenue recognition. For Enron to claim revenue (and, in this case, profits) from the call option it purchased from Merrill, Enron had to both earn and recognize the revenue (and profits).[85] But this was not the case because the contract allowed Merrill Lynch to opt out until September 2000—meaning that Enron could not properly claim revenues on the deal for 1999.

Shared Characteristics of Enron's Colluding Bankers

Enron created dozens of similar transactions with other banking institutions. The willingness of these investment bankers to actively participate in Enron's deception closely connects the Nahanni, Nigerian barge, and electricity transactions with their unnamed brethren. Citigroup and Donaldson, Lufkin & Jenrette (DLJ) designed some transactions, while Enron designed others.[86] None of the banks involved in Enron's accounting maneuvers likely set out to deceive the public. But whether acting as financial engineers or capital providers, all the banks had clear indications of Enron's intent.

All, including Merrill Lynch and Citigroup, knew that some of the transactions in which they engaged presented serious accounting problems. The bankers were aware that the transactions enabled Enron to adjust debt and cash flow on the company's balance sheet, and that Enron intended to shield substantive facts of the transactions from the public. The banks knew that outsiders would misinterpret the figures in Enron's financial statements, and believe the company to be much stronger than it actually was. The banks also understood that the transactions were pointless if they did not produce the balance-sheet results Enron wanted.

Merrill Lynch, for example, knew that Enron was going to book $12 million in revenue on the barge deal, even though Merrill was contributing only $7 million. Merrill Lynch also knew that the electricity trades would enable Enron to make its earnings targets for the quarter and year. That achieving those targets would enhance Enron executives' compensation was not lost on the Merrill bankers.[87] Enron's financial figures were also important to the company's credit rating, and Citigroup understood that rating agencies were paying attention to the balance between earnings and cash flow from operations.[88]

Because Enron's bankers did not want to assume the risks associated with particular transactions, Enron needed to retain those risks while giving the appearance of properly recorded gains. To support Enron's desired accounting benefit, a bank might accept a verbal agreement, or pass the risks back to Enron through simultaneous transactions with other parties. Despite these clear indications that Enron intended to disguise its true financial performance, the banks often acquiesced to its desires.

In the Nigerian barge deal, a final draft of the banking agreement omitted the guaranteed rate of return and Enron's promise to take Merrill Lynch out of the deal within six months. In the electricity trades, Merrill knew that Enron would want to unwind the options before either party had a chance to exercise them. Both parties also understood that the written agreement could not include the terms that were central to the deals.[89] Merrill Lynch has asserted that in both cases the concluding dates for the deals were not negotiated up front.[90] But significant evidence suggests that the termination points were part of an understanding between the parties when the deals were struck.[91]

Considerable evidence similarly suggests that the Canadian Imperial Bank of Commerce (CIBC) received guarantees that protected its equity investments.[92] Between 1998 and 2001, CIBC participated in at least eleven and as many as thirty-four so-called FAS 140 transactions with SPEs set up by Enron.[93]

CIBC was to provide the 3 percent independent at-risk equity needed to keep the SPEs off Enron's balance sheet. But like Merrill Lynch in the Nigerian barge transaction, CIBC received verbal assurances that Enron would repay its equity. In an e-mail referencing a transaction called Hawaii, Ian Schottlaender, a managing director in CIBC's Corporate Leveraged Finance Group, wrote: "I met with Andy Fastow . . . to get his assurance of support for our structured equity commitments. He is very aware of our commitments, acknowledges their importance to Enron and fully accepts our expectation of full repayment. While he cannot, for obvious reasons, guarantee repayment—he fully anticipates our repayment as scheduled."[94]

These verbal guarantees seem to have been the usual course of business between Enron and CIBC by the time CIBC presented the Hawaii project to its credit committee.[95] Approval of the project was made contingent on the Schottlaender-Fastow conversation.[96]

The bank understood why these assurances could not be committed to writing. In a June 2001 e-mail, a CIBC employee wrote: "Unfortunately, there can be no *documented* means of guaranteeing the equity or any short-fall or the sale accounting treatment is affected" (emphasis in original). An e-mail from the previous summer elaborates: "Under no circumstances can Enron provide any documentation or make any documented undertaking that this 3% equity will be 'taken out' in a reasonable period of time. As such it was complete 'trust me.'" "Trust me" was CIBC's internal shorthand for equity not covered by a documented repayment agreement but protected by verbal promises.[97]

The Nahanni project involved unshifted risk as well, although Citigroup, the structure's designer, hardly needed signals that Enron's accounting for the transaction was misleading.[98] According to the bankruptcy examiner, Citigroup was aware of the letter of credit protecting the supposedly independent at-risk equity.[99]

The knowledge they possessed is a primary basis for the SEC's allegations against these banks. These financial advisors understood the game being played, and, in joining it, became key participants in the delinquent society that grew up around Enron.

How Bankers Ignored Their Own Control Systems

Enron's bankers not only understood their client's unprincipled motives, and tended to resolve conflicts of interest in favor of self-serving gain, but also found ways to ignore their own control and risk-management systems. These bankers often deviated from normal business processes, or disregarded the warnings they generated, when entering into transactions with Enron. The spate of legal settlements dramatically illustrates the consequences of disregarding such internal controls.

For example, Enron's year-end 1999 deals with Citigroup did not pass unimpeded through the bank's approval structure. Citigroup executives were concerned that the Nahanni transaction exposed the bank to considerable risks, and might fail an internal "appropriateness" test often applied to structured transactions.[100] Most telling, Citigroup had to convince Enron to classify T-bills as merchant investments, to enable revenues from their sale to qualify as cash flow from operations. (The parties explicitly agreed to use government securities with maturities of more than ninety days, so the T-bills would not be considered cash-equivalents under GAAP.)[101] Before making this change, Enron likely would have counted the government securities as cash, and the sale would not have qualified as cash flow.[102]

Citigroup also disregarded calls for caution from its own executives when it helped create the Sundance partnership, designed to take parts of Enron's paper and pulp business off its balance sheet. Upper-level Citigroup executives advised against participating in this transaction. Wrote David Bushnell, head of risk management for Citigroup's Global Corporate and Investment Bank: "This is a complex structured transaction which I have refused to sign off on. . . . Risk Management has not approved this transaction for the following reasons: . . . The GAAP accounting is too aggressive and a franchise risk to us if there is publicity (a la Xerox)."[103]

Alan MacDonald, head of Citigroup's Global Relationship Bank, concurred with Bushnell: "We ([the head of Global Energy and Mining] and I) share Risk's view, and if anything feel more strongly, that suitability issues and related risks when coupled with the returns make it unattractive. It would be unfortunate if both GRB relationship management and Risk's views were ignored."[104] Despite these admonitions, the transaction proceeded.[105]

Citigroup seemed unable to refuse Enron's requests. Rather than simply limit the amount of credit it extended to Enron, Citigroup implemented an unusual insurance-like investment vehicle that would afford some shelter should Enron become unable to pay its debts. The bank designed and sold securities that derived their value from Enron's creditworthiness: as long as Enron continued to pay Citigroup, it continued to pay investors who purchased the securities. If Enron could not meet its obligations, Citigroup did not have to continue making payments. According to a class-action complaint filed by Enron shareholders, this was the largest such hedging program not just in Citigroup's history but ever.[106]

Citigroup was not the only bank whose employees expressed concern about the propriety of certain transactions with Enron. Royal Bank of Canada became aware that rating agencies had grossly miscalculated the amount of debt Enron held in off-balance-sheet SPEs, which presumably would affect the company's credit rating, and thus RBC's willingness to extend it further credit. However, RBC's risk-management group appears to have endeavored to keep this disparity quiet, and the company continued to participate in structured-debt transactions with Enron.[107]

A JPMorgan Chase executive who recognized that prepay transactions with Enron were actually loans suggested that JPMC keep an eye on them "so they don't disappear from [JPMC's] radar screen."[108] In essence, the executive was saying that JPMC had information about potentially illegal accounting that the market did not have. Rather than stopping the practice, this individual suggested considering it when evaluating Enron—to ensure that *the bank* did not get burned.

The two Merrill Lynch transactions from year-end 1999 offer a closer look at warnings from internal control groups that went ignored. Two Merrill Lynch committees, in reviewing these proposed deals independently, heard concerns from others (in the case of the Nigerian Barge deal) or expressed their own (in the case of the electricity trade). Yet neither committee saw fit to halt Merrill's involvement.

Red Flags in the Nigerian Barge Proposal

The Nigerian barge proposal ran into problems almost immediately. After receiving the initial proposal from Enron vice president McMahon, relationship manager Furst sought assistance from Merrill's Asset Lease and Finance group. James Brown, head of that group, initially rebuffed the transaction, because his group had no experience with that type of asset. Brown reconsidered only after Schuyler Tilney, another Merrill manager, convinced him that "the transaction was extremely important to Merrill Lynch's relationship with Enron." Brown remained opposed to the transaction, but agreed to help find it a forum.

On December 22, 1999, Merrill's Debt Markets Commitment Committee (DMCC) met to discuss the proposed transaction. Brown raised several concerns, including the propriety of Enron's intended accounting. He questioned (1) whether Enron could account for the transaction as a sale; (2) Merrill's lack of control over the barges, and Enron's intent to take Merrill out of the transaction quickly; (3) Enron's plan to book a $12 million gain, even though Merrill Lynch was investing only $7 million; (4) the risk to its reputation if Merrill was seen as aiding and abetting Enron in manipulating its income statement; and (5) the lack of a written agreement by Enron to buy back the barges.

Some DMCC members told Brown not to worry about Merrill Lynch's reputation, because the anticipated small gain was not really significant ("material") to Enron. Others observed that documents provided by Furst indicated that Enron had consulted with its accountants, and that Merrill Lynch was therefore protected from potential accounting problems.

But the DMCC was not excited about Enron's verbal assurances that it would buy back the barges. As a condition for not opposing the transaction, the committee required Dan Bayly, head of Merrill's Investment Banking Division, to secure confirmation from Fastow that Enron would take Merrill out of the transaction before the six-month period expired. The DMCC also wanted Bayly to impress on Fastow that this was not a transaction in which Merrill Lynch would normally participate, and that the bank expected to be rewarded with future business.

Thomas Davis, head of Merrill's Corporate and Institutional Client Group, ultimately approved the bank's participation in the transaction, whereupon Bayly secured the oral commitment from Fastow. Bayly then called Brown and instructed him to close the deal.

More Red Flags

With respect to the electricity trades, Merrill Lynch maintains that it "engaged in an extensive review and approval process designed to ensure that the [trades] (1) were legitimate 'at-risk' transactions, (2) were fully considered by senior Merrill Lynch personnel in every key area, and (3) were known and approved by senior Enron management and Arthur Andersen."[109] This is not inaccurate. However, Merrill Lynch failed to heed the warning signs generated by those processes.

The STRC evaluated the proposed electricity trades. Unlike the DMCC, the STRC appeared to have serious concerns when it considered the proposed transaction on December 30, 1999. Committee members were leery of the size of the gain Enron intended to book from the transaction, and its effect on the compensation and bonuses of senior Enron management. Committee members also raised doubts about the propriety and true nature of Enron's intended accounting.

To alleviate these concerns, the committee insisted on confirmation from Enron's accountant, Arthur Andersen, that it had approved the proposed accounting. The STRC meeting was adjourned to give Furst and Tilney, Merrill's relationship managers, time to contact Enron. When the committee reconvened, Enron chief accounting officer Richard Causey joined the meeting by phone, and assured members that Arthur Andersen had approved Enron's accounting in the matter.

Even this did not allay concerns, and some committee members asked to speak directly with Andersen. Causey opposed the request. The STRC then asked Causey to provide written confirmation that Andersen had approved the transaction, and to clearly state that Merrill had not provided any accounting advice to Enron in connection with it. Merrill Lynch's counsel prepared such a letter and forwarded it to Causey, who signed it and faxed it back to Merrill on December 31, 1999. The letter read in part:

This letter is to acknowledge and confirm that:

(i) Neither Merrill Lynch nor any of its affiliates or their respective employees (collectively, "Merrill Lynch") have provided accounting advice to Enron in respect of the Transactions;

(ii) Enron has reviewed the Transactions with its outside auditors, Arthur Andersen, and Arthur Andersen concurs with Enron's proposed accounting for the Transactions; and

(iii) Enron has not relied upon Merrill Lynch in any way to determine the appropriate market value of the Transactions.[110]

With the signed letter in hand, Merrill Lynch closed the electricity trade transactions with Enron on December 31, 1999.

How did Merrill justify going ahead with these deals in the face of so many red flags? From a broad perspective, it is unclear whether anyone at Merrill Lynch other than Furst and Tilney was aware of the concurrent transactions. There is no indication that the DMCC and STRC communicated with each other regarding either deal. If true, this reflects a fundamental problem with Merrill's relationship-management system, particularly given the apparent belief of some DMCC members that the gain from the barge transaction was not material to Enron.[111]

Although arguably immaterial when viewed alone, the Nigerian barge deal's importance becomes clear when placed in full context. First, the DMCC knew that without the $12 million in earnings Enron was planning to report from the deal, it would not make its fourth-quarter numbers.[112] Second, between the barge deal and the electricity trades, Merrill Lynch helped Enron book $62 million in fourth-quarter earnings—or 26 percent of its reported earnings that quarter.[113]

All told, Merrill Lynch's review committees raised red flags on these proposed transactions on *seven* distinct occasions:

Red Flag #1: The STRC asked for assurances from Enron that Arthur Andersen had approved the recording of the electricity trades as income from operations.

As noted, after reviewing the initial proposal, the STRC had enough reservations about the trades to insist on more information before it would allow the deal to proceed. Whether it asked for these assurances because it did not fully understand the accounting for the proposed trades, or because it actually knew (or believed) that they would violate GAAP, the committee was clearly uncomfortable with this unusual transaction.

Red Flag #2: When Causey, Enron's chief accounting officer, joined the committee by conference call to confirm that Andersen had approved the proposed trades, STRC members asked to speak directly to Andersen.

Enron's chief accounting officer should have known whether the deal violated accounting rules. The fact that members of the STRC did not take Causey at his word speaks to the magnitude of their suspicions that the proposed transaction potentially violated GAAP.

Red Flag #3: Causey opposed the committee's request for direct access to Andersen.

Why would a company's chief accounting officer impede a business partner's access to the company's auditor? The issue was certainly not privacy. Was it logistical? Perhaps the request came late in the process, and the trades needed to be closed before the end of business the following day. However, if Arthur Andersen was already up to speed on the deal, as Causey claimed, it could have joined the conference call. Or was Causey confirming a conversation he had never had with Andersen?

Red Flag #4: Denied direct access to Andersen, the STRC demanded that Causey sign a letter from Merrill's legal staff confirming that (1) Merrill had not provided any accounting advice to Enron, (2) Enron had reviewed the transaction with Andersen, and (3) Enron had determined the value of the transaction.

Why didn't Merrill Lynch simply refuse to participate in the deal, if the committee was so concerned that it required documentation denying culpability on Merrill's part? The answer would seem to be the $17 million fee Merrill expected for participating in the transaction. Merrill believed that the legal document signed by Causey shifted any legal risk back to Enron. Even if it did, the bank had a responsibility to protect the public by informing regulators such as the SEC. Merrill Lynch's principal business is predicated on trust. When Merrill decided to participate in the deal, it broke its commitment to its investors.

Red flags similarly signaled danger ahead in Merrill Lynch's participation in the Nigerian barge transaction:

Red Flag #5: James Brown, head of Merrill's Asset Lease and Finance Group, first turned down the deal on the grounds that his group had no experience with that type of asset.

Brown's reaction was sound: he knew that his group would need to rely on Enron to assess the deal's price, value, and risk. But Brown's sound business philosophy was overturned: he was told that the barge transaction had "relationship" ramifications, and that it was important to Enron.

Red Flag #6: When the DMCC convened to review the Nigerian barge proposal, Brown renewed his objections, this time adding that the lack of a written guarantee that Enron would either repurchase the barges or find a willing buyer added greatly to the risks of the transaction.

The DMCC was apparently almost as concerned as Brown about risks associated with the barges, and insisted on at least a verbal commitment from Enron's highest levels that Merrill Lynch would be taken out of the deal. Although Fastow gave his oral commitment to Bayly, Merrill's head of investment banking, two questions remain. Why was this verbal agreement not put in writing? And if Enron and Merrill executives knew that a written agreement would nullify the transaction's desired outcome, why would Andersen allow the deal, whether written or oral?

Red Flag #7: The DMCC made a point of directing Bayly to impress on Fastow and Enron that the transaction was not one in which Merrill Lynch would normally participate, and that the bank expected to be rewarded with future business.

The DMCC knew that the bank was not in a position to sell the barges, and would have to rely on Enron to secure a buyer and a return on its capital. To compensate for these uncertainties, Merrill Lynch explicitly asked that its participation be reciprocated. Here again, with a red flag flying, why not simply refuse to participate in the deal? Merrill Lynch stood to gain only $775,000. The allure of more lucrative future deals with Enron was apparently sufficient in the eyes of the Merrill executives to warrant the risk. Merrill Lynch may have again believed that Andersen would provide cover for any wrongdoing. However, the verdict in the trial—the jury found that Merrill Lynch knowingly and willingly colluded with Enron to defraud investors—suggests that no credible explanation was forthcoming.

In the face of its own beliefs about the impropriety of these transactions, Merrill Lynch chose to willingly participate in Enron's fraud. What's more, even though the bankers believed that the deals were material to the investor community, they informed no one. They chose instead to collect their fees, please their client, and invite further business.

Explaining the Bankers' Collusion

Why did so many red flags go unheeded? During a National Public Radio show on October 15, 2004, host Steve Inskeep spoke with *Fortune*'s Bethany McLean, one of the first business journalists to challenge Enron's strategy and results—in her case, six months before the company's collapse. Asked by Inskeep, "Why wouldn't Wall Street firms raise more red flags here?" McLean answered: "Specifically, in the case of Enron it was one of the highest fee-paying companies on Wall Street, so everybody wanted their business. And firms were willing to do whatever it took to get that business. The money came far ahead of the ethics."[114]

Enron in the late 1990s was one of the biggest catches among the Fortune 500, and, in the case of Merrill Lynch, an important prospect for its Houston office. Enron was also a splashy prospect. The company was famous for visiting top business schools and offering not only out-of-this-world compensation packages, but also opportunities to develop new ideas, experiment and take risks, and build new businesses. Jeff Skilling was a star in the making, and an Enron business card commanded respect. According to one Enron senior financial executive, "I believed I was working for a strong aggressive company that hires very smart people, some of the brightest minds around. And we solved extremely difficult problems."[115]

Merrill Lynch was not blind to Enron's star-quality status, and clearly wanted to join its inner circles. Merrill employees earned badges of honor in launching SPEs and helping engineer other creative financial transactions on behalf of Enron. They basked in the glow of being insiders, and surely used the opportunity to strengthen their personal networks. Nor was Merrill Lynch alone in wanting to enjoy the perks that accrued in being part of the team.

Indicative of Merrill's strong desire to increase its book of business, and the emotional satisfaction from being associated with Enron, are the striking speed and lack of deliberate consideration that characterize both the electricity trades and the Nigerian barge transaction. The highly complex electricity trades, which needed to be closed on December 31, 1999, were not presented to the STRC until December 30. If ever there was an instance of end-of-year management of earnings, this was it.

The Nigerian barge transaction was similarly presented to the DMCC on December 22, 1999. The deal closed five days later, on December 29, against a drop-dead deadline of December 31—again to enable Enron to book "revenues" for the calendar year. Neither deal could in any way have been construed as business as usual for Merrill Lynch, yet both were closed in record time.

Although Merrill seems to have had a solid policy for approving transactions, which included review panels composed of senior executives, hindsight leads us to question the strength of the process. It seems peculiar that no member of the review panels was an expert in financial accounting. At a minimum, the transactions should have received sign-off from both the legal and accounting departments. Although such measures might not have prevented either deal from being consummated, Merrill clearly cut many corners in the interest of both time and money.

A final factor helps explain Merrill Lynch's blind eye to the red flags raised by pending transactions: executive compensation. Public evidence is insufficient to document Merrill Lynch's compensation plan in detail. However, information suggests that the personal rewards available to employees who did not strictly comply with the spirit and technical details of accounting rules were significant. As an example, Daniel Bayly, one-time global head of Merrill Lynch's investment-banking division, made $10 million in salary and bonuses in 1999.[116]

Enron, too, was cast in this mold. Former Enron treasurer Glisan earned $100,000 in salary and a "modest" $20,000 in bonuses in 1996, his first year with the company. He ended his employment in 2001 with a salary of nearly $200,000 and $1 million in bonuses. From the witness stand he described how he saw the company manufacture earnings during his years at Enron.[117]

Enron's Bankers Routinely Failed to Address Conflicts of Interest

Like any other relationship, a banking relationship encompasses multiple interests beyond those of bank and client. When the client is a corporation, both parties are accountable to their respective shareholders. Many other groups and individuals, including suppliers, commodities traders, and the public at large, also have interests to varying degrees. Natural and healthy competition among these interests serves to balance the impact of any one decision.

In the case of Enron, two conflicts of interest undercut this natural competition, distorting the innate equilibrium and putting Enron and its banking partners and investors in severe danger. One involved bank employees who sought personal as opposed to institutional gain from their dealings with Enron. The other stemmed from institutional pressure to increase revenues from investment banking, even if that required muzzling astute financial analysts.

Enron's banks undoubtedly expected institutional interests to take precedence over their employees' personal interests. Yet employees of DLJ and Merrill Lynch invested their own money as well as personal time in ventures with Enron. Much as Enron employees such as Fastow and Kopper prospered at Enron's expense participating in the Chewco and LJM partnerships, individual bankers made personal investments that were diametrically at odds with their employers' best interests.

For example, ninety-five Merrill Lynch employees invested nearly $11 million in LJM2.[118] Among them were Furst and Tilney, the bank's key employees in the Houston area, who invested $200,000 and $750,000, respectively.[119] Merrill Lynch Investment Bank was also an investor in LJM2. Thus, when LJM2 purchased the bank's equity share of the barges, the bank was still indirectly invested in them.[120] Apparently, Merrill Lynch saw no problem with this arrangement, or with Fastow's dual role as buyer and seller in his positions with LJM2 and Enron, because the bank created the Merrill Lynch/LJM2 Co-Investment LP as an investment vehicle for its own executives. This seems odd, given the substantial fees Merrill was drawing from Enron. Like Fastow and Kopper, Merrill Lynch was now working both sides of the table.

DLJ employees also became personally involved in Enron-related entities on at least two occasions. According to Credit Suisse First Boston (CSFB), which purchased DLJ, Laurence Nath and Dominic Capolongo, both executives in DLJ's structured-finance group, served as directors of Atlantic Water Trust from November 2000 to November 2001, at Enron's request.[121] Atlantic Water Trust was the holding entity to which Enron shifted Azurix in the Marlin transaction—enabling Enron to move $1.9 billion in debt off its balance sheet and pay off $900 million of that indebtedness.[122]

What's more, during an October 2000 public stock offering, twelve DLJ employees, including Nath and Capolongo, personally invested $1 million in Osprey Trust.[123] Osprey Trust was one of the SPEs Enron used to raise money in the Whitewing transactions, designed to manage Enron's financial statement (see Chapter 3).[124] In all, DLJ's investments in Enron-related partnerships and SPEs totaled nearly $192 million, including a $5 million contribution to LJM2.[125]

Relationships between investment-banking and investment-advisory analysts gave rise to a second cluster of conflicts of interest. Despite supposed firewalls between the two groups and claims to the contrary, some banks appear to have pressured investment-research analysts to give Enron good ratings. One reason is that the banks wanted to obtain and retain Enron's banking business. A second reason is that Enron owed the banks a great deal of money. Knowing that they stood to lose significant sums if Enron went under, the banks worried that word would spread that Enron was on thin ice, jeopardizing investor confidence. All those verbal guarantees of repayment, they realized, would be worthless in bankruptcy court. Enron's banks therefore let their desire for profits undermine the objectivity of their own sell-side analysts. Those who produced reports that did not paint Enron in a most favorable light were pressured, threatened, and even terminated. And contact with Enron even influenced analysts who were not subject to such treatment.

The most blatant example of such destructive conflicts of interest occurred at Merrill Lynch. Equity analyst John Olson covered the energy sector for Merrill from 1992 through 1998.[126] In mid-summer 1997, Olson adjusted his intermediate-term rating on Enron stock from "accumulate" to "neutral," with a long-term "buy" designation.[127] This change did not go unnoticed by Enron, and would lead to Olson's termination a year later.[128]

In a memo dated April 1998, Schuyler Tilney and Rick Gordon, important Enron relationship managers, advised Merrill CEO Herb Allison that Andy Fastow had recently informed them that Enron would not select Merrill to participate in a large common-stock offering. Enron felt that the bank's inclusion "would effectively constitute an endorsement of Olson's valuation methodology of the Company, and, in particular of his negative valuation of Enron's burgeoning retail electricity and gas business."[129]

Tilney and Gordon wrote: "DLJ, whose top-ranked analyst has Enron's stock on his recommended list, will lead the offering and all of the co-managers have Buy ratings on Enron."[130] They went on to explain why they believed the relationship between Enron and Merrill Lynch had "been strained for a long period of time." "First," they maintained, "John [Olson] has not been a real supporter of [Enron], even though it is the largest, most successful company in the industry. Second, Enron views his research as flawed, particularly as it relates to a valuation of certain of its businesses (e.g., retail marketing). Finally, John often makes snide and potentially embarrassing remarks about [Enron] in meetings with analysts while in the presence of Ken [Lay] and Jeff [Skilling]."[131]

In response to the letter, Allison contacted Enron and asked the company to reconsider.[132] Enron agreed to use Merrill Lynch as comanager for 15 million shares of common stock Enron had decided to add to the offering.[133] Less than a month later, on May 22, Olson was fired.[134] After his termination, some within Merrill Lynch perceived that its relationship with Enron improved. Merrill Lynch soon received additional business from Enron worth $45 million to $50 million in fees, although it is unclear whether that business was conditional on Olson's removal.[135]

Another analyst apparently done in by a less-than-glowing review of Enron was Citigroup's Don Dufresne, who covered Enron between 1997 and 1999.[136] Dufresne "was not constructive in his views on Enron," according to Fastow, who further complained that during the previous equity offering Dufresne had not adequately supported the company.[137] Fastow cited Dufresne's position as one reason Citigroup had been relegated to a minor role in the Azurix initial public offering.

"Enron," Fastow remarked, "would like to see some progress in [Citigroup's] equity research view of Enron before the relationship with [Citigroup] can really progress."[138] Fastow made those comments in the spring of 1999. By the end of the year, Dufresne had been fired.[139] He was replaced by former Schroders analyst Raymond Niles. Citigroup purchased Schroders in 2000, and Enron's backing apparently landed Niles the position. Mark Koenig, head of Enron's investor-relations department, specifically requested the appointment.[140]

Though their experiences were less extreme than Olson's and Dufresne's, other analysts felt Enron's influence. The experiences of two CSFB analysts provide interesting cases. In 2001 Curt Launer, who had worked for DLJ when it was acquired by CSFB, headed the bank's energy-sector equity team.[141] His fixed-income counterpart was Jill Sakol.[142] The relationship between Enron and CSFB seems to have tainted their views in different ways.

In 1997, while he was still with DLJ, *Institutional Investor* named Launer the country's top natural gas analyst.[143] An article regaling his work described him as regretting maintaining a buy recommendation on Enron, because it had lagged the S&P 500 for the previous two years. "It had more issues than I ever bargained for when I recommended it," Launer told the magazine.

Yet seven months later, in April 1998, Launer was touting the stock in *Fortune*.[144] The following month, DLJ was the lead underwriter for Enron's offering of 50 million shares of common stock, which netted the bank more than $10 million—its largest one-time fee from Enron. From that point on, Launer was a staunch Enron supporter, and CSFB never publicly wavered in its support of Enron, despite apparent internal misgivings. In June 2001 CSFB managing directors told an Enron executive that they believed Enron was overvalued at $40 per share, yet CSFB analyst reports put Enron's target price at $84.[145] Only Lehman Brothers held a "strong buy" rating on Enron further into 2001 than CSFB.[146]

There are two implications here. First, Enron might have rewarded DLJ for changing its tune; and second, DLJ might not have wanted to underwrite an equity offering for a company that its own analysts did not support. In either case, the fact that Enron was a CSFB client did not help the objectivity of DLJ's research team. The Chinese Wall that purportedly existed between the banking and research departments was not holding up. On at least one occasion—for six weeks from September to October 2000—Launer was brought over the wall to work on an Enron-related project: the initial public offering of New Power Co. Launer himself invested $18,000 in New Power before giving it a positive recommendation.[147]

Jill Sakol's confidence in Enron was not quite as strong as Launer's. As 2001 moved from summer to fall, she felt that Enron's debt should be downgraded. As Enron executives apparently began to have problems with her coverage, Sakol's research began to receive extra attention from CSFB investment bankers. On at least one occasion, Michael Davis, a CSFB investment-banking vice president, edited her report before it was publicly released. He "added two paragraphs . . . that may help accounts in both the US and Europe get more comfortable with the share trust deals [such as Marlin and Osprey]."[148] Even the head of the CSFB analysis department, William Battey, reminded her that the Enron relationship was important to the bank. Sakol believed she could not provide an honest public review because it would upset people within CSFB for whom Enron was an important client. She was particularly troubled because CSFB traders relied on her research to sell off the bank's fixed-income stake in the Marlin structure.[149]

In the end, both Enron and its banking partners put profits ahead of their responsibility to be honest with investors. Thus it should not be surprising that no employees of Enron's banks made a real effort to push the company's murky accounting practices into the light. Bank employees could see that they would be rewarded for assisting in the deception, and that opposing voices were stifled and punished. They could not have detected much upside to strongly contesting obvious conflicts of interest.

What this piece of business history reveals is that responsibility for the Enron story is not limited to those who worked within the walls of the company's Houston headquarters every day, or those who populated the boardroom several times a year. Many actors outside of the corporate hierarchy enabled Enron's inept management and financial deception. We have seen that along with its accountants and lawyers, Enron's bankers played a prominent role. While some of Enron's bankers had only intermittent, superficial contact with the company, those discussed in this chapter spent a great deal of time working hand-in-hand with Enron executives providing infusions of cash through complex financial structures of questionable legality.

In addition to Enron's accountants, lawyers, and bankers, governmental entities such as the SEC and IRS—and quasigovernment groups such as the credit-rating agencies—must also shoulder some responsibility for failing to warn the public about the dangers Enron's business tactics posed to investors. These "public watchdogs" performed their duties torpidly, but are less culpable than Enron's "private watchdogs," because they were not active participants in the problematic arrangements. Yet, because of their complacency, they were vulnerable to manipulation and evasion at Enron's creative hands and incapable of detecting the problems that led to Enron's collapse and collateral social damage. It is to this failure that we now turn in Chapter 7.

Enron and Its Public Watchdogs

No more attentive to its conduct and investors' interests than its private bankers, Enron's public watchdogs included three federal regulatory agencies and three credit-rating agencies.[1] The regulatory agencies were the Securities and Exchange Commission (SEC), the Federal Energy Regulatory Commission (FERC), and the Commodities Futures Trading Commission (CFTC). Unresolved questions concerning the jurisdictions of these agencies—compounded by a lack of interagency communication, and inadequate review and enforcement procedures—enabled Enron to skirt regulatory limits, and critical information about its operations to go undetected.

Even more troubling was the remarkably ineffective job of the three quasi-public credit-rating agencies, Moody's, S&P, and Fitch. Although technically private enterprises, these agencies derive much of their power and income from their SEC designation as nationally recognized statistical rating organizations (NRSROs).[2] That designation—tantamount to a government-sanctioned license—has all but turned the rating industry into an oligopoly, and has arguably given these agencies greater public responsibility than other professional service providers, such as banks and accounting firms.

In assessing the credit risk Enron posed, the credit-rating agencies discharged that responsibility poorly. These agencies failed to publicly report—and to some extent even detect—Enron's deteriorating financial condition. They misunderstood the basic nature of Enron's business, and therefore assigned improper personnel to rating teams. They settled for incomplete explanations from Enron about confusing and incomplete data. And they isolated information within organizational silos, handicapping the work of everyone involved in the credit-rating process.

The conduct of the credit-rating agencies is central to the Enron story, and remains largely unexplained in the minds of many people, including professional investors. I therefore explore the conduct and performance of these quasi-public watchdogs before addressing why federal regulatory agencies—Enron's truly public watchdogs—did not fulfill their congressionally mandated task.

Quasi-Public Watchdogs: The Credit-Rating Agencies

The financial problems Enron had tried to keep private for years became public on October 16, 2001, when the company announced a $544 million charge against earnings and $1.2 billion write-down in shareholder equity.[3] The next day, the *Wall Street Journal* published a report detailing potential financial improprieties in connection with Enron's off-balance-sheet partnerships. But it was not until November 28—six weeks later, and just five days before Enron filed for bankruptcy—that the three major U.S. credit-rating agencies finally dropped Enron's rating below investment grade. This delay occurred despite the fact that Enron had notified Moody's and Standard & Poor's of impending "accounting adjustments" two weeks before it filed for bankruptcy, according to interviews conducted for the Senate Committee on Governmental Affairs.[4]

The public questioned the downgrade delay almost immediately. Why had these titans of credit analysis failed to warn the public earlier that Enron's ability to pay its creditors was in doubt? The credit-rating agencies responded that disclosing nonpublic information in advance—including accounting adjustments—would violate confidentiality agreements. Doing so would also discourage companies from providing important information to the agencies, undermining their ability to evaluate businesses' creditworthiness.

The credit-rating agencies also insist that Enron withheld important information from credit analysts—on everything from special-purpose entities to disguised loans to ratings triggers. Why would Enron risk the wrath of bodies with such enormous power to determine its future? As the company moved from a pipeline model to a trading model, it needed ready access to capital to cover its trading activities, and that access depended heavily on its credit rating.

Yet despite the withholding of information, had the raters seen the problem coming but held their tongues? If so, why should financial markets rely so heavily on private, profit-driven entities, rather than public-interest groups, to evaluate companies' credit strength? Numerous federal and state statutes mandate that regulated entities such as investment advisors and banks purchase only securities rated as "investment grade" by an NRSRO.[5] Issuers of stocks and bonds in U.S. capital markets therefore have little choice but to hire an NRSRO—and hope for an investment-grade rating.[6]

Their government-conferred status affords credit-rating agencies enormous influence in financial markets. Remarked author Thomas Friedman, discussing Moody's on *The News Hour* with Jim Lehrer: "There are two superpowers in the world today in my opinion. There's the United States, and there's Moody's Bond Rating Service. The United States can destroy you by dropping bombs, and Moody's can destroy you by downgrading your bonds. And believe me, it's not clear sometimes who's more powerful."[7]

Why Credit Ratings Were Important to Enron

Credit ratings influenced Enron's business in several ways. Because investors use ratings as a barometer of strength, Enron's credit rating affected its stock price.[8] This effect was magnified because Enron used its stock to support a number of structured-finance transactions, including the Rhythms hedge (see Chapter 4).[9] Enron relied on special-purpose entities (SPEs) to expand access to capital and manage debt—and, in turn, many of these SPEs relied on the parent company's creditworthiness as a selling point.[10] A drop in Enron's credit rating could therefore drive down the stock price in two ways.

Credit ratings also sometimes served as a repayment trigger. If, for example, Enron's rating fell below a certain level, the company had to meet accelerated financial obligations—which sometimes required almost immediate repayment of hundreds of millions of dollars. Moody's' November 2001 downgrade of Enron from BBB to BBB-, for example, tripped a ratings trigger in the Rawhide transaction that obligated Enron to repay $690 million within fifteen days.[11] That event was unusual not because such triggers were uncommon, but because BBB- was still an investment-grade rating.[12]

Perhaps most important, Enron's credit rating affected the interest rate the company paid on loans used to finance its growth. In addition to affecting the cost of borrowing, this rating also affected its availability. Indeed, in many transactions loans were callable if Enron's credit rating declined below some "trigger point."[13] But the most dramatic effects of Enron's credit rating was felt in its energy-trading business, Enron Wholesale Services, which accounted for 66 percent of Enron's earnings before interest and taxes as early as 1999. Because the unit required substantial lines of credit to cover its trades through EnronOnline, Enron's health was tightly tethered to its credit rating.[14]

These credit-rating concerns led to Enron's problematic use of SPEs.[15] Enron's large-scale power plant projects of the late 1990s were not yielding immediate dividends.[16] The credit-rating agencies noticed the burden of supporting these new businesses as early as 1999.[17] Because maintaining an investment-grade credit rating was vital to its energy-trading business, Enron's directors and executives were reluctant to issue new debt. Enron saw SPEs as a way to meet its capital needs without damaging its credit rating.[18]

Enron also used SPEs to curb the impact on its credit rating of mark-to-market accounting. Under such accounting, Enron had to record on its quarterly income statements shifts in the value of its energy contracts.[19] To soften the impact of these shifts and meet the criteria set by credit-rating agencies, Enron began to use transactions with SPEs to boost its cash flow, lower its debt, and smooth earnings reported on financial statements.[20]

Enron perceived its credit rating to be determined primarily by five credit ratios.[21] To control these ratios, Enron employed six transaction structures: FAS 140 transactions; tax transactions; noneconomic hedges; share trust transactions; minority-interest transactions; and prepay transactions (see Chapter 3).[22] Table 7.1 shows the impact of these transactions on the five key credit ratios, as reported by Enron and adjusted by the bankruptcy examiner. My analysis in Chapter 3 showed that the examiner's conclusions are exaggerated, so these numbers should be considered suggestive.

Table 7.1.   Impact of Enron's various transaction structures on reported credit ratios

Key Credit Ratio	2000 as Reported	2000 Adjusted	% Change
Funds flow interest coverage	4.07	0.90	(78%)
Pretax interest coverage	2.54	1.11	(56%)
Funds flows from operations/ total obligations	28.8%	(0.7%)	(102%)
Total obligations/total obligations plus total shareholders' equity and certain other items	41.4%	68.3%	65%
Debt / Total capital	40.9%	68.1%	67%

Had Enron not employed structured transactions to beautify its balance sheet, the credit-rating agencies might have had a difficult time maintaining its investment-grade rating. Perhaps the most telling statistics are the most basic: Enron originally reported net income for 2000 as $979 million. After adjusting for the impact of the structured transactions, the bankruptcy examiner put the figure at $42 million. The examiner also doubled Enron's reported 2000 debt, from $10.2 billion to $22.1 billion.[23] Although the examiner's calculations are open to dispute, the reasons that Enron's balance sheet was so attractive are not.

Everyone at Enron appears to have understood the importance of credit ratings.[24] Robert Belfer, a member of the finance committee of Enron's Board of Directors, told the bankruptcy examiner, "Let me put it to you this way. If it would be adversely viewed by the credit-rating agencies, it would certainly be a cause of concern to the Finance Committee."[25] The board reluctantly approved year-end deals on several occasions, to meet the necessary financial figures. Indeed, Enron generated 95 percent of its cash flow from operations in the fourth quarter, from 1998 to 2000.[26] Referring to a finance committee meeting in December 1999, Belfer noted the directors' concern: "It was a little disturbing having these come so close to the end of the year, but there was some discussion of that, as I recall, and the idea was to not put ourselves in that position again if we could avoid it."[27]

Even employees on the lower rungs of the corporate ladder knew that credit ratings drove many deals. One Enron officer, William Brown, told the bankruptcy examiner that he "understood the amount of any given prepay transaction was determined by the cash flow Enron wanted to show the rating agencies."[28] In his self-evaluation, another Enron employee, Joe Deffner, noted the connection between Enron's credit rating and the need to create funds flow without issuing more debt or equity: "To maintain our credit rating, if Enron were to finance itself primarily or solely through simpler, on-balance sheet reported structures, 40% of each transaction would be funded by the issuance of new debt and 60% through retained earnings or new equity."[29]

Some people outside Enron understood the financial ratios credit-rating agencies consider, and helped the company control them. For example, Citigroup designed the Nahanni structure (described in Chapter 6) with an eye toward balancing earnings and cash flow from operations—a ratio to which credit-rating agencies pay particular attention.[30] Royal Bank of Canada (RBC) was clearly aware that the rating agencies tracked the ratio of cash flow to total debt. Yet when it recognized that the agencies had underestimated the amount of debt Enron had moved into SPEs by as much as $13 billion, RBC did not share that information with them.[31] Instead, the bank helped Enron manufacture financial statistics by participating in dubious structured-finance transactions.[32] Had Enron not manipulated the financial data on which the credit-rating agencies depended, its rating would surely have suffered.[33]

Enron's Historic Credit Ratings

All three U.S. credit-rating agencies had begun rating Enron by 1995. However, except for a one-notch upgrade by Moody's in March 2000, Enron's credit rating showed virtually no movement before October 29, 2001. The following chronologies make this clear:[34]

S&P Enron Rating Chronology

12/95–11/1/01:	BBB+
10/25/01:	Changed outlook to "negative"
11/1/01:	Downgraded to BBB and put on CreditWatch negative
11/9/01:	Downgraded to BBB–, remained on CreditWatch negative
11/28/01:	Downgraded to B– (decided merger with Dynegy was unlikely to go through, but Enron hadn't officially collapsed)

Moody's Enron Rating Chronology

1989–3/23/00:	Baa2
3/23/00:	Upgraded to Baa1
10/16/01:	Placed on review for downgrade (publicly announced)
10/29/01:	Senior unsecured long-term debt downgraded to Baa2; placed long-term and short-term debt on review for further downgrade
11/8/01:	Privately decided to lower to Ba2 (below investment grade)
11/9/01:	Lowered long-term debt to Baa3, short-term debt from Prime-2 (investment grade) to Not Prime (speculative/noninvestment grade)
11/27/01:	Ratings committee voted to downgrade to B2 (below investment grade)
11/28/01:	Publicly announced downgrade

Fitch Enron Rating Chronology

1993–11/5/01:	BBB+
10/25/01:	Placed on Rating Watch negative
11/5/01:	Downgraded senior debt to BBB–, lowest investment-grade rating; remained on Rating Watch negative
11/9/01:	Rated Rating Watch evolving, based on merger negotiations, reflecting skepticism about the merger's prospects (would normally have been Rating Watch positive)
11/28/01:	Downgraded to CC

Although Enron continued to receive investment-grade ratings until shortly before it filed for bankruptcy, the agencies are quick to point out that the company was never in the upper range of that grade, owing largely to its dependence on structured transactions. For example, Ronald M. Barone, managing director of Standard & Poor's Corporate and Government Ratings Group, testified at a Senate hearing: "If you looked at Enron's financial profile on its face, you would have come to the conclusion that this could have been a company with a much higher credit rating, and yet [S&P takes] into account the aggressive use of financial structures and such."[35]

Fitch's Ralph G. Pellecchia similarly held that "the complexity of the company and the types of transactions that it entered into was a factor in keeping Enron's rating in the BBB category. I don't think there's any question about that."[36] Finally, John C. Diaz, Moody's managing director of investor services, acknowledged at the same Senate hearing that his rating agency was "aware of a lot of [Enron's] structured transactions."[37]

However, the rating agencies were more than just "aware" of Enron's propensity for structured finance: they rated debt connected to such transactions on several occasions. Enron spent considerable sums on these services. According to one estimate, Moody's earned $1.5 million to $2 million per year in fees for rating Enron's publicly and privately issued debt.

Whatever their knowledge of these transactions, the rating agencies' primary defense of their failure to downgrade Enron's credit has been fraud by the entities issuing the debt.[38] For example, according to Diaz, in testimony before the Senate committee:

We asked [Enron] at one point, to try to understand the scope of their off-balance-sheet obligations, to tell us everything they had—whether it was on-balance-sheet or off-balance-sheet, so that we could make a judgment as to how we would treat it. . . . And they gave us what they termed to be the kitchen sink of everything they had, but there was a lot of information that was just not given to us. So even when we were asking directly for information, they were just withholding it.[39]

At first blush, this defense seems credible: the agencies do not typically consider fraud in their credit evaluations.[40] Instead, the agencies perceive fraud as a risk inherent in any investment—one that they cannot always detect, particularly where the perpetrator's goal is to deceive them.[41]

Yet despite explicit denial of any responsibility to detect fraud, suspicions of irregularities might well have emerged from the agencies' in-depth analyses of Enron's cash flow and reported profits. After all, several groups of independent analysts managed to detect problems using the same publicly filed documents.[42]

Take, for example, financial analyses by the Off Wall Street Consulting Group (based in Cambridge, Mass.), performed during the same period when agencies were rating Enron's debt. Applying common analytical techniques and financial ratios to Enron's reported results, these researchers saw that profit margins were declining, return on capital was low, and earnings did not meet expectations. The latter was especially true if the analysts excluded transactions between related parties, which were essentially intracompany business dealings.[43] Based on these results, Off Wall Street believed that Enron stock was overvalued, and recommended selling it.

Similarly, Howard M. Schilit, Ph.D., president and founder of the Center for Financial Research & Analysis, found that a preliminary reading of Enron's filings raised a number of red flags: "I spent an hour of my time last night going through every quarterly filing proxy, no more than an hour, and I have three pages of warnings, words like 'non-cash sales,' words like '$1 billion of related party revenue.' . . . This was beginning in March 2000."[44] Schilit's condemnation of Wall Street analysts—"But for an analyst to say there were no warning signs in the public filings, they could not have read the same public filings I did"—presumably applies to credit-rating agency analysts as well. Even modest sensitivity to the financial facts of life would have led trained credit analysts to raise many questions about Enron's public reports.

The Critical Question

Why didn't the rating agencies detect Enron's financial problems earlier in the game? Did the agencies simply duck responsibility for detecting fraud by defining such investigation as off-limits, or were other factors at work as well? Perhaps the agencies thought they were not being paid to evaluate the investment merits of the debt they were rating, and their view of their professional role excluded any systematic attention to forensic accounting and reporting of financial results. However, although such self-perceptions might partially account for inattentive financial analysis, other influences also help explain this major oversight by the credit-rating industry.

First, like many companies, Enron lobbied the agencies for better ratings, and these attempts appear to have been moderately successful. For example, a report prepared by Enron for a January 29, 2000, conference with credit-rating agencies contends that the company should be considered an AA risk, given that "the off-balance sheet obligations are not material to Enron's consolidated credit analysis."[45] Less than two months after Enron's presentations to Moody's addressing transactions with off-balance-sheet entities, the agency upgraded Enron's rating from Baa2 to Baa1.[46] That upgrade is particularly curious given that fifteen months earlier, Moody's analysts had apparently been concerned that Enron was "pressured in its category."[47] It is unclear what changed in those five quarters to make a ratings bump seem prudent.

Second, raters also simply did not dig deeply enough into Enron's finances. For example, the rating agencies seem to have assumed that the vague references to related-party transactions in Enron's public filings provided all the information they needed—even though they admittedly did not completely understand the disclosures.[48] The cultural predispositions of the agencies simply did not include searching for and exposing problems. Internal trouble, financial or otherwise, is an important factor in ratings, but—unlike short-sellers—the rating agencies do not predicate their business on unearthing hidden surprises.

According to the International Organization of Securities Commissions, credit-rating agencies "attempt to make sense of the vast amount of information available regarding an issuer or borrower, its market, and its economic circumstances in order to give investors and lenders a better understanding of the risks they face when lending to a particular borrower or when purchasing an issuer's fixed-income securities."[49] With no particular motivation to examine Enron's representations more closely, the credit-rating agencies were not sensitive to potential disclosure and reporting irregularities. Their focus was on credit risk.

Rating analysts responded to others seeking explanations of Enron's businesses with comments such as, "Do you have a year?" and "When you find out, let me know." Whether these were weak attempts at humor or exaggerated versions of the truth, they reveal an underlying lack of understanding about how Enron made its apparent profits.[50]

How agencies staffed their rating teams also contributed to their failure to detect Enron's mounting problems and accounting disguises. One agency I consulted classified Enron as a traditional energy company—rather than a financial company with both innovative products and complicated accounting. That agency then assigned analysts who lacked the financial sophistication and experience to fully understand the company's activities. When agencies requested more information on Enron's business segments, the data provided had important gaps, making it even more difficult for inexperienced staff to ferret out problems that could affect the company's creditworthiness.

Analytical silos within the agencies also impeded the flow of information, and thus their ability to connect the dots concerning Enron's true financial condition. At the aforementioned agency, for example, corporate-finance units, which focused on clients' strategy and management, often worked independently of structured-finance units, which valued assets packaged into complicated financial transactions. The former were typically populated by generalists; the latter by financial technicians who tended to ignore the work of their less-technical colleagues. Information on Enron's strategy and financial status gathered by the corporate-finance group—based on traditional but informative metrics—does not seem to have reached the structured-finance group. Meanwhile the corporate-finance unit did not have easy access to information on Enron's transactions with SPEs gathered by the structured-finance unit. Indications of problems at Enron therefore went undetected or unattended.

These structural factors provide insight on why the rating agencies failed to notice signs of deception at Enron. However, they do not explain why the agencies maintained an investment-grade credit rating as the company's problems emerged into public view. Enron's financial troubles were well known by mid-October 2001, but six weeks passed before Enron's credit rating was finally dropped to junk status.

In hearings before Congress, representatives from the rating agencies identified the promise of the Enron-Dynegy merger as the reason for the delay.[51] The raters apparently believed that the post-merger entity would be creditworthy enough to remain above that important line of demarcation. When it became clear that Dynegy and the banks keeping Enron afloat were not going to consummate the deal, the rating agencies commenced firing, and the listing enterprise heeled over and slipped beneath the roiling waters into bankruptcy.[52]

Perhaps most important was the agencies' reticence to use their "execution power" to shut the company down. They certainly understood that Enron's business model lived or died on whether the company maintained its investment-grade rating. During the months leading up to Enron's collapse, rating agencies had little desire to sell what some industry participants refer to as a "gotcha" product. They therefore avoided tripping the credit-sensitive triggers embedded in off-balance-sheet transactions. The merger possibility gave the agencies a reason to withhold a devastating downgrade until it was unavoidable.

In the end, by failing to attend closely to their own sources of information, the credit-rating agencies, like the regulatory watchdogs, failed to perform according to their own standards. Indeed, the watchdogs most damaged by Enron's collapse—or, more precisely, by their failure to see it coming—might be these agencies whose reputation as accurate evaluators of companies' creditworthiness has been tainted.

Nevertheless, the fundamental problem does not lie within the walls of Moody's, Standard & Poor's, or Fitch. The credit-rating agencies' failure is notable because the government has delegated to these private, profit-driven organizations tremendous responsibility for the public welfare. Congress's intent in establishing the NRSRO designation was to afford investors a degree of protection. But as the Enron debacle shows, the financial market's growing dependence on credit-rating agencies poses a significant hazard. Whereas the SEC, FERC, and the CFTC are accountable to the American people through congressional oversight, the NRSROs are largely free from such review. If their reputations become too tarnished, the government may have to regulate or even withdraw their licenses. In either case, the rating agencies stand to lose.

The Public Watchdogs: Federal Regulatory Agencies

As noted, the most prominent government watchdogs responsible for monitoring Enron were the CFTC, FERC, and the SEC. None of these three watchdogs had jurisdiction over Enron in its entirety, but each was charged with overseeing portions of the company's business or its affiliates and subsidiaries.[53]

By its own account, the CFTC's role is to protect "market users and the public from fraud, manipulation, and abusive practices related to the sale of commodity and financial futures and options," and "foster open, competitive, and financially sound futures and option markets."[54] FERC "is an independent agency that regulates the interstate transmission of electricity, natural gas, and oil, and also reviews proposals to build liquefied natural gas terminals and interstate natural gas pipelines as well as licensing hydropower projects."[55] The SEC's self-described primary mission is "to protect investors and maintain the integrity of the securities markets."[56]

Unlike Enron's banking partners, which stood to gain materially from participating in its deceit, these watchdogs had nothing to gain from shielding Enron from the public light. Rather, much like Enron's Board of Directors, these agencies suffered from inadequate systems and shortsighted decision making.

For its part, Enron worked hard to make regulations and enforcement agencies serve its interests.[57] Recognizing that "politics shapes our markets as much as economics," the Enron Government Affairs group, in particular, worked "aggressively in policy arenas to create and protect commercial opportunities."[58] The unit variously sought to "maintain light handed regulation" of derivative energy products, to have Enron viewed as an environmentally conscientious company should oil and gas exploration on federal land be allowed, and to get Enron-backed nominees appointed to FERC.[59]

Enron executives, led by the politically connected Kenneth Lay, also actively lobbied. Among those who participated in high-level Washington conversations was Jeffrey Skilling, who met with Treasury Secretary Paul O'Neill in April 2001 to discuss the power issues that had plagued California the previous summer.[60] (Those issues included a tenfold increase in electricity, forcing blackouts and billions of dollars of damage to the regional economy. Federal prosecutors were alleging price manipulation by Enron and twenty-four of its trading partners.)[61]

Enron's political and business strategies were forged in an environment in which exploiting regulatory ambiguities and weaknesses were commonly viewed as admirable accomplishments.[62] What was special about Enron's behavior, however, was that the company used highly questionable tactics to take advantage of regulatory "opportunities." Consider Enron's maneuvering to comply with legal statutes governing ownership of facilities that produce alternative energy (see below). Rather than selling its wind farms to a third party, Enron merely transferred the *appearance* of ownership to a related party run by CFO Andy Fastow and his deputy, Michael Kopper. In so doing, Enron retained enough control to continue to record revenues from the wind farms on its books, while preserving its ability to "repurchase" the facilities when circumstances became more favorable (that is, when prices of wind farms were less inflated).[63]

The ambiguities and weaknesses of the regulatory system that enabled Enron to conduct such maneuvers fall into two categories:

GAPS AND OVERLAPS IN REGULATORY JURISDICTION: Gaps are areas not explicitly covered by regulation, while overlaps are areas potentially covered by more than one regulatory body—and hence, where jurisdiction is unclear. Jurisdictional ambiguities permitted some Enron activities to go unscrutinized by regulators. Coordination among the public watchdogs would have sealed these holes in the regulatory system, but the agencies communicated little, if at all.

WEAK REVIEW SYSTEMS: FERC and the SEC review companies' public financial filings for problematic assertions. However, the design of their review systems hampered the ability of these agencies to recognize indications of questionable activity by Enron. Limits on agencies' review time, staffing, and the scope of their reviews presented the most significant challenges. And neither watchdog had a system in place for ensuring that previous decisions remained appropriate as Enron's businesses evolved.

Absent concerted efforts to properly oversee companies' activities, and hampered by poorly designed review systems, the public watchdogs were repeatedly outwitted by companies with a penchant for pushing every perceived advantage. Enron was one of those companies.

Gaps and Overlaps in Regulatory Jurisdiction

Gaps and overlaps both concern activities that do not fall clearly into the jurisdiction of one agency. Gaps in the regulatory framework are essentially loopholes that are attractive to all businesses, even if those gaps are at odds with conceptions of the public interest. Overlapping responsibilities can be equally problematic if regulators at different agencies do not coordinate their efforts. If each of two agencies believes the other is regulating an activity, for example, that arena essentially goes unsupervised.

Enron was not loath to benefit from both gaps and overlaps. The following examples show how jurisdictional gray areas permitted Enron to act in some cases without regulatory oversight.

REGULATORY GAPS AND LACK OF COORDINATION BETWEEN FERC AND THE CFTC. Enron's Internet commodities-trading service, EnronOnline (EOL), from which participants could buy or sell natural gas or electric power, exploited one jurisdictional gap.[64] Enron did not simply facilitate commodities trades between parties in eBay fashion, but rather was a party—as either buyer or seller—to almost every trade.[65] It was this "one-to-many" nature of EOL that likely created the jurisdictional confusion between FERC and the CFTC.[66]

The CFTC oversees commodities exchanges, but takes action only against individual market participants (such as EOL) to prevent fraud or market manipulation.[67] FERC is responsible for regulating interstate energy trading. Because EOL was essentially an extension of Enron's trading units, FERC should have had primary monitoring and enforcement responsibility. It appears, however, that neither agency took steps to determine which should be responsible for EOL until a mid-2001 FERC inquiry.[68] Even then, FERC's investigation into EOL specifically excluded the question of jurisdiction, leaving that issue for later review.[69]

Enron actively protected EOL's unregulated status, developing a "strategy to defend regulatory structure surrounding EOL and EOL products."[70] This strategy apparently included misleading regulators about the amount of oversight EOL actually received. In response to regulators' questions in June 2001, the company contended that "there is no regulatory gap," meaning that EOL was indeed subject to government oversight.[71] Yet five months later, in a November internal report, Enron Government Affairs listed "preserve EnronOnline's unregulated status" as one of its current activities.[72] The disparity between its public and private positions suggests that Enron perceived confusion among regulatory agencies to be to its advantage.

With minimal government interference, EOL became "the overwhelmingly dominant e-trading platform for natural gas and electric power."[73] Concerns that Enron would use its dominant position to manipulate prices in energy markets proved well founded. In April 2004, Enron agreed to pay

$35 million in fines to settle charges by the CFTC. EOL energy traders had caused an artificial spike in natural gas prices on July 19, 2001, by purchasing large amounts of the commodity in a short period of time, and then quickly unwinding, or nullifying, those positions.[74]

After its own belated investigation, FERC concluded that EOL gave Enron knowledge of market conditions unavailable to its competitors. This informational trading advantage from EOL was highly lucrative for Enron, which could absorb losses in physical markets because of prices in financial markets. Enron manipulated thinly traded physical markets to profit in financial markets.[75]

For example, the energy traders who manipulated the market on July 19, 2001, coordinated their activities with Enron's traders of financial derivatives. The latter took short positions in natural gas as the spot price ran up, knowing that it would come back down almost immediately.[76] FERC also concluded that Enron used EOL to engage in numerous "wash trades," which deceived "EOL users by giving the impression of a much deeper and more developed market, thus increasing the industry's faith in EOL."[77] (FERC defines a wash trade as "a prearranged pair of trades of the same good between the same parties, involving no economic risk and no net change in beneficial ownership. These trades expose the parties to no monetary risk and serve no legitimate business purpose.") EOL made some of these wash trades with Enron affiliates.[78] Such manipulative activity was more difficult to detect because EOL "was operated entirely under Enron's discretion."

In light of EOL's potential for misuse, it is unfortunate that neither the CFTC nor FERC analyzed the jurisdictional question sooner. Had other questions regarding Enron not bubbled to the surface, perhaps neither agency would have taken any investigatory steps at all.

REGULATORY OVERLAPS AND LACK OF COORDINATION BETWEEN FERC AND THE SEC. Both the SEC and FERC—under different statutes and circumstances—are responsible for determining whether a firm is a public-utility holding company, and whether it qualifies for an exemption from that designation.[79] However, FERC often essentially delegated this responsibility to the SEC.

FERC policy was to accept SEC decisions on some exemptions for public-utility holding companies. If the SEC denied an application, FERC followed suit. If the SEC approved an application, FERC did likewise. As part of that policy, FERC treated as exempt any company with a "good-faith" application pending at the SEC.[80] However, because FERC refused to pursue any inquiry that might be seen as encroaching on the SEC, it considered every application to the SEC for an exemption—for all intents and purposes—to have been made in good faith.[81] What's more, neither agency communicated with the other about the jurisdictional question.[82] This is the sort of confusion from which Enron benefited.

The spring of 2000 found Enron in the middle of two related business negotiations. It was formally repurchasing the portion of the Zond Wind Energy Corp. it had sold to an SPE controlled by Fastow and Kopper, and it was also trying to sell Portland General Electric to Sierra Pacific Resources.[83] Zond, a producer of alternative energy, would be less valuable if owned by a public-utility holding company—because, in that case, the law would prohibit it from engaging in certain revenue-producing activities and charging higher rates.[84] FERC was responsible for enforcing this statute. If it owned Portland General, Enron would be considered a public-utility holding company, unless it could meet the criteria for exemption, or qualify for an SEC exemption recognized by FERC.

Enron did not qualify directly for the FERC exemption, but the jurisdictional overlap and the two agencies' failure to communicate enabled Enron to circumvent this regulatory impediment. Enron submitted an application for an exemption to the SEC on April 14, 2000.[85] When Enron filed for bankruptcy nearly two years later, the application was still pending.[86] Because of this, FERC accepted Enron's contention that it was entitled to an exemption.[87]

During those two years, FERC never contacted the SEC to discuss Enron's unresolved application or ask whether it had been made in good faith.[88] Nor did the SEC contact FERC. Of course, the SEC cannot contact every other agency its decisions might affect. However, two factors weighed in favor of reaching out to FERC in this case. First, Enron's application to the SEC made it clear that FERC had an interest in the outcome.[89] And second, the SEC had agreed to an Enron request to reserve its decision until Enron had divested itself of Portland General.[90] The SEC would have been well advised to notify FERC when two proposed sales of Portland General fell through.[91]

A post-mortem review of the performance of FERC and the SEC by the staff of the Senate Governmental Affairs Committee described the lack of communication on the appropriateness of Enron's application:

The SEC, for its part, observed that the decision to rely on a good faith application was FERC's and suggested that it was up to FERC to determine if the application met that agency's standards for good faith. FERC staff, for its part, argued that the application was made to the SEC and that an attempt by FERC to determine whether such an application was in good faith before the SEC had a chance to rule on it would be preemptively second guessing its sister agency's decision.[92]

FERC's approach of adopting SEC decisions is not inherently problematic. However, FERC should keep abreast of cases where it has essentially ceded its jurisdiction to the other agency.[93] For that reason alone, FERC should have initiated communication with the SEC regarding the status and good-faith nature of Enron's application. Instead, FERC kept silent.

With no regulatory agency examining Enron's status as a public-utility holding company or its ownership of Zond, the alternative energy producer continued to receive preferential treatment, as dictated by statute. The benefits of that preferential treatment, such as its freedom to charge higher rates for energy, flowed to Zond's owner, Enron.

Flawed Reviews by the SEC and FERC

By law, corporations must file certain documents with designated government agencies. The systems that the SEC and FERC used to review these documents for legal compliance were crippled by both volume and design. The systems therefore afforded the public watchdogs little opportunity to detect hints, clues, or even blatant announcements that Enron was testing the outer limits of the law through ever more daring strategies.

FERC and the SEC also lacked systems for ensuring that important decisions continued to be appropriate as time passed and Enron's businesses changed. The SEC simply had no process for reviewing earlier decisions. FERC had such a system, but it was driven by a company's peers: the agency reviewed an earlier decision only if another company brought a potential problem to its attention. Even then, the agency's participation might be best characterized as reluctant.

SEC REVIEW OF ENRON'S FILINGS.   Several of Enron's SEC filings contained elements that might have merited investigation.[94] In particular, the murky footnotes purporting to explain related-party transactions in Enron's 1999 and 2000 Form 10-K—and the many unconsolidated equity affiliates listed in its 2000 10-K—hint at deliberate attempts to keep information off its financial statements.[95] Despite these indications of wrongdoing, they slipped past the SEC undetected because of the agency's limited resources and the nature of its review process.[96]

The SEC's Division of Corporate Finance does not review every filing it receives.[97] The division gives priority to "transactional" filings—especially those related to initial public offerings. Such filings, which companies submit as needed, include "registration statements for newly-offered securities," "documents concerning tender offers," and "filings related to mergers and acquisitions." The division devotes little attention to periodic filings, which companies must submit on a schedule. These include "annual and quarterly filings (Forms 10-K and 10-Q)," "proxy materials sent to shareholders before an annual meeting," and "annual reports to shareholders."[98]

The SEC screens all transactional filings to determine whether they require closer examination. However, it subjects few periodic filings to such preliminary evaluation. Instead, the agency endeavors to "complete a full financial review of each issuer's filings in at least one of every three years— a review goal of about 30 to 35 percent of annual filings per year."[99] The SEC calculates this time period from the date of completion of the last review.[100] However, over the decade ending in 2000, growing disparity between the size of its workload and that of its workforce hampered the SEC's productivity.[101] In 2001, for example, the agency reviewed only 16 percent of all annual filings—half its stated goal.[102] The agency began its last financial review of an Enron annual report in 1997, and completed it in 1999; Enron was not due for another review until 2002.[103]

SEC staff members maintain that the fact that the agency screened periodic filings infrequently is irrelevant, because such a review would not have singled out Enron's 10-Ks and 10-Qs for further examination.[104] According to these staff members, "SEC reviewers may look at whether a company has clearly explained its accounting policies (e.g., how it calculates certain revenue or how it determines in what period it records that revenue), but they generally will not look at whether those policies have been applied appropriately in a particular instance."[105] This review process leaves many opportunities for misrepresentation wide open for exploitation.

FERC REVIEW OF ENRON'S FILINGS.   As noted, FERC is responsible for determining whether producers of alternative energy qualify for certain economic benefits, such as the ability to raise revenues in specific ways and charge higher rates. For an alternative energy facility to qualify, a public-utility holding company may not own more than 50 percent of it.[106] This provision prompted Enron to transfer half its ownership rights in Zond Wind Energy Corp. to RADR, a partnership run by Fastow and Kopper. Although the propriety of that transaction is questionable, an equally important question is why FERC found that such an ownership arrangement satisfied legal provisions.

The problematic answer is that FERC's process for reviewing the ownership of alternative energy producers is seriously flawed. Although the law details specific ownership rules, FERC largely ignores them. Instead, the agency focuses on ensuring that facilities use production techniques that qualify for the exemption:

> According to FERC staff, [applications to receive the statutory benefits] at the staff level are reviewed by engineers or others with technical experience to determine the [applicant facility's] compliance with technical requirements, but typically no one with financial expertise reviews the applications for conformity with the ownership requirements.[107]

Companies were thus free to claim whatever ownership arrangement they wanted. Enron simply asserted that RADR controlled 50 percent of the Zond wind farms, and FERC accepted the claim.[108] Enron executives were apparently so confident that FERC would not question the transaction and the resulting ownership that their presentation to Enron's board noted that it "satisfies FERC for transfer of ownership."[109]

ONGOING MONITORING.   The Investment Company Act of 1940 imposes special requirements on companies engaged primarily in "investing, reinvesting, or trading in securities."[110] However, the SEC may exempt a company from these requirements, "if and to the extent that such exemption is necessary or appropriate in the public interest and consistent with the protection of investors and the purposes fairly intended by the policy and provisions of [the Act]."[111] On March 13, 1997, the agency exempted Enron from the act's enhanced disclosure requirements, and from limits on investment activities and transactions by affiliates.[112]

However, the SEC had no way to monitor whether the evolution of Enron's business made the exemption inappropriate.[113] As Enron followed Skilling's asset-light strategy away from the pipeline business toward an energy-trading model, the company began to resemble the kind of firm that the Investment Company Act was designed to cover. This late-1990s metamorphosis—combined with Enron's staggering growth rate, and the SEC's earlier decision to allow Enron to use mark-to-market accounting—could have been grounds for revisiting the exemption.[114] But without any routine or required showing that the exemption should still apply, Enron remained free to engage in transactions denied other investment companies. Enron could also disclose less information than those companies. Having no standard follow-up process, the SEC did not review either of these practices.

Unlike the SEC, FERC occasionally did revisit some of its decisions on whether alternative energy producers qualify for economic benefits. However, FERC's approach to such review was hardly strenuous. In fact, FERC largely relied on the honesty of a company and the diligence of its peers in evaluating the appropriateness of previous decisions.

The SEC's process for reviewing ownership of qualifying facilities typically begins only when a facility experiences a material change in ownership. The owner must confirm that the facility remains qualified for its exemption. The owner can ask FERC to formally recertify the facility, or it can "self-certify," asserting that it still meets the criteria. Third parties can intervene in a formal FERC recertification, or petition the FERC for a declaratory order in the case of a self-certified facility.[115]

In Enron's case, FERC blunted the effectiveness of even this meager monitoring tool. Southern California Edison—an interested party in the recertification of Zond—cited Enron's failure to dispose of Portland General Electric in a motion to FERC for intervention. However, FERC noted that Zond had self-certified its ownership status, and thus that the agency had no formal action in which to intervene. Instead, FERC suggested that Southern California Edison pay a $16,000 filing fee and call its intervention motion a "petition for declaratory order."[116] Southern California Edison did not pursue this recommended intervention process. Still, its initial motion to FERC should have put the agency on notice that Zond's ownership might not satisfy legal requirements. But the agency apparently chose not to take any action until the Senate Committee on Governmental Affairs announced its investigation of FERC.[117]

Cleaning Up the Mess

Enron did not discriminate in its willingness to push legal limits. Rather than be satisfied with creating and dominating the online marketplace for electricity and natural gas, the company tried to wring every last advantage from its position. Even when it stood to gain relatively little in the grand scheme of its total business, as with the Zond wind farms, where all its maneuverings earned it only an additional $176 million, Enron did not play it safe. The implication is that it saw little risk of being caught.[118] Enron turns out to have been right.

Regulators were simply not up to the task. Regulations and oversight practices were porous; recognition and reaction slow. Just as Enron's control systems were left in the backwash of its turbocharged incentive system, so the regulatory framework was no match for the company's aggressive strategies. Even after it was notified that Enron's ownership of Zond might invalidate the wind farm's status as a qualifying facility, FERC resisted initiating an investigation until nearly ten months after Enron filed for bankruptcy. And it took prodding from the U.S. Senate to convince the agency to determine what role it should have played in overseeing businesses such as EnronOnline.[119]

The SEC and the CFTC fared as poorly, offering little resistance to Enron's manipulations. Had the regulators communicated in some way, their combined efforts and information might have sniffed out some improprieties and prevented others. Instead, acting alone, they could do little more than clean up the mess Enron left in its wake.

Enron executives were a bright, creative, aggressive lot. A patchwork regulatory system overseen by lenient public watchdogs was not sufficient to contain them. The watchdogs communicated inefficiently, had little time and inclination to adequately review public filings, and, perhaps most important, were inclined to take Enron at its word. There was little chance any would bark. Enron's people seem to have understood this. The first yelp did not emanate from any watchdog until the rating agencies lowered Enron to below investment grade, after the Dynegy merger disintegrated. By then, no one could protect Enron's investors.

By some estimates, Enron was functionally insolvent well before it announced formal bankruptcy. When it finally filed for bankruptcy protection, Enron defaulted on more than $10 billion worth of bonds. Had either government agencies or credit-rating agencies recognized and acted earlier on the company's growing financial dysfunction, the blow investors received on December 2, 2001, likely would have been tempered. Perhaps Enron would have created fewer structured-finance transactions, borrowed less money, or issued fewer bonds and shares. Or perhaps the company would have been a more attractive merger partner, and we would not be conducting a case study in forensic pathology on one of the largest bankruptcies in history.

PART II

Enron's Legacy

Five years after Enron's collapse, many facts about the case are still emerging and being contested, as criminal convictions of Enron executives await final appeal and adjudication in federal court. It is thus premature to try to identify the full legacy of the Enron case.

It is possible, however, to address three of the more obvious implications of the Enron story based on the analysis in the foregoing chapters. The first set of implications, addressed in Chapter 8, relates to the quality of corporate oversight and monitoring performed by boards of directors on behalf of shareholders. The second set of implications, addressed in Chapter 9, concerns the level and structure of management incentives approved by corporate boards. The third set of implications, discussed in Chapter 10, relates to ethical discipline within corporations—which I take to include not only the practical problems of handling conflicts of interest and truth-telling (disclosure), but also of choosing to live at the outer limits of the law, where what is legal and ethical is by definition never clear. Together these three chapters speak to some of the most critical aspects of contemporary corporate governance.

Because Enron's legacy is so intimately related to matters of corporate governance, a few definitions and clarifications are in order.

Corporate governance is commonly viewed as the set of institutional arrangements designed to align the interests of managers and shareholders.[1] When these interests are not perfectly aligned, which is often the case, so-called agency costs arise.[2]

When suppliers of capital invest in a business venture, they want to be sure that managers will be working in their interests and providing adequate returns. In a simple world, shareholders could be assured of such outcomes by signing a straightforward contract stipulating what managers should do with the invested funds, and how the returns are to be divided between both parties. However, in the real world it is hard to describe and foresee all future contingencies—hence shareholders and managers must rely on what could be called an "incomplete contract."[3]

In a world of incomplete contracts, shareholders cannot expect to retain the right to control decisions not stipulated in advance. These "residual rights of control" typically end up with managers, as shareholders are usually neither qualified nor sufficiently informed to decide what to do in the domain of everyday operations.[4] Here is where the agency problem is born, and why corporate governance is a day-to-day concern.

As the economic agents of shareholders, managers often have objectives that diverge, at least in part, from those who delegated them decision and control rights. This divergence of interest stems from the fact that self-interested behavior makes it nearly impossible for anyone to be a perfect agent for anyone else. Most rational men and women systematically make calculated decisions that increase their comfort or decrease their pain, and that otherwise provide personal gains.[5]

This aspect of human nature led Adam Smith, well over two hundred years ago, to recognize that managers will tend to be less vigilant in pursuing owners' interests than if they themselves were financing the business venture.[6] This agency problem can mean that managers maximize their own comfort and personal opportunities by slacking off, sitting on unproductive cash to insure themselves against unforeseen events, giving favorable prices to friends, underinvesting in assets or even selling them to make their returns on investment look good, or pursuing growth over profitability to maximize their own tangible and intangible rewards (as at Enron). Some of the worst agency problems occur in firms with excess cash, which managers invest in ever-declining rates of return rather than return the cash to shareholders (also an Enron phenomenon in the mid-1990s).[7]

Given the ubiquity of agency problems in organizations, much of the subject of corporate governance deals with constraints that managers put on themselves, or that investors put on managers, to minimize these problems. Toward that end, corporate boards and CEOs must devise administrative practices that minimize the ill effects of self-interested behavior and personal opportunism, and that foster cooperative behavior and compliance with organizational objectives and policies. This involves, among other things, designing and implementing a system of productive (as opposed to perverse) management incentives, a mechanism for top-level monitoring of corporate operations that protects the interests of shareholders, and reporting procedures that give shareholders an accurate picture of the true financial condition of their company.

Devising such governance mechanisms requires subtle judgments regarding how best to define and measure organizational performance, structure incentives, monitor ongoing operations, and report to shareholders. Designing such mechanisms also requires judgments about what ethical rules of the game should govern the conduct of the corporation on a day-to-day basis. Boards of directors of publicly listed companies have developed a variety of norms and practices for dealing with these complexities—with varying degrees of effectiveness. The Enron story provides rich evidence of just how ineffective such norms and practices can be.

Poorly designed management incentives, defective board oversight, and incomplete financial reporting combined to create a governance regime at Enron characterized by turbo-charged incentives without correspondingly powerful controls. For differing reasons, neither the board nor the capital market exercised its normal control function. The behavioral results were all but inevitable. Enron's exposure to agency problems was thus exacerbated rather than minimized.

A critical message of the Enron story is that the key to minimizing the agency problems of firms is an effective system of management incentives and board oversight. Under Enron's system of governance, the board (and the investing public) failed to detect and deter the distorted behavior that led to the company's corruption and massive destruction of value.

The Enron case, along with the recent history of other corporations, provides dramatic evidence that high-powered incentives require intensive monitoring by the board and its compensation and audit committees. And the bigger the management incentives and the larger the payoffs to executives, the greater the need for strong oversight and control. Because management incentives at Enron created the opportunity for executives to reap large gains by systematically overestimating the value of commodity contracts, turnkey power projects, and other investments, and by making short-term maneuvers to boost the company's stock price, the board had the responsibility to monitor management practice more intensively. The directors did not achieve this, if they even attempted it, before matters began to spin out of control.

If turbo incentives require turbo controls, Enron had the former without the latter. As time passed, a crash became inevitable. And because shareholders were oblivious to the true state of Enron's economic condition, when the company announced large initial write-offs in October 2001, triggering deep suspicions of its ethics and business acumen, it took only weeks to collapse as customers and trading counterparties defected. In light of this history, Part II of the book highlights the most important implications of Enron's governance breakdown for senior executives and directors of public corporations, and recommends effective solutions.

CHAPTER 8

Strengthening Board Oversight

Chapter 5 described directors' lack of effective oversight, which turned out to be very costly to shareholders and employees alike. That chapter also explored the many organizational factors that inhibited board oversight: the high level of executive turnover that accompanied Enron's frequent reorganizations; the distance of the CEO/chair from daily operations; the inability of Skilling and Lay to tolerate and learn from internal dissent; and critical lapses in the company's risk-management process. Add to this unhealthy organizational context the board's own inadequate processes, its apparent unresponsiveness to many red flags; its lack of broad-based mastery of Enron's financial techniques; and its notable lack of rigor in questioning management about the risks implicit in the use of off-balance-sheet partnerships, and in monitoring exceptions to the company's code of conduct. This mix—and its combined effect on the board's oversight capabilities—was toxic enough to put the company in mortal danger.

In the aftermath of Enron's collapse, Congress enacted new rules governing the composition and practices of boards of all publicly listed companies. These rules, embodied in the Sarbanes-Oxley Act of 2002, were designed to strengthen the monitoring and control of public companies by their boards of directors. Whatever the eventual impact of this supposed remedy to Enron-style breakdowns, we need not—and cannot—rely on the legislature (or the courts) to solve our long-run corporate governance problems. Indeed, Sarbanes-Oxley arguably has made it more difficult to recruit highly experienced executives and other professionals to board service, by threatening to increase the perils of lawsuits and the risks of damaged reputations.

Fortunately, remedies for the kind of governance breakdown that afflicted Enron as a *public company* can be found outside the legislative and legal arena, in the world of *private companies*. These remedies can be observed in businesses formerly owned by public companies that have been taken private with the help of professional buyout firms (commonly referred to as private-equity firms), and armed with active directors who pursue commonsense governance practices that have stood the test of time.

Before delving into this governance model, I want to be clear that my intent in describing board processes in the private-equity industry is not to suggest that buyout sponsors have an exclusive claim to effective corporate governance, or that boards of public companies should explicitly copy that model. The latter obviously work differently from the boards of professionally sponsored buyouts, because their ownership structures are so different. For example, in marked contrast to buyouts, the widely dispersed ownership of most public companies makes it difficult for owners to exercise their control rights in any concerted way. Similarly, while shareholders of buyouts are typically stable and focused for the most part on a four-to-ten-year payout, shareholders of public companies are an ever-changing, unstable lot, and largely unfocused owing to their diversity.

Boards of public and private companies also differ because owners of the latter are free to appoint as many nonindependent directors as they wish, while public companies work under a far more restrictive set of rules set by Congress, the New York Stock Exchange, and various industry organizations. (In contrast to independent directors, "nonindependent" directors may have, or have had, material relationships with the company, have been associated with the company during the last five years as an employee, be related to the board chairman or other board directors or corporate officers, and, as a voting member of the board's audit committee, hold a substantial block of company shares.) Given these fundamental differences, I am not suggesting that public companies can or should seek to *replicate* the private-equity governance model. I am suggesting, however, that directors who understand the unique features of the private-equity model (described below) can adopt and adapt many of its most salient characteristics, and in so doing minimize the principal-agent problems arising from the separation of ownership and control in large public firms and, in doing so, reduce the chance of Enron-type governance breakdowns.[1]

In light of the emerging debate over various practices of the booming private-equity industry—including the amount of fees charged by private-equity firms, the tax status of these fees, the investment time horizon of various buyout sponsors, and the implications of large public-equity firms issuing public shares—it might seem anomalous for me to hold up the private-equity industry as a model for effective governance and corporate control. While each of these subjects merits serious consideration, they do not in any way refute the proposition that over the past twenty years the private-equity industry has been, on balance, a highly effective repair shop for capitalism. My colleague Michael Jensen pointed out over a decade ago that a large proportion of American businesses fail to earn their cost of capital on a sustained basis and therefore systematically destroy economic value.[2] If this were not an enduring fact of economic life, there would few underperforming enterprises to repair, and the principal role of buyout firms as value-added, active investors would disappear. For interested readers, I explain in the endnote why the budding debate over industry practices has little to do with the efficacy of the private-equity governance model.[3]

Of course, as effective as the private-equity model of corporate governance may be, it is unlikely to be the source of reassurance to millions of American shareholders that Sarbanes-Oxley was designed to be. Yet, it is also unlikely that the oversight behavior of many public companies will change significantly unless they adopt something akin to the disciplined monitoring and control practices employed by the best private-equity boards.

Limits of Sarbanes-Oxley as a Tonic for Enron-Style Governance Breakdowns

Congress passed the Sarbanes-Oxley Act in July 2002, one year after the Enron scandal broke, but well before the full story of Enron's collapse was known. This was an emergency piece of legislation, passed with little considered discourse and even less involvement of the business community, during a collapsing stock market and a period of media frenzy over the massive WorldCom accounting scandal, in which reported earnings were allegedly inflated under instructions from CEO Bernie Ebbers by transferring line-cost expenses to capital accounts in conflict with generally accepted accounting principles (GAAP). (Ebbers was eventually sentenced to twenty-five years in prison.) The overall impact of Sarbanes-Oxley has been to substitute an increasingly rules-based system of corporate governance for the existing principles-based system.[4]

The rules imposed by the law placed special emphasis on the role of independent directors on corporate boards. All audit committees of the boards of public companies must be populated solely with independent directors, and the law encourages the New York Stock Exchange and Nasdaq to require that all listed companies be governed by a majority of independent directors. The law also requires CEOs to certify their companies' financial reports; accounting firms to report directly to the audit committee of the board, rather than to management; a mandatory code of ethics for directors and employees; federal protection of whistleblowers who report illegal or unethical behavior; and harsher penalties for white-collar crime. Perhaps most important, the act calls for management to document internal controls extensively, and for outside accountants to audit these controls annually. Finally, Sarbanes-Oxley established the Public Company Accounting Oversight Board to oversee accounting firms, which were formerly self-regulated, and establish rules for audits.

The assumptions underlying these new rules are noteworthy. Supporters assumed that the existing standards of fiduciary duty were not sufficient to deter breakdowns in corporate governance and control. They also assumed that the internal control systems of many U.S. corporations had failed to protect the interests of investors. Finally, they assumed that the best response was to strengthen external controls, by increasing the number of independent directors on corporate boards, improving the quality of information available to capital markets, and raising the penalties for self-dealing.

Although these assumptions are consistent with the Enron case, the irony of that legacy is that the new rules cannot—by themselves—prevent Enron-style debacles, because they do not address many of the causes of the company's breakdown. The vigilance of outside and part-time directors has surely increased in the wake of Sarbanes-Oxley. Reports suggest that the time audit committees spend fulfilling their mandate has risen substantially, with one such committee announcing a threefold increase in the frequency of its meetings since President Bush signed the law.[5] Sarbanes-Oxley may also strengthen the backbone of directors formerly less inclined to question business policies and practices. And the law has probably helped restore investor confidence in U.S. companies through the controversial and costly provision (section 404) requiring extensive documentation and external auditing of internal controls.

But alas, none of the legislation's new rules address the origins of Enron's collapse: the reckless gambling, perverse incentives, lack of accountability for one's decisions, culture of deceit, board-approved exemptions from the company's code of ethics, and ethical drift stemming from the pressure to "make the numbers look good"; the inability of the company's leadership to examine itself and face reality when painful problems emerged; and the collusion of financial intermediaries in managing and misrepresenting the company's financial position.

In light of the deviant behavior that precipitated Enron's collapse, it is unreasonable to expect formal CEO signoffs on financial statements—and annual assessments of companies' internal control systems by outside auditors, who are not in a position to observe managerial behavior—to protect shareholders from Enron-style breakdowns. The jury is still out, moreover, on whether independent directors, a cornerstone of the Sarbanes-Oxley Act, can actually stand up and hold senior corporate executives like Skilling and Lay accountable. What we do know is that little historical evidence shows a positive relationship between the percentage of outside independent directors and long-term corporate performance.[6] And although Sarbanes-Oxley does focus executives' and directors' attention on internal controls, the act is (appropriately) mute on the core issues of managerial competence, and has little to say about how to actually improve director oversight.

The Monitoring Challenge

Corporate boards of public companies often struggle to keep on top of their monitoring and oversight responsibilities. Despite their best intentions and honest labor, many sitting directors lack enough training in financial accounting, and the scientific, engineering, and other technical knowledge to effectively monitor the finances and oversee the strategic direction of their companies.[7]

Recent surveys show that many corporate directors apparently feel out of touch with their companies' prospects and problems. One study by McKinsey and Co. found that half of 1,016 public directors surveyed across industries and geographic regions had no clear sense of their companies' current strategy. Only 11 percent claimed to completely understand the risks their companies faced.[8] In another survey of board practices, conducted by Carter and Lorsch in North America, continental Europe, and Australia, a majority of CEOs lacked confidence that their independent directors understood their companies' businesses, regardless of the amount of time they spent.[9] It should not be surprising that under such conditions, many corporate directors are open to being "managed" by the people they are supposed to oversee.[10]

The obvious remedy for this skill deficit and knowledge gap is to improve board processes. As noted, a useful place to look is the private-equity industry. That industry, which includes venture-capital and buyout investments, has grown tremendously over the past fifteen years, with investments in private-equity partnerships climbing from less than $10 billion to more than $180 billion between 1991 and 2000.[11] And the U.S. industry's growth rate shows no sign of slowing; private-equity funds have raised over $400 billion of capital in the United States alone from 2002 to 2006.[12]

Private-equity firms typically serve as the general partner (GP) in investments pursued through a limited-partnership structure (typically referred to as a fund). The GP typically raises the bulk of a fund's required capital from institutional investors and wealthy individuals, who are referred to as limited partners. The GP identifies businesses in which to invest the fund's capital, and agrees to return that capital to the limited partners within a specified time period, usually ten to twelve years.[13] The GP then oversees these investment properties on behalf of its limited partners. Because the future of a private-equity firm depends on securing further investments, it has strong incentive to make each fund, and each company in which that fund invests, as successful as possible.

Despite this strong incentive, not all private-equity funds are successful. Returns to buyout funds have slightly exceeded returns to venture funds, but the returns to all such funds vary widely, especially venture funds. According to a recent study by Kaplan and Schoar, between 1980 and 2001 private-equity funds at the twenty-fifth percentile earned a cash-flow return (cash flow divided by the market value of capital employed) of 3 percent per year, while funds at the seventy-fifth percentile earned a cash-flow return of 22 percent per year.[14]

The 22 percent average annual return of the top quartile of performance for all private-equity firms is noteworthy. For illustration purposes it is consistent with the recent, publicly reported returns of The Blackstone Group in its June 25, 2007 prospectus. Blackstone's combined fund-level annualized returns in all its various businesses (buyout funds, real estate funds, and marketable alternate asset funds) from inception in 1989 to March 31, 2007 was 30.7 percent, or 22.6 percent net of fees. This contrasts with average annualized returns of the S&P 500 (adjusted for dividend reinvestment) of 10.9 percent.[15]

Although *average* returns of all private-equity funds before management fees are assessed exceed the returns of the Standard & Poor 500, this is typically not the case net of fees—which can run as high as 16–19 percent of committed capital for venture-capital funds.[16] In addition, if one were to saddle the S&P 500 with debt equivalent to that used in buyouts, the average returns of buyout funds before fees would probably no longer exceed those of the stock index.[17]

Still, as the Blackstone numbers suggest, the returns of the most successful private-equity funds tend to persist across generations. These high and recurring returns appear to reflect proprietary access by the top-performing funds to certain kinds of transactions (such as management buyouts where current managers invest alongside the large financial sponsors in the expectation of supernormal returns), and to knowledgeable, experienced GPs who provide advice and oversight to the companies in their portfolios.[18]

The private-equity approach to board oversight and control—sometimes referred to as the monitoring model of governance—has contributed to the performance of this surging industry.[19] The governance disciplines of leading private-equity firms, especially in the buyout sector, can go a long way toward smoking out the kind of reckless investing and unethical behavior seen at Enron, as well as providing a much-needed counterbalance to turbocharged financial incentives for executives. The ensuing discussion of board-level governance practices therefore refers to the buyout segment of the private-equity industry.[20]

The Private-Equity Model of Corporate Governance

I have mentioned that private-equity firms that specialize in buyouts play an important role as our repair shops of capitalism.[21] The major restructuring and extensive repairs needed to restore competitiveness to a faltering company (or division of a large company) is often best effected by taking the company private, and introducing the incentives and governance disciplines required to turn its operations around. These practices—repeated in many industries—are by no means uniform in design or effectiveness, and, like all models, the private-equity governance model may break down under the weight of exceptions and aberrations. Still, highly productive aspects of private-equity governance clearly differ from those typically associated with the boards of public enterprises:

- Private-equity boards typically reap the advantages of the in-depth due diligence that precedes a buyout, and use this highly specific knowledge to oversee and monitor the business.
- Private-equity directors typically spend more time—and often more informed time—with their companies post-buyout than many directors spend with their public companies. For example, after the normal due diligence process, and during the first one hundred days after gaining control, partners with the highest-performing private-equity funds often spend fifteen days a month with a company, assessing its management, formulating a strategy, and setting appropriate performance metrics.[22] Only after this burst of energy does involvement drop back to about two days per month—the amount of time Korn/Ferry reports that directors of large, public U.S. companies typically spend on board matters.
- Private-equity boards are typically small, working groups composed of individuals with continuing professional (as opposed to social) relationships. Directors often include buyout sponsors, other equity partners, perhaps an industry expert, sometimes a leading creditor, and the company CEO—all attuned by disposition to the rigorous monitoring of corporate affairs.

  A typical example is the board of Wisconsin Central Ltd. Railroad (WCL), a regional freight railroad established in a late-1980s leveraged buyout by Berkshire Partners, an early and distinguished buyout firm.[23] After the buyout, WCL's board included seven members: the company's CEO and CFO, along with two general partners from Berkshire and three outside investors who had participated in the buyout. One of the outside directors was also general counsel to WCL. These directors can be considered "active investors." Such investors tend to hold large equity or debt positions, be involved in the long-term strategic direction of the companies in which they invest, monitor and sometimes dismiss the managements of those companies, and may even manage the companies.[24]
- Members of private-equity boards typically have substantial wealth at risk. Even though the annual management fees that buyout sponsors collect are not linked to the performance of the companies in their

portfolios, the sponsors and their financial partners who sit on the boards have substantial equity ownership. The financial stakes of these partners vary widely, but their equity holdings represent an essential component of the private-equity governance model.

What's more, in contrast to the management of public corporations, senior managers in buyouts are also expected to invest a significant portion of their net worth in their companies. For example, Kohlberg Kravis Roberts (KKR), a prominent buyout firm, expects top managers to own 5–10 percent for large transactions, and as much as 25 percent for smaller ones, depending on their personal circumstances.[25] The idea is not only to convert managers into owners—thereby aligning their interests with those of other shareholders—but also to align *owners* with important managerial values, such as equating profitability with long-term strategies for investment and innovation.[26] Given the ownership stakes of both classes of directors, the personal costs of ratifying and pursuing policies that jeopardize either the short- or long-run condition of these companies are high.

- The best private-equity boards also know how to structure financial incentives to deter reckless gambling, and, in marked contrast to Enron, pay out only after managers have created real economic value. Indeed, attentive private-equity sponsors understand that management incentives are critical to the success of a buyout deal.

- Not that mistakes are never made in this domain. When KKR, Hicks Muse, another respected buyout firm, and an investor group that included a select group of managers paid $1.5 billion in May 1998 for Regal Cinemas, the nation's third-largest movie-theater chain, the buyers allowed the CEO and other operating managers to take personal equity stakes of $45 million and $225 million, respectively, off the table. This stock sell-off—which dropped management's ownership position in the company from 13.9 percent to just 2.9 percent—effectively left managers free to play roulette with other people's money. Although there were many reasons why this company joined a long list of theater chains that declared bankruptcy in the late 1990s, overspending by managers who had essentially liquidated their equity positions in the company was certainly high on the list. The failure of the Regal cinema buyout is compelling testimony to the importance of aligning the incentives of managers and investors.[27] Most private-equity firms routinely get this done.

- Private-equity boards have strong incentives to set aside enough time to monitor the business plans they approve, and to probe financial and operational issues. By design, most buyouts face cash-flow challenges related to their heavy debt-servicing obligations. And it takes only one unmonitored blowup for sponsors' flow of quality buyout opportunities to diminish. (In the case of Regal Cinemas, its board was slow to recognize changing industry conditions, management's flawed business assumptions, and the vulnerability of expected cash flows.) Thus experienced buyout boards rarely rely on quarterly or monthly meetings alone to monitor current cash flows and future prospects. These boards review a continuing stream of detailed monthly reports, and key directors often engage in weekly and sometimes even daily conversations with management. The idea is to pursue a candid, informal, and continuing dialogue with executives, rather than second-guess and overrule.
- Despite some notable examples of "flipping"—or reselling—buyouts after a rapid turnaround, most private-equity boards operate with a four-to-seven-year horizon, reflecting both the nature of corporate restructuring and the goal of securing future growth. This is far longer than the quarterly earnings horizon of public companies. Indeed, private-equity boards have none of the distractions associated with reporting quarterly financial results and monitoring a publicly quoted stock price.
- Finally, most private-equity boards are acutely aware of the need to establish effective checks and balances for CEOs and senior executives—offsetting high-powered financial incentives with the kind of continuous oversight and control noted above.

Private-equity directors are typically more informed, more hands-on, and more interventionist than more independent and distant public-equity directors. Because experienced private-equity boards—by virtue of their specialized investment philosophies and backing by professional risk capital—typically have the knowledge, information, power, motivation, and time to do a serious job of monitoring and control, they fulfill the indicators of effective organizations and boardrooms that researchers have identified over the years (see Table 8.1).[28] Though their directors may be of high quality, this is seldom the case for publicly owned companies, which stress director independence.

Table 8.1. Comparison of private-equity and public company directors

	Private-Equity Directors	Public Company Directors
Knowledge	Detailed knowledge of business as a result of due diligence conducted by buyout sponsor/directors.	Knowledge of the business not as detailed or deep. Highly variable knowledge among outside directors, depending on past business experience, length of service, and director education programs.
Information	Continuous, informal contacts between buyout sponsor/directors and top management, plus more formal weekly and monthly reviews. Information flows keyed to (a) the "business case" of the buyout prepared by the buyout sponsor/directors and (b) performance metrics dictated by the financial structure of the investment.	In the absence of recognized crises, formal business reviews prepared by management for monthly or quarterly board meetings according to their vision of the business, its value drivers, and current performance.
Power	CEO clearly works for the sponsor/director and is highly vulnerable to replacement. Directors have central role in designing incentive contracts for management.	Directors historically selected by CEO and are thus "beholden" to the CEO in the absence of crisis. CEO vulnerability to dismissal is low. Executive incentive contracts ratified but not typically designed by directors.
Motivation	Substantial personal wealth at risk and high stakes for the sponsor/director firm.	With the exception of founding directors (Google, The Home Depot, etc.), limited personal wealth at risk.
Time	Full-time commitment across portfolio companies. Extremely high during post-buyout and pre-liquidation stages. Ongoing oversight and control is part of a buyout sponsor/director's job.	Very part-time. Directors often hold member-ships on multiple corporate boards. Time commitment normally limited to monthly and/or quarterly meetings. Control function largely delegated to operating management.

To test the power of this private-equity governance model, ask yourself the following question: *Could Enron have happened if it had been a private-equity deal, governed by a small board composed of substantial investors (and their bankers), rather than a large, relatively uncommitted board representing dispersed public shareholders?*

If you answered "no" or "highly unlikely," you are assuming that private-equity boards know how to do something that many public-equity boards such as Enron's do not. That something relates, most likely, to the governance structure I have outlined above, as well as to the personal characteristics of effective directors.

Characteristics of Effective Private-Equity Directors

B. Charles (Chuck) Ames, a vice chairman of Clayton, Dubilier & Rice (a respected old-line buyout firm) and former CEO of two major public companies, has often been asked: What does it take to be a good director in today's world? Reflecting on his experience as both a sponsor of successful buyouts and a CEO, he ticks off five essential attributes of effective private-equity directors: common sense; a good nose that conducts frequent smell tests; a dogged determination to protect shareholder interests above all else; backbone, or the strength to dissent and even to resign to preserve integrity; and an unflinching commitment to ethical behavior.

Ames's elaboration on these attributes tends to focus on common sense. In fact, his ideas about common sense are so sensible—forged through decades as an operating manager, corporate director, and private-equity investor—that they strike me as defining uncommon common sense. Overall, this uncommon common sense involves rare skill in knowing when to ask the right questions about a business:

- How is the business performing against internal forecasts?
- What are the reasons for any variances?
- Are financial and management resources sufficient to execute the business plan?
- What is the short-term and long-term outlook for the business?
- What are the key drivers of that outlook?
- How are key business leaders responding to challenges?
- How is employee morale?

Common sense also involves asking the right questions about specific management proposals that will change the status quo:

- What are the costs?
- What are the benefits?
- What are the risks?
- What are the alternatives?
- Why is this alternative the best?
- What does it do for us competitively?
- Is it aligned with our vision and values?

Commonsense questions serve a critical function not only in the boardroom but also during meetings of the board's audit committee. One doesn't need to be a financial expert (as suggested by some corporate-governance reformers) to expect simple, revealing answers to questions such as:

- Is there anything we should do differently to increase transparency, or to more accurately reflect the company's true financial picture?
- Would you do or propose anything different if you were a member of the audit committee?
- Is our financial staff fully equipped to manage and control our company's financial affairs?
- Do our financial reporting and control structures have any weaknesses?

Ames encourages partners serving as directors of companies owned by his firm to ask such commonsense questions. In fact, his firm has codified these questions so up-and-coming partners can carry this commonsense discipline forward to the boards of their assigned companies. Most important, the firm trains these young partners to insist on receiving satisfactory answers to these questions and others like them.

Yet as Ames suggests, with his list of five attributes of successful private-equity directors, common sense is not a sufficient quality—especially in cases like Enron, where executives are not telling directors the full truth about a company's strategy and performance. Here is where "a good nose that conducts frequent smell tests," a strong backbone, and an "unflinching commitment to ethical behavior" come into play. As former President Reagan used to say, "Trust, but verify." The most direct way for directors to verify that strategies will be productive and outcomes appropriate is simply to meet complicated and suspicious explanations head on, with a battery of "why's?" For every answer to the first "why?" simply ask again why that answer makes sense. I guarantee—from years of Socratic instruction—that five successive "why's?" will reveal any weaknesses in a proposal, plan, or presentation. All that such an approach requires is the courage (and diligence) to ask, and the patience to wait for convincing answers.

There is nothing specific to the buyout business about this line of questioning. It is simply that the composition, structure, and incentives of private-equity boards have promoted the rigorous use of this Socratic method of interaction with operating executives. Had Enron's internal and external directors vigorously pursued questions such as these in their monitoring and oversight roles, chances are they would have gleaned information well beyond what management routinely offered.

They might also have delved into the reasons for Enron's first decline in profitability in 1997, and probed how management was preparing to get things back on track.

They might have looked at Enron's increasingly modest free-cash flow.

They might have examined the post-1997 flood of off-balance-sheet partnerships and transactions more carefully, and seen that too many were designed to manipulate Enron's financial results.

They might have examined current and alternate growth strategies, scrutinized the competitive and financial implications of following the existing course, and evaluated its compatibility with the company's espoused values and organizational rules of the game.

They might have smoked out whatever unresolved concerns Arthur Andersen might have had regarding the company's accounting and financial controls.

They might even have discovered the declining morale that gripped young and seasoned executives alike during 2000 and 2001.

Of course, we will never know for sure whether Enron's board would have detected the company's many instances of deceptive management, if directors had followed this commonsense line of questioning. But we do know that a little Socratic dialogue and cross-examination can go a long way toward breaking down whatever knowledge barriers might exist, and exposing fakery and lies.

For these reasons, we do not have to place all our hopes for improved corporate governance on the legislature or the courts—if the business community is willing to learn from experience. The incentive to do so is the likelihood of more legislated rules related to increased director liability if public corporations cannot regulate their own behavior—a truly bad idea if we want to attract highly qualified individuals to public company boards. The process of self-reflection and adaptation is long under way, as evidenced by the proposed governance reforms of the New York Stock Exchange and the ensuing debate pertaining to the role of independent directors in publicly listed companies, and the recommendations of the Blue Ribbon Commission on Board Leadership of the National Association of Corporate Directors (NACD) that address, among other things, how independent directors can be most effective in their oversight and board management roles.[29]

The well-established practices of private-equity directors—especially in holding out for satisfactory answers from senior executives and external auditors to fairly straightforward questions—provides experience on which the independent directors of public companies can reflect. While group norms and other social barriers often discourage confrontation among directors and board chairs of public companies, many private-equity directors have long been practicing the constructive engagement described by Chuck Ames.[30] Indeed, the ability of private-equity sponsors to raise vast amounts of capital rests largely on the implicit trust that sophisticated investors have in the rigorous approach of private-equity boards to internal governance and control.

Capturing the Full Benefits of the Private-Equity Governance Model

The common sense embedded in the private-equity model of corporate governance offers strong protection against Enron-style breakdowns. But we are still left with a critical practical question: how can we successfully transfer to boards of public companies the full benefits of deep knowledge, relevant information, motivation, power, and time commitment?

The answer to this question lies in five essential innovations in corporate governance:

- A different population of directors
- A different level of director compensation
- A greater degree of directors' wealth at risk
- A more arms-length relationship between directors and CEOs
- More shareholder influence on the nomination and removal of directors

These five conditions are closely related, and boards must adopt at least the first four collectively to produce any meaningful changes in outcomes.

As we will see, Enron's board satisfied some of these conditions, but missed others by a wide margin.

A Different Population of Directors

Because of the frequency and duration of scheduled board meetings and other professional obligations, many public directors simply cannot devote the time required to do an adequate job of monitoring and control. The McKinsey survey quoted earlier dramatically confirms this point.

In many respects, the ideal director for a company seeking to replicate some of the benefits of the private-equity model is a recently retired, technologically up-to-date senior executive with relevant operating or financial experience and the personal attributes articulated so succinctly by Chuck Ames. Many retired executives have significant corporate and governance experience, freedom from conflicts of interest, and the ability to devote the requisite time. And retired executives *are* found today in 95 percent of Fortune 1000 boardrooms, although we do not know the proportion of retired directors in the total pool of Fortune 1000 directors.[31]

What we do know, however, is that 82 percent of these boards include sitting CEOs and COOs of other companies. Experience and continued exposure to the daily challenges of business leadership make these directors excellent contributors and sounding boards, but their lack of time and limits imposed by their own boards restrict their participation in governance activities.[32] To the extent that these are also the circumstances of other sitting directors, the effectiveness of board oversight and control is severely diminished.

Only four of Enron's fifteen directors in 2001 were retired executives (or emeritus professors), meaning that apart from Skilling and Lay, most directors could devote little of their professional lives to Enron. Although several had twenty years or more experience on the board, and all were smart, accomplished people, the majority of Enron's nine fully employed outside directors likely never fully understood the company's complex strategies and operating risks.

We can observe the effects of professional constraints on Enron's directors in their repeated failure to challenge high-risk structured-finance transactions and questionable accounting practices, and to monitor the extensive off-the-books activities authorized by board resolutions. In contrast, boards put together by top-tier buyout firms are typically unencumbered by the constraints Enron's directors faced, as those boards are typically designed to have the time, knowledge, information, motivation, and power to provide the kind of oversight and control that Enron sorely lacked.

To replicate the essential features of the private-equity governance model, public corporations must reconsider the profile of their most desired directors. They need to expand efforts to recruit former executives of distinction (with or without broad name recognition), and successful entrepreneurs in their fifties, sixties, and seventies who have stepped down after decades of hard work and accomplishment, and thus have the time, energy, and interest to become truly focused directors. Whatever the demographics of this expanded cohort of potential directors, the kind of commonsense pursuit of the real story represented by Chuck Ames's line of questioning should be the most sought-after quality of mind.

Although we do not know the precise size and flow of this pool of potential directors, we do know that it is expanding because of the good health and longevity of aging of baby-boomers. We can also expect the pool of retired executives willing to serve as public directors to be determined not only by their intrinsic interest but also by the financial rewards. Unfortunately, data on directors' pay show that it is sufficient neither to lure large numbers of executives and entrepreneurs away from other endeavors nor to compensate them for rising legal risks and personal liabilities. In today's world of excessive *executive* compensation, arguing for increasing director compensation might be unfashionable. However, the fact is that most directors of public companies are seriously underpaid, given the work required by the private-equity governance model. Ironically, this was not was the case at Enron: its directors were well compensated according to the standards I suggest below. The fatal flaw in Enron's corporate-governance practices lay elsewhere.

A Different Level of Director Compensation

To expand the pool of desirable directors for public companies, compensation will have to rise significantly, especially for chairs of important committees with escalating responsibilities and burgeoning workloads. Yes, some have argued that some of the most desirable candidates for board positions probably do not need the money.[33] Nevertheless, it's safe to say that the risks and rewards of serving as a public director have become unbalanced, despite increases in average director pay of 25 percent in 2004–2005 alone.[34]

Higher pay notwithstanding, it is becoming increasingly difficult to fill boardroom vacancies with qualified directors. Some 70 percent of the Fortune 1000 directors polled by Korn/Ferry reported that board recruitment was becoming more difficult, with roughly one-third reporting that it had also become more difficult to recruit directors with extensive financial experience or proven general-management expertise. Moreover, nearly one-quarter of potential directors turned down a directorship during 2004—almost double the reported figure for 2003.[35] These recruiting difficulties are likely due to greater time commitments and personal legal risks, partly attributable to Sarbanes-Oxley.[36] Furthermore, the supply of competent directors appears to be dwindling, even as demand is, at a minimum, holding constant. The opportunity costs of failing to attract qualified directors to public companies must be judged significant, in light of the costs of the governance breakdown at Enron.

Although it is difficult to estimate the current pay of public directors precisely, because of differences in data across studies, a detailed study by the Investor Responsibility Research Center (IRRC) put total compensation for the average director of the S&P 1500 at $126,189 in 2004. For firms with revenues of $3 billion to $10 billion, average pay was reportedly $139,578; for firms with revenues greater than $10 billion, it was $169,342.[37] The NACD reported that average total director compensation at the top two hundred U.S. public corporations in 2000 was $138,747.[38]

Equity-based compensation has greatly expanded the financial remuneration of directors in recent years, often dwarfing cash compensation. The IRRC's reported average cash compensation of $46,703, for example, represented only 38 percent of directors' average total compensation. Other surveys have reported roughly comparable cash compensation. The Conference Board reported $50,000, and Korn/Ferry $56,970, for 2004.[39]

Since alternate computations and averages tend to disguise a good deal of pertinent information, I have built from the IRRC database my own estimate of the total compensation of the kind of highly engaged public directors that the private-equity governance model would require (see Table 8.2). My calculation assumes that the director is a member of a board's audit and compensation committees, has attended all committee and board meetings, and receives annual grants of either stock options or restricted stock.[40] The total annual compensation of such a director averages between $122,134 and $135,911.

This estimate is probably on the high side for many public directors, as not all the companies in the IRRC sample provided each of these types of compensation. For example, 27 percent of the companies surveyed did not pay their audit committee members a per-meeting fee, and 80 percent did not

Table 8.2.   Estimate of average compensation for public company directors

- Board retainer: $36,388
- Board meeting fees: $12,735 ($1,698 per meeting times an average of 7.5 meetings)
- Audit committee retainer: $8,531
- Audit committee meeting fees: $10,070 ($1,291 per meeting times 7.8 meetings)
- Compensation committee retainer: $7,402
- Compensation committee meeting fees: $6,804 ($1,251 times 5.6 meetings)
  Cash compensation subtotal: $81,930

- Stock Options: $53,981[a] *or*
- Stock Awards: $40,204[b]
  Equity compensation subtotal: $40,204–$53,981

Total annual compensation: $122,134–$135,911

Note: This analysis assumes companies that offered one form of equity-based compensation (say, options) to directors did not offer the other (restricted stock). The IRRC reports that only 66% of the companies that participated in its study offered some form of option grant and only 35% offered a stock award. See IRRC, pp. 78 and 83.

a. The IRRC estimates the present value of a stock option by multiplying the number of shares underlying each option by the company's fiscal year-end stock price and dividing the product by three. If a company discloses only the face value of the shares underlying the option grant, IRRC divides that value by three. If a company discloses only the option grant's Black Scholes value, IRRC uses that value as the present value. To annualize a one-time stock option grant, IRRC divides the present value by five. To annualize a periodic option grant, IRRC divides the present value by the period between the grants. For example, IRC divides the present value of an option granted every fourth year by four. If the company makes no indication of the frequency of an option grant, IRRC assumes the option is granted on an annual basis. IRRC, p. 91.

b. The value of a stock award is calculated by multiplying the number of shares awarded by the company's fiscal year-end stock price. If a company discloses only the face value of a stock award, IRRC uses that value. To annualize a one-time stock award, IRRC divides the calculated value by five. To annualize a periodic stock award, IRRC divides the calculated value by the period between the awards, as noted above. If the company makes no indication of the frequency of the stock award, IRRC assumes the award is granted on an annual basis. IRRC, pp. 91–92.

offer audit committee members a retainer. If I included these companies in my estimate, average pay would be significantly lower. Similarly, if my tally included companies that offered no annual stock options or stock awards, or only occasionally offered one or the other, the average annual compensation for this type of director would drop below the IRRC's average of $126,189.

Of course, serving as a public company director brings important *nonfinancial* benefits, such as prestige, business and social connections, and satisfaction from participating in an exciting venture. However, in trying to benchmark director pay, I have focused primarily on financial remuneration, because I assume that it is essential to attracting committed directors in the private-equity mode. More specifically, I assume that directors' financial benefits must meet or exceed those of other opportunities (which we can think of as directors' "reserve price").

Using the IRRC average of $126,189 in annual total compensation for S&P 1500 directors, and assuming that the average director spends 18 hours per month (or 216 hours per year) in preparation time, meeting attendance, and travel (as reported in the Korn/Ferry survey), I found that the corresponding per diem fee is about $4,674 ($126,189 ÷ [216 hours per year ÷ 8 hours per day]).[41]

Although this rate of pay might be enough for a relatively uninvolved director, I maintain that it is inadequate for highly engaged and heavily burdened chairs of critical board committees, who are increasingly exposed to legal liabilities that directors of private companies are not. It is certainly low relative to the hourly rates ($750–$900) charged by the top Wall Street lawyers often hired to advise board committees. It is low relative to the returns available to former CEOs from consulting for an equivalent number of days, and without the personal liability issues. It is also low compared with the financial and intellectual rewards from other uses of time, such as working with the portfolio companies of buyout firms, which offer substantial gains from equity participation.

Finally, this average pay is low relative to both the per diem compensation the directors received as senior executives at their own companies, and the per diem compensation of senior executives whose performance they pledge to monitor and evaluate. Although this last comparison is certainly not a perfect one, given that CEO pay has been skyrocketing, it does provide a crude benchmark for assessing the value of active directors of public companies.[42]

Tables 8.3 and 8.4 compare the total annual compensation of S&P 1500 directors and CEOs in 2004, broken down by company size. These tables show that the average director's per diem pay is 11–16 percent of that of the average sitting CEO. These tables also reveal that the higher a CEO's pay is, the lower a directors' pay is.

There are certainly arguments against making such direct comparisons between director and CEO pay—such as that high CEO compensation reflects the extreme difficulty of running large enterprises, and that the pay differential reflects an extreme shortage of executives capable of such leadership tasks. The counterargument says that many CEOs of large U.S. companies are simply overpaid because of windfall gains in share price unrelated to their actual operating performance. Nevertheless, despite this debate, there can be no ducking the fact that the relative pay of directors of public companies for their monitoring and control duties is a small fraction of the going rate for serious executive talent.

For example, were we to simply cut the market rate for the average S&P 1500 CEO in half, on the assumption that CEOs are seriously overcompensated, the per diem equivalent of an average director's pay would rise to only 33 percent of this revised rate for sitting CEOs. Were we to cut that rate in half yet again, public directors would still look underpaid, as their compensation would rise to only 60 percent of the rock-bottom rate for CEOs. And, in marked contrast to the payback to private-equity sponsors and directors, public-equity directors have no chance to participate in the often-large "backends"—or gains—realized after a public offering of shares or a strategic sale. (Returns on such deals can run as high as 20 percent above a preestablished threshold for limited partners.)

It should thus not be surprising that, given a choice, many respected, retired CEOs and senior executives of public corporations are opting out of the "public director market" to pursue other means of remaining active in the business community, such as associating with buyout or venture-capital firms. Both compensation and the potential to influence a private company's development often appear to be superior to the public-company alternative. That is why former GE chair Jack Welch, and ex-CEOs like him, have affiliated with leading private-equity firms over the past decade and eschewed new directorships on major public boards. As senior advisors to these firms and coinvestors, they stand to contribute much and earn a great deal, to everyone's benefit, including their own. And the Korn/Ferry poll noted earlier suggests that star CEOs are not the only ones declining directorships of public corporations.

With growing competition for talent and the rising risks of holding a board seat, it is a fair guess that the pool of experienced executives and successful

Table 8.3.   Public directors' total compensation: S&P 1500

	Mean Average	For Companies $3–10b Revenues	For Companies over $10b Revenues
Annual	$126,189	$139,578	$169,342
Per day equivalent[a]	$4,674	$5,170	$6,272

Note: Director compensation data from RRC's "Board Practices/Board Pay, 2005 Edition: The Structure and Composition of Boards of Directors at S&P Super 1,500 Companies." All data are for 2004. IRRC's universe is 1,275 companies of the S&P Super 1500. To calculate average Director Total Compensation, IRRC assumes the typical director sits on two committees, audit and compensation. The components of total compensation are retainers for board and committee service, fees for attending board and committee meetings, the estimated annualized dollar value of granted stock options, and the estimated annualized dollar value of restricted stock awards. "IRRC estimates the present value of a stock option by multiplying the number of shares underlying each option grant by the company's fiscal year-end stock price, and dividing the product by three," but uses the Black Scholes value if the company provides it. Stock awards are valued "by multiplying the number of shares awarded by the company's fiscal year-end stock price." Both option grants and restricted stock awards are annualized by dividing one-time grants and awards by five, and periodic grants and awards by the number of years in the period (e.g., options granted every fourth year are divided by four). If the frequency of a grant or award is unknown, IRRC assumes it to be annual. IRRC's total compensation figure does not include fees for serving as chairman of the board or a committee, nor does it include the value of benefits and perquisites.

a. For directors, per day equivalent is calculated by dividing the corresponding annual figure by 27 working-day equivalents per year. The number of working-day equivalents was derived from a finding in Korn/Ferry International's "31st Annual Board of Directors Study" that during 2004 board members spent an average of 18 hours per month on board-related activities such as review and preparation time, meeting attendance, and travel. That monthly figure was multiplied by 12 months to yield a total of 216 hours per year spent on board activities (18 hours per month × 12 months per year = 216 hours per year). The annual number of hours spent was divided by 8, the number of hours in the typical work day, resulting in the divisor of 27 working days per year (216 hours per year / 8 hours per working day = 27 working days).

entrepreneurs willing to spend the time to exercise effective oversight of public companies will expand only with significant increases in financial and other rewards. My sense is that a doubling of director compensation might be an absolute minimum—especially for important committee chairs at companies where traditional, episodic involvement morphs into a more continuous, highly informed engagement.[43] That compensation should be heavily equity based, to align directors' interests with those of shareholders. However, to guard against a short-term performance horizon, directors

Table 8.4.   CEO total compensation: S&P 1500

	Mean Average	For Companies $3–10b Revenues	For Companies over $10b Revenues
Annual	$6,393,625	$8,456,084	$12,692,880
Per day equivalent[a]	$28,416	$37,583	$56,413

Note: Chief Executive Officer compensation data are from Standard & Poor's Compustat® Execucomp data (http://wrds.wharton.upenn.edu/ds/comp/execcomp/), accessed November 2005. All data are for fiscal year 2004. CEO compensation figures are based on responses from 683 CEOs of S&P 1500 companies. CEO total compensation components are salary, bonus, debt forgiveness, signing bonus, severance payment, imputed interest, payment for unused vacation, 401k contributions, life insurance premiums, difference in value of stock purchased through stock purchase plan not available to other employees and the market price of that stock (does not include exercised options), tax reimbursements, perquisites and other personal benefits, long-term incentive plan payouts, any compensation due in 2004 but deferred by the CEO, value of restricted stock granted, and value of stock options granted. Restricted stock grants are valued by the grant date stock price. Stock option grants are valued through Black Scholes.

a. For CEOs, per day equivalent is calculated by dividing the corresponding annual figure by 225 working days per year (assuming 5 working days per week and accounting for vacations, holidays, and other time off).

should not receive any of the (greater) benefits of equity or option grants until they leave the board.[44]

To make the irony of Enron's case more explicit: the package of cash, stock options, restricted stock, and phantom-stock units (deferred cash payments linked to the value of Enron stock) awarded to its board members in 2000 was valued at $350,000. This is more than twice the national averages cited above, and just about on target with my recommended level of pay for directors serving in the private-equity mode.[45] A large portion of this value was due to a stock price that shot up after 1997 and became, in the light of subsequent analyses of Enron's true financial position, seriously overvalued. Nevertheless, the ample compensation of Enron's directors seems to conform to a critical design variable of the private-equity governance model. That this level of director pay did not have the model's intended effects should not be taken as an indication that directors' pay is irrelevant to board performance. Rather, it suggests two practical caveats: first, and most important, the first four elements of the private-equity governance model cannot be transferred piecemeal to a public-company context and, second, director compensation based largely on overvalued equity may actually diminish director discipline as they inadvertently or unconsciously work with management to support the market value of their company's stock (an issue discussed in Chapter 5).

A practical question regarding Enron is whether its directors would have behaved differently had they had enough "skin in the game"—or wealth at risk—to make a corporate loss a personal loss. In the next section, I argue that having personal wealth, as well as one's reputation, at risk is a powerful motivator consistent with the private-equity model of governance. This argument does not lack support in the business community and among governance experts. Still, Enron again seems to be an exception to the rule, as its nonemployee directors held, on average, more than $3 million in stock in the company. (Several directors' shareholdings substantially exceeded that figure, owing to long service with the company or pursuant to a merger transaction.) This suggests that director compensation and stock ownership are necessary but not sufficient conditions for fulfilling the private-equity governance model.

Putting a Higher Percentage of Directors' Wealth at Risk

Significant financial investments by private-equity directors in the companies they monitor provide strong motivation to spend whatever time it takes to effectively govern the firm. Directors of public companies, in contrast, typically have little real personal wealth at risk, because their companies have awarded them relatively insignificant amounts of options and stock grants. Thus they have little motivation to challenge proposals by senior executives and board chairs, or otherwise breach established norms of friendship, loyalty, collegiality, and team spirit.[46]

Directors' financial stakes have typically been defined by their shareholdings in a company, whether they acquired those shares through personal purchases on the open market or through stock-option or other award programs. One study in the late 1990s found that half of the public directors surveyed owned 0.005 percent or less of the companies on whose boards they sat.[47] Directors who hold such a negligible fraction of company ownership are hardly affected by the costs incurred by flawed management decisions that they fail to challenge.

Even at this low level of ownership, significant differences arise in the incentive effects of different methods of accumulating shares. Directors who have purchased stock risk declines in their equity stakes if a company's performance and long-term prospects fall. Stock options, in contrast, do not require recipients to put personal money on the table, and directors typically exercise their options only if the market price of the stock is above the strike price of the options, after they have vested. Thus directors who own stock options or hold stock awards risk no personal loss if the company's stock price declines. At worst, they are exposed to an opportunity cost—the loss of potential returns on their time spent as a board member.

Not all public companies are oblivious to the fact that director ownership of shares reduces the likelihood that directors will support unsound business policies and behave in ways that are inconsistent with the best interests of shareholders.[48] More than one-fifth of companies in the IRRC study maintain stock-ownership guidelines, in an attempt to align directors' and shareholders' interests. And nearly two-thirds of the directors polled in the Korn/Ferry study indicated that they must comply with stock-ownership guidelines.[49] Both percentages reflect significant increases over previous findings, indicating that more rigid rules governing stock ownership might be supplanting stock-option plans, which have been declining.

Stock-ownership guidelines typically stipulate that directors must hold a minimum number of shares, take a percentage of their retainer as stock, or hold a total dollar value of stock.[50] The IRRC reports that the average dollar value of stock held pursuant to such guidelines was roughly $175,000 in 2004, although how directors accumulated that amount (whether through stock purchases or stock grants) is unclear. However acquired, that amount is trivial compared with the at-risk capital held by directors of private-equity companies.

Growing attention is focusing on (1) how large a financial investment in a company, if any, directors should be required to make, and (2) how best to measure the size of that investment. These questions assume that director ownership of company stock benefits shareholders by minimizing the agency problem between directors and shareholders. The two basic measures of a director's equity holdings are the percentage of the company owned, and the dollars at stake as a percent of personal wealth.

At first blush, the first metric appears to be most consistent with the private-equity governance model. Directors who hold a significant, albeit fractional, share of a company would have significant control rights, as well as incentives to monitor the enterprise as rigorously as any private-equity director or owner. However, multibillion-dollar companies present a practical problem: independent directors could, at best, afford to purchase only a tiny fractional interest in them.

Fortunately, holding directors to this draconian standard is unnecessary. If the purpose of director ownership of company shares is to reinforce incentives to carefully monitor the enterprise, an equally strong incentive flows from the fraction of directors' personal wealth tied up in the firm. Although it is possible to estimate the non-firm wealth of some directors, breaching privacy norms would make it even more difficult to recruit them. Thus, some threshold commitment would seem to make sense—say, $250,000 to $500,000 for companies with $1 billion to $3 billion in revenues, and $500,000 to $1 million for directors of large companies with more than $3 billion in revenues. The personal stakes of these directors should motivate them to monitor public companies with as much energy as private-equity investors and directors would.[51]

Another approach might be a rule of thumb that directors' ownership stakes should be at least roughly equal to their level of compensation—at the higher level I have suggested. For comparison, boards are requiring a growing number of senior executives to hold several times their salaries in company stock. The General Motors board, for example, required CEO Richard Wagoner to hold seven times his 2004 salary of $2.2 million in GM stock. These requirements for personal commitments show that the stakes of private-equity directors can be replicated in the public-equity context.

To ensure a supply of independent directors, and encourage their purchase of meaningful equity stakes, public companies could facilitate borrowing for this purpose. The Sarbanes-Oxley Act generally prohibits company loans to directors and executives, partly because the prior practice was much abused as a way of compensating managers in a "performance-independent" way that was also invisible to outsiders. Bebchuk and Fried suggest another approach: companies could simply ask directors to secure bank loans at the market rate and commit to paying them, say, 2 percent of the outstanding balance each year until the loans are paid. Such subsidies would encourage share purchases but would not require companies to engage in actual lending, and directors might pay considerably more attention to their monitoring duties because they would have real skin in the game.[52]

Leveraged ownership of company shares could also help minimize the potential adverse effects of simply expanding costless equity grants to directors. One such impact is directors' inclination to focus (perhaps subconsciously) on remaining on the board and enjoying a stream of risk-free compensation, rather than on the difficult task of increasing share value. Some governance experts believe that this will continue to be a serious risk as long as board appointments depend on self-perpetuating nominating committees.[53]

Another potential adverse effect of simply expanding the size of equity grants and stock options is the inclination to focus on short-term changes in market value. Allowing directors to sell such stock only after they leave a board would discourage any actions that might jeopardize their long-term value.

Including loan-financed purchases of company shares in directors' compensation offers a further advantage. To the extent that conflict of interest arises stemming from the fact that directors essentially determine their own fees, a true "dollars-at-stake" feature could partially rescue directors' independence.

Many of Enron's directors met the wealth-at-risk standard of the private-equity governance model. Many nonemployee directors held significant amounts of the company's stock by virtue of their long tenure, or, in the case of one director, the sale of his company to Enron. But again, this should be construed not as a shortcoming of the private-equity governance model, but as a restatement of the great lesson of Enron's governance breakdown: that compliance with one or two features of a more promising approach does not ensure effective governance. Boards must adopt the complete menu of features to realize the benefits of private-equity monitoring and control. In Enron's case, the debilitating missing element was the lack of an arms-length relationship between the directors and Ken Lay in his dual roles as CEO and chair.

A More Arm's-Length Relationship between Directors and the CEO

In the world of private equity, the CEO of a buyout clearly works for the financial sponsors. The board continuously evaluates the CEO's performance, and that of the entire management team, based on cash flow and progress against a detailed business and financial plan that has been sold to the buyout's bankers and limited partners. In the private-equity context, the balance of power clearly lies in the hands of the nonexecutive directors.

This is not the usual pattern in large public corporations operating in the absence of some obvious life-threatening crisis. Under normal conditions, the board's agenda is often far broader than a buyout's business plan and current cash-flow forecast. What's more, the CEO typically secures power through his or her simultaneous tenure as board chair and central role in recruiting directors, naming committee chairs, setting the board's meeting agenda, running meetings, and generally controlling board discussions. In such a context, it is not always clear that the CEO works for the directors, who serve as the shareholders' economic agents.

In the wake of the many corporate scandals that followed the fall of Enron (Global Crossing, Adelphia Communications, WorldCom, Cendant, Tyco International, Qwest, Rite Aid, Computer Associates, HealthSouth, Hollinger International), numerous conversations have focused on how to make a board's internal processes more effective. Much of this focus has been on board structure—especially the question of whether it makes sense to separate the CEO and board chair roles, which are now combined in about 80 percent of U.S. companies. Proponents of separating those roles argue that together they concentrate too much power in the hands of the CEO, who may perform neither role effectively. The strongest proponents of separation argue that "it is contrary to human nature to expect total objectivity for the CEO regarding his or her performance relative to strategies he or she has helped to formulate."[54] They also note that one cannot expect a CEO, in the role of chairman, "to prepare the board to evaluate lapses and failures on his part, or on the part of his management."[55] Opponents to the complete separation of CEO and board chair roles maintain that the CEO is best placed to understand the business and guide nonexecutive directors' deliberations.[56]

Although no systematic research supports the claim that separating the CEO and board chair roles would, in and of itself, give rise to more effective corporate governance, a blue-ribbon commission assembled by the NACD recently recommended that when the chair and CEO roles are not separate, "there should be a designated leadership role for an independent director to serve as a focal point for the work of all independent directors."[57] The report notes that this role can be satisfied by either a nonexecutive chair or, in the combined CEO/chair model, by a "lead" or "presiding" director. This recommendation is evidence of mounting support in the world of public companies for shifting the balance of power back toward independent directors, as in the world of private equity.

While either arrangement proposed by the NACD would be a positive step forward, the complete separation of CEO and board chair roles is clearly more compatible with the private-equity governance model. Nonexecutive chairs are in the best position to apply the discipline of private-equity governance to public companies, and in doing so increase directors' strength and independence. This discipline involves:

- Surfacing the key issues and concerns of the independent directors
- Working with the CEO to set meeting agendas, which should include both issues and options central to the performance of the company
- Ensuring adequate time for full discussion of management proposals and important reports from board committees during meetings of the full board
- Calling meetings of nonemployee directors without the CEO present, either routinely or when doing so appears to be important
- Working to build consensus among the directors after they have expressed differences of opinion
- Perhaps most important, leading the process of evaluating the CEO and the board itself

This model of board leadership greatly reduces the danger that directors will fall victim to the CEO's power and charisma. Of course, implementing such a model requires careful planning. A board cannot simply strip a title from a sitting CEO/chair and hand it over to someone else. As MacAvoy and Millstein—two experienced directors, board advisors, and governance scholars—have noted, "Removing a title from such an individual looks like a demotion and sends a message that the board lacks confidence in the corporation's leadership. Instead, boards should view separation as a key issue to be resolved in succession, to be implemented when whoever is serving in both roles steps down. . . . While the appointment of a "lead" or "presiding" director may be the beginning of the process . . . it is not enough."[58]

The boards of buyouts almost always include a nonexecutive chair, to help counter social and psychological factors that dispose directors of all types of organizations to go along with policies and practices proposed or endorsed by the CEO and other senior executives. These factors may include feelings of friendship, loyalty, and reciprocity toward the CEO; norms of politeness and courtesy that preclude direct confrontation and interpersonal conflict; deference to the authority of the CEO as the most important figure; and the reticence of large shareholders to intervene in corporate affairs in the absence of a clear crisis.[59] As Chapter 5 noted, virtually all these factors were operating in the Enron case, and contributed directly to the company's governance breakdown. A nonexecutive chair or lead-director structure provides critical support for the highly disciplined monitoring that characterizes the work of experienced private-equity boards.

Greater Shareholder Influence over the Nomination and Removal of Directors

The final innovation required to transfer the full benefits of the private-equity governance model to the boards of public companies is the ability of dispersed shareholders to control those who nominally represent their interests. In a standard buyout, this is usually not a problem, because most major equity partners have seats on the board, and few reservations about removing senior managers who prove to be unimaginative, wrongheaded, or otherwise inept, including the CEO. Dissatisfied shareholders have a direct and swift means of protecting their interests.

This is not the case with shareholders of public companies, despite their legal right to turn their economic agents (the corporate directors) out if they are displeased with their actions. Instances where shareholders replace incumbents with a team that would do a better job are rare.[60] A recent study found that during a seven-year period (1996–2002), proxy contests involving attempts to replace a board occurred at only eighty of the thousands of publicly listed companies.[61] Only ten of these contests involved companies with market capitalizations in excess of $200 million.

The most commonly exercised option for disgruntled shareholders—to simply sell their shares (the so-called Wall Street Walk)—is a less-than-perfect solution if they are loath to incur substantial losses occasioned by flawed management. No mid-course corrections are available to such shareholders, save for expensive and time-consuming proxy contests aimed at removing unresponsive directors.

Incumbent directors who stand little chance of being removed have little incentive to focus fully on shareholder interests. The Securities and Exchange Commission (SEC) has responded by proposing, on several occasions, a simplified proxy-access policy for shareholders. Most recently, in October 2003, the SEC proposed a rather timid step toward improving shareholder access.

The proposal would allow shareholders and shareholder groups who own more than 5 percent of a public company's securities for at least two years to include their nominees in a board election, if one of two triggers occurred. The first trigger would be shareholder approval of a proposal to opt into the proxy system submitted by a shareholder who holds at least 1 percent of the company's equity. The other trigger would occur if 35 percent of the shareholders withheld votes for any particular candidate for director. Given either trigger, at the annual shareholders' meeting the following year, the company's proxy materials would have to include one (independent) candidate proposed by this 5 percent group. The number of such candidates would increase to two if the board is composed of nine to nineteen directors and votes are withheld from two management nominees, and to three if the board is composed of twenty or more directors.[62]

The Business Roundtable and other influential CEOs have persistently criticized the SEC for potentially opening corporate boards to activist institutional investors or single-issue advocacy, but their position is weak. The proposed proxy process involves far too many hurdles to expose corporate boards to obstructive, naïve, or uninformed radicals. Shareholders who are dissatisfied with the performance of incumbent directors would have to jump over at least five hurdles before gaining access to a small minority of board seats. These include (1) gaining enough support from fellow shareholders to reach one of the triggering thresholds, (2) waiting a year for the next election of directors, (3) satisfying the requirements for ownership and the holding period, (4) bearing the campaign costs of convincing other shareholders to vote for their candidate(s, and (5) actually gaining majority support for their candidate.[63]

Although the SEC proposal presents many opportunities for modification, in consultation with the business community, its basic thrust is a productive, if modest, step toward encouraging active, independent directors, and thus is entirely consistent with the private-equity governance model. If adopted, the process would provide at least a middling defense against compliant or captive directors, and encourage, if not promote, more rigorous board oversight of corporate affairs.

More radical proposals are afloat to increase shareholder influence over the nomination and removal of directors. In a lead article on March 11, 2006, the *Economist* proposed making an entire corporate board stand for re-election under majority voting every two or three years, while scrapping quarterly earnings reports. The article noted that "one of the reasons why private equity has become more popular in the corporate world" is that these enterprises have found a way of "restor[ing] the balance between owners and managers" and avoiding obsession with quarterly results, which "presses managers to pursue meaningless targets rather than think about what is best for the company."

This magazine's editors clearly understand the problem, as well as remedies based on the private-equity model. So, too, do many shareholders. More than a third of shareholders voting in the 2006 proxy season favored "majority-vote" proposals at Analog Devices, Capital One Financial, General Dynamics, Hewlett Packard, the United Health Group, and Wells Fargo.[64] Such proposals would require any sitting director who fails to secure a majority of votes in an election to tender his or her resignation, which the board would then decide whether to accept. Any new candidate for the board who failed to secure a majority of votes cast would simply not be elected.[65] Several companies, led by Pfizer, a leading pharmaceuticals company, have responded by adopting a formal majority-voting policy.

In the final analysis, the private-equity governance model shifts the structural, social, psychological, and power milieu of the board, so that directors no longer see themselves as employees or cheerleaders of the chair and CEO, when the same person holds the two positions, as is common in the United States. To many governance experts, this mindset has been one of the major sources of problems with corporate governance. Supporting the chair and CEO is clearly an important role for a board, but one that must be subordinated to its role as monitor.[66]

This is where Enron's governance system broke down, and where the private-equity governance model has particular relevance. As long as CEOs of public companies retain control of the recruitment and tenure of directors, the board's agenda, and the information that flows to the board, the power relationship between the board and CEO will tilt toward the CEO. Adopting the features of the private-equity governance model—in their entirety—can help shift power back toward the directors.

Is the Private-Equity Governance Model Sustainable for Public Corporations?

One of the most salient characteristics of private-equity boards is that directors' common task is well defined. That task is typically to prepare a company for a profitable "exit"—that is, its sale to a strategic investor or the public through a public issuing of shares. Private-equity directors can face a multitude of problems along the way, but the end game is always clear and the focus of everyone's energy.

In public corporations, the end game is rarely clear, and the directors' agenda is often more crowded than that of a buyout board. Beyond the standard responsibilities and compliance activities lies a rich mix of recurring agenda items, some of which are shared with private equity boards and some of which—especially those related to "earnings management" and corporate financial reporting—are not: overseeing longstanding conflicts of interest among the firms' principal constituencies; reviewing and ratifying various capital-expenditure requests and business plans; evaluating which parts of the business portfolio merit special support or a cut in resources; considering how best to drive future growth without sacrificing current profitability; ratifying or rejecting major acquisitions and divestitures; deciding, with the audit and finance committees, which profits to report or reserve in any quarter; approving dividend policy; reviewing various employment agreements with the compensation and governance committees; attending to management succession; and so forth. In working through such agendas, long-tenured directors on public boards run the risk of internalizing many of the cognitive biases of management, thereby complicating the monitoring process.

The practical question that intrudes on all the recommendations in this chapter is: What will prevent a public company that attempts to adopt the private-equity governance model from reverting to the "natural state" of a less-focused, more cognitively conditioned or compromised board? This is not an idle question, because anecdotal evidence suggests that when buyouts return to the public capital market, they often revert to more traditional governance practices and norms.

One way to prevent a regression is to ensure that a new public board understands and agrees to a well-defined set of corporate challenges on which all energies temporarily focus. While executing a profitable "exit" within a specified time may be a unique point of focus for private equity directors, comparable challenges of a concrete nature also exist once the company reenters the public capital market with a new, more independent board. These may include, for example, continuing to improve the company's competitive cost position or cash flow returns, or being first to market with the next generation of products and services. Such focal challenges may well change over time. However, without a specific task orientation, an essential private-equity characteristic will be missing, and that governance model will be exposed to the risks of dilution and dissipation.

CHAPTER 9

Avoiding Perverse Financial Incentives

Executive compensation is the acid test of corporate governance.
—Warren Buffett

Perverse financial incentives put in place or sanctioned by Enron's board compounded the company's governance problems. Financial incentives—especially those that pay for performance—can mesh the interests of managers and stockholders and focus attention on corporate goals. Enron's board of directors tried to achieve such alignment by making some 75 percent of senior executives' total compensation contingent on "increasing stockholder value."[1] However, the company's overall approach to financial incentives exerted a number of perverse side effects:

- It encouraged growth over profitability.
- It rewarded employees for closing commodity deals and power generation projects without concrete evidence of their future profitability.
- It deepened a deadly addiction to pumping up the company's stock price through a variety of obfuscating maneuvers.
- It helped create a corporate culture that tolerated and sometimes encouraged deception.

Many features of Enron's incentive system contributed to these outcomes. In fact, the system was a veritable archive of missteps and violations of basic, commonsense principles for financial incentives and pay for performance. Individually, these provisions would not have been devastating, but combined they proved deadly:

- Premature bonus payments
- Minimal use of comparative measures of performance
- Lack of disciplined, subjective performance measurement

- Failure to index executives' stock options
- Lack of constraints on the unwinding—or selling—of stock grants
- No provisions for "lookbacks" and "clawbacks" of bonuses and stock awards—that is, provisions for rescinding them if performance failed to meet expectations
- Unmonitored incentives to manage earnings
- An overall failure to balance turbo-charged incentives with adequate controls

Like many other public companies, the compensation committee of Enron's board did consult regularly with experienced executive compensation advisors—in this case, Hewitt Associates and Towers Perrin—on matters related to the design and levels of executive pay. However, whatever their advice, it did not forestall the disastrous results of Enron's breach of commonsense principles of financial incentives.

As Chapter 2 showed, Enron's leaders wanted the company to be a pay-for-performance shop. Corporate officers intended the compensation system to attract and retain the highest-caliber executives, provide "top quartile compensation for top quartile performance," mesh decision making with the company's espoused goals of innovation and growth, and align shareholders' and managers' interests.[2] However, in the hands of Enron's senior officers and directors, the pay-for-performance framework for corporate-level and operating executives became corrupted. This chapter outlines Enron's eight violations of commonsense principles for financial incentives and pay for performance, and suggests remedial action.

This analysis is timely, given widespread evidence that many companies tie executive compensation only weakly to financial performance, and that pay-for-performance schemes often reward short-term rather than long-term performance.[3] This pattern of executive pay is becoming less acceptable to shareholders, who perceive the absence of a clear link between executive compensation and performance as evidence of a massive failure of corporate governance. Indeed, the relationship between pay and performance is becoming a leading indicator of responsible (and irresponsible) corporate behavior.

Pay for Performance as a Framework for Financial Incentives

Pay for performance has many advantages as a framework for financial incentives. Leaders can design such plans to attract specific types of employees, and influence the quantity and quality of their work. Strong pay-for-performance plans and financial incentives also focus individuals on a firm's highest-priority tasks, so they work smarter, not just harder.

A clear link between performance measures and rewards provides the strongest incentives.[4] Rewards can be linked to quantitative measures or more subjective indicators. Bonuses can rise gradually or exponentially with performance, and may include guaranteed minimums as well as caps. The form of the measures and incentives should reflect the ends: that is, they should encourage or suppress the targeted behaviors.[5]

Incentive systems may also emphasize different time horizons, degrees of risk taking, and levels of teamwork and cooperation.[6] For example, annual cash bonuses tend to reward current performance, while deferred compensation, and stock options with long holding periods, reward the future results of today's actions. To encourage risk taking, boards often approve incentive systems that provide substantial payoffs for reaching predetermined, quantifiable objectives such as sales growth, percent of sales from new customers or new products, customer satisfaction, and incremental operating income—objectives for which there are clear performance measures and little ambiguity about desired results. However, attention to more qualitative objectives related to personal integrity and the protection of corporate reputation, which can only be assessed by informed judgment, can reassure boards that bonus awards will reflect an executive's total performance. Finally, incentive systems based on the performance of teams or subunits can emphasize group over individual accomplishments.

The history of Reckitt Benckiser—the Anglo-Dutch world leader in household cleaning products, with revenues of over £4 billion in 2005 and over 25,000 employees worldwide—shows how an effective pay-for-performance scheme can work.[7] To the company's board, pay for performance lies at the core of an organizational strategy intended to serve the best interests of shareholders and employees.

The company's annual reports continually emphasize that performance-oriented pay is "absolutely critical" to its success in competing against industry giants such as Procter & Gamble (U.S.), Unilever (Netherlands and U.K.), Colgate Palmolive (U.S.), Clorox (U.S.), Henkel (Germany), and Dial (U.S.). For example, Reckitt Benckiser's 2002 annual report stresses that the company puts "a heavy emphasis on winning," and that this orientation requires both a highly effective performance compensation system and high-quality people with "passionate commitment." Elsewhere the report refers to employees with a high propensity for achievement, commitment, entrepreneurship, and teamwork. John Beadle, the company's compensation and benefits director, maintains that the compensation policy attracts "a self-selected group of people who are motivated and excited by the remuneration system and who believe in themselves and in the system."

Key components of Reckitt Benkiser's pay-for-performance plan—and indeed all effective plans—include the types of rewards (salary, bonus, stock options, fringe benefits, quality of work environment, and time off); the size and range of those rewards (total value of the reward package); and the variability of rewards over time (how the level of compensation changes with performance, and how performance is measured). These basic elements encompass a plan's *composition, level,* and *functional form.*[8]

As Beadle suggests, plans that offer low salaries with potentially high bonuses tend to attract people with different risk profiles, energy levels, and entrepreneurial spirit from plans that offer higher salaries with no contingent payoffs. Reckitt Benckiser's plan emphasizes the former: it offers managers base pay that is "sufficient to live on"—plus a 40 percent bonus for meeting all growth and efficiency targets, such as growth in revenues and profits, and reductions in net working capital. Employees who substantially exceed these targets can earn bonuses of up to 140 percent of base salary; the CEO's bonus potential is 360 percent of base salary, and the CFO's is 270 percent. Employees who do not meet the targets receive no bonuses.

Reckitt Benckiser also provides long-term incentives in the form of stock options and restricted stock (securities with a contractual restriction, such as a lock up barring the resale of the stock for a specified period). Employees receive these rewards if the company meets three-year growth targets in earnings per share, set by the company's board of directors. The stock grants vest more quickly if the company meets annual growth targets. If the company does not reach these goals, the stock options and grants of restricted stock lapse. It is doubtful that executives looking for guaranteed remuneration at some market rate would take much comfort in this compensation plan.

Still, Reckitt Benckiser recognizes that it must offer employees their "opportunity cost" of not accepting another employer's offer, and expects its pay and contingent bonuses to influence the quality of the employees it attracts. Thus the board puts executives' base salaries near the mean of those of competitors, and pays cash bonuses for above-target performance that are double the industry median.

Reckitt Benckiser's experience attests to the efficacy of relying on strong performance incentives to create economic value. The company's 2002 annual report explicitly links its remuneration policy to its superior growth in market value over the preceding four years, compared with both the United Kingdom's most prominent stock index (UK FTSE 100) and a narrower peer group of direct competitors.

Another View

Not all organizational theorists agree that pay for performance works. Critics and proponents of other incentive plans argue that money is nowhere near the top of lists of factors that contribute to extreme job satisfaction or dissatisfaction. These critics also argue that incentives to increase productivity do not address underlying problems, and therefore fail to encourage meaningful change, and that performance incentives undermine intrinsic motivation and job interest. The latter claim assumes that individuals subject to excessive control lose interest, and that their performance declines.[9] Critics of pay for performance often cite studies that fail to find any strong, persistent correlation between cash compensation and managers' performance. These critics also note that stock options included as part of pay-for-performance plans often reward executives for market- and sector-wide movements unrelated to their efforts.[10]

However, each of these claims raises as many questions as it purports to answer. How does the relatively low ranking of money as a source of extreme satisfaction or dissatisfaction (sixth or seventh in one study) eliminate its motivational power?[11] Why would financial incentives undermine individuals' intrinsic motivation to do a good job; couldn't extrinsic rewards reinforce rather than replace internal motivation?[12] Does a lack of persistent correlation between executives' salaries and bonuses and performance discredit pay for performance, or merely signal its frequent misapplication?

The research underlying critics' claims is evidence not that pay-for-performance plans cannot work, but of serious implementation challenges. Indeed, research on employee behavior and compensation preferences suggests quite another perspective on the power of incentive pay. One consistent finding is that "when individual pay is clearly dependent on individual performance, job performance is higher than when pay and performance are not related."[13] Research also shows that managers prefer to have their pay tied to performance.[14] Although poorly designed and administered pay-for-performance plans can give rise to gaming behavior—wherein individuals try to make their performance look better than it is—it is precisely because incentives are so powerful that we see so many unintended and unwanted side effects of executive incentive plans.

Commonsense Principles of Pay for Performance

Serious design flaws in all three dimensions of Enron's pay-for-performance system—the level of compensation, the types and design of reward instruments, and the specific performance measures—keyed top executive pay to the wrong goals, and promoted excessive gambling with shareholders' money. These flaws are not unique to Enron, which is why they merit serious attention.

Level of Pay

By most measures, Enron was not a particularly profitable company. Throughout the 1990s, it never earned its cost of capital, which means that in a true economic sense it systematically destroyed value for its shareholders.[15] During the five years leading up to its bankruptcy, Enron's return on invested capital—operating profits after taxes divided by the total capital employed in the business—averaged only 6.4 percent. This metric actually overstates Enron's financial performance because of its negative tax rate in 1997 stemming from a $65 million write-off on a North Sea natural gas contract, which had the effect of increasing the company's reported return on invested capital in that year.

This extremely low level of economic performance did not keep Enron's executives from being highly paid. According to New York–based Charas Consulting, between 1996 and 2000 Enron paid its top executives nearly $600 million. In 2000 alone, Enron's top five executives received $283 million. Roughly 80 percent of the total compensation of these executives stemmed from cashing in stock options.[16]

The Charas study reported that Enron's pay scale exceeded that of its peers by a wide margin. In 2000, the company's executive salaries exceeded their peer-group average by 51 percent, while bonuses topped the average by 382 percent. Stock options granted that year (valued at the time of grant at $86.5 million) exceeded those of peers by 484 percent! Even if Enron's board felt that the company's peer group was higher-paying

Wall Street trading operations rather than traditional energy companies, Enron's substantial payouts to senior executives were remarkably uncorrelated with profitability.

Moreover, not only was senior executive pay excessive relative to that of peers, but the method for determining these payouts was limited in scope. Even as the salaries, bonuses, and stock grants of Enron's top five executives climbed, reflecting growth in the company's revenues and stock price, the productivity of capital invested in the business steadily declined. It is precisely this bias for growth over profitability—and the low return on capital in much of U.S. enterprise—that fuels criticism of management compensation, and raises questions about the effectiveness of firms' internal control systems.[17] Do corporate executives who fail to earn their cost of capital, and therefore systematically destroy real economic value, deserve such high levels of pay?

Ordinary U.S. citizens have generally tolerated high levels of executive pay and extreme wealth if earned on merit, because that means ordinary people can join the ranks of the wealthy. Thus for many Americans, the operative question is not "how much?" but "how?" At Enron, the "how" question is the most troubling, because of the perverse behavior it spawned.

Bonus Payments

Awarding bonuses up front—before cash and profits flow from commercial endeavors—invites employees to maximize their short-term pecuniary interests while compromising the company's long-term interests.

Premature award of executive bonuses was one of Enron's most serious violations of commonsense pay-for-performance principles, and the costs were enormous. As Chapter 2 noted, deal originators and commodity traders at Enron Wholesale Services could routinely earn as much as five times their salaries in cash bonuses for meeting targets based on the estimated present value of transactions executed within any given year. And these employees *themselves* estimated those present values, reviewed by an increasingly ineffective Risk Assessment and Control (RAC) group. Developers of large-scale power projects at Enron International also received a sizable portion of their large cash bonuses—some of which they could convert to shares of stock—when their projects were signed.

This approach to rewarding Enron's primary business developers had two notable effects. First, the bonus system encouraged deal originators and project developers—who ultimately were not held responsible for the profitability of their deals—to take on substantial risks. Second, the system perpetuated a corporatewide addiction to supernormal growth. In the early years, Enron's addiction to growth ensured that the innovative trading company gained first-mover advantage in newly deregulated energy markets. After 1997, however, when serious misrepresentations crept into Enron's accounting and reporting practices, the unfettered approach to both top-line (revenue) and bottom-line (profit) growth supported an increasingly overvalued stock price and fragile credit rating.

Cash bonuses awarded by the board to Enron's most senior executives—which ran from three to six times their salaries during the company's last three years of existence—reinforced this preoccupation with rapid growth. These cash bonuses also expanded exponentially with reported revenues and net income, even as the company's profitability dropped precipitously. For example, cash bonuses for the five most senior operating executives grew from just over $3 million in 1997 to more than $17 million in 2000—nearly a sixfold jump—while cash bonuses for Skilling and Lay skyrocketed more than twelve times. During that period revenues increased five times and reported profits nine times. The bad news was that the company's return on capital employed—the most economically robust measure of profitability—declined from a modest 9.38 percent to a meager 4.95 percent during the same period.

The practice of awarding bonuses to deal originators and traders based on the present value of deals closed within a year, and to senior executives based on growth rather than true profitability, compromised the company's long-term health. The failure of returns on risky commodity contracts, power projects, and merchant investments to meet both Enron's and Wall Street's expectations led senior executives to search out still more esoteric deals with even higher predicted returns and risks, and was further motivation for obfuscating the company's true financial condition. Many poorly performing commodity contracts, power projects, and merchant investments were eventually "sold" to off-balance-sheet entities (such as the Raptors partnerships) to avoid write-downs in fair market value in the company's financial reports, and to generate operating profits when expected returns failed to materialize from Enron's more traditional business.

Paying *before* performance is, of course, a far cry from paying *for* performance. The former is based on hope, the latter on results. Enron was not the only trading operation to pay bonuses based on expected values. However, three factors were notably absent that typically reduce the risks of cheating on such valuations. These include a strong culture of honesty and truth telling; longevity of traders in their positions; and clawback, or rescinding, of bonuses if expected results fail to materialize. In the latter case, bonus payments are often held in escrow and paid out over time, if a company and individuals meet expectations.

Comparative Measures of Business Performance

Reward systems that ignore comparative measures of business performance provide incentives for executives to do the wrong things.

In its proxy statements, Enron's board claimed that key performance measures for the most senior corporate officers included "funds flow, return on equity, debt reduction, earnings per share improvements, and other relevant factors" that help create "long-term shareholder value." However, many of these performance standards were not met, although other, growth-oriented targets clearly were.

For example, revenues grew from $13.3 billion in 1996 to $100.8 billion in 2000, while reported earnings grew from $584 million to $979 million, and earnings per share rose from $1.12 to $1.22. Enron's stock price also rose dramatically after 1997. Yet at the same time Enron was piling on debt, even if the total does not include the unreported debt buried in off-balance-sheet partnerships. Moreover, the company's earnings as a percent of capital invested declined every year that its asset base expanded.

Thus, despite the board's espoused approach to performance measurement, the directors appear to have defined performance of Enron's top executives, for all practical purposes, in terms of growth in revenue, earnings per share, and share price. The board apparently ignored or undervalued many important conditions for *sustaining* the price of Enron's shares, such as cash flow, return on invested capital, and balance-sheet strength, all of which deteriorated from 1997 onward.

The board also ignored comparative performance measures, such as the company's market share and profitability compared with that of its peers. For example, senior corporate executives and executives in Enron's Wholesale Services unit received bonuses even as other energy companies had begun imitating Enron's innovations in newly deregulated energy markets, putting severe downward pressure on trading margins. Comparative performance was similarly ignored at Enron International and NEPCO, Enron's power plant construction company, leaving these units to pursue ever more unpromising and unprofitable projects.

Like cash bonuses, Enron's stock options and grants of restricted stock were divorced from any comparative measures of performance. Executives received those rewards for meeting recurring after-tax income targets set by the board's compensation committee.[18] Only the company's performance unit plan included a comparative-performance feature.[19]

As noted, from 1996 through 2000, the combined pay of Enron's top five executives totaled nearly $600 million with stock options accounting for more than four-fifths of that amount. Enron was not alone, of course, in emphasizing equity-based pay. From 1990 through 2001, equity-based pay as a percentage of median CEO pay in the United States rose from 8 percent to 66 percent.[20] However, Enron's history of awarding a growing number of stock options at fixed prices to senior executives, without regard to the company's comparative performance, created several thorny problems as the stock price began to shoot up after 1997.

First and most important, the run-up in Enron's stock price had little to do with superior management performance. When a strong bull market takes hold, sparked by factors beyond the control of individual managers, executives holding fixed-price options enjoy huge windfalls. Under these conditions, the wealth effects of exercising these options create the illusion of enormous personal and corporate success, reinforcing whatever inflated self-image and hubris already exist.

Second, without comparative performance metrics for equity-based pay, the expertly promoted and overvalued share price may have lulled Enron into a false sense of security. This was evidenced by the triggers in various off-balance-sheet partnerships, which required Enron to top off its equity participation if its stock price fell below a given point. These provisions, of course, proved to be the undoing of many partnerships during the months before Enron's collapse.

Third, as senior executives received and exercised ever-larger stock-option grants without regard to the company's performance versus key competitors, the greatly enhanced wealth position of these executives separated them from the interests of the corporation and its shareholders. By 2001 both Ken Rice (most recently chair of Enron Broadband Services) and Lou Pai (most recently chair of Enron Accelerator, but the leader of various business initiatives during the 1990s) were spending little time in the office.

Before year-end they were gone, having accumulated such vast personal wealth that both had little incentive to remain.[21]

In 2000 alone, Rice received $2,170,000 in salary and bonus, plus a $4 million payout from the long-term incentive plan, and exercised stock options valued at more than $16 million. In all, at the end of his last full year at Enron, Rice took home nearly $22.5 million, and held exercisable options valued at more than $34 million.[22] Pai had sold more than $250 million in Enron stock by the time he left the company.[23] Jeff Skilling, who earned more than $20 million in salary and bonuses and resigned not long after Rice and Pai departed, sold more than $70 million in Enron stock between May 2000 and September 2001.[24] Like Pai and Rice, Skilling had amassed such wealth that he had little incentive to stay around once the headaches began piling up in 2001.

Finally, when share prices rise above normal valuations of reported earnings, the pressure to manage the company to maintain its high share price—and thus to preserve executives' wealth—becomes palpable. This pressure appears to have been part of Enron's motivation for inflating reported profits, and hiding poorly performing hedges and merchant investments in off-balance-sheet partnerships. Such pressure also helps explain the various efforts by Skilling and other Enron executives to promote the company's prospects and talk up the value of its stock from January 2001 onward, as alleged by the Securities and Exchange Commission (SEC).[25]

Cash bonuses and equity-based compensation linked to comparative performance might have restrained the hubris and feelings of superiority of Enron's most senior executives, and perhaps inhibited some of their gambling behavior. Had Enron subscribed to this principle of effective pay for performance, for example, senior executives at Enron Wholesale Services and Enron International would have been rewarded for contributing to superior stock-market returns to shareholders only when their performance equaled or exceeded that of executives in their peer group.[26] Because neither the company's bonuses nor its stock plans were based on this principle, the strongest signals from executives' paychecks were out of step with the realities of comparative performance.

Former SEC chair Arthur Levitt has proposed that companies' annual reports include a chart that plots their performance and top executives' compensation against those of a representative sample of peers. He has also proposed that the compensation committee of a company's board of directors justify, in writing, compensation greater than that paid by corporate peers.[27]

Given widespread failings in performance measurement and excessive rewards to senior executives, shareholders of public companies would be well served if corporate boards adopted those sensible suggestions.

Subjective Performance Measurement

Pay-for-performance systems that ignore rigorously applied subjective judgments often promote gaming behavior and provide insufficient direction to executives.

Not only did performance measures applied to Enron's corporate senior executives reflect a narrow set of financial metrics, but the quantitative measures used at lower management levels all but encouraged executives at Enron International and the Wholesale Services unit to game the bonus system. If only to forestall the destruction of value that occurs when managers overestimate returns on deals, bonus payments to new business developers and executives with oversight responsibility should reflect all dimensions of *real* performance. These should include the *quality* of deals, as well as the motives, work habits, and integrity of deal developers.

Senior executives are often disinclined to base bonuses on such measures, despite their obvious value. Subjective measures pick up where quantitative measures leave off by introducing knowledge of what actually happened to the equation. This helps distinguish the direct impact of employee behavior and decision making from that of uncontrollable events, and can contribute to a more meaningful measure of performance than the sole use of quantitative measures.

In practice, of course, it is difficult to rigorously apply subjective measures of individuals' performance. In business and academic settings alike, most people tend to receive good or outstanding reviews in the absence of incontestably bad performance. In a well-known study, Medoff and Abraham found that more than 94 percent of a sample of 7,629 managers in two large manufacturing firms received performance ratings of good or outstanding, as opposed to acceptable or unacceptable.[28] Another study in 1993 found that 91 percent of the grades of Harvard undergraduates were B– or higher, with Ds and Es *(sic)* virtually nonexistent. Some 43 percent of all grades that year were A and A–.[29]

There is considerable speculation as to why this pattern exists, though it is widely recognized that the personal discomfort associated with giving negative feedback can be high. Whatever the explanation, such pain-avoiding behavior by evaluators can smooth performance differences, making ranking impossible and blunting the motivational power of any evaluation system.[30]

Yet a focus on purely quantitative measures—whether revenues, current operating margins, present value of estimated future cash flow, or market value—can foster a narrow, self-centered view of success that distorts executive behavior. Absent the systematic application of subjective performance measures such as good business instincts, deep analytical skills, leadership potential, and ethical discipline—all of which Enron espoused in principle, even as it devalued them in practice—the tendency is to "play by the hard numbers." The Enron case is as good an example as any of what happens when subtler, more qualitative assessments of performance are crowded out or ignored.

Enron was among a handful of firms—including McKinsey and GE—that adopted the forced curve in evaluating individual performance and providing feedback. However, Enron's good intentions with respect to balancing objective and subjective performance measurement may have gone awry in its emphasis on individual over comparative business performance. Instances abound where the performance review committee (PRC) process evolved into a winner-take-all system—with employees' final rankings (and bonuses and promotion opportunities) determined more by supervisors' lobbying efforts than by peer assessments of innovativeness and entrepreneurship, analytical skills, communication, teamwork, and leadership potential. The widely perceived rank-and-yank system used within Enron Wholesale Services, along with the gradual breakdown of many other PRC processes, ended up demoralizing employees recruited and lauded as the industry's best.[31]

That Enron's introverted PRC process deflated many younger employees is not surprising, in light of the highly politicized ranking of up-and-coming executives, which reinforced the superstar culture within Wholesale Services. Nor is it surprising that it became easier to allocate bonuses based on the value of commodity contracts and power projects approved by RAC and other bodies in a given year, rather than on subjective judgments of the quality of trading strategies and development projects.

Lest we forget, Rebecca Mark, who was eventually forced to resign for her role in developing many of Enron's international power and water projects, received healthy bonuses while building her book of business. In their reported controversy over the company's international strategy, Mark and Skilling never resolved how to evaluate that strategy and assign performance-based rewards. The result was that Enron paid bonuses on several large power and water utility projects, and then, within a very few years, closed them down and wrote them off. Similarly, only a few years after paying large bonuses to deal originators and traders, Enron transferred many unprofitable commodity contracts and poorly performing hedges to off-balance-sheet entities, to dress up reported earnings and support the company's all-important credit rating.

The keys to successful implementation of subjective performance measurement are revealed in the history of Enron International. First, in the absence of a shared view of what constitutes a successful strategy or record of individual performance—as was the case between Skilling (Enron's chief operating officer) and Mark (the head of Enron International)—there is no chance that sufficient trust will exist to make discussions of performance either credible or palatable. As my colleague, Robert Simons, writes after a ten-year study of management control systems, "Subjective measures rely on the personal judgments of superiors and will be effective motivators only if the superior is capable of making an accurate and informed judgment about the subordinate and *only if trust between the superior and subordinate is high.*"[32] (Emphasis added.) In the absence of informed judgment *and* trust, subjective measures will simply not be seen as valid measures of accomplishment. Second, since by definition subjective performance measurement lacks credible objective metrics, making this process work requires textual descriptions of both expectations (by supervising bodies) and accomplishments (by reporting managers) for objectives that are difficult to quantify.[33] The rigor of subjective performance measurement depends entirely on the precision of these texts (or memos of understanding) and the attention devoted to their review.

Indexed Stock Options

Stock options that are not indexed to the movement of capital markets, and to gains in the price of competitors' stock, can give executives unearned windfalls for uncompetitive performance.

With fixed-price (as opposed to indexed) stock options, the exercise price is established at the market price on the day the options are granted, and remains fixed over the entire option period—typically seven to ten years. Executives thus benefit from any rise in the company's share price, even if it is less than that of competitors or the market as a whole.[34] One recent study of

U.S. stock prices over a ten-year period reported that only 30 percent of those price changes reflected corporate performance, with the remaining 70 percent driven by overall market conditions.[35] And that study was conducted before the strong bull market that drove Enron's rising share price and underlying valuations—even as profits as a percent of capital employed were steadily declining.

Awarding indexed rather than fixed-price stock options might have had a disciplining effect on managerial behavior at Enron. Indexed stock options are worth exercising only if a company's shares go up by more than some index of relative performance, such as the Standard & Poor 500. This approach prevents underperforming managers from being rewarded simply because the overall market is rising, and it avoids penalizing superior performers in a falling market. Indexing also eliminates the need for companies to react to market declines by issuing new or repriced options, in an effort to lift performance risk from executives' shoulders.[36]

In theory, the argument for indexed options makes sense. But in Enron's case its share price—based on highly misleading corporate reporting—outperformed the share price of many peers after 1997. Figure 9.1 shows that Enron's share price rose significantly faster than those of eleven peers from 1998 through 2000, just before the strong bull market began to subside and Enron's earnings were becoming suspect in some quarters.

Alternatives to the straightforward indexing options to the market performance of peers exist, but they have their own drawbacks. For example, under "performance-conditioned investing," which sets performance targets to an absolute increase in market value rather than an index of peers, managers who do not meet the targets forfeit their options—a serious penalty.

The "performance-accelerated" approach allows executives who meet their targets to accelerate the vesting of their stock options.[37] As Chapter 2 noted, Lay's 1996 employment agreement and stock-option plan included this provision. For every year (in any given year, or on a cumulative basis) that Enron's stock price outperformed the total return of the S&P 500 by 20 percent or more, one-third of Lay's options vested. This reduced the initial seven-year vesting period to as little as three years, providing strong incentive to push up Enron's short-term stock price.

The performance-based restricted stock issued to Skilling in 1998 (in lieu of performance units) also included accelerated vesting for meeting earnings targets.[38] Unhappily, this incentive (along with the triggers built into the debt covenants of many off-balance-sheet partnerships) might have fueled the efforts of Lay and Skilling and their most senior associates to boost Enron's stock price through overly optimistic depictions of the company's financial condition, limited transparency in financial reporting, and even deceptive accounting.

One way to minimize incentives to run up short-term stock price and compromise a company's long-term value is to lengthen the amount of time that executives must hold the stock options that they do exercise. Incentives to support a company's stock price are especially strong when its stock price is overvalued, as Enron's was during the late 1990s and into 2000. Many Enron senior executives sold massive amounts of stock during this period, suggesting that they intuitively knew that was the case. Longer holding periods—coupled with clawback provisions (see below)— would have been an effective antidote to the attitudes and behaviors that held sway at Enron, and that continue to reign at many public corporations.

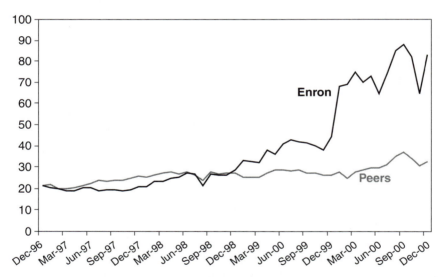

Figure 9.1 Stock prices of Enron and eleven peers, 1996–2001. The peer group, the same used in Enron's proxy statements, includes: AES Corp, BG Group, Coastal Corp (renamed El Paso CGP), Duke Energy, Dynegy, El Paso Energy Corp, Occidental Petroleum, Pacific Gas & Electric, and The Williams Companies. Two other firms included in the peer group were replaced during 2000 due to mergers: Columbia Energy Group was replaced by Level 3 Communications, Consolidated Natural Gas Co. by Dominion Resources.

A compatible approach, strongly argued by my colleague Michael Jensen, is to forget about both fixed-price and indexed options and rely instead on customized options, which become profitable only when share price appreciates by more than a firm's cost of capital. Under such a plan, the exercise price of executives' stock options would rise with a company's cost of capital.[39]

If the goal is to reward senior executives through grants of stock options or restricted stock only if they create real economic value, independent of short-term swings in stock prices—which I think *is* the proper goal—then Jensen's proposal has merit. However, the proposal sets a performance standard that is so high that it risks being rejected out of hand as simply noncompetitive in the market for senior executives.

The most practical way to capture the spirit of Jensen's proposal is to combine it with a more traditional indexed-option program. In that approach, executives could exercise their stock options only if the company's share price rose by more than some index over some extended period of time—*and* the company earned its cost of capital. Under that program, Enron executives would never have cashed in a single stock option. Such a program would also have clearly identified as unacceptable the enormous destruction of real economic value caused by the company's consistent failure to earn its cost of capital.

Enron's experience with fixed-price options shows how enormous payouts can be totally unrelated to economic and executive performance. Because Enron's board of directors and compensation consultants apparently ignored the fact that Enron never earned its cost of capital, and the factors contributing to that record, executives' stock options paid off handsomely, even as shareholders were earning less than the cost of capital on their investments. The board's message to management was simple: what counts is stock appreciation, not the true measure of sustainable corporate performance—conditions that foster returns that exceed the cost of capital.

Enron's experience also shows how, if options are not indexed, executives can reap windfall gains from stock market bubbles or short-term run-ups in stock price. Had Enron's stock options been indexed, the payoff to executives would have been far more modest, and far more representative of the company's true economic performance.

An effective indexed-option program must include two additional features. First, the number of options granted should reflect an executive's competence in building and supporting a sustainable business enterprise.

Second, because indexed options impose significant risks of nonpayment, I propose increasing the number awarded while lowering their exercise price.[40]

Although not a perfect science, the technology is in place to compensate executives for the added risk they incur under an indexed-option plan. Alfred Rappaport, who followed 170 companies from 1988 through 1997, showed that various combinations of larger option grants and discounted prices can enable executives of superior-performing companies to gain more with indexed than with conventional options.[41] I believe that the number of options and shares granted should rise proportionally with the degree of difficulty in meeting performance targets.

Few companies have adopted indexed or customized stock options. One recent study reports that only 5 percent of the largest fifty firms require executives to meet performance targets before their options vest.[42] This is probably due to the fact that indexed options must be marked to market on a regular basis, and "accrue an earnings charge reflecting the appreciation in the value of the option over the indexed exercise charge."[43] Simply put, indexed options, because they lack a fixed exercise price, fall outside the charge-free zone. Conventional stock options do not result in a charge to earnings.

Given an efficient stock market, these accounting peculiarities should not be important. That's because firms that issue conventional options must disclose their impact on net income and earnings per share in footnotes to their financial statements, and investors who read those footnotes should be able to figure out their effect on reported earnings. Fortunately, this issue is becoming moot, given the likelihood that companies will soon have to expense all options in some form on their published income statements.

Unwinding Stock Grants

Awarding stock grants without restricting the amount and timing of their sale weakens their incentive effects, allows executives to benefit from short-term rises in stock price, and puts corporate insiders in conflict with ordinary shareholders.

Companies typically grant executives considerable discretion in choosing how long to hold, and when to sell, exercised options and restricted stock, which are awarded as incentives to create value for shareholders. The Enron case reveals the adverse effects of this approach.

Options and restricted stock that have vested cannot, of course, be withdrawn. However, executives should not necessarily have unfettered freedom to sell stock grants that have vested according to plan. At Enron, executives might well have had strong reasons for cashing out, such as risk aversion and a desire for liquidity or diversification. But cashing out on the vesting date reduces executives' incentives to maximize long-term shareholder value. Although they periodically received new options and restricted stock, many Enron executives took significant amounts of money off the table, reducing their personal wealth at risk.

The lack of restrictions on the unwinding of incentives also weakened the bond of mutual interest between Enron managers and shareholders. Enron executives were like most corporate executives, who typically sell any stock they already hold when granted new options or restricted stock: many key Enron executives sold stock as its price surged after 1997. Thus the alignment of executives' and shareholders' interests was compromised to the extent that executives' financial security was assured.[44]

Perhaps more important, giving executives broad freedom to unwind their incentives reinforced Enron's preoccupation with short-term movements in its stock price. The shorter the required holding period for stock grants (three years was the general pattern at Enron), the greater the incentive for executives to pursue policies aimed at influencing short-term price movements and their personal wealth positions, without regard to the interests of long-term investors.

A final impact of the lack of a required holding period at Enron was a mismatch between the timing of financial rewards and the success or failure of its emerging business strategies. Although Enron's commodity-trading business might have been an early success until new competitors started beating down profit margins, not much else was: not the power plant development business after 1997, not the water utility business, not the broadband business, and not the merchant investment operation. Many executives who benefited from early exits were, in effect, rewarded for creating businesses well before anyone could tell whether they would be successful. Mostly they were not.

Perverse incentives are not the only byproduct of giving executives excessive discretion in selling stock grants. The absence of mandated holding periods beyond vesting dates can end up rewarding executives for short-term rises in the capital market that might be totally unrelated to corporate performance. Absent constraints on the sale of stock, recipients can reduce the incentive effects of indexed options at their discretion. The freedom to unwind incentive contracts is hardly a recipe for disciplined and effective pay for performance.

Finally, the freedom to sell exercised options and vested restricted stock at their discretion gives corporate insiders opportunities to earn above-average profits from trading the shares of their firms. These excess returns—which are unavailable to the public, and total about $5 billion per year, according to one estimate—represent a transfer of wealth from ordinary shareholders to corporate insiders.[45] Although executives may not use information they normally come across in their daily work to boost their personal profits, those they make by trading on "sub-material" insider information *are* legal. The distinction between "material" and "sub-material" information is subtle. However, whether or not such trading violates laws prohibiting insider trading, it is certainly unfair and inappropriate, according to principles of fiduciary duty, for corporate insiders to profit at the expense of less-informed shareholders.

Jesse Fried proposes a legal/regulatory remedy to such inappropriate profit taking: the simple requirement that executives disclose their intention to trade before doing so, which would not unduly constrain their liquidity.[46] I agree with my colleague Michael Jensen that such a solution is unnecessary. Wise boards can voluntarily require such disclosure.[47] More importantly, taking insider trading off a corporate board's agenda would only weaken its responsibility for enforcing executives' fiduciary duties.

Corporate boards have another good reason for monitoring the trading activities of corporate insiders. As Fried observes, "The prospect of insider trading profits may induce managers to engage in overly risky projects in order to generate large price swings" in share price.[48] Enron is a case in point. Avoiding such perverse incentives—however remote they might seem—should be a core responsibility of boards in overseeing strong pay-for-performance cultures.

Lookbacks and Clawbacks

Pay-for-performance systems that lack provisions for rescinding bonuses if companies revise their past or expected performance invite people to lie and game the system.

The history of Enron's collapse includes many episodes where executives and other employees overestimated returns from commodity contracts, power plant development projects, and merchant investments. Some of these errors reflected the natural enthusiasm that surrounds new business development, but others, especially at Enron Wholesale Services, were obvious attempts to game the system. Such behavior is not unique to Enron: virtually every performance measure is subject to gaming.

The implications should be clear. Every reward system that includes cash bonuses should, "if and when there is future revision of critical indicators on which bonus payments were based or received, provide for a review of past performance (a lookback) and the recovery of rewards (a clawback)."[49] Clawbacks can be based on formal accounting numbers such as earnings and revenues or other metrics. For such a program to work, a company would need to create bonus banks or other means of recovering deferred awards or retirement benefits. Such a program would also need to specify who decides whether the clawback provision is triggered, and the precise evidence on which such decisions are based.

Incentives to Manage Earnings

The higher the level of equity-based compensation, and the more sensitive total compensation is to reported earnings, the greater the incentives for executives to coordinate stock sales with decisions that affect reported earnings.

From 1997 onward, Enron executives used a variety of means to manage reported earnings, disguise the company's true financial condition, and support its credit rating and stock price. These included the sale of poorly performing assets and transfer of debt to off-balance-sheet partnerships, and the timely execution of asset swaps and prepaid commodity transactions with colluding financial institutions.

At the same time, from 1997 until the company's collapse in 2001, executives sold well over half a billion dollars' worth of stock. Not all—but clearly many—of these sellers participated in Enron's deceptive financial accounting and reporting. According to criminal indictments, plea bargains, and eventual convictions, the list of executives who both helped manage Enron's reported earnings and profited from stock sales included Causey, Fastow, Glison,[50] Rice, and Delainey,[51] among others at Enron headquarters and operating divisions.

Enron's senior executives are not alone in facing accusations of managing earnings. Evidence is mounting that the enormous increase in stock-based executive compensation in recent years is giving managers compelling incentive to manipulate their firms' reported earnings. Bergstresser and Philippson, for example, find that the more CEOs' overall compensation is tied to the value of stock, the more aggressively they use discretionary components of earnings not reflected in current cash flow, such as "accruals," to affect their firms' reported performance.[52] (Under accrual accounting, the performance of a company is measured by matching current and *expected future* revenues and expenses, rather than by simply matching revenues and expenses of transactions where there has been an exchange of cash. It is thought that this method gives a more accurate picture of a company's current financial condition.)

Bergstresser and Philippson's research is particularly relevant to Enron. We have known for some time that managers have many incentives to manipulate earnings, or hit explicit targets for reported income, to game bonus schemes.[53] However, evidence is accumulating that managers are now gaming capital markets as well, using accruals to manipulate the market valuations of their firms, and then profiting by selling some of their company stock.

Bergstresser and Philippson report that "accruals-based measures of earnings management are high at firms with high levels of stock based incentives," and that periods of high accruals coincide with unusually high levels of exercised stock options and stock sales by CEOs and other top executives. Bergstresser, Desai, and Rauth document a similar relationship between earnings manipulated through assumed rates of return on pension assets, and opportunistic stock sales by executives.[54] Although Enron brought new tools to managing reported earnings, recent research suggests that Enron is far from being an outlier in the world of equity-based executive compensation.

Just as Enron's (and other firms') problems with equity-based compensation stem largely from a lack of long-term time horizons supported by required holding periods for company stock, internal governance systems that essentially leave corporate executives unmonitored intensify these adverse effects. One egregious example was the repeated failure of the Enron board's compensation committee to keep tabs on Andy Fastow's compensation from the LJM partnerships, even though explicitly instructed by the full board to do so. The board's instructions followed its approval of an exception to the company's code of ethics on conflict of interest, stemming from Fastow's simultaneous service as Enron's CFO and managing partner of LJM, which had been set up to purchase assets from Enron.

The implications for corporate boards and their compensation and audit committees are straightforward. In companies where stock-based incentives are a major part of senior executives' compensation, corporate boards must heighten their monitoring of personal stock sales, to ensure that executives do not benefit from manipulating financial reports. Such oversight is consistent with the need to monitor the unwinding of stock grants. If voluntary oversight by corporate boards does not become more effective, regulators and legislatures are sure to impose their own controls.

Balancing Turbocharged Incentives with Turbocharged Controls

High-powered incentives require high-powered controls. However, relying primarily on formal controls is hazardous because they are subject to breakdowns and gaming. Effective control over the potentially perverse effects of high-powered management incentives requires a deeply infused organizational culture that includes shared beliefs and values.

Quite apart from the lax monitoring and control exercised by Enron's board, the company's efforts to control investment risk, employee performance, and financial reporting were, in the end, unsuccessful. Neither the sophisticated Risk Analysis and Control group (RAC), elaborate PRC process, large auditing staff, and corporate code of ethics—individually or collectively—protected Enron from the combined impact of unprofitable investments, dubious financial transactions designed to disguise the company's eroding profitability, and serious accounting errors. Although the company had devoted serious thought to designing its control processes, and taken them seriously for much of their existence, these systems nevertheless experienced critical breakdowns:

- RAC's critiques of off-balance-sheet hedging operations such as the Raptors fell on deaf ears. Risk controllers were unable to adequately assess many commodity deals rushed in for last-minute approval at the end of reporting periods. And the PRC process reportedly pressured risk controllers to cooperate with deal originators and commodity traders in valuing and approving uncertain contracts.
- The PRC process, which Skilling had hoped would "make clear what we value" and "what we compensate for," and enable Enron to move faster and communicate better, often ended up as a punitive process and source of conflict between traders and deal originators at Enron Wholesale Services. Worse, by accelerating promotions of highly rated employees and spurring rapid job changes, the PRC process had the

perverse effect of putting younger and less-experienced people in charge of new business units while reducing their accountability for prior investment decisions.

- Enron's internal auditing staff was blended with the company's external auditor, Arthur Andersen, blurring the lines between internal and external reviews of accounting transactions.

- Finally, the company's code of ethics was, in the end, honored in its breach through the culture of deceit, and the badly monitored, board-sanctioned exception to the code's self-dealing provisions affecting Fastow's dual role as CFO and managing partner of the LJM entities.

Weaknesses in board oversight and internal controls are certainly not unique to Enron, except perhaps in their collective impact. As noted by Robert Simons, a leading expert on management control whose research predates the Enron story, performance pressures on major corporations—together with high growth rates and inexperienced employees—typically cause inefficiencies, breakdowns, or both, as systems become overloaded and undermanaged.[55] Matters are made only worse, Simons maintains, when rewards for entrepreneurial behavior are high, internal competition is intense, and performance evaluation is based on forced rankings rather than individual merit. The problem worsens when only a handful of experts in an organization truly grasp the obligations and risks implicit in complex transactions, and the growing volume of such transactions puts serious pressure on internal reporting systems that track performance and value financial drivers.

As a defense against these risks, Simons offers a number of suggestions, including control systems designed to both monitor critical performance variables and stimulate organizational learning. Equally important is a well-understood set of values that clearly identifies specific actions and behaviors as off limits.[56]

What the Enron story reveals so dramatically is the importance of values and culture as the first line of defense against weak internal controls. Enron's RAC group, for example, was a highly sophisticated operation in its original design, and for much of its life. The part of Enron's control system that failed most and rendered RAC so ineffectual was its organizational culture—which valued entrepreneurship, innovation, and competitiveness, but set few explicit limits on activities such as those within Fastow's Global Finance unit, which operated in the gray zone where the borderlines between legal and illegal and ethical and unethical behavior were unclear.

Merriam-Webster defines culture as "the set of shared attributes, values, goals, and practices that characterizes a company or corporation."[57] Edgar Schein elaborates on organizational culture as a "pattern of basic assumptions that the group learned as it solved problems of external adaptation and internal integration that has worked well enough to be considered valid and therefore to be taught to new members as the correct way to perceive, think, and feel in relation to those problems."[58]

The behavior that shaped Enron's culture subverted truth telling to the promotion and preservation of the Enron story, through cover-ups and other means of disguising the company's true financial condition. In such an environment, turbocharged controls could never match Enron's turbocharged incentives. Leaders' preference for pushing the outer limits of accounting rules, discomfort with internal dissent, leniency in punishing blatant violations of generally accepted accounting practices and SEC rules, and tendency to confer propriety on what was done rather than stress what *should* have been done—in short, the company's noncompliant and defensive culture—poisoned the promise of an exemplary set of control processes run by the RAC and internal auditing groups.

In a world of turbocharged incentives, turbocharged controls can develop only from the long and steady focus of an organization's leaders on ethical habits of mind, the boundaries of acceptable behavior, and the core values of the business—which, as they gain force, become rules of conduct. In contrast to Johnson & Johnson, for example, where generations of leaders consciously communicated and reinforced the core values that ultimately saved the company during the Tylenol crisis (which started with an immediate and costly national recall of product after a woman in Chicago was inexplicably poisoned by a Tylenol tablet laced with arsenic), Enron could point only to its published code of ethics and a few public speeches by Ken Lay. In the absence of any commitment by Enron's leadership, few clear rules of conduct took hold, which helps explain why the company's pay-for-performance system generated so much perverse managerial behavior.

CHAPTER 10

Instilling Ethical Discipline

On May 25, 2006, Jeffrey Skilling and Kenneth Lay were convicted in federal court of nineteen counts of lying to investors, the Securities and Exchange Commission (SEC), and credit-rating agencies about the company's true financial position during the months leading up to Enron's bankruptcy.[1] They were also convicted of conspiracy to commit fraud, and using at least one cluster of off-balance-sheet entities—known as the Raptor partnerships—to fraudulently manage reported earnings. Not addressed in the criminal trial was the breakdown of administrative leadership at Enron that comprises much of the substance of this book but lies outside the jurisdiction of the courts.

Due to the legal ambiguities surrounding the various maneuvers that Enron used to disguise its true financial condition, the jury had to make many judgments in evaluating the opposing claims of the prosecution and the defense. Many of the allegedly fraudulent practices (such as the Raptor transactions discussed in Appendix A and many others that escaped attention in the trial) were actually close calls from a legal point of view. Despite these legal ambiguities, government lawyers were successful in convincing the jury that the details of Enron's compliance or noncompliance with legal rules were secondary to a pattern of deceptive behavior that was either masterminded or approved by Skilling and Lay.

In reaching this conclusion, the jury sent two strong messages to CEOs. The first was that CEOs can be convicted of conspiracy to defraud investors not only for making misleading statements to investors and the SEC, but also for financial policies and practices that might not be incontestable breeches of the law. In essence, the jury's verdict reflected the legal principle that in matters of alleged fraud, intent to deceive trumps the details of compliance with arcane legal rules.[2] This verdict is also consistent with the long-established

303

ethical principle that the moral status of an act should be judged not only by its consequences but also by the intentions of the actor.[3] The second message was that CEOs should not expect to escape responsibility for the devious or deceptive acts of others (such as Enron CFO Andrew Fastow), even though CEOs may not have been present when the offending acts were committed. In other words, the captain goes down with the ship.

The jury's messages are both appropriate and challenging for the business community. They are appropriate because the limits-testing behavior initially tolerated and encouraged by Skilling and Lay—only to be followed by claims of ignorance of subsequent misbehavior—is not unique to Enron. In many businesses, limits testing coupled with denials of wrongdoing have become standard practice. As former SEC chair Arthur Levitt has testified, many U.S. corporations have unfortunately developed a "culture of gamesmanship"—"where it is okay to bend the rules, to tweak the numbers, and let obvious and important discrepancies slide; where companies bend to the desires and pressures of Wall Street analysts rather than to the reality of the numbers" and where analysts and even auditors often overlook dubious accounting practices to better serve their own economic interests.[4]

The jury's messages are also a challenge because in much of the world of business Enron-type behavior falls into the shadowy space of legal ambiguity, where black-letter law and regulatory guidelines are not always reliable guides to appropriate conduct, and where the spirit of the law is open to interpretation. Managers must make repeated judgment calls in these murky borderlands, and face a very real chance of going to jail if the Justice Department and ordinary citizens perceive their judgments to be foul play.[5]

One of the greatest failings of Skilling and Lay is that they did not fully understand (or want to understand) the risks of leading Enron into the murky borderlands of the law—a territory characterized by newly deregulated energy markets, complex rules related to trading commodities and accounting for derivative contracts, and comparable uncertainties regarding increasingly intricate structured-finance transactions. To complicate matters, Enron's leaders were actively lobbying for further deregulation and more-limited federal oversight of the energy industry while pushing the company to exploit recent rule changes to its maximum advantage.

Pursuing such a strategy in a murky legal environment carried special obligations. The first was for Skilling and Lay to alert their organization to the survival risks of legal missteps. The second was for those leaders to pay sustained attention to nurturing a culture reflecting high ethical and legal standards. Unfortunately, neither obligation was met. Indeed, Skilling's and Lay's overconfidence in Enron's business model and discomfort with internal dissent, coupled with the huge financial and psychological rewards to those who bought into Enron's aggressive business model, severely compromised personal accountability for sustaining such ethical and legal standards.

Enron actually did not get around to publishing a code of ethics until July 2000. When finally published, the code emphasized a common theme of such statements: that compliance with the law and ethical standards were conditions of employment. All executives had to sign a certificate of compliance and periodically reaffirm their commitment to Enron's "principles of human rights" and underlying values, which included respect, integrity, communication, and excellence. Notably, however, executives returned their certificates of compliance to the deputy corporate secretary and director of stockholder relations, which effectively took Skilling and Lay out of the direct communication link.

In 2002 Ken Lay backed up this code by contributing a chapter to a book on business ethics titled *Ethical Leadership in Action.* In addressing what a CEO should expect from his board, he wrote, "The responsibility of our board—a responsibility which I expect them to fulfill—is to ensure legal and ethical conduct by the company and by everyone in the company. . . . That requirement does not exist by happenstance. It is the most important thing we expect from board members."[6] As laudable as Enron's code of ethics and Lay's public statements on values may have been, the management style of Skilling and Lay, combined with perverse incentives, costly breakdowns in internal controls, and ineffective board oversight, greased the wheels of Enron's ethical drift. In the end, the court held Skilling and Lay responsible for the disconnect between official policy (however late in its arrival) and the lack of day-to-day attention to ethical management.

Living in the Penumbra between Clear Rightdoing and Clear Wrongdoing

Eighty years ago, at the dedication of the Harvard Business School's new campus on June 24, 1927, Owen D. Young—a lawyer, visionary capitalist, founding chairman of RCA, and chairman of General Electric during the late 1920s—described the legally ambiguous territory in which Enron chose to live:

The law is not a satisfactory censor. It functions in the clear light of wrong-doing—things so wrong that the community must protect itself against them. Set over against the law on the opposite side is the clear light of right-doing—things which are so generally appealing to the conscience of all that no mistake could be made, no matter how complicated the business. The area of difficulty for business lies in the penumbra between the two.[7]

In Young's penumbra, or shadowed space, between the clear light of rightdoing and the clear light of wrongdoing lie many rules promulgated by a wide variety of bodies, including legislatures, courts, professional societies, industry associations, and religious institutions. However, many of these rules are not adaptable to specific business situations or are just plain ambiguous.[8] Rules governing Enron's use of off-balance-sheet partnerships to manage earnings, for example, or a legal sale of assets that enables a company to recognize profits on its financial statements, entailed enough ambiguity to pit Enron's most senior executives and their advisors against the Justice Department in criminal court. Enron's advisors thought the company was in legal compliance; government lawyers thought the opposite.

Further highlighting Young's penumbra, many rules—however specific or well written—serve as poor guides for decision making because they are advanced in isolation from one another, and thus are in conflict. In Enron's case, accounting rules governing a certain class of transactions known as prepays, which involved international parties, were subject to different rules in different national jurisdictions (see below and Chapter 3). Decision makers also may find that their duties conflict. For example, executives often cannot satisfy the interests of shareholders, employees, customers, and suppliers equally at particular points in time.

Finally, it is often unclear when executives cross the line between rightdoing and wrongdoing because that line is never precise, and no guidelines may exist to shed light on what will be overlooked or tolerated and what will be condemned and attacked.[9] Life in Young's penumbra therefore involves a steady stream of choices about what rules apply to a specific situation, whose interests executives should serve in which order, which duties they should attend to first, and when they should simply back off from a seemingly innovative idea that lies in uncertain legal and moral terrain.

Enron executives no doubt understood that they lived in a legal and moral gray area as they pushed financial structures and transactions to their legal limits, to serve their own idiosyncratic needs (perhaps pride and power) and protect Enron's vulnerable credit rating. And they no doubt understood that they were walking on unchartered and ambiguous legal ground when they designed new structured-finance vehicles and used complicated financial transactions that shielded debt from public view and enhanced reported earnings. Those executives did consult heavily with outside advisors and relied on their expert opinions, but evidence suggests that those advisors felt pressured to issue opinions favorable to Enron's interests.

Congressional investigating committees, forensic accountants and lawyers representing creditors, class-action suits representing shareholders, and ultimately Justice Department attorneys roundly criticized many of these practices. The actual legality of Enron's financial maneuvers was often unclear because so many employed structures in ways that had never been used or tested before. For this reason, Steven L. Schwarz, a structured-finance expert and professor of law and business at Duke University, felt called on to elaborate on the difficulties that Enron executives and their advisors faced in judging the appropriateness of certain structured-finance transactions:

> In perspective, therefore, Enron and its accountants were (in many cases) making exquisitely fine judgment calls—shades of gray that, for accounting purposes, must be rendered as black or white. Although, in retrospect, Enron may have misjudged, the culpability of its actions must be assessed ex ante, not ex post.[10]

In reviewing those exquisitely fine judgment calls, Michael Mulligan and Richard K. Rush—recognized authorities on accounting rules hired by Skilling's defense team—concluded that Enron's financial statements in no way violated generally accepted accounting principles (GAAP).[11] Of course, Mulligan and Rush were hired hands, but neither Professor Schwarz nor I can be so categorized. My own analysis in Chapter 1 of the uncertain illegalities surrounding the allegedly fraudulent Raptor partnerships, and my critique in Chapter 3 of the court-appointed examiner's claims of accounting fraud, support the view that many ambiguities surrounded the extent of Enron's compliance and noncompliance with GAAP and SEC rules.

Living in this ambiguous legal space required Enron's leaders to balance business judgments on building an innovative enterprise with ethical judgments on potentially injuring parties to whom they were in some way accountable. Unfortunately, it is precisely regarding these latter judgments that Enron's discipline broke down. After the business press started raising suspicions that Enron leaders did not fully and clearly disclose the company's financial strategy and, equally important, failed to carefully manage and monitor operations, customers in the wholesale trading operation progressively lost confidence in Enron and refused to deal with it. Within weeks the company collapsed as cash flow dried up and loans were called, causing enormous financial losses to shareholders and employees alike.

Table 10.1 shows how Enron's strategies and administrative practices encompassed these gradations of ethical and legal conduct. At one end of the spectrum, where no charges of either unethical or illegal behavior could possibly arise, lie many examples of highly innovative management: the successful intermediation of the natural gas market, the Gas Bank created by Jeff Skilling, the development of standardized commodity contracts, and the creation of EnronOnline, the Web-based trading platform that made Enron the leading buyer and seller of gas and electricity in the United States and Europe in its first year of operation.

This end of the spectrum also includes many examples of extremely inept management—activities for which there is no criminal liability: the unsuccessful extrapolation of the innovative natural gas strategy to the water and broadband businesses, the unprofitable international power plant development strategy, the perverse financial incentives for executives, the aggressive use of mark-to-market accounting, the performance guarantees in the power plant construction business, the noneconomic hedges, the breakdowns in the company's performance review and internal control processes, the intolerance of internal dissent, and the inability of Lay and Skilling to face Enron's true financial condition. U.S. law does not criminalize such bad management and poor business judgments, at Enron or elsewhere.

Toward the opposite end of the spectrum are many examples of devious management that were not clearly illegal in Enron's case: the use of off-balance-sheet partnerships and accounting reserves to manage reported earnings, the recategorization of investments to enable the company to book gains on its income statements, the reorganization of business structures to obfuscate line-of-business reporting, the use of prepay transactions that had the effect of bolstering reported earnings and minimizing reported debt, and the opaque disclosure and reporting of a wide variety of structured-finance transactions and related accounting practices, to name just a few.

I have termed many of these practices legal close calls because reasonable parties may differ about whether they are actually unlawful, based on different readings of an ambiguous rule or different interpretations of sworn testimony and intent. These practices exemplify what Owen Young was

Table 10.1 Range of management practices at Enron.

LEGAL			ILLEGAL
Innovative Management	Inept Management	Devious Management	Fraudulent Management
• Natural gas strategy (intermediation).	• Naïve extrapolation of a successful business model (reckless gambling).	• Use of nonindependent SPEs (LJM and Raptor entities) to meet cash flow and earnings targets, avoid booking large losses in asset values, and conceal debt burden.	• Fastow's admitted fraud.
• "Gas Bank."	• International strategy.		• Alleged conspiracy by top management to conceal the company's true financial position via false, misleading, and incomplete public statements to analysts, employees, and credit agencies and in SEC filings
• Standardized commodity contracts.	• Perverse incentives.	• Use of reserves, recategorization of investments (Nahanni), and corporate reorganizations (EES & EBS) to increase reported cash flow from operations and earnings-per-share.	
• EnronOnline: #1 buyer and seller of gas and electricity in U.S. and Europe.	• Aggressive use of MTM accounting.	• Use of "prepays" to bolster reported earnings.	
	• Performance guarantees.	• Parking poorly performing assets outside Enron by engaging in questionable asset sales (Nigerian Barges) designed to help Enron meet earnings targets.	
	• Noneconomic hedges.		
	• Breakdown in PRC process.	• "Bear hugs" assuring (but not "guaranteeing") LJMs would not lose money on its investments.	
	• Internal control failures.		
	• Intolerance of internal dissent.	• Opaque disclosure and reporting of off-balance partnerships and their role.	
	• Pain avoidance/denial.		
	• Exemptions from corporate Code of Ethics.		

No criminal charges could possibly arise out of these practices and outcomes. | *"Close calls." Reasonable parties may differ about legality and prospects for successful prosecution.* | *Clearly illegal, if true, resulting in criminal charges that should hold up in a court of law.*

talking about eighty years ago. Many of Enron's complex transactions, questionable accounting choices, vague disclosures, and corporate reorganizations lived in what he described as the penumbra between the clear light of wrongdoing and the clear light of rightdoing. While an alarming portion of Enron's financial maneuvers had an aroma of deception, lacked respect for the spirit of the law, and thus reflected ethical delinquency, much of this behavior was not clearly unlawful.[12]

The next section provides several examples of how Enron lived in this space, drawn from the criminal trial and earlier chapters. In later sections, I offer several ideas for creating an environment that encourages sound ethical judgment by those who find themselves in the penumbra defined by Owen Young in 1927 and inhabited by Enron decades later.

Examples from Enron's Life in the Penumbra

Corporate Reorganizations and Line-of-Business Reporting

One of the most controversial management decisions debated during the trial of Kenneth Lay and Jeffrey Skilling for criminal fraud was the reorganization of Enron Energy Services (EES), Enron's retail trading unit. The prosecution alleged that the company shifted EES contracts to Enron Wholesale Services (EWS) to hide $200 million in losses incurred by the retail division.[13] The defense claimed that "there were no such losses," just the possibility of them, and that consolidating the trading desks at EES and EWS allowed both to rely on the wholesale unit's superior risk-management group.[14] Enron reported retail earnings of $40 million for the quarter.[15]

Witnesses offered conflicting opinions on this maneuver. David Delainey, former EES president, called the decision "the worst conduct I had ever been a part of," and indicated that all involved knew the move was made to hide retail losses.[16] Skilling, in contrast, testified that "it was my state of mind at the time that EES was more likely to show a profit than to show a loss."[17] He also cited a discussion with Lou Pai, former head of EES, who told Skilling that the transferred contracts "were not losses."[18] Skilling said his own concerns about the propriety of the move prompted him to ask Delainey, "Are you sure you want to do this?"[19] Delainey, on the other hand, remembered the question as: "What do you want to do?" which he interpreted to mean, "Get in line."[20] Skilling attested that "my concern level dropped as I listened to the people that were actually involved in the issue."[21]

Characterizing this story as either clear wrongdoing or clear rightdoing requires discerning both the true financial condition of EES and the intent of executives responsible for the organizational change. Did they want to disguise losses or improve trading and risk management? Without knowing the true intent of decision makers, this seemingly devious decision remains in the penumbra.

Earnings Management

Earnings management, which entails manipulating financial information to achieve a desired earnings-per-share figure, was another battleground for the two legal teams at the criminal trial. Prosecutors charged that many of the company's transactions—particularly those involving Fastow-run partnerships—were fabricated strictly to help Enron to meet its estimates of earnings per share.[22] And when that wasn't enough, the company used funds from financial reserves to boost those earnings.[23] The defense argued that earnings numbers were in flux until finalized at the moment of disclosure, and that such adjustments were both a part and product of normal business practice.[24]

Former Enron personnel provided various explanations about how the company revised estimated earnings shortfalls to enable it to meet or exceed market predictions. Mark Koenig, the former head of Enron investor relations, testified about a conversation with Lay in early 2000 regarding earnings per share for the previous quarter: "[Lay] said he went to bed and we were at 30 cents and when he woke up we were at 31 cents."[25] The one-penny increase meant Enron had at the very last moment somehow achieved its forecasted figure for the fourth quarter of 1999.

A similar last-minute add-on occurred in the second quarter of 2000. Skilling explained that on returning from a brief safari vacation with his son, he learned that Enron might be able to report earnings of 34 cents per share—or 2 cents better than before he departed—because the company had just computed how it had benefited financially from the California energy crisis.[26] Documents detailing the numbers underlying Enron's earnings for that period back up the assertion that unfinished back-office work (financial analysis) rather than illicit accounting maneuvers created the change in reported earnings.[27]

From sworn testimony, it is difficult to make a confident judgment about the validity of claims that Enron manipulated its reported earnings, even though the jury found Skilling and Lay guilty of a conspiracy to deceive investors and other interested parties. Were unsettled earnings numbers that persisted until the final moments before a quarterly report a normal occurrence and accepted business practice, or should the company have known about them well in advance of disclosing them to the market? To the nonexecutive, the last-minute upward revision of these figures may look suspicious, but that does not necessarily make them improper. The process that produces reported earnings often involves last-minute trade-offs and judgments by senior managers as they close the books for the quarter or the year. During that process, decisions related to business development, legal compliance, and personal preference or intent often commingle, and are difficult to disentangle from the outside.

Accounting for Asset Sales

Undocumented side deals—wherein Enron allegedly agreed to help protect counterparties in asset sales from financial loss—were another popular topic at the Skilling/Lay trial. Fastow referred to these verbal assurances as "bear hugs."[28] If such assurances were a formal promise or pledge by Enron to protect a purchaser of assets from loss by agreeing to buy back the assets at a minimum price, then from a legal perspective this sales transaction was actually a loan, since no risk was ever transferred to the acquirer. However, if Enron's assurances were merely to help the purchaser find another party that *might* want to buy the asset, then risk did pass to the purchaser, and the transaction was a bona fide sale. Here's one disputed example.

In the 1999 Nigerian barge transaction discussed in Chapter 6, Merrill Lynch purchased from Enron the rights to energy produced by a power plant barge. In prosecuting executives involved in that transaction, the government contended that Enron CFO Andrew Fastow made a verbal promise to remove Merrill Lynch from the deal within six months by finding a new buyer or repurchasing the asset. In actuality, LJM2—an off-balance-sheet partnership controlled by Fastow—did end up repurchasing the asset from Merrill Lynch. In court, the defendants claimed that Enron had agreed only to help Merrill Lynch find a third-party purchaser, and that the transaction was thus a bona fide sale.

Once again, it is very difficult to determine the true intent of such verbal assurances. That determination depends largely on turns of phrase and subtle differences in meanings about what level of assistance Enron provided. It is a fine grey line. If verbal statements merely assure a potential buyer of an asset that the deal is a good one, they are hardly to be considered a guarantee that there is no way a buyer can lose. If, however, a written or oral statement gives the buyer a binding promise to buy back the asset at a price protecting the buyer from any loss, then a binding guarantee has been made and the transaction is not a bona fide sale (because there is no transfer of risk). The difficulty is identifying the line between normal transaction puffery and a formal guarantee. In the Nigerian barge trial, the jury stepped to the government's side of that line and sent five men to prison based, in large part, on its interpretation of a promise to provide assistance. While an appeals court later vacated the convictions of four Merrill Lynch executives on technical and procedural grounds (without suggesting "that no fraudulent, wrongful, or criminal act has occurred"), executives should find this case a harsh warning against leaving such unclear and undocumented assurances open to interpretation.[29]

Prepay Transactions

As businesses become increasingly global, companies face the ambiguities of discordant legal regimes. The opposing views of Enron's twelve Mahonia prepay transactions by the examiner appointed by the U.S. bankruptcy court and by the U.K.'s Commercial Court are a perfect example.

As Chapter 3 notes, the cash flows to Enron stemming from its commodity-trading business lagged the profits reported under mark-to-market accounting. Given this timing gap, Enron used prepay transactions to raise cash for current use.

Working with JPMorgan Chase and Citigroup, Enron developed a series of transactions in which banks advanced money equal to the funds that specific energy trades might realize in the future. Specifically, the banks agreed to prepay the purchase price of commodities such as oil and gas that Enron agreed to deliver in the future. These prepayments were typically routed through an intermediary or "conduit entity." Through a complex series of swap contracts, Enron effectively agreed to repay the prepayment over time, with interest. Both the bank examiner and a Senate subcommittee argued that Enron used these prepays to disguise the magnitude of its publicly disclosed debt, and inflate its reported net cash flow from operations.

However, assessments of these prepay transactions conflict. The examiner appointed by the U.S. bankruptcy court concluded that Enron's accounting treatment of the transactions did not comply with GAAP, since the prepays were recorded as price risk-management liabilities rather than debt. The examiner further concluded that Enron should not have reported the increases in the balances of its prepay transactions as net cash from operations rather than cash from financing activities.[30]

A British judge held the opposite. In a suit arising out of the Mahonia transactions, Justice Jeremy Cooke ruled that Enron "was justified in giving the prepays 'non-debt' treatment and accounting for them as Price Risk Management Activities." Cooke pointed out that Enron's choice of accounting for the prepays was a plausible interpretation of applicable accounting rules.[31]

There are explanations for these opposing views of Enron's prepays. Under U.S. legal norms, the transactions composing a Mahonia-type deal should be examined together, and when that occurs they appear to add up to a disguised loan. Under the British legal regime, each transaction in such a deal must be reviewed independently, meaning that as long as each individual transaction is properly accounted for, there can be no cumulative illegal effect. The only thing the two legal regimes agree on is that no GAAP rule is directly on point. This example shows how multiple legal frameworks create an unpredictability that executives must learn to navigate, adding depth to the moral deliberations that living in the penumbra entail.

Financial Disclosure

Disclosure decisions often revolve around how much to reveal about a company's financial condition. For competitive and other reasons, executives do not want to disclose every last detail about their operations, but they must provide enough information for investors to understand the company's financial position. Both the Powers committee convened by Enron's board and the court-appointed bankruptcy examiner criticized the footnotes to Enron's financial statements as "calculated to disclose as little as possible" and "fundamentally inadequate."[32] Yet while these criticisms strike me as valid, Enron's approach largely complied with rules regarding disclosure on proxy statements.

Such rules require companies to disclose information about insider interests in external ventures only "where practicable."[33] The footnote to Enron's 2000 proxy statement did not include details on Fastow's compensation from LJM2, a private investment company that primarily acquired and invested in energy and communications endeavors. Fastow was the managing director of LJM2's general partner, which was entitled to a percentage of any profits in excess of the general partners' proportion of the total capital contributed to LJM2.[34]

Enron in-house attorney Jordan Mintz noted that Enron relied on the "where practicable" clause to justify not disclosing the extent of Fastow's interest in LJM2. Because several LJM2 transactions had not been completed by the time the 2000 proxy statement was issued, Enron, in consultation with Arthur Andersen and Vinson & Elkins, decided that calculating Fastow's interest was not practicable, and therefore that interest did not need to be disclosed.[35] While this decision was "calculated to reveal as little as possible" about Fastow's external ventures, the guidelines seemingly permit it.[36] On the other hand, shareholders may have found details about the CFO's external activities critically important in judging the governance and control of their firm. The decision to withhold that information put Enron's executives well within the shadowed space of right and wrong.

Statements to Security Analysts

A conference call between Jeffrey Skilling and securities analysts on April 17, 2001, provides another example of the ethical and legal ambiguities surrounding financial disclosure. During that call, Skilling reportedly said that Enron Energy Services—Enron's newly launched, high-profile retail electricity unit—had earned $40 million in the third quarter before interest and taxes. According to testimony by Paula Reiker, Enron's former corporate secretary and deputy chief of investor relations, Skilling failed to mention that $30 million of that amount came from stock gains, rather than from operating earnings related to the core business of supplying energy and energy services to corporate and other customers. Reiker claimed that this "should have been disclosed."

Skilling's defense lawyer countered by calling attention to Enron's financial report for the first quarter of 2001, filed with the SEC one month after the conference call. In that report, a table summarizing the unit's results shows the $30 million in stock gains. Skilling's lawyer suggested that "this disclosure fulfilled any obligation Enron had to tell investors about the stock gains—particularly in the case of Wall Street analysts, whose jobs involved dissecting such SEC filings."[37] Under cross-examination, Reiker refused to budge. She pointed out that Enron's SEC filings were not available until weeks after the public announcement of earnings, and that "most analysts relied on the earnings release and the quarterly conference call" with Enron executives.[38]

Who is correct from a legal and ethical point of view? Is this an area where men and women of wisdom can differ, or does this question have a straightforward, incontestable answer? Here again, the ethics and legality of disclosure are a matter of degree.

Executives are obligated to provide all "material" information necessary to make a statement not misleading.[39] Skilling did not tell the analysts how much of the retail unit's earnings came from stock increases. That is clear.

For the sake of argument, let's assume that this information was material. The question remains whether Skilling acted inappropriately in keeping the details from analysts. One could argue that not providing a breakdown of the sources of earnings during the conference call gave the impression that the unit was more successful at its core business than it really was. But one could also argue that it was impractical to provide a lot of detail "under the circumstances"—in this case a conference call—and that it was reasonable to assume that analysts would peruse SEC filings for more information.

Executives often face this kind of dilemma. As indicated by "under the circumstances," the legal analysis of disclosure decisions is highly case-specific. For that reason, executives sometimes find it difficult to know when they can withhold certain information and when doing so will get them in trouble. This is the essence of the penumbra. In Enron's case, the jury sided with Paula Reiker.

Conflicts between Rules Compliance and Managerial Intent

Complying with accounting and SEC rules is often not sufficient from an ethical perspective. For example, Enron accounted for the majority of its SPE transactions correctly, yet some came under fire as intended to hide the company's true financial position. The most famous, or infamous, examples were the Raptor transactions, addressed in Chapter 1 and Appendix A. These complex and risky ventures had flaws—notably their reliance on the value of Enron stock to support noneconomic hedges—but it is not clear that Enron used them to intentionally mislead investors.

Skilling testified in criminal court that the Raptors were proper hedging vehicles.[40] The prosecution argued—and the jury agreed—that Enron also used these partnerships to manipulate reported earnings.[41] Perhaps the jury found the truth. However, without absolute knowledge of intent—what the law calls *scienter,* or the defendant's mental state regarding an intent to deceive, manipulate, or defraud—we cannot definitively judge Skilling's ethical standing in approving and using the Raptors. Much clearer is the fact that the Raptors simply did not work, because they were poorly designed, and because a careless accounting error in structuring them forced the company to write-down shareholder equity by $1.2 billion at the end of the third quarter of 2001. This write-down certainly clouded the public's judgment of an already-misunderstood hedging program. But the case of the Raptors shows that distinguishing an illegal maneuver from simply inept management by virtue of malevolent intent can be difficult in the penumbra.

Each of these examples reveals ambiguities surrounding decisions by Enron's senior executives and board of directors. Collectively, they define the morally gray space surrounding conflicting obligations and points of view, often without the possibility of clear resolution. The open question is how companies can exercise ethical discipline in such situations. Can they meet standards of ethical discipline through a transaction-by-transaction review of technical compliance with appropriate rules? Or is something more fundamental than a transactional, rules-based review essential to ethical discipline? The Enron case shows that the second question suggests the correct answer.

The Exercise of Ethical Discipline in Corporations

In 1977, political theorist and philosopher Hannah Arendt wrote a series of articles in the *New Yorker* about the utter thoughtlessness that often surrounds evil acts. She referred to this phenomenon as the "banality of evil."[42] One of her primary examples was the total lack of thought and reflection that characterized Adolph Eichmann's mindset during his trial for war crimes, held in Jerusalem in the early 1960s.

The notion that wrongdoing resides in thoughtlessness, as opposed to systematic attention to the consequences of one's decisions and acts, is relevant to the Enron case. While Enron's ethical drift may have been driven by personal predispositions "to win at all costs" and to "game the system," the available record does not convince me that this behavior resulted from a carefully orchestrated plan by Enron's leaders to defraud investors, even though they are ultimately and incontestably responsible for whatever damage this ethical drift created for investors and employees alike. Rather, as I have tried to explain, Enron's ethical drift—involving increasingly devious and deceptive behavior—unfolded in incremental steps over time as a result of increasing capital market pressures, hubris, careless mistakes, poorly designed and administered incentives, a culture that neither discouraged aggressive gaming nor tolerated internal dissent, breakdowns in the company's performance measurement and control systems, and the lack of attentive oversight by the board of directors. As Enron came under extraordinary pressure after a profit collapse in 1997 to reestablish a record of supernormal earnings growth, Enron's financial staff became increasingly adept at using otherwise legitimate structured-finance vehicles to dress up Enron's balance sheet and income statement while finding ways to reward limited partners and transaction counterparties. This financial maneuvering is evidence of extremely fertile minds at work on financial strategy. However, the administrative leadership that preceded this work, set the context for it, and approved it is also evidence of a fatal thoughtlessness about the potentially disastrous consequences of trying to exploit the arcane rules and regulations governing financial accounting and disclosure.

Enron's outside advisors reinforced this thoughtlessness. With the advice, support, and, in some instances, collusion of professional accountants, lawyers, and bankers, Enron slipped into the shadowed space between rightdoing and wrongdoing. One kind of financial ruse led to another, although many were not blatantly illegal. Such devious moves—involving a stunning array of mind-numbingly complex financial structures and transactions—soon became accepted as normal practice, until the company finally collapsed under the weight of careless accounting errors (in the Raptor partnerships) and subsequent public scrutiny. Along the way, standards of responsible judgment and action were lost amid the collective thoughtlessness of Enron's most senior executives, board of directors, and outside advisors.

Simple principles of common morality are, by themselves, inadequate protection against Enron-style thoughtlessness and ethical drift. Enron's published code of ethics reflected all the usual elements of ethical common sense: telling the truth, obeying the law, fulfilling contractual and promissory obligations, avoiding conflicts of interest, being fair in all business dealings, treating employees with dignity and respect, and so on. What was missing in Enron's case was not a code of ethics. Rather, it was a deep commitment to "quality" objectives—compliance with the law, the principles underlying the law, and high ethical standards—and thoughtful reflection on how best to achieve those objectives. Skilling's and Lay's lack of sustained commitment to these objectives—along with perverse incentives and a culture of deceit—created a lethal social pathology. By failing to provide clear guidelines for responsible action, Enron's leaders abandoned their more junior executives who operated in the penumbra between clear rightdoing and clear wrongdoing.

Kenneth Andrews, a distinguished Harvard Business School professor, observed many years ago that a commitment to quality objectives is an *organizational achievement,* while failure to pursue quality objectives is an *organizational failure*:[43]

> The moral person in the modern corporation is all too often on his or her own. This person cannot be expected to remain autonomous, i.e., acting on his or her best judgment, no matter how well endowed, without positive organized support. The stubbornness of corporate ethics as a problem obscures the simplicity of the solution that can be found once the leaders of a company decide to do something about their ethical standards. Ethical dereliction, sleaziness, or inertia is not merely an individual failure but a management problem as well.[44]

The "simplicity of the solution" to problems of corporate ethics that Andrews refers to lies in thoughtful attention to building a corporate environment conducive to the exercise of moral judgment. As Andrews points out, "When the persons whose moral judgment might ultimately determine the ethical character of their companies first come to work, they enter a community whose values will influence their moral judgment."[45]

At Enron, those institutional values included, most notably, innovation, freedom from bureaucratic inhibitors, continuous innovation, and maximization of shareholders' interests. Enron's espoused values also included meritocracy within the firm, civic philanthropy outside the firm, and all the usual standards of ethical conduct. However, incrementally and over time, Enron's values *in action* deviated from its espoused values.[46] Innovation mutated into reckless gambling, and top managers became careless or lazy in holding the company to strict ethical conduct, even as they began to receive enormous recognition and praise for their brilliant strategy and organizational prowess. Enron's commitment to quality objectives—already fragile owing to the culture of deceit that had grown up within the company—began to break down in ways that let its executives (and their advisors) follow their inclinations, and left thoughtful attention to ethics to chance.

The way aspiring and experienced managers were judged also influenced Enron's community values. The system of perverse incentives—which generously rewarded new-business originators, commodity traders, and project developers based on estimated rather than real returns, and which operated with short holding periods for stock options and grants and no lookbacks or clawbacks for outsized bonuses—tempted executives to pursue short-term personal gains for their own sake, sometimes at the expense of colleagues, and to hide or misrepresent mistakes. Under pressure to get ahead and get rich, many Enron executives were tempted to become thoughtless and careless, to seek to win at all costs, to sacrifice candor in communications with superiors, and to take advantage of the system that measured and rewarded performance.

In retrospect, this should not come as any great surprise. People will do what they are rewarded for doing. Corporate values other than maximum immediate returns will suffer if heavy incentives reward them for achieving precisely that. At Enron, top management's perpetual fear of a downgrade in its credit rating and a decline in its share price (used to capitalize many off-balance-sheet hedging vehicles) left little latitude for reported shortfalls in earnings and cash flow from operations. Every operating and financial executive felt this pressure. And as Enron expanded rapidly in scale and scope, the decentralization of authority across corporate functions and new business units provided greater latitude for error while increasing the risks of a breakdown in espoused values and standards of conduct.

The "simplicity of the solution" to the kind of ethical problems that Enron experienced and Andrews cites lies in organizational processes as well as commitment. Once leaders decide that they will actively manage ethical intention and performance—rather than leaving it untended in the corrosive environment of unprincipled competition and self-interest—they must put into place certain organizational features and policies.

Creating an Environment for Exercising Ethical Judgment.

There is little evidence in the recruitment, training, and performance assessment of Enron employees that the organization paid much attention on a regular basis to developing managers capable of identifying the ethical implications of a decision, thinking through the consequences of alternatives, seeking out different points of view, and deciding on the best course when lacking all the necessary information and answers. Indeed, in all my research into Enron's history, I have come across very little to do with how Enron backed up its nicely published code of ethics with organizational processes supportive of its espoused principles. Without such processes, there is scant hope that any organization can create an environment in which individuals can recognize and respond thoughtfully to ethical choices involving knotty conflicts of interest and conflicts of duty.[47]

In Enron's case, conflicts of interest occurred in clashes between managerial opportunism (in the form of personal gains and reputation) and the welfare of shareholders (in the form of knowledge about the true financial condition of their investment). Enron's conflicts of duty—so prevalent in the legal penumbra—involved the duty to comply with relevant accounting and SEC rules versus the perceived duty to deliver to shareholders (and credit-rating agencies) an unbroken stream of earnings growth. Indeed, what is so amazing about the history of Enron's rise and fall is the disconnect between Lay's public persona as a truly generous and socially responsive chief executive and his apparent lack of consistent, detailed attention to the development and support of responsible management within his organization.

Examples of Inadequate Organizational Processes

From the very beginning, Lay was a proponent of hiring "the best and the brightest" at Enron, and by the early 1990s he was paying special attention to building its intellectual asset base. I have described how Enron sought to recruit a deep reservoir of talent. Recruits were screened for intelligence, a strong work ethic, problem-solving ability, and a sense of urgency. An orientation and training program was designed not only to give recruits an overview of the business, but also a sense of superiority and good fortune in being asked to join such a remarkable company.

Once hired, Enron's approach to managing its talented employees was rooted in the 360-degree performance evaluation process modeled on the process Skilling had learned at McKinsey & Co. This biannual feedback system was based on reviews from peers, customers, and supervisors as well as those supervised. By 2001 about 8,000 of Enron's 24,000 employees were evaluated under this system, leaving the traditional pipeline, oil and gas exploration, and overseas operations to their own approach. The impact on organizational behavior was nevertheless significant, as this system encompassed the fastest-growing and most innovative portions of Enron's business.

Importantly, very little of the feedback provided by this process addressed an individual's compliance with ethical principles of the corporation. As a quick refresher, this performance-evaluation process began by aggregating individuals with similar job titles across the organization, and then assigning each job category its own performance review committee (PRC) composed of about twenty individuals in higher positions. Some thirty such PRCs operated throughout Enron, covering its energy trading businesses and corporate departments. PRCs met twice a year for as long as three weeks at a time to force-rank employees in their pools according to five key criteria: (1) innovation and entrepreneurship, (2) communication and setting direction, (3) teamwork and interpersonal skills, (4) leadership, vision, and values, (5) business and organizational skills, and (5) analytical and technical skills.

This process had many espoused advantages, including rewarding those who had contributed real economic value to the organization, serving as a safeguard against office politics by socializing the review process, promoting specific skills and abilities by making clear what Enron valued and rewarded, and improving communication, moving faster, and getting the right jobs done. Readers will remember, however, that this process sparked many complaints. Some characterized it as a ruthless rank-and-yank system with a short-term focus. Others complained that it conditioned success on making deals happen, not necessarily making them work. Still others felt that the process stunted teamwork and became a tool for rewarding loyalists and punishing dissenters (precisely what Skilling had hoped to avoid). According to testimony from one of my former students, "People were routinely treated as objects or commodities, loyalties were regularly sacrificed, and moral contracts were rarely honored."

Whatever the plusses and minuses of this process, there is little evidence that Enron used it to hold employees to the principles and values laid out in the company's code of ethics. For example, in defining what the "leadership/visions/values" criterion actually meant for an Enron vice president or managing director, instructional documents did not mention compliance with, or the embodiment of, Enron's espoused values.[48] A draft performance-feedback document was not much more inclusive or specific: only one out of forty-five measures related to Enron's stated values, and even that one did not explicitly refer to substantive ethical principles.[49] Finally, another internal document showing how to conduct feedback online does not refer to the company's published ethical values in describing performance in "leadership/visions/values."[50]

Neither is there strong evidence of swift discipline in the face of incontestable wrongdoing. The lack of severe punishment following the Valhalla trading scandal in 1987—along with several subsequent instances of cheating and wrongdoing—are all cases in point. Add to this record of ethical blindness Lay's and Skilling's inability to tolerate internal dissent, such as Vince Kaminski's repeated criticisms of financial transactions with off-balance-sheet entities (from his seat in Enron's Risk Analysis and Control group), and it is not difficult to conclude that few meaningful investments were being made in developing a culture conducive to ethical judgment. Indeed, an internal survey in April 2001 reported that "66% of employees responded that there is not good communication between business units and teams" on matters of company values. Other negative feedback on Enron's culture and related processes addressed ineffective coaching by the company's leadership, difficulties in challenging the status quo, and lack of clarity about how the performance review process worked.[51]

To create an environment conducive to the exercise of ethical judgment, organizations need precisely what Enron appeared to lack throughout its history—processes that support a commitment to quality objectives and high ethical standards. Despite the espoused objectives embedded in Enron's code of ethics, the company's organizational processes failed miserably in their supportive role. Indeed, evidence from preceding chapters suggests that important organizational processes actually sabotaged whatever quality objectives Enron's code was meant to promote.

Critical Organizational Processes

Organizational processes that support quality objectives and high ethical standards concern how senior executives and a company's board of directors measure performance, administer rewards and penalties, develop managers, and monitor behavior.

There is no question that Enron's financial targets and plans were extremely biased toward quarterly results, because the company's marginal credit rating was so dependent on current cash flow from operations. As trading margins began to decline, and as various diversification moves failed to deliver expected returns, this bias was reinforced. This short-term bias was, of course, exacerbated by the method by which business originators, commodity traders, power plant developers, and senior executives received bonuses. With only several visible exceptions, Enron's generous bonus plan related directly to short-term economic results.

Nothing will happen at companies like Enron to advance a doctrine of quality objectives and high ethical standards under such a performance-management regime. A bias toward short-term results is a gamble with the future of an enterprise, because managers who have little experience in balancing short-term, quantitative objectives with qualitative attention to long-term organizational values are not likely to make mature judgments in developing a sustainable business enterprise.

The "simplicity of the solution" to achieving quality objectives and high ethical standards lies in three organizational commitments: qualitative attention, balanced incentives, and decision audits. The only surprising feature of these required commitments is their collective undervaluation by Enron's leadership.

QUALITATIVE ATTENTION.   The Enron story shows that without persistent attention to qualitative aspects of individual and group performance, the chances of developing an organizational environment conducive to thoughtful social and ethical deliberation are minimal.[52] For this reason, negotiation and review of personal and business plans must include attention to the organization's qualitative objectives and ethical standards, such as the protection of corporate integrity and reputation, respectful behavior, truth telling, legal compliance, and host of other possible social goals. To be effective, this process must include qualitative measures related to these objectives and standards, in addition to whatever standard quantitative measures the plans may require.

One reason that formal performance-management plans such as Enron's so rarely include qualitative measures of integrity is that decision-making behavior and ethical ability are difficult to observe in practice. But where senior executives fail to give adequate attention to such qualitative indicators of management performance, or lack the courage to make subjective judgments based on these performance indicators, pressures to meet short-term economic targets will inevitably crowd out thoughtful reflection on how employees' decisions can best reflect the organization's ethical values.

One attractive byproduct of committing to difficult, subjective evaluations is that incentive rewards become easier to administer, and more defensible. Andrews and others have long argued that subjective evaluations are less susceptible to the kind of gaming associated with Enron-style, financially based performance measures. Qualitative performance measures also help individual managers see the full nature of their jobs more clearly.

Any effort to liberate an evaluation process by adding qualitative judgment to the numbers requires a parallel effort in managerial development—not so much through formal training as in how companies develop careers. If organizations elect to foster quality objectives and high ethical standards, then they will have to nurture the character and values of "promotable" managers. Somewhere in their early careers, promising managers must be exposed to important moral dilemmas in executive decision making. This book can provide many worthy case studies. The purpose of this mid-career education should be to emphasize breadth of perspective on how to make corporations moral, and the ethical imperatives for business leadership in contemporary society. These efforts need to emphasize thoughtfulness, not heroic action.[53]

BALANCED INCENTIVES.   A commitment to qualitative aspects of organizational performance requires a disciplined approach to incentives. One of the key lessons of Enron's history of perverse incentives and ethical drift is that every employee needs to know that the company's incentive system rewards accomplishments other than economic performance—*and penalizes failures.* This means that even if managers are successful in economic terms, they are still subject to forgone bonuses, demotion, or discharge for failure to fulfill the organization's qualitative objectives and ethical standards. Indeed, the most direct way of reinforcing commitment to such standards is to require employees to perform satisfactorily on qualitative measures before they can earn any incentive compensation. This constraint will motivate balanced performance across the full spectrum of managerial behavior.

An important corollary to this modified pay-for-performance principle is that when employees fall short of their personal or business targets—as they inevitably will, on occasion—inquiry into the reasons for these lapses, and how they can best meet their targets in the future, must precede adverse judgment and penalty. "Death penalties" for poor performance in the absence of due diligence will sabotage commitment to espoused social and ethical values.

DECISION AUDITS.   How many boards of directors routinely and systematically review the productivity of past capital expenditures? And how
many CEOs routinely and systematically review critical decisions by key
executives? At Enron, evidence suggests that such reviews were at best
episodic rather than routine, typically occurring after some fuss was raised
or startling problem developed. Even then, as in the Valhalla trading scandal, minimal follow-up ensued. In that case, the offending traders repeated
their fraudulent acts, this time prompting scrutiny from federal officials.

In contrast to Enron's record of careless and lazy management, frequent
decision audits and spot-checks are a necessary supplement to qualitative
objectives and balanced incentives. Indeed, one of the most effective deter-
rents of wrongdoing is heightened awareness of the probability of being
caught. This, it turns out, is actually a stronger deterrent than increasing the
severity of punishment for those who are caught. An example is the finding
that when police park an empty patrol car at locations where motorists are
likely to exceed the speed limit, the frequency of speeding is reduced.[54]
Whether or not frequent audits uncover deviant behavior is irrelevant. The
idea is to prevent, not just catch, misconduct.

Audits by boards of directors are as important as internal audits by management in building a strong organizational commitment to quality objectives and high ethical standards. In the post-Enron rush to revitalize board
oversight and control of corporate affairs, Section 404 of the Sarbanes-
Oxley Act required extensive and expensive documentation of internal controls by management, and annual review of these controls by outside
accountants. Whatever the expected benefits of documenting systems designed to inform and control corporate behavior, this is no substitute for actually looking at the behavior itself. Imagine the possibilities if internal
audit teams summarized for directors the actual behavior they observed and
the problems they uncovered related to qualitative objectives. Directors
could then strongly support a willing CEO in moderating management's un-
derstandable interest in short-term achievements and reinforcing attention
to the organization's highest long-term aspirations.[55]

Ethical Leadership

In his profoundly influential study of leadership in administration, Philip
Selznick begins by describing leadership as a "slippery phenomenon" that
eludes easy definition.[56] What leaders do is often difficult to explain, but

most of us would readily agree that much failure of leadership results from an inadequate understanding of its true nature and tasks. What little we do know is that leadership is work performed to meet the needs of a specific social situation (rather than a set of personality traits), and that it is not equivalent to holding high office or prestigious decision-making authority.

The notion of ethical leadership adds another level of complexity to our definition of administrative leadership, and certainly concerns the personal agenda and deportment of the chief executive. This behavior is far more influential in defining an organization's character and ethical predisposition than any policy issued over a CEO's signature. In the case of Enron, it is perhaps easiest to define ethical leadership by pointing to the crippling effects of its absence: the ethical drift described in Chapter 4, influenced by the combination of short-term financial pressures and personal opportunism.

The evidence presented here suggests that ethical leadership failed at Enron more by default than by positive error or sin. In fact, the behavior of Enron's CEOs maps Selznick's description of the most common failings of institutional leadership almost perfectly.

In the first instance, leadership defaults at Enron were rooted in the failure of Skilling and Lay to fully understand the source of Enron's institutional vulnerability (its organizational culture), and its potentially costly outcome (catastrophic loss of trust by Enron's trading counterparties, credit suppliers, and public investors). This failure was accompanied by a second one: the failure to define and actively promote purposes and values beyond becoming "the world's leading energy company—creating innovative and efficient energy solutions for growing economies and a better environment worldwide." Such a general statement did not provide clear decision-making premises and ethical guidelines for Enron employees.

Another leadership default is reflected in the fact that Enron's espoused values of respect, integrity, communication, and excellence enjoyed only superficial acceptance in its trading operations and financial office—two locales where personal opportunism ran rampant. Leaders' primary role is to prevent such aberrant behavior by working constantly to infuse the organization with values that have a disciplining effect on the attitudes and behavior of all employees, and that govern relationships with outside groups. Enron's leaders failed to provide a strong guiding hand in institutionalizing values that could meet these tests.

A third leadership default was the confounding of Enron's economic achievements with institutional success, by which I mean the accomplishment of purposes, the development of competencies, and the embodiment of values critical to the company's long-term survival. Skilling and Lay clearly needed to focus on fostering the minimum conditions for continued existence. However, once short-term economic success and a preoccupation with public relations began to crowd out the difficult work of promoting and protecting Enron's espoused values, the risks of ruthlessness, arrogance, secrecy, dishonesty, and general mediocrity multiplied. In the end, it was these values rather than those catalogued in Enron's code of ethics that did the company in.

If the history of leadership at Enron can be characterized as a default, then what guidelines for effective ethical leadership follow from Enron's story? Once again, Philip Selznick's remarkably insightful study of organizations and institutions provides practical guidance. "From a policy standpoint," Selznick writes, "most of the characteristics of the responsible leader can be summarized under two headings: the avoidance of personal opportunism and the avoidance of utopianism."

Personal opportunism, according to Selznick, is "the pursuit of immediate, short-run advantages in a way inadequately controlled by considerations of principle and ultimate consequence."[57] When the compensation of Enron's top 200 executives rose from almost $193 million in 1998 and to $1.4 billion in 2000 (including $1.06 billion in stock-option gains)—a sevenfold increase—even as reported net income grew by only 25 percent and Enron's return on equity was declining, the board sent a signal that it condoned personal gains far exceeding the company's true economic performance. So much for the principle of paying for true economic performance and for the notion of leadership as sacrifice.

This environment created strong incentives for employees to gamble in the name of innovation with shareholders' money for short-term personal advantage. These gambles included relentless diversification into businesses with only tenuous links to Enron's core competences in the natural gas business; massive product proliferation leading to 1,400 commodity and derivative products sold in thirty-five different countries, thirteen currencies, and scores of languages; investments in startups relying on unproven technologies; and excessive use of off-balance-sheet transactions to hide losses and corporate debt.

This mismatch between these deeply embedded commercial, organizational, and legal risks and the company's financial performance kindled the firestorm that erupted when it turned out that Enron's reported financial results were of doubtful dependability. Enron's highly compensated leaders were thus fully responsible for the run on the bank that Skilling correctly identified as the ultimate cause of the company's collapse. Opportunities for enormous personal gain distracted top executives from the essential tasks of maintaining institutional integrity and building stable relationships with shareholders and employees. These executives thus failed to heed Selznick's first guideline of effective leadership: avoid opportunism.

Nor did Enron's leaders fulfill Selznick's second guideline: avoid utopianism. Utopianism, according to Selznick, "hopes to avoid hard choices by a flight to abstractions."[58] In Enron's case, its stated purpose—at first, to be the world's best energy company, and later to be the world's best corporation—was too general to permit disciplined and responsible decision making in the face of difficulty. In this vacuum, abstract definitions of purpose unrelated to corporate ideals, distinctive competences, and organizational opportunities easily gave way to uncontrolled criteria as such personal preference and opportunism. As a natural result, immediate exigencies came to dominate actual choices. This loss of ideals sums up Enron's history and its enduring legacy.

Afterword

Despite years of intense investigative reporting, several descriptive narratives of Enron's rise and fall written by informed insiders and members of the business press, multiple investigations by Congress, an in-depth report by a special committee of Enron's board of directors, dozens of testimonies given by former Enron executives and directors under oath, extensive fact finding by the bankruptcy court examiner, the sixty-one-day trial of Kenneth Lay and Jeffrey Skilling during the spring of 2006, Skilling's 60,000-word appeal of his conviction for fraud and conspiracy to defraud filed in September 2007, and my own independent research, many important details of this remarkable story remain elusive.

There is still much that we do not know about the perceptions, intentions, thought processes, and apparent failings of Enron's leaders and their board of directors. For example why didn't Skilling and Lay see more clearly the risks and increasingly adverse effects of the extreme, performance-oriented management system that they had created? How could Skilling—a very public proponent of earning more money with less assets (the so-called "asset light" strategy)—rationalize Enron spending so heavily, and so beyond established capital budgets, on capital projects with highly speculative returns? According to what logic did Skilling and Lay, and ultimately the board, approve using the company's own stock to capitalize its own hedging counterparties—an extremely risky hedging arrangement that required Enron to issue more stock if either the current value of its stock or the future value of its commodity contracts declined and, in addition, left Enron with no effective hedge on its contracts if both values declined at the same time (which they did)? Why did Skilling, at critical moments, treat differences of opinion, pushback, and penetrating questions from both insiders and outsiders as either stupid comments or narcissistic insults rather than opportunities for constructive dialogue? Why did Skilling, Lay, and Enron's board of directors fail to understand and act decisively upon increasing internal evidence that Enron was financially distressed and heading toward insolvency? Why did Lay's espoused faith and Christian values fail to guarantee his moral leadership and protect the enterprise from increasing immoral behavior? How did Skilling and Lay imagine that their personal conduct could influence the behavior of others within the company? What internal images of personal leadership and stewardship did their behavior reflect? How did they reassure themselves that they were doing "the right things" all along?

Lingering questions of this nature suggest a kind of behavioral and psychological analysis that I neither set out to accomplish nor achieved. But this is not to say that I don't believe the mental attitudes and mindsets of Enron's leaders are among the most important and instructive aspects of this story. Indeed, I have a strong intuition that Enron, like many organizations, became a platform where powerful images of right and wrong, and of effective and ineffective leadership, were being acted out within the constellation of top executive roles and with the company's board of directors. Some of these internal images may have been driven by feelings of superiority and moral invulnerability or utopian visions of what Enron could be or, perhaps, excessive zeal masking feelings of self-doubt. Whatever the case, these personal images turned out to be profoundly destructive to both the individuals involved and the enterprise as a whole.

During the best of times, Kenneth Lay and Jeffrey Skilling were widely celebrated as innovative executives. Despite the denial and pain avoidance that Lay demonstrated at various times in his career at Enron, he was respected by many inside and outside the company as a leader who would not short-change values for profits. Jeffrey Skilling was viewed in many quarters as a visionary who saw natural gas as a model industry for perfecting an entirely new commodity-trading and financial regime. Those who worked with him or observed him from a distance saw, alongside his impatience and arrogance, a brilliant mind with an enormous capacity to synthesize data and ideas, to develop creative new ideas, and to communicate complex concepts with compelling simplicity and passion. Many other of the fifteen executives who entered guilty pleas were also talented individuals, including Andrew Fastow whose thievery and secret self-dealing were the most egregious crimes of those eventually indicted. That Lay and Skilling and some of their senior colleagues were found guilty of fraud and conspiracy to commit fraud (and, in Skilling's case, two counts of insider trading) suggests to me a far richer story line than weak management and profound lapses of judgment.

I strongly suspect that the full story of Enron—one that probes the psychology of Enron's leaders, their senior colleagues, and the company's board of directors—will reveal a more complete map of how they imagined Enron as a "great company," how they thought such a company should be managed and led, and how their self-interests and self-perceptions created individual and shared images of Enron as a highly functioning organization. In addition, a more complete account might explain why Enron's leaders were so unable to "see" the extremely dysfunctional organizational behavior that developed under their leadership. It is this self-declared blindness—and most particularly its sources—that should interest any of us who hold positions of administrative leadership in organizations. None of us are immune to this affliction. If we are to avoid the fate of Enron-type breakdowns, we need to understand the nature of this lack of acute vision, its causes, its developmental path, and ultimately its preventive therapies.

I have argued in this book that many social pathologies contributed to Enron's collapse—that before fraud, there was considerable innovation at Enron followed by a supreme overconfidence or grandiosity, which mutated into various forms of reckless gambling; that this grandiosity was reinforced by Enron's system of perverse incentives and facilitated by increasingly emasculated controls; that these perverse incentives festered in a developing culture of deceit; that this culture of deceit (and denial by Enron's leaders) fostered "ethical drift"; that deeply flawed board oversight failed to detect and deter this ethical drift; that this drift was aided and abetted by the collusion of financial intermediaries; and that the result of all this was a "normalization of deviant behavior" both inside and outside Enron. Yet the testimonies of both Lay and Skilling in federal court make it very clear that they would not view the Enron story in a similar light. Indeed, Enron's leaders have defiantly rejected the government's legal case against them and claimed no knowledge of any conspiracy to defraud investors and employees. Kenneth Lay maintained to his dying day that he was innocent of all charges brought against him. Jeffrey Skilling maintains a similar position, claiming that there was no conspiracy and no fraud and that Enron's collapse was caused by a "run on the bank" resulting from Fastow's lies to him, the board, and the credit-rating agencies. In addition, in his appeal filed on September 7, 2007, Skilling claimed profound weaknesses in the government's case against him, including its theories of criminality, its evidentiary proof, its unfair trial procedures, and its prosecutorial misconduct with respect to coerced plea agreements and the suppression of evidence. With respect to the latter, a supplemental appeal filed by Skilling on March 3, 2008, claimed government prosecutors suppressed evidence that prevented him from impeaching Fastow's trial testimony that asserted he and Skilling had several secret agreements that protected purchasers of troubled Enron assets from any losses, thereby enabling Enron to complete the sales and book earnings.

Skilling's September 7 appeal advanced four key arguments:

that the "right of honest services" theory used in the government's indictment as one basis for the conspiracy to defraud charge has been incorrectly applied;

that the judge issued flawed instructions to the jury on "materiality" and "deliberate ignorance";

that the decision not to move the trial outside Houston prejudiced Skilling; and

that the trial court did not give Skilling a fair chance to identify jurors who may have been capable of putting aside their biases on the case.

Early commentary by legal experts writing in white collar crime blogs suggested that Skilling's strongest argument was the first one, based on the decision of the Fifth Circuit Court of Appeals in *U.S. v. Brown*, issued in August 2006—three months after Skilling's conviction.[1] This decision overturned the fraud convictions of three defendants in the Enron Nigerian Barge trial—all Merrill Lynch employees who had been convicted of colluding with Enron in disguising the company's true financial condition. This reversal was based on the grounds that Merrill executives did not violate the "honest-services" provision of the Federal Criminal Code, as claimed by government prosecutors, because they believed they were acting in the best interests of Enron even while engaging in questionable transactions to bolster the company's balance sheet.

The "right of honest services" theory used to build the fraud conspiracy count against Skilling was one of three used by the government. According to this theory, the government claimed that Skilling, in conspiring to defraud Enron shareholders, unlawfully deprived Enron of its right to his "honest services."[2]

In the subsequent *U.S. v. Brown* case, however, the court held that an employee who believes his acts are for the benefit of the corporation cannot have the intent to deprive the company of the person's honest services. The effect of this decision was to vacate the conspiracy charges against four previously convicted Merrill employees.[3] This opinion essentially nullified one of the government's central legal theories used to charge Skilling and Lay with conspiracy to defraud. Predictably, this was Skilling's position, too. Skilling claimed in his appeal that his alleged actions were presumably not divergent from Enron's interests (maximizing share value and revenue) and that he should not have been convicted of "honest-services" fraud. In addition, since the "honest-services" theory was one of three used in the fraud conspiracy count and the jury did not identify which theory was the basis of its conviction, Skilling asked for a complete discharge of the fraud conspiracy charge.

The "honest-services" theory of fraud as articulated by the Fifth Circuit Court and promoted by Skilling's appeal to the same court seems quite odd to the layman. According to the court's interpretation of the "honest-services" theory, which is central to Skilling's appeal, even where an employee's act could be described as "dishonest, fraudulent, wrongful, or criminal," the act nevertheless "is not a federal crime *under the honest-services theory of fraud specifically*" (emphasis in original) if the employer created a set of incentives to achieve a corporate goal, the employee believed that his conduct promoted that goal to their mutual benefit, and the employee's conduct was consistent with that belief.

In other words, whatever can be said about Skilling's conduct—be it unscrupulous, immoral, or even criminal under some other statute—it is, according to the Fifth Circuit Court and Skilling's appeal, not a violation of the federal statute requiring employees to provide "honest services" to their employers. Skilling's conduct might violate other statutes, but not that one. Thus, whatever Skilling may have done—even if it involved lying, cheating, or misleading investors—it was not a violation of the "honest-services" statute as long as Enron had created incentives for a specific corporate goal, he believed he was pursuing that goal and that doing so would benefit both Skilling and Enron, and his conduct was consistent with this belief. Following this logic, Skilling claimed that the prosecution's "honest-services" allegations were incorrect, and the court erred in instructing the jury on an "honest-services" theory. It remains to be seen whether the courts will reach a different conclusion, perhaps in light of the fact that it was Skilling himself who set the corporate goals that he sought to achieve.

In light of precedent established by the Fifth Circuit Court in the *U.S. v. Brown* case, it nevertheless seems quite possible that the same court will agree with Skilling's argument, throw out the conspiracy charge, and reduce his twenty-four-year sentence. The government's Enron Task Force also seems ready to back down on its interpretation of the "right of honest services" theory and not appeal to the Supreme Court. Indeed, soon after the Fifth Circuit Court's explanation of the "honest-services" theory in *U.S. v. Brown*, government prosecutors acknowledged that the "honest services" provision *as interpreted in Brown* did not apply to four out of five of counts in a separate indictment of Kevin Howard, the former chief financial officer for Enron Broadband Services whom they accused of participating in activities leading to the falsification of Enron's earnings for the fourth quarter of 2000.[4]

Although the Fifth Circuit's narrow interpretation of "the right to honest services" legal theory seems to convert a statute requiring honesty in the conduct of corporate affairs into one requiring merely loyalty, the court's ruling on Skilling's appeal will not erase evidence that he played an important role in encouraging and tolerating a complex web of behaviors and dubious transactions whose combined effect was to mislead investors about Enron's true economic performance and prospects. Unfortunately, neither will the appeal process provide any new evidence about the thinking and beliefs that led to this behavior. Indeed, it is doubtful that any of my questions about the inner visions and motives of Enron's leaders can be answered without hearing directly from those who ultimately pleaded guilty to financial fraud or were convicted of fraud. Congressional hearings and courtrooms are not venues conducive to revealing deep insight to the interior images that shape our personal conduct as managers, leaders, and governors of human enterprise. A very different methodology and pubic record is required for such an analysis to be conducted. Yet, those of us working to fully understand the origins and implications of the Enron story for the governance of firms need this important missing chapter.

APPENDIXES

NOTES

BIBLIOGRAPHY

INDEX

The Raptor Structures and the
Surrounding Controversy

The espoused purpose of the Raptor structures was to hedge Enron's merchant investments—such as in telecommunications companies—to avoid having to report losses on these marked-to-market assets if their value declined.[1] Enron's contracts with the Raptors guaranteed that if the market value of a hedged asset did decline, the Raptors would pay Enron the difference between the previously recorded value and the new lower value.[2] Both the intent and the effect were to reduce, if not eliminate, fluctuations in Enron's reported net income.

Figure A.1 shows how the Raptor structures—actually special purpose entities, or SPEs—were capitalized, and what benefits each participant expected to realize. Figure A.2 illustrates two types of hedges transacted with the Raptor entities.

Once the Raptors were made public, they immediately sparked considerable controversy. In the criminal indictment of former CFO Andrew Fastow, CEO Jeffrey Skilling, and board chair Kenneth Lay, government prosecutors alleged that Enron used the Raptors to avoid public disclosure of declines in the value of merchant investments, and that Skilling had full knowledge of this purpose. Ben Glisan, Enron's former treasurer, testified during Skilling's criminal trial that he had outlined the Raptor transactions to Skilling in the spring of 2000, after which he and Skilling took them to the board's finance committee. He testified that he had informed the committee that the Raptors "had no economic value" as a hedging vehicle.[3]

David Delainey, a former trading and retail energy executive, echoed Glisan. Delainey testified that from his management position, the Raptors looked like "a pot of money we used to manipulate our income statement." Similarly and most important, Fastow testified that the Raptors were designed to help Enron keep earnings on the books by providing a hedging cushion, in case these assets had to be booked at their true lower values. He also testified that the LJM partnerships and the affiliated Raptors bought and warehoused Enron assets that no one else wanted, and acted as a middleman to allow Enron to receive certain accounting treatments on deals.

A deeper look at these allegations reveals a more nuanced picture of the Raptor entities. The LJM2 partnership—shown in Figure A.1 as an equity contributor to the Raptor SPEs—was controlled by Fastow, who appeared to have a conflict of interest. However, it is difficult to claim any foul because Enron's board of directors approved this arrangement.[4] In addition, Skilling presents arguments and evidence in his lengthy appeal that the Raptors had significant economic value as a hedging vehicle, that all relevant Raptors transactions were fully disclosed in Enron's public filings, and that government prosecutors' ("unfounded and unsupported") claims against him

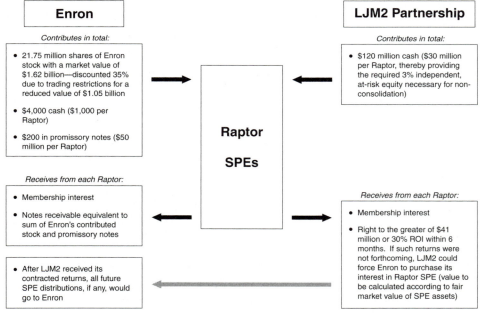

Figure A.1 Capitalization of Raptor special purpose entities (SPEs). For Raptor III only, Enron contributed warrants to purchase shares of The New Power Co. stock at $10.75 per share, or a cost of $259.1 million. TNPC's IPO price was $21.00 and the stock closed at $27.00 on its first day of trading, making Enron's contribution worth $650.7 million.

rested upon a "profound distortion of the applicable accounting rules and regulations" as well as the underlying economics and business rationale for the Raptor transactions."[5] What this unresolved conflict suggests is that while the Raptor structures were identified by Glisan as serving no economic purposes, and by government prosecutors as serving deceptive purposes, no consensus has emerged on whether or not the Raptor structures had a significant business purpose or violated any accounting rules.

Business Issues

The most important nonlegal criticism of the Raptor structures is that Enron's hedges with them were not real economic hedges at all. According to government prosecutors, this criticism has merit: Enron's hedges with three of the Raptors did not shift the risk of loss to a third party, because the only assets the Raptors held had been supplied by Enron itself—its own

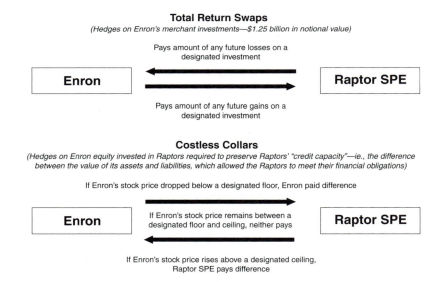

Total Return Swaps
(Hedges on Enron's merchant investments—$1.25 billion in notional value)

Pays amount of any future losses on a
designated investment

Enron   Raptor SPE

Pays amount of any future gains on a
designated investment

Costless Collars
(Hedges on Enron equity invested in Raptors required to preserve Raptors' "credit capacity"—ie., the difference between the value of its assets and liabilities, which allowed the Raptors to meet their financial obligations)

If Enron's stock price dropped below a designated floor, Enron paid difference

Enron   If Enron's stock price remains between a   Raptor SPE
          designated floor and ceiling, neither pays

If Enron's stock price rises above a designated ceiling,
Raptor SPE pays difference

Figure A.2 Two types of Raptors transactions. Total return swaps are arrangements whereby one party agrees to pay the other party the appreciation from an asset and receive payments from the other party for the depreciation of an asset. Collars are derivative transactions combining a put and a call that effectively set limits on the gain and loss that the holder of the call will realize. A costless collar includes premiums of equal value on the put and call, so neither party pays the other at the inception of the transaction.

shares. Essentially, in any payout under the hedging arrangement, regardless of direction, Enron would, in effect, be paying itself. Skilling, in his appeal, refutes this characterization of the hedge: "If the [Enron] stock remained at the same price or increased, the Raptors would be funded, which was the goal. If Enron's stock price dropped, LJM would have to pay Enron $30 million of LJM's *own* money." (Emphasis in original.)[6]

Raptor III was created to hedge Enron's investment in The New Power Co. (TNPC). This Raptor was capitalized with shares of TNPC, not Enron. This meant that Raptor III's ability to meet its obligations on the hedge depended on the value of TNPC stock, and that if TNPC's share price declined too far, Raptor III would not be able to pay Enron. The Powers report to the board of directors after Enron's bankruptcy called this "the derivatives equivalent of doubling down on a bet on TNPC."

Accounting Issues

Several accounting controversies surround the relationships between the LJM2 partnership and the Raptors. Setting up an SPE off Enron's balance sheet requires a 3 percent investment by an independent entity. LJM2 served that purpose. That partnership contributed $30 million to each Raptor SPE, and each Raptor later made a $41 million distribution to LJM2.[7]

These distributions raise two accounting issues. First, the Raptor payments can be seen as either a return *of* LJM2's equity investments, a return *on* those investments, or some combination of the two. If the payments were deemed to be a return of capital, then Enron would have had to include the Raptors and their debts in the company's financial statements, because the Raptors would no longer hold 3 percent independent at-risk equity. Under this assumption, the purpose of the structures would also have been lost.

Despite this possibility, considerable ambiguity persists about the true nature of the returns to LJM2. Glisan admitted in his negotiated plea bargain with government prosecutors that the $41 million distribution was both a return of and a return on capital, which invalidated the Raptor SPE as an independent entity; Skilling claims in his appeal that the $30 million contributed by LJM2 to the Raptor SPE remained at risk, thereby preserving that entity's independent status.[8] Thus any claim of accounting fraud from the classification of cash distributions must be considered hypothetical until some definitive, legal judgment is made.

Second, the $11 million difference between LJM2's $30 million investment in each Raptor and the $41 million return to LJM2 can be seen as a service fee for providing the appearance of independent, at-risk equity Enron needed to keep the Raptors off its balance sheet. If this were true, then that would be a clear accounting violation. However, once again we do not know the true intent of this payment.[9]

The Raptor structures also generated controversy about how the company treated increases in the value of its own stock in its financial reports. Accounting rules generally prohibit a company from recognizing increases in the value of its own stock as gains on its income statement. If we assume for the moment that Enron stock was rising in value, the company could have used that extra value to expand its hedging operations and reported net income. Here's how Enron could have used these hedging operations with the Raptors to affect its reported income.

The maximum cumulative value of hedging transactions that an entity can engage in depends on its "credit capacity." Here credit capacity refers to an entity's ability to meet its financial obligations: that is, the difference in value between the party's assets and liabilities. The only asset held by a given Raptor SPE was Enron stock (except for Raptor III, which was capitalized with TNPC stock). Thus the SPE's credit capacity would have increased as Enron's stock price rose.

As the SPE's credit capacity increased, Enron would have been able to hedge against larger investment losses. In effect, increases in Enron's stock price could have led to increased reported income from successful hedging transactions. But this did not actually happen. During the spring of 2001, Enron's stock was falling precipitously. So while Enron could have violated accounting rules by using gains in share value to generate gains in reported income, this situation never actually occurred.[10]

Yet another accounting complaint relates to Raptor-derived gains. Some commentators claim that it may have been inappropriate for Enron to use the cost method of accounting for Raptor-derived gains instead of the equity method, because Enron had significant influence over the Raptors. Under both methods, an investor records its investment at the original value paid. The cost method then allows the investor to hold off on reporting any investment gain or loss until receiving a distribution or closing out the investment. The equity method calls for the investor to adjust the value of the investment to recognize the investor's share of the entity's positive or negative earnings.

Had Enron used the equity method, the company would have had to report its pro rata share of Raptors' gains and losses. Enron would also have had to include losses in its financial statements—negating the essential purpose of the Raptors structure. By choosing the more controversial cost method of accounting, Enron in effect removed any interim Raptor-related losses from public view. Nevertheless, because there appears to be continuing ambiguity about the propriety of the cost method versus the equity method of accounting for SPE-related gains and losses, it is once again difficult to argue that Enron was clearly noncompliant with accounting rules.

Reporting Issues

Another criticism of the Raptors was that their disclosure was incomprehensible to even the most astute students of financial statements. The following excerpts from Enron's 2000 annual report, and a second-quarter submission to the Securities and Exchange Commission (SEC) that year, support that criticism:

> In 2000 and 1999, Enron entered into transactions with limited partnerships (the Related Party) whose general partner's managing member is a senior officer of Enron. The limited partners of the Related Party are unrelated to Enron. Management believes that the terms of the transactions with the Related Party were reasonable compared to those which could have been negotiated with unrelated third parties.
>
> In 2000, Enron entered into transactions with the Related Party to hedge certain merchant investments and other assets. As part of the transactions, Enron (i) contributed to newly-formed entities (the Entities) assets valued at approximately $1.2 billion, including $150 million in Enron notes payable, 3.7 million restricted shares of outstanding Enron common stock and the right to receive up to 18.0 million shares of outstanding Enron common stock in March 2003 (subject to certain conditions) and (ii) transferred to the Entities assets valued at approximately $309 million, including a $50 million note payable and an investment in an entity that indirectly holds warrants convertible into common stock of an Enron equity method investee. In return, Enron received economic interests in the Entities, $309 million in notes receivable, of which $259 million is recorded at Enron's carryover basis of zero, and a special distribution from

the Entities in the form of $1.2 billion in notes receivable, subject to changes in the principal for amounts payable by Enron in connection with the execution of additional derivative instruments. Cash in these Entities of $172.6 million is invested in Enron demand notes. In addition, Enron paid $123 million to purchase share-settled options from the Entities on 21.7 million shares of Enron common stock. The Entities paid Enron $10.7 million to terminate the share-settled options on 14.6 million shares of Enron common stock outstanding. In late 2000, Enron entered into share-settled collar arrangements with the Entities on 15.4 million shares of Enron common stock. Such arrangements will be accounted for as equity transactions when settled.

In 2000, Enron entered into derivative transactions with the Entities with a combined notional amount of approximately $2.1 billion to hedge certain merchant investments and other assets. Enron's notes receivable balance was reduced by $36 million as a result of premiums owed on derivative transactions. Enron recognized revenues of approximately $500 million related to the subsequent change in the market value of these derivatives, which offset market value changes of certain merchant investments and price risk management activities. In addition, Enron recognized $44.5 million and $14.1 million of interest income and interest expense, respectively, on the notes receivable from and payable to the Entities.[11]

In the second quarter of 2000, Enron entered into transactions with the Related Party to hedge certain merchant investments. As part of the transactions, Enron contributed to newly formed entities (the Entities) assets valued at approximately $800 million, including 3.7 million restricted shares of outstanding Enron common stock, $100 million in Enron notes payable and the right to receive up to 11.7 million shares of outstanding Enron common stock in March 2003 (subject to certain conditions). In return, Enron received non-voting interests in the Entities and a special distribution from the Entities in the form of $800 million in notes receivable, convertible into derivative instruments. In addition, Enron paid $82 million to purchase share settled options from the Entities on $14.6 million shares of Enron common stock.[12]

Despite the remarkable obscurity of Enron's expositions, they do not appear to violate generally accepted accounting principles (GAAP) or SEC rules. Indeed, Enron can rightly claim that it disclosed the existence of entities such as the Raptors, and transactions between these entities and Enron, even though it did not identify them by name.

Two other reporting controversies surround the Raptors, but the claimed violations were either approved by Arthur Andersen or remain ambiguous. For example, in its financial reports, Enron characterized transactions with the Raptors (unidentified as such) as "reasonable and are representative of terms that would be negotiated with unrelated third parties."[13] While this statement seems disingenuous, because Enron created the Raptor structures after it failed to find independent hedging partners for some of its investments, both Arthur Andersen and Vinson & Elkins, Enron's outside counsel, approved this language.

While other transactions may appear improper, they, too, were vetted and approved by Arthur Andersen. For example, on September 15, 2000, Enron allegedly backdated several transactions with the Raptors to August 3, 2000. This was supposedly justified as an administrative choice, to make calculating the required 3 percent at-risk, independent equity easier. But the August date is also when the value of a hedged asset—Avici Systems— reached its peak. The Powers report to the board notes that by treating the hedge as effective on August 3 rather than on September 15, when the hedging agreement was actually signed, Enron avoided recording a $75 million loss on its quarterly financial statements. However, Skilling's appeal claims that the Avici hedge was in fact executed on "August 3 or 4."

The Issue of the Raptor Put

A final controversy concerns the so-called Raptor put that was executed with three of the four Raptor entities (see Figure A.3). According to Skilling, Enron purchased a put on Enron stock from the Raptor entity for $41 million so that if Enron's stock dropped below a certain price, the Raptor would pay Enron the difference. As part of the hedging operation, once the put settled, the Raptor vehicle distributed the $41 million premium to LJM, and, in return, the Raptor would allow Enron to hedge volatile assets in the SPE.[14]

In the example shown, the Raptor put gave Enron the right to require the Raptor I SPE (Talon) to purchase 7.2 million shares of Enron common stock on October 18, 2000, six months after the effective date of the transaction, at a strike price of $57.50 per share. The closing price of Enron stock was $68 per share when Enron purchased the put.[15] In an economic sense, the put option was a bet by Enron that its own stock price would decline substantially. (In actuality, Enron's stock price increased during the summer of 2000, and the put option was settled between the two parties on August 3, 2000.)

One noteworthy aspect of this put was that its "strike price" was significantly below the market price of Enron's shares. To critics, this suggests that the contracting parties never expected to exercise the put. If true, the $41 million payment may have been a veiled payment to LJM2 for supplying the 3 percent independent, at-risk equity in the Raptors, thereby invalidating the Raptors as independent entities. However, this criticism has not been fully substantiated. On the one hand, Glisan's negotiated plea bargain is a heavy piece of evidence of the side of the put failing to serve as any true business purpose and causing the Raptor SPE (Talon) to fail to meet the minimum equity test as required by applicable accounting rules. On the other hand, Skilling has argued in his appeal that the true purposes of the put were to induce LJM2 to enter into risky hedging deals for Enron's benefit and, as was the practice or volatile dot-com companies at the time, to protect the company from a decline in its stock price. Thus, the "veiled

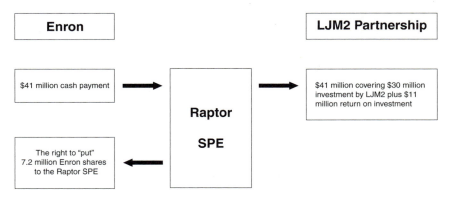

Figure A.3 The Raptor "put" transactions. Put transactions were executed with three of the four Raptor entities, making for a total cost of the combined 21.7 million Enron shares used for the puts equal to $120 million. As for the $41 million cash payment from Enron to the LJM2 partnership, the Powers report and Fastow's testimony in the Skilling/Lay criminal trial claim this payment had to be made before hedging operations could begin. In the end, all of the Raptor puts were settled early, with the Raptors returning roughly 14 percent of Enron's payments through increases to promissory notes held by Enron.

payment" claim remains at best a working hypothesis rather than a definitive violation of either GAAP or SEC rules.

Enron's puts with the Raptors were certainly unusual. Steven Stampf, head of the PricewaterhouseCoopers team that wrote Enron's fairness opinion (an assessment of the transaction's value and fairness for the transacting parties) for Raptor I, "conceded that he had never heard of a public company entering into a put transaction on its own stock." Some observers have suggested that Enron actually believed that its stock was going to decline in value, but no public statements by Enron officials support that theory. To the contrary, there is nothing in the physical capitalization of the Raptor structures that suggests they were created to serve any purpose other than making use of anticipated increases in Enron stock to fund a bona fide hedging operation. Neither is there any explicit, structural feature of the transaction suggesting that the puts were expected to produce income for Enron—or, for that matter that the puts were sham transactions designed to provide the Raptors with distributable income to pay off LJM2. Much has been left to claims and counter-claims of Skilling's intent in approving these transactions, and it is this respect that the true facts of the situation remain murky for any outside observer (and hotly contested by both government prosecutors and the Skilling defense team).

Termination of the Raptors

In the end, two separate problems with the Raptors did have a significant impact on Enron's financial statements.

The Raptors' credit capacity continued to diminish with the decline of Enron's share price through 2001. When cross-collateralization, restructuring, and additional Enron shares failed to fix the problem, Enron was forced to close the structures. On October 16, 2001, Enron announced that as a result, the company was recording an after-tax charge to earnings of $544 million. The termination also forced Enron to reduce shareholder equity by $200 million. This amount represents the difference between the fair value of stock and stock contracts that Enron owed the Raptors ($2.1 billion) and the value of Enron's notes receivable from the Raptors ($1.9 billion).

Around the same time, Anderson realized that mistakes had been made in accounting for the notes receivable (promissory notes) Enron had received from the Raptors in exchange for Enron shares. The notes were recorded as *increases* to shareholder equity, but should have been considered *decreases*—because, under GAAP, a note received in exchange for a company's own stock offsets shareholder equity until the note is paid. The errors required an additional $1 billion reduction in shareholder equity.

Because of business reasons and accounting errors, the Raptor structures failed to serve their espoused purpose. However, apart from obscure disclosure of the Raptors and the possible backdating of the Avici hedge in the third quarter of 2000, not much can be definitively cited as illegal about Enron's hedges with the Raptors. Yes, we can conclude that the Raptors were poorly designed, and in the end served as ineffective hedging vehicles. However, in light of enduring ambiguities, these outcomes appear to result primarily from poor business judgments. This inept management was then compounded by a serious accounting error, which, when discovered and reversed, crippled Enron's credibility in the capital market.

The Sithe Energies Deal:
How Enron Got Lucky on a
Risky Gamble

A twenty-year gas supply contract between Enron and Sithe Energies represented an extremely risky, long-term bet on the price of natural gas relative to the price of power in the northeastern United States.[1] Eight years into this contract, with the bet gone badly wrong, Enron and Sithe restructured the deal, erasing Enron's estimated $1.8 billion liability. Because Enron had used accounting methods to obscure the risks inherent in the deal, no mention of the restructuring appeared in its financial statements.

The Deal

In January 1992, Enron signed a twenty-year contract to provide all the natural gas for a 1,000-megawatt power plant that Sithe Energies, an operator of independent power plants, was building in Oswego, New York. The plant—which opened in January 1995 and cost more than $700 million to build—was owned by Sithe subsidiary Sithe/Independence Power Partners, L.P. (Sithe/Independence). News reports at the time estimated the value of the gas to be supplied by Enron over the life of the contract at $3.5 billion to $4 billion.

Enron Power Services had been the first to line up long-term gas supply contracts behind independent power plants. These plants could sell their power to local electric utilities at "avoided cost"—the cost the utilities avoided by not having to build more power-generating capacity. This arrangement promised to be highly profitable for many new power plants. The problem was that such plants required large amounts of financing, which banks were not eager to provide, because the price of fuel—the single biggest operating expense—was so volatile.[2] By offering innovative

351

long-term supply contracts, Enron stabilized the cost structure of these plants and made it easier for them to obtain financing.

Enron's Risky Bet

Under the original agreement between Enron and Sithe/Independence, the price for about 60 percent of the gas was fixed during the first five years. During the remaining fifteen years, the price paid by Sithe/Independence for almost all the gas supplied by Enron would fluctuate based on the market price of power in the Northeast.

The contract provided for a tracking account to monitor differences between Enron's contract price and spot gas prices. The account increased if the current spot gas price was greater than the contract price, and decreased if the current spot gas price was lower than the contract price.[3] Enron's claim on any positive balance in the tracking account was secured by a portion of the plant's cash flows. If the contract ended with a positive balance, Sithe/Independence would have to convey to Enron the lesser of (a) the balance in the tracking account, or (b) equity ownership in the plant based on the ratio of the tracking account balance to the plant's fair market value.

Enron had, in effect, placed a multibillion-dollar wager that the price of natural gas would stay lower than the price of power in the Northeast for twenty years. The deal was a very long bet on the "spark spread"—the difference between the price of input (fuel) and the price of output (electricity).

Why take such a big gamble? Hubris or nerve, very likely, is the answer, and a huge, immediate payoff. Enron stood to gain $3.5 billion to $4 billion from a single twenty-year contract—one of the largest contracts of that duration the gas industry had seen in many years.

The massive Sithe deal also became a showcase for Enron's gas supply business, cementing its reputation in the industry. In fact, Enron's pitch had convinced Sithe to burn gas instead of coal in the Independence plant. According to one account:

> To make the deal work, Enron had to combine gas supply commitments stretching from the Gulf of Mexico to Canada, and use derivatives to hedge its price risks. It was an aggressive and creative use of its financial capabilities. And while another company might have brought in partners to spread the risk, Enron was daring enough to handle the entire gas supply contract.

At a wine and cheese celebration of the deal's signing, Enron executives crowed that they had the only company that could pull together all the moving parts.[4]

Outside Enron, people were stunned at what Skilling had pulled off. The Sithe deal seemed to be ultimate proof that he could deliver on his big idea of supplying huge amounts of gas through long-term contracts.

Strong incentives likely also played an important role in this enormous gamble. When the deal was signed, Enron probably booked much of the estimated $3.5 billion to $4 billion under mark-to-market accounting, and paid the executives involved in the deal large cash bonuses up front. These incentives encouraged Enron dealmakers to place large, risky bets and worry about the consequences later.[5]

The Bet Goes Wrong

By year five of the twenty-year contract, it became clear that the relationship between gas supply costs and Northeast power prices was exactly the reverse of Enron's original forecasts. As a result, by mid-2001 the tracking account balance had grown to more than $419 million, and was reportedly rising by $25 million each quarter. At this rate, the tracking account balance would have reached $1.8 billion at the end of the contract.

The problem was that as the balance grew, the probability that Enron would collect fell. To see why, consider that the tracking account balance was ultimately secured by the value of the plant itself. As of mid-2001, a new 1,000-megawatt power plant could be built for $500 million to $600 million, making the existing Sithe/Independence plant worth considerably less. Thus a tracking account balance of $419 million could be considered roughly equivalent to the market value of the plant. According to Enron's Risk Analysis and Control group, continued depreciation of the plant and growth of the tracking account meant that Enron would receive an asset worth a small percentage of its total liability, at best, leaving the company with more than $1 billion in uncollectible IOUs.

The ballooning tracking account balance thus behaved like a ticking time bomb threatening to blow a huge hole in Enron's reported profits on the transaction. According to sources at Enron, this threat was not lost on Enron executives, who had been searching for a way out of the deal since late 1999.

Enron Gets Lucky

As it happened, Sithe/Independence also had a vested interest in restructuring the gas supply deal. An April 1999 court ruling had left the partnership exposed to market prices for the majority of the energy the plant sold. Power prices, and the plant's revenues, would fall as a result, imperiling the partnership's business plan, and the credit rating supporting three series of outstanding bonds.

On June 29, 2001, Sithe/Independence and Enron agreed to terminate the gas supply agreement. The $419 million balance in the tracking account was converted to a long-term subordinated loan due Enron. In a separate agreement, Sithe Energies, through an indirect, wholly owned subsidiary, sold a 40 percent limited partnership interest in Sithe/Independence to Oswego Cogen, an indirect, wholly owned subsidiary of Enron.

The restructuring of the Sithe transaction turned into an unqualified commercial success for Enron. But no mention of the restructuring appeared on Enron's third-quarter 2001 Form 10-Q, filed with the Securities and Exchange Commission. Why? According to sources at Enron, as a result of dubious financial reporting, the original liability associated with the gas deal was never reported, and a related charge to income never taken. Thus, even though the company successfully unwound the transaction and shed its unreported $1.8 billion liability, it could not publicly celebrate its success in avoiding both a financial disaster and an accounting scandal.

Excerpt from The Outside Directors' Response to "The Role of the Board of Directors in Enron's Collapse"

Executive Summary

The Report of the Permanent Subcommittee on Investigations of the Senate Governmental Affairs Committee, entitled "The Role of the Board of Directors in Enron's Collapse," unfairly accuses the Board of a fiduciary failure.[1] Enron's outside directors reject that accusation. These outside directors were independent, diligent, and in good faith and prudently performed their fiduciary duties based on the information provided to them.

- **The outside directors prudently executed their fiduciary duties to Enron shareholders.**

The Directors—as with any outside directors—needed reliable, complete information to execute their duties. They acted prudently, reasonably, and in good faith on the basis of the information that Enron management and outside advisors, including Arthur Andersen, provided to them. At the time, the Directors had no reason to suspect that Enron management or the company's advisors were withholding or distorting important information. As the PSI Report acknowledges, the Directors were misled and important information was withheld from them.

The Directors' reliance on internal and external advisors was necessary because the role of an outside director is limited by design. If outside directors were full-time employees and actively managed a corporation's day-to-day affairs, they would no longer be independent. In recognition of this limited role, the law fully authorizes and expects outside directors to rely on representations made to them by management and their outside experts. The Directors believe that if they had been provided with accurate information they requested or would have expected to receive from management, employees or advisors, this tragedy could have been avoided.

The PSI Report bases its conclusions on six factors that it contends demonstrate fiduciary failure. Each of these supposed factors rests on a skewed view of the facts or inappropriate conclusions.*

- **The Directors were not told that Enron was engaged in "high-risk" accounting practices that "push[ed] limits" or were " 'at the edge' of acceptable practice."**

The Report's conclusion that the outside directors were told that Enron was engaged in "high-risk" accounting practices that "push[ed] limits," or were " 'at the edge' of acceptable practice" (Report at 17–18) finds no legitimate support in the record. This conclusion is contradicted by the testimony of David Duncan and the documentary record in this matter.

- David Duncan publicly testified that "high-risk" meant that the client "had a very complex business model, engaged in very complex transactions with difficult . . . areas to reach accounting conclusions and that [Arthur Andersen] had a large amount of business with them." (*United States v. Arthur Andersen*, LLP, Criminal Action No. H-02–0121, Testimony of David Duncan, Trial Transcript at 2283–84 (S.D. Tex. 2002) ("Duncan Andersen Trial Testimony"). David Duncan testified that, out of about 3,000 publicly traded companies that were Andersen clients as of 2001, Andersen categorized "several hundred" as "high-risk." (Id. at 2285). David Duncan's testimony makes clear that "high-risk" did not mean Enron's accounting practices "push[ed] limits" or were " 'at the edge' of acceptable practice."
- The Arthur Andersen documents on which the Report relies do not in fact state that the company was engaged in high risk accounting practices that "push[ed] the limits" and were " 'at the edge' of acceptable practice." (Id.) Rather, as discussed below, that is an inference that the PSI drew based on the self-serving statements of outside counsel for Arthur Andersen and Arthur Andersen employees about an Arthur

---

*The Directors have tried to respond to the Report's allegations, which are largely supported by undisclosed materials, unidentified witness statements, and hearsay. The Directors do not have access to the documents and witness statements upon which the PSI relied, nor to information in the hands of the people who have asserted their Fifth Amendment rights.

Andersen employee's handwritten notation that was not shown or communicated to any Director.

- In the hundreds of pages of minutes of the Audit Committee meetings, which Arthur Andersen presumably reviewed, and Arthur Andersen presentations (prior to the Fall 2001 earnings correction), there is not a single occasion on which the Audit Committee was informed that Enron was engaged in high risk accounting practices that were inappropriate, "push[ed] the limits" and were " 'at the edge' of acceptable practice" (id.); to the contrary, in meeting after meeting, and in its formal representations in the Enron Annual Reports, Arthur Andersen continually assured the Audit Committee and the shareholders that it was comfortable with the complex accounting judgments being made and would stand behind them. Even now, David Duncan, the former Arthur Andersen partner on the Enron engagement, at his recent trial gave sworn public testimony that he was "not aware of any accounting improprieties at Enron." (Duncan Andersen Trial Testimony at 2020).

The Audit Committee knew that Arthur Andersen was paid specifically to ensure that the "innovative structures" conformed to GAAP, and hence took comfort that Arthur Andersen "was o.k." with them.

The Report cites three sources as support for its conclusion regarding the Directors' knowledge that Enron was engaged in high-risk accounting practices. None is reliable evidence of the Directors' knowledge:

- statements to PSI by outside attorneys for the now convicted Arthur Andersen, which faces exposure for its role in this matter and which is seeking to shift the blame;
- statements to PSI by outside counsel for Arthur Andersen employees who are also seeking to shift the blame and who refused to meet with the PSI because they asserted their Fifth Amendment right not to make statements that may incriminate themselves; and,
- internal Arthur Andersen memoranda discussing the accounting firm's discomfort over Enron's accounting practices—documents and concerns that should have been, but were not, raised in the strongest terms with the Audit Committee.

The Report's conclusion that the Directors knew that Enron was engaged in high risk accounting practices that "pushed limits" or were "at the edge" of acceptable practice (Report at 17–18) should not have been made.

- **The Directors' decision to approve the Chief Financial Officer's operation of the LJM partnerships was prudent in light of the strict controls the Board imposed, which would have been effective if management had implemented the controls and provided accurate information to the Board about the LJM transactions.**

The Report accuses the Directors of approving the CFO's participation in the LJM partnerships in the face of conflicts of interest. (Report at 3.) It also alleges that the "Board exercised inadequate oversight of [the] LJM transaction and compensation controls and failed to protect Enron shareholders from unfair dealing." (Id.) These findings ignore the clear evidence to the contrary. The Directors' ratification of the Office of the Chairman's decision to permit the Chief Financial Officer to establish and operate the LJM partnerships was based on the Directors' belief, after reviewing management's recommendation and receiving assurances from outside advisors about accounting for and control of these partnerships, that the partnerships were in the best interests of Enron and were designed to meet specific and important business purposes. The Directors understood at the time that Enron's inside and outside accountants and legal advisors had reviewed and approved the arrangement.

Under the Code of Conduct, the CFO's involvement in these partnerships required proper oversight by Enron management. The Directors certainly recognized that the CFO's participation in these arrangements presented conflict issues that needed to be addressed and managed. The Board understood that Enron's legal advisors had reviewed and approved of the LJM partnership structure, and had approved of Mr. Fastow's involvement in LJM as long as the Board ratified the Office of the Chairman's recommendation to allow Mr. Fastow to participate consistent with the Code of Conduct. As an additional "line of defense," the Board imposed a series of independent controls specifically assigned to numerous officers in the company who did not report to the CFO, including the CEO, COO, and the Chief Accounting and Risk Officers, as well as Arthur Andersen, to ensure that every transaction between the partnerships and Enron would be in the best interests of Enron. Arthur Andersen and Enron management assured the Board that the controls had been implemented and were effective, and the Directors had no reason to doubt those representations. At the February 12, 2001 Finance Committee meeting, Mr. Fastow reported that the controls "had been discussed with the Audit and Compliance Committee, and commented that the process was working effectively." (February 12, 2001 Finance Committee meeting minutes at 5; see also February 12, 2001 Audit Committee meeting minutes at 2–3). We now know that the controls were not followed, and the Directors were deprived of critical information about these transactions.

- **The outside directors did not make decisions designed to misrepresent the true financial condition of Enron.**

The Report's contention that the Board permitted Enron to engage in extensive "off-the-books" transactions to distort Enron's financial picture and thereafter failed to ensure adequate disclosure misstates both what Enron did disclose and the role of the outside directors in reviewing disclosures.

The Report continually uses the inflammatory term, "off-the-books." The Report, however, does not clarify that "off-the-books" does not mean "undisclosed." What it means is that the disclosures were in a different place in the company's annual report than the section setting forth the balance sheet. When the Report refers to "off-the-books," what it really means is "off-balance-sheet," and disclosed in footnotes to the balance sheet.

The Report's principal example of an improper "off-the-books" corporate strategy is a partnership called Whitewing. The Report's characterization of the accounting treatment of Whitewing shows that preparers of the Report do not fully understand financial reporting. The Report acknowledges that from 1997 to 1999, Whitewing was a consolidated entity. That means that Whitewing was consolidated on the balance sheet of Enron; in the Report's terms, "on-the-books," not "off-the-books." In 1999, Whitewing was deconsolidated and treated as an affiliate. When that occurred, Whitewing's assets and liabilities were included in the footnotes to the balance sheet in the Annual Report, and a single line item was reported on the balance sheet itself. Though "off-the-books" under the Report's definition, Whitewing was not "undisclosed."

The Report's discussion of these issues shows that the accurate classification and reporting of financial statements requires compliance with numerous laws, regulations and accounting conventions. The Directors were entitled to and did rely on Enron's outside experts on these matters. The outside auditor, Arthur Andersen, had to give its opinion on the validity of the financial statements, and did so year after year. The Directors also understood that Enron's auditors, Arthur Andersen, and its outside law firm,

Vinson & Elkins, had reviewed and approved the adequacy and complete-ness of Enron's disclosures. It is wrong to blame the Directors, who relied on what they believed at the time were two of the premier professional ser-vices firms in the world, for alleged inadequate disclosures.

- **The outside directors prudently approved compensation plans for Enron executives on the advice of outside experts to assure that the company would attract and retain what Enron be-lieved was its most valuable asset, its people.**

The Report criticizes the Compensation Committee for approving execu-tive compensation plans that had as their goal "keeping up with competitor pay." (PSI Report at 53.) The Report acknowledges that the Compensation Committee regularly sought advice from Towers Perrin, a highly respected executive compensation consulting firm. Towers Perrin advised the Com-pensation Committee of the need to offer compensation packages that were comparable to those offered by similarly situated companies and entities that recruited from the same talent pool.

The outside directors believed that attracting and retaining outstanding employees was critical to the success of the company. The Report seems to disparage the notion that pay packages comparable to opportunities that employees may obtain from other companies are necessary to this goal. Yet the Report cannot realistically contest, as one director testified at the hearing on May 7, 2002, that an employee who has better opportunities at another company would simply "walk across the street."

The criticism of the Compensation Committee for failing to supervise the Chief Executive Officer's use of his line of credit is also misplaced. At the time, a line of credit as part of CEO compensation was quite common. The Direc-tors had no reason to believe that Mr. Lay would misuse the line of credit and were not aware until recently that he had done so. The Directors agree that, by repeatedly using the line of credit to take out a loan and then immediately repaying it with stock, Mr. Lay was abusing this component of his compensa-tion package. Dipping into the line of credit in the morning and repaying it with stock in the afternoon many times over was a violation of the Board's in-tention when it approved this benefit. Some of the Directors have been pub-licly explicit in this regard. (May 7, 2002 PSI Hearing Transcript at 219–21.)

The Directors certainly would have expected Mr. Lay's conduct to have been brought to their attention by the employees, including those in legal, treasury, and control functions, who facilitated these sales. Every employee of Enron, including the CEO, had a fiduciary duty to the company as a whole.

- **The outside directors of the Board were independent of Enron. The Directors also believed that Arthur Andersen was independent of Enron. The outside directors exercised independent judgment about these matters.**

The Report contends that the Directors were too highly compensated. A contemporaneous independent study shows that the Directors' compensation was not excessive for a company of the size and complexity of Enron.

The Report also criticizes certain outside directors for having inappropriate financial ties to the company and alleges that the Board was not independent. Those ties were trivial, had no impact on the Directors' discharge of their duties, and did not affect the Board's independence.

The Chairs of the three most significant board committees did not receive any monies from Enron in addition to their director/committee chair compensation. Mr. John Duncan, who chaired the Executive Committee, and Dr. Jaedicke, who chaired the Audit Committee, do not appear on the Report's list at all. (PSI Report at 55–56.) Mr. Winokur, who chaired the Finance Committee, appears only because he is an outside director and shareholder of a company that occasionally sold oilfield equipment to subsidiaries of Enron in the ordinary course of business, on arms'-length terms. Those sales averaged approximately one-half of 1% of the annual revenues of that company.

Board members Dr. Mendelsohn and Dr. LeMaistre are the current and immediate past Presidents of the Houston-based M.D. Anderson Cancer Center ("the Center"), unquestionably one of the premier cancer centers in the world. During Dr. LeMaistre's tenure as President, Enron pledged $1.5 million as part of the Center's capital campaign. This amount is less than 1% of the total amount of money that the campaign raised from private sources and the Center staff. While Dr. Mendelsohn was an Enron director, the total Enron- and Lay-related contributions comprised less than 0.1 % of the private philanthropy raised by the Center during that period.

The relationship between the Enron contributions to the Mercatus Center at George Mason University, which employs former board member Dr. Gramm, is just as tenuous. Enron first contributed to the Mercatus Center before Dr. Gramm was employed there; since 1996, Enron's total contributions have been less than one-third of 1% of the Mercatus Center's budget.

Finally, Lord Wakeham received a $6,000 monthly retainer fee for the additional duties he performed in connection with Enron's European business and operations. The Board specifically was asked to and did take note of these facts and found Lord Wakeham independent.

The criticism of the Audit Committee for permitting Arthur Andersen to perform consulting services in addition to audit services for the company represents a condemnation of a widespread business practice, not a criticism of this Board. The members of the PSI may believe this practice should not be permitted. At the time, however, Enron and hundreds of other companies believed that companies could obtain more effective service if the work was centralized in one accounting firm.

The Directors do not accept the conclusion of the Report that they failed in their oversight duties. The two most significant conclusions of the Report are barely discussed. The Report (1) did not find that the outside Directors benefited personally from these transactions or that they acted in other than the utmost good faith, and (2) did find that the Directors were misled by people on whom they were entitled to rely.

The Directors particularly reject the suggestion in the Report that their culpability is demonstrated by their failure to acknowledge their responsibility. These directors executed their fiduciary duties prudently, responsibly, and in good faith.

Enron's Board of Directors

Table D.1 follows on pages 364–371.

Table D.1 Enron's Board of Directors, as of January 1, 2001

Name	Title	Age	Director Since	Share Holdings as of February 15, 2001[a]	Committee Assignments	Comments
Kenneth L. Lay	Chair of the board since 1986	59	1985	7,930,896	1	
Jeffrey K. Skilling	Former president and CEO, Enron Corp.	47	1997–2001	2,091,529	1	
Robert A. Belfer	Chair and CEO of Belco Oil & Gas Corp.; sold Belco Petroleum to Enron in 1985 for a large stake in Enron	65	1983	8,491,829	1, 3	Belco Oil & Gas had traded oil and gas contracts with Enron since 1996; Belfer sold more than 1 million shares in Enron but still retained a large stake.[c]
Norman P. Blake Jr.	Chair, president, and CEO of Comdisco, a diversified technical equipment leasing and information technology services company;	59	1993	24,611	3, 4	Blake also served on the board of Owens Corning Corp, which signed a $1 billion energy management deal with an Enron affiliate in 1999; sold $1.7 million of Enron stock in late 2000.[c]

	former chief executive of the U.S. Olympic Committee; served as a director of Owens-Corning				
Ronnie C. Chan	Chairman of Hang Lung Group, three publicly traded Hong Kong–based companies involved in property development, property investment, and hotels	51	1996	19,199	2, 3	Chan sold 8,000 shares ($337,250) of Enron stock in July 1999.[f]
John H. Duncan	Principal occupation since 1990 has been investments; also a director of EOTT Energy Corp and Azurix, two Enron subsidiaries, and of Group I Automotive	73	1985	233,837	1*, 4	Duncan sold $2 million of Enron stock in May 2000.[c]
Joseph H. Foy	Retired senior partner of Bracewell & Patterson, president	74	1985–2000		1, 2	Enron retained Foy's former law firm during 1998 and 1999,

Table D.1 (continued)

Name	Title	Age	Director Since	Share Holdings as of February 15, 2001[a]	Committee Assignments	Comments
	and chair of the Cowboy Artists of America Museum					and made $100,000 in donations to the Cowboy Artists of America Museum.[g]
Wendy L. Gramm	Director of the Mercatus Center at George Mason University, former chair of the Commodity Futures Trading Commission	56	1993	0	2, 5	Gramm is the wife of Senator Phil Gramm, Republican, of Texas.
Ken L. Harrison	Former chair and CEO, Portland General Electric	57	1997	954,692	None	Portland General Electric was acquired by Enron in 1997.
Robert K. Jaedicke	Professor (emeritus) of accounting at Stanford University Graduate School of Business; chair of audit committee,	72	1985	57,087	2*, 4	Jaedicke chaired the audit committees of six other corporations.[h]

	charged with overseeing Enron's financial operation					
Charles L. LeMaistre	President emeritus of the M.D. Anderson Cancer Center, University of Texas; president of the center for 18 years	77	1985	56,287	1, 4*	Enron had donated more than $600,000 to the Cancer Center since 1996.[c]
Rebecca Mark-Jusbasche	Chair and CEO of Azurix, Enron's international water business	46	1999–2000		None	Mark-Jusbasche sold 1,276,278 shares of Enron stock between 1997 and her departure from the corporation in 2000.[f]
John Mendelsohn	President of the M.D. Anderson Cancer Center, University of Texas	64	1999	5,563	2, 5	Enron had donated more than $600,000 to the Anderson Cancer Center since 1996.[c]
Jerome J. Meyer	Chair, Tektronix	64	1997–2001	17,400	3, 5	Meyer sold no shares of Enron stock between 1997 and 2001.[f]
Paolo V. Ferraz Pereira	Executive vice president of Group Bozano and former	46	1999	3,195	2, 3	Ferraz Pereira sold no shares of Enron stock between 1999 and 2001.[f]

Table D.1 (continued)

Name	Title	Age	Director Since	Share Holdings as of February 15, 2001[a]	Committee Assignments	Comments
	president of the State Bank of Rio de Janeiro					
Frank Savage	Chair of Alliance Capital Management International, a division of Alliance Capital Management L. P., also a director of Lockheed Martin Corporation, Alliance Capital Management L. P., and Qualcomm Corp.	62	1999	4,005	3, 4	Alliance, part of Axa Financial, was Enron's largest institutional shareholder, with about 43 million shares.[c]
John A. Urquhart	Senior advisor to the chair, Enron Corp.; president, John A. Urquhart Associates; and former senior vice	71	1990	47,795	3	As a consultant to Enron, Urquhart earned more than $6.5 million in fees and expense reimbursement beginning in 1991.[d]

	Age	Year(s)	Shares	Committees	Position	Enron relationship
					president of Industrial and Power Systems, General Electric	
Charles E. Walker	77	1984–1999		3	Founder and chair of the American Council for Capital Investment and the ACCF Center for Policy Research; senior advisor to the Center for Deliberative Polling at the University of Texas, and a principal with Walker/Free Associates and Walker/ Potter Associates	Enron paid Walker/Free Associates and Walker/ Potter Associates more than $70,000 for governmental relations and tax consulting ser- vices, and contributed up to $50,000 annually to ACCF.[i]
John Wakeham	68	1994	20,987	2, 5*	Chair of the U.K.'s Press Complaints Com- mission and chair or director of a number of publicly traded U.K. companies; former British secretary of state for energy and leader of the houses of Lords and Commons	Wakeham was paid $72,000 in 2001 as a consultant to Enron's European operations.

Table D.1 (continued)

Name	Title	Age	Director Since	Share Holdings as of February 15, 2001[a]	Committee Assignments	Comments
Bruce G. Willison	Dean of the Anderson School of Management, UCLA, since 1999	52	1997–1998		2,3	Willison sold no shares of Enron stock between 1999 and 2001.[f]
Herbert S. Winokur Jr.	Chair and CEO of Capricorn Holdings (a private investment company), and managing general partner of Capricorn Investors, L. P., Capricorn Investors II, L. P., and Capricorn Investors III, L. P.; also on the board of the Natco Group, an oil and gas wellhead equipment systems and services company	57	1985	119,755	1, 3*	Natco sold between $316,000 and $1,035,000 in equipment, parts, and service to Enron each year from 1996 till 2000.[e] Winokur sold no shares of Enron stock while serving as director.

Source: Enron Corp., 2000 Annual Report; Enron proxy statements filed May 2, 2000, and May 1, 2001.

a. Number of shares outstanding was 752,205,000, and share price was $83.13, as of December 31, 2000. As of May 1, 2001, the board of directors and executive officers (thirty in number) owned 3.44 percent of shares outstanding.

b. Belfer was both Enron's largest common stockholder and the majority owner of Enron's outstanding convertible preferred stock, of which he owned 17.66 percent.

c. Reed Abelson, "Enron's Collapse: The Directors," *New York Times (January 19, 2002).*

d. Mark Babineck, "Enron's Overseers Did Nothing as Creative Financing Wrecked Company," Associated Press Newswires, February 17, 2002.

e. U.S. Bankruptcy Court, Southern District of New York, *In re Enron Corp.,* Chapter 11, Case No. 01–16034 (AJG) "Final Report of Neal Batson, Court-Appointed Examiner" (November 4, 2003), Appendix D (Roles of Lay, Skilling and Outside Directors), p. 43 (citing Enron 1998 Proxy Statement, p. 28; Enron 1999 Proxy Statement, p. 28; Enron 2000 Proxy Statement, p. 26; Enron 2001 Proxy Statement, pp. 26–27).

f. Ibid., Attachment B (Outside Director Stock Sales 1997–2001).

g. Ibid., p. 41 (citing Enron 1998 Proxy Statement, p. 28; Enron 1999 Proxy Statement, p. 28; and Foy Sworn Statement).

h. Ibid., Attachment A (Biographies of Outside Directors, p. 6).

i. U.S. Senate, Permanent Subcommittee on Investigations on the Committee on Governmental Affairs, "The Role of the Board of Directors in Enron's Collapse," Hearing, S. Hrg. 107-511, 107th Congress, 2nd Session, May 7, 2002 (Exhibit 43, "Enron Board of Directors—Financial Ties to Enron).

1 = Executive Committee; 2 = Audit Committee; 3 = Finance Committee; 4 = Compensation Committee; 5 = Nominating Committee

*Denotes chair.

Finance Committee Meetings

Table E.1 follows on pages 374–376.

Table E.1 Finance Committee Meeting Information

Date	Duration	Absentees	Topics
10/11/99	1:30	Chan	• CFO report by Fastow including key ratios, long-term liabilities, and cash flow • Update on LJM1 • LJM2 presentation • Treasurer's report by McMahon including liquidity and financings • Proposed resolution that would allow a special committee of the board to approve issuance and sale of up to 500,000 shares of Enron common stock for the purpose of making acquisitions without full board approval • Chief Risk Officer's report by Buy including top twenty-five credit exposures, and top and bottom ten performing investments • Market risk update, including Enron's profit and loss and value at risk • Common stock dividend
12/13/99	1:15	None	• CFO report by Fastow including possible uses for proceeds from sale of Portland General Electric Company, stock repurchase program and recent activity, macro- and microeconomic financial issues for 2000 • Treasurer's report by McMahon • Proposed gas pipeline in the United Arab Emirates • Proposed prepaid gas deal with an independent oil and gas company • Proposed subsidiary preferred stock financing of up to $2.2. billion with unaffiliated investment group • Proposed sale of portion of Enron's Panama project • Chief Risk Officer's report by Buy including deal approval sheet relating to a contract extension with Eastern Power & Energy Trading Ltd.
5/1/00	1:30	Chan Meyer Pereiraon	• CFO report by Fastow including LJM2 update, LJM2's impact earnings and funds flow, Fastow's time commitment to

Date	Duration	Absentees	Topics
		Urquhart	LJM entities, and introduction of Glisan as McMahon's replacement • Glisan presented Raptor project including AA's review of Talon • Treasurer's report by McMahon including Enron's liquidity as of March 31, 2000 • Plan to monetize $1 billion in investments by year end • Current credit ratings • Need for additional borrowing flexibility • Proposed authorization for additional debt securities not to exceed $1 billion • Chief Risk Officer's report by Buy reviewed Enron's transaction approval process, proposed changes to risk management policy and the merchant portfolio • Review of certain EES transactions and the discrepancies between EES and RAC expected values including differences between the valuation models employed • RAC foreign exchange project • Market risk update • Commodity group returns on value-at-risk
8/7/00	2:00	None	• CFO report by Fastow including financial ratio deviations from those discussed with ratings agencies • Treasurer's report by Glisan including liquidity and condition of Raptors I and II • Raptor III proposed • Chief Risk Officer's report by Buy including merchant portfolio composition, credit exposure increases, Enron's top twenty-five credit exposures, nonperforming debt instruments, underperforming equity investments, top and bottom ten performing investments, proposed changes to risk management policy, and international investments • Proposed South America transactions • Ten-minute executive session covered Project Tammy including creation of Enron Finance

Date	Duration	Absentees	Topics
			Partners (EFP) with attendant asset contributions by Enron, assumption of $1.047 billion in debt by EFP, and related preferred securities sale of $500 million to outside investors
10/6/00	1:45	None	• CFO report by Fastow including proposed LJM3, benefits for Enron of doing business with LJM entities, Fastow's time commitment to LJM work, mitigations for conflicts of interest • Additional proposed LJM controls • Ratification of Office of the Chairman's finding that Fastow's LJM fund participation would not adversely affect Enron • Treasurer's report by Glisan regarding liquidity • Chief Risk Officer's report by Buy including RAC review of EES, a review of the transaction approval process, and doubling of average daily value-at-risk as a percentage
10/8/01	1:50	None	• CFO report by Fastow including liquidity risk ratio, asset monetization, importance of maintaining valuations for assets at least equal to the monetization values • Restructuring initiatives including Dabhol • Raptor description and termination including $1 billion reduction in Enron shareholder equity and $800 million reduction in expected third-quarter earnings • Whitewing update including that the bonds related to the structure would need funding in September 2002 • Azurix structure • Treasurer's report, credit-rating agency outlooks "stable" • Importance of straightforward financings in the marketplace • Chief Risk Officer's report including counterparty credit exposure concerns, market risk update • New market possibilities • Liquidity risk ratio analysis

Audit and Compliance
Committee Meetings

Table F.1 follows on pages 378–380.

Table F.1 Audit and Compliance Committee Meeting Information

Date	Duration	Absentees	Topics
2/7/99	1:35	None	• Arthur Andersen (AA) gives unqualified opinion on Enron's financial statements for 1998 including no changes in accounting policies and reviews status of Enron's internal controls • 1998 financial and internal controls audit update • 1998 financial statements draft • 1999 internal control audit plan • Update on market and credit risk including top twenty-five trade credit exposures, Enron's risk profile, limit violations, and stress test analysis , of trading portfolios • Annual report on taxable value of corporate aircraft used by officers and executives • "No significant areas of concern" covered in executive session
10/11/99	N/A	N/A	• Available minutes excerpt incomplete • AA indicates it spent considerable time during the third quarter reviewing a joint venture Enron was forming to monetize investments
2/7/00	1:10	None	• Update on regulatory initiatives • AA audit update: opinions on Enron's 1999 financial statements and internal controls would be unqualified; noted that Enron's "sophisticated business practices introduced a high number of accounting models and applications requiring complex interpretations and judgment"; presented 2000 audit plan • Discussion of 1999 financial statements including elimination of oil and gas reserve disclosures and footnotes to financial statements regarding related party transactions and asset impairments • Financial statements approved for inclusion in annual report and 10-K • Reference made to ACC's responsibility to review LJM1 and LJM2 transactions to make sure they are made on arm's-length basis

Date	Duration	Absentees	Topics
			• Causey reported on transactions asserting that all were made on arm's-length basis (the Powers Committee later determined that Causey's report did not include all of Enron's transactions with the LJM entities)
5/1/00	0:55	Chan Pereira	• AA reported on high-priority financial reporting areas including structured transactions regarding securitizations, syndication, and hedging vehicles; merchant portfolio; commodity trading; project development; and related party transactions that contain "inherent risks"
			• AA presented selected observations on Q1 2000 results
			• Business risk management analysis including review of trading controls showed no significant issues
			• Review of EES portfolio
			• Review of market risk including note that Enron's value at risk was higher than the industry norm because Enron used mark-to-market accounting for "a significantly larger number of contracts than most of the other companies"
			• Review of credit risk
			• Proposed changes to Enron's risk management policy
			• Review of proposed amended charter for ACC; approved for recommendation to full board
2/12/01	1:35	None	• AA opinions on 2000 financial statements and internal controls will be unqualified; no material weaknesses identified during audit
			• Review of reserves
			• Review of accounting procedures and financial reporting including the use of mark-to-market and fair-value-model accounting requiring significant judgment
			• Review of related party transactions
			• Credit risk related to 2000 financial statements

Date	Duration	Absentees	Topics
			• ACC report
			• Annual taxable value of corporate aircraft used by officers and executives
			• 2001 internal control audit plan
			• Policies and practices regarding management communication with analysts
			• Credit and market risk update to be discussed in finance committee
			• Enron transactions with LJM during 2000 including review of board's guidelines for LJM transactions and Enron's compliance with those guidelines
10/8/01	N/A	N/A	• Available minutes excerpt incomplete
			• AA presentation
			• Impact of FASB 142
			• Enron's earnings results for third quarter 2001
11/2/01	0:40	None	• Enron's response to formal SEC inquiry
			• AA's recent determination that Enron should restate $1.2 billion in equity
			• AA's work plan
			• Insufficient equity in Chewco to qualify for deconsolidation and links to Whitewing and other SPEs
			• Enron and AA responsibilities regarding Chewco
			• AA's error in accounting judgment regarding a 1999 LJM1 transaction that should be reviewed for restatement

Notes

Introduction

1. The phrase "murky borderlands" is from Saul W. Gellerman's famous article, "Why 'Good' Managers Make Bad Ethical Decisions," *Harvard Business Review* (July 1986).

2. The notion that intent can override compliance with esoteric rules is prevalent in U.S. jurisprudence. In reviewing a case of fraud, Judge Henry J. Friendly of the Second District Court of Appeals succinctly stated, "Proof of compliance with generally accepted standards was 'evidence which may be very persuasive but not necessarily conclusive that [the defendant] acted in good faith, and that the facts as certified were not materially false or misleading'" (*U.S. v. Simon*, 425 F.2d at 796, 805–806 [2d Cir. 1969]). Thus, the U.S. justice system is not a machine that plugs inputs into an equation and spits out a result. Following the rules is not enough. The spirit of the law is as important as its letter.

    Accounting and tax rules are rife with complexities subject to multiple interpretations beyond those envisioned by lawmakers. Businesses run afoul of such rules by attempting to maximize earnings (or reduce losses) through seemingly compliant structures that are actually mere subterfuge. Turning rules on themselves is accepted only to a point. At that point loopholes become nooses.

    Just as malicious intent can invalidate compliance and create liability, proper intentions can make up for legal shortcomings and fend off liability. The legal precept of good faith shelters those who wholeheartedly intend to do what the law prescribes, but fall short. Good faith protects parties that do not fulfill their end of a contract despite their best efforts, and it guards fiduciaries that make bad decisions despite proceeding cautiously. The good faith concept inserts humanity into the legal process.

    In many ways, intent is everything in the law. It separates fraud from an accounting mistake. It dictates how assets are distributed pursuant to a will. It is also the difference between first-degree murder and a horrible accident.

3. This is the "deontological" view of ethics (from the Greek word *deon*, which means binding duty). For a discussion of this and other ethical theories and

their relevance to economics, see Amitai Etzioni, *The Moral Dimension: Toward a New Economics* (New York: Free Press, 1988), especially chapter 1. Etzioni contrasts this view of ethics with utilitarianism, which regards two acts yielding similar results as equivalent, even if one involves a transgression, such as deception, and the other does not. See pp. 12–13.

4. This is a point that has been strongly and correctly made by John C. Coffee Jr., Adolf A. Berle Professor of Law, Columbia Law School, who has been a frequent commentator on the Enron case in both the print media and in academic papers. See, for example, John C. Coffee Jr., "What Caused Enron? A Capsule Social and Economic History of the 1990's," *Cornell Law Review* 89, no. 2 (2004).

5. Owen D. Young, "Dedication Address" (keynote address at the dedication of the new Harvard Business School campus on June 24, 1927). Reprinted in the July 1927 issue of *Harvard Business Review*, and available in the HBS Archives Collection (AC 1927 17.1). See also Rakesh Kuranna, Tarun Khanna, and Daniel Penrice, "Harvard Business School and the Making of a New Profession," HBS Case No. 9–403–105 (Boston: Harvard Business School Publishing, 2005), p. 15.

6. Jamie Dettmer and John Berlau, "Requiem for Enron," *Insight*, January 7, 2002.

7. April Witt and Peter Behr, "Dream Job Turns into a Nightmare: Skilling's Success Came at High Price," *Washington Post* (July 29, 2002). James W. Crowner, who hired Skilling at McKinsey's Houston office, remembered him as "outstanding in every respect," and "one of the most talented people we ever had."

8. Enron's outside directors have vigorously disputed the conclusions of both an investigation commissioned by the board itself (known as the Powers report) and of a report on the role of the board in Enron's collapse issued by the U.S. Senate. See William C. Powers Jr., Raymond S. Troubh, and Herbert S. Winokur Jr., *Report of Investigation by the Special Investigative Committee of the Board of Directors of Enron Corp.* (2002), available at www.enron.com; and U.S. Senate, Permanent Subcommittee on Investigations, Committee on Governmental Affairs, *The Role of the Board of Directors in Enron's Collapse*, S. Rep. No. 107–70 (2002). For the directors' response to the Senate critique, see W. Neil Eggleston and Dmitri Nionakis, *The Outside Directors' Response to the Permanent Subcommittee on Investigations of the Senate Governmental Affairs Committee Report: "The Role of the Board of Directors in Enron's Collapse"* (2002), available as an exhibit of *The Role of the Board of Directors in Enron's Collapse: Hearing before the Permanent Subcommittee on Investigations of the Senate Committee on Governmental Affairs*, 107th Cong. 715 (2002). The executive summary of the directors' response also appears as Appendix C.

Part I: The Origins of Enron's Collapse

1. For a discussion of the compliant behavior of directors toward unrestrained CEOs, see Randall Morch, "Behavioral Finance in Corporate Governance: Independent Directors and Non-Executive Chairs," Harvard Institute of Economic Research Discussion Paper No. 2037 (May 2004).

2. In his highly influential study of America's boards during the 1980s, Jay W. Lorsch observed that "directors must have enough power to influence the course of corporate direction, a power that is, at the least, slightly greater than the power of those the directors are to govern—the company's managers and the employees who report to them." Jay W. Lorsch, *Pawns or Potentates: The Reality of America's Corporate Boards* (Boston: Harvard Business School Press, 1989), p. 13.

3. Failure to take measures to prevent harm is an aspect of what the ethics literature calls "vicarious negligence." See Joshua D. Margolis, "Responsibility in an Organizational Context," *Business Ethics Quarterly* 11, no. 3 (July 2001): 438; and Larry May, *The Morality of Groups: Collective Responsibility, Group-Based Harm, and Corporate Right* (Notre Dame, Ind.: University of Notre Dame Press, 1987).

1. From Innovation to Reckless Gambling

1. Determining Enron's actual cost of capital is complicated by a lack of transparency in the company's financial reporting (such as inconsistent definitions of operating cash flows, and the true level of consolidated and unconsolidated debt). Indeed, internal documents and board minutes show that Enron's own estimates of its cost of capital varied rather widely from year to year.

2. Sanjay Bhatnagar and Peter Tufano, "Enron Gas Services," HBS Case No. 9–294–076 (Boston: Harvard Business School Publishing, 1994), 3.

3. This movement toward open access to pipelines was embedded in FERC Order 436 (1985). For an excellent summary of these and subsequent regulatory changes see Mary Lashly Barcella, "Natural Gas in the Twenty-First Century," *Business Economics* 31, no. 4 (October 1996): 19–24. FERC Order 436 is discussed on p. 21. See also John H. Herbert and Erik Kreil, "U.S. Natural Gas Markets: How Efficient Are They?" *Energy Policy* 24, no. 1 (1996): 1–5; and Gerald Granderson, "Regulation, Open-Access Transportation, and Productive Efficiency," *Review of Industrial Organization* 16 (2000): 251–266.

4. The story is actually a bit more complicated than this summary. With Order 636, FERC effectively "took itself out of the business of regulating gas commodity sales by taking regulated gas pipelines out of the commodity sales business." Order 636 required that gas commodity sales be unbundled from transportation transactions, which had the effect of transforming pipelines into what Barcella has aptly characterized as "time-share properties offering a variety of leasing arrangements." The separation of natural gas sales from the sales of transport services quickly led to the development of a highly competitive industry segment with no less than 264 natural gas marketers in the United States and Canada in 1995, broken down into a "core" group of 10 large marketers with a combined market share of 36 percent and a "fringe" group of more than 200 companies. This new industry structure enabled gas consumers to purchase gas from any one of a wide array of marketing companies who

could arrange for both the purchase and delivery of gas virtually anywhere in the country. See Barcella, "Natural Gas," pp. 21–22.

5. Skilling's vision of Enron's trading business is quoted in Bethany McLean, "Is Enron Overpriced?" *Fortune* (March 5, 2001).

6. Wendy Zellner, "Power Play," *Business Week* (February 12, 2001).

7. One problem was that the time lag between cash advances or loans to gas producers and cash receipts from gas buyers could be as long as two years. Enron could not finance such transactions on its own, so it set about creating financing vehicles to raise money for VPP. These vehicles—off-balance-sheet partnerships known as special purpose entities (or SPEs)—were legal, although they later became notorious for being used to disguise Enron's debt and losses. See Robert Bryce, *Pipe Dreams* (New York: Public Affairs, 2002), chapter 8; and Loren Fox, *Enron: The Rise and Fall* (Hoboken, N.J.: John Wiley, 2003); see pp. 31–32 and 63–64 for descriptions of Enron's Gas Bank and VPP program.

8. As noted, Enron used many types of derivatives in the conduct of its risk-management activities. In addition to futures and forward contracts, which became the "meat and potatoes" of Enron's trading business, some of Enron's most common derivatives included puts, calls, swaps, and collars. A *put* is an option that entitles the holder to sell to the counterparty a commodity, financial instrument, or other asset at an "exercise" or strike price throughout the option term, or at a fixed date (the expiration date). A *call* option has all the characteristics of a put option, except that it entitles the holder to buy rather than sell the commodity or financial instrument. A *swap* is a simple trading of assets or option contracts for a specified price. A total-return swap is an arrangement whereby one party agrees to pay the other the appreciation from an asset, and to receive repayments for its depreciation. A *collar* is a derivative transaction that combines a put and a call to effectively set a limit on the gain and loss the contract holder will realize. See www.investopedia.com for more detailed definitions and examples.

9. Phantom equity tracks the value of business units that have no stock of their own. At Enron, holders of phantom equity could convert it into Enron common stock or cash at certain times.

10. Skilling led the charge within Enron to convince regulators to permit the company to use mark-to-market accounting, previously an accepted technique for brokerages and trading companies who used it to record the value of their securities at the end of a trading day. Skilling convinced regulators to allow energy companies to adopt this accounting method as well. Skilling stood to benefit personally from this change in accounting, as his employment contract apparently guaranteed him as much as 3 percent of the value of his division's contracts, which mark-to-market accounting would greatly expand. See April Witt and Peter Behr, "Dream Job Turns into a Nightmare: Skilling's Success Came at a High Price," *Washington Post* (July 29, 2002): A01.

11. Skilling argued that mark-to-market was more appropriate than accrual accounting for matched purchases and sales, such as those Enron was creating,

because of the embedded hedge. He also argued that traditional accounting allowed companies with unmatched portfolios to create the financial outcome they wanted merely by selling winning positions while holding onto losers. See Kurt Eichenwald, *Conspiracy of Fools* (New York: Broadway Books / Random House, 2005), 59. If the value of mark-to-market contracts falls at some future date, they must be written down; that is, the company using them must report a charge to earnings. This can lead to extreme volatility in balance sheets. At Enron, to avoid such volatility, management pushed poorly performing assets to off-balance-sheet entities.

12. See Toni Mack, "Hidden Risks," *Forbes* (May 24, 1993). Although the use of mark-to-market accounting spread to other energy traders, Enron's chief accounting officer, Richard Causey, liked to claim that the company had developed these rules. See Jonathan Weil, "After Enron, 'Mark-to-Market' Accounting Gets Scrutiny," *Wall Street Journal* (December 4, 2001). Enron ignored the SEC's approval date and instituted mark-to-market a full year earlier. See Bryce, *Pipe Dreams*, p. 67.

13. Peter Coy, Stephanie Anderson, Dean Foust, and Emily Thornton, "Enron: How Good an Energy Trader?" *Business Week* (February 11, 2002).

14. Vince Kaminski and John Martin, "Transforming Enron: The Value of Active Management," *Journal of Applied Corporate Finance* 13, no. 4 (Winter 2001): 45.

15. "Enron's Ghost: Recharging," *Economist* (April 20, 2002):72.

16. Eventually, Williams Cos., Coastal Corp., Atlantic Richfield Co., Mobil Corp., Bankers Trust, Morgan Stanley, AIG, and Natural Gas Clearinghouse competed with Enron in trading natural gas in North America.

17. Under Skilling's influence, Enron's hard-asset revenues declined from 80 percent of reported revenues in 1990 to only 3 percent in 2000, but nevertheless provided one-third of Enron's cash flow in 2000. Industry experts estimated that profits from the company's traditional gas pipeline business were growing at an annual rate of 18–20 percent during this period. See "Strength of Enron's Cash Position May Be Moot, Given Its Spiraling Stock Slide," *Global Power Report* (November 9, 2002).

18. Kristen Hays, "Pipelines, Power Plants Keeping Enron Afloat," *Commercial Appeal Memphis* (February 23, 2002).

19. Bryce, *Pipe Dreams*, p. 217.

20. Margaret M. Carson, "Enron and the New Economy," *Competitiveness Review* 11, no. 2 (2001): 2. Carson was Enron's director of corporate strategy and competitive analysis.

21. Carson, "Enron and the New Economy," p. 1.

22. Fox, *Enron: The Rise and Fall*, pp. 166–167. This and the following two paragraphs draw heavily from this account of EnronOnLine.

23. Enron Corp. 2000 Annual Report, p. 3; and Fox, *Enron: The Rise and Fall*, p. 169.

24. The use of mark-to-market accounting afforded Enron "huge latitude for deciding when to include as current earnings profits they expect[ed] to realize in future periods from energy-related contracts and other 'derivative' instruments."

See U.S.-Senate, Committee on Governmental Affairs, *Financial Oversight of Enron: The SEC and Private-Sector Watchdogs,* 107th Congress, S. Rpt. 107-75 (Washington, D.C.: Government Printing Office, 2002), p. 44; and Jeanne Cummings et al., "Enron Lessons," *Wall Street Journal* (January 15, 2002).

25. For more on estimating forward commodity prices, see Jonathan R. Laing, "The Bear that Roared," *Barron's* (January 28, 2002). Enron's use of mark-to-market accounting for long-term commodity contracts has been called "mark-to-guess." See, for example, Eichenwald, *Conspiracy of Fools,* p. 56. "Many of the contracts covered companies in states that had not yet deregulated their power markets. In those cases, Enron forecasted when the states would deregulate those markets and then projected what prices would be under the currently nonexistent deregulated market. Then, based on its projections, Enron would calculate its total profit over the life of the contract. After discounting that figure for the risk that its customers would default and the fact that it would not receive most payments for years, Enron would book the profit immediately." Floyd Norris and Kurt Eichenwald, "Fuzzy Rules of Accounting and Enron," *New York Times* (January 30, 2002).

26. Vince Kaminski and John Martin, "Transforming Enron," p. 45.

27. Paul Beckett, Jathon Sapsfor, and Alexei Barrionuevo, "Power Outage: How Energy Trades Turned Bonanza into an Epic Bust," *Wall Street Journal* (December 31, 2000): A1.

28. I computed ROCE by dividing Enron's net operating income (after taxes) by its long-term assets plus net working capital.

29. Enron's profitability might also have been adversely affected by its seemingly unregulated expense-account spending, liberal use of corporate aircraft, and the exorbitant real estate costs associated with its Houston and London headquarters—all of which its business units had to absorb.

30. Jeff Skilling, videotaped interview by Robert Bruner, Darden School of Business, University of Virginia, May 25, 2001.

31. Mimi Swartz and Sherron Watkins, *Power Failure: The Inside Story of Enron* (New York: Doubleday, 2003), p. 13.

32. The recent books by Bryce, Fox, Swartz and Watkins, and McLean and Elkind are full of unidentified quotes and testimonies to Enron's arrogant managerial behavior. Although these accounts are entertaining, they do not distinguish fact from hearsay. Bethany McLean and Peter Elkind, *The Smartest Guys in the Room: The Amazing Rise and Scandalous Fall of Enron* (New York: Portfolio, 2003).

33. Fox, *Enron: The Rise and Fall,* p. 72.

34. Electricity prices were more than twice as volatile as gas prices, which themselves could swing by as much as 40 percent per year. See Fox, *Enron: The Rise and Fall,* p. 67. The inability to store electricity may contribute to its price volatility, but the exact impact of that factor is difficult to determine. Besides price volatility, the main difference between power and gas trading lies with the instrument used to trade them. The main instrument for gas trading is the monthly futures contract that clears on the NYMEX, priced at the Henry Hub

delivery point in Louisiana. For example, if a business in Boston wants to hedge its gas price for next July, it can buy a futures contract for delivery at Henry Hub. The "basis differential" between Henry Hub and Boston is relatively stable; and if the business is worried about basis, it can hedge that, too, by purchasing pipeline capacity. (Gas markets are fairly well integrated coast-to-coast, while power prices tend to vary much more by location.)

In contrast to gas, electric power is usually traded through brokers, and on a more local basis. If the hypothetical Boston business wants to hedge its power costs for July, it has to buy a forward contract for delivery at Boston. Virtually no power derivatives are traded on exchanges, so the company must buy power directly from a broker, over the counter, or from other such sources.

35. Barcella reported that by1996 natural gas marketers had begun to market electric power "to arbitrage across fuels by taking advantage of the ability of electric power producers to use a variety of fuels." Barcella writes, "deals have been reported in which a marketer bought power that had been generated from coal and traded this power to an electric utility for gas that the electric utility now did not need for its own generating plant. The marketer took that gas and sold it to another gas consumer, making a profit on the entire series of transactions." Barcella, "Natural Gas," pp. 22–23.

36. Carson, "Enron and the New Economy," p. 1.

37. Bob Williams, "Enron Looking to International Arena for Growth Via Hydrocarbon/Power Schemes," *Oil & Gas Journal* (June 29, 1998): 61–63.

38. V. Kasturi Rangan and Krishna G. Palepu, "Enron Development Corporation: The Dabhol Power Project in Maharashtra, India (A)" (Boston: Harvard Business School Publishing, 1996), 8 (HBS Case No. 9–596–099).

39. In the end, MSEB could afford only a 15 percent stake.

40. This $900 million figure is the amount that Enron eventually wrote off for the Dabhol project, after a full review of its impaired assets after Enron declared bankruptcy. Previous estimates of Enron's equity stake in Dabhol were in the $550 million range. These estimates reflected the following logic: Assuming that 67–75 percent debt is common in an electric power project such as Dabhol, the debt portion probably ran between $1.9 billion and $2.2 billion, and the equity portion, between $700 million and $1 billion. At a 65 percent share of the equity, Enron's portion was probably close to $550 million. See Josey Puliyenthuruthrl, "Enron Inches Toward India Plant Sale," *Daily Mail* (November 14, 2002), for an early external estimate of Enron's equity stake. Such estimates proved to be substantially short of the mark.

41. See McLean and Elkind, *The Smartest Guys in the Room,* p. 259.

42. See Eichenwald, *Conspiracy of Fools,* pp. 188–190, for more on this acquisition.

43. Ibid., p. 214.

44. Other big players in the power industry, such as Southern California Edison and Virginia's Dominion Resources, and industry outsiders such as Dow Chemical, also moved to exploit the new opportunities. Fox, *Enron: The Rise and Fall,* p. 61.

45. According to a leading study, one of the crucial features of electricity markets—which differentiates it from other commodity markets—is the need for real-time balancing of locational supply and demand. "This requirement flows from the technological characteristics of supply and distribution. Since electricity cannot be stored, instantaneous supply and demand must always be in balance; otherwise the integrity of the whole system might be compromised." See http://media.wiley.com/product_data/excerpt/00/04711040/0471104000.pdf, chapter 1, p. 8. Because electricity cannot be stored, several services have developed to ensure reliability, the most important of which is the "spinning reserve." To avoid a system breakdown, supply and demand must be balanced in real time. Spinning reserve is best understood as unused capability (the difference between the amount of electricity a generator can produce and the amount it actually does produce), which can be instantly deployed to maintain that balance. To maintain the balance, a generator does not operate at full capacity until needed. Power producers can decide to allocate their capacity to the energy (primary) market or the ancillary services market, which includes spinning reserve. Other ancillary services aimed at maintaining system reliability include nonspinning reserves, operating reserve, energy imbalance, regulation, and reactive power supply. While the spinning reserve and ancillary services presumably can be used to back up short-term supply contracts, writing long-term electricity contracts that depend on unknown future spinning reserves would appear to be far more difficult.

46. The industry has developed "wheeling" to facilitate the transmission of electric power over long distances. Wheeling involves using the transmission facilities of one utility system to transmit power to another system, or to transmit power between customer facilities within a single system or between systems. In wheeling, the entity transmitting the power does not own or use it directly. Executing long-term supply contracts that rely on wheeling is more complicated than delivering natural gas through pipelines owned or controlled by the shipper.

47. Swartz and Watkins, *Power Failure*, p. 113.

48. Ibid., p. 68.

49. Ibid., p. 71.

50. Ibid., p. 172.

51. Enron Corp. 10-Q filing to SEC (September 30, 2001), pp. 31 and 52. See also Swartz and Watkins, *Power Failure*, p. 173.

52. In a June 30, 2003, disclosure to the bankruptcy court, the Enron estate announced that a professional advisor had assigned a current value of $1.2 billion to Portland General. Because Enron had carried the utility on its books at $3 billion at the time of bankruptcy, the final write-down totaled $1.8 billion. On November 19, 2003, the *Wall Street Journal* reported that Enron had agreed to sell Portland General Electric to Texas Pacific Group, a buyout firm, for $1.25 billion in cash plus the assumption of debt, thereby confirming the June valua-

tion. Rebecca Smith, "Enron Set to Sell Oregon Utility to Texas Pacific," *Wall Street Journal* (November 19, 2003): A8.

53. Fox, *Enron: The Rise and Fall,* p. 173.

54. McLean and Elkind, *The Smartest Guys,* p. 174.

55. Ibid., p. 178.

56. Ibid., p. 300.

57. Ibid., p. 273. This unit's West Coast traders also stupidly took advantage of badly designed trading rules to profit from the California energy crisis, and in doing so created serious political and legal problems for the company and made a mockery of Lay's espoused commitment to high ethical standards.

58. Ibid., p. 303.

59. Described in McLean and Elkind, *The Smartest Guys,* pp. 243–244.

60. Quoted in Fox, *Enron: The Rise and Fall,* p. 239.

61. In 2000, the business lost $60 million on revenues of $408 million. In the first quarter of 2001, it reported losses of $35 million on revenues of $83 million. In the second quarter, the company lost $102 million on revenues of only $16 million. In the third quarter, the business reported losses of $357 million on *negative* revenues of $125 million—with much of the loss related to starting up content delivery. According to Enron's 10-Q filing on September 30, 2001, broadband's negative revenues reflected a valuation adjustment on a derivative instrument associated with its content systems business, code-named Project Braveheart (see Chapter 4). The actual capital loss was $1.3 billion, minus some $300 million in recovered cash and cash-equivalents. See Enron Corp., 8-K Filing to SEC (April 17, 2003). Seven senior executives of Enron Broadband Services were later indicted for securities fraud for issuing allegedly false and misleading statements and press releases to security analysts, and failing to disclose information about broadband's poor business performance. *United States of America v. Kenneth Rice et al.,* "Superseding Indictment," U.S. District Court, Southern District of Texas, Houston Division, Cr. No. H-03-93–01, April 29, 2003.

62. Quoted in Bryce, *Pipe Dreams,* p. 278.

63. Enron Corp., 10-K Filing to SEC (March 31, 1999), p. 12.

64. Bryce, *Pipe Dreams.* See pp. 278–280 for more on the similarities and differences between Enron's broadband and energy-trading businesses.

65. Ibid., p. 277.

66. David Kirkpatrick, "Enron Takes Its Pipeline to the Net," *Fortune* (January 24, 2000).

67. According to one class-action suit filed against Enron, the company claimed in its 2000 annual report and elsewhere that its network included twenty-five pooling points in eighteen U.S. cities plus Tokyo, Brussels, Paris, and Amsterdam. The suit held that only New York, London, Las Vegas, and Los Angeles had pooling points up and running as of December 2000. See *Newby et al. v. Enron Corp.,* "Class Action Complaint," U.S. District Court, Southern District of Texas, Civil Action No. H-01-3624, April 8, 2002 and summarized in Fox,

Enron: The Rise and Fall, p. 239. It is not clear why Enron issued these false claims, or indeed whether the misrepresentations described in the class-action suit are true. However, we do know that only a small portion of Enron's lines were actually "lit," meaning that they could transmit the light waves required to carry Internet data.

68. Swartz and Watkins, *Power Failure*, p. 202.

69. Enron's foray into home delivery of video was noteworthy not only because of its commercial failure, but also because of its circumvention of established accounting rules. See Chapter 4.

70. Brad Foss, "How Fledgling Water Business Named Azurix Foreshadowed Fall of Energy Giant Enron," Associated Press Newswires, February 3, 2002.

71. Ibid. See also Eichenwald, *Conspiracy of Fools*, p. 187; and Bryce, *Pipe Dreams*, p. 177. Long after Enron's collapse, Mark told me that the company's water business was not built around a trading model. These claims notwithstanding, the road show that preceded a public offering often mentioned this model. And one of Enron's U.S. units, which ran the Water2Water.com Web site, created a database of excess demand and water rights in five or six states, and tried to invest in those rights at just the right time. Rebecca Mark, interview with the author (June 10, 2003).

72. When asked how such a large, risky portfolio of bets could pass Enron's internal risk management screen, an M&A executive explained that the Risk Assessment and Control group, headed by Rick Buy, could not assess a strategy's risk: all it could do was assess tradable assets. That's because the group had no expertise in evaluating operating assets, their cost structure, potential efficiency gains and synergies, and profit potential. The risk assessment was thus perfunctory, focusing mainly on foreign-exchange risks and "filling out the paperwork." I have also been told that the Enron board was wary of the Wessex transaction, but that Lay persevered on the grounds that the new water strategy was partly compensation (and support) for Mark for not being designated Enron's next COO and CEO-apparent.

73. Enron Corp., 10-K Filing to SEC (April 2, 2000), p. 195; and Bryce, *Pipe Dreams*, pp. 136–137.

74. Enron Corp., 8-K Filing to SEC (April 1, 2002).

75. Foss, "Water Business."

76. Interview with the author (October 14, 2003).

77. See Michelle Wallin, "Enron to Drop Utility Deal in Argentina," *Wall Street Journal* (March 1, 2002): A7, for how Azurix won a thirty-year concession from Buenos Aires province in June 1999 with a bid that was more than three times the offer of the second-place contender. A more recent account places Azurix's bid at twice the offer of the second-place contender. See Eichenwald, *Conspiracy of Fools*, p. 190.

78. Bryce, *Pipe Dreams*, p. 186.

79. See explanatory notes to the monthly operating statement for December 2 through December 31, 2001, submitted by Enron Corp. to the U.S. Bankruptcy

Court: Enron Corp., "Monthly Operating Statement for December 2 through December 31, 2001," Submitted to the U.S. Bankruptcy Court, Southern District, April 22, 2002.

80. The estimated write-downs in Stephen Cooper's April 22, 2002, report to the U.S. Bankruptcy Court (ibid.) might be a conservative view of Enron's capital losses. Enron's 10-Q for September 30, 2001, showed some $60 billion in assets on its balance sheet. Based on interviews with Enron executives on May 6–8, 2003, it appeared that the total recovery of Enron's assets would be in the $23 billion to $30 billion range made up of $15 billion to $20 billion of cash, trading book liquidation, and tangible asset sales, and another $7 billion to $10 billion of assets being staged for sale or spin off (including Portland General, gas transmission pipelines, and certain international assets). According to this calculation, between $30 billion and $40 billion in equity and asset values was lost in the bankruptcy.

81. A. C. Cooper, W. C. Dunkelberg, C. Y. Woo, and W. J. Dennis, Jr., "Entrepreneurs' Perceived Chances for Success," *Journal of Business Venturing* 3, no. 2 (1988): 97–108; and L. E. Palich and D. R. Bagby, "Using Cognitive Theory to Explain Entrepreneurial Risk-Taking: Challenging Conventional Wisdom," *Journal of Business Venturing* 10, no. 6 (1995): 425–438; Andrew L. Zacharakis and Dean A. Shepherd, "The Nature of Information and Overconfidence in Venture Capitalists' Decisionmaking," *Journal of Business Venturing* 16, no. 4 (2001): 311–322; and Y. Trope, "Uncertainty-Reducing Properties of Achievement Tasks," *Journal of Personality and Social Psychology* 37 (1979): 1505–1518.

82. H. E. Aldrich and C. M. Fiol, "Fools Rush In? The Institutional Context of Industry Creation," *Academy of Management Review* 19, no. 4 (1994): 645–670; cited and discussed in Shailendra Raj Mehta and Arnold C. Cooper, "God Rewards Fools: Optimism as a Predictor of New Firm Success" (working paper, Krannert School of Management, Purdue University, 2003). The Mehta and Cooper paper summarizes the literature on optimism, and presents interesting research results on the positive effects of optimism on new business creation.

83. Swartz and Watkins, *Power Failure*, p. 13.

84. McLean and Elkind, *The Smartest Guys*, p. 226. Many experts apparently echoed Skilling's hubris. Gary Hamel, a reigning management guru and best-selling author, raved: "Like Microsoft created DOS, Enron is creating MOS: the market operating system. And they can apply it everywhere." Ibid.

85. Enron Corp., 1999 Annual Report, p. 2.

86. A cursory review of Lay's personal investment behavior reveals a reckless investor who borrowed extensively against Enron stock, and who drew on multiple lines of credit to invest $62 million in risky private equity deals, mutual funds, and other public securities; real estate; and a share of the Houston Texans football team. When Enron's stock price began to fall during the spring and summer of 2001, Lay was left with too little collateral to back up his margin calls. Executives who were directly responsible for extending Enron's business model into new markets, and for monitoring its increasingly diverse and risky

operations, apparently shared this personal appetite for risk. For one interpretation of Ken Lay's personal investment behavior, based on interviews with his investment advisors, see Kurt Eichenwald, "Company Man to the End, After All," *New York Times* (February 9, 2003), section 3, p. 1.

87. U.S. Senate, Permanent Subcommittee on Investigations, Committee of Governmental Affairs, "The Role of the Board of Directors in Enron's Collapse," 107th Congress, S. Rep. No. 107–70 (2002), p. 19.

88. See, for example, Lisa Ordonez Schweitzer, and Bambi Douma, "The Dark Side of Goal Setting: The Role of Goals in Motivating Unethical Decision-Making," *Academy of Management Proceedings* (2002) MOC: B1–B6."

89. Although the Rhythms hedge failed in the end, it temporarily kept losses associated with the collapsing market value of Rhythms off Enron's balance sheet. According to government investigators, the temporary rise in Enron's stock price, which more than covered the liability of the Rhythms put, led two of Enron's bankers, Fastow, and friends of Fastow who had invested in the deal to bilk a temporary surplus in the Swap Sub.

90. This description of internal criticism of the Rhythms hedge by members of RAC relies on reports in Eichenwald, *Conspiracy of Fools,* pp. 240–250, and Fox, *Enron: The Rise and Fall,* pp. 150–154. The former report is particularly well referenced.

91. McLean and Elkind, *The Smartest Guys in the Room,* p. 192.

92. Fox, *Enron: The Rise and Fall,* p. 154.

93. See note 8.

94. This description of the New Power hedge leaves out several financial details that are not relevant here. See Fox, *Enron: The Rise and Fall,* pp. 206–207, and the Powers report: William C. Powers Jr., Raymond S. Troubh, and Herbert S. Winokur Jr., *Report of Investigation by the Special Investigative Committee of the Board of Directors of Enron Corp.* (2002), available at www.enron.com.

95. U.S. Bankruptcy Court, Southern District of New York. *In re Enron Corp.,* Chapter 11, Case No. 01–16034 (AJG), "Second Interim Report of Neal Batson, Court Appointed Examiner" (January 21, 2003), p. 7, note 16.

96. As part of their standard contractual arrangements, Enron and its trading counterparties regularly posted cash deposits or letters of credit to collateralize a portion of their trading obligations. A downgrade to below investment grade could lead to a substantial increase in the cash required for collateral and margin deposits with Enron's wholesale trading partners. The best credit rating, held by only about a dozen U.S. companies, is AAA. Enron never achieved higher than a BBB+ rating—just a few levels above junk-bond status. The level of debt required to grow the business as fast as top management intended kept Enron from receiving a higher rating. This created a difficult balancing act: the company had to try to maintain its credit rating while taking on increasing amounts of debt to finance growth. Not surprisingly, Enron's credit rating became a major preoccupation of both the corporate office and the board. See Chapter 4.

97. Enron's 10-K filing with the SEC on September 30, 2001, explains this potential "note trigger event" in detail (see p. 12). Besides credit related to its wholesale trading business, Enron and its subsidiaries had outstanding guarantees or surety bonds related to construction projects and other performance obligations. Under certain circumstances, the issuers of such sureties could request collateral.

98. Enron's asset-light business essentially involved wholesaling risk, intermediating liquidity, and arbitrage. This and the following characterizations of Enron's trading operations are drawn from André F. Perold, unpublished paper, December 11, 2001.

99. How does a synthetic matched book differ from a simple matched book of investments (or hedges)? In the simple model, Enron might exploit arbitrage opportunities between fixed and floating interest rates through traditional interest rate swaps. (A swap is a simple trading of assets or option contracts at a specified price.) Enron would enter into one interest rate swap as a floating-rate payor, and a second interest rate swap as a fixed-rate payor. Under the synthetic model, Enron might decide to match with its own energy sales in London a weather derivative sold to a London outdoor restaurant that required Enron to pay the restaurant if the temperature fell below a specific "strike" level for a specified period of time. If London dropped below the strike temperature, Enron would pay the restaurant but also sell more energy at higher prices during the unexpected cold weather, thereby covering the cash payment to the restaurant. If the weather were unusually warm and Enron ended up selling less than the usual amount of energy in London, its diminished energy profits would presumably be compensated by the premium earned on the contract sold to the restaurant. This synthetic hedge presumes, of course, a relationship between London weather and energy *prices* as well as demand. Were energy prices to decline in the face of localized energy demand during a few cold weeks, this synthetic matched book could fail. A presentation by William H. Widen to the Enron Panel (a faculty study group) at Harvard Law School modeled this example. See "Enron's Most Problematic Derivatives Transactions" (undated draft).

100. Chris Argyris, "A Next Challenge in Organizational Leadership," mimeo, November 2002, and conversations with the author.

101. A. Twersky and D. Hahnemann, "Judgment under Uncertainty," *Science* 185 (1974): 1124–1130. For a summary of defective decision-making strategies, see Irving L. Janis and Leon Mann, *Decision Making* (New York: Free Press, 1977), 14–17.

2. The Impact of Perverse Incentives

1. Jeffrey Skilling, "Enron's Transformation: From Gas Pipelines to New Economy Powerhouse." Speech at Harvard Business School (April 26, 2001) (hereafter referred to as "Skilling videotape").

2. Kenneth Lay, Videotape Interview, Harvard Business School (January 11, 2001) (hereafter referred to as "Lay videotape").

3. Skilling videotape and Christopher A. Bartlett and Meg Glinska, "Enron's Transformation: From Gas Pipelines to New Economy Powerhouse," HBS Case No. 9–301–064 (Boston: Harvard Business School), 9.

4. Skilling videotape. To underscore his commitment to a dynamic workplace, Skilling eliminated Enron's dress code when he took over as COO, reconfigured offices and space, and replaced walls with glass or write-and-wash capabilities to facilitate brainstorming and spontaneous diagramming. Screens in elevators showing CNN constantly also contributed to a high-energy, high-tech environment. Some employees found this environment invigorating and some found it scary. See Robert Preston and Mike Koller, "Enron Feels the Power," *InternetWeek* (October 20, 2000); and Samuel Bodily and Robert Bruner, "Manager's Journal: What Enron Did Right," *Wall Street Journal* (November 19, 2001).

5. Hillary Durgin, "The Guru of Decentralisation," *Financial Times* (June 26, 2000). This pattern tended to vary from business unit to business unit, of course. In Enron International, for example, which focused largely on developing large-scale power projects, the rules of the game were more standardized and uniformly applied.

6. Christopher Koch, "Reinvent Now," *CIO* (August 15, 1999). This pattern did not hold at Enron International, where the board was generally notified and given a chance to halt progress once a project incurred $100,000 in early expenses. Board members could later veto a project after it had incurred $1 million to $2 million in expenses.

7. Ibid.

8. Lay videotape.

9. Global Change Associates, *Enron 2001: An Inside View*, pp. 27–28.

10. Skilling videotape.

11. Julian E. Barnes et al., "Investigative Report: How a Titan Came Undone," *U.S. News & World Report* (March 18, 2002).

12. Advocates of 360-degree review claim that it generates a more accurate picture of an employee's performance and development needs, and provides more thorough and helpful feedback, than the traditional "one-sided" appraisal by a single supervisor. Enron's 360-degree system was supported by a Web-based Performance Evaluation Process, which included training for human relations staff and other employees, training in data inputs and reports, training for facilitators of Performance Review Committee meetings, and detailed guidelines on providing employee feedback. See Enron internal document, "Enron Global Performance Measurement," undated, p. 4.

13. Joint Committee on Taxation, *Report of Investigation of Enron Corporation and Related Entities Regarding Federal Tax and Compensation Issues, and Recommendations*, vol. 1, p. 550.

14. From June 2000 to April 2001, 511 Enron employees were redeployed in the process of building new businesses. See Enron internal document

(prepared by Corporate Analysis and Reporting), "Enron's Culture," April 2001, p. 17.

15. Jeff Skilling, "Enron's Transformation: From Gas Pipelines to New Economy Powerhouse." Speech at Harvard Business School, April 26, 2001.

16. Jeff Skilling, Interview at Darden Business School, videotape, May 25, 2001.

17. Skilling videotape.

18. Ibid.

19. Author's interview with anonymous Enron executive, May 7, 2003.

20. Eichenwald, *Conspiracy of Fools* (New York: Broadway Books / Random House, 2005), pp. 120–121.

21. Barnes et al., "Investigative Report."

22. Joshua Chaffin and Stephen Fidler, "The Enron Collapse," *Financial Times* (April 9, 2002).

23. Eichenwald, *Conspiracy of Fools*, pp. 212–214, 255–257, and 462–463.

24. U.S. Senate, Permanent Subcommittee on Investigations, Committee on Governmental Affairs, "Frank Luntz of the Luntz Research Companies to Ken Lay, Greg Whalley, and Mark Frevert," exhibit #34. Memorandum dated October 19, 2001, presented at hearings before the 107th Congress, 2nd Session, July 23 and 30, 2002, p. 342.

25. Global Change Associates, *Enron 2001*, p. 34.

26. Skilling videotape.

27. Vince Kaminskiand John Martin, "Transforming Enron: The Value of Active Management," *Journal of Applied Corporate Finance* 13, no. 4 (Winter 2001): 49.

28. Bartlett and Glinska, p. 9.

29. Ibid., p. 341.

30. John Schwartz, "As Enron Purged Its Ranks, Dissent Was Swept Away," *New York Times* (February 4, 2002): 135.

31. U.S. Senate, Committee on Governmental Affairs, "The Fall of Enron: How Could It Have Happened?" Hearing, 107th Congress, 2002, p. 340; available at www.gpoaccess/congress/senate/homeland/index.html.

32. Brad Foss, "How a Fledgling Water Business Helped Sink Enron," *Associated Press* (February 3, 2002).

33. Schwartz, p. 135.

34. Bethany McLean and Peter Elkind, *The Smartest Guys in the Room: The Amazing Rise and Scandalous Fall of Enron* (New York: Portfolio, 2003), 63.

35. Ibid.

36. Ibid., p. 55.

37. These economists focus on the principal-agent problem as the central challenge of internal control. According to this view, since people tend to be self-interested, there is no such thing as a "perfect agent." Thus principals and owners must put in place incentives (usually monetary) to minimize the risk that divergent interests and loyalties will develop between themselves and their agents, to whom they generally delegate significant decision rights. See Michael C. Jensen, "Self-Interest, Altruism, Incentives, and Agency Theory,"

Journal of Applied Corporate Finance 7, no. 2 (Summer 1994): 40–45; reprinted in Michael C. Jensen, *Foundations of Organizational Strategy* (Cambridge: Harvard University Press, 1998).

38. Brian Cruver, *Anatomy of Greed: The Unshredded Truth from an Enron Insider* (New York: Carroll & Graf, 2002), 78–79.

39. While it is not entirely clear what proportion of Enron's trading book was comprised of long-term contracts (and what the frequency distribution of long-term contracts were by length of contract), Enron's 1992 Annual Report clearly stated that a key goal of the Enron Gas Services unit was to place greater reliance on long-term, fixed-price contracts. At that time, less than 10 percent of all natural gas sales were on a long-term, fixed-price basis (see Sanjay Bhatnagar and Peter Tufano, "Enron Gas Services" [Boston: Harvard Business School Publishing, 1994] HBS Case No. 294–076, p.5). Based on consultations with former Enron financial executives and other knowledgeable professionals, my sense is that during the late 1990s the distribution of Enron's risk management contracts by contract length was roughly 70 percent below two to three years, 20 percent between three to five years, and 10 percent for contracts greater than five years. At the long end of the spectrum, natural gas and electricity contracts were reported in Enron's 2000 10-K as having maximum terms of twenty-three and twenty-four years, respectively. Bandwidth contracts went out as long as eleven years. Also reported in the 10-K was the fact that as of December 31, 2000, the volumetric weighted average maturity of Enron's fixed-price portfolio was approximately one and a half years. All this suggests, of course, that a large proportion of contracts was at the short end. Nevertheless, it was at the longer end—between five years and twenty+years—that much of Enron's trading profits were made. It is also where most of Enron's trading risks and contract valuation abuses lay.

40. See McLean and Elkind, *The Smartest Guys in the Room*, pp. 62–63, for a description of how originators, traders, and finance executives would divvy up the value of a long-term commodity transaction.

41. Testimony of John Arnold before the Commodity Futures Trading Commission in the Matter of Enron Corp., Ref. No. 44916, August 19, 2002.

42. Ibid., p. 122.

43. Agis Salpukas, "Firing Up an Idea Machine: Enron Is Encouraging the Entrepreneurs Within," *New York Times* (June 27, 1999).

44. Skilling videotape.

45. Bartlett and Glinska, p. 9.

46. Christopher Koch, "Reinvent Now," *CIO* (August 15, 1999).

47. Kaminski and Martin, p. 45.

48. Gallagher Polyn, "Getting a Better Risk Picture," *Risk* (August 2001): 33.

49. See the Powers report, William C. Powers Jr., Raymond S. Troubh, and Herbert S. Winokur Jr., *Report of Investigation by the Special Investigative Committee of the Board of Directors of Enron Corp.* (2002), available at www.enron.com, pp. 170–171.

50. McLean and Elkind, p. 116.
51. Ibid.
52. Ibid., p. 117.
53. Enron Corp., Minutes of the Audit Committee of the Board of Directors (February 12, 2001), p. 3.
54. Author interviews with anonymous Enron executives, corroborated with evidence in McLean and Elkind, p. 130.
55. Author's interview with anonymous Enron personnel, May 6, 2003.
56. McLean and Elkind, p. 118.
57. Rebecca Smith and John R. Emshwiller, *24 Days* (New York: HarperBusiness, 2003), 348–349.
58. Skilling claims that he was never supposed to sign off on LJM deals, even though his signature sometimes appears on deal approval sheets. See Eichenwald, *Conspiracy of Fools,* p. 624.
59. Chaffin and Fidler, "The Enron Collapse."
60. Ibid.
61. Cruver, p. 274.
62. Ibid., pp. 79–80.
63. See Enron Corp. 8-K Filing to SEC, April 22, 2002. Because the company's revenues jumped by $70 billion from 1998 to 2000, overstatements of commodity contracts were probably much greater than $4 billion. Enron's new management explicitly identified another $8 billion to $10 billion in "potential downward adjustments of certain price risk assets and collateral" (such as forward contracts, swaps, options, energy transportation assets utilized for trading activities, and other activities) that would have been required due to the commencement of the Chapter 11 bankruptcy cases. In other words, Enron's bankruptcy either invalidated many contracts or transaction counterparties simply refused to stay in the game. Enron Wholesale Services, the Houston-based commodity trading operation, negotiated most of these overvalued contracts.
64. Joint Committee on Taxation, p. 566.
65. See Enron Corp. May 1, 2001 Proxy Statement. Houston, Enron Corp., p. 22.
66. Enron proxies 1995–2000, as reported in Robert Bryce, *Pipe Dreams* (New York: Public Affairs, 2002), 315.
67. Executives at Enron International received bonuses under a Project Participation Plan, which tied extra compensation to completion of power projects and other deals, not to Enron's earnings.
68. Joint Committee on Taxation, pp. 569–570.
69. Ibid., p. 571. The bonus for Enron International CEO Rebecca Mark was calculated as 1 percent of EI's net income, "subject to the sole discretion of Enron's Chairman and CEO." See ibid., Appendix A, Executive Employment Agreement, Enron Corp. and Rebecca P. Mark (May 4, 1998).
70. Ibid., p. 569.
71. Author's interview, June 5, 2003. When Wing first worked at Houston Natural Gas in the mid-1980s, his contract for the Bayonne, New Jersey, project gave

him 0–1.5 percent of free cash flow after projects reached a 17 percent internal rate of return, or IRR. (IRR is the interest rate that makes the net present value of all cash flow equal to zero and is a measure of an investment project's profitability.) Wing's payout was 0.25 percent of free cash flow at 17 percent IRR, rising to 1.5 percent at 25 percent IRR.

When Houston Natural Gas merged with InterNorth to create Enron, Wing resigned because he didn't get the job he wanted, and set up a consultancy called the Wing Group. Enron soon hired Wing back as an independent power project consultant, and then again as an employee. Although his contract changed, it remained performance oriented. For developing the highly successful Teesside power project in Great Britain, for example, Wing and his associates received a 5 percent carry (or claim on the project's future earnings), later reduced to 3 percent as the project expanded. For the most part, neither he nor his team received bonuses or extra compensation unless their fully operational projects cleared performance hurdles.

72. Project Participation Plan, Enron Development Corp., undated mimeo, and Joint Committee on Taxation, pp. 581–582. An important wrinkle in this plan created a fair amount of anxiety among project developers: the board could change the rules or amend this plan at any time. A committee appointed by the board could also determine which executives could participate, the size of each participant's award, and a project's net value based on virtually any factors the committee deemed relevant, although most of the information submitted to the committee came from project teams. In addition, the costs of contesting the committee's project valuations were high. To do so, executives would have to convince 50 percent or more dissenting participants to file a written notice of dissent within fifteen days, and bear all the costs of the dispute resolution process.

73. Joint Committee on Taxation, pp. 581–582.

74. Indeed, no power projects other than Dabhol actually failed.

75. The EDC bonus scheme eventually shifted to pay 4 percent of a project's net present value at closing, and the remaining 4 percent one to four years later, depending on the deal. The costs of failed projects as well as a capital charge were deducted from the bonus pool. However, development teams still earned significant bonuses.

76. Other motives besides the high bonuses payable in both cases may have been at work. Wessex was one of the few well-respected public companies that Mark could get her hands on, so this property probably looked critical to the launch of her water strategy. Similarly, in the Argentinean case, Mark might have felt that she needed to move quickly in light of the Azurix IPO to prove her claim that EDC had the skills to expand water utility management on a global scale. The acquisition in Argentina was closed a few days before the Azurix IPO.

77. David Barboza, "Officials Got a Windfall before Enron's Collapse," *New York Times* (June 18, 2002): C1.

78. "Enron Ex-Officials Receive Indictments in U.S. Fraud Case," *Wall Street Journal* (March 27, 2003): C10.

79. Enron Corp., May 6, 1997 Proxy Statement, Houston: Enron Corp., p. 28, n6 to the Summary Compensation Table on p. 26; Enron Corp., May 5, 1998 Proxy Statement, Houston: Enron Corp., p. 27, n6 to the Summary Compensation Table on p. 25; and Enron Corp., May 4, 1999 Proxy Statement, Houston: Enron Corp., p. 29, n6 to the Summary Compensation Table on p. 27.

80. Eichenwald, *Conspiracy of Fools*, p. 59. This argument assumes adequate (and clear) disclosure of the methodology and its impact on reported earnings, which does not seem to have occurred. For example, mark-to-market accounting can lead to extreme volatility in balance-sheet values, which provided incentives for Enron management to push poorly performing assets to off-balance-sheet entities.

81. Enron ignored the SEC's approval date and instituted mark-to-market a full year earlier. See Bryce, *Pipe Dreams*, p. 67.

82. Joint Committee on Taxation, Appendix D, pp. 166–170.

83. Jason Leopold and Jessica Berthold, "Enron's Filings Show Lavish Compensation Was Awarded to Many Senior Executives," *Wall Street Journal*, March 18, 2002.

84. Jeffrey K. Skilling 1996 Employment Agreement with Enron Capital Trade & Resources Corp.

85. Leopold and Berthold, "Enron's Filings." According to this article, Skilling's attorney, Bruce Hiler, said that Skilling actually collected on only a third of the $100 million because he "didn't need all that money." Lou Pai, the former chair and chief executive of Enron Energy Services, owned a 3 percent phantom equity stake in that unit. (See *Wall Street Journal*, March 27, 2002, correction to Leopold and Berthold's March 18 article citing Pai's holdings.) Pai converted his stake in EES to Enron common stock over a four-year period, accounting for the bulk of the $268 million in shares he sold before leaving the company in June 2001. Other senior executives benefited from similar arrangements.

86. See Descriptions of Long Term Incentive Plans in Enron Corp., 1997 Proxy, p. 31; 1998 Proxy, p. 31; 1999 Proxy, pp. 33–34 (included as footnote 1 to Long-Term Incentive Plan—Awards in 1998); and Enron Corp., May 1, 2001, Proxy Statement, Houston, Enron Corp., p. 23 (the account of Lay's payout also explains the plan's basic structure).

87. Enron Corp., 1998 proxy, p. 31.

88. See Enron Corp., 1997 proxy, p. 25, and 1999 proxy, p. 26.

89. The compensation committee explained the change as follows: "Although Enron's relative performance to its peers is an important measure, it has become more difficult to identify the most appropriate peer group for a company with Enron's diversified lines of business. Also, due to the changes associated with increased merger and acquisition activity, peer group performance is much more volatile without directly being tied to the efforts of executive

management. . . . As a result, for the 1999 long-term grants to corporate and certain operating executives, performance based restricted stock and stock options have been utilized. . . . The ultimate value of the performance based restricted stock awards to executives depends upon the achievement of recurring after-tax net income targets established by the committee for the years 1999, 2000, and 2001 and Enron's stock price. Stock options are granted at market price; therefore, for any compensation to be realized pursuant to stock options, the market price of common stock must increase." See Enron Corp., 1999 Proxy, p. 21.

90. Enron Corp., May 2, 2000, Proxy Statement, Houston, Enron Corp., p. 28, footnote 5 to Summary Compensation Table on p. 26. Enron met its earnings targets for 1999, so one-third of the restricted stock grants became vested in January 2000. The 2001 proxy does not clearly address the issue, so it is unclear whether another third became vested because of performance in 2000. Because of shortcomings in the performance of Enron's stock, Lay did not receive a cash payout under PUP or its successor plan(s) in 1997, 1998, or 1999, but he did receive $1,218,750 in 2000 and $3,600,000 in 2001 under the plan. PUP units granted in 1998 would have been eligible for payout after 2001, but the company filed for bankruptcy in late 2001. However, Ken Lay and Jeff Skilling were awarded 2.5 million PUP units and 1 million units, respectively, in 1998 (the basis for future cash bonuses). See Enron Corp., 1997 Proxy, p. 23; 1998 Proxy, p. 22; 1999 Proxy, pp. 33–34; 2000 Proxy, p. 23; and 2001 proxy, p. 23.

91. For a discussion of accelerated vesting based on performance, see Stuart L. Gillan and John D. Martin, "Financial Engineering, Corporate Governance, and the Collapse of Enron," Center for Corporate Governance, University of Delaware, Working Paper 2002–001, p. 30ff.

92. McLean and Elkind, p. 93.

93. Even when the requirements for accelerated vesting were not met, the board's compensation committee provided another bite at the apple. For example, when Enron failed to achieve the requisite performance in 1997, the committee amended the terms of Lay's 1994 option award so that his options would fully vest if Enron met its goal for recurring earnings per share in 1998. See Enron 1997 Proxy, p. 22.

94. Kenneth L. Lay 1996 Employment Agreement, effective December 9, 1996. This agreement defined "total shareholder return" as the sum of appreciation or depreciation in the price of a share of Enron's common stock and the dividends paid, expressed on a percentage basis.

95. See Lucian Bebchuk and Jesse Fried, *Pay without Performance: The Unfulfilled Promise of Executive Compensation* (Cambridge: Harvard University Press, 2004), 139–143.

96. Gillan and Martin, p. 31.

97. Jeffrey N. Gordon discusses this point in "Governance Failures of the Enron Board and the New Information Order of Sarbanes-Oxley," *Connecticut Law Review* (Spring 2003): 1130.

98. A growing body of empirical work supports the view that managers' freedom to unload options and shares provides incentives to manipulate earnings and engage in fraud. See Bebchuk and Fried, *Pay without Performance,* p. 184, for a summary of this research.

99. Joint Committee on Taxation, p. 657.

100. Loren Fox, *Enron: The Rise and Fall* (Hoboken, N.J.: John Wiley & Sons, 2003), p. 94.

101. The differences in the totals for Lay and Skilling in Tables 2.3 and 2.4 reflect different data sources and estimation methods. Because I developed the totals in Table 2.4 from SEC filings, Table 2.3 probably underestimates the gross proceeds for Lay and Skilling.

102. See http://transcripts.cnn.com/TRANSCRIPTS/0102/05/mlld.00.html.

103. Rebecca Smith, "Sale of Enron Unit to Sierra Pacific Becomes Unlikely," *Wall Street Journal,* March 26, 2001.

104. See U.S. Bankruptcy Court, Southern District of New York, Official Committee of Unsecured Creditors of Enron Corp. et al. vs. Kenneth L. Lay and Linda P. Lay, Case No. 01–16034 (AJG), p. 7. An Enron internal document, "Investment Portfolio: Lessons Learned, November 2000," comes to similar conclusions.

105. Because Enron established a Special Assets Group in late 2000 to review and monitor merchant assets, Skilling must have been aware of problems with the large portfolio of such assets.

106. John R. Emshwiller, "Enron's Skilling Cites Stock-Price Plunge as Main Reason for Leaving CEO Post," *Wall Street Journal* (August 16, 2001): A2.

107. "Enron's Ken Lay: 'There's No Other Shoe to Fall,'" *Business Week,* August 24, 2001.

108. Floyd Norris and David Barboza, "Enron's Many Strands: Ex-Chairman's Finances," *New York Times* (February 16, 2002).

3. The Evolving Culture of Deceit

1. For publicly listed companies, the Securities and Exchange Commission (SEC) generally recognizes GAAP rules, and those of other standard-setting bodies meeting specified conditions, for the purposes of enforcing security laws. See U.S. Securities and Exchange Commission, *Securities Act of 1933,* Sec. 19 (b).

2. United States District Court, Southern District of Texas, Houston Division. Complaint. Superseding Indictment. *U.S. v. Richard A. Causey, Jeffrey K. Skilling, and Kenneth L. Lay,* July 7, 2004, Cr. No. H-04–25 (S-2). For at least one of these alleged violations—involving so-called prepay transactions—there is a difference of legal opinion over the application of GAAP to these transactions. See the discussion of "prepays" later in this chapter. In contrast, the conclusion of a court-appointed examiner (Neal Batson) that Enron violated GAAP in five other types of transactions designed to obfuscate Enron's true financial

condition and manage its credit rating has not been contradicted in any legal proceeding that I am aware of.

3. Kurt Eichenwald and John Markoff, "Deception, or Just Disarray," *New York Times* (June 8, 2003): Sec. 3, p. 1.

4. Kurt Eichenwald, *Conspiracy of Fools* (New York: Broadway Books / Random House, 2005), pp. 397 and 457–458.

5. Ibid., p. 288.

6. Enron was not the only company in this boat. The Williams Companies, Inc., was also experiencing serious cash management problems at this time and for similar market-related reasons. See Joshua A. Corval, Robin Greenwood, and Peter Tufano, *Williams, 2000*, HBS Case 9-203-068 (rev. February 7, 2006).

7. These instances of financial disorganization are discussed in Eichenwald, *Conspiracy of Fools*, pp. 429–430 and 560.

8. U.S. Senate, Permanent Subcommittee on Investigations, Committee on Governmental Affairs, "Frank Luntz of the Luntz Research Companies to Ken Lay, Greg Whalley, and Mark Frevert," exhibit #34. Memorandum dated October 19, 2001, presented at hearings before the 107th Congress, 2nd Session, July 23 and 30, 2002.

9. Executives typically cashed in their holdings of Enron stock when they resigned. Rebecca Mark, who led Enron's international initiatives and served as a vice-chair of the board, and Lou Pai, former head of the failed Enron Energy Services, reportedly netted $80 million and $354 million, respectively, from liquidating their Enron stock. See Scott Sherman, "Enron: Uncovering the Uncovered Story," *Columbia Journalism Review* (March-April 2002): 25.

10. These two were Stan Horton, CEO of Enron Transportation Services, and Mark Frevert, of Enron Wholesale Services, Enron's commodity-trading operation.

11. "Enron Selects Kinder to Be Its President and Operating Chief," *Wall Street Journal* (October 12, 1990).

12. Harry Hurt III, "Power Players: Enron Has Shaken Up the Sleepy Gas Pipeline and Power Businesses by Aggressively Embracing Risk and Continually Remaking Itself, so What's Not to Like?" *Fortune* (August 5, 1996).

13. See the Powers report, William C. Powers Jr., Raymond S. Troubh, and Herbert S. Winokur Jr., Report of Investigation by the Special Investigative Committee of the Board of Directors of Enron Corp. (2002), available at www .enron.com, p. 170.

14. Julie Mason, "Enron's Former Chairman Repeatedly Tells Probers He Didn't Know about Deals," *Houston Chronicle* (February 20, 2002).

15. *Fortune* also named Enron its Most Innovative Company for six straight years, and ranked it number two in employee talent in 1999. *Fortune* further ranked Enron first among energy companies on its list of most admired companies, while the *Financial Times* named Enron Energy Company of the Year for 2000. See Vince Kaminski and John Martin, "Transforming Enron: The Value of Active Management," *Journal of Applied Corporate Finance* 13, no. 4 (Winter 2001): 39–49.

16. This and the following paragraphs are adapted from Jeffrey McMahon's testimony. Hearing before the U.S. House Energy and Commerce Subcommittee on Oversight and Investigations, Committee on Energy and Commerce, "The Financial Collapse of Enron—Part ," 107th Congress, 2nd Session (February 7, 2002).

17. Ibid., pp. 55, 59, 60, and Exhibit 9.

18. The Powers report, pp. 166–167.

19. The emotional discomfort and suffering that attend problems and their avoidance are key sources of mental illness. Inasmuch as most of us have this tendency to a greater or lesser degree, according to Peck, most of us are, to a greater or lesser degree, mentally ill. M. Scott Peck, M.D., *The Road Less Traveled* (New York: Simon & Schuster, 1978), 16.

20. Irving L. Janis and Leon Mann, *Decision Making* (New York: Free Press, 1977), 50, 82.

21. Michael C. Jensen and William H. Meckling, "The Nature of Man," *Journal of Applied Corporate Finance* (Summer 1994); and Michael C. Jensen, "Self-Interest, Altruism, Incentives, and Agency Theory," *Journal of Applied Corporate Finance* (Summer 1994).

22. Daniel Goleman, *Emotional Intelligence* (New York: Bantam Books, 1995), 13–65; and Joseph LeDoux, *The Emotional Brain* (New York: Simon & Schuster, 1996), ch. 6.

23. Chris Arygyris and Donald A. Schoen, *Organizational Learning II: Theory, Method, and Practice* (Boston: Addison-Wesley, 1996).

24. Bethany McLean and Peter Elkind, *The Smartest Guys in the Room: The Amazing Rise and Scandalous Fall of Enron* (New York: Portfolio, 2003), 90.

25. I have borrowed the term "non-productive behavior" from Chris Argyris's work on productive versus defensive reasoning, elaborated in Chris Argyris, "A Next Challenge in Organizational Leadership" (mimeo, November 2002).

26. Large-sample surveys show that very few people rank themselves below the fiftieth percentile of their peers. For more on this phenomenon, see George P. Baker, Michael C. Jensen, and Kevin J. Murphy, "Compensation and Incentives: Practice vs. Theory," *Journal of Finance* 43, no. 3 (July 1988).

27. Ibid., p. 17.

28. Joseph L. Badaracco, *Defining Moments* (Boston: Harvard Business School Press, 1997), 57, 59, and 64.

29. Several chroniclers have told the story of how Lay chose to handle the fraud discovered at Enron's Valhalla oil-trading operation. This account relies heavily on Robert Bryce, *Pipe Dreams* (New York: Public Affairs, 2002), 36–43; McLean and Elkind, *The Smartest Guys in the Room*, pp. 15–26; and Eichenwald, *Conspiracy of Fools*, pp. 35–39.

30. McLean and Elkind, *The Smartest Guys in the Room*, p. 19.

31. Ibid., p. 39.

32. Ibid., p. 18.

33. "Doubling down" involves purchasing more shares of a security already held in an investment portfolio when prices are falling, thereby reducing the average

cost of the investment and creating the opportunity to regain paper losses when and if the share price rebounds.

34. This summary draws heavily from Mimi Swartz and Sherron Watkins, *Power Failure: The Inside Story of Enron* (New York: Doubleday, 2003), 69–70; and McLean and Elkind, *The Smartest Guys in the Room*, p. 95.

35. Even if Alexander had been trying to strengthen his bargaining power with Enron or, as some former executives claim, to boost his own profit-based compensation, he deserved a direct response to his request for intervention by the CEO.

36. Swartz and Watkins, *Power Failure,* p. 79.

37. Ibid., p. 80.

38. Ibid., p. 88. This summary draws heavily from pp. 88–94.

39. Ibid., p. 92.

40. The House Energy and Commerce Committee released the full text of Watkins' letter on January 15, 2002, after her testimony. The *New York Times* reprinted the letter in full on January 16, 2002, p. C6. See also Swartz and Watkins, *Power Failure,* Appendix A, pp. 361–362; and Eichenwald, *Conspiracy of Fools,* p. 486.

41. April Witt and Peter Behr, "Dream Job Turns into a Nightmare: Skilling's Success Came at a High Price," *Washington Post* (July 29, 2002); and Swartz and Watkins, *Power Failure,* Appendix C, pp. 363–368.

42. The Powers report, p. 173.

43. These quotes from the Vinson & Elkins report, along with the description of the Watkins incident are from the Powers report. See, especially, pp. 174–176.

44. Ibid., pp. 176–177.

45. John R. Emshwiller, "Enron Official Gave Warnings as Early as '99," *Wall Street Journal* (March 18, 2002).

46. See the Powers report. This story emerged in interviews between Kaminski and the Powers committee, confirmed in interviews conducted by this author.

47. Judith Burns, "Enron Lawyer Says Tried to Work 'Within System,'" *Dow Jones News Service* (February 2, 2002).

48. Ibid.

49. Professor Bala G. Dharan of Rice University developed this point in testimony prepared for the U.S. House Energy and Commerce Committee, "Enron's Accounting Issues: What We Can Learn to Prevent Future Enrons" (Federal News Service, February 6, 2002).

50. Ibid., p. 4.

51. See U.S. Senate, Committee on Government Affairs, *Financial Oversight of Enron: The SEC and Private-Sector Watchdogs,* 107th Cong., S. Prt. 107–75 (Washington, D.C.: Government Printing Office, 2002), 24–25; and U.S. Bankruptcy Court, Southern District of New York, *In re Enron Corp.,* Chapter 11, Case No. 01–16034 (AJG), "Final Interim Report of Neal Batson, Court-Appointed Examiner" (November 4, 2003).

52. Eichenwald, *Conspiracy of Fools,* pp. 596, 599, 608, and 624.

53. Investigative reporters from the *Wall Street Journal,* the *New York Times,* the *Washington Post, Fortune,* and *Newsweek* developed much of the data in the following discussion. Other data are from Congressional testimonies and Enron's 8-K filing with the SEC on November 8, 2001. When information in these sources differed from the Powers report (supra note 13), I have tended to rely on the latter as the final authority.

    This section does not detail alleged practices related to the management of Enron's earnings. It is widely known, however, that Enron lived in a quarter-to-quarter scramble to post ever-higher profit numbers. This allegedly led some traders to establish "prudence reserves" that they could tap when needed. Investigative reporting by the *Wall Street Journal* and unconfirmed discussions with Enron employees suggest that when a quarter looked tight, some analysts simply adjusted forward price curves to make long-term energy contracts look more attractive. See Julian E. Barnes, Megan Barnett, Christopher H. Schmitt, and Marianne Lavelle, "Investigative Report: How a Titan Came Undone," *U.S. News and World Report* (March 18, 2002); and the foregoing discussion of earnings management at Enron Capital & Trade.

54. The description of the Braveheart partnership relies heavily on investigative reporting by Rebecca Smith, "Blockbuster Deal Shows Enron's Inclination to All-Show, Little-Substance Partnerships," *Wall Street Journal* (January 17, 2002); and a summary of alleged violations of U.S. securities laws in the (superseding) indictment of Kenneth Rice et al: U.S. District Court, Southern District of Texas, Houston Division. Complaint. *United States of America v. Kenneth Rice et al.* Cr. No. H-03–93–01.

55. Enron could have ended up as the controlling partner of Thunderbird if it had not found enough truly independent, third-party investors.

56. This section draws on the Powers report, pp. 41–67; U.S. Bankruptcy Court, Southern District of New York, *In re Enron Corp.,* Chapter 11, Case No. 01–16034 (AJG), "Second Interim Report of Neal Batson, Court-Appointed Examiner," (January 21, 2003), Annex 1 to Appendix L; the reporting of John Emshwiller and Rebecca Smith, "Enron Jolt: Investments, Assets Generate Big Loss," *Wall Street Journal* (October 17, 2001); Allan Sloan, with others, "Digging into the Deal that Broke Enron," *Newsweek* (December 17, 2001); and Peter Behr, "Hidden Numbers Crushed Enron," *Washington Post* (January 12, 2002).

57. Andersen also discovered problems associated with unrecognized fee income and "required payments" from Chewco to Enron; and with revenues from price increases in Enron's own stock, which accounting rules usually preclude.

58. Kopper's management fees and a $10 million cut of the repurchase transaction suggests theft or embezzlement, as well as a major misrepresentation of Enron's current earnings and outstanding debt.

59. Swartz and Watkins, *Power Failure,* p. 139.

60. Ibid., p. 140.

61. U.S. Securities and Exchange Commission, Staff Accounting Bulletin Release No. SAB-51, 7 Se. L. Rep. (CCH) ¶ 75, 721, at 64, 262 (March 29, 1983).

62. This summary is based on U.S. Bankruptcy Court, "Second Interim Report," Appendix O, pp. 13–15.

63. See U.S. District Court, Southern District of Texas, Houston Division. Complaint. *U.S. v. Andrew S. Fastow et al.*, Cr. No. H-02–0665. This indictment superseded an earlier one.

64. U.S. Bankruptcy Court, "Second Interim Report," p. 36. Although the SPEs the examiner selected for review were the most important in contributing to Enron's downfall, his analysis excluded many others. This portion of the examiner's work cost more than $20 million in professional fees, billable to the Enron estate.

65. See U.S. Bankruptcy Court, Southern District of New York, *In re Enron Corp.*, Chapter 11, Case No. 01–16034 (AJG), "First Interim Report of Neal Batson, Court-Appointed Examiner" (September 21, 2002), p. 10.

66. Statements such as "the evidence is sufficient for a finder of fact to conclude," and that a certain conclusion is "likely," make that clear. The first phrase is peppered throughout Batson's reports. For examples, see U.S. Bankruptcy Court, "Third Interim Report," Appendix G, pp. 14 and 92; and U.S. Bankruptcy Court, "Final Interim Report," Appendix D, p. 180.

67. Ibid., Appendix M, pp. 1 and 8.

68. Ibid., p. 38, note 102. A swap is a simple trading of assets or option contracts for a specified price. In a total-return swap, one party usually agrees to pay another if an asset appreciates in value, and receives repayments from the other party if the asset depreciates in value. It is unclear whether Enron's characterization of its contractual agreements as total-return swaps meets the standards of the International Swaps and Derivatives Association.

69. Ibid., p. 39.

70. Ibid., Appendix M, pp. 4–5.

71. Ibid., Appendix J, p. 4.

72. Ibid., p. 6.

73. Lindy L. Paull, chief of the Joint Committee on Taxation, is reported to have told the Senate Finance Committee that Enron's tax department "was converted into an Enron business unit, complete with annual revenue targets." See David Cay Johnston, "Wall St. Banks Said to Help Enron Devise Its Tax Shelters," *New York Times* (February 14, 2003), p. C1.

74. April Witt and Peter Behr, "Enron's Other Strategy: Taxes," *Washington Post* (May 21, 2002): A1.

75. U.S. Bankruptcy Court, "Second Interim Report," Appendix J, p. 11.

76. Ibid., p. 10.

77. U.S. Bankruptcy Court, "Second Interim Report," p. 41.

78. Here is how the court-appointed examiner summarized Enron's use of the share trusts technique:

"Enron formed a holding company for Azurix that was jointly owned by Enron and MarlinWater Trust ("Marlin"), a Delaware business trust that was funded primarily by debt and a small amount of equity raised from third parties. The proceeds of the debt and equity were contributed to the holding company and used to repay a portion of Enron's acquisition debt. Enron indirectly guaranteed Marlin's debt by agreeing to sell Enron stock for proceeds sufficient to repay the debt, and if sufficient proceeds could not be raised from the sales of the Enron stock, then to repay the debt with cash.

"Although Enron held the controlling financial interest in the holding company, by bestowing upon Marlin the right to appoint half of the directors of the holding company and certain of its subsidiaries, Enron contended, and Andersen agreed, that the holding company did not have to be consolidated with Enron. This technique, using GAAP rules that were approved only weeks before the structure was implemented, was designed by Enron and Andersen to remove the $900 million acquisition debt and the Azurix assets from Enron's balance sheet. While in this instance a narrow application of the GAAP rules may have permitted off-balance-sheet treatment of the debt, Enron failed to properly disclose its contingent liability to provide funds to repay the debt. Although Enron described the arrangements in general in notes to its financial statements, it was not until it filed its third quarter 2001 Form 10-Q just prior to its bankruptcy that Enron clearly disclosed the amount of its obligation and revealed that it could be called upon to satisfy that amount in cash under certain clearly foreseeable circumstances." Ibid., pp. 41–42.

79. Ibid., Appendix G, pp. 138–139.
80. Ibid., pp. 123–126.
81. Ibid., p. 43.
82. U.S. Senate, Committee on Governmental Affairs, *The Role of the Financial Institutions in Enron's Collapse—Volume 1: Hearing before the Permanent Subcommittee on Investigations of the Senate Committee on Governmental Affairs,* 107th Congress (July 23, 2002) (the PSI Prepay Report).
83. U.S. Bankruptcy Court, "Second Interim Report," Appendix E, p. 2. Calculating the exact amount or "extent" of Enron's obligations under prepay transactions is a very complicated matter, so the $5 billion obligation claimed by the bankruptcy court could be reduced by alternate computational methods.
84. In the first transaction, a bank made a cash payment to a conduit entity equal to the amount that Enron wanted to borrow, in return for the conduit's promise to deliver to the bank a specified quantity of commodities in the future. Second, the conduit entity made the same current cash prepayment to Enron or an affiliate, in return for a promise from Enron to deliver commodities under a forward contract with terms identical to the original contract between the bank and the conduit entity. Third, Enron agreed to deliver cash to the bank in the future, and the bank agreed to deliver the specified commodity to Enron in the future, on the same terms as in the preceding steps. The value exchanged in the first two legs of the prepay transaction was identical, but the value of the third contract, between Enron and the bank, included an additional amount that was roughly equivalent to interest. Credit risk plays an

important role in these prepays, because where there is credit risk, the perfect cycle composing the prepay collapses. Ibid., pp. 1–2.

85. Ibid., p. 5.

86. Cooke held that Enron "was justified in giving the prepays 'non-debt' treatment and accounting for them as Price Risk Management Activities." Thus, in his opinion, GAAP had not been violated. "Whilst therefore there may be other ways in which the transactions could properly be accounted, on the evidence before me, I cannot conclude that the accounting treatment actually adopted was contrary to GAAP." *Mahonia Ltd. v. JPMorgan Chase and WestLB*, QBD (Commercial Court), ¶ 221, 228. In later analysis, Cooke eliminated any lingering doubt about his position.

   Cooke was not alone in his position. The prior Congressional testimony of Ronald M. Barone, the manager of Standard & Poor's ratings work for Enron, supports the proposition that cash from prepay transactions was properly reported as cash flow from operations. In his testimony Barone said that he concluded that Enron was using prepay transactions on a regular basis for "strategic reasons" (such as "smoothing out cash flows or earnings" under the company's price risk management program) and that, accordingly, the funds from these transactions were "to be more akin to operational cash flow" than a source of financing. See U.S. Senate, Committee on Governmental Affairs, "Rating the Raters: Enron and the Credit Rating Agencies," 107th Congress 62–63, 2002. Testimony of Ronald M. Barone, Managing Director, Standard and Poor's. Available at www.gpoaccess.gov/congress/senate/homeland/index .html.

87. U.S. Bankruptcy Court, "Second Interim Report," Appendix E (Prepay Transactions), p. 29. ("No specific comprehensive accounting guidance for prepay transactions exists."); *Mahonia*, ¶ 176 and 196.

88. U.S. Bankruptcy Court, "Second Interim Report," Appendix E (Prepay Transactions), pp. 20–29 and 45.

89. Cooke concluded that "a faithful representation of those contracts required them to be treated as the contracts they were and not on some composite basis, as if they constituted a single loan, simply because the economic effect of them, if they . . . were fully performed, was similar or identical to that of a loan. They contained provisions which made them swap contracts with margin obligations and obligations to make payments which depended on the market movement of gas prices. There was price risk in each both on a performance basis and on a default basis." *Mahonia*, ¶ 191, 192, 220, and 236.

90. In *U.S. v. Sarno*, the 9th Circuit ruled that "adherence to GAAP would obviously qualify as weighty exculpatory evidence; it does not, however, necessarily shield one from criminal liability." *U.S. v. Sarno*, 73 F.3d 1470, 1482 n.6 (Ninth Cir. 1995). See also *U.S. v. Simon*, 425 F.2d 796, 805–806 (Second Cir. 1969), *cert. denied*, 397 U.S. 1006 (1970).

91. Ibid., pp. 47–48.

92. In its SEC 10-Q filing for the third quarter of 2001, Enron admitted that the number of SPE transactions was not in accordance with GAAP rules. The examiner's report shows how extensive Enron's deception was.

93. Swartz and Watkins, *Power Failure*, p. 135.

94. U.S. District Court, Southern District of Texas, Houston Division, Complaint. *U.S. v. Andrew S. Fastow et al.* Cr. No. H-02–0665, Exhibit A to Plea Agreement, p. 1. Similarly, the guilty plea bargain of Timothy Despain, Enron's former assistant treasurer, specifically identified prepay transactions as serving debtlike obligations, a conclusion that was not disclosed to credit ratings agencies. See *U.S. v. Timothy Despain*, Cr. No. H-04, Sentence Data Sheet, pp. 2–3.

95. My analysis is based on information made available to the bank examiner in 2003 and his own analysis. My revised calculations for the Type A transaction in the table's upper panel may prove too generous, pending future revelations.

96. U.S. District Court, *U.S. v. Fastow et al.*, p. 55.

4. Ethical Drift

1. In early April 2007, one of the fifteen plea bargainers, Christopher Calger, was successful in withdrawing his guilty plea to wire fraud in connection with an asset sale in 1990 and 2000. U.S. District Judge Lee Rosenthal approved Calger's request to withdraw his guilty plea after an appeals panel reversed fraud and conspiracy convictions in a separate 2004 Enron case in which government prosecutors used a theory that turned out to be central to Calger's case. See Kristen Hays, "Judge OKs Withdrawal of Enron-Related Guilty Plea," *Houston Chronicle* (April 2, 2007).

2. Neal Batson's final report discusses findings related to Skilling's and Lay's breach of fiduciary duties. The report focuses particularly on the duties of care, candor, and loyalty. See U.S. Bankruptcy Court, Southern District of New York, *In re Enron Corp.*, Chapter 11, Case No. 01–16034 (AJG), "Final Interim Report of Neal Batson, Court-Appointed Examiner" (November 4, 2003).

   A fiduciary's duty of care entails making informed judgments. That duty encompasses both process and substance. Fulfilling due care in process relates to the decision-making method. Fulfilling due care in substance means ensuring that proposals have a rational business purpose. In Enron's case, the uneconomic, or "dirty," hedges described in Chapter 1 appeared to have had no rational business purpose. The duty of candor involves reporting material information to shareholders and other interested parties as required by law. Chapter 3 showed the degree to which Enron abrogated that fiduciary responsibility. The duty of loyalty entails not putting self-interest over the interests of the corporation and its owners. In its indictment of Andrew Fastow, the government claimed, among other things, that he had breached that duty.

3. This chapter focuses on transactions with SPEs after 1997, at least some of which represent fraudulent behavior. This is not to dismiss the unethical behavior of deal originators and developers (outlined in earlier chapters) who

overvalued commodity contracts and development projects under mark-to-market accounting, to meet their bonus targets and allow Enron to meet its earnings targets.

4. U.S. Bankruptcy Court, "Final Interim Report," discusses Enron's conflicting business goals in assessing how the company's fraud could have occurred. See pp. 83–89.

5. In other words, a restatement of Enron's November 8, 2001, balance sheet in accordance with GAAP would have required a $8 billion to $10 billion write-down of risk-management assets accounted for under mark-to-market accounting. See Stephen Cooper, Report to the U.S. Bankruptcy Court, Southern District of New York, April 22, 2002.

6. Senior research associate Perry Fagan helped pinpoint the moment when Enron drifted into a situation where only deceptive accounting and financial reporting could mask reality.

7. "Gambling to survive" is a type of wager that Professor Donato Masciandaro of Universita Luigi Boconi has referred to as "betting for resurrection." See Luigi Donato and Domato Masciandoro, "Putting the Crooks Out of Business: The Emerging Role of Integrity in Banking Supervision and Regulation: The Italian Case (1991–2001)," undated mimeo. More directly relevant to the U.S. setting is B. C. Esty, "A Case Study of Organizational Form and Risk Sharing in the Savings and Loan Industry," *Journal of Financial Economics* 44, no. 1 (1997): 57–76.

8. Bethany McLean and Peter Elkind, *The Smartest Guys in the Room: The Amazing Rise and Scandalous Fall of Enron* (New York: Portfolio, 2003), 119.

9. Ibid.

10. Robert Bryce, *Pipe Dreams* (New York: Public Affairs, 2002), 134.

11. McLean and Elkind, *The Smartest Guys in the Room,* p. 119.

12. Loren Fox, *Enron: The Rise and Fall* (Hoboken, N.J.: John Wiley & Sons, 2003), 103.

13. Interview with the author, June 10, 2003.

14. The head count of Skillingites is from McLean and Elkind, *The Smartest Guys in the Room,* p. 105.

15. In June 1997 Enron paid Phillips Petroleum, owner of the so-called J-Block gas field in the North Sea, $440 million as part of a settlement that would allow Enron to exit a contract committing Enron to pay twice the price of gas available on the open market.

16. Bryce, *Pipe Dreams,* p. 135.

17. In late October 2001 the Chewco transaction was reviewed by both Enron and Andersen accountants and judged to be an SPE without sufficient outside equity and therefore improperly deconsolidated from Enron's financial statements. As a result Enron announced in November that it would restate its prior period financial statements from 1997 through 2001. This retrospective restatement had a huge impact. Enron's reported net income for the period was reduced by more than $400 million and the company's reported debt for these years was increased from $561 million (1998) to $711 million (1997),

depending on the year. See the Powers report: William C. Powers Jr., Raymond S. Troubh, and Herbert S. Winokur Jr., Report of Investigation by the Special Investigative Committee of the Board of Directors of Enron Corp. (2002), available at www.enron.com, p. 42.

18. Ibid., p. 58; and Fox, *Enron*, p. 127.

19. According to the Powers report (p. 59) (and based on working papers from Arthur Andersen), Enron recorded in the first quarter of 2000 as much as $126 million gains from in-stock appreciation on Enron shares held by JEDI.

20. Enron Corp., Minutes of the Executive Committee of the Board of Directors, November 5, 1997, p. 1.

21. Rebecca Smith and John R. Emshwiller, *24 Days* (New York: HarperBusiness, 2003), 311, citing November 7, 1977 board minutes.

22. According to the Powers report, "There is little doubt that Kopper (who signed all of the agreements with Barclays and the December 30 letter) was aware of the relevant facts. The evidence also indicates that Enron Treasurer Ben Glisan, who had principal responsibility for Enron's accounting for the transaction, attended meetings at which the details of the reserve accounts and the cash collateral were discussed. If Glisan knew about the cash collateral in the reserve accounts at closing, it is implausible that he (or any other knowledgeable accountant) would have concluded that Chewco met the 3% standard."

The report concluded: "Largely because Kopper, Glisan, and Andersen declined to speak with us on this subject, we have been unable to determine why the parties utilized a financing structure for Chewco that plainly did not satisfy the SPE non-consolidation requirements. Enron had every incentive to ensure that Chewco was properly capitalized. It is reasonable to assume that Enron employees, if motivated to protect only Enron's interests, would have taken the necessary steps to ensure that Chewco had sufficient outside equity. We do not know whether Chewco's failure to qualify resulted from bad judgment or carelessness on the part of Enron employees or Andersen, or whether it was caused by Kopper or other Enron employees putting their own interests ahead of their obligations to Enron." See pp. 52–54.

23. Fastow told Enron employees that Skilling, then Enron's president and chief operating officer, had approved his participation in Chewco as long as it would not have to be disclosed in Enron's proxy statement. Skilling told the Powers committee that he recalled Fastow's reporting that the Chewco outside investors were members of Fastow's wife's family, and that Skilling told Fastow he did not think that was a good idea. The Powers report, pp. 43–44 and n7.

24. U.S. District Court, Southern District of Texas, Houston Division, Complaint. *United States of America v. Andrew S. Fastow et al.*, Cr. No. H-02-0665.

25. See the Powers report, pp. 68–76, and McLean and Elkind, *The Smartest Guys in the Room*, pp. 189–197, for a more detailed description of the creation and conduct of the LJM1 partnership.

26. According to one unidentified Enron source reported in Smith and Emshwiller, *24 Days*, senior Enron officials asked Fastow to head up the partnership. See

p. 43. In this role, Fastow reportedly received an annual fee equal to 2 percent of the money he raised. Having raised $300 million to $400 million by May 2000 for LJM2, his partnership fee could have run as high as $8 million a year. See p. 51. These fees were in addition to his profit participation.

27. Enron's Code of Ethics allowed a senior officer to participate in a transaction in which he has a conflict of interest with Enron if the office of the chairman determined that this would not adversely affect the interests of the company.

28. Quoted from the LJM2 placement memo, as reported in McLean and Elkind, *The Smartest Guys in the Room,* p. 198. The LJM2 team included Fastow and his two deputies from Enron Global Finance, Michael Kopper and Ben Glisan.

29. Ibid., p. 199.

30. Enron's appetite for international power projects and acquisitions was fed by its success in 1997 in winning an exemption from the Investment Company Act of 1940. The provisions of this act would have prevented the company's foreign operations from shifting debt to off-balance-sheet partnerships, and barred executives from investing in partnerships affiliated with Enron. The exemption cleared the path for the company to both expand overseas and make greater use of the special partnerships that eventually caused it so much turmoil. Although lawyers who approved the exemption viewed it "as narrow because it applied only to the foreign operations of Enron and some of its subsidiaries," Enron pushed the limits of the ruling. As noted in Chapter 1, a former SEC official characterized the ruling as giving Enron "carte blanche to go all over the world and set up subsidiaries and affiliated entities that would have been prohibited under the act." See Stephen Labaton, "Enron's Collapse: Regulations," *New York Times* (January 23, 2002).

31. Skilling actually began using SPEs earlier than 1997. When he set up Enron Capital & Trade in the early 1990s, COO Kinder told Skilling that he wanted ECT to finance itself, and that any capital Enron put into ECT would count against the phantom equity (or capital stake in the division) held by top executives. These provisions spurred Skilling to search for ways to raise capital that would allow ECT to grow quickly without drawing on the Enron bank account and diluting his capital stake. He created his first SPE, called Cactus, in 1991. See McLean and Elkind, *The Smartest Guys in the Room,* pp. 66–67.

32. Enron Corp., PowerPoint Bank Presentation, Waldorf Astoria, New York, November 19, 2001; cited in U.S. Bankruptcy Court, Southern District of New York, *In re Enron Corp.,* Chapter 11, Case No. 01–16034 (AJG), "Second Interim Report of Neal Batson, Court-Appointed Examiner" (January 21, 2003), p. 11.

33. Enron put total off-balance-sheet obligations at the end of 1997 at $1.43 billion, and total obligations (which included debt on the balance sheet) at $7.68 billion. According to the bankruptcy examiner, a portion of Enron's off-balance-sheet debt might have appeared on the balance sheet classified as something other than debt. See Enron Rating Agency Presentation for Moody's Investors Services, February 17, 1998, as cited in Appendix D to U.S. Bankruptcy Court, "Second Interim Report," p. 82.

34. Ibid., p. 78.

35. Enron was sometimes quite open about using off-balance-sheet partnerships to hide debt and manage earnings. For example, at the annual LJM partnership meeting on October 26, 2000, Fastow (then Enron CFO and managing partner of LJM) explained that new energy and communications projects typically do not generate earnings or cash flow in the first one to three years. Such investments therefore would improve current earnings and credit ratios. The solution, Fastow told the limited partners, was to move merchant investments off the books and create structures to accelerate earnings and cash flows, presumably by applying mark-to-market accounting. Fastow added that in accommodating Enron's needs, the LJM partnership offered its investors unusual profit opportunities. See U.S. Senate, Permanent Subcommittee on Investigations, Committee on Governmental Affairs, "LJM Investments Annual Partnership Meeting Presentation, October 26, 2000," Exhibit #25, presented May 7, 2002.

36. SPEs were not the only means Enron used to cover up its increasingly troubled financial performance. A former Enron executive who was especially critical of leadership told me that the company merged the trading books of the commodities-trading operation (Enron Energy Services) and wholesale operation (Enron Wholesale Services) in 2000 not to boost efficiency, as advertised internally, but to cover up a $1 billion shortfall in operating cash from EES trading losses. (I could not verify this.) I was also told that some of the gains from California energy trades were reserved and later released in 2001, further misrepresenting Enron's true operating results.

37. Ironically, 1997 was the year when Skilling tried to strengthen Enron's risk management. In the wake of the J-Block loss (see note 15 above), he assembled a collection of financial and risk-assessment analysts, business managers, and lawyers into the independent group known as Risk Assessment and Control. RAC was responsible for analyzing the financial and nonfinancial risks of all significant contracts, projects, and businesses.

38. Lisa Ordonez Schweitzer and Bambi Douma, "The Dark Side of Goal Setting: The Role of Goals in Motivating Unethical Decision-Making," *Academy of Management Proceedings* (2002): MOC: B1–B6.

5. The Directors' Failure

1. Excerpt from "What Should a CEO Expect from the Board of Directors?" by Kenneth Lay. Lay contributed one of several chapters in a corporate governance booklet distributed at the November 2002 luncheon at which Houston-area businessman Jack Blanton received the Ethical Leadership in Action Award from the Center for Business Ethics at St. Thomas University. The statement appears to have originated in a speech delivered in the mid-1990s. See Eric Berger, "Lay Pens Chapters on Ethics," *Houston Chronicle* (November 11, 2002), 21.

2. I would like to acknowledge the valuable assistance of research associate Jason Mahon in drafting significant sections of this chapter. His close reading and careful summary of the record related to legally mandated fiduciary duties of Enron's directors were important contributions, as was his research assistance and role as a discussion partner.

3. Enron shareholders and former employees did, however, file civil suits against the company's directors seeking compensation for alleged violations of (1) Section 10(b) of the Securities Exchange Act of 1934 (related to material misrepresentation and omission of facts about the company's financial performance) and (2) the federal Employee Retirement Income Security Act (ERISA). It is interesting that the plaintiffs in the Section 10(b) suit did not assert claims alleging violations of fiduciary duty under state law, even though the facts that would need to be proved to support the stated claims of Enron shareholders and employees would also offer support to claims of a fiduciary breach. For example, if a plaintiff could establish sufficient facts to satisfy a material misrepresentation claim, that same information would also likely support a claim for a breach of the fiduciary duty of candor. This legal possibility is unlikely to be pursued, however, since the judge overseeing the shareholder's class action against Enron's directors threw out all Section 10(b) claims.

As to the ERISA claims, former Enron employees alleged breaches of fiduciary duty based on the directors' role in overseeing Enron's retirement plans, but these are specific to that statute and are distinguishable from the general fiduciary duties owed under state law. The employees alleged that Enron's directors failed to appoint and monitor retirement plan fiduciaries, and failed to disclose material facts about the company's financial condition to such fiduciaries.

4. The reports from these investigations—as well as the responses of the outside directors—must be read with care, because they naturally reflect the partisan interests of their authors. My analysis of the directors' breach draws on this large body of information, as well as many other publicly accessible sources.

The Powers report, produced by the Special Investigative Committee of the Board of Directors of Enron Corporation several months after Enron's collapse and bankruptcy filing, details many of the intricate transactions the company used to buoy its financial statements. Herbert S. Winokur Jr., the only member of the investigative committee to serve on Enron's board during the time frame in question, did not participate in the portion of the report that evaluates the performance of the directors. See William C. Powers Jr., Raymond S. Troubh, and Herbert S. Winokur Jr., *Report of Investigation by the Special Investigative Committee of the Board of Directors of Enron Corp.* (2002), available at www.enron.com, p. 31, n3 (hereafter the Powers report).

One of two Senate committees that examined the board's responsibility for Enron's demise, reported the findings of hearings held in May 2002 in: U.S. Senate, Permanent Subcommittee on Investigations, Committee on Governmental Affairs, "The Role of the Board of Directors in Enron's Collapse," 107th Cong., S. Rep. No. 107-70 (2002) (hereafter Senate Board Report). The subcommittee's report reaches a number of insightful conclusions that, unfortunately, are tainted by the shock, anger, and political posturing with which Enron's bankruptcy was met. A more straightforward, comprehensive report issued one year later by the Senate's Committee on Finance reviewed directors' compensation and incentive plans. See U.S. Senate, Joint Committee on Taxation, "Report of Investigation of Enron and Related Entities Regarding Federal Tax and Compensation Issues, and Policy Recommendations," 108th Cong., JCS-3-03 (2003) (hereafter Taxation Report).

Finally, Neal Batson, the examiner appointed by the New York Bankruptcy Court, produced a four-volume report (three interim reports and one final report) that included many technical financial and accounting appendices. The final 1,117-page volume included a detailed appendix specifically dealing with the behavior of Enron's board of directors. See U.S. Bankruptcy Court, Southern District of New York, *In re Enron Corp.*, Chapter 11, Case No. 01–16034 (AJG), "First Interim Report of Neal Batson, Court-Appointed Examiner"(Bankr. S.D.N.Y. September 21, 2002), "Second Interim Report of Neal Batson Court-Appointed Examiner" (January 21, 2003), "Third Interim Report of Neal Batson, Court-Appointed Examiner" (June 30, 2003), "Final Report of Neal Batson, Court-Appointed Examiner" (November 4, 2003). All are available at www .enron.com. These reports, which summarized a lengthy investigation of Enron's collapse on behalf of the company's creditors and are vast in scope, are estimated to have cost more than $90 million in professional fees. See John R. Emshwiller and Mitchell Pacelle, "In His Own Defense: Enron Inquiry Worth $90 Million?" *Wall Street Journal* (March 18, 2004), C1.

The reports commissioned by the New York Bankruptcy Court and transcripts of the hearings of the Senate Investigations Subcommittee are particularly important because they include subpoenaed documents related to an array of board activities, including corporate memos, presentations, and board committee minutes. Together these documents provide a picture of what the board knew and did not know about Enron's operations, and how the board conducted its affairs. The transcripts of subcommittee hearings are among the most important sources of information because they include sworn statements from Enron directors made under pain and penalty of perjury.

5. The board's assertions are correct to a degree. Careful reading of the Senate report reveals that some of the directors' claims are based on evidence that is accurately portrayed in the report—for example, that Enron's directors "knowingly allowed Enron's use of high risk accounting practices," based partly on a note by Arthur Andersen executive David Duncan and a written statement on behalf of Tom Bauer, an Arthur Andersen partner.

More generally, Enron's directors' claimed that the board was not informed of critical information related to a variety of matters, including the Chewco, Rhythms, and Raptor transactions. See the prepared statement of Herbert S. Winokur Jr., chairman of the board's finance committee in U.S. House, Energy and Commerce Committee, Oversight and Investigations Subcommittee, "The

Financial Collapse of Enron," 107th Congress 124, February 7, 2002. See also U.S. Senate, Permanent Subcommittee on Investigations, Committee on Governmental Affairs, "Letter from W. Neil Eggleston, Partner, Howrey Simon Arnold & White, LLP, to The Honorable Carl Levin, Chairman, Senate Permanent Subcommittee on Investigations of the Committee on Governmental Affairs, United States Senate, and The Honorable Susan Collins, Ranking Subcommittee Minority Member, U.S. Senate," U.S. Government Printing Office, S. HRG. 107–511, August 1, 2002; and U.S. Senate, Permanent Subcommittee on Investigations, Committee on Governmental Affairs, "The Outside Directors' Response to: The Role of the Board of Directors in Enron's Collapse" U.S. Government Printing Office, S. HRG. 107–511, August 1, 2002 (hereafter the Outside Directors' Response). This response, it should be noted, followed Winokur's initial Senate testimony by six months.

Despite the February 2 testimony of Winokur and other directors (which was consistent with the subsequent Outside Directors' Response) the Senate report condemned the board for "fiduciary failures" and came close to claiming that the directors breached their fiduciary duty—albeit through a superficial analysis that was careful not to allege an actual violation.

6. The distinction between a legal standard and a legal principle is noteworthy because violation of the former results in a monetary fine, probation, or even incarceration. Violation of the latter carries no mandated penalty; instead, the offender's price is disgrace and a sullied reputation.

7. See, for example, the Business Roundtable, *Statement on Corporate Governance* (September 1997), 10; Council of Institutional Investors, *Corporate Governance Policies* (September 2002); and TIAA-CREF, *Policy Statement on Corporate Governance* (January 2004), 12. General Electric prefers that its board include about fifteen directors, "given the size and breadth of GE and the need for diversity of board views." General Electric Co., *Governance Principles* (July 22, 2004). Morgan Stanley prefers a board of between ten and twelve members. See Morgan Stanley, *Morgan Stanley Board of Directors Corporate Governance Policies* (December 9, 2003), 21.

8. See, for example, The Business Roundtable, "Statement on Corporate Governance," p. 1; American Law Institute, *Principles of Corporate Governance: Analysis and Recommendations* (St. Paul, Minn.: American Law Institute, 1994), §§ 3.05 ("Audit Committee in Large Publicly Held Corporations"), 3A.04 ("Nominating Committee in Publicly Held Corporations: Composition, Powers, and Functions"), and 3A.05 ("Compensation Committee in Large Publicly Held Corporations: Composition, Powers, and Functions"). Each calls for the respective committee to be comprised of nonemployees, including a majority with "no significant relationship with the corporation's senior executives."

9. Despite the fact that ten of Enron's nineteen directors agreed on January 6, 2005 to settle a class action claim that the board unintentionally misled shareholders in SEC filings pursuant to an underwriting of notes, no violations of

fiduciary duty were either alleged or admitted. The ten directors had sold stock during the notes underwriting.

10. Bryan A. Garner, ed., *Black's Law Dictionary, 7th ed.* (St. Paul, Minn.: West Publishing, 1999).

11. Fiduciary relationships, including the duties owed between the parties, are creatures of state law. Because no federal statute directly governs fiduciary duties (see Hillary A. Sale, "Delaware's Good Faith," *Cornell Law Review* 89 [2004]: 456, 457 n.9), when a plaintiff brings a suit against a director for breach of a fiduciary duty, the claim is governed by state law even if filed in federal court. See, for example, *Bianco v. Erkins*, 243 F.3d 599 (2d Cir. 2001); *BBS Norwalk One, Inc. v. Raccolta, Inc.*, 205 F.3d 1321 (2d Cir. 2000); *Hollis v. Hill*, 232 F.3d 460 (5th Cir. 2000).

Applying the law of the appropriate state is important because states tend to have at least slight differences in their statutory laws as well as case law. Case law precedents may be binding or persuasive, depending on the relationship between the two forums.

To help courts determine which state law to apply, state and federal courts have derived rules from statute or case law. These rules vary from state to state and circuit to circuit, but most apply the "internal affairs doctrine." Under this doctrine, claims that arise out of the internal affairs of a corporation, such as a suit against an individual in his or her capacity as a director on a corporate board, are governed by the state in which that corporation is incorporated. Enron was incorporated in Oregon, so fiduciary duty claims against its directors were subject to Oregon law, specifically Oregon Revised Statutes § 60.357(1) (2005). ("A director shall discharge the duties of a director, including the duties as a member of a committee, in good faith, with the care an ordinarily prudent person in a like position would exercise under similar circumstances and in a manner the director reasonably believes to be in the best interests of the corporation.")

When an area of state law is not well developed, the courts may consider opinions from other jurisdictions. Such is the case here. Oregon courts do not have a particularly thorough history of analyzing corporate law. Delaware, on the other hand, is widely regarded as having the most complete body of corporate law. The courts of Oregon and other jurisdictions often look to Delaware's interpretations in reaching opinions on their own corporate statutes.

12. *Malone v. Brincat*, 722 A.2d 5, 10 (Del. 1998). ("Although the fiduciary duty of a Delaware director is unremitting, the exact course of conduct that must be chartered to properly discharge that responsibility will change in the specific context of the action the director is taking with regard to either the corporation or its shareholders.")

13. See Oregon Revised Statutes §60.357 (2005). This is one area in which the laws of Oregon and Delaware diverge. Whereas the Oregon statute and case law articulate an ordinary negligence standard of care (see *Devlin v. Moore*, 130 P.35, 45 [Or. 1913]), the Supreme Court of Delaware has set a "gross

negligence" standard for its jurisdiction (see *Aronson v. Lewis*, 473 A.2d 805, 812 [Del. 1984]). Ordinary negligence is a higher standard—that is, easier to violate. Gross negligence involves recklessness, or the conscious disregard of a danger, whereas ordinary negligence involves the objective failure to act as a prudent person would under the circumstances. The latter does not require a showing that the actor was subjectively aware of the given risk.

14. See *Gagliardi v. TriFoods Int'l Inc.*, 683 A.2d 1049, 1051 n.2 (Del. Ch. 1996); see also *Miller v. AT&T*, 507 F.2d 759, 762–763 (3d Cir. 1974).

15. *Klinicki v. Lundgren*, 695 P.2d 906, 910 (Or. 1985).

16. See *Aronson v. Lewis*, at 812 ("directors have a duty to inform themselves, prior to making a business decision, of all material information reasonably available to them").

17. *West Point-Pepperell, Inc. v. J.P. Stevens & Co.*, 542 A.2d 770, 780 (Del. Ch. 1988). See also *Sinclair Oil Corp. v. Levien*, 280 A.2d 717, 720 (Del. 1971) ("A board of directors enjoys a presumption of sound business judgment, and its decisions will not be disturbed if they can be attributed to any rational business purpose").

18. *Malone v. Brincat.*

19. See *Devlin v. Moore*, at 45; see also *Hoye v. Meek*, 795 F.2d 893, 896 (10th Cir. 1986) and *In re Caremark Int'l Inc.*, 698 A.2d 959, 971 (Del. Ch. 1996).

20. See *In re Caremark*, at 969–970, and *Graham v. Allis-Chalmers*, 188 A.2d 125, 130 (Del. 1963).

21. *Zidell v. Zidell*, 560 P.2d 1086, 1089 (Or. 1977).

22. R. Franklin Balotti and Joseph Hinsey IV, "Directors Care, Conduct, and Liability: The Model Business Corporation Act Solutions," *The Business Lawyer* 56, no. 1 (November 2000): 35–58; and conversations with Professor Hinsey.

23. Historically, courts have hesitated to base liability solely on a breach of the fiduciary duty of good faith. In recent years, however, the judiciary, including the de facto jurisdictional standard bearer for corporate law—Delaware—has sustained alleged violations based only on the duty of good faith. Whether attributed to judicial activism or the natural progression of case law, the duty of good faith has become a useful statutory weapon for aggrieved shareholders. See, for example, *In re Walt Disney Co. Derivative Litigation, Consolidated C.A. No. 15452*, 2005 Del. Ch. LEXIS 113, 191 n.487. "It is precisely in this context—an imperial CEO or controlling shareholder with a supine or passive board—that the concept of good faith may prove highly meaningful. The fiduciary duties of care and loyalty, as traditionally defined, may not be aggressive enough to protect shareholder interests when the board is well advised, is not legally beholden to the management or a controlling shareholder and when the board does not suffer from other disabling conflicts of interest, such as a patently self-dealing transaction. Good faith may serve to fill this gap and ensure that the persons entrusted *by shareholders* to govern Delaware corporations do so with an honesty of purpose and with an understanding of whose interests they are there to protect." Ibid., at 191 n487 (emphasis in original).

For more analysis of claims based on breaches of good faith see Sale, "Delaware's Good Faith."

24. Although directors are agents of the owners, according to the property model of the firm, directors' duties are technically owed directly to the corporation and indirectly to the shareholders. However, a corporation is nothing more than a paper entity, so shareholders are the effective recipients of any duties or benefits that flow to the corporation. For example, in derivative suits, shareholders are bringing suit on behalf of the corporation, because the institutional representatives—the board of directors—are arguably not reliable and fail to perform their duties. When derivative suits are successful, the benefits generally flow directly to the corporation, not the shareholders. The shareholders, as owners of stock, benefit indirectly through increases in share value. See *Ross v. Bernhard*, 396 U.S. 531, 534 (1970).

25. American Bar Association, Section of Business Law, Committee on Corporate Laws, "Revised Model Business Corporation Act" (RMBCA) (2002) § 8.30 cmt. 2 (regarding §8.30(b)).

26. A more complete legal analysis than the one presented here would also consider the so-called director exculpation clause. In many states, including Oregon and Delaware (Delaware being where most large U.S. companies are incorporated), corporations are free to hold directors blameless for negligent breaches of fiduciary duty. See Oregon Revised Statutes § 60.047(2)(d). This statute covers both ordinary negligence and gross negligence (reckless behavior). The difference between negligent, reckless, and intentional behavior is most easily described by analogy. A driver who hits a pedestrian while fiddling with the radio has acted negligently in not watching the road. Drivers are expected to take care to avoid hitting pedestrians, and are liable for the products of their negligent actions. A driver who strikes a pedestrian while driving on the sidewalk for fun has acted recklessly. The driver knew that driving on the sidewalk involved a high risk of causing bodily harm to pedestrians, but did so anyway. The driver did not intend to injure anyone, but disregarded the higher probability that damage would be done. If the driver steered onto the sidewalk for the purpose of striking the pedestrian, the act was intentional. Causing bodily harm to the pedestrian was the goal of the action, and that goal was achieved.

  Exculpation provisions do not protect directors from liability based on acts that they know contravene corporate interests. Because Enron provided its directors with such a clause, they would face legal liability only if their actions can be shown to breach the good faith duty. The clause is contained in § A, Article VII of Enron's Articles of Incorporation.

27. See, for example, the Conference Board, *Commission on Public Trust & Private Enterprise: Findings and Recommendations* (January 9, 2003), 20. ("In fulfilling its oversight function, boards must monitor management's operating performance as well as ethical and legal compliance. In approving strategies, boards need to understand, among other things, the corporation's capital allocation, debt levels, risks and vulnerabilities, compensation strategy, and growth opportunities.

Importantly, they must engage management on the central issues facing the company and have a firm grasp of the tradeoffs that lie at the heart of a corporate enterprise.")

28. For a detailed definition of decision control, see Michael C. Jensen, *Foundations of Organizational Strategy* (Cambridge: Harvard University Press, 1998), 175–198; originally published as Eugene F. Fama and Michael C. Jensen, "Separation of Ownership and Control," *Journal of Law and Economics* 26 (June 1983).

29. These tasks—which Robert Simons calls "diagnostic controls"—are central to corporate control in settings where significant decision rights over the use of resources have been delegated to operating managers. See Robert Simons, "Control in an Age of Empowerment," *Harvard Business Review* (March-April 1995): 80–88.

30. *In re Walt Disney Co. Derivative Litigation, Consolidated C.A. No. 15452,* 2005 Del. Ch. LEXIS 113. One of the most well-publicized fiduciary cases in recent years pitted Walt Disney stockholders against the company's directors. The plaintiffs alleged that in the process of hiring Michael Ovitz as president and firing him less than two years later, the defendants breached their fiduciary duties of care and good faith. The plaintiffs contended that the board did not spend enough time reviewing relevant information or discussing the details before validating CEO Michael Eisner's decision to hire Ovitz. Furthermore, they argued that the lack of deliberation constituted a failure to act in the best interests of the corporation. Chandler held that while the board's performance fell short of corporate governance ideals, it was not so lacking as to violate duties owed shareholders by the directors as fiduciaries of the corporation. Ibid., at 3.

Of the governance shortcomings he found, Chandler took particular umbrage with Eisner's control over the Disney empire, commenting: "Eisner . . . enthroned himself as the omnipotent and infallible monarch of his personal Magic Kingdom" (Ibid., at 199). Chandler cited the Disney CEO as a source of the board's problems: "By virtue of his Machiavellian (and imperial) nature as CEO, and his control over Ovitz's hiring in particular, Eisner to a large extent is responsible for the failings in process that infected and handicapped the board's decision-making abilities. Eisner stacked his (and I intentionally write 'his' as opposed to 'the Company's') board of directors with friends and other acquaintances who, though not necessarily beholden to him in a legal sense, were certainly more willing to accede to his wishes and support him unconditionally than truly independent directors" (ibid., at 191).

The facts from the Disney case are comparable to those of the Enron situation in some respects. In both cases, charismatic executives dominated the boardroom (Disney's Eisner and Enron's Lay and Skilling). These executives controlled board membership (by selection, and in some cases ejection), resulting in stables of directors whose independence was compromised because they hesitated to challenge management. These "sycophantic tendencies" hampered the board's ability to fully consider information before making decisions (ibid., at 191 n.488).

31. For a complete description of the entities and financial transactions involved in the Rhythms hedge, see Annex 2 to Appendix L to the U.S. Bankruptcy Court, "Second Interim Report," pp. 5–37, and the Powers report, pp. 79–85. For a complete description of the entities and financial transactions involved in the Raptors transactions, see Annex 5 to Appendix L to the U.S. Bankruptcy Court, "Second Interim Report," pp. 3–32, and the Powers report, pp. 99–128.

  See materials for the meeting of the board's finance committee on May 1, 2000 (Project Raptor Presentation, p. 23: U.S. Senate, Permanent Subcommittee on Investigations of the Committee on Governmental Affairs, "The Role of the Board of Directors in Enron's Collapse," Hearing. S. Hrg. 107-511, 107th Congress, 2nd Session, May 7, 2002, Exhibit 28, p. 306) (hereafter Senate Hearing 107-511). Handwriting next to the second bullet point ("i.e., UBS forward position") indicates a comparison to the Rhythms hedge structure. For a complete description of the entities and financial transactions involved in the Rhythms hedge, see Annex 2 to Appendix L to the U.S. Bankruptcy Court, "Second Interim Report," pp. 5–37, and the Powers report, pp. 79–85. For a complete description of the entities and financial transactions involved in the Raptors transactions, see Annex 5 to Appendix L to the U.S. Bankruptcy Court, "Second Interim Report," pp. 3–32, and the Powers report, pp. 99–128.

32. See Annex 2 to Appendix L to the U.S. Bankruptcy Court, "Second Interim Report," p. 3 (citing Rhythms S-1, Principal Stockholders Table, and Draft Project Martin Fairness Analysis, August 13, 1999—the PWC Fairness Analysis).

33. Enron also sought a way to utilize the "embedded" value of forward contracts on its own stock with UBS AG. See the Powers report, p. 78. See also Annex 2 to Appendix L to U.S. Bankruptcy Court, "Second Interim Report," p. 4. Enron stock closed at $81.75 on June 30, 1999. At that time, Enron's forward contract with UBS obligated it to purchase its own shares at a strike price of $45.00.

34. See Appendix D to U.S. Bankruptcy Court, "Final Report," p. 107.

35. The Powers report, p. 42. Also cited in Jeffrey N. Gordon, "Governance Failures of the Enron Board and the New Information Order of Sarbanes-Oxley," *Connecticut Law Review* 35 (2003): 1125, 1133. Enron and LJM2 completed twenty-one transactions, including four Raptors hedges, between December 1999 and mid-2001. See Appendix D to U.S. Bankruptcy Court, "Final Report," p. 107.

  Only three of four transactions with the Raptor partnerships were actually presented for board approval. (Raptor III was never presented. See Outside Directors' Response, p. 21.) Raptors I, II, and IV had essentially the same structure, and, like the Rhythms transactions, were funded almost entirely by Enron. In Raptor I, for example, Enron contributed $537 million in company stock and stock contracts to its hedging partner, an SPE called Talon that was controlled by Fastow's LJM2 partnership, and served as a hedging mechanism for underperforming merchant investments that Enron wanted off its balance sheet. LJM2 put up $30 million—equivalent to the 3 percent of at-risk equity in Talon that Enron needed to deconsolidate the SPE under accounting rules(see the Powers report, p. 101). For an expanded explanation of the 3 percent rule, see Appendix B (Accounting Standards) to the U.S. Bankruptcy Court, "Second Interim Report," pp. 29–39 and Chapter 2.

In a new wrinkle, Raptor I included an unwritten agreement that LJM2 would receive $41 million before Talon began any of its hedging activities—a handsome return on LJM2's $30 million investment. Neither Talon documents nor board presentation materials indicate that this was to be a part of the deal. According to critics of the Raptor transactions, Enron all but guaranteed the deal for the LJM partnership through a put purchased from Talon: that is, Enron paid exactly $41 million for the right to put shares of its own stock to Talon at a later date (the Powers report, pp. 101–103).

Raptor III—designed to hedge Enron's considerable investment in The New Power Company (TNPC)—was different from the other Raptors in one significant respect: it was supported not by Enron but by TNPC stock, the investment the arrangement was designed to hedge. The Powers report described the hazard of this strategy this way: "If the value of TNPC stock decreased, the vehicle's obligation to Enron on the hedge would decrease in direct proportion. At the same time, its ability to pay Enron would decrease. Raptor III was thus the derivative's equivalent of doubling-down on a bet on TNPC." The Powers report, p. 114. See also Appendix D to U.S. Bankruptcy Court, "Final Report," p. 66.

36. This conclusion assumes, of course, that the directors approved the partnerships and hedging transactions in good faith. A decision is presumed to have been made in bad faith if it has no "rational business purpose"—that is, it is "so beyond the bounds of reasonable judgment that it seems essentially inexplicable on any [other] ground." See *West Point-Pepperell, Inc. v. J.P. Stevens & Co.,* at 780 and *Litwin v. Allen,* 25 N.Y.S.2d 667, 700 (N.Y. Co. Sup. Ct. 1940). ("Whichever way we look at this transaction, therefore, it was so improvident, so dangerous, so unusual and so contrary to ordinary prudent banking practice as to subject the directors who approved it to liability in a derivative stockholders' action.")

See also *In re Walt Disney Co. Derivative Litigation,* 2005 Del. Ch. LEXIS 113 (Del. Ch. 2005). In his opinion, Judge Chandler addressed the effect of the business judgment rule (2005 Del. Ch. LEXIS at 179–180). ("Plaintiffs must prove by a preponderance of the evidence that the presumption of the business judgment rule does not apply either because the directors breached their fiduciary duties, acted in bad faith or that the directors made an 'unintelligent or unadvised judgment,' by failing to inform themselves of all material information reasonably available to them before making a business decision."). He also addressed the Delaware director exculpation provision (ibid., at 168) ("[8 *Del. C.* § 102(b)(7)] prohibits recovery of monetary damages from directors for a successful shareholder claim, either direct or derivative, that is exclusively based upon establishing a violation of the duty of due care.").

Judge Chandler summarized the combined impact thusly: "Because duty of care violations are actionable only if the directors acted with gross negligence [that is, the board is required only to consider material facts which are reasonably available], and because in most instances money damages are unavailable to a plaintiff who could theoretically prove a duty of care violation, duty of care violations are rarely found." Ibid., at 162.

37. One notable example where the board was kept in the dark about investment risks and accounting shenanigans relates to Enron's investment in Mariner Energy, an oil and gas company that did deepwater exploration. Enron bought Mariner in 1996 for $185 million. Enron North America executives later revalued this highly speculative investment upward to convert these valuation increases into mark-to-market income. By the second quarter of 2001, the Mariner asset was assigned a carrying value of $376 million based on a model that was not supported by Enron's Risk Analysis and Control (RAC) group. In fact, RAC then valued Mariner at $47.3 million to $195.9 million. By the third quarter, the difference between RAC's average valuation of Mariner and that shown as its book value was nearly $230 million. (Enron eventually took a $257 million write-off on Mariner.)

Despite this enormous, undocumented write-up in value by Mariner executives, RAC's chief risk officer Rick Buy did not bring this unusual departure from established risk management accounting to the board's attention. According to interviews with knowledgeable Enron executives, Buy did not disclose many other such violations to the board. See corroborating evidence in Bethany McLean and Peter Elkind, *The Smartest Guys in the Room: The Amazing Rise and Scandalous Fall of Enron* (New York: Portfolio, 2003), 130.

38. See Enron Corp., Minutes of the Board of Directors, June 28, 1999.

39. Appendix D to U.S. Bankruptcy Court, "Final Report," pp. 59–60. See also Enron, Board Minutes, June 28, 1999, pp. 1, 13.

40. Ibid., p. 59 n.278 (citing Wakeham sworn statement).

41. Ibid., p. 59 n.278 (citing Gramm sworn statement).

42. Enron Corp., Minutes of the Finance Committee of the Board of Directors, May 1, 2000.

43. Appendix D to U.S. Bankruptcy Court, "Final Report," p. 73 (citing board minutes, May 2, 2000).

44. Enron Corp., Minutes of the Board of Directors, May 2, 2000.

45. Appendix D to U.S. Bankruptcy Court, "Final Report," p. 74 (citing executive committee minutes, June 22, 2000).

46. Enron Corp., Minutes of the Board of Directors, August 6–8, 2000, p. 28. (In presenting Raptor III, Skilling notes that the executive committee had approved Raptor II on June 22, 2000.)

47. The presentation materials for the May 1, 2000, meeting show that the board received information about Enron's likely financial commitment, as well as several risks and mitigating factors. The minutes indicate that Rick Causey informed the board that Andersen "was comfortable with the proposed

transaction," and that the project sponsored by Andrew Fastow and his Global Finance Group was approved for recommendation to the board after a discussion. Though the duration of this discussion is unclear, the board likely spent no more than ten minutes on the entire topic, including the presentation, given that the ninety-minute meeting covered ten primary topics plus at least four lesser ones.

48. If Judge Chandler's *Disney* opinion is any guide, the Enron board likely satisfied its duty of care in that it considered all reasonably available information, even though the directors do not appear to have spent much time discussing the details of the Rhythms and Raptors transactions. Enron executives did not present the transactions as imperative to the company's survival, and they were likely similar in many respects to other transaction proposals the directors had seen. See *In re Walt Disney Co. Derivative Litigation, Consolidated C.A. No. 15452,* 2005 Del. Ch. LEXIS at 212–213.

  While the board apparently spent little time considering the information on the two transactions available to them, it is not clear that the time they did spend was insignificant. Ibid., at 216. The initial presentations were part of crowded agendas, but the length of the meetings provided some opportunity for discussion. Ibid., at 215. With respect to the later Raptors transactions, any legal analysis would likely weigh the board's prior knowledge of the general structure. Ibid., at 216. In the case of the Rhythms transaction, the board knew it would be a topic of conversation and had received related materials ahead of time. Ibid., at 216–217. Because senior managers made the presentation, the directors likely understood that management supported the projects. Ibid., at 219. While other information may have been material, it is not clear that it was readily available, so the board was under no obligation to search it out. Ibid., 219–220 and 227. In sum, Enron's directors appear to have approved these transactions with the best interests of the corporation in mind, given the circumstances as they understood them. Ibid., at 223, 227.

49. Appendix D to U.S. Bankruptcy Court, "Final Report," p. 48: "Enron's Board . . . had been told about contractual and market restrictions on Enron's ability to sell or hedge the stock." See also p. 49: "[Board Secretary Rebecca C. Carter] again pointed out to the Board members that Enron was subject to a 'six month hold requirement on the stock.'" This cites a memorandum from Rebecca C. Carter, Senior Vice President, Board Communications, Enron, to Enron Board of Directors regarding weekly update, April 23, 1999, p. 1.

  For general mention of the hedging prohibition, see Annex 2 to Appendix L to U.S. Bankruptcy Court, "Second Interim Report," p. 13. See also Appendix D to U.S. Bankruptcy Court, "Final Report," p. 47 (citing letter from Gil Melman, Sr. Counsel, Enron Communications Investment Corp., to Rose Stroud, Legal Transfers Area, American Securities & Trust, Inc., March 20, 2000). See also the Powers report, p. 77: ("Enron was prohibited [by a lock-up agreement] from selling its shares before the end of 1999.").

50. On June 30, 1999, Enron and Swap Sub reached an agreement whereby Enron held put options exercisable on June 29, 2000. See Annex 2 to Appendix L to U.S. Bankruptcy Court, "Second Interim Report," pp. 12–13, citing ISDA Master Agreement between Enron and Swap Sub dated June 21, 1999. See also Confirmation between Enron and Swap Sub, June 30, 1999. (Neither document appears to have been made public.)

51. Appendix D to U.S. Bankruptcy Court, "Final Report," p. 53 n.251: ("Lay stated that the Board discussion focused more on Fastow's conflict than the economics of the transaction.") See also p. 54: ("The 'hold' restriction on the Rhythms stock, which had been mentioned to the Outside Directors in two communications prior to the Board meeting, was apparently not discussed."). See also pp. 55–58, though no specific reference is given as to what elements of the conflict issue were discussed; and the Powers report, p. 69: ("After a discussion, the Board adopted a resolution approving the proposed transaction with LJM1. The resolution ratified a determination by the Office of the Chairman that Fastow's participation in LJM1 would not adversely affect the interests of Enron." No specific details of the conversation are given.).

52. U.S. Senate, Permanent Subcommittee on Investigations, Senate Committee on Governmental Affairs, *The Role of the Board of Directors in Enron's Collapse*, S. Rep. No. 107–70 (2002), p. 28. Enron's Code of Ethics (sometimes referred to as Enron's Code of Conduct) suggests that it was the duty of the chair and CEO to determine whether officers' and employees' conflicts adversely affected the company's interests, and to approve or disapprove any waiver of the code based on that determination. In this case, the Enron board may have been asked to ratify the chair's decision, to inoculate the proponents against future complaints.

This action has been alternatively characterized as an application of the Code of Ethics and a waiver of the Code of Ethics. In a substantive sense, it makes no difference what the action is called. To determine whether an individual may do something otherwise prohibited by the Code of Ethics—that is, whether that individual should receive an exception—the determining party must apply the code, or consider the relevant criteria. For examples of applications, see the testimony of former Enron director Herbert S. Winokur Jr. before the Senate (Senate Hearing 107-511, pp. 17–18, 59–60).

For examples of references to a waiver, see the June 28, 1999, "Project LJM Board Presentation," which lists "Waiver of Code of Conduct" as the first of several "Key Elements of Transaction to be Approved" (June 28, 1999 Project LJM Board Presentation, p. 8; Exhibit #19) in Senate Hearing 107-511. See also Enron Corp., Minutes of the Finance Committee of the Board of Directors, October 11, 1999, in which Fastow "noted that [the relevant section of the Code of Ethics] would prohibit him from participating in LJM2 as managing partner due to his position as Executive Vice President and Chief Financial Officer of the Company absent appropriate reviews and waivers from the Board and a finding that such participation does not adversely affect the best interests of the Company." p. 2; Exhibit #56b to Senate Hearing 107–511). See also "LJM2 Summary" presented at that meeting, which contains a request that the Finance Committee and Board of Directors "Ratify decision of Office of the Chairman to waive Code of Conduct in order to allow A. Fastow participation in LJM2 as General Partner." (Exhibit #20, p. 271 in Senate Hearing 107-511). Mr. Winokur served as finance committee chair at that time. The board approved a Code of Ethics waiver for a third partnership, LJM3, that was never formed. See Appendix D to U.S. Bankruptcy Court, "Final Report," p. 112.

53. The Powers report, p. 166.

54. Enron Corp., Enron's Code of Ethics, July 2000, p. 57. Available at www .thesmokinggun.com/graphics/packageart/enron/enron.pdf (accessed November 27, 2007).

55. See Appendix D to U.S. Bankruptcy Court, "Final Report," p. 58 (citing internal Andersen e-mail from David B. Duncan to Benjamin S. Neuhausen and copy to John E. Stewart, June 1, 1999).

56. Several directors recognized that the idea should have received greater scrutiny. Ibid., pp. 55–56 (citing Winokur, Jaedicke, and Savage sworn statements). Some directors believed that the Rhythms transaction was to be the only deal between Enron and LJM, even though the presentation materials clearly anticipated other collaborations.

57. In his *Disney* opinion, Judge Chandler explained why directors' failure to achieve these principles did not expose them to liability. "This Court strongly encourages directors and officers to employ best practices, as those practices are understood at the time a corporate decision is taken. But Delaware law does not—indeed, the common law cannot—hold fiduciaries liable for a failure to comply with the aspirational ideal of best practices, any more than a common-law court deciding a medical malpractice dispute can impose a standard of liability based on ideal—rather than competent or standard-medical treatment practices, lest the average medical practitioner be found inevitably derelict." *In re Walt Disney Co. Derivative Litigation,* 2005 Del. Ch. LEXIS at 4–5.

58. Annex 2 (Rhythms) to Appendix L to U.S. Bankruptcy Court, "Second Interim Report," pp. 7–9, 13: ("No other party had assets at risk."). See also Annex 5, pp. 3–4, 48–49 (Raptors): ("Enron never escaped the risk of loss since it provided all of the capital with which the Raptors could pay Enron on the derivatives."). See also the Powers report, p. 97; and Chapter 2.

59. Appendix D to U.S. Bankruptcy Court, "Final Report," pp. 47, 155 (Rhythms), and p. 70 (citing finance committee meeting materials, May 1, 2000) (Raptors). See also the Powers report, pp. 157–158.

60. *U.S. v. Glisan,* Plea Agreement, No. 02-CR-665 (S.D. Tex. Sept. 10, 2003), at Ex. 1 (Glisan Statement—Count Five), available at http://news.findlaw.com/hdocs/ docs/enron/usglisan91003plea.pdf (accessed November 27, 2007).

61. The Powers report, p. 157.

62. Outside Directors' Response, p. 20.

63. Appendix D to U.S. Bankruptcy Court, "Final Report," p. 54 n.257; Or. Rev. St. § 60.397(2). See also RMBCA § 8.30 cmt. 4.

64. Outside Directors' Response, p. 9.

65. Enron Board Minutes, June 28, 1999, do not refer to Andersen.

66. Enron Finance Committee minutes, May 1, 2000, p. 3.

67. Appendix D to U.S. Bankruptcy Court, "Final Report," p. 53 (citing Gramm and Meyer sworn testimony and Lay interview). The directors apparently did not discuss the discrepancy between the investment and the expected return. In each transaction, the best result Enron could hope for was return of the assets minus the costs and fees associated with the transfers. Ibid., p. 155 (Rhythms), and p. 158 (Raptors). Under the terms of the Rhythms hedge, for example, Enron transferred $234 million in exchange for, at best, $167 million. Ibid., p. 155: ("According to the information provided to the board when it approved the Rhythms transaction, Enron gave up $234 million, and the most it could receive in return was one-half of that value plus payment under a $50 million promissory note."). In fact, Enron lost $69 million on the deal. Ibid., p. 53.

68. Ibid., p. 73 (citing board minutes, May 2, 2000), and p. 75 (citing executive committee minutes, June 22, 2000).

69. *Malone v. Brincat*, at 10.

70. According to the Delaware Supreme Court, directors should use materiality as a measuring stick when determining whether to disclose information. See *Stroud v. Grace*, 606 A.2d 75, 84 (Del. 1992). By itself, materiality is a loose standard, but the U.S. Supreme Court tightened it a bit, holding that a fact is material if there is "a substantial likelihood that the disclosure of [that] omitted fact would have been viewed by the reasonable investor as having significantly altered the 'total mix' of information made available." See *TSC Industries, Inc. v. Northway Industries, Inc.*, 426 U.S. 438, 449 (1976).

71. *Herzfeld v. Laventhol, Krekstein, Horwath & Horwath*, 378 F.Supp. 112, 121 (S.D.N.Y. 1974).

72. Disclosures include those made in proxy statements and footnotes to financial statements. For more on the disclosure review and approval process, see the Powers report, pp. 181–184.

73. The Powers report, pp. 181–183. See, for example, Enron Corp., Minutes of the Audit Committee of the Board of Directors, February 12, 2001, p. 3.

74. See Appendix D to U.S. Bankruptcy Court, "Final Report," p. 82 (citing memorandum from Lowry A. Crook, Wilmer Cutler, to Enron Files, regarding interview of Gary Peng, January 19, 2002). ("After Peng (the Director of Financial Reporting) prepared the draft 10-Q or 10-K, he distributed it for comments to approximately 50 people. . . . A small group were required to sign off on the 10-Qs and 10-Ks before release. These included the Chief Accounting Officer (Rick Causey), the Legal Department, Jeff Skilling, and, under new disclosure rules, Enron's Board.") See also the Powers report, p. 182: ("Causey signed the Forms 10-Q and 10-K as the Chief Accounting Officer. All of the Directors and Fastow signed the 10-Ks as well.").

75. The Powers report, p. 187. Enron's outside directors seem to have misconstrued their duty as requiring them to simply make the reader aware of the company's state of affairs. The directors pointed out that "many transactions cited by the [Senate] Report . . . were disclosed in Enron's public filings with the SEC." Outside Directors' Response, p. 23. However, the cited disclosures do not explain the transactions, despite their clear importance to the corporation's overall well-being. See also the Powers report, p. 197, and Senate Board Report, p. 51. For additional examples, see the Powers report, pp. 192, 199.

76. Enron's outside directors contend that the company's (purportedly) independent auditor and its outside legal counsel repeatedly assured them that the disclosures of Enron's off-balance-sheet transactions were adequate under GAAP and SEC rules. See Outside Directors' Response, pp. 23–24. However, case law requires more. See *Schlossberg v. First Artists Production Co.*, No. 6670, 1986 WL 15143, 15 (Del. Ch. December 17, 1986): ("It may be that in certain circumstances, financial information stated in accordance with generally accepted accounting principles would have to be explained or supplemented in order to satisfy the standard of complete candor."). See also *Lynch v. Vickers Energy Corp.*, 383 A.2d 278, 281 (Del. 1977): (In the context of explaining a majority shareholder tender offer, "completeness, not adequacy, is both the norm and the mandate under the present circumstances."). See also *U. S. v. Simon*, 425 F.2d 796 (2d Cir. 1969): (in the context of fraud, GAAP compliance is merely persuasive evidence that financial statements are not materially false or misleading, not conclusive).

77. For example, Enron's 10-K for 1999 includes the statement: "Enron Management believes that the terms of the transactions with related parties are representative of terms that would be negotiated with unrelated third parties." Enron Corp., 10-K Filing to the SEC, December 31, 1999, p. 106, available from Thomson Research, http://research.thomsonib.com (accessed November 27, 2007).

78. See Financial Accounting Standards Board, "Statement of Financial Accounting Standards No. 57: Related Party Disclosures," (Norwalk, Conn.: Financial Accounting Standards Board, 1982), § 3. ("Transactions involving related parties cannot be presumed to be carried out on an arm's-length-basis, as the requisite conditions of competitive, free-market dealings may not exist. Representations about transactions with related parties, if made, shall not imply that the related-party transactions were consummated on terms equivalent to those that prevail in arm's-length transactions unless such representations can be substantiated.")

79. Appendix D to U.S. Bankruptcy Court, "Final Report," p. 48 (references made in weekly board updates to market restrictions on Enron's ability to hedge the Rhythms investment).

80. Or. Rev. Stat. §60.301(2). ("All corporate powers shall be exercised by or under the authority of, and the business and affairs of the corporation

managed under the direction of, the board of directors, subject to any limitation set forth in the articles of incorporation or in an agreement authorized by ORS 60.265.") See also RMBCA § 8.01 and official comments.

81. See *Hoye v. Meek,* at 896 (bank president liable for duty to monitor violation because he delegated all responsibilities, and did not keep informed about bank's investments).

82. *In re Caremark,* at 971 ("In my opinion only a sustained or systematic failure of the board to exercise oversight—such as an utter failure to attempt to assure reasonable information and reporting systems exist—will establish the lack of good faith that is a necessary condition of liability.").

83. *Francis v. United Jersey Bank,* 432 A.2d 814, 822 (N.J. Sup. Ct. 1981).

84. Revised Model Business Corporation Act (RMBCA), § 8.30 cmt. 2.

85. Appendix D to U.S. Bankruptcy Court, "Final Report," pp. 37–38 (citing sworn statements of Belfer, Chan, Duncan, Foy, Gramm, LeMaistre, Meyer, Savage, Wakeham, and Winokur).

86. Ibid., p. 37 (citing sworn statements of Gramm, Meyer, LeMaistre, Savage, Chan, Willison, and Blake).

87. Ibid., p. 37 n. 182 (citing Gramm sworn statement: "I would say that the finance committee would have up to a foot of documents, sometimes even more, because I wouldn't necessarily see everything that they got beforehand that they read while they were at home. . . . The audit committee got a substantial amount of, I would say, several inches of documents.").

88. Ibid., p. 37 n.183 (citing sworn statements of LeMaistre, Savage, Meyer, Chan, Periera, and Duncan).

89. Ibid., p. 36 n.179. These findings by the bankruptcy examiner appear to be based on information and documents collected during his investigation that are not available to the public.

90. Ibid., p. 87. Complete verification of these calculations by the bankruptcy examiner is not possible, as the underlying data are in documents not made available to the public.

91. Appendix D to U.S. Bankruptcy Court, "Final Report," p. 88 (citing meeting materials from the Enron nominating committee, February 12, 2001; part of 2001 board assessment). Also see p. 37 n.183 (citing Savage sworn statement: "I thought the board was a very strong board, very intelligent, asked a lot of questions. And we met frequently. So I didn't have any concerns about the board or the board structure or the board practices.").

92. Appendix D to U.S. Bankruptcy Court, "Final Report," p. 57 (citing board minutes of June 28, 1999, pp. 6–8). Although an excerpt from these minutes is included as Exhibit 56(a) to the Senate hearing on the role of the board of directors, the pages cited by the bankruptcy examiner are not yet available to the public. See Senate Hearing 107-511, p. 432.

93. Enron Corp., Minutes of the Board of Directors, October 11–12, 1999. pp. 17–18.

94. Finance Committee minutes, October 11, 1999, pp. 1–2.

95. This director was more concerned about the liability exposure Fastow was assuming than about any risk to Enron. Appendix D to U.S. Bankruptcy Court, "Final Report," p. 109 (citing Foy sworn statement).

96. Enron Corp., Minutes of the Finance Committee of the Board of Directors, October 6, 2000, p. 2.

97. Attachment A (Biographies of Outside Directors) to Appendix D to U.S. Bankruptcy Court, "Final Report," p. 2 (citing Blake sworn statement) and p. 16 (citing Winokur sworn statement of November 20, 2002).

98. Enron Finance Committee minutes, October 6, 2000, pp. 2–3.

99. Ibid., p. 2.

100. Enron Audit Committee minutes, February 12, 2001, p. 3.

101. Enron Finance Committee minutes, February 12, 2001, p. 5.

102. Appendix D to U.S. Bankruptcy Court, "Final Report," pp. 112–113 (citing e-mail from Jordan Mintz to Ron Baker, "the 2/12/01 Mintz E-mail").

103. Enron Corp., Minutes of the Audit Committee of the Board of Directors, February 7, 2000, p. 4; Enron Audit Committee minutes, February 12, 2001, pp. 2–3; Enron Finance Committee minutes, October 11, 1999, p. 2; Enron Finance Committee minutes, October 6, 2000, pp. 2–3. See also Appendix D to U.S. Bankruptcy Court, "Final Report," pp. 109–110 (citing audit committee minutes of February 7, 2000, and Chan sworn statement); and pp. 112–113 (citing audit committee minutes of February 12, 2001, finance committee minutes of February 12, 2001, and e-mails from Jordan Mintz to Enron executives).

104. Enron Finance Committee minutes, October 6, 2000, p. 2; U.S. House, Energy and Commerce Committee, Oversight and Investigations Subcommittee, "The Financial Collapse of Enron," 107th Cong. 124 (February 7, 2002) (hereafter HEC Hearing Transcript).

105. See Enron Finance Committee minutes, October 6, 2000, and HEC Hearing Transcript, pp. 125–126, 129.

106. Appendix D to U.S. Bankruptcy Court, "Final Report," p. 142 (citing Mintz and Wilmer Cutler interview, January 4, 2002).

107. U.S. Department of Justice, Enron Trial Exhibits and Releases, Exhibit 3586, available at www.usdoj.gov/enron/exhibit/04-06/BBC-0001/OCR/EXH047 -00086.TXT accessed January 5, 2008.

108. Ibid., p. 142.

109. Ibid., pp. 146–147 (citing Lay interview). See also the Powers report, p. 164.

110. Ibid., p. 57 (citing board minutes, June 28, 1999).

111. Ibid., p. 116 (citing Duncan and LeMaistre sworn statements); and p. 118 (citing Richard N. Foster, McKinsey consultant, sworn statement). Section 16(a) of the Securities Exchange Act of 1934 requires executive officers and directors, as well as persons who own more than 10 percent of a registered class of the corporation's equity securities, to file reports of ownership and changes in ownership with the SEC and the stock exchange on which the corporation is registered. Foster, a McKinsey executive present at many Enron board meetings in an advisory role, testified that the Enron board felt it was not proper for

the company to know how Fastow was compensated by LJM, because such knowledge could damage the arm's-length nature of the transactions.

112. See *Devlin v. Moore,* at 45 ("If nothing has come to the knowledge to awaken suspicion that something is wrong, ordinary attention to the affairs of the institution is sufficient. If, on the other hand, directors know, or by the exercise of ordinary care, should have known, any facts which would awaken suspicion and put a prudent man on his guard, then a degree of care commensurate with the evil to be avoided is required, and a want of that care makes them responsible."). See also Melvin Aron Eisenberg, ed., *Corporations and Other Business Organizations* (New York: Foundation Press, 2001), 700 (editor's note 1(f) regarding RMBCA § 8.31).

113. See *Graham v. Allis-Chalmers,* at 130. See, generally, *McCall v. Scott,* 250 F.3d 997 (6th Cir. 2001) *(McCall II).*

114. See *Devlin v. Moore,* at 45. See also Eisenberg, *Corporations,* p. 700 (editor's note 1(f) regarding RMBCA § 8.31). Under fiduciary law, the depth and scope of the required investigation depend on the perceived danger. See *Devlin v. Moore,* at 45. See also *Fitzpatrick v. FDIC,* 765 F.2d 569 (6th Cir. 1985) (director must be personally satisfied with the adequacy of the investigation). It should be noted that where a director exculpation provision is in force—as it was at Enron—directors who miss a red flag because of negligence do not violate their duty to inquire. See *McCall II,* at 1001. To establish liability, plaintiffs must show that the directors acted without good faith. See *McCall v. Scott,* 239 F.3d 808 (6th Cir. 2001) (McCall I). See also *In re Abbott Laboratories Derivative Shareholder Litigation,* 325 F.3d 795, 809 (7th Cir. 2003). Directors do so if they consciously disregard red flags of which they are aware. *McCall v. Scott* 250 F.3d 997 (6th Cir. 2001) (McCall II) at 1001. See also *In re Abbott Laboratories,* at 809.

115. *McCall I,* at 819.

116. Ibid., at 819. See also *In re Abbott Laboratories,* at 809.

117. Outside Directors' Response, p. 16. ("Each and every year Arthur Andersen expressed three important opinions to the public and to Enron's Accounting Committee about Enron's financials: Enron's financials presented fairly, in all material respects, the financial condition of the company; Enron's internal controls were adequate; and Andersen had no disagreements with Enron management concerning its accounting practices.")

118. Appendix D to U.S. Bankruptcy Court, "Final Report," p. 122 (citing board minutes, December 9, 1997, and December 8, 1998; and finance committee minutes, December 13, 1999, and December 11, 2000).

119. Appendix D to U.S. Bankruptcy Court, "Final Report," p. 122 (citing finance committee minutes, December 13, 1999, May 1, 2000, August 7, 2000, and December 7, 2000).

120. Ibid., p. 162.

121. Ibid., p. 123 n. 549 (citing Skilling's SEC testimony, November 1, 2002).

122. Appendix D to U.S. Bankruptcy Court, "Final Report," p. 126 (citing Belfer's sworn statement).

123. Senate Hearing 107-511, p. 61 (testimony of Dr. Robert Jaedicke, Enron director).

124. For instance, an Enron employee told a Senate subcommittee staffer that director Norman Blake had commented that Fastow ought to get a patent on the Raptor structures to sell to other companies. His comment indicates that the board understood that Enron was at the frontier of creative accounting. Senate board report, p. 21 n.47.

125. Appendix D to U.S. Bankruptcy Court, "Final Report," p. 139 (citing Skilling, Wilmer Cutler interview, on November 27, 2001, and SEC testimony, December 5, 2001). The audit and finance committees were also told on multiple occasions that the accounting for structured transactions posed a risk because the intricate "rules always changed" (finance committee minutes, December 13, 1999, Major 2000 Finance Issues; and audit committee minutes, May 1, 2000); that Andersen's interpretations of those rules required "significant judgment" (audit committee minutes, February 7, 1999, May 1, 2000, and February 12, 2001); and that the company was heavily dependent on these types of transactions (finance committee minutes, December 13, 1999; audit committee minutes, February 12, 2001). All minutes are from Senate Hearing 107-511, various exhibits.

126. The Powers report, p. 4. See also Senate Board Report, p. 21. See also Appendix D to U.S. Bankruptcy Court, "Final Report," p. 120 (citing Winokur's sworn statement of November 21, 2002, and Lay interview).

127. For a general discussion of compliant behavior of directors towards unrestrained CEOs see Randall Morch, "Behavioral Finance in Corporate Governance—Independent Directors and Non-Executive Chairs," Harvard Institute of Economic Research, Discussion Paper No. 2037 (May 2004).

128. In his highly influential study of America's boards during the 1980s, Jay W. Lorsch observed that "directors must have enough power to influence the course of corporate direction, a power that is, at the least, slightly greater than the power of those the directors are to govern—the company's managers and the employees who report to them." Jay W. Lorsch, *Pawns or Potentates: The Reality of America's Corporate Boards* (Boston: Harvard Business School Press, 1989), 13.

129. As Lorsch pointed out in *Pawns or Potentates,* pp. 142, 146, and 152, directors' emotional attachment to what has historically been their company's primary business impedes them from changing their approach.

130. Colin B. Carter and Jay W. Lorsch, *Back to the Drawing Board* (Boston: Harvard Business School Press, 2004), 21. Carter and Lorsch suggest four causes of this state of affairs. First, boards pay too little attention to their own design, and how they will perform their job and meet their obligations. Second, board empowerment creates tension with the CEO, but boards rarely recognize or address this tension. Third, time and knowledge limit a board's ability to accomplish its job. The more complex a company becomes, the further behind the board falls. Finally, additional statutory requirements have made the job of

boards harder, but most have not changed the manner in which they conduct business. Ibid., p. 19–20. Carter and Lorsch suggest that boards spend more time determining their optimal design, rather than continuing to conduct business the way they have for the past century. Ibid., p. 58.

131. Enron's directors might have also suffered from the common tendency of corporate boards to compartmentalize and isolate the information they receive from meeting to meeting. According to Lorsch: "Directors and managers alike have trouble recognizing that a series of specific, year-to-year failures adds up to a long-term trend, and tend to view each event as independent and temporary, or cyclical. Recognizing the pattern is even harder for time-pressed directors, depending as they do on the CEO and management for information." Lorsch, *Pawns or Potentates,* p. 141.

132. In most agency relationships, in which principals (such as a corporation's shareholders) engage others (such as a corporation's elected directors and appointed managers) to perform a service, efforts to manage conflicting interests create costs. Stock-based compensation is widely considered in the U.S. context to limit these costs. See Michael C. Jensen and William H. Meckling, "Theory of the Firm: Managerial Behavior, Agency Costs, and Ownership Structure," *Journal of Financial Economics* 3, no. 4 (October 1976): 305–360.

133. For more on this phenomenon, see Michael C. Jensen, "Agency Costs of Overvalued Equity," Harvard NOM Research Paper No. 04–26, 2004, p. 4.

134. U.S. Senate, Joint Committee on Taxation, *Report of Investigation of Enron Corporation and Related Entities Regarding Federal Tax and Compensation Issues, and Policy Recommendations,* 108th Congress, (2003), 584 (hereafter Taxation Report).

135. The purpose of deferred compensation plans is usually to reduce participants' current compensation and thus their taxable income, to earn tax-free growth of deferred monies or assets, and to accumulate funds for retirement or other future objectives on a tax-favored basis.

136. Taxation Report, p. 586.

137. Ibid., p. 589.

138. Jensen, "Agency Costs of Overvalued Equity," p. 4.

139. Ibid.

140. Even Carter and Lorsch recognize that regardless of design and statutory requirements, boardroom performance rests on individuals (see *Back to the Drawing Board,* p. 164): "In reality, no one—except the directors in attendance—will ever find out whether or not the meetings are actually serving their intended purpose. The behavior of the board members cannot be controlled from outside the boardroom. The directors might meet for a few minutes or many hours. They may or may not deal with significant matters. Their leader may or may not have a deep grasp of the issues or the skill to help them reach a consensus. As important as [the suggested requirement that would record the names of presiding directors in proxy statements] is, all that it can do is give boards the opportunity to do the right thing. What actually happens behind closed doors depends upon the directors in the room."

141. Appendix D to U.S. Bankruptcy Court, "Final Report," p. 52.

142. Senate Board Report, p. 61. (Jaedicke's testimony). See also Appendix D to U.S. Bankruptcy Court, "Final Report," p. 60 (citing Blake sworn statement and Lay interview).

143. Ibid., pp. 70–71 (citing Lay interview).

144. Ibid., p. 71 (citing Winokur sworn statement).

145. Ibid., p. 71 n.333 (citing Blake sworn statement).

146. Ibid., p. 73 (citing board minutes, May 2, 2000).

147. Ibid., p. 53 (citing Gramm and Meyer sworn statements).

148. Ibid., pp. 56–57.

149. Ibid., pp. 57–58.

150. Appendix D to U.S. Bankruptcy Court, "Final Report," pp. 57–58 (citing Mendelsohn and Winokur sworn statements). See also the Powers report, p. 150.

151. Appendix D to U.S. Bankruptcy Court, "Final Report," p. 57.

152. Project LJM board presentation materials, in Senate Hearing 107-511, p. 7 ("General Partner [Fastow] will not receive any current or future (appreciated) value of ENE stock.").

153. The Powers report, p. 151.

154. Enron Finance Committee minutes, October 6, 2000, p. 3; and Appendix D to U.S. Bankruptcy Court, "Final Report," p. 116 (citing LeMaistre sworn statement).

155. Appendix D to U.S. Bankruptcy Court, "Final Report," p. 147 (citing Wilmer Cutler interview with Lay, January 16, 2002).

156. Appendix D to U.S. Bankruptcy Court, "Final Report," pp. 145–146 (citing Skilling interview with Wilmer Cutler, November 27, 2001, and December 5, 2001, SEC testimony).

157. The Powers report, p. 171.

158. Outside Directors' Response, pp. 20–22.

159. The directors' widespread lack of mastery of Enron's financial strategy was also reflected in the work of the Compensation Committee. For example, some members of the committee interviewed by the Senate's Joint Committee on Taxation were not fully aware of issues for which they were responsible and often made decisions. One former member did not know whether Enron offered nonqualified deferred compensation. Another could not remember whether the committee approved qualified retirement plans, while yet another did not know what a qualified retirement plan was. In a similar vein, former compensation committee members interviewed by the Joint Committee could not explain why Enron purchased two annuities from Lay and his wife in 2001, although they knew that an outside consultant, Towers Perrin, had issued an opinion providing justification for the transaction. Taxation Report, pp. 553 and 557.

160. Irving Janis, *Groupthink* (Boston: Houghton Mifflin, 1982). See also Marleen A. O'Connor, "The Enron Board: The Perils of Groupthink," *University of Cincinnati*

Law Review 71 (Summer 2003): 1233, for a detailed discussion of Enron's board based on theories of social psychology, including that proposed by Irving Janis.

161. Lorsch, *Pawns or Potentates*, p. 91 ("Despite an appearance of openness and candor, the reality is often different. A subtle set of unspoken norms, in fact, dictates the actual course of behavior in the boardroom. Even the ideal outward behavior of the CEO doesn't necessarily result in effective contributions from directors.").

162. Meyer reported that Lay accepted his resignation and said: "Jeff thinks you're one of a couple of directors that are too negative in your questioning and he thinks we need some folks that maybe have a background much more aligned with the trading business." U.S. Bankruptcy Court, *In re Enron Corp.*, Chapter 11, Case No. 01–16034 (AJG); Appendix D (Roles of Lay, Skilling, and Outside Directors) to U.S. Bankruptcy Court, "Final Report," p. 90, n430, citing Meyer sworn statement at 27.

163. See Scott Plous, *The Psychology of Judgment and Decision Making* (New York: McGraw-Hill, 1993); L. Babcock and G. Lowenstein, "Explaining Bargaining Impasse: The Role of Self-Serving Biases," *Journal of Economic Perspectives* (Winter 1997); and Max H. Bazerman, G. Lowenstein, and Don A. Moore, "Why Good Accountants Do Bad Audits," *Harvard Business Review* (November 2002).

164. Lorsch, *Pawns or Potentates*, p. 66 ("But dissatisfied directors are rarely openly critical"); and p. 93.

165. Ibid., p. 93 ("Since directors shouldn't openly criticize the CEO, or the CEO's positions, the accepted way of objecting is to ask penetrating questions. If other directors join in and the tone of the discussion becomes increasingly critical, the message sent is one of disapproval").

166. Ibid., p. 57.

167. Ibid., pp. 84–86.

168. See Appendix D to U.S. Bankruptcy Court, "Final Report," p. 88 n.418.

169. Ibid.

170. See biographical information for Robert K. Jaedicke and John H. Duncan, Attachment A (Biographies of Outside Directors) to Appendix D to U.S. Bankruptcy Court, "Final Report," at pp. 3, 6. See also p. 88 n418 (citing Gramm's sworn statement that she had no particular expertise in accounting or auditing).

171. See, for example, ibid., p. 37 ("In advance of each regularly scheduled meeting, Enron usually provided to each Outside Director a package containing the meeting agendas and voluminous amounts of preparatory materials, often exceeding several hundred pages in length"); n.182, citing statements by Wendy Gramm that the finance and audit committees received "several inches" or "up to a foot of documents" in advance of meetings; and pp. 98–99 ("Fastow, Glisan, and others often used misleading or unclear terms or jargon. For example, CFO Reports and Treasurer Reports used terms like 'balance sheet management' transactions and 'funds flow management transactions' to describe

SPE transactions generally, but with no explanation of the 'management' those transactions might have affected").

172. In materials of the nominating committee that were part of a board assessment from February 12, 2001, several directors anonymously indicated that the board was deficient in financial and accounting areas. Ibid., p. 89.

173. Ibid., p. 88.

174. Lorsch, *Pawns or Potentates*, p. 82. ("One basic difficulty is that directors see most problems through the eyes of the CEO, who, like a multitalented film-maker, writes the script, assigns the roles, directs the production, and has the starring role!")

175. See Appendix D to U.S. Bankruptcy Court, "Final Report," pp. 18–19 ("As a top executive officer, Lay was also active in matters involving the Enron Board, including determining what information would be presented to the Board and making certain he had a detailed understanding of that information. He presided at all Board meetings, and he developed the agendas for the Board meetings. In addition, he and Skilling held a rehearsal several days in advance of each meeting to review with the presenters the business unit presentations. According to Rebecca Carter, who served as corporate secretary from 1999 to 2001, at these review sessions, Lay and Skilling 'went through every slide, so it was pretty—fairly detailed.' Lay said that he would often make comments and suggestions on the presentations during this review.")

176. The first published report on Enron's deteriorating investment portfolio appeared in November 2000. The RAC group prepared this report during the summer of 2000 and subsequently briefed their boss, Rick Buy, along with Rick Causey, Enron's chief accounting officer. This report was not presented to the board until the February meeting. Why the substance of this report failed to move to the board more expeditiously in unknown. See Enron report, "Investment Portfolio: Lessons Learned," November 2000.

177. Lorsch, *Pawns or Potentates*, pp. 80–83, 101–102, 153.

178. Ibid., p. 13: ("The directors' only power advantage [over the CEO] is their capacity to act as a group by reaching a consensus"), and p. 95: ("When eight or ten outside directors agree on an issue, it is difficult for any but the most intransigent CEO to resist").

179. Ibid., p. 101. This is a point also developed by Irving Janis, *Groupthink*.

180. This is consistent with Lorsch's more general findings. See *Pawns or Potentates*, pp. 49 and 94.

181. Regarding their lack of financial expertise, the directors wrote anonymously that the board "need[s] more technology/risk management and finance skills;" that the "board is too large, but missing skills in technology and very sophisticated finance;" and that "another person with strong background on financial derivatives may also help." Nominating committee materials (part of 2001 board assessment), quoted in Appendix D to U.S. Bankruptcy Court, "Final Report," p. 89.

6. The Collusion of Financial Intermediaries

1. I want to acknowledge the assistance of research associate Jason Mahon in re-searching and drafting this chapter, and of Byron Morgan, an MBA student at Harvard Business School, who prepared an initial write-up of the Merrill Lynch story under my supervision.

2. Andersen's objectivity was probably compromised by the $121 million in fees it earned from Enron between 1998 and 2000. In 1999 Andersen called Enron its "largest client . . . by a wide margin," after posting $46.4 million in fees, nearly double the 1998 total. In 2001 Andersen accumulated some $50 million in fees from Enron-related work—almost a million dollars per week. Cross-pollination between Enron and Andersen working groups may have also contributed to Andersen's permissive tone with Enron. Between 1989 and 2000, Enron hired eighty-six accountants away from Andersen. It is not a stretch to conclude that together, these two factors diminished Andersen's corporate will to object to Enron's questionable choices. See U.S. Bankruptcy Court, Southern District of New York, *In re Enron Corp.*, Chapter 11, Case No. 01–16034 (AJG) "Final Report of Neal Batson, Court-Appointed Examiner" (November 4, 2003), Appendix B (Role of Andersen) p. 29 (citing numerous Andersen reports in footnote 79).

3. U.S. Bankruptcy Court, "Final Report," p. 50. Vinson & Elkins was not the only group of attorneys that abetted Enron's various schemes. Andrews & Kurth played a pivotal role in twenty-eight of Enron's FAS 140 transactions, preparing opinions attesting to the true sale, true issuance, or substantive consolidation of those transactions, in some cases with full knowledge that these representations were inaccurate. See ibid., pp. 50–51. Enron's in-house attorneys also supported its efforts to deceive the public. See ibid., pp. 51–55.

4. Ibid., p. 48. Like Andersen, Vinson & Elkins was well compensated by Enron. Between 1997 and 2001, the law firm collected more than $162 million in legal fees from Enron. See Appendix C (Role of Enron's Attorneys) to U.S. Bankruptcy Court, "Final Report," p. 21 (citing letter from John K. Villa, Williams & Connolly LLP, to Rebecca M. Lamberth, A&B, October 24, 2003, p. 1).

5. See U.S. Senate, Committee on Governmental Affairs, *The Role of the Financial Institutions in Enron's Collapse—Vol. 2: Hearing before the Permanent Subcommittee on Investigations of the Senate Committee on Governmental Affairs*, 107th Congress (2002), available from www.gpoaccess.gov, p. 271 (written testimony of Lynn Turner) (hereafter U.S. Senate, *The Role of the Financial Institutions*).

6. See Adam Levy, "The Deal Machine," *Bloomberg Markets* 11, no. 1 (January 2002): 33–34.

7. These figures were derived from information available through Thomson's SDC Platinum database.

8. Enron-related revenues, 1997–2001 (in millions): Citigroup: $188.3; CSFB: $94.1; JPMorgan Chase: $92.3; BT/Deutsche: $72.0; Merrill Lynch: $63.3;

Royal Bank of Scotland: $60.0 (1998–2001); DLJ: $47.9 (1997–2000); Barclays: $40.0; CIBC: $30.0; Toronto Dominion: $29.2.

These figures are drawn from the banks' submissions to the U.S. Senate's Permanent Subcommittee on Investigations in connection with hearings on the role of financial institutions in Enron's collapse, and from the Enron bankruptcy examiner's appendix reports on individual banks: U.S. Bankruptcy Court, "Final Report." Exact amounts vary slightly, depending on the source.

9. Mitchell Pacelle and Robin Sidel, "Citigroup Accord to End Enron Suit May Pressure Others," *Wall Street Journal* (June 13, 2005): C1; and U.S. Securities and Exchange Commission Press Release No. 2003–87, July 28, 2003, "SEC Settles Enforcement Proceedings against JPMorgan Chase and Citigroup." According to the release, the SEC intended to direct money obtained through settlements to victims of the fraud pursuant to the Fair Fund provisions of Section 308(a) of the Sarbanes-Oxley Act of 2002.

10. U.S. Securities and Exchange Commission Press Release No. 2003–32, March 17, 2003, "SEC Charges Merrill Lynch, Four Merrill Lynch Executives with Aiding and Abetting Enron Accounting Fraud."

11. *Regents of the University of California v. Credit Suisse First Boston (USA) Inc.*, F.3d (5th Cir. 2007).

12. This total is based on information from various press releases available through the SEC Web site (www.sec.gov/spotlight/enron.htm), the University of California Board of Regents Web site (www.universityofcalifornia.edu/news/enron/welcome.html), and the Enron Web site (www.enron.com/corp/pressroom/releases/2005/press_chron2005.html). In a February 15, 2002, ruling, U.S. District Court Judge Melinda Harmon designated the University of California Board of Regents as the lead plaintiff in the class-action lawsuit brought by Enron investors. In March 2007, the U.S. Court of Appeals for the 5th Circuit reversed Judge Harmon's ruling that Enron's shareholders could sue as a class or pool their resources as a group in suing the banks. In disallowing the class-action status, the appeals panel also erased the shareholders' ability to allege that Merrill Lynch & Co., Credit Suisse First Boston, and Barclay's were primary participants in a fraud that helped fuel Enron collapse. Participants in the class action suit appealed to the U.S. Supreme Court to reverse the ruling by the appeals panel.

13. For a detailed review of the Nahanni transaction, see U.S. Bankruptcy Court, Southern District of New York, *In re Enron Corp.*, Chapter 11, Case No. 01–16034 (AJG) "Second Interim Report of Neal Batson Court-Appointed Examiner" (January 21, 2003), Annex 3 (Nahanni Transaction) to Appendix I (Minority Interest Transactions).

14. See www.citigroupgcib.com/our_businesses/h_global_relationshi.jsp. The unit describes itself as providing expertise in "cash management, foreign exchange, custody, clearing, and loans, to capital markets, derivatives, and structured products."

15. See U.S. Senate, *The Role of the Financial Institutions* (Testimony of Maureen Hendricks, Senior Advisory Director, Salomon Smith Barney/Citigroup, and James F. Reilly, Managing Director, Global Power & Energy Group, Salomon Smith Barney/Citigroup).

16. U.S. Bankruptcy Court, Southern District of New York, *In re Enron Corp.,* Chapter 11, Case No. 01–16034 (AJG) "Third Interim Report of Neal Batson, Court-Appointed Examiner" (June 30, 2003), Appendix D (Citigroup), p. 1.

17. Ibid., p. 11 (citing Enron's July 2000 relationship review; and p. 37: "As early as 1993, Citigroup was aware that Enron had significant amounts of off-balance sheet obligations that were not included in Enron's publicly disclosed debt"); (citing CASH 3 approval memo, p. 15: "at year-end 1993, as Enron's total debt (not including off-balance sheet items of $2.6 billion) was at $2.805 billion").

18. Ibid., p. 109 (citing Citigroup execution approval memo from Otto Jager et al., to GCS Commitment Committee, December 14, 1999, regarding Nahanni execution approval). The memo read, in part, "The Nahanni transaction allows Enron to reduce volatility of operating cash flow (at the expense of greater volatility in its cash flows from financing activities), while avoiding an increase in leverage. In effect, Nahanni allows Enron to balance the cash impact of the merchant asset/investment accounts, providing a *bridge* to the sale of merchant assets" (emphasis added). In other words, the transaction created the appearance that Enron had achieved certain cash-flow figures through the sale of merchant assets, when in fact the source of the cash was a Citigroup loan.

19. Ibid., p. 90 (citing Citigroup exposure spreadsheet, p. 28).

20. See ibid., p. 35 (citing Sumit Mathai inter-Citigroup e-mail, November 5, 1999); and U.S. Bankruptcy Court, "Second Interim Report," p. 15.

21. U.S. Bankruptcy Court, "Third Interim Report," Appendix D (Citigroup), p. 88. The other two were Nighthawk, in 1997, and Rawhide, in 1998.

22. Ibid., pp. 88–89.

23. Ibid., p. 91.

24. Under GAAP, a corporation can opt not to consolidate an SPE on its financial statements if 3 percent of the SPE's assets is equity contributed by an independent party that remains at risk over the life of the SPE. For a more detailed explanation of the 3 percent equity test, see U.S. Bankruptcy Court, "Second Interim Report," Appendix B (Accounting Standards), pp. 29–39.

25. U.S. Securities and Exchange Commission, *In the Matter of Citigroup, Inc.,* Securities Exchange Act Release No. 48230, SEC Administrative Proceeding File No. 3–11192, "Order Instituting a Public Administrative Proceeding Pursuant to Section 21C of the Securities Exchange Act of 1934, Making Findings, and Imposing a Cease-and-Desist Order and Other Relief" (2003), available at www .sec.gov/litigation/admin/34-48230.htm, § 3(D)(1) Discussion: Enron-Related Conduct (hereafter SEC 2003 Citigroup Order). Note that the minority interest is the source of the transaction's cash flow to Enron.

26. U.S. Bankruptcy Court, "Third Interim Report," Appendix D (Citigroup), p. 88: "Citigroup developed the idea for the Minority Interest structure and considered it to be a proprietary product."

27. SEC 2003 Citigroup Order, § 3(D)(1) Discussion: Enron-Related Conduct.

28. U.S. Bankruptcy Court, "Third Interim Report," Appendix D (Citigroup), p. 34 (citing Nahanni global loans approval memo, December 7, 1999, p. 13: "In recent years, rating agencies have focused on 'managing to cash' the profits earned under MTM accounting: that is, insuring earnings were a reflection of cash received."). See also SEC 2003 Citigroup Order, § 3(A)(1) Introduction: Enron Corp.: "A mismatch between earnings and cash flow from operating activities could have raised questions about the quality and sustainment of Enron's fair-value earnings; in other words, it could have created uncertainty over whether those earnings would ultimately convert to cash."

29. U.S. Bankruptcy Court, "Third Interim Report," Appendix D(Citigroup), p. 110 (citing Jager sworn statement, pp. 37–38). See also SEC 2003 Citigroup Order, § 3(A)(1) Introduction: Enron Corp.

30. U.S. Bankruptcy Court, "Third Interim Report," Appendix D (Citigroup), p. 110 (citing sworn statements of Elliot Conway, a managing director in Citigroup's Global Capital Structuring Group, and Otto Jager, a Citigroup employee in that group). The transaction relied on T-bills with maturities of 120 days rather than cash to further obfuscate its true character. SEC 2003 Citigroup Order, at n.10, supra note 7.

31. Compare the broader definition of permissible assets in Enron's 1999 annual report with the narrower definition in the 1998 annual report. See SEC 2003 Citigroup Order, at n.10, supra note 7. The sale of the assets was executed on December 29, 1999. SEC 2003 Citigroup Order, § 3[D][1], Discussion: Enron-Related Conduct.

32. U.S. Bankruptcy Court, "Second Interim Report," Annex 3 (Nahanni) to Appendix I, p. 1 (citing Citibank Execution Approval Memorandum from Otto Jager, Alfred Griffin, and Genevieve Gervais, regarding Project Nahanni Execution Approval, December 14, 1999, pp. 6–7: "Enron is uniquely required to report the cash flows associated with its merchant activities in 'Cash Flow from Operating Activities' on its cash flow statement."). Enron's reported cash flow from operations for 1999 was $1.228 billion (citing Enron Corp., 1999 Annual Report, p. F-6). See also SEC 2003 Citigroup Order, § 3(D)(1) Discussion: Enron-Related Conduct, July 28, 2003.

33. SEC 2003 Citigroup Order, § 3(D)(1) Discussion: Enron-Related Conduct, supra note 7.

34. U.S. Bankruptcy Court, "Second Interim Report," Annex 3 (Nahanni) to Appendix I, pp. 5, 12. The letter of credit from West LB was for the benefit of Yukon, a subsidiary that was wholly owned by Enron's majority-owned subsidiary, Marengo.

35. See U.S. Bankruptcy Court, "Third Interim Report," Appendix D (Citigroup), p. 113. In a December 14, 1999, e-mail to other Citigroup employees, Conway

wrote: "Enron has requested the ability to borrow the funds raised in the structure over year end." The SEC contends that the use of the T-bill sale proceeds was part of the Nahanni plan all along. "As originally contemplated, Enron could withdraw the proceeds of the T-bill sales by borrowing from [the subsidiary] Marengo, after contributing sufficient assets to insure eventual redemption of [the minority shareholder] Nahanni's interest." See also SEC 2003 Citigroup Order, § 3(D)(1) Discussion: Enron-Related Conduct, supra note 7.

36. U.S. Bankruptcy Court, "Second Interim Report," Annex 3 (Nahanni) to Appendix I, p. 1 (citing Enron 1999 annual report, p. F-4).

37. U.S. Bankruptcy Court, "Third Interim Report," Appendix D (Citigroup), p. 90 (citing Citigroup exposure spreadsheet, p. 28).

38. U.S. Bankruptcy Court, "Second Interim Report," Annex 3 (Nahanni) to Appendix I, p. 1.

39. See SEC 2003 Citigroup Order, § 3(D)(1) Discussion: Enron-Related Conduct, supra note 7.

40. U.S. Bankruptcy Court, "Third Interim Report," Appendix D (Citigroup), pp. 114–115. In the Nighthawk transaction, Enron used a surety bond, a costless collar, and a put option to protect the 3 percent equity investment that should have been at risk. Ibid., p. 96.

41. Merrill Lynch, 1999 Annual Report, pp. 1–2.

42. U.S. Senate, *The Role of the Financial Institutions,* p. 2079, ex. 212, p. 23 of fax from Merrill's Robert Furst to Jim Brown, December 21, 1999 (Nigeria Barge Project Sell Down Transaction and Shareholder Structure) cites "allowing Enron to book a gain based on the sale of [projected] cash flows" as a reason to engage in the transaction; p. 2360, ex. 264 (Enron Risk Assessment and Control Deal Approval Sheet for Nigeria Barges Equity Sell Down): "The primary objectives of the sale are to accelerate earnings into 1999 (approximately $124.5 million) and to reduce Enron's capital exposure in Nigeria."

43. U.S. Bankruptcy Court, "Second Interim Report," Appendix I, p. 30: "As a result of [the Nigerian Barge deal], Enron booked $12 million in earnings for the fourth quarter of 1999" (citing memo from Eric Boyt, Enron, to the files, regarding Nigerian Barge Transaction—Accounting Issues, March 15, 2000, pp. 5–6); and p. 41: "Enron recorded a gain of approximately $50 million from the electricity trade transactions" (citing updated Entries to Record Unrealized PRM Value; and Kronthal sworn statement, pp. 64–65, 82).

44. See U.S. District Court, Southern District of Texas, Houston Division. Complaint. *U.S. Securities and Exchange Commission v. Merrill Lynch & Co., Inc., Daniel H. Bayly, Thomas W. Davis, Robert S. Furst, Schuyler M. Tilney,* Cr. No. H-03-0946 (hereafter *U.S. SEC v. Merrill Lynch*), paragraph 52. See also U.S. Bankruptcy Court, "Third Interim Report," Appendix I (Merrill Lynch), p. 6 n. 14. Merrill's fee for the electricity trade was originally to be $17 million, but when it unwound the transaction in June 2000, Enron refused to remit any fee at all. The parties settled on half the original figure. Merrill Lynch collected a total of $775,000 through the Nigerian barge deal: Enron paid $250,000 as an advisory

fee, and Merrill Lynch made $525,000 on its $7 million investment when LJM2 purchased Merrill Lynch's equity in the barges for $7.5 million.

45. Ibid., p. 16. Internal Merrill Lynch documents conflict regarding the exact amount Merrill received from Enron-related business in 1999, but $40 million appears to be the midpoint figure.

46. Other evidence shows that Merrill Lynch consistently considered the impact of its investment-banking decisions on its relationship with Enron, even when they were on questionable ethical ground. For example, when Fastow sought investment capital from Merrill Lynch for his LJM2 partnership, Merrill considered it in part because "Enron is an excellent client," and because Merrill saw that "Andy Fastow is in an influential position to direct business to Merrill Lynch." See U.S. Senate, *The Role of the Financial Institutions,* p. 2200, ex. 233 (Merrill Lynch interoffice memo, July 2000, Davis from Sullivan/Tilney/Furst).

47. U.S. Bankruptcy Court, "Third Interim Report," Appendix I (Merrill Lynch), p. 25 (citing Furst/Bayly memo, December 1999located at U.S. Senate, *The Role of the Financial Institutions,* p. 2064, ex. 208).

48. Ibid., p. 2059, ex. 207 (Appropriation Request Appendix, Part III Enron Overview).

49. U.S. Bankruptcy Court, "Third Interim Report," Appendix I (Merrill Lynch), p. 12 (citing Enron relationship review, January 2000).

50. Ibid., p. 16 (citing fax from James Brown to Gerard Haugh and Joseph Valenti) (the Brown/Haugh fax).

51. *U.S. SEC v. Merrill Lynch.*

52. U.S. Securities and Exchange Commission, Litigation Release No. 18038, paragraph 2, March 17, 2003 (hereafter SEC Litigation Release).

53. U.S. Senate, *The Role of the Financial Institutions,* p. 2059, ex. 207 (Merrill Lynch appropriation request cover page).

54. U.S. Bankruptcy Court, "Third Interim Report," Appendix I (Merrill Lynch), p. 24.

55. U.S. Senate, *The Role of the Financial Institutions,* p. 2,059, ex. 207 (Merrill Lynch appropriation request cover page).

56. Ibid.

57. U.S. Bankruptcy Court, "Third Interim Report," Appendix I (Merrill Lynch), pp. 26–27 (citing Brown sworn statement).

58. U.S. Senate, *The Role of the Financial Institutions,* p. 2,064, ex. 208 (Merrill Lynch interoffice memo from Robert Furst to Dan Bayly et al., p. 2: "The following transaction structure has been developed to allow Purchaser to purchase 90% of the projected after tax cash flow to be generated over three (3) years by the 90 MW Nigeria Barge Project").

59. Merrill Lynch invested the $7 million through an SPE, Ebarge, LLC, which it had created specifically for this transaction. The remaining $21 million was loaned to Merrill Lynch by Enron through Enron Barge Holding, Ltd. U.S. Bankruptcy Court, "Third Interim Report," Appendix I (Merrill Lynch), p. 31 (citing December 29, 1999, E-Barge, LLC Share Purchase Agreement, pp. 1, 4–5).

60. U.S. Senate, *The Role of the Financial Institutions,* p. 2,164, ex. 222 (Share Purchase Agreement between Merrill Lynch and LJM2).

61. Ibid., p. 2,173, ex. 223 (e-mail from Joseph Valenti to Kira Toone-Meertens, January 17, 2002).

62. Ibid., p. 2,071, ex. 210 (draft of Merrill Lynch agreement letter to Jeff McMahon, Enron Corp., December 23, 1999, p. 1). However, in testimony to the bankruptcy examiner, James Brown indicated that Merrill did not help create the structure. Instead, this was an up-front fee to appease Merrill, which wanted some of its payment before the transaction was concluded. U.S. Bankruptcy Court, "Third Interim Report," Appendix I (Merrill Lynch), pp. 31–32 (citing Brown sworn statement, pp. 114–115).

63. U.S. District Court, Southern District of Texas, Houston Division, Complaint, Third Superceding Indictment, *U.S. v. Bayly, Boyle, Brown, Fuhs, Furst, Kahanek* (Cr. No. H-03-363).

64. See U.S. Securities and Exchange Commission. Staff Accounting Bulletin Release No. 101, "Revenue Recognition in Financial Statements." Available at www.sec.gov/interps/account/sab101.htm. See also U.S. Senate, *The Role of the Financial Institutions,* p. 2,051, ex. 204a (Factors Leading to Non-Recognition of Revenue in a Sales Transaction Under Generally Accepted Accounting Principles, chart prepared by the Permanent Subcommittee on Investigations). Under SEC guidelines, a sales transaction cannot be recognized as such if "(1) the seller has significant obligations for future performance to directly bring about resale of the product by the buyer, (2) the risks of ownership did not pass from the seller to the buyer, and (3) the seller provides interest-free or significantly below market financing to the buyer beyond the seller's customary sales terms and until the products are resold."

   Interestingly, no accounting expert addressed the at-risk concept during the Nigerian barge trial. However, expert testimony from another Enron proceeding offers a framework for evaluating the transfer of risk. In the so-called broadband trial, executives from Enron Broadband Services (EBS) were charged with fraud. In testimony for the defense regarding the impact of a hypothetical guarantee by EBS to pay back an investor's equity, accounting expert Michael Mulligan testified, "But let me say that, if there was a guarantee by EBS to buy back at a fixed price and a determined amount, then the equity would not be at risk and you would not be able to deconsolidate and this transaction would fail." (*U.S. v. Hirko et al.,* Criminal Action No. H-03-93-05, Transcript, p. 11,679, lines 4–7.) Mulligan further stated that a guarantee would have that effect even if it were made only orally rather than in writing. (Ibid., lines 9–14.) However, Mulligan also indicated that a promise to find a third-party purchaser would not destroy the at-risk quality of an equity investment, because such a promise "lacks definiteness. There's no third party that's actually giving the guarantee. And, so it would not have the defined nature of what's required to be a guarantee. Consequently, you'd have to conclude that the equity remains at risk until that third party comes forward and makes the guarantee themselves." (Ibid., p. 11,680, lines 3–12.)

Applying Mulligan's analysis to the Nigerian barge transaction suggests that Merrill's equity investment was never at risk, and therefore that Enron should not have characterized the transaction as a sale. Merrill participants have stated that they believed Enron was obligated only to make its best efforts to remove Merrill from the deal within six months. U.S. Bankruptcy Court, "Third Interim Report," Appendix I (Merrill Lynch), pp. 36–37, citing Brown sworn statement, p. 64; and Bayly SEC Testimony, pp. 102, 137). However, considerable written and verbal evidence seems to indicate that Enron promised to take Merrill out of the deal by June 30, 2000, by either finding a third-party purchaser or, if one could not be found, repurchasing Merrill's equity investment (see note 66 for a list of evidence). If true, this would eliminate the "definiteness" problem that Mulligan testified was present in the broadband trial. Evidence also suggests that the parties agreed to provide Merrill with a set interest rate on the alleged equity—the "fixed price" and "determined amount" Mulligan mentioned—making the transaction more a loan than an investment.

65. Ibid., pp. 36–37 (citing Brown sworn statement and Bayly SEC testimony).

66. For instance, at trial, Ben Glisan, the former Enron treasurer, testified that "he believed Enron would have made Merrill Lynch whole and that Merrill never took any real risk" (Mary Flood, "Enron Judge Rules Criminal Conspiracy Likely," *Houston Chronicle* (October 8, 2004), www.chron.com/cs/CDA/ssistory .mpl/special/enron/2836656, accessed November 29, 2007). Several documents included as exhibits at the Senate hearing on financial institutions show that Enron made two promises to Merrill Lynch regarding the Nigerian barge transaction. First, Enron promised to take Merrill Lynch out of the deal by the end of June 2000. Second, Enron guaranteed Merrill Lynch a specific rate of return. Both terms were part of Jeff McMahon's initial appeal to Robert Furst. In a December 21, 1999, e-mail notifying Dan Bayly and Jim Brown, among others, about McMahon's proposal, Furst wrote that "Enron is viewing this transaction as a bridge to permanent equity and they believe our hold time will be for less than six months. The investment would have a 22.5% return." (Furst e-mail to Bayly et al., December 21, 1999, in U.S. Senate, *The Role of the Financial Institutions*, p. 2,064, ex. 208.)

The two terms were also included in the December 23, 1999 draft of the transaction agreement. "The SPE [formed by Merrill Lynch] or its equity interest in [the barges] will be subsequently sold to third party investors or purchased by Enron or an affiliate." (Letter from Merrill Lynch to Jeff McMahon, Executive VP and Treasurer, Enron, Senate Financial Institutions Hearings, December 23, 1999, in ibid., p. 2,071, ex. 210.) The omission of the terms from the final draft dated December 29, 1999 (letter from Merrill Lynch to Andrew Fastow, Executive VP and CFO, Enron, December 29, 1999, in ibid., p. 2,074, ex. 211) is likely attributable to the fact that their inclusion would destroy Enron's intended accounting treatment. (See reference to EITF Abstract 88–18 and SFAS No. 66 in U.S. Bankruptcy Court, "Third Interim Report," Appendix I (Merrill Lynch), p. 29 n.131.)

Regardless, in a December 22, 1999, phone call, Andrew Fastow promised Dan Bayly that Enron would take Merrill Lynch out of the deal within six months. Ibid., p. 28 (citing Bayly's SEC testimony, pp. 95–99, 101–103, 129), and p. 33 (citing Brown/Lyons e-mail and Brown/Haugh fax). As indicated by Michael Mulligan, the defense's accounting expert in the Broadband trial, this verbal promise destroyed the equity's at-risk quality.

Additional evidence suggests that the parties understood that Enron was making two unwritten promises as part of the transaction:

- The appropriation request cover page submitted to Merrill Lynch's debt markets capital committee before the deal was approved includes the notation "Project Start/Finish: Needs to Close by 12/31/99—Takeout by 6/30/00" (U.S. Senate, *The Role of the Financial Institutions*, p. 2059, ex. 207). In his own sworn testimony to the bankruptcy examiner, James Brown stated that he told the DMCC of Enron's intent to take Merrill out of the deal quickly U.S. Bankruptcy Court, "Third Interim Report," Appendix I (Merrill Lynch), p. 26 (citing Brown sworn statement, pp. 62–64). A contemporaneous memo from Brown, Tilney, and Furst (as well as two other Merrill employees, Brad Bynum and Mark DeVito) to the DMCC summarized the transaction. Under "Fees" they wrote, "Proposed $250,000 plus 15% per annum or a flat 22.5% return per annum" and under "Maturity" they wrote, "Less than six months." U.S. Senate, *The Role of the Financial Institutions*, p. 2,429, ex. 269.
- In a review of his year 2000 achievements, an Enron executive stated that he had "negotiated and executed the sale of the Merrill Lynch equity to LJM, fulfilling [Enron's] obligation to Merrill Lynch." Ibid., Dan O. Boyle, 2000 Deals and Accomplishments, p. 2,364, ex. 265.
- Kira Toone, a Merrill investment-banking employee, wrote two e-mails implying that the undocumented promises were part of the agreement. Her May 4, 2000, e-mail calculates income accrued on the barge investment using the 15 percent annualized figure. Ibid., Toone e-mail to Gary Carlin, p. 2163, ex. 221. On June 13, 2000, she wrote, "As we approach June 30, 2000 I am getting questions concerning Ebarge, LLC (the SPE through which Merrill Lynch made its supposed equity contribution). It was our understanding that Merrill Lynch IBK positions would be repaid its equity investment as well as a return on its equity by this date. Is this on schedule to occur?" Ibid., Toone e-mail to Joseph Valenti, among others, p. 2,158, ex. 218.
- A January 2002 e-mail from Curt Cariddi, a Merrill Lynch private equity finance employee, includes a description of the barge deal. He wrote that "the arrangement called for [Enron] to pay 15% per annum on [the barge] investment." Ibid., Cariddi e-mail to Jospeh Valenti, among others, p. 2,161, ex. 220.
- A memo entitled "Benefits to Enron, Summary," written by LJM2 employee Ace Roman, notes Enron's promise to remove Merrill Lynch from the

Nigerian barge transaction. "Enron sold barges to Merrill Lynch (ML) in December of 1999, promising that Merrill would be taken out by sale to another investor by June 2000. The project could not be sold by June, so without LJM2's purchase Enron would have had to strain the ML/Enron relationship or repurchase the assets and reverse earnings and funds flow in the original transaction." Ibid., p. 2,157, ex. 217. The participation of LJM2, an Enron-related party, appears to fit within the parameters of the take-out promise as described in the December 23, 1999, draft agreement.

- A June 14, 2000, letter apparently drafted by Geoffrey Wilson of Merrill Lynch Investment Bank's Strategic Asset Lease and Finance Group indicates that Enron was prepared to repurchase Merrill Lynch's interest in the Nigerian Barges before LJM2 became involved. "On December 29, 1999, Ebarge LLC, a limited liability company controlled by Merrill Lynch ('Ebarge'), purchased [an interest in] Enron Nigeria Barge Ltd. . . . Enron has agreed to purchase the shares from [Merrill Lynch] by June 30, 2000 for a purchase price . . . of $7,510,976.65." Ibid., letter drafted by Geoffrey Wilson, from Robert Furst, Merrill Lynch, to Dan Boyle, Enron, June 14, 2000, pp. 2, 159, 160.

- Enron actually kept its promises. On June 29, 2000, one day before the take-out deadline, Merrill Lynch received $7.525 million from LJM2 for its share of the Nigerian Barges. U.S. Bankruptcy Court, "Third Interim Report," Appendix I (Merrill Lynch), p. 30 (citing LJM2-Ebarge, LLC Share Purchase Agreement). Merrill was also paid $250,000 for what Enron called an "advisory fee," though it is not clear that Merrill provided any service other than a willingness to participate. Ibid., p. 31 (citing letter from Merrill Lynch to Jeff McMahon, Executive VP and Treasurer, Enron, December 23, 1999). The total of $775,000 that Merrill Lynch made on the deal was a 22.14 percent annualized return on the $7 million it contributed, or just under the 22.5 percent return McMahon mentioned in his initial conversation with Furst.

In Enron's defense (and his own), Jeffrey Skilling might believe or argue that every one of Enron's contracts had a so-called integration clause that essentially negated any prior history of comments or indications of side deals or guarantees. While that might well have been the case, it is unclear to me how such a clause would make any substantive difference. In my opinion, I do not think Merrill Lynch would ever have sued Enron for reneging on a side deal or guarantee because, in doing so, they would be admitting to fraud. Further, Merrill Lynch and Enron executives could still have exchanges of winks, nods, or code language that could be as important as the contracts themselves.

67. Mary Flood and Tom Fowler, "5 Guilty in Enron Barge Scheme," *Houston Chronicle,* November 4, 2004, available at www.chron.com/cs/CDA/ssistory .mpl/special/enron/barge/2883572, accessed November 30, 2007.

68. Mary Flood, "Former Merrill Lynch Executives Get Less Prison Than Requested," *Houston Chronicle,* April 23, 2005, available at www.chron.com/cs/ CDA/printstory.mpl/special/enron/barge/3146490, accessed November 30, 2007. Mary Flood, "Ex-Enron, Merrill Execs Sentenced," *Houston Chronicle,*

May 13, 2005, available at www.chron.com/cs/CDA/ssistory.mpl/special/
enron/barge/3180226, accessed November 30, 2007.

69. Loren Steffy reported Judge Jolly's disclaimer in "From Ruling Quagmire, Honest Dishonesty Emerges," *Houston Chronicle,* April 3, 2006. For Judge Werlein's order, see Kristen Hays, "Judge Orders Retrial in Enron Barge Case," *Houston Chronicle,* April 4, 2007.

70. U.S. Senate, *The Role of the Financial Institutions,* p. 2,064, ex. 208 (citing letter from James B. Weidner, Clifford Chance US LLP, to the Honorable Carl Levin, Chairman, and the Honorable Susan Collins, Ranking Member, Permanent Subcommittee on Investigations, Committee on Governmental Affairs, U.S. Senate, September 13, 2002, p. 6). U.S. Bankruptcy Court, "Third Interim Report," Appendix I (Merrill Lynch), p. 37 (citing e-mail from Dan Gordon to Christine Gonzalez and Jeff Kronthal et al., Merrill Lynch, December 29, 1999).

71. Ibid., p. 41, citing Jeff Kronthal's sworn statement.

72. U.S. Senate, *The Role of the Financial Institutions,* p. 2,064, ex. 208 (Weidner letter, September 13, 2002, p. 7): "Specifically, Mr. Baxter explained that Arthur Andersen had determined that Enron could continue to maintain off-balance sheet treatment of certain power facilities by selling the output of those facilities to Merrill Lynch through the call options."

73. Ibid., p. 6. See also U.S. Bankruptcy Court, "Third Interim Report," Appendix I (Merrill Lynch), p. 38 (citing Gordon e-mail, December 29, 1999).

A call option gives the holder the right to buy a certain quantity of a security or an underlying asset (in this case, electricity) at a specified price (called the strike price) until a specified date (called the expiration date). For example, Merrill Lynch could buy a call option on electricity from Enron. Assume that the strike price of this call is $10, with an exercise date of January 1. In this example, Merrill is betting that the price of electricity on January 1 will be more than $10, so it will be buying electricity at a discount. The seller of the call option bets the opposite. If the cost of electricity is less than $10, Merrill will not exercise the call option, and will instead buy electricity on the open market.

74. Ibid., p. 38 (citing call option confirmation letters from Enron Power Marketing, Inc. to Dan Gordon, Merrill Lynch, and John Protano, Merrill Lynch, December 28, 1999). See also U.S. Senate, *The Role of the Financial Institutions,* p. 2,064, ex. 208 (Weidner letter), p. 6.

75. U.S. Bankruptcy Court, "Third Interim Report," Appendix I (Merrill Lynch), p. 39 (citing Gordon e-mail, December 29, 1999).

76. Ibid., p. 38 (citing Jeff Kronthal sworn statement, pp. 109–110, 112). There are indications, however, that the matching options were not completely offsetting. See ibid., p. 42 n. 213, stating that some evidence suggests that "the market moved against Enron" in the electricity trades (citing e-mail from Gordon to Tilney and Furst, May 30, 2000, p. 2; and Weidner letter, September 13, 2002, p. 8: "By June 2000, Merrill Lynch's mark-to-market profit on the trades had increased by more than $2 million").

77. Ibid., p. 39 (citing Gordon e-mail, December 29, 1999). See also *U.S. SEC v. Merrill Lynch*, at paragraph 40: "Enron was initially surprised regarding the size of the fee because the transaction posed little risk to Merrill Lynch, but ultimately agreed to pay a $17 million fee given the importance of the transaction to its year end earnings." Enron might also have agreed knowing that it would seek a renegotiated fee during the next calendar year.

78. U.S. Bankruptcy Court, "Third Interim Report," Appendix I (Merrill Lynch), p. 38 (citing Jeff Kronthal sworn statement, pp. 109–110; and Enron Power Marketing confirmation letters).

79. In a May 2000 e-mail to Dan Gordon, Schuyler Tilney, relationship manager with Enron, implies that when Merrill agreed to the electricity trades, it was aware that Enron would probably want to unwind the transaction. "This is not that great a surprise as Cliff Baxter indicated to Rob [Furst] and me at year end when we did this trade that he thought they would want to unwind it at some point" U.S. Bankruptcy Court, "Third Interim Report," Appendix I (Merrill Lynch), p. 44. Merrill has refuted contentions that the unwinding was part of the deal from its initiation. (See Weidner letter, September 13, 2002, p. 8: "Merrill believes there was nothing improper about the transactions, nor was there any pre-arrangement to cancel them.")

80. U.S. Bankruptcy Court, "Third Interim Report," Appendix I (Merrill Lynch), p. 41 (citing e-mail from Rodney Malcolm, Enron, to David Delainey, Enron, May 31, 2000; and Gordon e-mail, May 30, 2000). The cited e-mails indicate that the fee was renegotiated in May, but other evidence indicates that Enron contacted Merrill about unwinding the trades as early as February. See Weidner letter, September 13, 2002, p. 8.

81. Ibid., p. 6. Gordon and Merrill's risk-management team "concluded the trading risks were significant." "[Jeff Kronthal, head of Merrill Lynch's Global Derivatives Group] believed . . . Merrill Lynch faced significant operational risks should [Enron Power Marketing] decide to satisfy its obligations through delivery of the output of Enron's power facilities." Gordon and Kronthal concluded that Merrill Lynch would need to charge a relatively large premium to compensate for these trading and operational risks. (Eventually, Enron agreed to structure the trades, consistent with normal market practice, such that there was a $17 million net present value difference between the options premiums to be paid by the respective parties over the course of the trades in Merrill Lynch's favor.)

82. U.S. Bankruptcy Court, "Third Interim Report," Appendix I (Merrill Lynch), p. 39 (quoting Gordon e-mail, December 29, 1999).

83. Ibid., p. 42 (quoting Gordon e-mail, May 30, 2000).

84. Ibid., p. 42 (citing Merrill Lynch CS/EPMI memorandum agreement, p. 1; Kronthal sworn statement, pp. 42–43).

85. Under FASB and SEC guidelines, revenue should not be recognized until it is realized, or realizable and earned. Statement of Financial Accounting Concepts (SFAC) No. 5, paragraph 83(b) states that "an entity's revenue-earning activities

involve delivering or producing goods, rendering services, or other activities that constitute its ongoing major or central operations, and revenues are considered to have been earned when the entity has substantially accomplished what it must do to be entitled to the benefits represented by the revenues." Paragraph 84(a) continues "the two conditions (being realized or realizable and being earned) are usually met by the time product or merchandise is delivered or services are rendered to customers, and revenues from manufacturing and selling activities and gains and losses from sales of other assets are commonly recognized at time of sale (usually meaning delivery)." In addition, paragraph 84(d) states that "if services are rendered or rights to use assets extend continuously over time (for example, interest or rent), reliable measures based on contractual prices established in advance are commonly available, and revenues may be recognized as earned as time passes." See Financial Accounting Standards Board, "Statement of Financial Accounting Concepts No. 5, Recognition and Measurement in Financial Statements of Business Enterprises" (Norwalk, Conn.: Financial Accounting Standards Board, 1984).

86. U.S. Bankruptcy Court, "Third Interim Report," Appendix D (Citigroup), p. 88 n. 346. The minority-interest transaction was designed by Citigroup's Capital Restructuring and Equity Derivatives groups. See also SEC 2003 Citigroup Order, § 3(D) (Discussion), paragraph 2: "Citigroup developed Project Nahanni and presented it to Enron as a financial statement solution to that operating cash flow shortfall."

Donaldson, Lufkin & Jenrette supposedly designed the share trust structures used in Enron deals such as Marlin and Whitewing, though Fastow claimed that Enron actually created those models. See Joshua Chaffin and Stephen Fidler, "Enron's Alchemy Turns to Lead for Bankers," *Financial Times* (February 28, 2002): " 'Chase and Citi both underwrote a lot, but the advisory work and the real brains behind [the partnerships] was from CSFB and DLJ,' says a former Enron employee," but "Some CSFB bankers say the partnerships had been 'fully baked' by Enron's finance team, and that the former DLJ bankers were merely brought in to execute them. Indeed, Mr. Fastow claimed in 1999 that Enron had been responsible for Marlin, created to help finance its purchase of Wessex Water, the UK utility. Several banks not involved in the transaction 'came back and marketed it to us' as their own creation, he told *CFO Magazine*." Available at http://specials.ft.com/enron/FT3E9GX09YC.html, accessed December 3, 2007. See also U.S. Bankruptcy Court, "Third Interim Report," Appendix G (Role of BT/Deutsche and its Affiliates), p. 11 (citing e-mail from George Tyson, Deutsche Bank, to Marcus Tarkington, Deutsche Bank, November 29, 2000: "As a Tier 1 Bank, [BT/Deutsche and its affiliates] are frequently brought into unique and lucrative transactions for Enron, such as the highly successful Marlin and Osprey Trust transactions that we developed with DLJ.").

87. Ibid., Appendix I (Merrill Lynch), p. 26 (citing Brown sworn statement, pp. 62, 65–67).

88. Ibid., Appendix D (Citigroup), pp. 108–109 (citing Citigroup's Nahanni Capital Structuring Transaction Execution Approval Package, December 14, 1999).
89. Ibid., Appendix I (Merrill Lynch), pp. 26, 32–37, 44.
90. Merrill Lynch's assertion is not implausible, yet not conclusive either. Regarding the Nigerian barge deal, see ibid., pp. 36–37 (citing Brown sworn statement, pp. 64, 103–104; and Bayly SEC Testimony, pp. 102, 137: "Merrill Lynch has denied that anyone at Enron ever guaranteed that Enron would take Merrill Lynch out of the transaction. Rather, Brown testified that Enron simply committed to use its best efforts to locate a purchaser for Merrill Lynch's interest in the barges. Similarly, Bayly has contended that he understood Fastow's commitment to be only a best efforts commitment.") Regarding the electricity trades, see Weidner letter, September 14, 2002, p. 8: "Merrill Lynch believes there was nothing improper about the transactions, nor was there any pre-arrangement to cancel them. As to the latter issue, the negotiations that occurred in the first quarter of 2000—when no agreement could be reached regarding the termination—confirm that there was no such pre-arrangement."
91. Regarding the barge deal, see ibid., Appendix I (Merrill Lynch), pp. 33–36. As noted, evidence obtained by the bankruptcy examiner suggests that the negotiations during the first quarter of 2000 regarding the unwinding of the electricity trades were necessitated by Enron's refusal to pay Merrill Lynch the agreed $17 million fee for entering the transaction. The sides eventually settled on $8.5 million, and the transactions were unwound on June 30, 2000. See ibid., p. 42 (citing Merrill Lynch CS/EPMI memorandum agreement, p. 1; and Kronthal sworn statement, pp. 42–43).
92. See U.S. District Court, Southern District of Texas, Houston Division, Complaint, *U.S. Securities and Exchange Commission v. Canadian Imperial Bank of Commerce, Daniel Ferguson, Ian Schottlaender, Mark Wolf,* Case No. H-03-5785, paragraphs 27–36 (especially 32, 34–35, referring to Enron's inability to document the guarantee). See also U.S. Bankruptcy Court, "Third Interim Report," Appendix H (Role of CIBC and Its Affiliates), pp. 20–24, 54–57: "By the time the Credit Committee began to evaluate Hawaii, it had come to expect the verbal assurances of repayment of CIBC's 3% equity from Enron." Ibid., p. 46.
93. These transactions derive their moniker from Statement of Financial Accounting Standards No. 140, which covers transfers and servicing of financial assets and extinguishment of liabilities. The transactions were designed to move illiquid assets off Enron's balance sheet. See *SEC v. Canadian Imperial Bank,* paragraph 17; and U.S. Bankruptcy Court, "Second Interim Report," Appendix M (FAS 140 Transactions), p. 1.

    See U.S. Bankruptcy Court, "Third Interim Report," Appendix H (Role of CIBC and Its Affiliates), p. 4: "CIBC engaged in at least eleven FAS 140 Transactions with Enron"; and *SEC v. Canadian Imperial Bank,* paragraph 17: "Enron and CIBC . . . entered into approximately 34 transactions that were purportedly asset sales but in reality were CIBC loans to Enron."
94. Ibid., paragraphs 11 and 32 (quoting Schottlaender e-mail, October 23, 2000).

95. U.S. Bankruptcy Court, "Third Interim Report," Appendix H (Role of CIBC and Its Affiliates), p. 46: "By the time the Credit Committee began to evaluate Hawaii, it had come to expect the verbal assurances of repayment of CIBC's 3% equity from Enron."

96. Ibid., pp. 46–47 (citing Mercedes Arango's sworn statement, then executive director in CIBC's Corporate Leveraged Finance Group).

97. *SEC v. Canadian Imperial Bank,* paragraph 35 (quoting e-mail by unnamed CIBC employee, July 11, 2001), and paragraph 33.

98. U.S. Bankruptcy Court, "Third Interim Report," Appendix D (Citigroup), p. 88 n. 346. The structure of the minority-interest transaction was designed by Citigroup's Capital Restructuring and Equity Derivatives Groups. Before marketing the product to clients, Citigroup presented it to Arthur Andersen's Professional Standards Group and to Moody's, to ensure that the structure would achieve the desired accounting and credit rating outcomes. Ibid., p. 92.

99. Ibid., p. 112 (citing Irrevocable Letter of Credit No. 22703100654WLB,December 29, 1999: "Citigroup knew that the debt in the Nahanni structure would be repaid no later than January 27, 2000 because the letter of credit, which was required to be in place at all times while the debt existed, expired by its terms on that date."). The examiner's conclusion depends on whether Citigroup knew about the letter of credit. If Citigroup had such knowledge, it also knew that the accounting treatment was incorrect.

100. Ibid., pp. 24–25 (discussing exposure limits), and pp. 27–29 (discussing the appropriateness test).

101. Ibid., p. 111.

102. Compare the description of merchant activities in Enron's 1998 and 1999 financial statements. Enron Corp. 10-K Filing to the SEC, December 31, 1998, Notes to Consolidated Financial Statements, Note 4; and Enron Corp. 10-K Filing to the SEC, December 31, 1999, Notes to Consolidated Financial Statements, Note 4.

103. U.S. Senate, Permanent Subcommittee on Investigations, Committee on Governmental Affairs. "Fishtail, Bacchus, Sundance, and Slapshot: Four Enron Transactions Funded and Facilitated by U.S. Financial Institutions," S. Prt. 107-82 (2003), p. 23 (citing Bushnell's memo to Michael Carpenter, head of Citigroup's Global Corporate and Investment Bank, May 30, 2001).

104. Ibid. (citing MacDonald's e-mail to Michael Carpenter, head of Citigroup's Global Corporate and Investment Bank, May 31, 2001).

105. Ibid., pp. 23–24. (citing Shawn Feeney e-mail to Andrew Lee, Citigroup, June 29, 2001).

106. See U.S. District Court, Southern District of Texas, Houston Division, *In re Enron Corporation Securities Litigation,* Civil Action No. H-01-3624, "First Amended Consolidated Complaint for Violation of the Securities Laws" (S.D. Tx, May 14, 2005), ¶ 681.

107. U.S. Bankruptcy Court, Southern District of New York, *In re Enron Corp.,* Chapter 11, Case No. 01-16034 (AJG), "Report of Harrison J. Goldin, the

Court-Appointed Examiner in the Enron North America Corp. Bankruptcy Proceeding, Respecting His Investigation of the Role of Certain Entities in Transactions Pertaining to Special Purpose Entities" (November 14, 2003), pp. 101–102.

108. U.S. District Court. Southern District of Texas, Houston Division, Complaint, *U.S. SEC v. J.P.Morgan Chase,* July 2003, paragraphs 27–28.

109. U.S. Bankruptcy Court, "Third Interim Report," Appendix I (Merrill Lynch), p. 7, supra note 57 (citing Weidner letter, September 13, 2002).

110. U.S. Bankruptcy Court, "Third Interim Report," Appendix I (Merrill Lynch), p. 41 (citing letter from Richard Causey, Enron, to Merrill Lynch Capital Services, December 30, 1999).

111. Ibid., p. 27 (citing Brown sworn statement, p. 77).

112. Ibid., p. 5 (citing e-mail from Schuyler Tilney, Merrill Lynch, to Dan Gordon and Robert Furst, Merrill Lynch, May 30, 2000).

113. See Enron Corp., 1999 Annual Report, p. 41 (Earnings on Common Stock for the Year Ended December 31, 1999, reported as $827million); and Enron Corp., 10-Q Filing to SEC, September 30, 1999, p. 3 (earnings on common stock for nine months ended September 30, 1999, reported as $592 million).

114. Bethany McLean, interviewed by Steve Inskeep, *Morning Edition,* National Public Radio, October 15, 2004, ("Putting Corporate Executives on Trial"). Audio available at www.npr.org/templates/story/story.php?storyId=4110551 accessed January 5, 2008.

115. Kris Axtman, "Inside the Culture and Collapse of Enron: In the Trial of Corporate Titans, Witnesses Describe a World of Brains, Skill, and Deception," *Christian Science Monitor* (October 12, 2004).

116. Mary Flood, "Houston Jurors to Hear Closing Arguments Today in Enron Barge Case," *Houston Chronicle* (October 27, 2004).

117. Kris Axtman, "Inside the Culture and Collapse of Enron."

118. U.S. Senate, *The Role of the Financial Institutions,* p. 2,352, ex. 261 (Senate PSI List of Merrill Lynch Employees Investing in LJM2).

119. U.S. Bankruptcy Court, "Third Interim Report," Appendix I (Merrill Lynch), p. 17 (Subscription Agreement for Merrill Lynch/LJM2 Co-Investment, Inc. of Schuyler Tilney, March 31, 2000, p. 7; and Subscription Agreement for Merrill Lynch/LJM2 Co-Investment, Inc. of Robert Furst, March 31, 2000, signature page only). The Senate PSI put their investments at lesser amounts: Furst, $130,000, and Tilney, $487,500. U.S. Senate, *The Role of the Financial Institutions,* p. 2,352, ex. 261 (Senate PSI List of Merrill Lynch Employees Investing in LJM2).

120. Ibid., p. 2,192, ex. 229 (Merrill Lynch e-mail, June 2000).

121. Charles Gasparino and Randall Smith, "CSFB Bankers Served as Directors of Enron Entity," *Wall Street Journal* (April 5, 2002): C1. CSFB purchased DLJ in November 2000. Nath and Capolongo—both of whom moved from DLJ to CSFB after the takeover—began serving as directors for Atlantic Water Trust that same month.

122. U.S. Bankruptcy Court, "Second Interim Report," Appendix H (Marlin Transaction), pp. 3–4.

123. See U.S. Senate, *The Role of the Financial Institutions,* p. 1991, ex. 194g (April 24, 2002 letter from Gary G. Lynch, CSFB Global General Counsel and Executive Board Member, to The Honorable Carl Levin, Chairman, Senate Permanent Subcommittee on Investigations of the Committee on Governmental Affairs, Appendix 3). This was the third offering (resulting in the name Osprey III) made to finance the Osprey SPE. Nath invested $150,000 and Capolongo, $75,000.

124. Whitewing Associates was among the boldest of Enron's off-balance-sheet deals (SPEs). Formed as an Enron subsidiary in December 1997, Whitewing was initially funded with $579 million from Enron and $500 million from an unnamed outside investor. Whitewing was removed from the books in 1999 when Enron sold half of the partnership. Thereafter, Whitewing was no longer controlled by Enron.

   Whitewing borrowed billions of dollars from investors in the United States and overseas (including Wall Street investment banks) to buy power plants, pipelines, and other of Enron's international assets. In return for loaning the money to Whitewing, the investors received interest-bearing promissory notes from Osprey, a trust controlled by Whitewing, to be paid back in 2003. Whitewing was then to resell Enron's assets on the open market.

   Enron guaranteed that if the assets were sold at a loss, it would make up the shortfall with shares of its own common stock. Therefore, Enron would be on the hook if the assets Whitewing bought from it declined in value. Investors were further assured that if its shares fell below $48.55, Enron would distribute extra stock to Whitewing investors to cover any losses. The deal with Osprey also required Enron to issue more stock if its stock price fell below $47.00.

   If Enron had to issue stock to prop up these two entities, the additional shares would dilute the holdings of existing shareholders, leading to drops in the stock price.

   It was eventually revealed that Enron had used Whitewing and Osprey to buy some of its overseas assets at inflated prices, to make financial statements look better. See U.S. Bankruptcy Court, "Second Interim Report," Appendix G (Whitewing Transaction).

125. U.S. Senate, *The Role of the Financial Institutions,* Appendix 2, p. 4 (Lynch letter, April 24, 2002).

126. U.S. Bankruptcy Court, "Third Interim Report," Appendix I (Merrill Lynch), p. 19 (citing Olson sworn statement, pp. 6–7, 11).

127. Ibid., pp. 19–20 (citing John E. Olson, Merrill Lynch, comment: "Enron Corp.—ENE Will Rise Again and Fight Another Day: But Not Today," July 17, 1997).

128. See U.S. Senate, *The Role of the Financial Institutions,* p. 2,406 (Olson/Melnick e-mail, May 22, 1998), ex. 269 (letter between Merrill Lynch and Permanent Subcommittee on Investigations, and additional materials); and U.S. Bank-

ruptcy Court, "Third Interim Report," Appendix I (Merrill Lynch), pp. 21–22 (citing Olson sworn statement; and Olson/Melnick e-mail, May 22, 1998).

129. U.S. Senate, *The Role of the Financial Institutions*, p. 2,206, ex. 239 (interoffice memo from Tilney and Gordon to Herb Allison, CEO of Merrill Lynch, April 18, 1998, p. 2).

130. Ibid.

131. Ibid.

132. U.S. Bankruptcy Court, "Third Interim Report," Appendix I (Merrill Lynch), p. 3 (Weidner letter, September 13, 2002).

133. Ibid., p. 21 (citing Gordon e-mail to the Merrill Lynch Equity Strategy Board and Equity Commitment Committee, April 23, 1999).

134. See U.S. Senate, *The Role of the Financial Institutions*, p. 2,406, Ex. 269 (Olson/Melnick e-mail, May 22, 1998).

135. Ibid., p. 2,209, ex. 240 (Tilney/Allison e-mail, January 15, 1999: "On a positive note, I want to update you on recent developments in our relationship with Enron since you spoke to their CEO, Ken Lay, last spring regarding our difficult relationship in Research. It is clear that your responsive message was appreciated by the Company and any animosity in that regard seems to have dissipated in the ensuing months. To that end, we have recently been awarded two significant mandates by Enron: the first to lead manage the $1.5 billion IPO of their water company [Azurix], which is expected to file in late February; and the second to raise a $1 billion private equity fund on behalf of the parent, which is expected to kick-off in early March. Total fees to Merrill for these two transactions alone should be $45–50 million.").

136. U.S. Bankruptcy Court, "Third Interim Report," Appendix D (Citigroup), p. 30 (citing memo from Michael Carpenter, Citigroup, to Dean Keller, Citigroup, December 15, 1999, p. 4).

137. Fastow communicated this to Citigroup's Robert Holloman, who reported the conversation in an e-mail. See ibid., p. 30 (citing Holloman e-mail to James Reilly, Citigroup, March 16, 1999).

138. Ibid.

139. Ibid., p. 31 (citing memo from Michael Carpenter, Citigroup, to Dean Keller, Citigroup, December 15, 1999, p. 4).

140. Ibid. (citing memo from Maureen Hendricks, Citigroup, to Michael Carpenter, Citigroup, March, 8, 2000, p. 1).

141. U.S. Bankruptcy Court, "Final Report," Appendix F (CSFB), p. 29 (citing Launer sworn statement).

142. Ibid., p. 30 (citing Sakol sworn statement). Sakol replaced Terran Miller in April 2001.

143. "1997 All-America Research Team: Energy," *Institutional Investor* 31 (October 1, 1997).

144. Erin Davies, "Enron: The Power's Back On. Rousing a $20 Billion Giant," *Fortune* (April 13, 1998). To be fair, Launer was not the only analyst to change his mind about Enron at that time. Prudential analyst Carol Coale is quoted as

feeling positive about Enron, and the article implies that other analysts shared Launer's and Coale's view in the spring of 1998.

145. See U.S. District Court, Southern District of Texas, *In re Enron Corporation Securities Litigation,* Civil Action No. H–01-3624, "First Amended Consolidated Complaint for Violation of the Securities Laws," ¶ 56 (May 14, 2005).

146. U.S. Senate, Committee on Governmental Affairs, *The Watchdogs Didn't Bark: Enron and the Wall Street Analysts: Hearing before the Senate Committee on Governmental Affairs,* 107th Cong. (2002), available from Government Printing Office, www.gpoaccess.gov (accessed July 11, 2006), p. 127 (Chart: "Enron Stock Recommendations by Broker").

147. Ibid. (testimony of Curt Launer, managing director, Global Utilities Research Group, Credit Suisse First Boston).

148. U.S. Bankruptcy Court, "Final Report," Appendix F (CSFB), p. 31 n. 111 (citing Sakol sworn statement; e-mail from Michael Davis, VP, CSFB, to Peter O'Malley, VP, CSFB, August 31, 2001, regarding research issues to be discussed with Enron Treasurer Ben Glisan; and Lauren Pugliese e-mail to Paul Davis, director, and Jamie Welch, managing director, November 11, 2001).

149. Ibid., pp. 32–33 (citing Sakol sworn statement).

7. Enron and Its Public Watchdogs

1. I want to acknowledge the assistance of research associate Jason Mahon in researching and drafting this chapter.

2. See U.S. Securities and Exchange Commission, "Report on the Role and Function of Credit-Rating Agencies in the Operation of the Securities Markets (as Required by Section 702(b) of the Sarbanes-Oxley Act of 2002)" (January 2003), available at http://sec.gov/news/studies/credratingreport0103.pdf, accessed December 5, 2007 (hereafter SEC Credit-Rating Agency Report), p. 6. The SEC first used the NRSRO designation in 1973, in a proposed amendment to the "net capital rule" (17 C.F.R. § 240.15c3–1). That rule requires broker-dealers to deduct certain percentages of the market value of their securities positions when calculating net capital. Under the proposal, the deduction percentage corresponded to the issuer's credit rating, as determined by an NRSRO. The SEC adopted these changes in 1975. See Richard M. Levich, Giovanni Majnoni, and Carmen Reinhart, eds., *Ratings, Rating Agencies, and the Global Financial System* (Boston: Kluwer, 2002), p. 74 n. 38.

3. U.S. Senate, Committee on Governmental Affairs, *Financial Oversight of Enron: The SEC and Private-Sector Watchdogs,* 107th Congress, S. Prt. 107-75 (Washington, D.C.: Government Printing Office, 2002), pp. 109–110. "In early October 2001 Enron's assistant treasurer, Timothy DeSpain, called Moody's and Enron to tell them that Enron would soon announce: (1) a $1 billion write-down on after-tax income due to bad investments, and (2) a $1.2 billion reduction in shareholder's equity which DeSpain described only as an accounting adjustment. . . . On October 16, Enron made the earnings announcement

about which it had advised Moody's and S&P nearly two weeks earlier." See also Enron Corp., press release, October 16, 2001, available at www.enron .com/corp/pressroom/releases.

4. U.S. Senate, *Financial Oversight of Enron,* p. 109.

5. For a sample list of regulations incorporating the NRSRO designation, see Levich et al., *Ratings, Rating Agencies,* pp. 74–75.

6. Andrew Fight, *The Ratings Game* (New York: Wiley, 2001), p. 224. See also Steven L. Schwarcz, "Private Ordering of Public Markets: The Rating Agency Paradox," *University of Illinois Law Review* 1, no. 3 (2002).

7. This widely quoted remark was made on the February 13, 1996, edition of *The News Hour* with Jim Lehrer.

8. U.S. Senate, Permanent Subcommittee on Investigations, Committee on Governmental Affairs, *The Role of the Board of Directors in Enron's Collapse,* 107th Congress, S. Rep. No. 107–70 (2002), p. 45. (When Enron was downgraded and put on watch for additional downgrades, "investors reacted by selling Enron stock.") Rating agencies discourage the use of their opinions in this manner. In fact, the *Code of Conduct Fundamentals for Credit-Rating Agencies* clearly states, "credit ratings are not recommendations to purchase, sell, or hold any security." International Organization of Securities Commissioners, Technical Committee, "Code of Conduct Fundamentals for Credit-Rating Agencies" (December 2004), p. 1. Academics and other market participants use credit ratings in more technical endeavors such as rating migration matrices, predicting credit spreads and analyzing relative value, determining the depth of financial review required on a loan application, and triggering debt repricing, refinancing, and collateralization. See Richard Cantor, "Recent Advances in Credit Risk Research," *Role of Internal and External Ratings in the Credit Process,* conference paper, Moody's Corporation and NYU Salomon Center Inaugural Credit Risk Conference, May 20, 2004, pp. 4–5.

9. U.S. Bankruptcy Court, Southern District of New York, *In re Enron Corp.,* Chapter 11, Case No. 01–16034 (AJG) "Second Interim Report of Neal Batson Court-Appointed Examiner" (January 21, 2003), Annex 2 (LJM1 Rhythms Transactions) to Appendix L (Related Party Transactions), p. 7. (Enron contributed 6,755,394 shares of Enron common stock to LJM1 in return for the hedge and $64 million in LJM1 notes.)

10. Ibid., p. 48.

11. U.S. Senate, Committee on Governmental Affairs, "Rating the Raters: Enron and the Credit-Rating Agencies," 107th Congress (2002). See also Kurt Eichenwald, *Conspiracy of Fools* (New York: Broadway Books / Random House, 2005), 610–612.

12. Eichenwald, *Conspiracy of Fools,* p. 612. See also U.S. Bankruptcy Court, "Second Interim Report," Annex 1 (Mahonia) to Appendix E (Prepays), pp. 11–12, for examples of credit ratings as triggers in Enron deals. The "margin agreement" of the Mahonia prepay transaction included such a trigger. See also U.S. Senate, "Rating the Raters," p. 26. (The testimony of Standard & Poor's Ronald

Barone indicates that the deals related to Marlin, Osprey I, and Osprey II contained ratings triggers.)

13. U.S. Bankruptcy Court, "Second Interim Report," Appendix N (Bammel Transactions), p. 9 (citing section 3.04(a)(iv) of the Bammel Participation Agreement).

14. U.S. Bankruptcy Court, "Second Interim Report," pp. 18–19.

15. Ibid., p. 15: "Two key factors drove Enron's management of its financial statements: (i) its need for cash, and (ii) its need to maintain an investment grade rating."

16. William C. Powers Jr., Raymond S. Troubh, and Herbert S. Winokur Jr., *Report of Investigation by the Special Investigative Committee of the Board of Directors of Enron Corp.* (2002), available at www.enron.com, p. 42 (the Powers report).

17. See U.S. Bankruptcy Court, "Second Interim Report," p. 19 n. 51: "The rating agencies cite [Enron's] strong market position and diversified assets, mitigated partly by the risks associated with its aggressive expansion plans and related effects on the company credit measures. Moody's specifically stated in its last ratings review (December 21,1999) that [Enron's] rating is pressured in its category," quoting a Merrill Lynch analyst. Despite this concern, Moody's upgraded Enron from Baa2 to Baa1 less than fifteen months later.

18. The Powers report, p. 42 (Enron executives did not want to dilute EPS by issuing additional equity either). See also U.S. Senate, *The Role of the Board of Directors,* p. 8: "All of the Board members interviewed by the Subcommittee were well aware of and supported Enron's intense focus on its credit ratings, cash flows, and debt burden."

19. See U.S. Bankruptcy Court, "Second Interim Report," p. 23.

20. U.S. Senate, *The Role of the Board of Directors,* p. 7.

21. Enron Corp., 2000 Annual Report.

22. U.S. Bankruptcy Court, "Second Interim Report," p. 35.

23. All data and calculations are from ibid., p. 49.

24. U.S. Bankruptcy Court, Southern District of New York, *In re Enron Corp.,* Chapter 11, Case No. 01–16034 (AJG) "Final Report of Neal Batson, Court-Appointed Examiner" (November 4, 2003), Appendix D (Roles of Lay, Skilling, and Outside Directors), p. 128.

25. Ibid., p. 124 (Belfer sworn statement, at pp. 104–105).

26. See chart "Reported Cash Flows from Operations," in U.S. Bankruptcy Court, "Final Report," Appendix D, p. 125.

27. Ibid., p. 126.

28. U.S. Bankruptcy Court, "Second Interim Report," p. 62 (citing December 4, 2002 Brown telephone interview; Brown was involved in the Yosemite I and II prepays). See also n. 144 (citing e-mail between JPMorgan employees noting Ben Glisan's comments about Enron's need to match cash flow and mark-to-market earnings for better evaluations from rating agencies).

29. Ibid., p. 22 (citing Enron interoffice memo from Joe Deffner to David Delainey regarding year-end accomplishments and overall accomplishments).

30. U.S. Bankruptcy Court, "Final Report," Appendix D (Role of Citigroup and its Affiliates), pp. 108–109 (citing Citigroup's Nahanni Capital Structuring Transaction Execution Approval Package, December 14, 1999).

31. U.S. Bankruptcy Court, Southern District of New York, *In re Enron Corp.*, Chapter 11, Case No. 01-16034 (AJG), "Report of Harrison J. Goldin, the Court-Appointed Examiner in the Enron North America Corp. Bankruptcy Proceeding, Respecting His Investigation of the Role of Certain Entities in Transactions Pertaining to Special Purpose Entities" (November 14, 2003), pp. 101–102.

32. Ibid., at 102.

33. U.S. Bankruptcy Court, "Second Interim Report," p. 62 (citing Senate hearing testimony of John Diaz and Pamela Stumpp, Moody's, at ¶ 4, and Ronald Barone, S&P, at 13).

34. U.S. Senate, "Rating the Raters," pp. 64–69 and 121–127.

35. Ibid., p. 36.

36. Ibid.

37. Ibid.

38. Ibid., p. 25. (Ronald M. Barone, Standard & Poor's, "Senator, this was not a ratings problem. This was a fraud problem.")

39. U.S. Senate, Committee on Governmental Affairs, *The Role of the Financial Institutions in Enron's Collapse, Vol. 2: Hearing before the Permanent Subcommittee on Investigations of the Senate Committee on Governmental Affairs*, 107th Congress (2002), available from www.gpoaccess.gov, p. 44.

40. U.S. Senate, "Rating the Raters," p. 25: Steven L. Schwarcz, professor of law, Duke University School of Law: "Furthermore, ratings do not cover the risk of fraud. To the extent Enron provided the rating agencies with insufficient or fraudulent information, that would explain their failure to predict Enron's demise."

41. John Rutherford Jr., "Securities Regulation and Stability: Learning the Lessons of Recent Corporate Failures," International Organization of Securities Commissioners, Technical Committee Meeting, Panel 5, Frankfurt, Germany, October 6, 2005, p. 18.

42. U.S. Senate, "Rating the Raters," pp. 62 and 83 (Standard & Poor's), pp. 120–121 (Moody's), and p. 129 (Fitch). See also U.S. Senate, *Financial Oversight of Enron*, p. 77 (independent investment and research groups).

43. Off Wall Street Consulting Group, "Enron Corp. Report," May 6, 2001.

44. U.S. Senate, Committee on Governmental Affairs, *The Watchdogs Didn't Bark: Enron and the Wall Street Analysts*, 107th Congress (2002), p. 40.

45. See U.S. Senate, "Rating the Raters," pp. 92–115.

46. Ibid., p. 122.

47. See U.S. Bankruptcy Court, "Second Interim Report," p. 19 n. 51; and note 17 in this chapter.

48. U.S. Senate, *Financial Oversight of Enron*, p. 116.

49. International Organization of Securities Commissioners, Technical Committee, "Report on the Activities of Credit-Rating Agencies," September 2003, p. 1.

50. U.S. Senate, *Financial Oversight of Enron*, p. 119.

51. U.S. Senate, "Rating the Raters," p. 27. (Moody's John Diaz testified that three elements of the proposed merger prompted Moody's to retain Enron's investment-grade rating. The "merger would give [Enron] the capital to survive; the probability that the merger would go through based on the changes they made; and that the combined entity would be investment grade because of the structural changes made to the deal.")

52. U.S. Senate, *Financial Oversight of Enron*, p. 115.

53. For example, FERC's jurisdiction included Enron subsidiaries that engaged in energy generation, transmission, or marketing. U.S. Senate, Committee on Governmental Affairs, Hearing, *Asleep at the Switch: FERC's Oversight of Enron Corporation, Vol. 1*, 107th Congress, 2002, Exhibit A: Majority Staff, "Staff Memorandum: Committee Staff Investigation of the Federal Energy Regulatory Commission's Oversight of Enron Corp.," p. 7. See also the prepared statement of FERC chair Patrick H. Wood, "FERC's regulatory jurisdiction extends to a number of Enron subsidiaries. However, the Commission does not regulate the parent corporation, Enron Corporation, as it does not engage in activities which are under FERC jurisdiction," p. 131.

54. See CFTC Web site at www.cftc.gov/cftc/cftcabout.htm, accessed December 5, 2007.

55. See "What FERC Does," available on the FERC Web site at www.ferc.gov/about/ferc-does.asp, last updated November 27, 2007. More specifically, the agency's responsibilities include regulating the transmission and sale of natural gas for resale in interstate commerce; regulating the transmission of oil by pipeline in interstate commerce; regulating the transmission and wholesale sales of electricity in interstate commerce; licensing and inspecting private, municipal, and state hydroelectric projects; approving the siting of and abandonment of interstate natural gas facilities, including pipelines, storage, and liquefied natural gas; ensuring the reliability of high voltage interstate transmission systems; monitoring and investigating energy markets; using civil penalties and other means against energy organizations and individuals that violate FERC rules in the energy markets; overseeing environmental matters related to natural gas and hydroelectricity projects and major electricity policy initiatives; and administering accounting and financial reporting regulations and conduct of regulated companies.

56. See SEC Web site at www.sec.gov/about/whatwedo.shtml.

57. See Chapter 1.

58. U.S. Senate, *Asleep at the Switch, Vol. 1*, p. 295.

59. Ibid., pp. 274–275 (Enron Federal Government Affairs, Outlook & Goals for 1999):

> 3) *Commodity Futures Trading Commission (CFTC)/Derivatives:* Recent CFTC "concept release" has raised new questions about who has the authority to regulate derivatives. CFTC to be reauthorized before 2000. *Goal:* Obtain a statutory exemption from CFTC regulation for energy derivatives, prevent a movement of regulatory authority over energy derivatives to other

financial regulatory agencies (Fed, Treasury, SEC). Maintain light handed regulation.

13) *Opening of federal lands to oil & gas exploration and development:* Position Enron to take advantage of possible trend developing within Department of Energy, Department of Interior, U.S. Forest Service to allow drilling on federal lands. *Goal:* Work with environmental community and Congress to highlight the advantages Enron brings as a "green" company toward being a good environmental steward for such projects on federal land.

See also ibid., "Staff Memorandum," pp. 43–45.

60. Ibid. (citing letter from John Duncan, assistant secretary for legislative affairs, Department of the Treasury, to Senator Joseph I. Lieberman, chair, Committee on Governmental Affairs, April 22, 2002, p. 1).

61. Enron's West Coast Power Division, located in Portland, Ore., had been identified by federal prosecutors as a major disruptor in California's "day-ahead" and "hour-ahead" energy market. As reported by Mary Flood in a *Houston Chronicle* report ("Ex-trader pleads guilty to schemes," February 5, 2003), Enron trading practices were designed to increase prices in selected markets. In one scheme (called "Get Shorty") Enron traders first sold ficti- tious emergency backup power it didn't have at a high price in the "day- ahead" market and then collected the money, cancelled the contracts, and covered the commitment by purchasing lower priced power in the "hour- ahead" market and profiting from the difference. Another ruse (called "Load Shift") involved submitting fraudulent energy schedules and bids to the Cal- ifornia market "to create the appearance of congestion on a transmission line. This would trigger payments attached to easing congestion and let Enron profit from its own lies when it used its transmission rights to ease the sham congestion."

62. Former SEC Chair Arthur Levitt observed in U.S. corporations what he charac- terized as a " 'culture of gamesmanship'—a gamesmanship that says it is okay to bend the rules, to tweak the numbers, and let obvious and important dis- crepancies slide; a gamesmanship where companies bend to the desires and pressures of Wall Street analysts rather than to the reality of the numbers; where analysts more often overlook dubious accounting practices and too often are selling potentially lucrative investment banking deals; where auditors are more occupied with selling other services and making clients happy than detecting potential problems; and where directors are more concerned about not offending management than with protecting shareholders. U.S. Senate, Committee on Governmental Affairs, "The Fall of Enron: How Could It Have Happened?" 107th Congress, (2002), pp. 26–27.

63. See U.S. Senate, *Asleep at the Switch, Vol. 1,* pp. 374–386 (finance committee minutes, May 5, 1997. Conclusions regarding proposed transfer of wind farms to RADR include, "Not a sale for book purposes; thus, continued recognition of project revenues" and "Call option to repurchase the assets in the future and sell in 'non-fire sale' environment.").

64. See ibid., "Staff Memorandum," p. 19. (In connection with EnronOnline, Enron offered a variety of financial products such as "swaps, caps, floors, and collars" for purchasers of more than twenty types of energy and plastics commodities, including polyethylene, PVC, propane, and methanol.)

65. See U.S. Senate, *Asleep at the Switch*, Vol. 1, ex. A-28, p. 808. (Inquiry into EnronOnline, August 16, 2001: "On EOL, Enron marketers are on one side of every trade just as they are when they use phone and fax to trade.")

66. See ibid., "Staff Memorandum," pp. 24–25.

67. See ibid., and www.cftc.gov/cftc/cftcabout.htm. The CFTC's jurisdiction is generally laid out in 7 U.S.C. § 2(a)1(A): "The Commission shall have exclusive jurisdiction . . . with respect to accounts, agreements (including any transaction which is of the character of, or is commonly known to the trade as, an 'option,' 'privilege,' 'indemnity,' 'bid,' 'offer,' 'put,' 'call,' 'advance guaranty,' or 'decline guaranty'), and transactions involving contracts of sale of a commodity for future delivery, traded or executed on a contract market, or derivatives transaction execution facility . . . or any other board of trade, exchange, or market, and transactions subject to regulation by the Commission."

See also, 7 U.S.C. §§ 2(h)(1) , 2(h)(2)(B), and 2(h)(2)(C). These sections describe the types of transactions between private parties that are exempt from some requirements under Title 7 of the U.S. code, and explain that the CFTC retains some oversight and enforcement responsibilities with respect to such transactions.

68. See U.S. Senate, *Asleep at the Switch*, Vol. 1, "Staff Memorandum," p. 19. Enron Online opened for business in October 1999, but "it was not until May 2001 that FERC's General Counsel initiated a staff-level inquiry into the status of electronic trading in the electric power and natural gas markets, in general, and the role played by Enron Online, in particular."

69. Ibid., ex. A-28, p. 808 (Inquiry into EnronOnline, August 16, 2001: "The Office of the General Counsel is currently drafting a comprehensive memorandum concerning the Commission's jurisdiction over online trading.").

70. Ibid., "Staff Memorandum," p. 25 (citing Enron Corp., "Update on Federal Government Affairs Energy Crisis Campaign," July 27, 2001).

71. Ibid., p. 25. U.S. Senate, Committee on Governmental Affairs, *Asleep at the Switch: FERC's Oversight of Enron Corporation*, Vol. 2. Available at http://www.gpoaccess/congress/senate/homeland/index/html, p. 190. ("Electronic Platforms and Energy Trading, Talking Points addressing Common Misperceptions." The talking point at the top of p. 190 lays out Enron's explanation of EOL's regulatory coverage by the CFTC and FERC. Though the document is undated, Enron used this explanation almost exactly in responding to FERC inquiries submitted on June 14, 2001, and included on page 196.)

72. Ibid. See also U.S. Senate, *Asleep at the Switch*, Vol. 1, p. 295 (Government Affairs, November 2001).

73. Ibid., ex. A-28, p. 809 (Inquiry into EnronOnline, August 16, 2001).

74. Wall Street Journal, "Business in Brief—Enron Corp.: Price-Manipulation Allegations Are Settled for $35 Million," *Wall Street Journal* (April 29, 2004). See

U.S. District Court, Southern District of Texas, Houston Division, Complaint. *U.S. Commodity Futures Trading Commission v. Enron Corp. and Hunter Shively,* H-03–909 (March 12, 2003); available at www.cftc.gov/files/enf/03orders/ enfenron-complaint.pdf.

75. See Federal Energy Regulatory Commission, Staff Report, "Price Manipulation in Western Markets: Findings at a Glance," available at www.ferc.gov/ industries/electric/indus-act/wec/enron/summary-findings.pdf.

76. See Federal Energy Regulatory Commission, Staff Report, "Final Report on Price Manipulation in the Western Markets," Docket No. PA02–2–000, March 2003, p. III-36. Available at www.ferc.gov/industries/electric/indus-act/wec/ enron/enrondata.asp#skipnavsub.

77. Ibid., pp. VII-1 and 13.

78. Ibid., pp. VII-12–13 (analyzing trades on Enron OnLine between Enron and EPMI Long Term Southwest, an Enron affiliate, on August 14, 2001).

79. FERC oversees the Public Utilities Regulatory Policies Act of 1978 (commonly known as PURPA). The SEC oversees the Public Utilities Holding Company Act of 1935 (commonly known as PUHCA).

80. See U.S. Senate, *Asleep at the Switch,* Vol. 1, "Staff Memorandum," p. 14; U.S. Senate, *Financial Oversight of Enron,* p. 55.

81. See ibid., p. 16 n. 41.

82. Ibid., p. 16: "According to their own accounts, at no point did either agency contact the other to discuss the pending application."

83. U.S. Senate, *Financial Oversight of Enron,* p. 53. See also U.S. Senate, *Asleep at the Switch,* Vol. 1, "Staff Memorandum," p. 10. In May 1997, Enron sold a 50 percent interest in Zond to an SPE called RADR. See also U.S. District Court, Southern District of Texas, Houston Division, Complaint. *U.S. SEC v. Kopper,* Civil Action No. H-02–3127 (August 21, 2002); U.S. District Court, Southern District of Texas, Houston Division, Complaint. *U.S. SEC v. Fastow,* Civil Action No. H-02–3666 (October 2, 2002). Whether this transaction should have qualified as a true sale is also subject to debate. For all intents and purposes, Enron retained control of the wind farms.

See also Enron Corp., Form U-1, Application Under the PUHCA of 1935 (April 14, 2000), Item 1, §B: Reasons Enron Is Seeking an Alternative Exemption (hereafter Enron's Application for Alternative PUHCA Exemption), Appendix B (Proposed Notice).

84. 16 U.S.C. § 2601.

85. See Enron's Application for Alternative PUHCA Exemption.

86. See U.S. Senate, *Asleep at the Switch,* Vol. 1, "Staff Memorandum," p. 15.

87. See U.S. Senate, *Financial Oversight of Enron,* p. 54.

88. See U.S. Senate, *Asleep at the Switch,* Vol. 1, "Staff Memorandum," p. 16: "According to their own accounts, at no point did either agency contact the other to discuss the pending application."

89. Enron filed two applications with the Securities and Exchange Commission that requested an exemption from provisions of the Public Utility Holding

Company Act of 1935 as a means of obtaining relief from PUHCA's "qualifying facility" or "QF" ownership restrictions. See U.S. Securities and Exchange Commission, Administrative Proceeding File No. 3-10909, available at www .sec.gov/rules/other/35-27574.htm, accessed January 6, 2008.

90. Enron made a presentation to the SEC in July 2001 on its application. The two parties agreed that the application would not be reviewed until after Enron completed its pending sale of Portland General, which would render the application moot. U.S. Senate, *Financial Oversight of Enron*, p. 55 n. 198 (citing interview by Senate staff members of SEC staff, September 3, 2002).

91. The original deal between Enron and Sierra Pacific broke down on April 26, 2001. A second potential buyer, Northwest Natural Gas, backed out on October 8, 2001. Ibid., p. 55.

92. Ibid., p. 56 n. 20q.

93. Ibid., p. 55. Incidentally, Southern California Edison, not FERC or the SEC, was the first party to push for a review of Enron's PUHCA application and attendant PURPA exemption. Even then, FERC informed SC Edison that it would not consider the company's contentions unless it submitted a "petition for declaratory order," with the $16,000 filing fee. U.S. Senate, *Asleep at the Switch*, Vol. 1, "Staff Memorandum," p. 16.

94. U.S. Senate, *Financial Oversight of Enron*, pp. 36–39.

95. Enron Corp., 10-K Filing to the SEC, 1999, item 14, footnote 16; Enron Corp., 10-K Filing to SEC, 2000, item 14, footnotes 9 and 16. See also U.S. Senate, *Financial Oversight of Enron*, p. 38 n. 131.

96. Although this subsection focuses on the SEC's review of public filings, similar complaints could apply to the agency's review of its own decisions. As noted, the SEC had no processes in place to ensure that its decisions approving Enron's use of mark-to-market accounting, and exempting Enron from the Investment Company Act of 1940, remained appropriate years later.

97. The SEC employs three levels of review: A "full review, a full financial review, or certain filings may be monitored for specific disclosure items. A full review involves an in-depth examination of the accounting, financial, and legal aspects of an issuer's filing. A full financial review involves an in-depth accounting analysis of an issuer's financial statements and management's discussion and analysis or business plan disclosure." U.S. General Accounting Office, *SEC Operations: Increased Workload Creates Challenges*. GAO-02–302 (2002), p. 22 n. 26.

98. See SEC Web site at www.sec.gov/about/whatwedo.shtml.

99. U.S. GAO, *SEC Operations*, p. 23.

100. U.S. Senate, *Financial Oversight of Enron*, p. 36.

101. U.S. GAO, *SEC Operations*, pp. 11, 22. Between 1991 and 2000, annual corporate filings increased by 59 percent (from 61,925 in 1991 to 98,745 in 2000), but the staff responsible for that workload expanded by only 29 percent. The same period saw an explosion of initial public offerings.

102. Ibid., p. 23.

103. U.S. Senate, *Financial Oversight of Enron*, pp. 31, 34, and 36.
104. Ibid., p. 36. Aside from the time since the last review, screening criteria are confidential. Ibid., p. 10.
105. Ibid., p. 12.
106. Public Utility Regulatory Policy Act of 1978 (PURPA), 18 C.F.R. § 292.206(b).
107. U.S. Senate, *Asleep at the Switch*, Vol. 1, "Staff Memorandum," p. 12.
108. Ibid., p. 13.
109. See U.S. Senate, *Asleep at the Switch*, Vol. 1, pp. 374–386 (ex. A-9: minutes of the meeting of the finance committee of Enron's Board of Directors, May 5, 1997, "Enron Renewable Energy Corp." presentation).
110. 15 U.S.C. § 80a-3(a)(1)(A); (2004).
111. 15 U.S.C. § 80a-6(c); (2004).
112. U.S. Senate, *Financial Oversight of Enron*, p. 59. Experts disagree about whether Enron needed the exemption at all. The Investment Company Act applies if more than 40 percent of a company's assets are invested in securities. If the company owns the majority of a subsidiary, those assets are not considered investments for the purpose of determining the 40 percent line. Enron applied for the exemption because the company was increasingly relying on SPEs in connection with overseas projects. However, Enron was a minority owner of those SPEs, meaning that those assets would be considered investments for determining whether the Investment Company Act applied to Enron. See ibid., p. 57. Even if Enron had not received the exemption, it likely would have reorganized itself to stay outside the purview of the act. See ibid., p. 60.
113. Ibid.
114. Ibid., pp. 35, 42. (The SEC approved Enron's use of mark-to-market accounting beginning in the first quarter of 1992. In what turned out to be typical Enron style, the company responded by using the accounting method to report its financial information a full year earlier.)
115. U.S. Senate, *Asleep at the Switch*, Vol. 1, "Staff Memorandum," pp. 10, 16.
116. Ibid., p. 16.
117. Ibid.
118. See ibid., p. 17 n. 45: "So CalEd estimates that from July 1997 to April 2002, the wind farms at issue have been able to collect as much as $176 million more than if they had not had QF status. E-mail from Susan Kappelman, Southern California Edison Co. to David Berick, Professional Staff, Senate Committee on Governmental Affairs, dated September 6, 2002. Committee Staff has not attempted to independently confirm this number nor have we been able to quantify other financial benefits, such as tax credits and depreciation, that Enron may have received from its ownership interests in these projects."
119. See ibid., p. 16. On two occasions in the spring of 2002, Southern California Edison petitioned FERC to review Enron's PUHCA exemption application, to ensure that it remained a good-faith application. The Senate began its review of Enron, including FERC's performance, in January 2002. Ibid., p. 2. "The memorandum [which included analysis of the FERC's jurisdiction over EOL]

was not completed until July 2002; in fact nothing was done about it until Chairman Lieberman raised questions about it in his May 15, 2002 letter to [FERC] Chairman Wood." Ibid., p. 24.

Part II: Enron's Legacy

1. In most developed economies, these institutional arrangements include (1) rules addressing the protection of shareholder rights; (2) arrangements affecting the exercise-of-control rights held by owners and their delegated agents (corporate directors); (3) procedures for transferring these control rights; and (4) society's juridical framework for redressing grievances and resolving disputes. See the *OECD Principles of Corporate Governance* (Paris: Organisation for Economic Co-operation and Development, 1999) for more on these arrangements.

2. Berle and Means, in their classic study of the modern corporation, refer to this phenomenon as the separation of ownership and control. Adolf A. Berle and Gardiner C. Means, *The Modern Corporation and Private Property* (New York: Harcourt, Brace & World, 1932).

3. Andrei Shleifer and Robert W. Vishny, "A Survey of Corporate Governance," *Journal of Corporate Finance* 52, no. 2 (June 1997): 740–741. Much of the language in my summary of the agency problem comes from this source.

4. Sanford Grossman and Oliver Hart, "The Cost and Benefits of Ownership: A Theory of Vertical and Lateral Integration," *Journal of Political Economy* 94 (1986): 691–719.

5. Michael C. Jensen and William H. Meckling, "The Nature of Man," *Journal of Applied Corporate Finance* 7, no. 2 (Summer 1994): 4–19.

6. Adam Smith, *An Inquiry into the Nature and Causes of the Wealth of Nations,* ed. Edwin Cannan (Chicago: University of Chicago Press, 1976) [1776].

7. Michael C. Jensen, "Agency Costs of Free Cash Flow, Corporate Finance, and Takeovers," *American Economic Review* 76 (1986): 323–329.

8. Strengthening Board Oversight

1. The so-called principal-agent problem was first identified by Berle and Means in the 1930s (Adolf A. Berle and Gardiner C. Means, *The Modern Corporation and Private Property* (New York: Harcourt, Brace & World, 1932). Mark S. Mizruchi has cogently summarized this problem in "Berle and Means Revisited: The Governance and Power of Large U.S. Corporations," University of Michigan Working paper, April 2004, p. 2: "Berle and Means began by arguing that capital in the U.S. had become heavily concentrated during the previous few decades and that this vested a relatively small number of companies with enormous power. As these firms grew, it became increasingly difficult for the original owners to maintain their majority stockholdings, and stocks became dispersed among a large number of small shareholders. The consequence of

this dispersal, Berle and Means suggested, was the usurpation, by default, of power by the firm's managers, those who ran the day-to-day affairs of the firm. These managers were seen as having interests not necessarily in line with those of the stockholders. Whereas owners preferred that profits be returned to them in the form of dividends, for example, managers preferred to either reinvest the profits or, in more sinister interpretations, to further their own privileges, in the form of higher salaries or "perks." Removed from the pressures of stockholders, managers, for Berle and Means, were now viewed as a self-perpetuating oligarchy, unaccountable to the owners whom they were expected to represent."

More recently, Mark Roe of the Harvard Law School has defined the combination of the separation of the ownership and control of large firms and weaknesses arising from America's decentralized system of regulation as the two "core instabilities" in America's system of corporate governance. See "The Inevitable Instability of American Corporate Governance, Harvard Law and Economics Discussion Paper No. 493, July 2007.

2. Michael C. Jensen, "The Modern Industrial Revolution, Exit and the Failure of Internal Control Systems." *Journal of Finance* 48 (July 1993): 831–880.

3. The emerging debate surrounding private-equity can be summarized as follows. Some observers question whether the annual, 2 percent management fee and the one-time, 20 percent participation (or "carried interest") in realized gains flowing to private-equity firms at the sale of portfolio companies are excessive. Others challenge the seemingly advantageous tax treatment of "carried interest" at the long-term capital gains rate of 15 percent rather than ordinary income rate (about twice that much)—a policy that has facilitated the accumulation of great wealth by the partners in successful private-equity firms. Still others claim that buyout firms are, at base, financial predators engaging in "rip, strip, and flip" operations that impose significant pain on laid-off employees, while paying current investors handsomely. Finally, there is a concern in some quarters that if private-equity firms, like The Blackstone Group, choose to sell shares in public market, the essential advantages of private-equity investing will be seriously compromised as public investors substitute their short-term investment objectives for the more long-term perspective of the private-equity community.

None of these issues threaten the fundamental proposition that the governance practices of highly skilled private-equity firms provide an effective, value-creating function for both investors and the economy as a whole. Indeed, what professional investors have clearly understood is that the classic private equity governance model, in the hands of experienced and serious operators, serves an important remedial role. Thus, in response to questions pertaining to the size of front-end and back-end fees charged by private-equity firms, I should point out that if the chances of achieving above-average returns by renewing underperforming corporate assets were low, no investors would be willing to live with the current management fees and carried interest fee structure, and no investors would stick around to give the private-equity investment and governance model a chance to work. On this issue, the market has already "spoken" and the message appears to be that investors are willing to pay premiums for the chance to earn above-average returns.

With respect to the question of whether the private-equity firm's carried interest or 20 percent participation in all realized gains should be taxed at a capital gains rate or the higher income rate, men and women of wisdom, both in and out of Congress, differ on this point. That these differences of opinion over tax policy exist does nothing to negate the fact that significant gains on private-equity portfolios have been achieved over a sufficiently long period to make an informed judgment. (Relevant evidence is presented in this chapter.)

As for adherents to the "rip, strip, and flip" school of thought, they have typically generalized from a few notable examples of rapid cost cutting followed by quick sales of portfolio companies to secondary financial or strategic buyers. What these concerned observers fail to understand, however, is that most buyout candidates offer significant opportunities for increased operating efficiencies, that in the world of business everything is for sale at the right price (even the venerable *Wall Street Journal*), that there is little evidence that R&D and other growth-oriented expenditures are cut by buyout sponsors (which would be a totally irrational move given the need to sell the buyout to knowledgeable investors at a significant premium over cost in order to achieve expected returns), and that, in any case, the average holding period for buyouts is over four years—hardly suggesting that private-equity firms systematically flip assets.

Finally, on the issue of private-equity firms issuing public shares and the possible adverse effects of such public ownership on firm performance, I hasten to point out that the shares offered to the public in the first transaction (The Blackstone Group) are only in the management company (The Blackstone Group LLP) not the private-equity *funds* themselves (Blackstone Holdings), which are funded outside of the public capital markets by qualified professional investors of many stripes. This should have no meaningful impact on the traditional governance and control practices of the very large private-equity firms (the ones presumably considering public offerings) because they have a sufficiently steady flow of cash-outs and sales of "restored" properties to meet investors' expected returns. This, by the way, is not the case for relatively small private-equity shops. However, if the public were allowed to participate in the actual funds sponsored by large private-equity firms, then there would be, of course, a very legitimate question about their ability to maintain their long-term investment time horizon in the face of the notoriously short-term orientation of many participants in the public capital market. But this is not going to happen.

While short-termism is a risk for private-equity firms with public shareholders, Blackstone for one is certainly aware of it. In its prospectus, filed on June 25, 2007, the company explicitly sought to advise its public shareholders that it intended to maintain its long-term investment perspective: "As a public company we do not intend to permit the short-term perspective of the public markets to change our own focus on the long-term in making investment, operational and strategic decisions. Because our businesses can vary in significant and unpredictable ways from quarter to quarter and year to year, we do not plan to provide guidance regarding our expected quarterly and annual operating results to investors or analysts after we become a public company. . . . Accordingly, we expect to take actions regularly with respect to the purchase or sale of investments and the structuring of investment transactions for our investment funds to achieve this objective, even if these actions adversely affect our near-term results. We believe that optimizing returns for the investors in our funds will create the most value for our common unitholders over time." The Blackstone Group Prospectus, Filed (with SEC) Pursuant to Rule 424, Registration No. 333-141504, July 25, 2007 (p. 11).

4. The law has also forced public accounting firms to pay paramount attention to their auditing (rather than their advisory and consulting) business. In a speech at the Isenberg School of Management at the University of Massachusetts–Amherst, then-Senator Paul Sarbanes (D-Md.) observed that Congress was concerned that accounting firms had lost sight of their central mission, in their quest to win consulting work at the companies they audited: "There was concern that auditors were pulling their punches to get consulting fees." Joseph Nocera, "For All Its Cost, Sarbanes Law Is Working," *New York Times* (December 3, 2005): B12.

5. Colin B. Carter and Jay W. Lorsch, *Back to the Drawing Board* (Boston: Harvard Business School Press, 2004), p. 38.

6. Some early studies show that having more outside independent directors improves performance, but many later studies show the opposite. See Steven T. Petra, "Do Outside Independent Directors Strengthen Corporate Boards?" *Corporate Governance* 5, no. 1 (2005): 55–64. For example, one of the most recent comprehensive, statistical studies shows that firms with more independent board members do not have higher profitability or otherwise perform better. Indeed, there is evidence that such firms perform worse than other firms, according to market-based performance measures, as opposed to accounting measures. See Sanjai Bhagat and Bernard Black, "The Non-Correlation between Board Independence and Long-Term Firm Performance," *Journal of Corporate Law* 22, no. 1 (Winter 2002): 231ff.

7. See the survey reported in Carter and Lorsch, *Back to the Drawing Board,* pp. 23–28. Stanley Gold, CEO of Shamrock Holdings and a director of Walt Disney and other public companies, also argues this point incisively in "Corporate Boards: A Director's Cut," Manager's Journal, *Wall Street Journal,* February 18, 2003, p. B2.

8. Robert F. Felton and Pamela Keenan Fritz, "The View from the Board Room," *McKinsey Quarterly,* 2005 Special Edition: Value and Performance, pp. 54–55.

9. Carter and Lorsch, *Back to the Drawing Board,* p. 38.

10. This is another trenchant observation by Stanley Gold. Presumably referring to his work as a director at Disney, he asks, "How is a director with no scientific background to understand complex formulations in biology, physics, or engineering, or one without manufacturing experience to assess the quality of children's merchandise?" Gold, "Corporate Boards," p. B2.

11. Steve Kaplan and Antoinette Schoar, "Private-Equity Performance: Returns, Persistence, and Capital Flows," MIT Sloan School of Management Working Paper 4446–03 (November 2003), p. 2; and *Journal of Finance* 60 (August 2005): 1791ff.

12. Blackstone Group Prospectus, filed June 25, 2007, p. 149.

13. Kaplan and Schoar, "Private-Equity Performance," p. 5.

14. Ibid., p. 10.

15. Blackstone Group Prospectus, p. 158.

16. Paul Gompers and Josh Lerner, "An Analysis of Compensation in the U.S. Venture Capital Partnership," *Journal of Financial Economics* 51 (1999): 3–44.

17. The Blackstone Group Prospectus provides an excellent explanation of how the use of leverage (or debt financing) affects private equity returns: "A significant reason why many private equity funds may deliver superior returns on equity relative to traditional equity investments is the benefit of leverage. In the typical transaction effected by a private equity fund—a leveraged buyout acquisition of a company—the private equity fund borrows most of the purchase price and thereby magnifies the gain on its investment if the company's value appreciates (or its loss if the company's value declines). If a private equity fund were to acquire a company today with a total enterprise value of $1 billion, a typical capital structure for the transaction would be an equity investment of $300 million and $700 million of debt (generally consisting of senior loans from commercial banks and high yield bonds issued in the public market). If the private equity fund is successful in its objective of improving the operating performance of the acquired company over the period of its ownership of the company so that five years later it can effect a sale of the company at a total enterprise value of $1.3 billion, a 6% annual appreciation over the price it paid, it will have achieved a doubling of its equity investment or a gross annual internal rate of return of 15%. If over that period of time the company has used its operating cash flow to repay $300 million of the acquisition borrowings, the private equity fund will have tripled its equity investment and achieved a gross annual internal rate of return of 25%. Alternatively, if the acquired company were to encounter operating difficulties resulting in a 15% decline in its total enterprise value to $850 million and had not been able to use operating cash flow to repay any acquisition debt, the private equity fund would lose half of its equity investment if the company were to be sold at that price." (Blackstone Group Prospectus, p. 149.)

18. Kaplan and Schoar, "Private-Equity Performance," p. 4.

19. See, for example, a speech by SEC Commissioner Harvey J. Goldschmid, "Remarks before the Council of Institutional Investors," Washington, D.C., April 11, 2005, p. 3.

20. Many of these practices have been documented in case studies, teaching notes, working papers, and books developed for the Harvard Business School course "Coordination, Control, and the Management of Organizations." See, for example, Michael C. Jensen, William A. Meckling, Carliss Y. Baldwin, George P. Baker, and Karen H. Wruck, "Course Notes for Coordination, Control and Management of Organizations" (Fall 1995); Karen H. Wruck, "The Ownership, Governance and Control of Organizations," Course Module Overview Note, Harvard Business School (April 1997); Michael C. Jensen, *Foundations of Organizational Strategy* (Cambridge: Harvard University Press, 1998); George P. Baker and George David Smith, *The New Financial Capitalists: Kohlberg Kravis Roberts and the Creation of Corporate Value* (Cambridge: Cambridge University Press, 1998); and Malcolm S. Salter, "Notes on Governance and Corporate Control," *Journal of Strategic Management Education* 1, no. 1 (2003): 5–54.

21. The private-equity model characterized here reflects neither the potential innovations nor the potential risks of the blind pools of private-equity investments recently created to accommodate the enormous flow of risk capital seeking above-average returns. Indeed, the jury is still out regarding the capacity of traditional buyout sponsors to monitor and control large portfolios of private companies effectively.

22. Joachim Heel and Conor Kehoe, "Why Some Private Equity Firms Do Better than Others," *McKinsey Quarterly* 1 (2005): 24–26.

23. Michael C. Jensen, Willy Burkhardt, and Brian K. Barry, "Wisconsin Central Ltd. Railroad and Berkshire Partners (A): Leveraged Buyouts and Financial Distress," Harvard Business School Case 9–190–062.

24. Michael C. Jensen, "Eclipse of the Modern Corporation." *Harvard Business Review* 89, no. 5 (September-October 1989): 65.

25. Baker and Smith, *The New Financial Capitalists*, p. 96.

26. Ibid., p. 97.

27. Malcolm S. Salter and Daniel B. Green, "Regal Cinemas LBO (A)," Harvard Business School Case 9–902–019; and "Regal Cinemas LBO (B)," Harvard Business School Case 9–902–020.

28. These five indicators of effectiveness are reported in Jay A. Conger, David L. Finegold, and Edward E. Lawler III, "Appraising Boardroom Performance," *Harvard Business Review* (January-February 1998), 136–148. I have found them particularly useful in analyzing the performance of Enron's board of directors. See also Edward E. Lawler III, George S. Benson, David L. Finegold, and Jay A. Conger, "Corporate Boards: Keys to Effectiveness," *Organizational Dynamics* 30, no. 4 (2002): 310.

29. See New York Stock Exchange, "NYSE Listed Company Manual Section 303A, Corporate Listing Standards" (updated February 13, 2004), available at www.nyse.com/pdfs/section303Afaqs.pdf (accessed December 11, 2007), and David Nadler, and Jay W. Lorsch, *Report of the NACD Blue Ribbon Commission on Board Leadership* (Washington, D.C.: National Association of Corporate Directors, 2004).

30. For a detailed discussion of the social barriers to frank and open discussion on corporate boards, see Jay W. Lorsch, *Pawns or Potentates: The Reality of America's Corporate Boards* (Boston: Harvard Business School Press, 1989); and Myles L. Mace, *Directors: Myth and Reality* (Boston: Division of Research, Graduate School of Business Administration, Harvard University, 1971).

31. Korn/Ferry International, *31st Annual Board of Directors Study,* 2004.

32. Ibid., p. 11.

33. See, for example, Joseph Hinsey, "Pssst . . . Wanna Be a Director?" (mimeo, March 23, 2005). Hinsey is the H. Douglas Weaver Professor of Business Law, emeritus, at Harvard Business School.

34. Investor Responsibility Research Center, "Board Practices/Board Pay, 2005 Edition: The Structure and Composition of Boards of Directors at S&P Super 1,500 Companies," (Washington, D.C.: IRRC, 2005), 77. This study included data on 1,275 companies in the sample of 1,500.

35. Korn/Ferry International, *31st Annual Board of Directors Study.*

36. At a conference on private equity at Harvard Business School on January 10–11, 2006, a comment was made to a wave of nodding heads that virtually no director (or sponsor) of a portfolio company sold through an initial public offering would volunteer to remain on the board, in light of current litigation risks.

37. Ibid., p. 94.

38. National Association of Corporate Directors, "Director Compensation: Purposes, Principles, and Best Practices," Report of the Blue Ribbon Commission of the NACD (Washington, D.C.: NACD, 2001), p. v.

39. Conference Board, "Directors' Compensation and Practices in 2004" (Conference Board, 2004). This study reports data for 510 public companies (212 manufacturers, 88 financial firms, and 210 service companies).

Only the IRRC and the Conference Board break out data on equity-based compensation in their surveys of directors. Although both studies reported about the same average value of restricted-stock grants ($40,000), the Conference Board reported a significantly lower average value for stock-option grants than the IRRC ($24,000 versus $53,981).

The IRRC segments its data by companies' market capitalization. According to this analysis, the larger the company, the lower the likelihood that it offers stock options to its directors; the inverse is true for stock awards. The trend appears to favor awards of deferred or restricted stock over stock options. Compared with 2000 levels, the prevalence of option grants dropped (70 percent of companies offered them in 2000, versus 66 percent in 2004), while the prevalence of stock awards rose (29 percent of companies offered them in 2000, versus 35 percent in 2004).

The Conference Board study puts the percentage of companies offering equity compensation to directors at 89 percent; 65 percent of those companies granted stock options, 27 percent offered restricted stock, and 15 percent made annual stock grants. Because the study does not indicate whether respondents in these categories overlap, it is impossible to tell what percentage of companies offer more than one type of equity compensation. According to this study, the median value for stock-option grants was $24,000, while the median value of restricted-stock grants was $40,000. However, those figures are based on small sample sizes—202 companies and 95 companies, respectively—and thus are probably not particularly useful other than as a loose comparison.

By way of comparison, the Korn/Ferry study (of 904 companies from the Fortune 1000) found that 79 percent of these companies offer some form of equity compensation. Among those 714 companies, the most common practice was to offer options only (46 percent), followed by restricted-stock grants (37 percent); 9 percent offered both grants and options, while 8 percent offered unrestricted-stock grants only. This study did not attempt to estimate values for equity compensation. (The differences in the numbers reported by these surveys reflect differences in the universe of corporations and the underlying data.)

In reporting average cash compensation for directors, the IRRC and Korn/Ferry provided mean averages, whereas the Conference Board provided medians. The Conference Board broke out all data by three major-industry categories, but did not supply aggregate statistics or the underlying data. Thus the figures reported here are estimated medians—which assume that the median of the three reported numbers would be the actual median if the categories were combined. Though this method is inexact, it seems reasonable to assume that these estimated medians are at least near the actual figures.

40. I wish to acknowledge the many contributions of Jason Mahon in helping prepare the following analyses of director compensation and stock ownership.

41. Korn/Ferry International, *31st Annual Board of Directors Study*, p. 26.

42. The pay of CEOs of S&P 500 companies quadrupled between 1992 and 2000, owing mainly to a ninefold jump in stock options. Brian J. Hall and Kevin J. Murphy, "The Trouble with Stock Options," *Journal of Financial Perspectives* 17 (2003): 51.

43. From both a practical and theoretical perspective, it is important to identify the marginal effects of doubling directors' fees. Will director performance double with a doubling of fees? What behavior will such rewards improve? These are important questions because, to use a simple example, directors cannot simply show up twice as often to scheduled board meetings (unless they have missed a lot of past meetings).

The marginal effects on behavior are expected to be (1) greater preparation for board meetings, (2) more time devoted to meeting with key operating managers and visiting key operating facilities, (3) more active and informed participation in board meetings based on a greater familiarity with the company's challenges and prospects, and (4) a greater propensity among good directors to remain on boards rather than defecting to other rewarding opportunities. As director pay rises, it makes sense for public companies to report more fully to shareholders about how the board organizes its work of reviewing and ratifying management proposals and monitoring corporate performance and conduct.

44. Coca-Cola's novel director-compensation plan, which awards directors $175,000 in stock each year—payable only if the company meets earnings-per-share targets—is a courageous attempt to link director interests with shareholder interests. However, the lack of a long-term holding period for this stock puts a great deal of pressure on the board to tolerate aggressive earnings management. For a description of this plan, see Floyd Norris, "Coke's Board to Get Bonus or Nothing," *New York Times,* April 6, 2006, p. C1.

45. See U.S. Senate, Permanent Subcommittee on Investigations, Committee on Governmental Affairs, "The Role of the Board of Directors in Enron's Collapse," S. Rep. 107-70, 107th Congress, 2nd Session, p. 11. Also Hearings exhibits 35a and 35b on compensation of Enron board members, based on information in Enron filings with the SEC: U.S. Senate, Permanent Subcommittee on Investigations on the Committee on Governmental Affairs, "The Role of the Board of Directors in Enron's Collapse," Hearing. S. Hrg. 107-511, 107th Congress, 2nd Session, May 7, 2002.

46. See Lucian Bebchuk and Jesse Fried, *Pay without Performance: The Unfulfilled Promise of Executive Compensation* (Cambridge: Harvard University Press, 2004), p. 23 and following, for a discussion of director pay and performance.

47. John E. Core, Robert W. Hothausen, and David F. Larker, "Corporate Governance, Chief Executive Officer Compensation, and Firm Performance," *Journal of Financial Economics* 51 (1999): 371–406.

48. According to agency theory, financial incentives, especially equity-based incentives, can play an important role in bridging the gap between the interests of managers and shareholders by aligning their rewards for success and penalties for failure. The same notion applies to the relationship between directors and shareholders. See Michael C. Jensen and William M. Meckling, "Theory of the Firm: Management Behavior, Agency Costs and Ownership Structure," *Journal of Financial Economics* 3, no. 4 (October 1976); and Jensen, *Foundations of Organizational Strategy,* chapter 3.

49. Korn/Ferry's survey of individual directors does not supply the actual numbers of respondents, only these percentages.

50. IRRC, "Board Practices/Board Pay," p. 86.

51. For many retired CEOs, the $500,000 to $1 million requirement for investment might be far too low to replicate the incentives of private-equity partners. I have suggested this number so as not to deter qualified directors from considering such service.

52. Bebchuk and Fried, *Pay without Performance,* p. 114.

53. See ibid., p. 205, for a discussion of this point.

54. Paul W. MacAvoy and Ira M. Millstein, *The Recurring Crisis in Corporate Governance* (New York: Palgrave Macmillan, 2003), p. 100.

55. Ibid., p. 4.

56. Nick Bradey, "Board Structure and Effectiveness," in George S. Dallas, ed., *Governance and Risk* (New York: McGraw-Hill, 2004).

57. See New York Stock Exchange, "NYSE Listed Company Manual Section 303A," and Nadler and Lorsch, *Report of the NACD Blue Ribbon Commission on Board Leadership*.

58. MacAvoy and Millstein, *Recurring Crisis*, p. 118.

59. Bebchuk and Fried, *Pay without Performance*, pp. 31–34.

60. Ibid., p. 208.

61. Lucian Bebchuk, "The Case for Shareholder Access to the Ballot," *Business Lawyer* 59 (2003): 43–66. Also cited in Bebchuk and Fried, *Pay without Performance*, p. 208.

62. This summary is from SEC Commissioner Roel C. Campos, "The SEC's Shareholder Access Proposal" speech delivered at the Yale Law School Center for the Study of Corporate Law, New York City, January 10, 2005.

63. These hurdles are discussed in Bebchuk and Fried, *Pay without Performance*, p. 209.

64. Gretchen Morgenson, "Finally, Shareholders Start Acting Like Owners," *New York Times*, June 11, 2006, p. C1.

65. "The Shareholders' Revolt," *Economist*, June 17, 2006, p. 71.

66. See Michael C. Jensen, Kevin J. Murphy, and Eric G. Wruk, "CEO Pay . . . and How to Fix It," Harvard Business School NOM Research Paper No. 04–28, revised 2005, p. 54.

9. Avoiding Perverse Financial Incentives

1. Enron Corp., May 6, 1997, Proxy Statement, p. 14.

2. Ibid.

3. Lucian Bebchuk and Jesse M. Fried, *Pay without Performance: The Unfulfilled Promise of Executive Compensation* (Cambridge: Harvard University Press, 2004), 121–122, citing the work of Kevin J. Murphy, "Executive Compensation," *Handbook of Labor Economics*, vol. 3, ed. by Orley Ashenfelter and David Card (New York: Elsevier, 1999), 2535.

4. Of course, rewards can take many forms, ranging from praise and public recognition to promotions and cash rewards. This discussion focuses on monetary rewards "because individuals are willing to substitute non-monetary rewards for monetary rewards and because money represents a generalized claim on resources and is therefore in general preferred over an equal dollar-value payment in kind." Ibid., pp. 594–595.

5. Michael C. Jensen, "Self-Interest, Altruism, Incentives, and Agency Theory," *Journal of Applied Corporate Finance* 7, no. 2 (Summer 1994): 42.

6. See Malcolm S. Salter, "Tailor Incentive Compensation to Strategy," *Harvard Business Review* (March–April 1973): 94–102, for a detailed discussion of this point.

7. See Jay W. Lorsch, V. G. Narayanan, and Krishna Palepu, "Executive Remuneration at Reckitt Benckiser plc," Harvard Business School Case No. 9–104–062, January 27, 2004.

8. George P. Baker, Michael C. Jensen, and Kevin J. Murphy, "Compensation and Incentives: Practice vs. Theory," *Journal of Finance* 43, no. 3 (July 1988): 612.

9. Edward L. Deci and Richard M. Ryan, *Intrinsic Motivation and Self-Determination in Human Behavior* (New York: Plenum Press, 1985).

10. Bebchuk and Fried, *Pay without Performance,* pp. 121–122, citing the work of Kevin J. Murphy, "Executive Compensation," in Orley Ashenfelter and David Card, eds., *Handbook of Labor Economics,* vol. 3, bk. 2 (New York: Elsevier, 1999), 2,535.

11. Frederick Herzberg, B. Mauser, and B. Snyderman, *The Motivation to Work* (New York: Wiley, 1959).

12. Osterloh and Frey argue that extrinsic motivation is not simply additive to in- trinsic motivation, but often crowds it out altogether. They also hold that when an organizations needs to transfer tacit forms of knowledge seamlessly, the use of extrinsic rewards and other market-like elements such as profit centers is counterproductive. See Margit Osterloh and Bruno S. Frey, "Motivation, Knowledge Transfer, and Organizational Forms," *Organizational Science* 11, no. 5 (September-October 2000): 538–550.

13. Edward E. Lawler III, *Pay and Organizational Effectiveness: A Psychological View* (New York: McGraw-Hill, 1971), 132.

14. I. R. Andrews and M. M. Henry, "Management Attitudes Toward Pay," *Indus- trial Relations* 3 (1963): 29; and Edward E. Lawler III, "Managers' Attitudes Toward How Their Pay Is and Should Be Determined," *Journal of Applied Psy- chology* 50 (1966): 273.

15. Many startups fail to meet this test of creating real economic value during their early years, as heavy investments are being made, new products launched, and the foundations for future profitability put in place. Enron, however, had deep roots and a respectable history as an old-line, asset-rich pipeline and gas distri- bution enterprise. It is thus a stretch to characterize Enron—a merger between two established energy companies—as a new venture. Even the newer, asset- light side of the business, which pioneered innovative trading platforms and energy contracts, had few structural barriers to near-term profitability, as long as the pricing and risks of commodity contracts were prudently managed. In- deed, during its earliest years, when Enron was the sole innovator, one would have expected its margins to be quite high. By the time it was imitated by other energy companies, Enron had advantages of both experience and scale to minimize the impact of narrowing profit margins on individual commodity transactions.

16. The top five executives were Jeffrey Skilling; Kenneth Lay; Stanley Horton, CEO of Enron Transportation Services; Mark Frevert, CEO of Enron Wholesale Services; and Kenneth Rice, CEO of Enron Broadband Services. The results of the Charas study were reported in Dan Ackman, "Pay Madness at Enron," *Forbes* (March 22, 2002). In this study, equity-based pay included granted but unexercised stock options, and the net value of exercised stock options.

17. Michael C. Jensen, "The Modern Industrial Revolution: Exit and the Failure of Internal Control Systems," *Journal of Finance* 48 (July 1993): 831–880.

18. Enron Corp., May 4, 1999 Proxy Statement, 27.

19. Under this plan, executives received stock grants at the beginning of each fiscal year, and each unit was assigned a value of $1. The units were subject to a four-year performance measurement period, during which Enron's total stockholder return was compared with that of eleven peer companies (the peer group). The units were then assigned a value ranging from $0 to $2 based on Enron's rank within the peer group. Enron had to rank first for the units to be valued at $2, and it had to rank third for them to be valued at $1. Regardless of its rank, Enron's stockholder return had to be above that of ninety-day U.S. Treasury bills over the same period to be assigned any value at all.

    In 1997, for example, Lay did not receive any payment under the performance unit plan for the 1993–1996 period, because the company's total stockholder return did not meet performance standards. From 1993 to 1996, Enron's return to its stockholders was 80.59 percent, compared with 81.21 percent for its industry peers. The 1997 proxy statement indicated a targeted payout for the top two corporate officers in the $700,000–$800,000 range, and $225,000 for the next level down—far below expected (and realized) gains from grants of stock options and restricted stock. However, in 2000 Kenneth Lay received a cash payment of $1,218,750 for the 1996–1999 performance period, and in 2001 he received another cash payment of $3,600,000 for the 1997–2000 performance period. See Enron 1997 Proxy Statement, pp. 23 and 31; and Enron Corp., May 1, 2001 Proxy Statement, p. 23.

20. Brian J. Hall, "The Six Challenges of Equity-Based Pay Design," *Journal of Applied Corporate Finance* 15, no. 3 (2003): 49–70. See also Brian J. Hall and Kevin J. Murphy, "The Trouble with Executive Stock Options," *Journal of Economic Perspectives* 17, no. 3 (2003).

21. Bethany McLean and Peter Elkind, *The Smartest Guys in the Room: The Amazing Rise and Scandalous Fall of Enron* (New York: Portfolio, 2003), 333–335.

22. Enron 2001 Proxy Statement, pp. 18–22. Rice also held options that he could not yet exercise valued at more than $41 million. He was granted nearly $1.8 million in options in 2000 as part of his compensation for moving from Enron Commodity & Trade to Enron Business Services. McLean and Elkind, *The Smartest Guys in the Room*, p. 187. Other reports put Rice's earnings for 2000 at $47.3 million, but that figure appears to include some stock options granted in 2000 that he could not immediately exercise. See Bill Murphy, "Fast Living, Quick Riches Filled Enron Exec's Days," *Houston Chronicle* (May 18, 2003): 1.

23. McLean and Elkind, *The Smartest Guys in the Room*, p. 334. Reported as $270 million by Peter Behr and Robert O'Harrow Jr., "$270 Million Dollar Man Stays in the Background," *Washington Post* (February 6, 2002), A1. This figure is likely drawn from the class-action lawsuit filed by investors. See U.S. District Court, *In re Enron Corporation Securities Litigation*, Class Action Complaint, available online at */www.universityofcalifornia.edu/news/enron/welcome.html*. The bulk of Pai's stock sales occurred in 2000 as Enron's stock price was still climbing and he was finalizing his divorce. McLean and Elkind, *The Smartest Guys in the Room*, p. 302.

24. Enron Corp., May 5, 1998 Proxy Statement, p. 18; Enron 1999 Proxy Statement, p. 17; Enron May 2, 2000 Proxy Statement, p. 18; and Enron 2001 Proxy Statement, p. 19. Skilling's precise base compensation for 2001 is not known, but an executive compensation "stress test" commissioned by the compensation committee of Enron's board, and performed by Towers Perrin, suggested that he received about $8 million in cash. Staff of the Joint Committee on Taxation, *Report of Investigation of Enron Corporation and Related Entities Regarding Federal Tax and Compensation Issues, and Policy Recommendations,* 108th Congress, JCS-3-03, February 2003, Volume III, Appendix D, p. 166. See also David Barboza, "Officials Got a Windfall Before Enron's Collapse," *New York Times* (June 18, 2002), 1 (which reported that in 2001 Skilling received $7.5 million in cash bonuses and incentives). See Chapter 2, Table 2.4, for my calculations of the net cash generated from Skilling's sales and swaps of Enron stock; and McLean and Elkind, *The Smartest Guys in the Room,* p. 350.

25. See United States District Court, Southern District of Texas, Houston Division, Complaint, *U.S. Securities and Exchange Commission v. Jeffrey K. Skilling and Richard A. Causey,* Case No. H-04-0284 (Harmon), February 19, 2004, for alleged actions to prop up Enron's stock price.

26. For extensive discussion of this point, see Alfred Rappaport, "New Thinking on How to Link Executive Pay with Performance," *Harvard Business Review* (March–April 1999): 91–101; and Bebchuk and Fried, *Pay without Performance,* pp. 139–144. The following section draws heavily on these excellent sources.

27. Arthur Levitt Jr., op ed opinion, *Wall Street Journal* (November 22, 2004). This suggestion goes beyond SEC Release No. 33-8732A, dated August 29, 2006, which amends disclosure requirements in proxy and information statements, periodic reports, current reports, and other filings under the Securities Exchange Act of 1934 and in registration statements under the Exchange Act and the Securities Act of 1933. This amendment is intended to make proxy and information statements, reports, and registration statements easier to understand and to provide investors with a clearer and more complete picture of the compensation earned by a company's principal executive officer, principal financial officer, highest paid executive officers, and members of its board of directors. While this 436-page amendment requires companies to provide investors material information necessary for understanding compensation polices and decisions, there is no requirement or even discussion of comparisons with corporate peers.

28. James Medoff and Katharine Abraham, "Experience, Performance, and Earnings," *Quarterly Journal of Economics* 95, no. 4 (December 1980): 703–736.

29. Craig Lambert, "Desperately Seeking Summa," *Harvard Magazine* (May–June 1993): 36.

30. The "forced curve" at Harvard Business School is one response to grade inflation in university settings.

31. Global Change, *Enron 2001: An Inside View,* p. 34.

32. Simons, Robert, *Levers of Control* (Boston: Harvard Business School Press, 1995), 76.

33. For further discussion, see M. Beer, R. Eisenstadt, and R. Biggadike, "Developing an Organization Capable of Strategy Implementation and Reformulation," in *Organizational Learning and Competitive Advantage*, ed. B. Moingnon and A. Edmonson (London: Sage, 1996).

34. Rappaport, "New Thinking," p. 93.

35. A study by SCA Consulting reported by Simon Patterson and Peter Smith, "How to Make Top People's Pay Reflect Performance," *Sunday Times* (London) (August 9, 1998), business section, p. 8; also cited in Bebchuk and Fried, *Pay without Performance*, p. 138.

36. See Rappaport, "New Thinking," p. 94; and Bebchuk and Fried, *Pay without Performance*, p. 142.

37. Bebchuk and Fried identify these variants of indexed options as ways to reduce windfall gains to executives who hold conventional stock options. See *Pay without Performance*, p. 142.

38. Enron 2000 Proxy Statement, p. 28, fn. (5).

39. "Consider an example where the cost of capital's 10% net of dividend yield, the current stock price is $10 and the exercise price of the option is $10. Such options would pay managers nothing if the stock price failed to rise over any period by an amount greater than the cost of capital less the dividend yield. [If the stock price in our example rises to $11 over the first year, it is still exactly equal to the new exercise price, and the exercise value of the option is still zero.] This means managers earn nothing on their options unless shareholders do better than break even. Since cost of capital options are less valuable, firms can award more of them to managers for the same cost to the firm and thereby create more high-powered incentives for the same cost." Michael C. Jensen, Kevin J. Murphy, and Eric G. Wruk, "CEO Pay . . . and How to Fix It," Harvard Business School NOM Research Paper No. 04–28, revised 2005, pp. 61–62.

40. Kevin J. Murphy, "Explaining Executive Compensation: Managerial Power versus the Perceived Cost of Stock Options," *University of Chicago Law Review* 69 (2002): 863.

41. Rappaport, "New Thinking," pp. 95–96.

42. Alan Levinsohn, "A Garden of Stock Options Helps Harvest Talent," *Strategic Finance* 82 (2001): 81, cited in Lucian Bebchuk, Jesse M. Fried, and David I. Walker, "Managerial Power and Rent Extraction in the Design of Executive Compensation," *University of Chicago Law Review* 69 (Summer 2002): 36, 41.

43. Ibid.

44. See Eli Ofek and David Yermack, "Taking Stock: Equity-Based Compensation and the Evolution of Managerial Ownership," *Journal of Finance* 55 (2000): 1367.

45. Jesse Fried, "Reducing the Profitability of Corporate Insider Trading through Pretrading Disclosure," *Southern California Law Review* 71 (1998): 303–392, especially p. 322.

46. Ibid., especially p. 349ff.

47. Jensen, Murphy, and Wruk, "CEO Pay," p. 67.

48. Fried, "Reducing the Profitability," p. 305.

49. This is another on-target recommendation by Jensen, Murphy, and Wruk, "CEO Pay," p. 79.

50. Ben Glisan Jr. was treasurer of Enron in 2000. He pleaded guilty to commit wire and security fraud in September 2003 but did not agree to cooperate with prosecutors and went straight to prison for the maximum five-year term.

51. David Delainey was the chairman and CEO of Enron Energy Services, the retail contracting arm of the company. He pleaded guilty to one count of insider trading in October 2003 and agreed to cooperate with government investigations of Enron. According to his plea bargain, Delainey paid the government $4.2 million and was sentenced to two years in prison. As part of his settlement with the SEC, he handed over another $3.7 million.

52. Daniel Bergstresser and Thomas Philippson, "CEO Incentives and Earnings Management," *Journal of Financial Economics* (June 2006): 511.

53. Such behavior has been well documented by Healy and others. See Paul Healy, "The Effect of Bonus Schemes on Accounting Decisions," *Journal of Accounting and Economics* 7 (1985): 85–107.

54. Daniel Bergstresser, Mihir Desai, and Joshua Rauh, "Earnings Manipulation, Pension Assumptions, and Managerial Investment Decisions," *Quarterly Journal of Economics* 121, no. 1 (February 2006): 157–195.

55. Robert Simons, "How Risky Is Your Company?" *Harvard Business Review* (May–June 1999): 86.

56. Simons, *Levers of Control;* and Robert Simons, "Control in an Age of Empowerment," *Harvard Business Review* (March–April 1995): 80–88.

57. Merriam-Webster Online, *Online Dictionary,* at www.m-w.com.

58. Edgar H. Schein, *Organizational Culture and Leadership,* 2nd ed. (San Francisco: Jossey-Bass, 1992), 12.

10. Instilling Ethical Discipline

1. In addition to one charge each for securities fraud involving the Raptor transactions, conspiracy to commit securities fraud, and insider trading, Skilling was convicted on six counts of filing false financial statements, four counts of making false and misleading statements during telephone calls with financial analysts, one count of making similar false statements at a conference for financial analysts, and of making five false statements to auditors in quarterly and annual representation letters.

2. The notion that intent can override compliance with esoteric rules is prevalent in U.S. jurisprudence. In reviewing a case of fraud, Judge Henry J. Friendly of the Second District Court of Appeals succinctly stated, "Proof of compliance with generally accepted standards was 'evidence which may be very persuasive but not necessarily conclusive that [the defendant] acted in good faith, and that the facts as certified were not materially false or misleading.'" (*U.S. v. Simon,* 425 F.2d 796, 805–806 [2d Cir. 1969].) Thus the U.S. justice system is

not a machine that plugs inputs into an equation and spits out a result. Following the rules is not enough. We require fellow citizens to respect the purpose behind laws as much as the laws themselves. The spirit of the law is as important as its letter.

Accounting and tax rules are rife with complexities subject to multiple interpretations beyond those envisioned by lawmakers. Businesses run afoul of this intent-compliance balance by attempting to maximize earnings (or reduce losses) through seemingly compliant structures that are actually mere subterfuge. Turning rules on themselves is acceptable only to a point. At that point, loopholes become nooses.

Just as malicious intent can invalidate compliance and create liability, proper intentions can compensate for legal shortcomings and fend off liability. The legal precept of good faith shelters those who wholeheartedly intend to do what the law prescribes but fall short. Good faith protects parties who do not fulfill their end of a contract despite their best efforts, and guards fiduciaries who make bad decisions despite proceeding cautiously. The good-faith concept inserts humanity into the legal process.

In many ways, intent is everything in the law. It separates fraud from an accounting mistake. It dictates how assets are distributed pursuant to a will. It is also the difference between first-degree murder and a horrible accident.

3. This is the "deontological" view of ethics (from the Greek word *deon,* which means binding duty). For a discussion of this and other ethical theories and their relevance to economics, see Amitai Etzioni, *The Moral Dimension: Toward a New Economics* (New York: Free Press, 1988), especially chapter 1. The definition of a moral act presented here comes directly from Etzioni's description of deontological ethics on p. 12. Etzioni contrasts this view with that of utilitarians, who regard two acts yielding similar results as equivalent, even if one involves a transgression, such as deception, and the other does not. See p. 13.

4. U.S. Senate, Committee on Governmental Affairs, "The Fall of Enron: How Could It Have Happened?" 107th Congress (2002), pp. 26–27.

5. The phrase "murky borderlands" is from Saul W. Gellerman's famous article "Why 'Good' Managers Make Bad Decisions," *Harvard Business Review* (July 1986).

6. Privately distributed booklet printed by the Center for Business Ethics at the University of St. Thomas, 2002.

7. Owen Young delivered these comments as part of his keynote address at the dedication of the new campus of Harvard's Graduate School of Business Administration on June 24, 1927. See Young, Owen D., "Dedication Address" (keynote address at the dedication of the new Harvard Business School campus on June 24, 1927). Reprinted in the July 1927 issue of *Harvard Business Review,* and available in the HBS Archives Collection (AC 1927 17.1).

8. For an excellent discussion of the inadequacy of rules in guiding decision making, see Etzioni, *The Moral Dimension,* pp. 173–176.

9. Saul W. Gellerman made this point in the article cited earlier, reprinted in Kenneth R. Andrews, *Ethics in Practice* (Boston: Harvard Business School Press, 1989), 18–26.

10. Steven L. Schwarz, "Fifteenth Annual Corporate Law Symposium: Corporate Bankruptcy in the New Millennium—Enron and the Use and Abuse of Special Purpose Entities in Corporate Structures," *University of Cincinnati Law Review* 70 (2002): 1309, 1313.

11. Roger Parloff, "Credibility GAAP," CNNMoney.com, April 7, 2006, available at http://money.cnn.com/2006/04/07/news/newsmakers/pluggedin_enron _fortune/index.htm, accessed December 14, 2007.

12. Ethics shares certain features with the law (such as forbidding murder), but it also differs in "not being created or changeable by anything like a deliberate legislative, executive, or judicial force or the threat of it but, at most, praise and blame and other such signs of favor or disfavor." William K. Frankena, *Ethics* (Englewood Cliffs, N.J.: Prentice-Hall, 1973), 7.

13. U.S. District Court, Southern District of Texas, Houston Division, Complaint. *U.S. v. Skilling and Lay.* H-CR-04–025SS, prosecution's opening statement, January 31, 2006, , at 360–361; Alexei Barrionuevo, "Ex-Enron Chief Defends Shift of Contracts," *New York Times* (April 13, 2006): 5.

14. Alexei Barrionuevo, "Witness Says Enron Hid Huge Loss From Investors," *New York Times* (February 3, 2006): 3. See also John R. Emshwiller and Gary McWilliams, "Skilling Defends His Statements of Enron's Financial Situation," *Wall Street Journal* (April 20, 2006): C3; and Bethany McLean and Peter Elkind, *The Smartest Guys in the Room: The Amazing Rise and Scandalous Fall of Enron* (New York: Portfolio, 2003), 303.

15. John R. Emshwiller and Gary McWilliams, "Enron Testimony Focuses on Disclosure Timing," *Wall Street Journal* (February 24, 2006): C3. Also see McLean and Elkind, *The Smartest Guys in the Room,* p. 303 (profits of $40 million).

16. Barrionuevo, "Ex-Enron Chief Defends Shift of Contracts."

17. U.S. District Court, *U.S. v. Skilling and Lay,* transcript of Jeff Skilling's testimony, April 19, 2006, at 13814–13816.

18. Barrionuevo, "Ex-Enron Chief Defends Shift of Contracts."

19. U.S. District Court, *U.S. v. Skilling and Lay,* Skilling testimony, at 13844–13846.

20. Ibid. See also Barrionuevo, "Ex-Enron Chief Defends Shift of Contracts."

21. Barrionuevo, "Ex-Enron Chief Defends Shift of Contracts."

22. U.S. District Court, *U.S. v. Skilling and Lay,* Skilling testimony, at 13844–13846. See also prosecution's opening statement, at 366.

23. Ibid. See also John R. Emshwiller and Gary McWilliams, "Accountant Says Enron Dipped into Reserves to Pad Earnings," *Wall Street Journal* (April 20, 2006): C3.

24. Alexei Barrionuevo and Kurt Eichenwald, "Skilling Denies Arranging Secret Side Deals at Enron to Benefit Fastow," *New York Times* (April 12, 2006): 3.

25. Alexei Barrionuevo, "Ex-Executive Says Enron Fudged Data," *New York Times* (February 2, 2006): 1.

26. U.S. District Court, *U.S. v. Skilling and Lay,* Skilling testimony, at 13594.

27. In his appeal Skilling identified this unfinished back office work as being related to (a) assessing the real litigation claims following the California energy
crisis and (b) determining how much expected costs to reserve and current
profits to report. Reply *Brief of Defendant-Appellant Jeffrey K. Skilling* at 57, *U.S. v.
Skilling* (5th Cir. 2007)(06-20885).

28. U.S. District Court, *U.S. v. Skilling and Lay,* Andy Fastow testimony, March 9,
2006, at 7063–7064.

29. In the criminal case against Jeffrey Skilling, government prosecutors argued
that Skilling was actually the source of binding "side deals" or guarantees
that masked phony sales of assets and that these "side deals" were the principal device used by Skilling to perpetuate his scheme to defraud. Skilling's
appeal provides a detailed discussion of the difficulties involved in determining when normal negotiations with a potential buyer of an asset reach the ·
level of an actual guarantee. Brief of Defendant-Appellant Jeffrey K. Skilling
at 107-122, U.S. v Skilling (5th Cir. 2007)(06-20885). Based on this discussion, Skilling argues that the government's factual showing on this issue was
"thin and ambiguous" and that the judge's guidance to the jury on this complicated matter was virtually nonexistent and therefore extremely prejudi-
cial to his defense. Finally, Skilling argued that there was, in fact, no irregu-
larity in Enron's accounting treatment of such transactions as the Nigerian
Barges, "no error in its financial reports, no omissions in its public disclosures, no false statements to its auditors—in short no violation of the law."
See p. 9.

30. U.S. District Court, *U.S. v. Skilling and Lay,* Andy Fastow testimony, March 9,
2006, at 5.

31. *Mahonia Ltd. v. JPMorgan Chase and WestLB,* QBD (Commercial Court), ¶
221, 228.

32. U.S. Bankruptcy Court, Southern District of New York, *In re Enron Corp.,* Chapter 11, Case No. 01–16034 (AJG) "Second Interim Report of Neal Batson
Court-Appointed Examiner" (January 21, 2003), Appendix B (Enron's Disclosure of Its SPEs), p. 117; and William C. Powers Jr., Raymond S. Troubh, and
Herbert S. Winokur Jr., *Report of Investigation by the Special Investigative Committee
of the Board of Directors of Enron Corp.* (2002), available at www.enron.com,
p. 187 (the Powers report).

33. The Powers report, p. 188.

34. Enron Corp., May 2, 2000 Proxy Statement (Houston: Enron Corp, 2000), 25.

35. U.S. Bankruptcy Court, "Second Interim Report," Appendix B, p. 58, and the
Powers report, p. 187.

36. According to U.S. Bankruptcy Court, "Second Interim Report," Appendix B,
p. 117.

37. As reported by Emshwiller and McWilliams, "Enron Testimony."

38. Ibid.

39. The U.S. Supreme Court has held that information is material if there is "a
substantial likelihood that the disclosure of [that] omitted fact would have

been viewed by the reasonable investor as having significantly altered the 'total mix' of information made available." *TSC Industries, Inc. v. Northway Industries, Inc.,* 426 U.S. 438, 449 (1976). Furthermore, in disclosing information, executives must not make "any untrue statement of a material fact or any omission to state a material fact necessary in order to make the statements made, in light of the circumstances under which they were made, not misleading." Section 17(a)(2) of the Securities Act of 1933. 15 U.S.C. 77q(a)(2) (2006).

40. U.S. District Court, *U.S. v. Skilling and Lay,* Skilling testimony, at 13492–1397. For broader discussion of the Raptors, see pp. 13492–13564.

41. U.S. District Court, *U.S. v. Skilling and Lay,* Fastow testimony, (describing the illicit purpose of Raptor transactions), at 6553.

42. Hanna Arendt, "Thinking," *New Yorker* (November 21, 1977): 65–140; (November 28, 1997): 135–216; (December 5, 1977): 135–216. Referenced and summarized in Kenneth E. Goodpaster, "Ethical Imperatives and Corporate Leadership," in Kenneth R. Andrews, ed., *Ethics in Practice* (Boston: Harvard Business School Press, 1989), pp. 214–215.

43. Kenneth R. Andrews, ed., *Ethics in Practice* (Boston: Harvard Business School Press, 1989), p. 10.

44. Ibid., p. 6.

45. Ibid., p. 8.

46. This notion of major differences between the values an organization espouses versus those it practices is developed extensively in Chris Argyris and Donald A. Schoen, *Theories in Practice: Increasing Professional Effectiveness* (San Francisco: Jossey-Bass, 1974).

47. See Andrews, *Ethics in Practice,* pp. 1–11. See also William K. Frankena, *Ethics,* p. 3.

48. Enron internal document, "Skills/Behaviors Descriptors: Vice President/Managing Director," March 30, 2001.

49. This performance measure reads as follows: "Embodies Enron Vision and Values: Inspires excellence in others, by example and integrity. Articulates Vision and Values: demonstrates respect in interacting with others." See Enron internal document, "DRAFT: Performance Feedback," March 30, 2001.

50. Enron internal document, "Enron: Global Performance Management," p. 13, undated.

51. Enron internal document, "Enron's Culture," prepared by Corporate Analysis and Reporting, April 2001, p. 4.

52. The phrase "qualitative attention" is from Andrews, *Ethics in Practice,* p. 263.

53. This is a familiar refrain to those who worked with Kenneth Andrews and read his reflections on the purposes and prospects of moral education for managers.

54. This description of deterrence through internal audit, and the patrol car example, are from Gellerman in ibid., p. 24)

55. The time is ripe for revisiting this practical idea, first proposed by Andrews in ibid., p. 265.

56. The following definitions and discussion of administrative leadership are drawn directly from Philip Selznick, *Leadership in Administration* (New York:

Harper & Row, 1957), 22–28. This widely known and respected essay provides an almost perfect lens through which to view both Enron's leadership default and pathways to effective institutional leadership.

57. Ibid., p. 143.
58. Ibid., p. 148.

Afterword

1. *U.S. v. James A. Brown, Daniel Bayley, Robert S. Furst, William R. Fuhs,* 459 F.3d 509 (U.S. Court of Appeals for the Fifth Circuit filed August 1, 2006), No. 05–20319.

2. The relevant statute is the federal wire fraud statute, which makes it a federal crime to form a "scheme or artifice to defraud" and to use the wires in further-ance of the scheme. 18 U.S.C. §1343. Congress has specifically provided that a " 'scheme or artifice to defraud' includes a scheme or artifice to deprive an-other of the intangible right of honest services." 18 U.S.C. § 1346.

3. "We do not presume that it is in a corporation's legitimate interests ever to mis-state earnings—it is not. However, where an employer intentionally aligns the interests of the employee with a specified corporate goal, where the employee perceives his pursuit of that goal as mutually benefiting him and his employer, and where the employee's conduct is consistent with that perception of the mutual interest, such conduct is beyond the reach of the honest-services the-ory of fraud as it has hitherto been applied." *U.S. v. Brown,* at 22. The court supported, however, the conviction of Brown for perjury and obstruction of justice pertaining to his grand jury testimony related to his knowledge of the Nigerian Barge transaction and, in particular, "whether there was an oral buy-back guarantee between Enron and Merrill and if there was such an agree-ment, who was culpable" at 38. The court's decisions were not, however, unanimous. One judge dissented on the vacated conspiracy charge; another judge dissented on the upheld perjury and obstruction of justice charge.

4. U.S. District Court, Southern District of Texas, Houston Division. *U.S. v. Howard,* United States' Response to Defendant's Motion to Vacate Convictions, Docket Entry 1247, Cr. No. H–03–0093, at 6.

Appendix A

1. Unless otherwise noted, this appendix draws on the following sources: Enron Interoffice Memorandum, Corporate Tax Department, April 19, 2000; William C. Powers Jr., Raymond S. Troubh, and Herbert S. Winokur Jr., *Report of Investi-gation by the Special Investigative Committee of the Board of Directors of Enron Corp.* (2002), available at www.enron.com (hereafter the Powers report), February 2003, Vol. 2, Appendix B, Section XVI, "Off Balance Sheet Partnerships," pp. 569–576; and U.S. Bankruptcy Court, Southern District of New York, *In re Enron Corp.,* Chapter 11, Case No. 01-16034 (AJG), "Report of Harrison J.

Goldin, the Court-Appointed Examiner in the Enron North America Corp. Bankruptcy Proceeding, Respecting His Investigation of the Role of Certain Entities in Transactions Pertaining to Special Purpose Entities" (November 14, 2003)(hereafter the Goldin report).

The Powers report claimed that the Raptor structures were needed because Enron's merchant investments "could not be practically hedged through traditional transactions with third parties," because of the size and illiquidity of these investments.

2. The actual details were more complex. The Raptor structures were designed to offset market-to-market gains and losses on Enron's equity position using hedges that also had to be marked to market for accounting purposes. The combined effect of these two positions was to allow Enron to reduce, if not eliminate, its exposure to fluctuations in reported net income. Another important accounting nuance was that Financial Accounting Standards (FAS) rules allowed hedgers to "park" gains and losses on hedges in the part of the income statement called Other Comprehensive Income, until it was time to recognize them in current income—that is, when a hedge option lapsed or was exercised.

3. In September 2003, Glisan had pleaded guilty to conspiracy charges that included development of the Raptor structures to help manipulate Enron's books.

4. Similarly, even though the terms of the LJM2 partnership disproportionately favored the partnership over Enron in dealings with the Raptors—suggesting self-dealing by Fastow, who served as LJM2's managing partner—neither Skilling, Lay, nor the corporation have any clear legal liability vis-à-vis Enron's shareholders. Fastow may have struck a rich compensation deal for himself, but in the absence of Skilling's and Lay's knowledge, there is no corporate fraud.

5. Reply Brief of Defendant-Appellant Jeffrey K. Skilling, *U.S. v. Skilling* (5th Cir. 2007)(06-20885), at 9–12.

6. Ibid., at 11.

7. LJM's rich arrangement with the Raptors can be summarized as follows: while LJM2 contributed a relatively small sum to the Raptors, it was entitled to all distributions from the Raptors up to the greater of $41 million or a 30 percent annualized return on investment within six months. Only after that obligation was fulfilled could the Raptors distribute funds to Enron. Similarly, if a Raptor was liquidated, LJM2 was entitled to repayment of its original $30 million investment. If the Raptor's assets were worth less than that, LJM2 received their entire value. Enron received its original investment only if assets remained beyond $30 million. This arrangement was slightly different for the Raptor III entity.

8. Plea Agreement, *U.S. v. Glisan* (U.S. District Court for the Southern District of Texas)(H-02-0665), at 11; and Reply Brief of Jeffrey K. Skilling, at 12.

9. The $11 million payment was not specifically addressed in the Glisan plea agreement.

10. The Powers report commented on another hypothetical aspect of this accounting issue: "Were this permissible, a company with access to its own outstanding stock could place itself on an ascending spiral: an increasing stock price would enable it to keep losses in its investments from public view; which, in turn, would spur further increases in its stock price; which, in turn, would increase its capacity to keep investments from public view."

11. Enron Corp., 2000 Annual Report (Houston: Enron Corp., 2000), 48, footnote 16 (Related Party Transactions).

12. Enron Corp., 10-Q Filing to SEC, March 31, 2002, footnote 7 (Related Party Transactions).

13. Ibid.

14. Ibid., p. 10.

15. news.findlaw.com/hdocs/docs/enron/sicreport/chapter 5, p. 103.

Appendix B

1. Senior research associate Perry Fagan prepared this appendix.

2. See Loren Fox, *Enron: The Rise and Fall* (Hoboken, N.J.: Wiley, 2003), 32–33.

3. The tracking account bore an interest rate of 1 percentage point over prime.

4. Fox, *Enron: The Rise and Fall*, pp. 32–33.

5. Bethany McLean and Peter Elkind, *The Smartest Guys in the Room: The Amazing Rise and Scandalous Fall of Enron* (New York: Portfolio, 2003), 61. The Sithe deal made Skilling a big winner. In 1992, the net income of Enron Capital and Trade more than doubled, making it the second-largest contributor to Enron's earnings. When Enron bought out 30 percent of the phantom equity Skilling received when he set up ECT, he reaped $4.7 million in cash, and his two-year-old company was valued at $650 million.

Appendix C

1. W. Neil Eggleston and Dimitri J. Nionakis, Howrey Simon Arnold & White, LLP, 1299 Pennsylvania Avenue, N.W., Washington, D.C. 2004, August 1, 2002. For full text see Eggleston and Nionakis, The Outside Directors' Response to the Permanent Subcommittee on Investigations of the Senate Governmental Affairs Committee Report: "The Role of the Board of Directors in Enron's Collapse," available as an exhibit in *The Role of the Board of Directors in Enron's Collapse: Hearing before the Permanent Subcommittee on Investigations of the Senate Governmental Affairs Committee,* 107th Congress (2002).

Bibliography

In re Abbott Laboratories Derivative Shareholder Litigation. 325 F.3d 795, 809 (7th Cir. 2003).

Abelson, Reed. "Enron's Collapse: The Directors." *New York Times,* 19 January 2002.

Ackerill, J. L., ed. *A New Aristotle Reader.* Princeton, N.J.: Princeton University Press, 1987.

Ackman, Dan. "Pay Madness at Enron." *Forbes,* 22 March 2002.

Aldrich, H. E., and C. M. Fiol. "Fools Rush In? The Institutional Context of Industry Creation." *Academy of Management Review* 19, no. 4 (1994): 645–670.

American Bar Association. Section of Business Law. Committee on Corporate Laws. "Revised Model Business Corporation Act" (RMBCA) (2002).

American Law Institute. *Principles of Corporate Governance: Analysis and Recommendations.* St. Paul, Minn.: American Law Institute Publishers, 1994.

Andrews, I. R., and M. M. Henry. "Management Attitudes towards Pay." *Industrial Relations* 3 (1963).

Andrews, Kenneth R. *Ethics in Practice.* Boston: Harvard Business School Press, 1989.

Arendt, Hannah. "Thinking." *New Yorker,* 21 November 1977, 28 November 1977, 5 December 1977.

Argyris, Chris. "A Next Challenge in Organizational Leadership." November 2002. Mimeo.

Argyris, Chris, and Donald A. Schoen. *Organizational Learning II: Theory, Method, and Practice.* New York: Addison-Wesley, 1996.

———. *Theories in Practice: Increasing Professional Effectiveness.* San Francisco: Jossey-Bass, 1974.

"Aristotle's Ethics." *Stanford Encyclopedia of Philosophy.* Available at http://plato.stanford.edu/entries/aristotle-ethics/.

Arnold, John. Testimony before the Commodity Future Trading Commission in the Matter of Enron Corp., Ref. No. 44916, 19 August 2002.

Arnold v. Society for Savings Bancorp, Inc. 650 A.2d 1270 (Del. 1994).

Aronson v. Lewis, 473 A.2d 805 (Del. 1984).

Axtman, Kris. "Inside the Culture and Collapse of Enron: In the Trial of Corporate

Titans, Witnesses Describe a World of Brains, Skill, and Deception." *Christian Science Monitor,* 12 October 2004.

Babcock, L., and G. Lowenstein. "Explaining Bargaining Impasse: The Role of Self-Serving Biases." *Journal of Economic Perspectives,* Winter 1997.

Babineck, Mark. "Enron's Overseers Did Nothing as Creative Financing Wrecked Company." Associated Press, 17 February 2002.

Badaracco, Joseph L. *Defining Moments.* Boston: Harvard Business School Press, 1997.

Baker, George P., Michael C. Jensen, and Kevin J. Murphy. "Compensation and Incentives: Practice vs. Theory." *Journal of Finance* 43, no. 3 (July 1988).

Baker, George P., and George David Smith. *The New Financial Capitalists: Kohlberg Kravis Roberts and the Creation of Corporate Value.* Cambridge: Cambridge University Press, 1998.

Balotti, R. Franklin, and Joseph Hinsey IV. "Directors Care, Conduct, and Liability: The Model Business Corporation Act Solutions." *The Business Lawyer* 56, no. 1 (November 2000).

Banerjee, Neela. "Who Will Needle Regulators Now that Enron's Muzzled?" *New York Times,* 20 January 2002.

Banerjee, Neela, David Barboza, and Andrey Warrant. "Enron's Many Strands: Corporate Culture." *New York Times,* 28 February 2002.

Barboza, David. "Enron Sought to Raise Cash Two Years Ago." *New York Times,* 9 March 2002.

———. "Officials Got a Windfall before Enron's Collapse." *New York Times,* 18 June 2002.

Barcella, Mary Lashly. "Natural Gas in the Twenty-First Century." *Business Economics* 31, no. 4 (October 1996): 19–24.

Barnes, Julian E., Megan Barnett, Christopher H. Schmitt, and Marianne Lavelle. "Investigative Report: How a Titan Came Undone." *U.S. News & World Report,* 18 March 2002.

Barrionuevo, Alexei. "Ex-Enron Chief Defends Shift of Contracts." *New York Times,* 23 May 2006.

———. "Ex-Executive Says Enron Fudged Data." *New York Times,* 2 February 2006.

———. "Questioning the Books." *Wall Street Journal,* 26 February 2002.

———. "Witness Says Enron Hid Huge Loss from Investors." *New York Times,* 23 February 2002.

Barrionuevo, Alexei, and Kurt Eichenwald, "Skilling Denies Arranging Secret Side Deals at Enron to Benefit Fastow." *New York Times,* 12 April 2006.

Bartlett, Christopher A., and Meg Glinska. "Enron's Transformation: From Gas Pipelines to New Economy Powerhouse." HBS Case No. 9–301–064. Boston: Harvard Business School, 2001.

Bazerman, Max H., G. Lowenstein, and Don A. Moore. "Why Good Accountants Do Bad Audits." *Harvard Business Review,* November 2002.

BBS Norwalk One, Inc. v. Raccolta, Inc. 205 F.3d 1321 (2nd Cir. 2000).

Bebchuk, Lucian. "The Case for Shareholder Access to the Ballot." *Business Lawyer* 59 (2003): 43–66.

Bebchuk, Lucian, and Jesse Fried. *Pay without Performance: The Unfulfilled Promise of Executive Compensation.* Cambridge: Harvard University Press, 2004.

Bebchuk, Lucian, Jesse M. Fried, and David I. Walker. "Managerial Power and Rent Extraction in the Design of Executive Compensation." *University of Chicago Law Review* 69 (Summer 2002).

Beckett, Paul, Jathon Sapsfor, and Alexei Barrionuevo. "Power Outage: How Energy Trades Turned Bonanza into an Epic Bust." *Wall Street Journal,* 31 December 2000.

Beer, M., R. Eisenstadt, and R. Biggadike. "Developing an Organization Capable of Strategy Implementation and Reformulation." In *Organizational Learning and Competitive Advantage,* edited by B. Moingnon and A. Edmonson. London: Sage, 1996.

Behr, Peter. "Hidden Numbers Crushed Enron." *Washington Post,* 12 January 2002.

Behr, Peter, and Robert O'Harrow Jr. "$270 Million Dollar Man Stays in the Background." *Washington Post,* 6 February 2002.

Behr, Peter, and April Witt. "Concerns Grow amid Conflicts: Officials Seek to Limit Probe, Fallout of Deals." *Washington Post,* 30 July 2002.

Berger, Eric. "Lay Pens Chapters on Ethics." *Houston Chronicle,* 11 November 2002.

Bergstresser, Daniel, Mihir Desai, and Joshua Rauh. "Earnings Manipulation, Pension Assumptions, and Managerial Investment Decisions." *Quarterly Journal of Economics* 121, no. 1 (February 2006): 157–195.

Bergstresser, Daniel, and Thomas Philippson. "CEO Incentives and Earnings Management." *Journal of Financial Economics,* June 2006.

Berle, Adolf A., and Gardiner C. Means. *The Modern Corporation and Private Property.* New York: Harcourt, Brace & World, 1932.

Bhagat, Sanjai, and Bernard Black. "The Non-Correlation between Board Independence and Long-Term Firm Performance." *Journal of Corporate Law* 22, no. 1 (Winter 2002).

Bhatnagar, Sanjay, and Peter Tufano. "Enron Gas Services." HBS Case No. 294–076. Boston: Harvard Business School Publishing, 1994.

Bianco v. Erkins. 243 F.3d 599 (2nd Cir. 2001).

The Blackstone Group Prospectus. Filed (with SEC) Pursuant to Rule 424, Registration No. 333-141504. 25 July 2007.

Bodily, Samuel, and Robert Bruner. "Manager's Journal: What Enron Did Right." *Wall Street Journal,* 19 November 2001.

Bradey, Nick. "Board Structure and Effectiveness." In *Governance and Risk,* edited by George S. Dallas. New York: McGraw-Hill, 2004.

Brehm v. Eisner. 746 A.2d 244, 264 (Del. 2000).

Bryce, Robert. *Pipe Dreams.* New York: Public Affairs, 2002.

Burns, Judith. "Enron Lawyer Says Tried to Work 'within System.'" *Dow Jones News Service,* 2 February 2002. Business Roundtable. *Statement on Corporate Governance.* The Business Roundtable, September 1997.

Campos, Roel C. "The SEC's Shareholder Access Proposal." Speech delivered at the Yale Law School Center for the Study of Corporate Law, New York City, 10 January 2005.

Cantor, Richard. "Recent Advances in Credit Risk Research." *Role of Internal and External Ratings in the Credit Process,* conference paper, Moody's Corporation and NYU Salomon Center Inaugural Credit Risk Conference, 20 May 2004.

Caremark Int'l Inc. 698 A.2d 959, 971 (Del. Ch. 1996).

Carney, Dan. "How Enron Alienated Just About Everyone." *BusinessWeek Online,* 17 January 2002.

Carson, Margaret M. "Enron and the New Economy." *Competitiveness Review* 11, no. 2 (2001).

Carter, Colin B., and Jay W. Lorsch. *Back to the Drawing Board.* Boston: Harvard Business School Press, 2004.

Catanach, Anthony H., and Rhodes, Shelley C. "Enron: A Financial Reporting Failure." *Villanova Law Review* 48, no. 4 (2003).

CFTC Web site at www.cftc.gov/cftc/cftcabout.htm (accessed 9 January 2008).

Chaffin, Joshua, and Stephen Fidler. "The Enron Collapse." *Financial Times,* 9 April 2002.

———. "Enron's Alchemy Turns to Lead for Bankers." *Financial Times,* 28 February 2002.

Charas Consulting Study. Submitted to Enron Corp.

Chiles v. Robertson. 767 P.2d 903 (Or. Ct. App. 1989).

Citigroup. "Global Corporate Banking," Citigroup Corporate and Investment Banking Web site. www.citigroupcib.com (accessed 9 January 2008).

Coffee, John C. Jr. "Understanding Enron: It's about the Gatekeepers, Stupid." Columbia Law School, The Center for Law and Economics, Working Paper No. 207, 30 July 2002.

———. "What Caused Enron? A Capsule Social and Economic History of the 1990's." *Cornell Law Review* 89, no. 2 (2004).

Columbus Dispatch. "Enron: A Primer." 26 January 2002.

Compustat North America database, available at www2.standardandpoors.com (accessed 9 January 2008).

Conference Board. *Commission on Public Trust & Private Enterprise: Findings and Recommendations.* The Conference Board, 9 January 2003.

———. "Directors' Compensation and Practices in 2004." The Conference Board, 2004.

Conger, Jay A., David Finegold, and Edward E. Lawler III. "Appraising Boardroom Performance." *Harvard Business Review,* January-February 1998: 136–148.

Cooper, A. C., W. C. Dunkelberg, C. Y. Woo, and W. J. Dennis, Jr. "Entrepreneurs' Perceived Chances for Success." *Journal of Business Venturing* 3, no. 2 (1988): 97–108.

Cooper, Stephen. Report to the U.S. Bankruptcy Court. Southern District of New York. 22 April 2002.

Core, John E., Robert W Hothausen, and David F. Larker. "Corporate Governance,

Chief Executive Officer Compensation, and Firm Performance." *Journal of Financial Economics* 51 (1999): 371–406.

Corval, Joshua A., Robin Greenwood, and Peter Tufano, *Williams, 2000.* HBS Case 9-203-068 (rev. 7 February 2006).

Council of Institutional Investors. *Corporate Governance Policies.* Council of Institutional Investors, September 2002.

Coy, Peter. "Exploiting Uncertainty: The 'Real-Options' Revolution in Decision-Making." *BusinessWeek,* 7 June 1999.

Coy, Peter, Stephanie Anderson, Dean Foust, and Emily Thornton. "Enron: How Good an Energy Trader?" *BusinessWeek,* 11 February 2002.

Cruver, Brian. *Anatomy of Greed: The Unshredded Truth from an Enron Insider.* New York: Carroll and Graf, 2002.

Cummings, Jeanne, John R. Emshwiller, Tom Hamburger, Scot J. Paltrow, Jathon Sapsford, Ellen E. Schultz, Randall Smith, and Rebecca Smith. "Enron Lessons." *Wall Street Journal,* 15 January 2002. Available from www.factiva.com (accessed 20 July 2006).

Davies, Erin. "Enron: The Power's Back On. Rousing a $20 Billion Giant." *Fortune,* 13 April 1998.

Deci, Edward L., and Richard M. Ryan. *Intrinsic Motivation and Self-Determination in Human Behavior.* New York: Plenum Press, 1985.

Dettmer, Jamie, and John Berlau. "Requiem for Enron." *Insight,* 7 January 2002.

Devlin v. Moore. 130 P.35, 45 (Or. 1913).

Donato, Luigi, and Domato Masciandaro. "Putting the Crooks Out of Business: The Emerging Role of Integrity in Banking Supervision and Regulation. The Italian Case (1991–2001)." Undated mimeo.

Durgin, Hillary. "The Guru of Decentralisation." *Financial Times,* 26 June 2000.

Economist. "Enron's Ghost: Recharging." 20 April 2002.

Economist. "The Shareholders' Revolt." 17 June 2006.

Eggleston, W. Neil, and Dmitri J. Nionakis. The Outside Directors' Response to the Permanent Subcommittee on Investigations of the Senate Governmental Affairs Committee Report: "The Role of the Board of Directors in Enron's Collapse." Available as an exhibit in *The Role of the Board of Directors in Enron's Collapse: Hearing before the Permanent Subcommittee on Investigations of the Senate Governmental Affairs Committee,* 107th Congress (2002).

Eichenwald, Kurt. "Company Man to the End, after All." *New York Times,* 9 February 2003.

———. *Conspiracy of Fools.* New York: Broadway Books / Random House, 2005.

Eichenwald, Kurt, and John Markoff. "Deception, or Just Disarray, at Enron?" *New York Times,* 8 June 2003.

Eisenberg, Melvin Aron, ed. *Corporations and Other Business Organizations.* New York: Foundation Press, 2001.

Emshwiller, John R. "Enron Official Gave Warnings as Early as '99." *Wall Street Journal,* 18 March 2002.

———. "Enron's Skilling Cites Stock-Price Plunge as Main Reason for Leaving CEO Post." *Wall Street Journal,* 16 August 2001.

Emshwiller, John R., and Gary McWilliams. "Accountant Says Enron Dipped into Reserves to Pad Earnings." *Wall Street Journal,* 20 April 2006.

———. "Enron Testimony Focuses on Disclosure Timing." *Wall Street Journal,* 24 February 2006.

———. "Skilling Defends His Statements of Enron's Financial Situation." *Wall Street Journal,* 20 April 2006.

Emshwiller, John R., and Mitchell Pacelle. "In His Own Defense: Enron Inquiry Worth $90 Million?" *Wall Street Journal,* 18 March 2004.

Emshwiller, John, and Rebecca Smith. "Enron Jolt: Investments, Assets Generate Big Loss." *Wall Street Journal,* 17 October 2001.

Enron Corp. Annual Report, 1998.

———. Annual Report, 1999.

———. Annual Report, 2000.

———. Code of Ethics, July 2000.

———. 8-K Filing to SEC, 8 November 2001.

———. 8-K Filing to SEC, 1 April 2002.

———. 8-K Filing to SEC, 17 April 2003.

———. 8-K Filing to SEC, 22 April 2002.

———. Enron's Articles of Incorporation.

———. Form U-1: Application Under the PUHCA of 1935. 14 April 2000.

———. Internal document. "DRAFT: Performance Feedback," 30 March 2001.

———. Internal document. "Enron: Global Performance Management," undated.

———. Internal document. "Investment Portfolio: Lessons Learned, November 2000."

———. Internal document. Jeffrey K. Skilling 1996 Employment Agreement, effective 1 January 1996, with Enron Capital Trade & Resources Corp.

———. Internal document. Kenneth L. Lay 1996 Employment Agreement, effective December 9, 1996.

———. Internal document (prepared by Corporate Analysis and Reporting). "Enron's Culture," April 2001.

———. Internal document. "Skills/Behaviors Descriptors: Vice President/Managing Director," 30 March 2001.

———. Interoffice Memorandum. Corporate Tax Department, 19 April 2000.

———. Minutes of the Audit Committee of the Board of Directors, 7 February 2000.

———. Minutes of the Audit Committee of the Board of Directors, 1 May 2000.

———. Minutes of the Audit Committee of the Board of Directors, 12 February 2001.

———. Minutes of the Board of Directors, 28 June 1999.

———. Minutes of the Board of Directors, 11–12 October 1999.

———. Minutes of the Board of Directors, 2 May 2000.

———. Minutes of the Board of Directors, 6–8 August 2000.

———. Minutes of the Executive Committee of the Board of Directors, 5 November 1997.

———. Minutes of the Executive Committee of the Board of Directors, 22 June 2000.

———. Minutes of the Finance Committee of the Board of Directors, 11 October 1999.

———. Minutes of the Finance Committee of the Board of Directors, 13 December 1999.

———. Minutes of the Finance Committee of the Board of Directors, 1 May 2000.

———. Minutes of the Finance Committee of the Board of Directors, 7 August 2000.

———. Minutes of the Finance Committee of the Board of Directors, 6 October 2000.

———. Minutes of the Finance Committee of the Board of Directors, 7 December 2000.

———. Minutes of the Finance Committee of the Board of Directors, 12 February 2001.

———. "Monthly Operating Statement for December 2 through December 31, 2001." Submitted to the U.S. Bankruptcy Court, Southern District, 22 April 2002.

———. Payment to Insiders, Schedule of Financial Affairs. Submitted to New York Bankruptcy Court, 17 May 2002. Case No. 01–16034.

———. PowerPoint Bank Presentation. Waldorf Astoria, New York, 19 November 2001; cited in U.S. Bankruptcy Court. Southern District of New York. *In re Enron Corp.*, Chapter 11, Case No. 01–16034 (AJG), "Second Interim Report of Neal Batson, Court-Appointed Examiner" (Bankr. S.D.N.Y. 21 January 2003), p. 11.

———. Press releases. Available at www.enron.com/corp/pressroom/releases (accessed 11 November 2003).

———. Proxy Statement. 6 May 1997.

———. Proxy Statement. 5 May 1998.

———. Proxy Statement. 4 May 1999.

———. Proxy Statement. 2 May 2000.

———. Proxy Statement. 1 May 2001.

———. Special Investigative Committee of the Board of Directors. *Report of Investigation,* 2002.

———. 10-K Filing to SEC, 31 December 1998.

———. 10-K Filing to SEC, 31 December 1999.

———. 10-K Filing to SEC, 31 December 2000.

———. 10-Q Filing to SEC, 31 March 1999.

———. 10-Q Filing to SEC, 30 June 1999.

———. 10-Q Filing to SEC, 2 April 2000.

———. 10-Q Filing to SEC, 30 September 2001.

———. 10-Q Filing to SEC, 31 March 2002.

Enron Corp. to the United States Bankruptcy Court, Southern District of New York, 22 April 2002.

"Enron Development Corporation: The Dabhol Power Project in Maharashtra, India (A)." Harvard Business School Case, Rev. 8 July 1998.

Enron Web site. www.enron.com/wholesale/petro/price.html; http://www.enron.com/wholesale/petro/trading.html (accessed 11 November 2003).

Esty, B. C. "A Case Study of Organizational Form and Risk Sharing in the Savings and Loan Industry." *Journal of Financial Economics* 44, no. 1 (1997).

Esty, Benjamin, and Peter Tufano, with Matthew Bailey. "Contractual Innovation in the U.K. Energy Markets: Enron Europe, The Eastern Group, and the Sutton Bridge Project." Harvard Business School Case N9–200–051.

Etzioni, Amitai. *The Moral Dimension: Toward a New Economics.* New York: Free Press, 1988.

Fama, Eugene F., and Michael C. Jensen. "Separation of Ownership and Control." *Journal of Law and Economics* 26 (June 1983).

Fastow, Andy. Transcript of Testimony. *U.S. v. Lay and Skilling,* H-CR-04–025SS (S.D. Tex. 2006). 7 and 9 March 2006.

Federal Energy Regulatory Commission. Staff Report. "Final Report on Price Manipulation in the Western Markets." Docket No. PA02–2–00, March 2003. Available at www.ferc.gov/industries/electric/indus-act/wec/enron/enrondata .asp#skipnavsub (accessed 10 January 2008).

———. Staff Report. "Price Manipulation in Western Markets: Findings at a Glance." Docket No. EL00-95-000. April 13, 2005.

———. "What FERC Does." Available at www.ferc.gov/about/ferc-does.asp (accessed 14 January 2008).

Felton, Robert F., and Pamela Keenan Fritz. "The View from the Board Room." *McKinsey Quarterly,* 2005 Special Edition: Value and Performance.

Fight, Andrew. *The Ratings Game.* New York: John Wiley and Sons, 2001.

Financial Accounting Standards Board. "Statement of Financial Accounting Concepts No. 5: Recognition and Measurement in Financial Statements of Business Enterprises." Norwalk, Conn.: Financial Accounting Standards Board, 1984.

———. "Statement of Financial Accounting Standards No. 57: Related Party Disclosures." Norwalk, Conn.: Financial Accounting Standards Board, 1982.

———. "Statement of Financial Accounting Standards No. 140: Accounting for Transfers and Servicing of Financial Assets and Extinguishments of Liabilities—a Replacement of FASB Statement No. 125." Norwalk, Conn.: Financial Accounting Standards Board, 2000.

Fitzpatrick v. FDIC, 765 F.2d 569 (6th Cir. 1985).

Flood, Mary. "Enron Judge Rules Criminal Conspiracy Likely." *Houston Chronicle on the Web,* 8 October 2004, www.chron.com (accessed 12 November 12 2004).

———. "Ex-Enron, Merrill Execs Sentenced." *Houston Chronicle on the Web*, 13 May 2005. Available at www.chron.com/cs/CDA/ssistory.mpl/special /enron/barge/ 3180226 (accessed 19 May 2005).

———. "Ex-trader pleads guilty to schemes." *Houston Chronicle,* 5 February 2003.

———. "Former Merrill Lynch Executives Get Less Prison than Requested." *Houston Chronicle on the Web,* 23 April 2005. Available at www.chron.com/cs/CDA/printstory.mpl/special /enron/barge/3146490 (accessed 19 May 2005).

———. "Houston Jurors to Hear Closing Arguments Today in Enron Barge Case."

Houston Chronicle on the Web, 27 October 2004. Available at www.factiva.com (accessed 12 November 2004).

Flood, Mary, and Tom Fowler. "5 Guilty in Enron Barge Scheme." *Houston Chronicle on the Web,* 4 November 2004, www.chron.com/cs/CDA/ssistrory.mpl/special/enron/barge/2883572 (accessed 2 June 2005).

Foss, Brad. "How a Fledgling Water Business Helped Sink Enron." Associated Press, 3 February 2002.

———. "How Fledgling Water Business Named Azurix Foreshadowed Fall of Energy Giant Enron." Associated Press, 3 February 2002.

Foster Electric Report. "EEI Report Reveals Power Marketers' Sales Increased over 400 Percent in 1997; Less Domination by the Top 10 Sellers." 5 August 1998.

Fox, Loren. *Enron: The Rise and Fall.* Hoboken, N.J.: John Wiley & Sons, 2003.

Frammolino, Ralph, and Jeff Leeds. "Andersen's Reputation in Shreds." *Los Angeles Times,* 30 January 2002.

Francis v. United Jersey Bank, 432 A.2d 814, 822 (N.J. Sup. Ct. 1981).

Frankena, William K. *Ethics.* Englewood Cliffs, N.J.: Prentice-Hall, 1973.

Freedenthal, Carol. "Leadership: A Critical Element in Restructuring." *Pipeline & Gas Journal,* August 1998.

Fried, Jesse M. "Reducing the Profitability of Corporate Insider Trading through Pretrading Disclosure." *Southern California Law Review* 71 (1998): 303–392.

Friedman, Thomas. Interview by Jim Lehrer. *News Hour with Jim Lehrer,* 13 February 1996.

Gagliardi v. TriFoods Int'l Inc., 683 A.2d 1049, 1051 n.2 (Del. Ch. 1996).

Garner, Bryan A., ed. *Black's Law Dictionary,* 7th ed. St. Paul, Minn.: West Publishing, 1999.

Gasparino, Charles, and Randall Smith. "CSFB Bankers Served as Directors of Enron Entity." *Wall Street Journal,* 5 April 2002.

Gellerman, Saul W. "Why 'Good' Managers Make Bad Decisions." *Harvard Business Review,* July 1986.

General Electric Co. *Governance Principles.* 22 July 2004.

Ghemawat, Pankaj, and David Lane. "Enron: Entrepreneurial Energy." HBS Case No. 9–700–079. Boston: Harvard Business School Publishing, 2000.

Gibney, Frank Jr. "Enron Plays the Pipes." *Time,* 28 August 2000.

Gillan, Stuart L., and John D. Martin. "Financial Engineering, Corporate Governance, and the Collapse of Enron." Center for Corporate Governance, University of Delaware, Working Paper 2002–001.

Glass, John. "Enron's Power Play Gives IPPs an Edge." *Boston Business Journal* 2 (September 1991).

Glater, Jonathan, and Michael Brick. "Enron's Collapse: The Overview." *New York Times,* 22 January 2002.

Global Change. *Enron 2001: An Inside View.*

Gold, Stanley. "Corporate Boards: A Director's Cut." Manager's Journal, *Wall Street Journal,* 18 February 2003.

Goldschmid, Harvey J. "Remarks before the Council of Institutional Investors."

Speech, Washington, D.C., 11 April 2005. Available at www.sec.gov/news/speech/speecharchive/2005speech.shtml (accessed 14 January 2008).

Goleman, Daniel. *Emotional Intelligence.* New York: Bantam Books, 1995.

Gompers, Paul, and Josh Lerner. "An Analysis of Compensation in the U.S. Venture Capital Partnership." *Journal of Financial Economics* 51 (1999): 3–44.

Goodpaster, Kenneth E. "Ethical Imperatives and Corporate Leadership." In *Ethics in Practice,* edited by Kenneth R. Andrews. Boston: Harvard Business School Press, 1989.

Gordon, Jeffrey N. "Governance Failures of the Enron Board and the New Information Order of Sarbanes-Oxley." *Connecticut Law Review,* Spring 2003.

Graham v. Allis-Chalmers. 188 A.2d 125, 130 (Del. 1963).

Granderson, Gerald. "Regulation, Open-Access Transportation, and Productive Efficiency." *Review of Industrial Organization* 16 (2000): 251–266.

Granof, Michael H., and Stephen A. Zeff. "Unaccountable in Washington." *New York Times,* 23 January 2002.

Greaney, Thomas L. "Editorial: Lining Up the Suspects in the Great Enron Caper." *St. Louis Post-Dispatch,* 15 January 2002.

Grossman, Sanford, and Oliver Hart. "The Cost and Benefits of Ownership: A Theory of Vertical and Lateral Integration." *Journal of Political Economy* 94 (1986).

Hall, Brian J. "The Six Challenges of Equity-Based Pay Design." *Journal of Applied Corporate Finance* 15, no. 3 (2003): 49–70.

Hall, Brian J., and Kevin J. Murphy. "The Trouble with Executive Stock Options." *Journal of Economic Perspectives* 17 (2003).

Hays, Kristen. "Judge OKs Withdrawal of Enron-Related Guilty Plea." *Houston Chronicle,* 2 April 2007.

———. "Judge Orders Retrial in Enron Barge Case." *Houston Chronicle,* 4 April 2007.

———. "Pipelines, Power Plants Keeping Enron Afloat." *Commercial Appeal Memphis,* 23 February 2002.

Healy, Paul. "The Effect of Bonus Schemes on Accounting Decisions." *Journal of Accounting and Economics* 7 (1985): 85–107.

Heel, Joachim, and Conor Kehoe. "Why Some Private Equity Firms Do Better than Others." *McKinsey Quarterly* 1 (2005): 24–26.

Herbert, John H., and Erik Kreil. "U.S. Natural Gas Markets: How Efficient Are They?" *Energy Policy* 24, no. 1 (1996): 1–5.

Herrick, Thaddeus, and Alexei Barrionuevo. "Were Auditor and Client Too Close-Knit?" *Wall Street Journal,* 21 January 2002.

Hertz, D. B. "Investment Policies that Pay Off." *Harvard Business Review* 46 (January-February 1968): 96–108.

Herzberg, Frederick. "One More Time: How Do You Motivate Employees?" *Harvard Business Review,* January-February 1968.

Herzberg, Frederick, B. Mauser, and B. Snyderman. *The Motivation to Work.* New York: Wiley, 1959.

Herzfeld v. Laventhol, Krekstein, Horwath & Horwath. 378 F. Supp. 112, 121 (S.D.N.Y. 1974).

Hill, Patrice. "Clinton Helped Enron Finance Projects Abroad." *Washington Times,* 21 February 2002.

Hiltzik, Michael. "The Fall of Enron." *Los Angeles Times,* 31 January 2002.

Hinsey, Joseph. "Pssst . . . Wanna Be a Director?" (mimeo, 23 March 2005).

Hollis v. Hill. 232 F.3d 460 (5th Cir. 2001).

Hoye v. Meek. 795 F.2d 893, 896 (10th Cir. 1986).

Hunt, Albert R. "A Scandal Centerpiece: Enron's Political Connections." *Wall Street Journal,* 17 January 2002.

Hurt, Harry III. "Power Players." *Fortune,* 5 August 1996.

International Organization of Securities Commissioners. Technical Committee. "Code of Conduct Fundamentals for Credit Rating Agencies," December 2004.

———. "Report on the Activities of Credit Rating Agencies." September 2003, p. 1.

Investor Responsibility Research Center. "Board Practices/Board Pay, 2005 Edition: The Structure and Composition of Boards of Directors at S&P Super 1,500 Companies." Washington, D.C.: IRRC, 2005.

Janis, Irving L. *Groupthink.* Boston: Houghton Mifflin, 1982.

Janis, Irving L., and Leon Mann. *Decision Making.* New York: Free Press, 1977.

Jensen, Michael C. "Agency Costs of Free Cash Flow, Corporate Finance, and Takeovers." *American Economic Review* 76 (1986): 323–329.

———. "Agency Costs of Overvalued Equity." Harvard NOM Research Paper No. 04.26, 2004.

———. "Eclipse of the Modern Corporation." *Harvard Business Review* 89, no. 5 (September-October 1989).

———. *Foundations of Organizational Strategy.* Cambridge: Harvard University Press, 1998.

———. "The Modern Industrial Revolution, Exit and the Failure of Internal Control Systems." *Journal of Finance* 48 (July 1993): 831–880.

———. "Self-Interest, Altruism, Incentives, and Agency Theory." *Journal of Applied Corporate Finance* 7, no. 2 (Summer 1994).

Jensen, Michael C., Willy Burkhardt, and Brian K. Barry. "Wisconsin Central Ltd. Railroad and Berkshire Partners (A): Leveraged Buyouts and Financial Distress." Harvard Business School Case 9–190–062.

Jensen, Michael C., and William H. Meckling. "The Nature of Man." *Journal of Applied Corporate Finance,* Summer 1994.

———. "Theory of the Firm: Managerial Behavior, Agency Costs, and Ownership Structure." *Journal of Financial Economics* 3, no. 4 (October 1976): 305–360.

Jensen, Michael C., William A. Meckling, Carliss Y. Baldwin, George P. Baker, and Karen H. Wruck. "Course Notes for Coordination, Control, and Management of Organizations." Harvard Business School, Fall 1995.

Jensen, Michael C., Kevin J. Murphy, and Eric G. Wruk. "CEO Pay . . . and How to Fix It." Harvard Business School NOM Research Paper No. 04–28, Revised 2005.

Johnston, David Cay. "Wall St. Banks Said to Help Enron Devise Its Tax Shelters." *New York Times,* 14 February 2003.

Kadlec, Daniel. "Who's Accountable?" *Time,* 21 January 2002.

Kaminski, Vince, and John Martin. "Transforming Enron: The Value of Active Management." *Journal of Applied Corporate Finance* 13, no. 4 (Winter 2001).

Kaplan, Steve, and Antoinette Schoar. "Private Equity Performance: Returns, Persistence and Capital Flows." MIT Sloan School of Management Working Paper 4446–03 (November 2003), and *Journal of Finance* 60 (August 2005).

Kapner, Suzanne. "A Rush to Hire Enron Employees." *New York Times,* 8 March 2002.

King, Julia, and Gary H. Anthes. "Enron Hits the Gas." *Computerworld,* 20 November 2000.

Kirkpatrick, David. "Enron Takes Its Pipeline to the Net." *Fortune,* 24 January 2000.

Klinicki v. Lundgren. 695 P.2d 906, 910 (Or. 1985).

Koch, Christopher. "Reinvent Now." *CIO,* 15 August 1999.

Kohn, Alfie. "Why Incentive Plans Cannot Work." *Harvard Business Review,* September-October 1993.

Korn/Ferry International. "31st Annual Board of Directors Study," 2004.

Kuranna, Rakesh, Tarun Khanna, and Daniel Penrice. "Harvard Business School and the Making of a New Profession." HBS Case No. N9–403–105. Boston: Harvard Business School Publishing, 2005.

Labaton, Stephen. "Enron's Collapse: Regulations." *New York Times,* 23 January 2002.

Laing, Jonathan R. "The Bear that Roared." *Barron's,* 28 January 2002.

Lambert, Craig. "Desperately Seeking Summa." *Harvard Magazine,* May-June 1993.

Lawler, Edward E. III. "Managers' Attitudes Toward How Their Pay Is and Should Be Determined." *Journal of Applied Psychology* 50 (1966).

———. *Pay and Organizational Effectiveness: A Psychological View.* New York: McGraw-Hill, 1971.

Lawler, Edward E. III, George S. Benson, David L. Finegold, and Jay A. Conger. "Corporate Boards: Keys to Effectiveness." *Organizational Dynamics* 30, no. 4 (2002).

Laxmi, John. "Enron: Restructuring an Energy Company." *Global Finance,* May 2000.

Lay, Kenneth. Videotape interview, Harvard Business School, 11 January 2001.

LeDoux, Joseph. *The Emotional Brain.* New York: Simon & Schuster, 1996.

Leopold, Jason, and Jessica Berthold. "Enron's Filings Show Lavish Compensation Was Awarded to Many Senior Executives." *Wall Street Journal,* 18 March 2002.

Levich, Richard M., Giovanni Majnoni, and Carmen Reinhart, eds. *Ratings, Rating Agencies, and the Global Financial System.* Boston: Kluwer Academic, 2002.

Levitt, Arthur Jr. "Op Ed Opinion." *Wall Street Journal,* 22 November 2004.

Levinsohn, Alan. "A Garden of Stock Options Helps Harvest Talent." *Strategic Finance* 82 (2001).

Levy, Adam. "The Deal Machine." *Bloomberg Markets* 11, no. 1 (January 2002): 33–34.

Litwin v. Allen. 25 N.Y.S.2d 667, 700 (N.Y. Co. Sup. Ct. 1940).

Lorsch, Jay W. *Pawns or Potentates: The Reality of America's Corporate Boards.* Boston: Harvard Business School Press, 1989.

Lorsch, Jay W., V. G. Narayanan, and Krishna Palepu. "Executive Remuneration at

Reckitt Benkhiser plc." Harvard Business School Case 9–104–062, 27 January 2004.

Lynch v. Vickers Energy Corp. 383 A.2d 278, 281 (Del. 1977).

M&A executive, Azurix international development team. Interview with author, 28 July 2003.

MacAvoy, Paul W., and Ira M. Millstein. *The Recurring Crisis in Corporate Governance.* New York: Palgrave Macmillan, 2003.

Mace, Myles L. *Directors: Myth and Reality.* Boston: Division of Research, Graduate School of Business Administration, Harvard University, 1971.

Mack, Toni. "Hidden Risks." *Forbes,* 24 May 1993.

Macy, Jonathan R. "Efficient Capital Markets, Corporate Disclosure and Enron." *Cornell Law Review* 89, no. 2 (2004): 394–422.

Mahonia Ltd. v. JPMorgan Chase and WestLB, QBD (Commercial Court).

Malone v. Brincat. 722 A.2d 5, 10 (Del. 1998).

Margolis, Joshua D. "Responsibility in an Organizational Context." *Business Ethics Quarterly* 11, no. 3.

Mason, Julie. "Enron's Former Chairman Repeatedly Tells Probers He Didn't Know about Deals." *Houston Chronicle,* 20 February 2002.

May, Larry. *The Morality of Groups: Collective Responsibility, Group-Based Harm, and Corporate Right.* Notre Dame, Ind.: University of Notre Dame Press, 1987.

McCall v. Scott (McCall I). 239 F.3d 808 (6th Cir. 2001).

McCall v. Scott (McCall II). 250 F.3d 997 (6th Cir. 2001).

McKinnon, John D. "Enron Tried to Delay Paying Taxes on Foreign Profit, Documents Show." *Wall Street Journal,* 4 March 2002.

———. "Questioning the Books: Enron Hasn't Fulfilled Promise to Disclose Tax Records to Congress." *Wall Street Journal,* 26 February 2002.

McLean, Bethany. Interviewed by Steve Inskeep, *Morning Edition,* National Public Radio, 15 October 2004.

———. "Is Enron Overpriced?" *Fortune,* 5 March 2001.

McLean, Bethany, and Peter Elkind. *The Smartest Guys in the Room: The Amazing Rise and Scandalous Fall of Enron.* New York: Portfolio, 2003.

McMahon, Jeffrey. Testimony. "Enron Bankruptcy." U.S. House. Energy and Commerce Committee, Oversight and Investigations Subcommittee. 107th Congress. 7 February 2002.

Medoff, James, and Katharine Abraham. "Experience, Performance, and Earnings." *Quarterly Journal of Economics* 95, no. 4 (December 1980): 703–736.

Mehta, Shailendra Raj, and Arnold C. Cooper. "God Rewards Fools: Optimism as a Predictor of New Firm Success." Working Paper, Krannert School of Management, Purdue University, October 2003.

Merrill-Lynch. 1999 Annual Report.

Miller, William H. "Vision Vanquisher." *Industry Week,* 18 May 1998.

Miller v. AT&T. 507 F.2d 759, 762–763, 3d Cir. 1974.

Mizruchi, Mark S. "Berle and Means Revisited: The Governance and Power of Large U.S. Corporations." University of Michigan Working Paper, April 2004.

Morch, Randall. "Behavioral Finance in Corporate Governance—Independent Directors and Non-Executive Chairs." Harvard Institute of Economic Research Discussion Paper No. 2037, May 2004.

Morgan Stanley. *Morgan Stanley Board of Directors Corporate Governance Policies.* Morgan Stanley, 9 December 2003.

Morgenson, Gretchen. "Finally, Shareholders Start Acting Like Owners." *New York Times,* 11 June 2006.

Murphy, Bill. "Fast Living, Quick Riches Filled Enron Exec's Days." *Houston Chronicle,* 18 May 2001.

Murphy, Kevin. "Explaining Executive Compensation: Managerial Power versus the Perceived Cost of Stock Options." *University of Chicago Law Review* 69 (2002).

Murphy, Kevin J. "Executive Compensation." In *Handbook of Labor Economics,* vol. 3, bk. 2, edited by Orley Ashenfelter and David Card. New York: Elsevier, 1999.

Murray, Allan. *Revolt in the Boardroom.* New York: HarperCollins Publishers, 2007.

Nadler, David, and Jay W. Lorsch. *Report of the NACD Blue Ribbon Commission on Board Leadership.* Washington, D.C.: National Association of Corporate Directors, 2004.

National Association of Corporate Directors. "Director Compensation: Purposes, Principles, and Best Practices." Report of the Blue Ribbon Commission of the NACD, 2001.

New York Stock Exchange. "NYSE Listed Company Manual Section 303A, Corporate Listing Standards" (updated February 13, 2004), available at www.nyse.com/pdfs/section303Afaqs.pdf (accessed 11 December 2007).

New York Times. "The Rise and Fall of Enron." Editorial. 2 November 2001.

"A Next Challenge in Organizational Leadership." November 2002. Mimeo.

"1997 All-America Research Team: Energy." *Institutional Investor* 31 (1 October 1997).

Nocera, Joseph. "For All Its Cost, Sarbanes Law Is Working." *New York Times,* 3 December 2005.

Norris, Floyd. "Coke's Board to Get Bonus or Nothing." *New York Times,* 6 April 2006.

Norris, Floyd, and David Barboza. "Enron's Many Strands: Ex-Chairman's Finances." *New York Times,* 16 February 2002.

Norris, Floyd, and Kurt Eichenwald, "Fuzzy Rules of Accounting and Enron." *New York Times,* 30 January 2002.

O'Connor, Marleen A. "The Enron Board: The Perils of Groupthink." *University of Cincinnati Law Review* 71 (Summer 2003).

OECD Principles of Corporate Governance. Paris: Organisation for Economic Co-operation and Development, 1999.

Ofek, Eli, and David Yermack. "Taking Stock: Equity-Based Compensation and the Evolution of Managerial Ownership." *Journal of Finance* 55 (2000).

Off Wall Street Consulting Group, Inc. "Enron Corp. Report," 6 May 2001.

Oil & Gas Investor. "Enron Producer Services." 1 April 2001.

Omaha World-Herald. "Nation's Largest Natural Gas Company Turns to the Sun's Light." 25 November 1994, quoted from *New York Times.*

Oregon Revised Statutes, c. 60.047(2)(d), 60.301(2), 60.357(1).

O'Reilly, Brian. "The Power Merchant." *Fortune,* 17 April 2000.

Osterloh, Margit, and Bruno S. Frey. "Motivation, Knowledge Transfer, and Organizational Forms." *Organizational Science* 11, no. 5 (September-October 2000): 538–550.

Pacelle, Mitchell, and Robin Sidel. "Citigroup Accord to End Enron Suit May Pressure Others." *Wall Street Journal,* 13 June 2005.

———. "J. P. Morgan Settles Enron Lawsuit—Payment of $2.2 Billion Tops Recent Citigroup Deal; Move Shifts Strategic Plan." *Wall Street Journal,* 15 June 2005.

Palich, L. E., and D. R. Bagby. "Using Cognitive Theory to Explain Entrepreneurial Risk-Taking: Challenging Conventional Wisdom." *Journal of Business Venturing* 10, no. 6 (1995): 425–438.

Parloff, Roger. "Credibility GAAP." CNNMoney.com, 7 April 2006, http://money.cnn.com/2006/04/07/news/newsmakers/pluggedin_enron_fortune/index.htm (accessed 10 January 2008).

Patterson, Simon, and Peter Smith. "How to Make Top People's Pay Reflect Performance." *Sunday Times* (London), 9 August 1998.

Peck, M. Scott, M.D. *The Road Less Traveled.* New York: Simon & Schuster, 1978.

Perold, André F. Unpublished paper, 11 December 2001.

Petra, Steven T. "Do Outside Independent Directors Strengthen Corporate Boards?" *Corporate Governance* 5, no. 1 (2005).

Plous, Scott. *The Psychology of Judgment and Decision Making.* New York: McGraw-Hill, 1993.

Pollick, Mike, and Chris Davis. "A Primer on Enron's Connections to Florida." *Sarasota Herald-Tribune,* 9 February 2002.

Polyn, Gallagher. "Getting a Better Risk Picture." *Risk,* August 2001.

Powers, William C. Jr., Raymond S. Troubh, and Herbert S. Winokur Jr. *Report of Investigation by the Special Investigative Committee of the Board of Directors of Enron Corp.,* 2002.

Preston, Robert, and Mike Koller. "Enron Feels the Power." *InternetWeek,* 30 October 2000.

Prosecution's Opening Statement. *U.S. v. Skilling and Lay,* H-CR-04–025SS (S.D. Tex. 2006), 31 January 2006.

Public Citizen. "Blind Faith: How Deregulation and Enron's Influence over Government Looted Billions from Americans." December 2001.

Public Utility Regulatory Policy Act of 1978 (PURPA). 18 C.F.R. § 292.206(b).

Puliyenthuruthrl, Josey. "Enron Inches toward India Plant Sale." *Daily Mail,* 14 November 2002.

Rangan, V. Kasturi, and Krishna G. Palepu. "Enron Development Corporation: The Dabhol Power Project in Maharashtra, India (A)." Boston: Harvard Business School Publishing, 1996. HBS Case No. 9–596–099.

Rappaport, Alfred. "New Thinking on How to Link Executive Pay with Performance." *Harvard Business Review,* March-April 1999: 91–101.

*Regents of the University of California v. Credit Suisse First Boston (USA) Inc._*F.3d (5th Cir. 19 March 2007).

Revised Model Business Corporation Act, 8.30 cmt.2.

Roe, Mark. "The Inevitable Instability of American Corporate Governance." Harvard Law and Economics Discussion Paper No. 493, July 2007.

Ross v. Bernhard, 396 U.S. 531, 534 (1970).

Rutherford, John Jr. "Securities Regulation and Stability—Learning the Lessons of Recent Corporate Failures." IOSCO Technical Committee Meeting, Panel 5, Frankfort, Germany, 6 October 2005.

Sale, Hillary A. "Delaware's Good Faith." *Cornell Law Review* 89 (2004).

Salpukas, Agis. "Firing Up an Idea Machine: Enron Is Encouraging the Entrepreneurs Within." *New York Times,* 27 June 1999.

Salter, Malcolm S. "Notes on Governance and Corporate Control." *Journal of Strategic Management Education* 1, no. 1 (2003): 5–54.

———. "Tailor Executive Compensation to Strategy." *Harvard Business Review,* March-April 1973: 94–102.

Salter, Malcolm S., and Daniel B. Green. "Regal Cinemas LBO (A)." Harvard Business School Case 9–902–019.

———. "Regal Cinemas LBO (B)." Harvard Business School Case 9–902–020.

Schein, Edgar H. *Organizational Culture and Leadership,* 2nd ed. San Francisco: Jossey-Bass, 1992.

Schlossberg v. First Artists Production Co. No. 6670, 1986 WL 15143, 15 (Del. Ch. 17 December 1986).

Schonfeld, Erick. "The Power Brokers." *Business 2.0,* January 2001.

Schroeder, Michael. "Accounting for Enron." *Wall Street Journal,* 21 January 2002.

———. "Enron's Board Was Warned in '99 on Accounting." *Wall Street Journal,* 8 May 2002.

———. "Questioning the Books." *Wall Street Journal,* 11 February 2002.

Schwarcz, Steven L. "Fifteenth Annual Corporate Law Symposium: Corporate Bankruptcy in the New Millennium: Enron and the Use and Abuse of Special Purpose Entities in Corporate Structures." *University of Cincinnati Law Review* 70 (2002).

———. "Private Ordering of Public Markets." *University of Illinois Law Review* 1, no. 3 (2002).

Schwartz, John. "As Enron Purged Its Ranks, Dissent Was Swept Away." *New York Times,* 4 February 2002.

Schwartz, John, and Richard A. Oppel Jr. "Enron's Collapse: The Chief Executive." *New York Times,* 29 November 2001.

Schweitzer, Lisa Ordonez, and Bambi Douma. "The Dark Side of Goal Setting: The Role of Goals in Motivating Unethical Decision-Making." *Academy of Management Proceedings* (2002).

Selznick, Philip. *Leadership in Administration.* New York: Harper & Row, 1957.

Sherman, Scott. "Enron: Uncovering the Uncovered Story." *Columbia Journalism Review,* March–April 2002.

Shleifer, Andrei, and Robert W. Vishny. "A Survey of Corporate Governance."
    Journal of Corporate Finance 52, no. 2 (June 1997).
Simons, Robert. "Control in an Age of Empowerment." *Harvard Business Review,*
    March–April 1995: 80–88.
———. "How Risky Is Your Company?" *Harvard Business Review,* May–June 1999.
———. *Levers of Control.* Boston: Harvard Business School Press, 1995.
Sinclair Oil Corp. v. Levien. 280 A.2d 717, 720 (Del. 1971).
Skilling, Jeffrey K. Brief of Defendant-Appellant Jeffrey K. Skilling. *U.S. v. Skilling.*
    5th Cir., 17 September 2007 (06-20885).
———. "Enron's Transformation: From Gas Pipelines to New Economy Power-
    house." Speech at Harvard Business School, 26 April 2001.
———. Reply Brief of Defendant-Appellant Jeffrey K. Skilling. *U.S. v. Skilling.* 5th
    Cir. December 21, 2007 (06-20885).
———. Testimony before Panel V of Oversight and Investigations Subcommittee,
    U.S. House. Energy and Commerce Committee. 7 February 2002.
———. Transcript of Testimony. *U.S. v. Skilling and Lay,* H-CR-04–025SS (S.D. Tex.
    2006). 18 & 19 April 2006.
———. Videotaped interview by Robert Bruner. Darden School of Business, 25 May
    2001.
Sloan, Allan, with others. "Digging into the Deal that Broke Enron." *Newsweek,*
    17 December 2001.
Smith, Adam. *An Inquiry into the Nature and Causes of the Wealth of Nations.* Edited by
    Edwin Cannan. Chicago: University of Chicago Press, 1976 (1776).
Smith, Christopher L. E-mail to author, 19 March 2003.
Smith, Rebecca. "Blockbuster Deal Shows Enron's Inclination to All-Show, Little-
    Substance Partnerships." *Wall Street Journal,* 17 January 2002.
———. "Enron Set to Sell Oregon Utility to Texas Pacific." *Wall Street Journal,*
    19 November 2003.
———. "Sales of Enron Unit to Sierra Pacific Becomes Unlikely." *Wall Street Journal,*
    26 March 2001.
Smith, Rebecca, and John R. Emshwiller. "Enron Attempts to Show Investors a
    Softer Side." *Wall Street Journal,* 28 August 2001.
———. *24 Days.* New York: HarperBusiness, 2003.
Staff of the Joint Committee on Taxation. "Report of Investigation of Enron Corpo-
    ration and Related Entities Regarding Federal Tax and Compensation Issues, and
    Policy Recommendations." 108th Congress, JCS-3–03, February 2003.
Standard & Poor's Compustat Execucomp database, available at http://wrds
    .wharton.upenn.edu/ds/comp/execcomp/ (accessed 10 January 2008).
"Strength of Enron's Cash Position May Be Moot, Given Its Spiraling Stock Slide."
    *Global Power Rep*ort, 9 November 2002.
Stroud v. Grace, 606 A.2d 75, 84 (Del. 1992).
Swartz, Mimi, and Sherron Watkins. *Power Failure: The Inside Story of Enron.* New
    York: Doubleday, 2003.

Tempest, Rone. "With the Theater or PACs, Texans Saw Kenneth Lay as 'On Top of the World' Influence." *Los Angeles Times,* 25 January 2002.

Thomas, Evan, and Andre Murr, with others. "The Gambler Who Blew It All." *Newsweek,* 4 February 2002.

TIAA-CREF. *Policy Statement on Corporate Governance.* TIAA-CREF, January 2004.

Trope, Y. "Uncertainty-reducing Properties of Achievement Tasks." *Journal of Personality and Social Psychology* 37 (1979): 1505–1518.

TSC Industries, Inc. v. Northway Industries, Inc. 426 U.S. 438, 449 (1976).

Twersky, A., and D. Hahnemann. "Judgment under Uncertainty." *Science* 185 (1974): 1124–1130.

U.S. Bankruptcy Court. Southern District of New York. *In re Enron Corp.,* Chapter 11, Case No. 01–16034 (AJG), "First Interim Report of Neal Batson, Court-Appointed Examiner" (Bankr. S.D.N.Y. 21 September 2002).

———. *In re Enron Corp.,* Chapter 11, Case No. 01–16034 (AJG), "Second Interim Report of Neal Batson, Court-Appointed Examiner" (Bankr. S.D.N.Y. 21 January 2003).

———. *In re Enron Corp.,* Chapter 11, Case No. 01–16034 (AJG), "Third Interim Report of Neal Batson, Court-Appointed Examiner" (Bankr. S.D.N.Y. 30 June 2003).

———. *In re Enron Corp.,* Chapter 11, Case No. 01–16034 (AJG), "Final Report of Neal Batson, Court-Appointed Examiner" (Bankr. S.D.N.Y. 4 November 2003).

———. *In re Enron Corp.,* Chapter 11, Case No. 01–16034 (AJG), "Report of Harrison J. Goldin, the Court-Appointed Examiner in the Enron North America Corp. Bankruptcy Proceeding, Respecting His Investigation of the Role of Certain Entities in Transactions Pertaining to Special Purpose Entities" (Bankr. S.D.N.Y. 14 November 2003).

———. *The Official Committee of Unsecured Creditors of Enron Corp. et al. vs. Kenneth L. Lay and Linda P. Lay.* Entered at Case No. 01–16034 (AJG).

U.S. Court of Appeals for the Fifth Circuit. *U.S. v. James A Brown, Daniel Bayley, Robert S. Furst, William R. Fuhs.* 459 F.3d 509 (1 August 2006) No. 05-20319.

U.S. Department of Justice. Enron Trial Exhibits and Releases, Exhibit 3586. Available at www.usdoj.gov/enron/exhibit/04-06/BBC-0001/OCR/EXH047-00086 .TXT (accessed 5 January 2008).

U.S. District Court, Southern District of Texas, Houston Division. *In re Enron Corporation Securities, Derivatives, and "ERISA" Litigation, Memorandum and Order Regarding Outside Director Defendants' Motions.* Civil Action No. H-01–3624 Consolidated Cases, 12 March 2003.

———. Complaint. Superseding Indictment. *U.S. v. Richard A. Causey, Jeffrey K. Skilling, and Kenneth L. Lay.* Cr. No. H-04–25 (S-2). (7 July 2004,)

———. Complaint. Third Superceding Indictment, *U.S. v. Bayly, Boyle, Brown, Fuhs, Furst, Kahanek.* Cr. No. H-03–363.

———. Complaint. *U.S. Securities and Exchange Commission v. Canadian Imperial Bank of Commerce, Daniel Ferguson, Ian Schottlaender, Mark Wolf.* Case No. H-03–5785.

———. Complaint. *U.S. Securities and Exchange Commission v. Fastow.* Civil Action No.

H-02–3666. (2 October 2002.) Available at www.sec.gov/litigation/complaints/ comp17692.htm.

———. Complaint. *U.S. Securities and Exchange Commission v. Jeffrey K. Skilling and Richard A. Causey.* Case No. H-04–0284 (Harmon). (19 February 2004.)

———. Complaint. *U.S. Securities and Exchange Commission v. J.P. Morgan Chase,* July 2003.

———. Complaint. *U.S. Securities and Exchange Commission v. Kopper.* Civil Action No. H-02–3127. (21 August 2002.) Available at www.sec.gov/litigation/complaints/ comp17692.htm.

———. Complaint. *U.S. Securities and Exchange Commission v. Merrill Lynch & Co., Inc., Daniel H. Bayly, Thomas W. Davis, Robert S. Furst, Schuyler M. Tilney.* Case No. H-03–0946.

———. Complaint. *U.S. v. Andrew S. Fastow et al.* Cr. No. H-02–0665.

———. Complaint. *U.S. v. Kenneth Rice et al.* Cr. No. H-03–93–01.

———. *In re Enron Corporation Securities Litigation.* Class Action Complaint. Available at www.universityofcalifornia.edu/news/enron/welcome.html.

———. *In re Enron Corporation Securities Litigation.* Civil Action No. H-01–3624. "First Amended Consolidated Complaint for Violation of the Securities Laws." (14 May 2005.)

———. *Mark Newby et al. v. Enron Corp. et al.* Civil Action No. H-01–3624. (8 April 2002.)

———. *U.S. v. Glisan.* Plea Agreement, No. 02-CR-665 (10 September 2003).

———. *U.S. v. Hirko et al.* Criminal Action No. H-03–93–05.

———. *U.S. v. Howard.* United States' Response to Defendant's Motion to Vacate Convictions. Docket Entry 1247, Cr. No. H-03-0093.

———. *U.S. v. Timothy Despain.* Cr. No. H-04, Sentence Data Sheet.

———. Complaint. *U.S. Commodity Futures Trading Commission v. Enron Corp. and Hunter Shively.* H-03–909. (12 March 2003.) Available at www.cftc.gov/files/enf/ 03orders/enfenron-complaint.pdf.

U.S. General Accounting Office. *SEC Operations: Increased Workload Creates Challenges.* GAO -02–302, 2002. Available at www.gao.gov/new.items/d02302.pdf.

U.S. House. Committee on Education and Workforce. Subcommittee on Oversight and Investigations. "On the Subject of Innovative Workplace for the Future." Testimony of Elizabeth A. Tilney (Senior Vice President for Advertising, Communications and Organizational Development, Enron Corp.). 20 May 1997.

———. Energy and Commerce Committee. "Enron's Accounting Issues: What We Can Learn to Prevent Future Enrons." Testimony of Bala C. Dharan, 6 February 2002 (see LexisNexis Congressional transcript, Federal News Service, 6 February 2002).

———. Oversight and Investigations Subcommittee. "The Financial Collapse of Enron." 107th Congress, Second session. 7 February 2002.

U.S. Securities and Exchange Commission. Administrative Proceeding File No. 3 10909. Available at www.sec.gov/rules/other/35-27574.htm (accessed 6 January 2008).

———. Credit Rating Agency Report, p. 6.

———. *In the Matter of Citigroup, Inc.* Securities Exchange Act Release No. 48230. Securities and Exchange Commission Administrative Proceeding File No. 3–11192. "Order Instituting a Public Administrative Proceeding Pursuant to Section 21C of the Securities Exchange Act of 1934, Making Findings, and Imposing a Cease-and-Desist Order and Other Relief." (2003). Available at www.sec.gov/litigation/admin/34–48230.htm.

———. Litigation Release No. 18038, 17 March 2003.

———. Press Release No. 2003–32. "SEC Charges Merrill Lynch, Four Merrill Lynch Executives with Aiding and Abetting Enron Accounting Fraud." 17 March 2003.

———. Press Release No. 2003–87. "SEC Settles Enforcement Proceedings against J. P. Morgan Chase and Citigroup." 28 July 2003.

———. Press releases (various). Available at www.sec.gov/spotlight/enron.html and University of California Board of Regents Web site: www.universityofcalifornia.edu/news/enron/welcome.html.

———. "Report on the Role and Function of Credit Rating Agencies in the Operation of the Securities Markets (as Required by Section 702(b) of the Sarbanes-Oxley Act of 2002." Available at www.sec.gov/news/studies/credratingreport0103.pdf.

———. *Securities Act of 1933.*

———. Staff Accounting Bulletin Release No. 101. "Revenue Recognition in Financial Statements." Available at www.sec.gov./interps/account/sab101.htm.

———. Staff Accounting Bulletin Release No. SAB-51, 7 Se. L. Rep. (CCH) (29 March 1983).

———. Web site: www.sec.gov/about/whatwedo/shtml.

U.S. Senate. Committee on Commerce, Science, and Transportation. Hearing. 107th Congress, Second Session. 12 February 2002.

———. Committee on Governmental Affairs. *Asleep at the Switch: FERC's Oversight of Enron Corporation, Vol. 1—Hearing.* 107th Congress (2002). Available at www.gpoaccess/congress/senate/homeland/index/html.

———. *Asleep at the Switch: FERC's Oversight of Enron Corporation, Vol. 2—Hearing.* 107th Congress (2002). Available at www.gpoaccess/congress/senate/homeland/index/html.

———. "The Fall of Enron: How Could It Have Happened?" Hearing, 107th Congress, 2002. Available at www.gpoaccess/congress/senate/homeland/index.html.

———. *Financial Oversight of Enron: The SEC and Private-Sector Watchdogs.* S. Prt. 107–75 (2002). Available from Government Printing Office, www.gpoaccess.gov (accessed 11 July 2006).

———. "Rating the Raters: Enron and the Credit Rating Agencies." 107th Congress 62–63 (2002). Testimony of Ronald M. Barone, Managing Director, Standard and Poor's. Available at www.gpoaccess.gov/congress/senate/homeland/index.html.

———. *The Role of the Financial Institutions in Enron's Collapse—Vol. 1: Hearing before the Permanent Subcommittee on Investigations of the Senate Committee on Governmental*

Affairs. 107th Congress (2002). Available from Government Printing Office, www.gpoaccess.gov (accessed July 11, 2006).

———. *The Role of the Financial Institutions in Enron's Collapse—Vol. 2: Hearing before the Permanent Subcommittee on Investigations of the Senate Committee on Governmental Affairs.* 107th Congress (2002). Available from Government Printing Office, www.gpoaccess.gov (accessed July 11, 2006).

———. *The Watchdogs Didn't Bark: Enron and the Wall Street Analysts: Hearing before the Senate Comm. on Governmental Affairs.* 107th Congress (2002). Available from Government Printing Office, www.gpoaccess.gov (accessed July 11, 2006).

U.S. Senate. Permanent Subcommittee on Investigations. Committee on Governmental Affairs. "Fishtail, Bacchus, Sundance, and Slapshot: Four Enron Transactions Funded and Facilitated by U.S. Financial Institutions," S. Prt. 107–82 (2003). Available from Government Printing Office, www.gpoaccess.gov (accessed July 11, 2006).

———. "Frank Luntz of the Luntz Research Companies to Ken Lay, Grey Whalley, and Mark Frevert," Exhibit #34. Memorandum dated 19 October 2001. Presented at hearings before the 107th Congress, 2nd Session, 23 & 30 July 2002.

———. "Letter from W. Neil Eggleston, Partner, Howrey Simon Arnold & White, LLP, to the Honorable Carl Levin, Chairman, Senate Permanent Subcommittee on Investigations of the Committee on Governmental Affairs, U.S. Senate, and the Honorable Susan Collins, Ranking Subcommittee Minority Member, U.S. Senate." U.S. Government Printing Office. S. Hrg. 107–511. 1 August 2002.

———. "LJM Investments Annual Partnership Meeting Presentation, October 26, 2000," Exhibit #25. Presented at hearing on 7 May 2002.

———. "The Outside Directors' Response to: The Role of the Board of Directors in Enron's Collapse." U.S. Government Printing Office. S. Hrg. 107–511. 1 August 2002.

———. "The Role of the Board of Directors in Enron's Collapse." S. Hrg. 107–511, 107th Congress, 2nd Session. 7 May 2002.

———. "The Role of the Board of Directors in Enron's Collapse." S. Rep. 107–70, 107th Congress, 2nd Session (2002).

———. "Testimony of Robert Jaedicke," 107th Congress, 2nd Session, 7 May 2002.

U.S. Supreme Court. *Dirks v. SEC.* 463 U.S. 646 (1983).

———. *Santa Fe Industries v. Green.* 430 U.S. 462 (1977).

U.S. v. Reyes. 239 F.3d 722, 736 (Fifth Circuit 2001).

U.S. v. Sarno. 73 F.3d 1470, 1482 n.6 (Ninth Circuit 1995).

U.S. v. Simon. 425 F.2d 796 (Second Circuit 1969).

Vaughan, Dianne. "The Trickle-Down Effect: Policy Decisions, Risky Work, and the Challenger Tragedy." *California Management Review* 39 (Winter 1997): 80–103.

Wall Street Journal. "Business in Brief—Enron Corp.: Price-Manipulation Allegations Are Settled for $35 Million." 29 April 2004.

———. "Corporate Boards: A Director's Cut." Manager's Journal, 18 February 2003.

———. "Enron Ex-Officials Receive Indictments in U.S. Fraud Case." 27 March 2003.

———. "Enron Lessons." 15 January 2002.

———. "Enron Selects Kinder to Be Its President and Operating Chief." 12 October 1990.

Wallin, Michelle. "Enron to Drop Utility Deal in Argentina." *Wall Street Journal,* 1 March 2002.

In re Walt Disney Co. Derivative Litigation. Consolidated C.A. No. 15452 (Del. Ch. 2005).

Washington Post. "Investigating Enron." Editorial. 6 January 2002.

Watkins, Sherron S. Unsigned letter to Ken Lay. *New York Times,* 16 January 2002.

Weil, Jonathan. "After Enron, 'Mark-to-Market' Accounting Gets Scrutiny." *Wall Street Journal,* 4 December 2001.

West Point–Pepperell, Inc. v. J. P. Stevens & Co. 542 A.2d 770, 780 (Del. Ch. 1988).

Williams, Bob. "Enron Looking to International Arena for Growth Via Hydrocarbon/Power Schemes." *Oil & Gas Journal,* 29 June 1998: 61–63.

Witt, April, and Peter Behr. "Dream Job Turns into a Nightmare: Skilling's Success Came at a High Price." *Washington Post,* 29 July 2002.

———. "Enron's Other Strategy: Taxes." *Washington Post,* 21 May 2002.

Wruck, Karen H. "The Ownership, Governance and Control of Organizations." Course module overview note. Harvard Business School, April 1997.

Young, Owen D. "Dedication Address." Keynote address at the dedication of the new Harvard Business School campus, June 24, 1927. Reprinted in the July 1927 issue of *Harvard Business Review,* and available in the HBS Archives Collection (AC 1927 17.1).

Zacharakis, Andrew L., and Dean A. Shepherd. "The Nature of Information and Overconfidence in Venture Capitalists' Decisionmaking." *Journal of Business Venturing* 16, no. 4 (2001): 311–322.

Zellner, Wendy. "Power Play." *BusinessWeek,* 12 February 2001.

Zidell v. Zidell. 560 P.2d 1086, 1089 (Or. 1977).

Zirn v. VLI. 681 A.2d 1050, 1062 (Del. 1996).

Index